Magic, Texts and Travel

Homage to a Scholar, Will Ryan

edited by
Janet M. Hartley
and
Denis J. B. Shaw

Study Group on Eighteenth-Century Russia
London, 2021

ISBN 978-0-9503314-8-5
Study Group on Eighteenth-Century Russia
www.sgecr.co.uk

Contents

TEXTS AND TRANSLATIONS

TRAVEL, TECHNOLOGY AND EXPLORATION

Will Ryan

Introduction

WILL RYAN learnt his Russian at school (Bromley Grammar School for Boys), then in the joint services programme for linguists during national service in the Royal Navy and finally at Oxford. The greatest intellectual influences on him at Oxford were Boris Unbegaum and John Simmons;[1] they instilled a love of the Russian language and the need for a meticulous approach to sources which has stayed with him throughout his career. He spent one year in Leningrad as a British Council postgraduate student in 1962–63 (during the Cuban missile crisis, at a time when he was still in the naval reserve). While studying manuscripts in the Manuscript Department of what is now the National Library of Russia he made the acquaintance of Dmitrii Sergeevich Likhachev. Likhachev immediately recognized a true scholar, took a serious interest in his work and they became friends. Will's postgraduate work led to a DPhil in 1970 on 'Astronomical and Astrological Terminology in Old Russian Literature'. By this time he had already been employed by the Clarendon Press and had worked as an assistant curator at the Museum of the History of Science in Oxford. There followed eight years as a lecturer in Russian language and literature at the School of Slavonic and East European Studies (University of London, and now part of University College London), where he served as chairman of the staff assembly and editor of the *Slavonic and East European Review*. But the main part of his career was spent at the Warburg Institute where he was the academic librarian for twenty-six years and is now an honorary fellow (and whose contribution, both intellectual and practical, to the Institute is described here by Charles Burnett).

This volume honours and celebrates Will's contribution to scholarship. The range of expertise demonstrated by the contributors reflects the breadth of Will's own scholarship, which encompasses magic, folklore, linguistics, textual analysis, and the history of science and exploration. His postgraduate work evolved into a far wider interest in magical texts and spells which led to the publication of many articles and chapters and culminated in 1999 in his magisterial book, *The Bathhouse at Midnight: An Historical Survey of Magic and Divination in Russia*. The book is encyclopaedic in coverage and is divided into the following sections: popular magic; wizards and witches; popular divination; signs, omens, auguries; calendar predictions; predictions

---

[1] John Simmons, librarian and scholar, loved cats; Will's article 'Russia and the Magic of Cats' was written in his honour in a special edition of the journal *Solanus*.

from dreams and the human body; spells, curses and magic prayers; talismans and amulets; *materia magica*; texts on amulets; magic of letters and number; geomancy; alchemy and the virtues of stones; Byzantine and post-Byzantine astrology; magic, the Church, the law and the State. The book has been described as 'impressive in its scope, its thoroughness, and its phenomenal basis in knowledge' [...] 'a work of incomparable import'[2] and as a 'fundamental reference work on magic in Russia for generations to come'.[3] Many reviewers commented, almost in awe, that the book was the product of over thirty years of scholarship, all too rare today when so many of us are required to write to meet targets in five-year plans.

The book appeared at a time when the constraints of Soviet scholarship were ending and a new generation of Russian scholars was turning its attention to Russian magic. Will's book was acknowledged in Russia as of fundamental importance and *The Bathhouse at Midnight* appeared in Russian translation in 2006 as *Bania v polnoch': istoricheskii obzor magii i gadanii v Rossii* (Aleksei Chernetsov was the main editor and Elena Smilianskaia was one of the translators). A generous tribute to Will's contribution to Russian cultural history written by Andrei Toporkov and Aleksei Chernetsov was published to celebrate his eightieth birthday.[4]

Magic is well represented in this volume by the chapters on Russian spells by Val Kivelson (on animal magic) and Andrei Toporkov (on love spells) and on Russian amulets by Aleksei Chernetsov. Will's book demonstrated that the boundaries are porous between magic, science, religion and traditional beliefs (Will was also an active member, and president, of the British Folklore Society). The chapters by Eve Levin on blood-letting, by Gary Marker on the Talitskii case and by Florentina Badalanova Geller on the mythographies of the demonic discuss the complexity of beliefs in the context of medicine, religion and customs in Russia and Bulgaria. As a librarian, Will had few PhD students but Yuri Stoyanov was jointly supervised with Charles Burnett on the topic of 'Apocryphal Themes and Apocalyptic Elements in Bogomil Dualist Theology and their Implications for the Study of Catharism'; Yuri currently works on Freemasonry and has contributed a chapter here from his latest research on Russian Freemasonry.

---

[2]   Valerie Kivelson, review in *American Historic Review*, 105, 2000, 5, pp. 1834–35.
[3]   Eve Levin, review in *Slavic Review*, 59, 2000, 4, p. 931.
[4]   A. L. Toporkov, A. V. Chernetsov, 'Iubilei. Vil'iamu Frensisu Raianu – 80 let', *Nauchnyi al'manakh traditsionnaia kul'tura*, 2 (66), 2017, pp. 187–91.

Will's first job was to revise and copy edit the *Oxford Russian–English Dictionary*. His interest in linguistics and translations has remained and evolved throughout his career. His first publication, 'Rathbone's Surveyor', in 1964, discovered the first translation of part of an English book into Russian in the early seventeenth century. He jointly wrote the *Penguin Russian Dictionary*, which appeared in 1995, and has translated a number of important articles by Russian scholars into English. His work is founded on a meticulous and erudite analysis of texts, of which particular mention should be made of the pseudo-Aristotelian *Secret of Secrets* alleged to be the advice given by Aristotle to Alexander the Great, which has been described as the most popular non-religious text of the Middle Ages and which could be found in royal libraries all over Europe, including Russia. Will first discovered the Russian version of this document in the Bodleian Library when he was an undergraduate; he wrote many articles on the subject but it would be some sixty years before this important but immensely difficult text with annotated translation was to be published jointly with Moshe Taube as *The* Secret of Secrets*: The East Slavic Version* (2019). Moshe has added to this work in his analysis of the Slavic translations from Hebrew in this volume. Translations of foreign legal texts were important to the tsars as Bill Butler's paper on Peter I demonstrates. Will's meticulous approach to textual analysis is shared by Ralph Cleminson and Sergei Bogatyrev who both use their expertise in this volume to challenge legends — the former looking at classical writers on the land of Serica and the latter analysing Russian chronicles on the golden belt incident in 1433. Adelina Angusheva-Tihanov thoroughly examines Slavonic renditions of the text of the *Vita* of St Basil. Will has known Boris Uspenskij for many years and the topic of his contribution here on royal titles and forms of address reflects their shared interest in the meaning of words and the possible misinterpretations which can arise from their use.

Will liked to discover things. His own view is that one of his most important publications was a short article on 'John Tradescant's Russian Abacus' published in 1972. Will had discovered when working at the Museum of the History of Science that the abacus in the collection was in fact Russian and wrongly labelled (it was a compulsory part of visits to Oxford that his children had to be taken to the Museum to see the abacus, now of course correctly labelled). His interest in science and naval technology stems not only from his employment at the Museum but also from his national service in the navy. He will be pleased, therefore, to see the inventions of Samuel Bentham described in Roger Bartlett's paper and the account of the exploits of Lord Effingham with the Russian navy in the joint paper by Elena Smilianskaia and Julia Leikin. The latter stems from a project being prepared for the Hakluyt Society, of which Will had been the series editor for many years and then vice president and president. This volume includes chapters on Russian exploration by Jim Gibson on the river Amur and Alexey Postnikov on the Arctic and North Pacific coasts; Jim published a massive two-volume study of Russian California with the Hakluyt Society, and Alexey is the Russian representative of the Society in Russia. Will devoted much scholarly activity to the Hakluyt Society because of his interest in the history of travel and exploration (and his relationship with the Society is discussed further by Jim Bennett). This volume is rich on travel accounts within the Russian Empire, or at least its extremities — in Siberia (Denis Shaw) and the Crimea (Tony Cross) — and beyond — in Jerusalem (Simon Dixon) and Manchuria (Paul Dukes). It is fitting that so many British members of the Study Group on Eighteenth-Century Russia feature in this section of the volume, as Will was one of the earliest members of the Group and has been a regular participant and contributor to the annual meetings in the United Kingdom and to the Group's international conferences. It is perhaps also fitting that the final paper in the collection is on Manchuria — Will's teacher at his grammar school, Freddie May, had learnt his Russian in Harbin under extraordinarily difficult circumstances.

Will's contribution to scholarship has been given formal recognition: he was elected Fellow of the British Academy in 2000 and was awarded an honorary doctorate by the Russian Academy of Sciences in 2007. Will has always been generous in sharing his scholarship, in encouraging younger scholars and in taking an interest in the work of colleagues. His contributions to discussions, whether it has been at seminars at the School of Slavonic and East European Studies and the Warburg Institute or at meetings of the Slavonic and East European Medieval Studies Group and the Study Group on Eighteenth-Century Russia, have been erudite, and often have been witty, but have always been kind and supportive to young scholars. He is a firm believer that the most valuable discussions take place outside the lecture theatre — whether over meals or at the bar in conferences or, best of all, at home with generous supplies of food and drink on the table. Will is a wonderful host and an excellent cook and his *kotlety po-Raianskii* (Ryan meatballs) are legendary.

This volume is a reflection of the deep respect in which Will is held and of his friendship with so many colleagues in so many countries. It was completed under difficult circumstances as COVID-19 closed archives and libraries and restricted travel. Several contributors had to overcome these unexpected problems and did so with fortitude. We are also grateful to Barbara Wyllie for preparing this difficult and complex text for publication. The publisher is the Study Group on Eighteenth-Century Russia. We have followed the style of the Modern Humanities Research Association and used the Library of Congress transliteration scheme. Above all, we should like to thank all the contributors; they have made this volume not only possible but a pleasure and a privilege to edit.

Janet M. Hartley and Denis J. B. Shaw
October 2020

Will Ryan and the Warburg Institute

THIS book is dedicated to Will Ryan. In all his publications and official documents Will Ryan has preferred to call himself W. F. Ryan. He was never 'William' and the F (for 'Francis') was rarely spelt out. But as 'Will' he was ever present, and ever busy, at the Warburg Institute, as the academic librarian from 1976 to 2002. The Library is the heart of the Warburg Institute: the continuation of the collection originally assembled in Hamburg by Aby Warburg himself according to his ideals of the history of culture and civilization, and progressively developed by his librarians and their successors following Warburg's conception. Will inherited a great responsibility in taking on the Library. Like previous librarians, he preserved the traditional organization of its holdings, in which the reader, in browsing the shelves, was led from magic to natural science, from numerology to arithmetic, and from alchemy to chemistry, and could find books and offprints shelved according to similarity of subject — the principle of the good neighbour. But he also oversaw the transition from the Warburg card catalogue to the computer catalogue shared with the other libraries of London University's School of Advanced Study, which entailed changing from the 1899 Prussian Instructions, used by the Library since its Hamburg days, to Anglo-American Cataloguing Rules. Under his direction the Library was expanded and refurbished in the 1990s, with the stacks changing orientation in order to provide much-needed additional shelf space.

As well as managing all aspects of the Library, Will acquired a reputation for his practical skills, especially with his Black and Decker drill. When an ancient power guillotine in the bookbindery was condemned by a health and safety inspector for having a completely unguarded steel flywheel, Will came in the next day with a large cake tin, a few screws and his trusty drill — the cake tin was still firmly in place when the machine was finally replaced many years later. When the brushes which were supplied to 'push' the water away in the event of flooding were found to be too large to fit between the stacks, Will sawed them down to the right size.

In addition to looking after the Library, Will was the guardian of the separately housed Yorke Collection, consisting of the books and manuscripts of the learned magician and occultist, Aleister Crowley. Will had to make sure that no one who might be susceptible to malign spirits issuing from the books gained access to the collection (an offshoot of this role was his 1992 article: 'The Great Beast in Russia:

Aleister Crowley's Theatrical Tour in 1913 and his Beastly Writings on Russia').

Magic and the occult have been well represented in the Warburg Institute ever since Aby Warburg and Wilhelm Prinz discovered that the Latin manual of magic called *Picatrix* was a translation of the Arabic *Goal of the Wiseman*, written by Maslama al-Qurṭubī. The ascent of knowledge advocated by Maslama — through the theoretical disciplines until one achieved the ability to put one's knowledge into action — coincided with the idea behind the ascent through the floors of the Warburg Library, starting from Image, then progressing to Word, Orientation (philosophy, theology and science) and finally arriving at Action on the fourth floor. Will contributed to this field in his two most substantial books: *The Bathhouse at Midnight: An Historical Survey of Magic and Divination in Russia* (1999), and *The* Secret of Secrets: *The East Slavic Version* (2019), together with Moshe Taube. As a leading figure (including being president) in the Folklore Society (which also had a corner in the basement of the Warburg Institute), he arranged public lectures and several conferences on folk magic and charms, one of which was published as *The Power of Words: Studies on Charms and Charming in Europe* (2013), edited by him together with James Kapaló and Éva Pócs.

Another major role within the Institute was his editorship of the Warburg's publication series (with Jill Kraye and, later, myself), which, on his watch, produced books on pseudonymous writings — *Pseudo-Aristotle's* Secret of Secrets (1982), Pseudo-Bede, *De mundi celestis terrestrisque constitutione* (1985), *Pseudo-Aristoteles Latinus: A Guide to Latin Works Falsely Attributed to Aristotle before 1500* (1985) and *Pseudo-Aristotle in the Middle Ages: The* Theology *and other Texts* (1986) — and the colloquium proceedings: *Magic and the Classical Tradition* (2006) — which he co-edited with me. His characteristic hands-on approach meant that he also took charge of the typesetting of each volume, so all that remained was to send the book to the printers. Outside the Institute he was for many years the Series Editor of the books of the Hakluyt Society (serving for a while as its president), which reflected his own interest in travel literature.

Will's writing is full of fascinating anecdotes (whether the workings of charms to ensure safe childbirth, Peter the Great's English yacht or the involvement of cats in magic), and these anecdotes often regaled his fellow diners in the Institute's common room: a tale of his guiding a Russian delegation round the remote Scottish nuclear power station of Dounreay sticks in my mind.

Through his own writings, Will has contributed more than any other scholar in English to our understanding of magic and the occult, astrology and astronomy, in pre-modern Russia. But he has also provided immense aid and support to other scholars and researchers, in his roles as librarian, editor, adviser and friend. The following papers are a fitting tribute from some of these friends.[1]

Charles Burnett
Warburg Institute, October 2020

---

[1] I am grateful to Jill Kraye and Ian Bavington Jones for supplying information.

Will Ryan and the Hakluyt Society

WILL RYAN's long, distinguished and affectionate relationship with the Hakluyt Society has thrived on its particular set of virtues: a love of books and of learning, respect for record made accessible through editorship, an interest in people in their historical circumstances, and the simple pleasure of knowing things and sharing them. These features made the Society a natural locus for Will and he in turn has upheld its values and character.

The Hakluyt Society has maintained a core purpose since its foundation in 1846: to publish scholarly editions of primary accounts of voyages and other travels in durable volumes and to distribute these to subscribing members and through the book trade generally. Will joined the Society in 1975. He translated and annotated Abbot Daniel's *Pilgrimage* from the old Russian original (the previously published translation having been from an unreliable French translation), which appeared as part of the Hakluyt Society volume *Jerusalem Pilgrimage, 1099–1185* in 1988. It was the longest of the assembled texts and Daniel and Will have given us a charming, lively and (for Daniel) personal story: 'I travelled that holy road unworthily, with every kind of sloth and weakness, in drunkenness and doing every kind of unworthy deed.'

Will became an 'honorary secretary' in 1990, a post which he held jointly with Sarah Tyacke and which included what would later be the duties of the 'series editor', a title adopted for Will and Sarah in 1995. Will would be a series editor, either on his own or jointly with Robin Law or Michael Brennan, through to his election as president in 2008. In 2007 he was joined by two 'honorary assistant series editors', Gloria Clifton and Joyce Lorimer, who continue as series editors today. This means that Will shouldered this central responsibility at the Society for eighteen years. He then was president until 2011 and continues now as an active vice-president.

Will's period as series editor saw many important volumes published and some major projects brought to fruition. The three volumes of *Olaus Magnus, A Description of the Northern Peoples, 1555* spanned 1996–98 and the volume editor, Peter Foote, recorded that: 'Will Ryan has seen these difficult volumes through the press. They could not have been in more capable hands.' Will had the distinction of seeing the fifth and final volume published of a work that had required the attentions of many an honorary secretary or series editor, having spanned

1957–2000, after an initial proposal in 1922; this was *The Travels of Ibn Battuta, A.D. 1325–1354.*

The Malaspina Expedition 1789–1794 in three volumes fell to Will's watch and the editors acknowledge that his 'meticulous overseeing' created a text for the printer from 'contributions reaching him in no particular order from the [four] different editors'. The outstanding achievement of Will's stamina and perseverance, however, is surely *Russian California, 1806–1860: A History in Documents.* This was published in two very large volumes in 2014, after Will was no longer series editor, but the series editorial work had definitely fallen to him. Former president Glyn Williams has mentioned to me that he has always noted that Will's many commitments to the Society were carried out when he was a very busy and prestigious academic librarian, with his own commitments in research and publication.

In 2013 Will was awarded the President's Medal of the Hakluyt Society. In making this award, the president, Michael Barritt, quoted the opinion of Roy Bridges, Will's immediate predecessor as president, which is worth recording here:

> [...] few of those who have served as Honorary Secretaries and latterly Series Editors, vital as their contributions have been, were quite able to match the linguistic and technical skills as well as cultural awareness which Will has so devotedly deployed for our collective benefit.

So it is appropriate to end with a small instance of these skills. We give the last word to Abbot Daniel, in Will's translation, who in the early twelfth century wrote what could be the *credo* of the Hakluyt Society: 'I have set down everything which I saw with my own eyes, so that what God gave me, an unworthy man, to see may not be forgotten.'

Jim Bennett
The Hakluyt Society, October 2020

MAGIC AND BELIEFS

A Contribution to the Study of Russian Amulets

A. V. Chernetsov

Academy of Sciences, Institute of Archaeology, Moscow

THE literature on Russian amulets in the medieval and early modern period is rich and extensive. Of particular importance is the ground-breaking book by Will Ryan which gives a scholarly overview of Russian magic, including amulets.[1] Our knowledge of this area, however, is still inadequate. Information on East Slavic amulets can be found in a variety of sources: amulets are well represented in archaeological finds;[2] they are reported and described in medieval and late medieval manuscripts (in particular, in medical texts and herbals); they are also included in ethnographic observations and collections. These sources, however, have often been studied in isolation by separate groups of specialists. Analytical research on pendants commonly found in archaeological collections is difficult, for example, because in many cases it is hard to distinguish between amulets and items of decoration.

The study of amulets is particularly complicated because outside influences and importations from other cultures are common in superstitious beliefs (cultural phenomena of exotic origin were often regarded as more powerful than what was traditional and local). Many amulets of Finno-Ugric origin[3] are found in a number of regions in

---

[1]   See W. F. Ryan, *The Bathhouse at Midnight: An Historical Survey of Magic and Divination in Russia*, University Park, PA, 1999: 'Talismans and Amulets', pp. 217–68, 'Materia magica', pp. 269–92, and 'Texts as amulets', pp. 293–308. The book was published in Russian in 2006 under my editorship. See also the bibliography in particular in the brief encyclopaedic guide to amulets: N. I. Tolstoi, 'Amulet', *Slavianskie drevnosti. Etnolingvisticheskii slovar'*, ed. N. I. Tolstoi, Moscow, 1995, vol. 1, pp. 105–06.

[2]   V. V. Gol'msten, 'Lunnitsy Rossiiskogo istoricheskogo muzeiia', in *Otchet Istoricheskogo muzeia za 1913 g.*, Moscow, 1914, pp. 89–106; M. V. Sedova, 'Amulet iz drevnego Novgoroda', *Sovetskaia arkheologiia*, 1957, no. 4, pp. 166–67; N. P. Zhurzhalina, 'Drevnerusskie priveski-amulety i ikh datirovka', *Sovetskaia arkheologiia*, 1961, no. 2, pp. 122–40; V. P. Darkevich, 'Topor kak simvol Peruna v drevnerusskom iazychestve', *Sovetskaia arkheologiia*, 1961, no. 4, pp. 90–101; A. V. Uspenskaia, 'Nagrudnye i poiasnye priveski', in *Ocherki po istorii russkoi derevni v X–XIII vv.: Trudy Gosudarstvennogo Istoricheskogo muzeia*, Moscow, 1967, vyp. 43, pp. 88–133; V. V. Sedov, 'Amulety-kon'ki iz drevnerusskikh kurganov', in *Slaviane i Rus'*, Moscow, 1968, pp. 151–57; E. A. Riabinin, 'Zoomorfnye ukrasheniia drevnei Rusi X–XIV vv.', in *Svod arkheologicheskikh istochnikov*, Leningrad, 1981, vyp. E1–60; idem, 'Iazycheskie priveski-amulety drevnei Rusi', in *Drevnosti slavian i Rusi*, Moscow, 1989, pp. 55–63; N. A. Makarov, 'Drevnerusskie amulety-topariki', *Rossiiskaia arkheologiia*, 1992, no. 2, pp. 41–56.

[3]   L. A. Golubeva, 'Zoomorfnye ukrasheniia finno-ugrov', in *Svod arkheologicheskikh*

medieval Russia but it is interesting that they can also be found in areas that did not have a Finno-Ugric substrate population. Amulets of Scandinavian origin[4] have also been found in Eastern Europe. There was, of course, a strong Byzantine cultural influence on medieval Russian society and some Byzantine medieval superstitions and amulets related to such superstitions spread among the East Slavs.

My own academic interest in the study of medieval Russian amulets associated with the cultural influence of Byzantium arose after the death of Tat'iana Vasil'evna Nikolaeva (1921–84), a leading expert on medieval Russian Christian antiquities. In her final years she was engaged in preparing a corpus of serpent amulets (the so-called *zmeeviki*), a topic to which B. A. Rybakov had introduced her. The seemingly paradoxical nature of the amulets explains their fascination. One side (the obverse) of these medallions can credibly be regarded as a Christian icon whereas the motif on their reverse side, which is often accompanied by a Greek inscription, is magical and features a sickness demon. While this type of amulet is not the only example of Christian piety intermingled with superstitious beliefs condemned by the Church, it is nevertheless a striking visual manifestation of this symbiosis. In this regard, it is important to note that such amulets survived in Russia for an exceptionally long period. Because of Professor Nikolaeva's illness, and then her death, her work was not completed, and the Institute of Archaeology of the USSR Academy of Sciences asked me to complete it. The sections written by Nikolaeva in the original book were retained and my contribution was to rectify any omissions and add relevant comments. The book was published in 1991.[5]

At the time of publication of that book we were not fully aware of the range of Byzantine amulets that were prototypes of the Russian variants. An extensive collection of Byzantine amulets was analysed by the American scholar Jeffrey Spier shortly after our book was published.[6] Materials from his paper added substantially to the information included in our book and, to some extent, confirmed a

istochnikov, Moscow, 1979, vyp. E1–59; Riabinin, 'Zoomorfnye ukrasheniia'; P. M. Aleshkovskii, 'Iazycheskii amulet-priveska iz Novgoroda', *Sovetskaia arkheologiia*, 1980, no. 4, pp. 284–86.

    [4] G. L. Novikova, 'Skandinavskie amulety iz Gnezdova', in *Smolensk i Gnezdovo (k istorii drevnerusskogo goroda)*, Moscow, 1991, pp. 175–79; E. A. Mel'nikova, E. N. Nosov, 'Amulety s runicheskoi nadpis'iu s Gorodishcha pod Novgorodom', in *Drevneishie gosudarstva na territorii SSSR: Materialy i issledovaniia 1986*, Moscow, 1988, pp. 210–22.

    [5] T. V. Nikolaeva, A. V. Chernetsov, *Drevnerusskie amulety-zmeeviki*, Moscow, 1991 (reviewed by A. Frank, *Slavic Review*, 54, 1995, 1, pp. 169–70).

    [6] J. Spier, 'Medieval Byzantine Amulets and their Tradition', *Journal of the Warburg and Courtauld Institutes*, 56, 1993, pp. 25–62.

number of our statements. Since 1991, some new Russian finds have also been discovered and analysed.[7] I started work on this important but problematic subject on the basis of my own earlier research on medieval Russian superstitions.[8]

This paper examines medieval Russian amulets which display external influences and/or were related to manuscripts. I have described many of these amulets in earlier papers, but as I continued my research I was able to find some additional analogies and parallels that threw light on the origin of these items and their functions.[9]

Some late classical Greek and medieval amulets are in the form of seals, signets and signet rings. Sometimes the word 'seal' is used to describe specific magic drawings that include magic symbols and inscriptions usually inside a circle.[10] Magic symbols of this sort of Western origin can be found in a manuscript of the second half of the seventeenth century that contains a selection of incantations and descriptions of the miraculous properties of precious stones.[11] In another manuscript dated 1689, known as the Pskov Chronicle, the magical signs used in mathematical divination and linked to astrology (geomancy) seem to have been used as property marks and seals by the first Russian princes[12] and were apparently used in the procedure of signing treaties and entering into tributary arrangements.

[7] V. Iu. Koval', 'O drevnerusskikh amuletakh-zmeevikakh', *Kratkie soobshcheniia Instituta arkheologii*, 2007, vyp. 221, pp. 54–63; O. M. Oleinikov, 'Novye nakhodki amuletov-zmeevikov v Velikom Novgorode', *Rossiiskaia arkheologiia*, 2016, no. 4, pp. 273–83

[8] A. V. Chernetsov, 'Medieval Russian Pictorial Materials on Paganism and Superstitions', in *Symposium International et pluridisciplinaire sur la paganism slave. Contributions,* Brussels–Gand 21–24 May 1980; *Slavica Gandensia,* Gand, 7/8, 1980–81, pp. 99–112; A. A. Turilov, A. V. Chernetsov, 'Otrechennaia kniga Rafli', in *Trudy Otdela drevnerusskoi literatury Instituta russkoi literatury (Pushkinskogo Doma) AN SSSR,* Leningrad, 1985, vol. 40, pp. 260–344. See also Ryan, *The Bathhouse at Midnight,* pp. 338–56.

[9] This paper is based on earlier Russian publications with additions and further analysis: A. V. Chernetsov, 'K izucheniu drevnerusskikh amuletov', in *De mare ad mare: Arkheologiia i istoriia: sbornik statei k 60-letiiu N. A. Krenke,* Moscow and Smolensk, 2017, pp. 106–18.

[10] Henricus Cornelius Agrippa ab Nettesheym, *De occulta philosophia libri tres,* Paris, 1567 (ed. pr. 1531), pp. 39–93; H. A. Winkler, *Siegel und Charaktere in der Muhammedanischen Zauberei,* Berlin and Leipzig, 1930.

[11] A. L. Toporkov (ed.), *Russkie zagovory iz rukopisnykh istochnikov XVII–pervoi poloviny XIX v.,* Moscow, 2010, p 348, fig. 3.

[12] A. A. Turilov, A. V. Chernetsov, 'Deianiia kniagini Ol'gi v "Pskovskom Kronike" 1689 g.', in *Drevniaia Rus'. Voprosy medievistiki,* 65, 2016, no. 3, pp. 57–75 (62, fig. 6); A. V. Chernetsov, A. A. Turilov, 'An Occult Version of the Early Medieval History of Russia and Description of Arctic Navigation Routes in the *Pskov Chronicle* of 1689', *The Journal of the Hakluyt Society,* January 2017 (http://www.hakluyt.com/journal_index.htm), p. 4, figs 2, 3, p. 6.

During the transition from the non-Christian age to the Christian epoch a particular variety of amulets became popular; they were the so-called gnostic gems, that is, carved stones, usually inserts of signet rings, which reflected syncretistic Greek and oriental religious cults of the eastern provinces of the late Roman empire.[13] They chiefly feature Graeco-Egyptian, Graeco-Syro-Mesopotamian, Graeco-Asia Minor and other motifs, in particular Graeco-Judaic and Graeco-Early Christian. It should be also noted that such amulets were distributed throughout the northern Black Sea region.[14] Further analysis clearly demonstrates the paramount importance of the late Classical and early Byzantine glyptics of this type for medieval Russia.

The so-called curse tablets which spread across the whole Mediterranean area are another well-known variety of amulets in the late Classical world.[15] These tablets are typically made of lead and have a text scratched on them. They were often rolled or folded and used in malefic magic. The curse tablets were tossed surreptitiously into graves or the sanctuaries of chthonic deities to bring misfortune on the person being cursed. Tablets exist which list the targets of curses, such as rivals and, in particular, athletes, gladiators, equestrians and even racehorses about to enter a race. In many cases such tablets reveal traces of intentional damage and piercing (tablets embedded with nails or rods have been found). Metal sheet amulets with magical inscriptions were widespread in antiquity and the medieval period. They were often made as pendants. Such amulets are known in particular in the early Byzantine[16] and Scandinavian[17] traditions.

In recent years, a serious study has been made of the very distinctive Bulgarian amulets, some of which have been dated to the tenth century, and contain Glagolitic letters, which indicates an early date. These

[13] C. Bonner, *Studies in Magical Amulets, chiefly Graeco-Egyptian*, University of Michigan Studies, Humanistic Series 49, Ann Arbor, MI, and London, 1950; A. Delatte, Ph. Derchain, *Les Intailles magiques greco-egyptiennes*, Paris, 1964.

[14] O. Ia. Neverov, 'Gnosticheskie gemmy, perstni i amulety iuga SSSR', *Vestnik drevnei istorii*, 1974, no. 1, pp. 95–103.

[15] John G. Gager (ed.), *Curse Tablets and Binding Spells from the Ancient World*, New York, 1992; E. G. Kagarov, *Grecheskie tablichki s prokliatiiami (defixionum tabellae)*, Khar'kov, 1918; T. A. Mikhailova, N. Iu. Chekhonadskaia, 'Gall'skaia "tablichka iz Larzaka". Pragmatika i zhanr', in *Zagovornyi tekst. Genezis i struktura*, Moscow, 2005, pp. 73–92; S. Iu. Saprykin, A. A. Maslennikov, 'Svintsovaia plastina s grecheskoi nadpis'iu iz Fanagorii', *Vestnik drevnei istorii*, 2007, no. 4, pp. 50–61; A. V. Mikhailenko, 'Tablichki prokliatii kak istochnik dlia izucheniia sotsial'noi zhizni v drevnei Gretsii', in *Vestnik Sankt-Peterburgskogo universiteta*, series 2, Istoriia, 2013, vyp. 2, pp. 60–68.

[16] Spier, 'Medieval Byzantine Amulets', plates 6, *c, d, f*.

[17] Mel'nikova, Nosov, 'Amulety s runicheskoi nadpis'iu'.

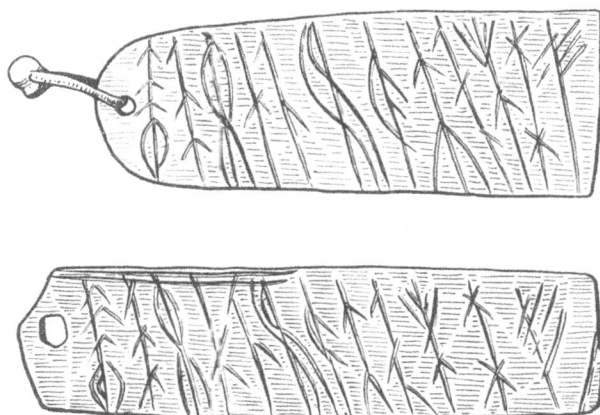

Fig. 1. A Scandinavian pendant amulet of the tenth century from the archaeological excavations at Riurikovo Gorodishche near Novgorod (from Mel'nikova, Nosov, 'Amulety s runicheskoi nadpis'iu', see footnote 4).

amulets are rolled metal sheets (typically made from lead) with magical texts.[18] Such finds (around several dozens) serve to establish direct linkage between archaeological materials and manuscripts. There is a clear link between the South Slav amulets and the earlier Mediterranean tradition, in particular curse tablets. Many Bulgarian tablets contain curses directed to a *nezhit* (personification of illness, supernatural evil being). It is important to note that apocryphal prayers against the *nezhit*, the *triasavitsa* (fever demon), the *hystera*-дъна (a demon personifying the womb, or an illness or even death, which was depicted on Byzantine and medieval Russia *zmeeviki* or 'serpent amulets') represent a closely-related group of texts. These malicious demons causing illness, which threatened the reproductive cycle and killed children and women in childbirth in the Byzantine tradition, are often personified as Gello (Gyllou).[19]

Finds of amulets similar to these Bulgarian amulets have to date not been found in Russia, but texts similar to the incantations inscribed on the Bulgarian metal scrolls can be found in medieval Russian manuscripts and birch-bark letters. However, there is one text in the

[18] K. Popkonstantinov, V. Konstantinova, 'Olovni plastini s nadpisi', in *Kirilo-Metodievska entsiklopediia*, Sofia, 1995, vol. 2, pp. 850–53; Popkonstantinov, 'The Letter of Abgar on a Tenth-Century Amulet', in Karsten Grünberg, Wilfried Potthoff (eds), *Ars Philologica. Festshrift für Baldur Panzer zum 65. Geburtstag*, Frankfurt, Brussels, Bern, New York, Vienna, 1999, pp. 649–54.
[19] Nikolaeva, Chernetsov, *Drevnerusskie amulety-zmeeviki*, pp. 16, 17.

Russian chronicles that contains an entry suggesting that the pagan East Slavs had a tradition of making metallic (in this case, gold) curse tablets in the period when the medieval Russian state was being established.

The entry in question reports on the treaty of 971 between the Kievan Prince Sviatoslav and Byzantium. The text declares 'If we violate this treaty, we shall be pierced like gold.'[20] As explained by I. I. Sreznevskii, the crux in the text is '*budem koloti*' 'we shall be pierced' (*koloti* is used in the earliest version of the text; later copies of the text use *zoloti* 'gold', which would make the sentence read 'We shall be gold like gold') but is related to a Scandinavian mythological motif and is basically a reference to Gullveig, a wicked witch (the first part of her name means 'gold') who was responsible for the outbreak of hostilities between the Vanir and the Aesir. She was pierced by spears, but reborn three times to sow the seeds of discord and war (The Elder Edda, Völuspá, The prophecy of the seeress, 21):

> She that remembers the war, the first on earth,
> when Gullveig [which means gold-draught] they with lances pierced,
> and in the high one's [Odin's] hall her burnt,
> thrice burnt, thrice brought forth,
> oft not seldom; yet she still lives.
> (Translation by Benjamin Thorpe)[21]

On the one hand, the obscure reading 'We shall be gold like gold' (*zoloti*) used in the treaty of 971 is found in most copies of the text while 'We shall be pierced like gold' (*koloti*) is used only once (in the earliest copy of the text), which seems to support the suggestion that *zoloti* is the correct word. On the other hand, the phrase 'We shall be pierced like gold and be slain with our own weapon' contains two synonymous verbs used in parallel and is absent in the copies of the text with *zoloti*.

Describing how the treaty of 971 was concluded, the later copies of the *Primary Chronicle* sometimes contain an obscure addition: 'and we have now made a *pinekhrusa* (*pinechrosa*) for this purpose', which

---

[20] *Polnoe sobranie russkikh letopisei* (hereafter *PSRL*), Moscow, 1962, vol. 1, column 73; I. I. Sreznevskii, *Materialy dlia slovaria drevnerusskogo iazyka*, St Petersburg, 1893 (reprint Moscow, 1958), vol. 1, columns 995, 996; A. A. Romenskii, '"koloti iako zoloto": k interpretatsii formuly kliatvy rusov v dogovore s Vizantiei 971 g.', in *Istoriia romeev vo vremeni i prostranstve; tsentr i periferiia. Tezisy dokladov XXI Vserossiiskoi nauchnoi sessii vizantinistov, Belgorod, 20–25 aprelia 2016 g.*, Belgorod, 2016, pp. 170–72.
[21] *The Elder Edda. A Book of Viking Lore*, trans., introduction, notes by A. Orchard, London, 2011, p. 432.

follows the phrase 'as it is inscribed upon this charter [parchment] and sealed with our seals'.[22] The word *pinekhrusa* has a clear Greek etymology (*pinax* means 'writing or votive tablet', *chrysos* means 'gold'). Apparently, when a covenant was signed, a metal (gold) 'curse tablet' was used, and this tablet could be pierced to bring punishment on the oath breaker. The use of a curse tablet during the execution of the treaty of 971 is quite convincing, all the more so as the curse, or the oath, is mentioned in the text of the treaty: 'We shall be damned by the god in whom we believe — Perun and Volos the god of beasts (cattle).'[23] If this (the most substantiated) interpretation of the word *pinekhrusa* is right, then it confirms that the use of *koloti* ('pierced like gold') is correct. Agreeing with the interpretation proposed by I. I. Sreznevskii, A. S. Orlov, a distinguished scholar of medieval Russia culture, seemingly thought this syncretism of a pagan culture to be quite natural when he wrote that, for the Kievan prince: 'the Varangian (Scandinavian) Sviatoslav [...] held dear his native mythology which is known to us from the treaty Sviatoslav signed with the Greeks (971), and perhaps also from such works as the Edda or Nibelungenlied.'[24]

Ritual curses (spells) have been known in the medieval Russian tradition since the earliest treaties with the Byzantine Empire dated by chronicles to 907–971.[25] Such spells written on objects turn the latter into a sort of amulet. For example, the precious cross of St Euphrosynia decorated with gold, gemstones and cloisonné enamel, made in 1161, bears an inscription that includes curses prescribed against those who will dare take out, give away or sell this relic from the monastery to which it was presented.[26] The curse contains Christian motifs. Despite the curse, the cross was removed to various places from the thirteenth century onwards. This precious and unique relic was lost during the Second World War. Another example is a fragment of a clay pot carrying a curse against those who violate the rights of the owner inscribed on the pot-sherd found in the minor town of Rostistavl'-Riazanskii.[27]

---

[22] *PSRL*, vol. 6, vyp. 1, Moscow, 2000, p. 62; F. P. Sergeev, 'Iz istorii slov "napisanie", "kharatiia", "pinekhrosa" (po materialam dogovorov russkikh s grekami)', *Izvestiia Volgogradskogo gos. ped. universiteta*, 68, 2012, vyp. 4, pp. 112–15.

[23] *PSRL*, vol. 1, column 73.

[24] A. S. Orlov, *Drevniaia russkaia literatura XI–XVI vv.*, Moscow and Leningrad, 1937, p. 58.

[25] *PSRL*, vol. 1, columns 32, 33, 47, 48, 54, 73.

[26] B. A. Rybakov, *Russkie datirovannye nadpisi XI–XIV vv., Arkheologiia SSSR. Svod arkheologicheskikh istochnikov*, Moscow, 1964, pp. 32–33.

[27] V. Iu. Koval', A. A. Medyntseva, A. A. Eremeev, 'Gorshok s nadpis'iu iz Rostislavlia Riazanskogo', *Rossiiskaia arkheologiia*, 2013, no. 3, pp. 137–43 (141, fig. 7).

Fig. 2. A fragment of a pot with a magic inscription from archaeological
excavations in Rostislavl'-Riazanskii (from Koval', Medyntseva, Eremeev,
'Gorshok s nadpis'iu iz Rostislavlia Riazanskogo', see footnote 27).

The inscription, which is only partially preserved, dates to the
twelfth–thirteenth centuries and is translated as 'NN has given this
pot to Iurii, any [other] person who takes it will be [will not be ...].'
The inscription was made before the pot was fired (in medieval Russia
pots mostly contain inscriptions scratched on fired clay pottery). The
purpose of this inscription is not clear because a household pot was of
no value. Apparently, the inscription was made to ensure the safety of
its contents. Such apotropaic inscriptions are found on other objects as
well, for example, a bone handle of a knife from the medieval Russian
town of Drogichin (Drohiczyn) in present-day Poland which dates to
the end of the eleventh/early twelfth centuries.[28] The inscriptions on the
pot and the knife handle do not have Christian motifs.

In 1998 the sites of several medieval Russian dwellings were
excavated in a trench parallel to the western façade of the cathedral
of the St Michael Golden-Domed Monastery in Kiev founded by Grand
Prince Sviatopolk II Iziaslavich in honour of his patron saint in 1108. The
cultural deposit, dating to the end of twelfth/first half of the thirteenth
centuries, yielded a fragment of a Chalcolithic axe (approximately 4000
BC) with Christian motifs, apparently engraved in the twelfth century.[29]

The stone is very hard and resembles the microgabbro-diorite that
is found in central Ukraine. This find has been published several times.
One side of the axe displays a scratched figure of 'Our Lady of the Sign'
(37 mm high). Her hands are raised with the palms upwards and the

[28] K. Musianowicz, 'Sprawozdanie z prac wykopaliskowych w roku 1954 w
Drohiczynie pow. Siemiatycze', *Wiadomości archeologiczne*, 12, Warsaw, 1956, 2, pp.
343–44, table 46.
[29] See G. Iu. Ivakin, A. V. Chernetsov, 'Unikal'nyi amulet iz raskopok v Kieve', in
A. L. Toporkov, A. A. Turilov (eds), *Otrechennoe chtenie v Rossii XVII–XVIII vekov*,
Moscow, 2002, pp. 521–32.

Fig. 3. A polished stone Chalcolithic axe with later Christian motif, Kiev.

Fig. 4. Pattern outlining of the images on the stone axe (both from Ivakin, Chernetsov, 'Unikal'nyi amulet iz raskopok v Kieve', see footnote 29).

folds of the omophorion are well defined. Our Lady stands on a rectangular piece of fabric and wears a pectoral medallion featuring a schematic shoulder-length image of the infant Jesus. There is an MP monogram with a diacritic abbreviation mark to the left of her head. The other side features the archdeacon St Stephen wearing a long sticharion (30 mm high). On his right arm, which is slightly bent, he holds a thurible suspended on three chains. In his left hand he holds an object that is usually depicted in the pictures of this saint. Some scholars identify it as a martyr's crown, while others interpret it as a model of a church or pyx for consecrated bread, or a zion (a tabernacle for incense). The vertical inscriptions 'CTE' and 'ФANOC' flank the figure.

It is a well-known fact that in the early Iron Age and the medieval period stone implements were regarded as miraculous objects and could be used as amulets. In homilies and sermons they are called 'thunder arrowheads and axes, a wicked and ungodly thing'.[30] However, they were also in use in medieval Russia and could be decorated with motifs from Christian iconography as well.

A number of polished stone axes with images and inscriptions added much later have been described in earlier publications (examples come mainly from a publication by H. Obermeier). One of the axes carries a magical inscription in Greek and therefore can be categorized as a gnostic amulet.[31] This set of analogies can be enlarged by adding to the list a polished stone weapon featuring an image and a gnostic inscription described in a well-known paper by C. Bonner.[32]

More evidence of the re-use of prehistoric stone weapons in medieval Russia can be found in a fragment of a polished stone shaft-hole battle-axe dating to the Bronze Age discovered during excavations in the Tver' kremlin, a fragment of which was retrieved from the layers dating to the mid-fourteenth century. It is a fragment of a weapon made from white marl, a stone which is not suitable for making weapons. Apparently this artifact symbolized wealth and a high status. The surface of the stone axe is formed of facets, and its midrib running along the longitudinal axis of the axe imitates a casting joint. This weapon, made from a more archaic and cheaper material, is therefore an imitation of a more perfect and prestigious metal item (imitations of this type are well known to archaeologists). One of its facets carries letters of the Cyrillic script (the first few characters placed in alphabetical order) scratched

---

[30] N. I. Tolstoi, 'Gromovaia strela', in *Slavianskie drevnosti*, vol. 1, pp. 561–63; see also *Domostroi po Konshinskomu spisku i podobnym*, Moscow, 1908, p. 22.

[31] Ivakin, Chernetsov, 'Unikal'nyi amulet iz raskopok v Kieve', p. 526, drawing 21, 5.

[32] Bonner, *Studies in Magical Amulets*, p. 238, plate XXV, fig. 7 (Berlin museum).

on it in the fourteenth century.[33] The Cyrillic script on this prehistoric artifact seems to incorporate an object of superstitious worship into Christian culture, whereas the visualization of the alphabet reflects the perception of basic literacy elements as something sacral. It should be remembered that the so called 'alphabet prayer' is part of the medieval Slavic manuscript tradition.[34] Some other concepts related to stones, or other objects regarded as stones, are reviewed in my publication dedicated to a unique sorcerer's recipe from a manuscript dating to the first half of the sixteenth century discovered and published by A. A. Turilov.[35]

Gnostics gems could feature Greek and oriental deities depicted according to traditional iconography. At the same time, some of such gems display images that have no analogues in pictorial representations on any other objects. One of them is a very specific image of an anguiped, which is a snake-legged creature with a rooster's head; this creature wears armour and holds a whip and a shield in its hands.[36] Sometimes instead of a rooster's head the creature has a different zoomorphic head. Quite often this image is accompanied by the inscription Αβρασαξ (the sum of the numerical values of the letters in this name corresponds with the number of days in the year). In some cases, this image has an inscription that reads ΙΑΩ (cf. Yahweh). Such gems were still in use in the medieval period. Their impressions are found on wax and mastic seals applied to Russian documents. For example, this image can be seen on the seal affixed to the will of the Prince Ivan Iureevich Patrikeev written in 1498.[37] The seal belonged to his wife Ovdotiia. The zoomorphic head of the creature is indeterminable. Another similar seal was applied by the Prince P. I. Shuiskii to the charter of 1542.[38] The head of the creature is ornithomorphic with a pronounced rooster's

[33] T. V. Rozhdestvenskaia, 'Nadpisi na predmetakh', in *Tverskoi kreml'. Kompleksnoe arkheologicheskoe istochnikovedenie (po materialam raskopa Tverskoi kreml' 11, 1993–1997 gg.)*, St Petersburg, 2001, pp. 211, 214, fig. 2, 1.

[34] Ryan, *The Bathhouse at Midnight*, p. 293, note 2; K. Kuev, *Azbuchnita molitva v slavianskite literaturi*, Sofia, 1974.

[35] A. A. Turilov, 'Kamen' dlia vyzyvaniia dozhdia i vetra', *Zhivaia starina*, 2000, no. 3, pp. 16–18; A. V. Chernetsov, 'The Sorcerer's Stone: Magic of Water and Blood', *Russian History*, 40, 2013, pp. 515–31.

[36] Bonner, *Studies in Magical Amulets*, plate VIII, pp. 162–76; plate IX, pp. 177–85; Delatte, Derchain, *Les intailles magiques*, pp. 25–39, nos. 1–33; H. Mode, *Stwory mityczne i demony*, Warsaw, 1977 p. 222.

[37] *Sobranie gosudarstvennykh gramot i dogovorov*, Moscow, 1813, vol. 1, p. 338.

[38] P. Ivanov, *Sbornik snimkov s drevnikh pechatei, prilozhennykh k gramotam i drugim iuridicheskim aktam, khraniashchimsia v Moskovskom arkhive Ministerstva iustitsii*, Moscow, 1858, table V, 72; Nikolaeva, Chernetsov, *Drevnerusskie amulety-zmeeviki*, p. 114, table XXI, 4.

comb. The legend inscribed around the image is in Russian (apparently, the inscription was placed on a metallic setting of a signet ring into which an ancient carved stone was inserted). A collection of similar carved stones is known to have been owned by Catherine II.[39] In the first half of the nineteenth century sceptical scholars did not believe that these gemstones were ancient ('We must agree that archaeologists overestimated the importance of these gemstones' stated an encyclopedia entry in 1835)[40] and ascribed them to medieval artisans. It is difficult to say how the creature depicted on such gemstones was perceived in medieval Russia. Given its extremely specific and undoubtedly fantastic appearance, most likely it was interpreted correctly as magical.

Serpent amulets (*zmeeviki*) form the largest, and very important, proportion of Russian amulets in the context of religious and superstitious beliefs. [41]

Fig. 5. A stone serpent amulet from Suzdal' twelfth–thirteenth centuries Jasper (from Nikolaeva, Chernetsov, Drevnerusskie amulety-zmeeviki, see footnote 5).

The hypothesis of a linkage between serpent amulets and a gnostic legacy is the most convincing; one may cite as evidence the gnostic gemstones decorated with the head of the Gorgon Medusa[42] (there is no need to prove that the iconography of the serpent motif on such amulets is related to this figure from Greek mythology). The initial connection

---

[39] Ryan, *The Bathhouse at Midnight*, p. 221.

[40] 'Abraksas', in *Entsiklopedicheskii leksikon*, St Petersburg, 1835, vol. 1, p. 41.

[41] Nikolaeva, Chernetsov, *Drevnerusskie amulety-zmeeviki*; Ryan, *The Bathhouse at Midnight*, chapter 8, 6.6, pp. 241–53.

[42] Delatte, Derchain, *Les intailles magiques*, pp. 224–27, N 306–12.

between serpent amulets and specific female health problems is clear in the light of a frequently found Greek inscription associating this demonic creature with ὑστέρα, which means uterus (some Slavic texts and Russian serpent amulets use the word дъна that has the same meaning as the Greek word). Gnostic gemstones include a significant group of amulets that protect against these illnesses. The word inscribed on these amulets is μήτρα which is another Greek word for uterus. Such amulets feature a schematic motif representing this female organ.[43] It is difficult to describe it as anatomically precise; it is rather an ideogram or a pictogram, whereas the serpent motif is an allegorical representation of this organ.

More clarity on the original purpose of serpent amulets can be found in the publication of J. Spier who found a Byzantine bronze amulet depicting Christ healing the woman 'with an issue of blood' (Matthew 9: 20–22; Mark 5: 25–34). [44]

There is one more feature that links together serpent amulets and gnostic glyptics, namely Byzantine amulets with a scene featuring King Solomon (or some other character) depicted as a rider trampling down a female demon.[45] The female figure in this scene belongs to the same group of demons as the *hystera*-дъна, the *triasavitsa* fever demoness and the *nezhit*. Such images are not known in Russia while in Byzantium they are found as stand-alone scenes or in combination with a serpent motif.[46]

The serpent motif is not a mandatory feature of the serpent type of amulets which combine Christian and non-Christian (or apocryphal) motifs. M. N. Speranskii in his work compared the Byzantine amulet published by Charles du Cange with Russian serpent amulets.[47] The serpent motif does not appear on this amulet; instead, along with a scene featuring Our Lady and the St Seven Sleepers of Ephesus, it also displays St Sisinnius with Archangel Sikhail who is defeating (flagellating) naked shivering fevers (fever demons). The motif of seven sleepers supervised life-giving and peaceful sleep for the subject. For this reason, a famous folded icon made by the artisan Lukian dating

---

[43] Ibid., pp. 245–58, N 336–63; Bonner, *Studies in Magical Amulets*, plate VI, pp. 129–40; plate VII, pp. 141–47. On amulets with the inscription μητρα see M. I. Sokolov, 'Novyi material dlia ob"iasneniia amuletov, nazyvaemykh zmeevikami', in *Drevnosti. Trudy Slavianskoi komissii MAC*, Moscow, 1895, vol. 1, pp. 177–78.

[44] Spier, 'Medieval Byzantine Amulets', plate 3, d, N 38.

[45] A. V. Bank, 'Gemma s izozrazheniem Solomona', *Vizantiiskii vremennik*, 1956, no. 8, pp. 331–37; Spier, 'Medieval Byzantine Amulets', plate 6, e.

[46] Spier, 'Medieval Byzantine Amulets', plate 2, b, N 21; plate 3, a, N 33.

[47] M. N. Speranskii, 'O zmeevike s sem'iu otrokami', *Arkheologicheskie izvestiia i zametki*, Moscow, 1893, no. 2, p. 59.

to 1412 which depicts seven sleeping youths as well as Sisinnius and Sikhail might be ascribed to the same type of amulets.[48] Contemporary descriptors often include words that have lost links with their original meaning; for example, some 'deer-stones' (*stelae*) frequently found across the Eurasian steppe sometimes have no images of the deer at all.

Fig. 6. A Byzantine amulet featuring an angel beating demons who send ailments (from Speranskii, 'O zmeevike s sem'iu otrokami', see footnote 47).

A pectoral stone icon of the thirteenth century which is a peculiar analogy to serpent amulets because of Christian motifs on the front combined with a non-Christian symbol on the reverse (Fig. 7) was first published by A. S. Uvarov.[49]

He pointed out that this small icon depicting the ascension of Alexander the Great to heaven on the reverse side was used as a pendant to an icon in a cathedral in Zaraisk (which was a part of the Riazan' principality). Later scholars could not reference this artistic work because its location remained unknown. Later this icon was discovered in a Riazan' museum collection and was described in detail in the publication by T. M. Pankova[50] and, along with other contemporary

[48] T. V. Nikolaeva, 'Ikona-skladen' 1412 g. mastera Lukiana', *Sovetskaia arkheologiia*, 1968, no. 1, pp. 89–102; A. A. Turilov, 'K voprosu datirovki i proiskhozhdeniia skladnia mastera Lukiana', in *Neischerpaemost' istochnika. K 70-letiiu V. A. Kuchkina*, Moscow, 2005, pp. 151–60.

[49] A. S. Uvarov, 'Vzgliad na arkhitekturu XII veka v Suzdal'skom kniazhestve', in *Trudy I Arkheologicheskogo s"ezda v Moskve 1869*, Moscow, 1871, vol. 1, pp. 252–66 (p. 265).

[50] T. M. Pankova, 'O dvukh proizvedeniiakh melkoi kamennoi plastiki XII – nachala XIII veka (ob ikonakh domongol'skogo perioda s siuzhetami "Deisus. Voznesenie Aleksandra Makedonskogo", "Apostol Petr"', in *Trudy Riazanskogo gosudarstvennogo istoriko-arkhitekturnogo muzeia-zapovednika. Sbornik statei*, Riazan', 1998, pp. 138–48.

stone icons, in the publication by V. G. Putsko.[51] Pankova was the first to provide a detailed and exhaustive description. At the same time, the semantics of this mixture of the Christian motif on one side with the non-Christian depiction of the ascension of Alexander the Great depicted on the reverse side remains still unresolved.

Fig. 7. A pectoral stone icon depicting the ascension of Alexander the Great on the reverse side, Zaraisk (reproduced in Chernetsov, 'Polet Aleksandra Makedonskogo', see footnote 52).

The motif of the ascension of Alexander the Great to heaven was very popular in medieval Russia and reproduces Byzantine images.[52] One such object of Byzantine applied art dating to the thirteenth century is a silver cup featuring this motif which has been found in north-west Siberia.[53] In medieval Russia this scene was also depicted on the façade reliefs of the Cathedral of St Demetrius (1194–97) in Vladimir, on a gold diadem of the thirteenth century decorated with cloisonné enamel found near Kiev, on goldwork embroidery of the twelfth/thirteenth centuries on a shirt from a rich grave in the Cathedral of St Sophia in Novgorod and so on. It is also represented on

[51] V. G. Putsko, 'Iz istorii russkoi kamennoi plastiki XIII v.: riazanskie ikony s izobrazheniem Deisusa', in *Velikoe kniazhestvo Riazanskoe: istoriko-arkheologicheskie issledovanniia i materialy*, Moscow, 2005, pp. 569, 573–76.

[52] A. V. Chernetsov, '"Polet Aleksandra Makedonskogo": novye materialy k ikonografii', in *Moskovskaia Rus': problemy arkheologii i istorii arkhitektury*, Moscow, 2008, pp. 52–63.

[53] B. Marshak, M. Kramarovskii (eds), *Sokrovishcha Priob'ia*, St Petersburg, 1997, pp. 149–57.

a miniature from the Illustrated Chronicle of Ivan the Terrible.[54] It is important that this motif is depicted on the coins of the Grand Prince Boris Aleksandrovich of Tver' (1427–61),[55] which is evidence of its links with the state, monarchic symbolism (and monetary regalia).

Narrative scenes close to Byzantine prototypes, as well as those that bear the marks of the severe deterioration of the initial motif features, can be found among medieval Russia artifacts. The ascension of Alexander the Great as depicted on the pectoral icon in question is regarded as one of the closest to the Byzantine originals. It is interesting to note the absence of one element, namely the wheels of the chariot which is taking the 'aeronaut' up to the heaven. In this icon the central figure sits on something that resembles a box or a basket. Alexander is shown wearing a crown with tines which means that the depicted figure is a monarch. Small animals used as baits to lure griffins are shown as spoils of the chase; they hang with their heads down while the flying griffins stretch their necks towards them.

Alexander the Great is linked in a certain way with biblical tradition. This historical figure is mentioned in 1 Maccabees (1:5); this is an apocryphal book, though it is included in the Septuagint and the Slavic Bible. Versions of the *Alexander Romance* composed by an unknown writer designated subsequently as Pseudo-Callisthenes, which underwent changes in the medieval period, interpreted the story of this great conqueror in a Christian context. Some Byzantine emperors associated their activities with the deeds of this great conqueror of antiquity. At the same time, images of Alexander the Great in medieval Russia cannot be regarded as images of a saint (although in the Church calendar in the Ethiopian tradition Alexander is a righteous man).[56] According to a medieval legend, Alexander claimed to be the son of a pagan deity, and this tradition results in a clear pagan element in Alexander's image. Notably, in the first Slavic version of Palladius, *De gentibus Indiae et Bragmanibus*, the Slavic chief pagan deity is described as Alexander's father ('the son of the god, Great Porun (Perun), King Alexander, the ruler of all people'),[57] and in this text the name of

---

[54] St Petersburg, Rossiiskaia natsional'naia biblioteka, chronograph volume 17.17.97, f. 729v.

[55] A. V. Chernetsov, 'Types on Russian Coins of the XIV and XV centuries. An Iconographic Study', *British Archaeological Report (BAR)*, International series, 167, Oxford, 1983, pp. 71–72, plates VIII, 12, 13.

[56] S. B. Chernetsov. 'Puteshestvie Aleksandra Velikogo iz Ierusalima v raj i obratno', *Zhivaia starina*, 1997, no. 3, p. 28.

[57] V. Mansikka, *Religiia vostochnykh slavian*, Moscow, 2005, p. 223. The first edition of this work was published in German: V. Mansikka, *Die Religion der Ostslaven. I. Quellen*, Folklore Fellows Communications 43, Helsinki, 1922.

the Slavic deity corresponds to Zeus-Amon in the original version of the legend. Interestingly, B. A. Rybakov, who attempted to show the connections between the motif of the ascension of Alexander the Great and Slavic mythology, did not discuss this text and compared the image of the great conqueror with another Slavic deity — Dazhdbog (the god of the sun).[58] Meanwhile the aforesaid quotation and the likening of Alexander to the prophet Elijah in another text (see below) demonstrate that this Macedonian conqueror was probably associated with the Thunderer, chief of the pagan gods.

The question is how to explain and justify in theological terms the Alexander the Great motif combined with sacred images on the same object. The Zaraisk icon displays the Deisis on the front. Therefore, it shows three figures that are the most revered in Christianity. The importance of the images of Jesus Christ and Our Lady needs no comment. John the Baptist is also a figure of paramount importance because in the Scripture it is reported that 'among those that are born of woman there hath not risen a greater than John the Baptist' (Matthew 11: 11), and he appears as the prophet Elijah from the Old Testament risen from the dead (Matthew 11: 14; 17: 11–14; Mark 9: 11–13). St Thomas Aquinas declared that the wearing of medals bearing scriptural sacral quotations and images must not be confused with non-Christian symbols.[59] As a result, in accordance with this doctrine, the combination in question was condemned by medieval theologians.

The image of the ascension of Alexander the Great to heaven is typical of the so-called triumphal scenes which were common in medieval art.[60] A triumphal chariot is a key, though not a mandatory, element. Such images have been known in Russia since the eleventh century. Of particular note is a famous Kievan relief featuring a triumphal chariot of Dionysus (or Rhea-Cybele).[61] All scenes depicting the ascension of Alexander the Great as well as those with the chariots of the sun and the moon, which have been known in medieval Russia from the end of the fourteenth century,[62] are part of this group of narrative scenes.

---

[58] B. A. Rybakov, *Iazychestvo Drevnei Rusi*, Moscow, 1987, p. 640.

[59] Ryan, *The Bathhouse at Midnight*, p. 228.

[60] R. van Marle, *Iconographie de l'art profane au Moyen Age et à la Renaisance*, The Hague, 1931, 1932, vols 1–2; Hoffmann, *Die Welt der Spielkarte*, Leipzig, 1972, pp. 15–19, plates 14–19.

[61] A. V. Chernetsov, 'K interpretatsii odnogo rel'efa Lavrskoi tipografii', in *Kul'turnii shar. Statti na poshanu Gliba Iur'ovicha Ivakina*, Kiev, 2017, pp. 464–70.

[62] *Kievskaia Psaltyr' 1397 g.*, Moscow, 1979, fol. 188.

According to Pseudo-Callisthenes, the ascension of Alexander the Great was not a triumph in the full meaning of the word as it was a not very successful experience in aeronautics because it demonstrated Alexander's limited abilities. However, in medieval art this motif was definitely a manifestation of the triumph that glorified the great conqueror. In the Slavic version of the pseudo-Aristotelian *Secret of Secrets*, which dates to the fifteenth century, the ascension of Alexander the Great is directly associated with the ascension of the prophet Elijah to heaven in a chariot of fire ('some people say that he was exalted like [prophet] Elijah in the chariot'),[63] which apparently is a rethinking of this popular motif in works of art; the mention of a chariot is important. Interestingly, in this paragraph Alexander the Great has the sobriquet 'Two-Horned' which is consistent with the Arabic tradition according to which the great conqueror is called Iskander Zul-Qarnain or Zulqarnain (the Two-Horned One). The popularity of the prophet Elijah in the Christian world, and in particular in medieval Russia, was enormous. The ascension of the prophet Elijah to heaven in a chariot of fire is certainly close to the ancient and the medieval triumphal scenes.

In the Russian text dated to the twelfth century the griffin harnessed to Alexander's chariot was associated with an angel sent to carry the prophet Habakkuk to Daniel (Daniel 14:31–37, apocryphal part 'Bel and the Dragon'). The ascension of Alexander the Great in medieval iconography was a distinct apotheosis of monarchic power as evidenced by the reproduction of this motif on cathedral walls, diadems, and even on coins in Tver'.

However, the idea of the triumph that is undoubtedly present in the composition featuring the ascension of Alexander the Great as such does not offer an answer to the question why this motif is combined with venerated Christian images, or how this relates to the purpose of the icon. A plausible explanation is that the image of Alexander the Great is combined with the Deisis when the meanings of these images coincide in a particular context. The most likely reason for such coincidence is the apotropaic nature of the image which could be ascribed both to Christian and non-Christian motifs.

The image of Alexander the Great is frequently encountered in Russian magic texts related to warfare. For example, a number of incantations of a Christian nature directed against enemy weapons

---

[63] M. N. Speranskii, *Iz istorii otrechennykh knig. IV Aristotelevy vrata ili Tainaia Tainykh*, St Petersburg, 1908, p. 135. See the critical edition by W. F. Ryan and Moshe Taube of this text: *The Secret of Secrets: The East Slavic Version*, Warburg Institute Studies and Texts 7, London, 2019.

appear in manuscript collections of the first half of the seventeenth century and the 1730s as 'the prayer of Alexander of Macedon'.[64] The manuscript collection of the first half of the seventeenth century mentions invincibility as a quality of Alexander the Great ('you cannot destroy me and injure me as you could not destroy and injure King Alexander of Macedon'),[65] whereas the manuscript collection of the early eighteenth century originating in Siberia mentions his bravery and physical strength ('give me, my Lord [...] Alexander's bravery and strength').[66] The prayer asking the God to help Russian princes to acquire 'Alexander's bravery' re-occurs in some versions of the *Supplication* (var. *Epistle, Word) of Daniel the Exile*.[67]

The magical meaning of Alexander the Great is also reflected in a translated divination text included in the pseudo-Aristotelian *Secret of Secrets* known in Russia from the fifteenth century. The onomantic table in this treatise (onomantic tables use the numbers formed by the letters of the names of contestants or military commanders for predicting the outcome of a contest or a battle) contains the names of Alexander and his enemy King Porus of the Paurava kingdom symbolizing victory and defeat.[68] The legend of the battle between Alexander and Porus who died in this battle is present in the Russian versions of the *Alexandria* (the Slavic *Alexander Romance*), although in reality Porus was not killed and surrendered to Alexander. Similar narratives associated with Alexander the Great are found in other medieval traditions, for instance, a Syrian divination text of the twelfth century also mentions Alexander, although in this text his antagonist is another historical figure — the Persian King Darius.[69]

Perceptions of Alexander's invincibility are related to a legendary tale from the *Alexandria* and the *Physiologus* about the conqueror getting hold of the Gorgon head ('and Alexander got hold of it [the Gorgon head] and conquered all peoples').[70] The invulnerability and invincibility of Alexander were explained by the fact that he possessed the Gorgon head. This motif is known both in medieval Russian and Byzantine traditions.

[64] *Otrechennoe chtenie v Rossi, XVII–XVIII vekov*, Moscow, 2002, pp. 187, 208, 209, 332, 231.

[65] Ibid., p. 182.

[66] Ibid., p. 265.

[67] N. N. Zarubin, *Slovo Daniila zatochnika po redaktsiiam XII i XIII vv. i ikh peredelkam*, Leningrad, 1932, pp 34, 35, 73, 119.

[68] Ryan, *The Bathhouse at Midnight*, p. 315.

[69] Ibid., p. 316, n. 62.

[70] A. Karneev, *Materialy i zametki po literaturnoi istorii Fiziologa*, St Petersburg, 1890, p. xi.

This narrative directly links the image of Alexander the Great to the motif of the Gorgon head which appears on serpent amulets in a modified version. Since these characters to a certain extent are antagonists (like Perseus, Alexander beheads the Gorgon Medusa), this similarity has to be further examined and the links identified. According to late Greek sources, gorgons are water demons, the sisters of Alexander the Great.[71] The South Slavic version of this legend known from a Russian manuscript dating to the end of the fifteenth century gives an account of Alexander's daughter who came into the possession of life-giving water by deceit and became an immortal and invisible demon (the latter trait is quite consistent with the 'ugliness' of the Gorgon and the serpent motif). Subsequently Alexander's daughter became a *samovila*, which is a popular character of South Slavic folklore.[72]

Alexander, however, is not only the antagonist of the Gorgon but he also wears a Gorgoneion, which is an amulet that bears the head of a Gorgon; he can also act as her next of kin. A talisman depicting Alexander the Great, and in particular his ascension to heaven, was worn to render its possessor brave, invincible and invulnerable. These functions largely coincide with those of serpent amulets. The use of coins featuring Alexander the Great as protective amulets was mentioned in one of the texts written by John Chrysostom in the fourth century.[73]

Comparing the motif featuring the ascension of Alexander the Great and the compositions depicting serpents, we can say that the former was more prestigious, oriented to feudal (warrior) values and valour targeting directly the princely and boiar audience whereas, according to their original purpose, the scenes depicting serpents performed primarily protective, curative and physiological functions. This difference, however, is unlikely to have been fundamental from the point of view of amulet wearers. Indeed, serpent amulets could be owned by men, in particular, princes (for example, the famous Chernigov *grivna* (a *grivna* in medieval Russia is normally a silver ingot payment, but this is a *zmeevik* pendant dating to the end of the eleventh century that belonged to Vladimir Monomakh). T. V. Nikolaeva put forward convincing arguments in support of the use of some serpent amulets as special amulets for warriors.[74]

---

[71] Ryan, *The Bathhouse at Midnight*, p. 264, n.238.
[72] Ia. S. Lur'e, 'Literaturnaia i kul'turno-prosvetitel'naia deiatel'nost' Efrosina v kontse XV v.', *Trudy Otdela drevnerusskoi literatury Instituta russkoi literatury*, Leningrad, vol. 17, 1961, p. 162.
[73] Ryan, *The Bathhouse at Midnight*, p. 143.
[74] T. V. Nikolaeva, 'Zmeeviki s izobrazheniem Fedora Stratilata kak filakterii

It is significant that in the *Philopatris*, a tenth-century Byzantine satirical dialogue, the symbolism of the Gorgon head upon the Goddess Athena's breast manifests itself not only as something protective but also as ensuring victory in battle:

> 'What is the use of the Gorgon, and why does the goddess wear it on her breast?' — 'To intimicate and avert dangers; with its help Athena strikes terror in the hearts of her enemies and decides who will win [...]. The Gorgon [...] cannot, like gods, render help from afar, and can protect only the one who wears it.'[75]

This excerpt demonstrates the military symbolism of the Gorgon head motif and also gives valuable information on belief in the powerful properties of amulets depicting the Gorgon, and belief in chief deities living in the sky versus belief in mythological characters of lower ranking.

It should be noted that in a number of cases the image of Alexander the Great could be likened to the images of saints. For example, as attested in the chronicles, Prince Aleksandr Nevskii had the same name as Alexander the Great.[76] The images of the ascension of Alexander the Great depicted on the coins of Prince Boris Aleksandrovich of Tver' and the wax seal of the boiar Mikhail Aleksandrovich Nagoi that hangs on the charter of 1615[77] can be interpreted as patronymic images relating to the prince on whose behalf the coins were minted and the seal owner (both had the patronymic of Aleksandrovich). However, the image on the Zaraisk icon can hardly be regarded as a patronymic since the name of Aleksandr is not encountered among the names of the Riazan' princes (if we disregard princes of the appanage principality of Pronsk).

Another artifact that will be described below is a privately owned silver signet ring.[78] Its owner, G. I. Dagirov, who provided a photograph of the signet ring which was passed down to him from his family members, sought professional advice to clarify the dating of the signet ring and interpret the inscription on it. L. A. Zavadskaia from the State Hermitage Museum dated the signet ring to the sixteenth/seventeenth centuries and suggested it had been made by Western European artisans and that the Slav Cyrillic inscription had been added on the top of the

preimushchestvenno dlia voinov', in *Slovo o polku Igoreve i ego vremia*, Moscow, 1985.

[75] *Vizantiiskii satiricheskii dialog*, Leningrad, 1986, p. 10.

[76] PSRL, 1851, vol. 5, p. 176; PSRL, 1959, vol. 26, p. 77.

[77] Ivanov, *Sbornik snimkov s drevnikh pechatei*, tables IX, 18.

[78] See A. V. Chernetsov, 'Eshche odna Solomonova pechat'', *Zhivaia Starina*, 2004, no. 3, pp. 28–30.

ring later. I agree in general with this interpretation; in all likelihood, both the signet ring and the inscription it bears are dated to the middle or the second half of the seventeenth century.

R. M. Munchaev, a well-known Russian archaeologist, asked me to help in interpreting this inscription. A six-line inscription in an octagonal frame is on the reverse on the top of the signet ring:

Fig. 8. An inscription on the top of the silver ring (the text from Old Testament) (from Chernetsov, 'Eshche odna Solomonova pechat', see footnote 78).

TPEMI
ЗЫБЛЕТ
СЯ И ТРЯСЕ
ТСЯ А ЧЕТВ
ЕРЬТАГО НЕ
МОЖЕ

(The inscription, 'Треми зыблется и трясется, а четверьтаго не може', reads as, 'For three things [it] is disquieted and [it] quakes and for four it cannot [bear]'; there is an overdot after the last letter 'e' in the last line, possibly, replacing the word ending 'тъ'.)

It is fair to say that this inscription is an enigma. Taken at face value, it is incomprehensible; the subject in this phrase is absent; the meaning linked to the numerals 'three' and 'four' remains unclear. Apparently, what we have here is a play on words associated with number symbolism which was quite common in written traditions and folklore. Many nations have a huge number of sayings involving combinations of twosomes, threesomes (triads), foursomes, 'sevens', and so on. One can recall Russian proverbs such as: 'You can forgive three times, but the fourth time you must castigate', 'Measure seven times, and cut once'.

In the Russian written tradition number symbolism sometimes becomes exceptionally flowery. Writing his will in 1407, Cyprian, the Metropolitan of Kiev and all Rus', at the end of the document 'wrote philosophically': 'How the double collapsed, the triple was hidden soon, the fourth died, the fifth was breathless and turned to dust [...] Alas the double ten [twentieth] perished; the eighth following after the seventh demonstrates future decomposition.'[79] The overall meaning of this lamentation that 'everything will turn to dust and ashes' and explanation of all these 'threes' and 'tens' requires a sophisticated knowledge of the written traditions of that period.

Regarding the inscription on the signet ring which is modelled on the phrase 'three is this and this, and four is not possible'; or 'three is this and this, and four is even more so', we shall note its similarity with a well-known passage on Moscow as the third Rome which reads as follows: 'Two Romes have fallen. The third stands. And there will never be a fourth.' The owner of the signet seal was tempted to use this comparison as well; however, there is only a general similarity rather than a precise and unquestionable analogy.

A whole string of 'fours' (as well as 'threes') can be found in the 'Ascetic Discourses of Abba Isaiah to his Disciples' (known as the *Asceticon*), which is an early Christian text dating to the fourth century AD (The Seventh Discourse: On Virtues).[80] In the medieval Russian written tradition of the late seventeenth century there is a text which specifically focuses on 'fours'. It is 'Czwartak' (four things), a poem written by a Polish poet Jan Żabczyc and translated into Russian. The following maxim appears in this poem: 'Every person has four things he can never satisfy to the full: the ear, the tongue, the hand and also the

---

[79] *PSRL*, 1965, vol. 11, p. 197.
[80] *Dobrotoliubie. V russkom perevode sviatitelia Feofana, zatvornika Vyshenskogo.* expanded edition, Moscow, 2010, vol. 1, pp. 278–80. On the significance of the *Dobrotoliubie* (*Philokalia*) florilegium for later Orthodox piety and asceticism see *The Way of a Pilgrim and The Pilgrim Continues His Way*, trans. R. M. French, introduction Huston Smith, San Francisco, CA, 1991 (reprint of 1954 edition).

heart.'[81] However, these 'fours' which are typical products of Western rhetoric and scholastic, are not close analogies to the inscription on the signet ring.

The examination of all similar motifs in medieval writings naturally suggests that we should go to their source, that is, chapter 30 of the Proverbs of Solomon, where number symbolism is also well represented. In the aforesaid chapter we find the closest analogy to the inscription on the signet ring. It should be noted that in the ancient Hebrew (the Masoretic Text) and Protestant versions of the Bible this chapter is attributed to another author, Agur the son of Jakeh who 'spake unto Ithiel, even unto Ithiel and Ucal' (Proverbs 30:1). The Septuagint and the translation of the Bible into Church Slavonic do not contain this attribution. Therefore in medieval Russia this text was attributed to Solomon.

The biblical text explains what is meant in this case by the numbers 'three' and 'four'. The relevant biblical text is provided below (the English version is on the left, and the Church Slavonic version which is the Bible of 1581 printed by Ivan Fedorov in the town of Ostrog, Ukraine, is on the right):

21. For three things the earth is disquieted and for four which it cannot bear:
22. For a servant when he reigneth; and a fool when he is filled with meat;
23. For an odious woman when she is married and a handmaid that is heir to her mistress.

21. Треми трясется земля, четвертаго же не может понести:
22. Аще раб въцарится, и безумный исполнится пищею;
23. И раба, аще ижденет свою госпожду, и мръзка жена аще ключится добру мужу.

The inscription on the signet ring is, in fact, identical to the Church Slavonic text of the Bible, but still there are some significant differences that require explanation. The first feature is the absence of the subject 'the earth'. This can be explained by the intention to make the 'philosophical' inscription as mysterious as possible. The second less important feature is the word 'зыблется' (quakes) next to 'disquieted'; зыблется is a synonym used to make the text more expressive and can

---

[81] S. I. Nikolaev, 'Proizvedeniia Iana Zhabchitsa v russkikh perevodakh XVII v.', *Trudy otdela drevnerusskoi literatury*, Leningrad, 1981, vol. 36, pp. 163–92.

also be taken as a hidden allusion to the missing word 'earth', as the Church Slavonic letter 'з', which the word 'зыблется' begins with, is called 'земля' (earth). These deviations from the biblical text, however, do not affect the interpretation of the inscription on the signet ring.

A possible interpretation of this inscription is the glorification of virtue. The inscription was, probably, selected based on some particular circumstances of the life of the signet ring owner (verse 23). Condemnation of impostors of the Time of Troubles (verse 22) is a possible political allusion. It seems that the quotation from the book attributed to King Solomon inscribed on the signet ring was intended to make this signet ring resemble the legendary Seal of Solomon that Solomon used to command demons and genies. In medieval Russia such legends were widespread; some seals associated with the names of King David[82] and King Solomon are known (they depict Solomon's Wise Judgment; I Kings 3: 16–28);[83] as well as a magical square containing a palindrome:

Fig. 9. Motifs associated with legendary rings of biblical kin:
1. Solomon's Wise Judgment on the top of the seal ring of the seventeenth century (from Snimki drevnikh russkikh pechatei, see footnote 83);
2. A lead seal of Dmitrii Donskoi (1359–89) with a scriptural quotation ascribed to King David (from Ianin, 'Redchaishii pamiatnik moskovskoi sfragistiki XIV v.', see footnote 83).

[82] V. L. Ianin, 'Redchaishii pamiatnik moskovskoi sfragistiki XIV v.', in Kratkie soobshcheniia Instituta istorii material'noi kul'tury, Moscow, 1954, vyp. 53, pp. 148–50; A. A. Turilov, ' "Vse sia minet". Otgoloski legendy o tsare Davide v russkoi sfragistike i knizhnosti', in Slaviane i ikh sosedi, Moscow, 1994, vyp. 5, pp. 107–13; A. V. Lavrent'ev, 'Pechat' velikogo kniazia Dmitriia Ivanovicha Donskogo i russkie fobii XIV v.', Studia Slavica et Balcanica Petropolitana, 19, 2016, 1, pp. 110–30.
[83] Ivanov, Sbornik snimkov s drevnikh pechatei, plate 19, 315; Snimki drevnikh russkikh pechatei, Moscow, 1882, plate 114.

S A T O R
A R E P O
T E N E T
O P E R A
R O T A S

This is known in Russia as the Seal of Solomon.[84] As we have seen, some inserts on the Byzantine seal rings depicted King Solomon. As the legend has it, Solomon (Sulaymān in Arabic tales) commanded demons with the help of his ring. Images of the demons that Solomon summoned and made do his bidding are known both in the Western European tradition[85] and the Eastern tradition (the image engraved on the insert for the seal ring).[86] The motif of Solomon commanding demons vividly manifested itself in a Russian spell of the first half of the seventeenth century: 'King Solomon ruled forty satans, those forty satans had fire burning in their mouths, let the heart of this God's servant burn like this [...].'[87] The magic Sator square, as explained by a Russian sorcerer who lived in Kursk province at the end of the nineteenth century, contains an incantation in the 'Egyptian' language that is not comprehensible to anyone.[88] Meanwhile transparent words — 'tenet', 'opera', 'sator' — clearly indicate that the talisman is of Latin origin.

The seals of Solomon in medieval Russia are notable in that some of such seals carry a misspelled word, i.e. TERET instead of TENET (from Latin *tenere* — to hold).[89] The most plausible explanation of this conversion of N into R is a flawed version of the imprint originating from a Glagolitic source (in the Glagolitic script the letter Ⱂ which stands for N resembles the Russian letter R [Р]). Since Glagolitic books were rewritten in the Cyrillic script not later than the eleventh century; this mistake shows that the Seal of Solomon came to medieval Russia with the adoption of Christianity and the spread of Slavic writings.

---

[84] A. I. Sobolevskii, *Perevodnaia literatura Moskovskoi Rusi XIV–XVII vv.*, St Petersburg, 1903, p. 226; W. F. Ryan, 'Solomon, SATOR, Acrostics and Leo the Wise in Russia', *Oxford Slavonic Papers*, new series 19, 1986, pp. 46–61; Ryan, *The Bathhouse at Midnight*, pp. 431–33.

[85] Émile Angelo Grillot de Givry, *Le Musée des sorciers, mages et les alchemists*, Paris, 1927, p. 90, fig. 70, p. 93, figs 71, 72.

[86] E. C. F. Babelon, *La Gravure en pierres fines camées et intailles*, Paris, 1894, p. 204, fig. 154.

[87] Toporkov (ed.), *Russkie zagovory*, p. 106.

[88] Speranskii, 'O zmeevike', p. 51, n.3.

[89] A. A. Romanov, *Drevnerusskie kalendarno-khronodicheskie istochniki XV–XVII vv.*, St Petersburg, 2002, p. 64.

The magic inscription in question was used in the medieval period throughout many centuries and was written with letters of various scripts.[90] This runic inscription has been made, for instance, on a silver vessel of the eleventh century found on the island of Gotland.[91]

The suggested earlier date of the appearance of the Sator square in medieval Russia corrects some misconceptions about the earliest Slavonic texts. Indeed, the latter included mainly *minimum minimorum* of the Byzantine tradition, that is Christian liturgical texts intended, primarily, for monastic use. Interestingly, elements of an occult nature became entangled in this quasi-clerical tradition from the very beginning as evidenced not only by the Seal of Solomon. From the eleventh century, serpent amulets with a Greek magic inscription (incantations against diseases) which were of Byzantine origin became common in Russia. A Slavic version exists of this incantation dating to the eleventh century in Glagolitic script.[92]

The magic force attributed in Russia to the Seal of Solomon is described in a book of home remedies of the seventeenth century:[93] 'Anyone who writes wonderful words from the Seal of Solomon on his hand with the blood of a bat and lays this hand upon a sleeping person [...] will be liked by this person as he wishes.'[94] The key text of Russian late medieval occultism ('[When'] Solomon [...] was strengthened in his kingdom', II Chronicles 1: 1) gives a detailed account of the Seal of the King.[95] In this case, the book mentions a ring decorated with a stone (called *anthrax*, which is the Greek word for coal) with a carved inscription. This complex text with many coded abbreviations and cabbalistic numbers demonstrates the importance attached to the Seal of Solomon in medieval Russia and at the same time demonstrates the difficulties faced by scholars in interpreting such texts and objects.

(Translated by L. I Matkina)

---

[90] Ryan, *The Bathhouse at Midnight*, p. 302.

[91] A. Andersson, *Medieval Drinking Bowls of Silver Found in Sweden*, Stockholm, 1983, pp. 56, 85, plate 15F.

[92] Nikolaeva, Chernetsov, *Drevnerusskie amulety-zmeeviki*, pp. 17, 49, 50.

[93] Moscow, Rossiiskaia gosudarstvennaia biblioteka, f. 310, Undolskii collection, no. 696.

[94] A. L. Toporkov, 'Sueveriia v lechebnikakh XVII–XVIII vv.' in *Otrechennoe chtenie v Rossii XVII–XVIII vekov*, Moscow, 2002, pp. 376–93 (p. 381).

[95] Sobolevskii, *Perevodnaia literatura Moskovskoi Rusi*, p. 428.

Animal Magic: Uses and Abuses in Muscovite Rituals and Spells

Valerie A. Kivelson
University of Michigan

Spell so that your horse doesn't run away: Feed bread to your
horse and say: 'As this stone doesn't move from its place,
so may the horse not leave me, forever and ever.'
Olonetskii sbornik (second quarter, 17th century)

There is a sacred sea-ocean, and in that sacred sea-ocean is
a stone, in the depths of the sea. Under that stone stands a
pike-fish made of iron, and her teeth are iron. She eats up
the sea foam, and just so may that pike eat up cunning
women and witches, and sorcerers, both black and red.
Olonetskii sbornik (second quarter, 17th century)

And as the cuckoo bird grieves for her nestlings and
cries for them, so may that female slave of god
grieve and cry for me.
(1663)

And he told him to say the incantation while taking
an eye from a live chicken. Then he should crush it
and give it to women to drink.
(1668/69)[1]

THE *Volkhovnik*, a book of divination condemned by the mid-sixteenth
century Stoglav Church Council, described omens associated with
cats. The seventeenth-century *Zhitie* of Sergei Nuromskii mentioned
that devils had a habit of taking the form of cats. These nuggets, along
with other feline-related beliefs and practices, we know thanks to a
festschrift article that our current honouree, W. F. Ryan, offered to
his friend and colleague John Simmons in 2005. A short piece, 'Russia
and the Magic of Cats' is filled with the astonishing range, profound
erudition, warmth and humour characteristic of Will Ryan in his

---

[1] A. L. Toporkov (ed.), *Russkie zagovory iz rukopisnykh istochnikov XVII–pervoi
poloviny XIX v.*, Moscow, 2010, pp. 113–14, no. 53; p. 135, no. 114; Moscow, Rossiiskii
gosudarstvennyi arkhiv drevnikh aktov (hereafter RGADA), f. 210, Prikaznyi stol, stlb.
653, l. 29; Sevskii stol, ed. khr. 230, l. 2.

magisterial work and in his personal interactions. In the spirit of fun so palpable in Will's publications, and as a tribute to a valued friend and respected colleague, I offer this exploration of animals in Russian spells in the seventeenth and early eighteenth centuries.[2]

Cats, Ryan notes, appear rarely in Russian magical spells. Given this dearth, he will surely appreciate a spell from the second half of the seventeenth century that offers protection from 'tom cats and female cats and kittens', along with other dangerous beings such as sorcerers, spell-casters, malevolent people, 'pigs and piglets, dogs and puppies, all kinds of birds and beasts'. A scary list indeed.[3]

While cats (and kittens) play only a minor role in the Russian magical canon, other animals occupy prominent positions. An examination of about 200 spells from the seventeenth century determines that over a third involve animals in one way or another. Of those included in A. L. Toporkov's collection of spells from manuscript sources, the *Olonetskii* collection, with 132 spells in total, includes 42 referring to animals; a book of cures (*lechebnik*) from the 1670s refers to animals in seven of its twenty-six articles; and the spell book of Semen Vasil'evich Aigustov from his 1688–89 trial mentions animals in nine of its sixteen spells.[4] Animals were star players on the magical stage.

Many spells are directed toward animals, that is, animals are their object. Such spells promise to keep livestock from straying, to find missing animals, to prevent wolves or other predators from attacking flocks. Others invoke animals as mythic beings, like the iron pike-fish of my epigraph. These fabulous creatures may serve as animal helpers, devouring ailments or driving off hostile forces. A third group of spells developed the human-animal bond more profoundly, and touchingly. These spells, exemplified by the third of our epigraphs, folded the animal world into the human, eliminating any categorical separation between the two. They drew on a shared experience of love, sorrow and

[2] W. F. Ryan, 'Russia and the Magic of Cats', *Solanus*, new series, 19, 2005, pp. 7–13. See also his *The Bathhouse at Midnight: An Historical Survey of Magic and Divination in Russia*, University Park, PA, 1999, pp. 282–85.

[3] Ryan, 'Russia and the Magic of Cats', p. 9 n.11. Toporkov (ed.), *Russkie zagovory*, p. 345 no. 4.

[4] Ibid., pp. 87–144, 324-30, 331–41. The other seventeenth-century texts included in this anthology have fewer spells, but mention animals in half of their entries. The 200 spells are assembled from Toporkov's publications of texts, texts published by N. Ia. Novombergskii in the early twentieth century, my own archival work, and scattered texts published in other works, including Ryan's. See N. Ia. Novombergskii, *Koldovstvo v Moskovskoi Rusi XVII vek*, St Petersburg, 1906; idem., *Materialy po istorii meditsiny v Rossii*, 4 vols, St Petersburg, 1905; idem., *Vrachebnoe stroenie v do-Petrovskoi Rusi: Materialy po istorii meditsiny v Rossii*, vol. 4, Tomsk, 1907.

loss. The anguish of a mother cuckoo bird as she grieves for her lost chick, or of a mare as she mourns the loss of her foal, are summoned to evoke the equivalent sentiment in the human target. There is something beautiful and moving in this comprehension of a unified biosphere, in which humans resist the urge to lord it over the natural world. The poetics of animal emotion shows a kind of empathy, a recognition of kinship, that connect humans with the creatures around them.

If the first three categories of animal-related spells suggest an integrated natural world in which humans lived at one with nature, aware of the dangers each posed to the other but equally aware of each other's needs and feelings, the fourth category of spells confounds that harmonious picture. These spells required animals, or more commonly animal parts, as elements of their ritual enactment. These animal sacrifices may involve explicit acts of cruelty, such as the requisite 'eye from a live chicken' demanded in the 'spell for women' quoted in the epigraph. Others merely called for animal body parts — bears' heads or paws, eagles' eyes or feathers or talons, reptiles' skins — without specifying the particular means for obtaining them. Here animals figure as resources to be killed, dismembered, utilized. They suggest not oneness with but domination over nature. In these spells, the practitioners assert an unquestioned right to kill, dissect, and exploit fish and fowl, cattle and 'every creeping thing that creepeth upon the earth', in whatever way suits their purpose.[5]

In the remainder of this paper, I will expand on each of these four aspects of animal magic. The specific examples examined here all derive from manuscripts of the seventeenth and very early eighteenth centuries, although, as Will Ryan reminds us, many of the same tropes and practices continued into the nineteenth and early twentieth centuries, and some even to today. Toward the end of the paper, I will situate this inquiry in the historical debates about human-animal relations, and then turn in closing to questions of meaning and consider what, if anything, this variety of attitudes can tell us about Muscovites views of themselves and the natural world.[6]

---

[5] The fundamental expression of this position of absolute dominance over nature in the Christian tradition is set forth in Genesis 1:26–28.

[6] In the relatively undeveloped field of Russian animal studies, a pioneering work is Jane Costlow and Amy Nelson (eds), *Other Animals: Beyond the Human in Russian Culture and History*, Pittsburgh, PA, 2010. In the even less developed area of Muscovite animal studies, the key contributions to date come from Charles Halperin and Ann M. Kleimola: Charles J. Halperin, 'Royal Recreation: Ivan the Terrible Goes Hunting', *Journal of Early Modern History*, 14, 2010, pp. 293–316; idem., 'Did Ivan IV's *Oprichniki* Carry Dogs' Heads on Their Horses?', *Canadian-American Slavic Studies*, 46, 2012, pp. 40–67; Ann M. Kleimola, 'Good Breeding, Muscovite Style:

Spells Directed toward Animals

The first category of spells, those in which animals were the primary object of concern, generally aspired to protect precious domestic animals from the depredations of other creatures, people, or circumstances, such as disease or loss. Ryan quotes a lovely one from the *Olonetskii* spell book, which protects cattle from danger. Arising before dawn, the owner should walk around his cattle three times, holding a spear that had penetrated a bear, and recite: 'May an iron fence encircle my herd, as many as are sent [...]. My cattle, may you look like tree stumps, logs and stones to all black, grey and hunting wild beasts, from this day for the whole summer until the first snow.'[7] Another from the same spell book appeals for protection 'from any black or grey beast, and from the lion'. It calls on Jesus Christ to protect the spellcaster's 'horses and cows, sheep, and goats and any mute creature', and to raise his right hand to guard those flocks from 'any ferocious creature, from the lion and the wolf, from the bear, from all sorts of rioters and thieves'. It appeals to St George to call off his 'grey and black hounds, and to put them in iron chains and to hold them back'.[8]

Protective spells and rites to protect livestock were often performed on 6 May, St Egor's Day, the first day cattle could be driven out to pasture each spring. A spell book turned in as evidence in a trial in 1688–89 dictated the following words and ritual:

> Cut two switches from a year-old willow tree and take some moss from a church and feed it to your cattle. And drive the cattle out on Egor's Day, and go around with an icon and candles. And take some wool from each animal and touch it with a cross, and let them graze together. [And say:] 'As that wool will never scatter for all eternity, so may my livestock never scatter, for all eternity.' And when you start to drive them out, drive the animals forward, poke them with two of the switches and drive them forward with a third.[9]

"Horse Culture" in Early Modern Rus", *Forschungen zur osteuropäischen Geschichte*, 50, 1995, pp. 199–238; idem., 'Hunting for Dogs in Seventeenth-Century Rus', *Kritika: Explorations in Russian and Eurasian History*, 3, 2010, pp. 467–88; idem., '"Ni pes ni vyzhlets ni gonchaia sobaka": Images of Dogs in Rus', in Brian Boeck, Russell E. Martin and Daniel Rowland (eds), *Dubitando: Studies in History and Culture in Honor of Donald Ostrowski*, Bloomington, IN, 2012, pp. 427–42, and Charles J. Halperin and Ann M. Kleimola, 'Beastly Humans and Humanly Beasts in Seventeenth-Century Russia', *Vivliofika: E-Journal of Eighteenth-Century Russian Studies*, 6, 2018, pp. 46–57.

  [7] Ryan, *The Bathhouse at Midnight*, p. 195.
  [8] Toporkov (ed.), *Russkie zagovory*, p. 115 no. 56, see also p. 101 no. 25, p. 116 no. 57.
  [9] Valerie A. Kivelson and Christine D. Worobec (eds), *Witchcraft in Russia and Ukraine: A Sourcebook, 1000–1930*, Ithaca, NY, 2020, p. 324; see also Toporkov (ed.), *Russkie zagovory*, p. 336 no. 8.

More specific spells could be used to ensure that a new-born foal would live or to revive one born dead, to make sure a horse would not run away or jump over one's fence.[10]

Sometimes the danger posed to domestic animals and livestock might derive from human malice, as seen in a feud that landed two dragoons from Sokol'skoi *ostrog* in court in 1660. A certain Fedor Koloukhov reported that his fellow dragoon Karpik Lomakin had threatened him with a curse, apparently blaming Koloukhov for the death of his chickens. Koloukhov testified that:

> Karp brought to me a dead chick. He appeared and said, 'Whoever would harm my nestling should know that I will protect that nestling. I will bury this chick in the ground and place a candle on it, and the one who harmed my nestlings will die just like this chick.' And that's what I heard.[11]

Suspicion of magical assault on livestock was common enough, or at least credible enough that religious authorities expressed concern and tried to root out the problem. A mid-sixteenth-century confessional guide recommended that priests inquire of their parishioners: 'Have you bewitched a person or animal to cause them death, or have you bewitched grain?'[12]

Yet another group of spells directed toward animals, in this case not domestic but wild ones, were the ever-popular spells for successful hunting, fishing and trapping, such as the following from 1688–89:

> As you flow swiftly, glorious River Luzha, as you flow quickly, day and night, not hearing and not stopping, without twists and turns, all the way to the glorious ocean-sea, so may the white beasts — hares and red foxes and black martens, without hearing and without stopping, without twists and turns, day and night, run into my silken winding traps. Like you, glorious Luzha River, never turn away from the ocean-sea and without hearing and without stopping, without twists or turns, day and night, so may the white beasts, hares, and red foxes and black martens not turn from and not hear and not stop until they run into my silken traps.[13]

---

[10] Toporkov (ed.), *Russkie zagovory*, p. 119 nos. 68, 69, 70, p. 120 nos. 71, 72, p. 325 no. 6.

[11] RGADA, f. 210, Prikaznyi stol, stlb. 595, ll. 599–626. Quotation on l. 605.

[12] Kivelson, Worobec, *Witchcraft in Russia and Ukraine*, p. 104.

[13] Ibid., pp. 322–33, 431–32; Toporkov (ed.), *Russkie zagovory*, p. 335, no. 6, p. 321 no. 1, pp. 357–58 nos. 1–2, p. 427 no. 4.

Animals, of course, could endanger not only livestock and crops but humans themselves. A sizable subset of spells confronted the problem of snake bites. A spell against snake bite written in Karel'sko-Vepskian language, but included in the Russian *Olonetskii* collection, addresses the snake:

> Reptile, reptile, I know, reptile, snakes in a faraway land: the female snake is your mother; the chief snake is your father with his blue head. The mother snake slithers into a hole in the ground. In the heart of the stone, you build your home. With this silken belt I will remove your pain, in the heart of the stone I will place it, your wound in a tussock with willow.[14]

Spells also targeted animals less ferocious than the lions and bears and hostile neighbours mentioned above, but equally dangerous and equally feared. Numerous spells promised to stop worms from feasting on cabbage plants, mice from devouring stored harvests, or ants from whatever mischief they might wreak.[15] The humble ant shows up in a surprising number of spells. Anthills featured as auspicious sites for the performance of magical rituals.

This more or less exhausts the spells directed toward animals, whether protectively, defensively, or reactively. These, clearly, were the bread-and-butter spells in a world where livestock provided many of the valuable calories and much of the labour power required for subsistence, and where predatory and destructive wildlife, from wolves to ants, threatened survival of both humans and livestock.

Animals as Mythic Beings

If the spells directed toward animals reflect the very real concerns of a society reliant on agriculture and animal husbandry, they also draw on the mythical imagery and language that make the Russian magical tradition so fantastical and lyrical. Here animals take on a very different role. Rather than being the passive targets of magic, they elevate the tone and substance of the spells, they transport the action to a fabulous folkloric realm. They invoke imaginary creatures such as the 'Sirin' or Paradise bird, or a golden squirrel, or 'a basilisk, an asp, a snake that looks like a cloud, a snake that slithers up an oak tree, a fiery snake, a hairy snake, [...] a woman-eating snake, a copper Echidna-

---

[14] Ibid., pp. 132–33 no. 109, translation into Russian provided. On snake bites see also p. 328 no. 18; p. 329 no. 21, p. 330 no. 26, p. 367, p. 369 no. 2.

[15] Ibid., p. 119 nos 66, 67, p. 120 no. 84 (commentary on pp. 245–46), p. 124 no. 84, p. 130 no. 103, pp. 139–40, no. 121. anthills: p. 111 no. 45, p. 325 no. 3, p. 328 no. 19.

snake'.[16] These creatures may simply set the scene, or they may perform key functions, animating or realizing the spell's action. These spells are so enchanting that it is hard to limit oneself to only one or two. A simple spell to heal wounds, for instance, requires that the following be repeated three times:

> Across the sea, across the blue sea, stands the oak of moist mother earth. Up flies an eagle, across the blue sea. In its claws it carries a golden needle, in its wings, silken thread. It sews up and bewitches away all wounds, whether wooden or iron, and with whispered spells, all injuries.[17]

Another, again translated from Karel'sko-Vepskian, develops the poetry of these mythic creatures more extensively. Intended as a means to cure stomach pain, the spell invokes a ritual threesome of marvellous beasts:

> From the black sea emerges a black horse with hooves of iron, and the black horse kicks with iron hooves, and the sufferer will hear that he has recovered his health [...]. From the black sea emerges a big black dog with teeth of copper, and with teeth of copper the big black dog bites the person suffering from pain in his stomach, and let him hear, the sufferer, that he has recovered his health [...].
> From the black sea emerges a black falcon with golden talons, with a golden beak. The falcon beats the sufferer with its golden talons and its golden beak, so that the one suffering from pain in his stomach recovers his health. Bone to bone, vein to vein, sinew to sinew, seventy lived as one.[18]

Like the obliging creatures in this spell, mythic animals often bring about the desired result. Animals proved particularly helpful in the constant struggle with *gryzha*, that is, hernias. Remedies for *gryzha* in children and adults abound in Muscovite healing practices and spell books. Folk healers might succeed in 'untying' hernias, though sometimes they came under suspicion of having 'tied the hernia on' in

---

[16] Kivelson, Worobec, *Witchcraft in Russia and Ukraine*, p. 345; Toporkov (ed.), *Russkie zagovory*, pp. 128–29 no. 98, p. 367, p. 369 no. 2.

[17] Ibid., p. 98 no. 17. See also, ibid., p. 96 no. 9. Early eighteenth-century examples are also quite common. See, for instance, Kivelson, Worobec, *Witchcraft in Russia and Ukraine*, pp. 340–47, 443. On mythic animals in other contexts, see Ol'ga Valdislavovna Belova, *Slavianskii bestiarii. Slovar' nazvanii i simvoliki*, Moscow, 2001; Aleksandr Viktorovich Gura, *Simvolika zhivotnykh v slavianskoi narodnoi traditsii*, Moscow, 1997; E. V. Pchelov, *Bestiarii moskovskogo tsarstva: zhivotnye v emblematike moskovskoi Rusi kontsa XV–XVII vv.*, Moscow, 2011.

[18] Toporkov (ed.), *Russkie zagovory*, pp. 107–08 no. 36.

the first place.[19] Often the cure involved a spell that implores a magical beast eat up or gnaw away (*gryzhit'*) the hernia. 'There is a whale-fish in the depths of the sea, and it eats up hernia and illness from slave of God So-and-so.'[20] In the same voracious spirit, the iron-pike of the epigraph devours witches and ill-wishers with her iron teeth to protect the spell-caster from harm.

Animal Qualities and Animal Emotions as Magical Power
Spells frequently build analogies to work their magic, and animal imagery abounds in these analogies. 'Like ferocious bees root about and swarm, so may buyers swarm these merchants for their goods.'[21] Sometimes they pack the animal analogies in as thick and fast as the swarms of bees just mentioned:

> Make my enemies as meek as sheep before a wolf. Make me strong against them like the lion and the wolf, pouncing and roaring at them [...]. May they have the tongues of oxen and the whiskers and mind of a grouse. May they panic like a grey hare, and may they run from me like grey hare and sheep, and I would chase after them like the grey wolf, and bite them on their hind legs.[22]

Most interesting, perhaps, of the uses of animals in spells is the evocation of animals' (imputed) emotional states. Beyond colourful similes and references to characteristic traits such as ferocity or timorousness, spells also draw force from animals' interiority. This pattern shows up most commonly in love spells and the class of spells called 'spells to power', that is, spells intended to win the mercy or even the love of powerful people. In these verses, the love and longing, grief and anguish of mother animals upon losing their offspring is turned to the interest of the spell-caster. The spell's target should pine and weep except in the presence of the spell-caster. By the same token, the target should revel in the spell-caster's company, as animals rejoice in the natural richness of their environment.

---

[19] RGADA f. 210, Prik. Stol., stlb. 268, ll. 209–2280b.; Prikaznyi stol, st. 564, ll. 197–209; Kivelson, Worobec, *Witchcraft in Russia and Ukraine*, pp. 213–20.

[20] Toporkov (ed.), *Russkie zagovory*, p. 134 no. 111. See also ibid., p. 361.

[21] Ia. A. Kantorovich, *Srednevekovye protsessy o ved'makh. Reprintnoe vosproizvedenie izdaniia 1899 goda*, Moscow, 1990, pp. 173–74; Novombergskii, *Koldovstvo*, pp. 112–34, no. 33; Ryan, *The Bathhouse at Midnight*, p. 199; L. N. Maikov, *Velikorusskoe zaklinanie. Sbornik L. N. Maikova*, 1869, reprint, St Petersburg, 1994, no. 326.

[22] Toporkov (ed.), *Russkie zagovory*, p. 125 no. 87. See also ibid., pp. 125–26 no. 88, pp. 315–17 no. 1, p. 346 no. 5.

A spell addressed to the tsar and authorities contained in the *Olonetskii* spell book develops the joyous side:

> As a bird sings as it soars through the fresh air, rejoicing in the morning sunrise and the red sun and the white world, and as any beast in the field cries out in joy, and as a fish rejoices in the water, and as any animal moving on earth rejoices, so may they [powerful people] take joy in me, slave of God So-and-so. Amen.[23]

A spell book from the second half of the seventeenth century develops the theme of inconsolable animal grief and yearning in a spell to power:

> There is on this earth a stone asp, and to that stone asp swallows fly. They fly to their nests and to their babies, who have flown away. As swallows cannot forget their nests or their nestlings, so may princes and boiars and magnates and all Orthodox Christians be unable to forget me, slave of God So-and-so.[24]

These two affective vocabularies — of joy and anguish — structure most spells to power and spells for love and sexual passion. Both rest on an understanding that animals and humans share a common emotional life, the strands of which can be braided across species' lines. Emotion can even be gathered up from animals across the globe and injected in a concentrated dose into a human victim. 'A spell to send misery to a girl', jotted down in Semen Aigustov's notebook in 1688 or 1698, worked according to this principle:

> You, Woe (*toska*), go around the hamlets and villages and collect the grief from every kind of livestock, and from every wild beast, and from every person, and from every grass or plant, and from every flower, and from every reptile. Bring that grief and woe to the slave of God So-and-so. Set fire to her heart with her liver and her hot blood for me, So-and-so, every day and every hour, from sunrise to sunset.

Further elaborating the varieties of misery and woe common to humans and animals, the spell continues, enumerating further hardships drawn from the animal world:

---

[23] Ibid., p. 106 no. 32. See also, p. 344 no. 2, and A. L. Toporkov, 'Verbal Charms against Authorities and Judges in Seventeenth- and Eighteenth-Century Russia', in *Witchcraft Casebook: Magic in Russia, Poland, and Ukraine, 15th–21st Centuries, Russian History/Histoire russe*, 40, 2013, 3–4, pp. 532–39.

[24] Toporkov (ed.), *Russkie zagovory*, p. 343 no. 1.

In an oak tree on Oak island in the ocean sea sits a bird without feathers or wings. Fly to her, bird, many birds, bring her woe, keys. As breathless and bitter as birds without feathers, without wings, just so breathless and just so bitter should that slave of God So-and-so be for me, slave of God So-and-so, and as breathless and bitter as a beluga-fish in a river without water, just so airless, just so bitter may that slave So-and-so be for me, for slave So-and-so.[25]

Fantastic scenarios like those conjured forth by these spells demand empathy with non-human creatures. They represent sympathetic interpretation of the joys and suffering, both physical and psychic, of wild animals. Without anthropomorphizing the creatures of the air, forest and river, the spells reflect imaginative forays into the hearts and minds of animals. They respect the creatures' emotional experiences in terms appropriate to each species (birds long to fly; fish need water to breathe, beasts flourish in open spaces) but with an essence that is transferrable to human beings. A lovely spell from the late seventeenth or early eighteenth century underscores the comparability and transferability of human and animal longings and desires:

Like a little baby pines for its mother, reaching out for her in the daytime, waking in the night for its mother's breast, and like a fish longs for water, and like a beast for the forest, and like a caged bird pines for the open air, and like a person in prison yearns for release, and like a dear friend longs for another, and cries, and grieves, so may that beautiful girl So-and-so.[26]

The girl, the prisoner, the infant, the bird, the fish and the beast all long for love and freedom and to be at home in their element. Such cross-species empathy and awareness of a shared, exchangeable set of needs and desires sometimes opens ideas of reciprocity between humans and animals. For instance, a spell intended to protect fields from the depredations of birds offers mutual assurances of non-aggression:

You, birds of Christ, swift hunting dogs, you have your own property (*sobina*), so don't trample my property, don't stamp on it. I sow for you in the dark forests, on the green meadows, and you can trample

---

[25] Kivelson, Worobec, *Witchcraft in Russia and Ukraine*, p. 326; Toporkov (ed.), *Russkie zagovory*, pp. 338–39 no. 12.

[26] Ibid., p. 370. Kleimola finds fleeting flashes of empathy: 'Muscovite icon painters did not portray dogs as savage beasts or mankillers but seemingly empathized with fellow creatures.' See her 'Hunting for Dogs', p. 486.

and stamp on your own property. And don't think any ill toward me
or toward my property, and I won't think any ill toward you, birds of
Christ.[27]

Empathy and reciprocity suggest a harmony between humans
and animals, a respectful, compassionate understanding and even
identification across species divides. The next category of spells dashes
that charming picture and leaves it butchered into fragments.

Dismembering Animals

Magic drew not only on the resonant sympathies that united humans
with animals but also on the utterly unsentimental sacrifice of beasts in
the service of human wants and needs. This Janus-faced attitude lurks
under the surface of the lovely, affecting spells presented in the previous
section, where it is so often sacrifice, loss, or pain that powers the
magic. Whether pictured as bereaved mother bird or yearning human
lover, the actors and subjects of those spells were meant to suffer.

Magic transferred physical suffering across the human-animal
divide. Spells might instruct pain or illness to leave the body of the
human sufferer and to afflict an animal instead: 'Hernia (*gryzha*) don't
gnaw (*gryzhit*') this baby, but chew on the mare's bone or the dog's.'[28]
Animals served as convenient receptacles of human pain, places to
deposit affliction.

Muscovite magic visited violence on the bodies of animals more
directly as well. A protective charm against bewitchment invokes a
mythic copper man who shoots a golden squirrel and 'takes out its
heart of iron. He chops it in three pieces and incants and enchants with
three whispered words. Forever and ever.'[29] This particular spell leaves
unstated how much of its narrative action was to be ritually performed
to activate its magic. Others, however, are utterly explicit. To cure
toothache, the instructions list only actions, without any accompanying
words: 'Take from a marten its penis (*muzheski posik*), dry it, and then
stick it in your teeth.' A remedy for childhood insomnia specifies that
one should take the liver of a hare and dry it in a towel: 'Then put it
under the child's head, and if necessary, you should hold the child's
head.'[30]

---

[27] Toporkov (ed.), *Russkie zagovory*, p. 336 no. 7.
[28] Ibid., p. 126 no. 90.
[29] Ibid., p. 129 no. 98. See discussion of animal parts in V. L. Kliaus, 'Serdtsa
ptits i polovye organy zhivotnykh', in A. L. Toporkov (ed.), *Seks i erotica v russkoi
traditsionnoi kul'ture*, Moscow, 1996, pp. 313–22.
[30] Toporkov (ed.), *Russkie zagovory*, p. 110 no. 40; p. 118 no. 62.

Animal parts feature in countless spells. The right eye of an eagle could be worn as a talisman to avert the anger of the tsar. Its right wing eased childbirth, and its left leg could help with advantageous purchases, sales, and accumulation of wealth. A dead swallow tucked under a sleeping person's armpit could bring back memories of earliest childhood. 'Of the bear's head: bury it in the middle of the courtyard and livestock will be found.'[31] A ritual to protect cattle on St Egor's Day prescribes circling one's cattle, walking around them three times, following the direction of the sun. One should carry a candle and an egg, and hold a black grouse by the neck. After intoning the requisite incantation three times, 'put down the burning candle and the egg as before, but kill the grouse with a little knife.'[32] In each of these prescriptions, animal life must be sacrificed in order to animate the desired magic. Death and dismemberment pave the way to human success, knowledge, or control.

How the bear's head appeared in the courtyard, by what hunting practices the great creature was killed and decapitated, remains unstated, as do the details of obtaining the eagle parts. Some spells came with more or less explicit instructions for obtaining and extracting the necessary body parts. The means were sometimes calculated to cause pain. In 1668/69, when being tried for sorcery, Vaska Ivanov, son of a deacon in the town of Solikamsk, admitted under torture that he knew two spells and had taught them to others. For one of the spells, a would-be seducer was 'to say the incantation while taking an eye from a live chicken. Then he should crush it and give it to women to drink.'[33] A spell from the 1670s meant to fend off crickets recommends that you burn a cricket's head with coal, but you should stop short of burning it to death. And you should say: 'Tell your comrades that you shouldn't come here; and I'll give you three hours.'[34] To discover someone's secrets, 'pull out the tongue of a snake and of a big toad, put them wrapped in a deerskin under the head of him as he sleeps, and you will know everything he has done concerning you since your birth, and what he will think in the future.'[35]

---

[31] RGADA, f. 210, Prikaznyi stol, op. 13, stlb. 734, ll. 115–203. See also stlb. 749, l. 189 (1677). On talismanic use of animal parts, see Ryan, *The Bathhouse at Midnight*, pp. 183, 282, 284–85; A. V. Chernetsov, 'The Sorcerer's Stone: Magic of Water and Blood', in *Witchcraft Casebook*, pp. 519–31; V. L. Kliaus, 'Zagovory i magicheskie sredstva', in A. Toporkov (ed.), *Russkii eroticheskii fol'klor*, Moscow, 1995, pp. 344–61.

[32] Toporkov (ed.), *Russkie zagovory*, pp. 101–02 no. 25.

[33] RGADA, f. 210, Razriadnyi prikaz, op. 14, Sevskii stol, ed. khr. 230, l. 2.

[34] Toporkov (ed.), *Russkie zagovory*, p. 325 no. 4.

[35] Ibid., p. 91 no. 2.

The deliberate dismembering of animals is key to the potency of these and many other spells. The fact that the chicken must be alive when its eye is pulled out of its head, or that the cricket must be allowed to survive its ordeal by fire acknowledges in a backhanded way that the victim is a living being, capable of experiencing pain. In a perverse way, the spells mobilize that same empathy across species that we have seen earlier. This time, however, the rituals mobilize animals' capacity for suffering to power the magic. In the logic of the spells, it is crucial that animals retain feeling: their agony, like that of the grieving cuckoo, is key to the success and power of the spell.

To add one final note to this section on dismembering animals in spells, we should mention that spells sometimes draw on magic force derived from *re*assembling fragmented animal body parts. This fusion power emerges most clearly in a poetic trope that appears in numerous spells, usually apotropaic spells against hostile weapons:

> Guide arrows with their shafts [back] into the tree, glue to the fish, feather to the bird, bird to the sky, and the fish to the sea, and iron and bullets and buckshot and shells to your mother in the earth. Guide [them], Lord, away from me, slave of God So-and-so.

Or similarly:

> Go, iron, to your mother the earth, away from me [...] and tree, go to the woods, and you, feather, go to your mother bird, bird to the sky, and you, glue, go to your mother fish, and fish to the sea.[36]

Whether through fission or fusion, animal parts and the process of dismemberment drew on a profound sense of the commonalities between humans and animals. Even when it was pain, and what would count today as cruelty, that energized a ritual performance, it drew its force from awareness of the animals' capacity for experiencing pain. Living in close proximity to animals, both domestic and wild, Muscovites demonstrated in their magical practices a keen sense of shared wants and needs.

Muscovites, Animal Studies, and the Human-Animal Divide

Poring over collections of spells and sorting them into categories reveals a great deal about Muscovite attitudes toward the natural world in which they were so deeply enmeshed. Might this exercise connect in

[36] Ibid., pp. 353, 355 no. 12, p. 341 no. 16.

any way with broader questions about human-animal interactions or with the recent development of the field of animal studies? Certainly the answer must be affirmative.

An early pioneer in this area among early modernists was Keith Thomas, who identified an early modern watershed in English attitudes toward animals. In this era, he says, the English erected a mental divide between pets — beloved, named, and sentimentalized — and other animals, including farm animals and game. The former were coddled, and the later were designated as comestibles, commodities. In either case, the animals in question were stripped of any spiritual force or association that may have clung to them in earlier centuries. Like the rest of the world, they were disenchanted.[37] As is the way of things Thomas's early forays have been subject to critical re-examination and modification, but for many authors, his work remains the dominant framework to be tested or questioned.[38]

Given its lasting relevance, then, it is significant that his model seems to have no purchase at all in the Muscovite case. The idea of pets seems not to have coalesced yet by the sixteenth or seventeenth centuries, so the integration of a certain subset of creatures into family life was for the time being a non-starter. Although a few noblewomen may have kept lapdogs toward the end of the seventeenth century, the practice was not widespread. Charles J. Halperin finds that even prized hunting dogs were not named (or their names went unrecorded), and Ann M. Kleimola notes that the two named dogs she can find in the huge array of sources she examined were not complimentary: Stinker (*Smerd*) and Dummy (*Durak*).[39] As for the other pole of Thomas's duality,

---

[37] Keith Thomas, *Man and the Natural World: Changing Attitudes in England 1500–1800*, London, 1983.

[38] A few of the many works that consider the implications of Thomas's model: Richard W. Bulliet, *Hunters, Herders, and Hamburgers: The Past and Future of Human–Animal Relationships*, New York, 2005; Erica Fudge, *Perceiving Animals: Humans and Beasts in Early Modern English Culture*, Chicago, IL, 2002; eadem, 'A Left-Handed Blow: Writing the History of Animals', in Nigel Rothfels (ed.), *Representing Animals*, Bloomington, IN, 2002, pp. 3–17; Adrian Franklin, *Animals and Modern Culture: A Sociology of Human-Animal Relations in Modernity*, London, 1999; Helen Parish, '"Paltrie Vermin, Cats, Mise, Toads, and Weasils": Witches, Familiars, and Human-Animal Interactions in the English Witch Trials', *Religions*, 10, 2019, pp. 134–48; Boria Sax, 'The Magic of Animals: English Witch Trials in the Perspective of Folklore', *Anthrozoös*, 22, 2009, 4, p. 317; James A. Serpell, 'Guardian Spirits or Demonic Pets: The Concept of the Witch's Familiar in Early Modern England. 1530-1712', in Angela N. H. Craeger, William Chester Jordan and Shelby Cullom (eds), *The Animal–Human Boundary: Historical Perspectives*, Rochester, NY, 2002, pp. 157–90. Important articles in animal studies are collected in Linda Kalof and Amy J. Fitzgerald (eds), *The Animals Reader: The Essential Classic and Contemporary Writings*, New York, 2007.

[39] Kleimola, Halperin, 'Royal Recreation', p. 292; Kleimola notes that in his treatise

livestock and wild animals certainly figured prominently in Muscovite lives and imagination, but as the spells demonstrate beyond a doubt, there was not a move to strip them of their spiritual power. Quite the contrary, their animal essence was understood as pulsing with magical power. The force of their being, of their pain, their grief and their joy, persisted undiminished in the Muscovite mental universe. If Thomas's characterization of seventeenth-century England is correct, and can be extended more broadly to other parts of Europe, then we can safely identify attitudes toward animals as yet another instance in which Russia's path diverged from the European model.

In the growing field of animal studies, other scholars have approached human-animal relations with quite a different set of questions in mind. In particular, a major strand in the literature questions the entire premise of a clear-cut division between the two categories. Our examination of Muscovite spells serves as a case in point. In Muscovite magic, distinctions between humans and animals blurred and experiences overlapped to the degree that it becomes hard to maintain any sharp sense of a binary division. In a study of 'Beastly Humans and Humanly Beasts' Halperin and Kleimola find that 'The boundary between human and animal in seventeenth-century Russia was more porous than has been realized.' Muscovites 'in text and art could not sustain the sharp differentiation between human and animal'.[40]

A productive strand in animal studies has explored thinking about this dividing line in various cultures. The general scholarly consensus seems to be that early modern European societies experienced profound anxiety when their efforts to set humans apart from dumb beasts were revealed to be unstable. Such apprehensions could lead to draconian penalties for crossing the line. Trials of 'wolfmen', the essential fantasy of categorical mixing, occurred across Europe, though not in Muscovy.[41]

---

on falconry, Tsar Aleksei Mikhailovich recommended noble names for hunting birds: 'Hunting for Dogs', p. 481. For an example of an aristocratic lady with a pet, see the tiny hand-held lapdog in the portrait of Marfa Apraksina, first wife of Tsar Fedor Alekseevich, 1681–82: https://rusmuseumvrm.ru/data/collections/painting/17_19/ neizvestniy_hudozhnik_portret_marfi_matveevni_apraksinoy_1681_1682_zh_3985/ ?lang=en (accessed 8 January 2020).

[40] Halperin, Kleimola, 'Beastly Humans and Humanly Beasts', pp. 46, 56. Halperin and Kleimola conclude that the condemnations of crossing the line between human and beast 'ultimately demonstrate the Muscovite premise of human superiority over animals', p. 57.

[41] Laura Stokes, *Demons of Urban Reform: Early European Witch Trials and Criminal Justice, 1430–1530*, New York, 2011; Jan Machielsen, 'The Making of a Teen Wolf: Pierre de Lancre's Confrontation with Jean Grenier (1603–10)', *Folklore*, 130, 2019, 3, pp. 237–57; Johannes Dillinger, '"Species", "Phantasia", "Raison": Werewolves and

Bestiality, that is, sexual intercourse with animals, drew the harshest punishment — burning at the stake — across the German and Swiss lands from the mid-fifteenth century. It constituted a capital offence throughout Europe and colonial America. In Russia, however, of the 101 cases identified by Marianna Muravyeva between 1648 and 1800, not a single one resulted in the death penalty. In fact, she argues that early modern Russian courts, both secular and ecclesiastical, viewed the essence of the crime as violation of property and degradation of humanity. She finds little expression of concern with the dangers of hybridity or the confusion of kinds. Muravyeva follows Eve Levin in finding that bestiality was seen as a less heinous infraction than those that disrupted social relations.[42]

Intermixing across species lines seems to have evoked less outrage than in other societies, perhaps because it was so deeply engrained in the Muscovite mythic, magical imaginary. The evidence of the spells suggests not anxiety but rather a degree of comfort with the ambiguities of the human-animal divide. Spells take the fungibility of characteristics across categorical divides as their operating premise. Transference of traits is their essential methodology. How meaningful could taxonomical divisions be, if a single spell promised protection from bewitchment for a class of beings made up of 'children, adults, or livestock'?[43]

Deeply embedded in the natural world, Muscovite spells evinced little interest in shoring up the boundaries or patrolling the borders. Rather, they revelled in the possibilities of experiencing life and the world through the eyes of beasts. The lyrical logic of spells allowed Muscovites to unleash their imaginations, letting them soar on the wings of the bird flying free in the air, or swim with the fins of fish gulping in water through their gills, happy and at home in their natural element.

Shape-Shifters in Demonological Literature', in Willem de Blécourt (ed.), *Werewolf Histories*, Basingstoke, 2015, pp. 142–58. Evidence of belief in human transformation into animals is scant in Muscovite sources. See Kivelson, Worobec, *Witchcraft in Russia and Ukraine*, pp. 37, 40; Ryan, *The Bathhouse at Midnight*, pp. 81, 91, 414; Maureen Perrie, *The Image of Ivan the Terrible in Russian Folklore*, Cambridge, 1987, pp. 178–79.

[42] Marianna Muravyeva, 'Sex with Animals in Early Modern Russia: Legal Spaces of Negotiating the Boundaries of Humanity', *Vivliofika: E-Journal of Eighteenth-Century Russian Studies*, 7, 2019, pp. 108, 106; Eve Levin, *Sex and Society in the World of the Orthodox Slavs, 900–1700*, Ithaca, NY, 1989, pp. 205–07.

[43] Toporkov (ed.), *Russkie zagovory*, p. 112 no. 49.

Blood-Letting as a Therapy in Muscovy

Eve Levin

University of Kansas

In Russia in the era before Peter the Great's reforms, Western-style medicine had already gained a significant presence. In the seventeenth century, the Muscovite government's Apothecaries' Chancellery (*Aptekarskii prikaz*) hired medical professionals from abroad to provide care to the imperial court, key government personnel and the army.[1] Although these medical professionals varied in their conceptual approaches to healing — humoral, miasmic, chemical, and astrological medicine — they all saw blood-letting as an accepted therapy. Indigenous folk healers also adopted blood-letting as a treatment, plying their trade surreptitiously because of laws forbidding witchcraft.

It is surprising that pre-modern Russians accepted bleeding as a therapy, because their traditional conception of the causes of disease did not encompass the system of humours. Instead, Russians conceived of disease as sentient beings who invaded the body. A variety of methods, including prayers, spells, herbal potions, and baths could be invoked to draw the invader from the body of the patient. However, bleeding was not among traditional remedies.

Sources of Russian Blood-letting Texts

Unlike most European cultures, Russia had little exposure to the legacy of ancient medicine. Medieval Russians rarely learned Greek or Latin, and classical secular texts appeared infrequently amongst the materials translated into Slavonic. Consequently, only two short passages presented the idea of humours and the practice of blood-letting, both intended as philosophical edification rather than as an instruction manual for medical practitioners.

The first, a Slavic translation of the pseudo-Aristotlian book *Secret of Secrets*, talks briefly about the value of blood-letting for the

---

[1] On the history of medicine in pre-modern Russia see: Wilhelm Michael Richter, *Geschichte der Medicin in Russland*, 3 vols, Moscow, 1813–1817; N. Novombergskii, *Vrachebnoe stroenie v do-Petrovskoi Rusi*, Tomsk, 1907; Mikhail Sokolovskii, *Kharakter i znachenie deiatel'nosti Aptekarskago prikaza*, St Petersburg, 1904; M. B. Mirskii, *Meditsina Rossii XVI–XIX vekov*, Moscow, 1996; Sabine Dumschat, *Ausländische Mediziner im Moskauer Russland*, Stuttgart, 2006; Eve Levin, 'The Administration of Western Medicine in Seventeenth-Century Russia', in Jarmo Kotilaine and Marshall Poe (eds), *Modernizing Muscovy: Reform and Social Change in Seventeenth-Century Russia*, London, 2004, pp. 363–89.

maintenance of health, referring to humours in passing.[2] The second, entitled 'Galen on Hippocrates', presented the concept of humours in more detail. It appeared in two variants — a longer version of about ten manuscript pages, and a shorter and more widespread version of three manuscript pages — preserved in monastic miscellanies dating to the fifteenth century and later.[3] It was found among readings concerning monastic spirituality, as a treatise on the nature of the body as a reflection of the created world — similar to others texts that connected the body with the four elements and Christian creation myths.[4] It was not intended to serve as a guide for the actual treatment of patients.

According to the Galen text, the humours reflected the elements of fire, air, earth, and water, as well as the properties of heat, dryness, cold, and wetness.[5] The long version associated the dominance of certain humours with stages of life and times of the year: blood in a child up to age 14 in the spring; red bile in a youth up to age 30 in the summer; red bile in a man of 45 years in the autumn; and phlegm in a man of 80 years in the winter.[6] Already the original Galenic system was corrupted here with the confusion of the two types of bile.[7] The substitution of red for black is easily explained; the words in Old Slavonic for red (*chermnaia*) and black (*chernaia*) were very similar. However, the mistakes indicate that the copyists did not understand the principles of the humoral system. The long version of the Galen text specified that illness arises from imbalance in the humours:

> Question: When is a person healthy and when is he ailing?
> Answer: He is healthy when the aforementioned four humours stand joint in strength and balance in everything.[8]

Next, the long version affirmed the skill of the physician (*vrach'*). Both versions of the text then designated the appropriate seasons of the year for blood-letting to maintain health — spring and autumn.

---

[2]   W. F. Ryan and Moshe Taube, *The Secret of Secrets: The East Slavic Version: Introduction, Text, Annotated Translation, and Slavic Index*, London, pp. 340–47.

[3]   For a scholarly publication of this text, see V. V. Mil'kov, *Drevnerusskie apokrify*, St Petersburg, 1999, pp. 450–73.

[4]   Ibid., pp. 440–42.

[5]   For a summation of the theory of humours see Vivian Nutton, 'Humoralism', in W. F. Bynum and Roy Porter (eds), *Companion Encyclopedia of the History of Medicine*, 2 vols, London, 1993, 1, pp. 281–91. On the history of blood-letting as a therapy, see K. Codell Carter, *The Decline of Therapeutic Bloodlettinng and the Collapse of Traditional Medicine*, New Brunswick, NJ, 2012.

[6]   Mil'kov, *Drevnerusskie apokrify*, pp. 455–56.

[7]   Compare Nutton, 'Humoralism', p. 286.

[8]   Mil'kov, *Drevrerusskie apokrify*, p. 459.

The year has four seasons: spring, summer, autumn, and winter. Spring begins from 25 March to 25 June. There is a multiplication of blood. It is appropriate therefore to let blood and to conduct a cleaning of the belly with a substance [...].[9]

Recommendations about diet accompanied the guidance about blood-letting. In summer, readers were advised, to 'flee from the letting of blood', while in autumn blood-letting and purging was permissible when 'the moon is waning'.[10]

Beginning in the late fifteenth century, other texts intended as guides for healing came to the Russian reading audience from Western Europe. Imported and translated texts were recombined with indigenous written and oral material, often of apocryphal or folkloric origin.[11] To judge from those medicinal manuscripts that included ownership information, most were the property of literate Russians of middling social status.[12] Some books were prepared for the Russian staff of the Apothecaries' Chancellery.

The earliest known translation of a Western European medical text into Russian has been dated to 1487. According to an inscription preserved in a later manuscript, the translator used Latin and Polish originals. Linguistic features indicate that the translator was from an East-Slavic speaking region of Lithuania.[13] The extant manuscript intermixed this text with others, including the short redaction of 'Galen on Hippocrates'. The first section was organized by type of medicinal plant, but only one plant is used in connection with blood-letting. The first use for '*kaogan*' (ginger), described as 'warm and dry, advantageous', reads 'Whoever wants to let blood, then take ginger in one's mouth and with this use drive evil blood from a person and leave

---

[9]   Ibid. Instead of the usual word for 'substance', the translator transliterated the Greek '*to boifima*' to become the Slavonic '*voifima*', which would probably be understood to be a specific sort of medicinal potion rather than a general term.

[10]   Ibid., pp. 460, 468–69.

[11]   For information on the content of Russian medical manuscripts, see V. M. Florinskii, *Russkie prostonarodnye travniki i lechebniki: sobranie meditsinskikh rukopisei XVI i XVII stoletiia*, Kazan', 1879; V. F. Gruzdev, *Russkie rukopisnye lechebniki*, Leningrad, 1946; N. A. Bogoiavlenskii, *Drevnerusskoe vrachevanie v XI–XVII vv.*, Moscow, 1960; A. A. Turilov, 'Narodnye pover'ia v russkikh lechebnikakh', in A. L. Toporkov and A. A. Turilov (eds), *Otrechennoe chtenie v Rossii XVII–XVIII vekov*, Moscow, 2002, pp. 367–75.

[12]   For an example, see the 'Travnik' ('Herbal'), Moscow, Russian State Library (hereafter RGB), f. 310, Undol'skogo, no. 1072, which belonged to a sub-clerk, Pavel Kurochkin.

[13]   L. N. Pushkarev, 'Vvedenie', in A. A. Novosel'skii and L. N. Pushkarev (eds), *Redkie istochniki po istorii Rossii*, Moscow, 1977, pp. 5–12 (pp. 9–11).

the good'.[14] This provision indicated a different understanding of the purpose of blood-letting — not to even out the balance of humours by removing excess blood, but rather to separate out 'bad' blood from 'good' blood.

The second section of the text was organized around types of illness. In a few cases, bleeding was listed among the therapies, which more often involved herbal medicines, foods, amulets, or prayers. A chapter entitled 'On many medicines, and for which diseases to let blood' listed three uses:

> If a person is scabby, let blood on 20 May.
> If a person [has] fear, sorrow, or excitement, let blood on 15 August from the left hand.
> If the throat is swollen, let [blood] from the head vein above the heart [vein].[15]

In a different chapter, blood-letting was recommended for a variety of ailments: poor eyesight, discharge from the eye, mental illness, coughs, blood flow, a variety of mouth ailments, nightmares, withered limbs, and diseases of the ribs, thighs or internal organs.[16] Blood-letting was also part of the therapy: 'if blood boils in a person, or bitterness', from the nose, or 'if it is serious', from the hand.[17]

The Astrology of Blood-letting

In Russia, the practice of blood-letting as recorded in the medical literature was closely connected with astrology. Although astrology in its classical form first came to Russia from Bulgarian or Serbian translations from the Greek,[18] its use in the medical setting in Russia derived from Western Europe.[19] The innovation in both spheres was connected with Nicolaus Bulow, a German Catholic from Lübeck, who translated Johannes Stöffler's almanac into Russian. A practitioner

---

[14] *Redkie istochniki*, p. 18. For the identification of 'kaogan' see p. 140.

[15] Ibid., p. 34. A similar passage is found in a calendar manuscript: Oxford University Bodleian Library, MS Bodl. 945 (SC 9347), Psalter with appendices, fol. 623v. However, the ideal date for relief of scabies is 1 May. Instead of treatment for a swollen throat, the Oxford Psalter specifies treatment for a person who is 'cold and dry', with blood-letting advised on 15 May.

[16] *Redkie istochniki*, p. 115.

[17] Ibid., p. 121.

[18] W. F. Ryan, *The Bathhouse at Midnight: An Historical Survey of Magic and Divination in Russia*, University Park, PA, 1999, pp. 383–85, 392–94, 399–403.

[19] Michael MacDonald, 'The Career of Astrological Medicine in England', in Ole Peter Grell and Andrew Cunningham (eds), *Religio Medici: Medicine and Religion in Seventeenth-Century England*, Aldershot, 1996, pp. 62–90.

of astrological medicine himself, Bulow translated instructions on auspicious and inauspicious days for blood-letting.[20] However, Bulow was not the only source of this information; Ivan Rykov, a Russian scholar from Pskov, also compiled an astrologically-based guide to blood-letting.[21]

The use of astrology in determining medical treatment, as in everything else, remained controversial in Muscovy. Zodiac texts were explicitly banned at the Moscow Church Council of 1551.[22] Nonetheless, astrological medicine became entrenched at the imperial court in Moscow.[23] Mark Ridley, the author of *A Short Treatise of Magneticall Bodies and Motions*, served as a court physician to Tsar Fedor and his wife Irina Godunova.[24] The noted English proponent of astrological medicine, Arthur Dee, composed his tract *Fasciculus chemicus, or, Chymical collections* while living in Moscow as a physician of the Apothecaries' Chancellery.[25] Specifically to the point, Samuel Collins' treatise on blood-letting, produced for the Apothecaries' Chancellery in May 1664, specified auspicious days for the procedure. On one of those days, 3 June 1664, he supervised Tsar Aleksei's blood-letting.[26]

Pre-modern Russian culture had a long tradition of listing lucky and unlucky days, according to either the solar calendar or the lunar cycle.[27] However, the lists of generally auspicious and inauspicious days did not match up directly with recommendations concerning blood-letting. Indeed, the lists of 'good' and 'bad' days for blood-letting varied, and the same manuscript could include more than one list, thus offering inconsistent guidance. This pattern was common in pre-modern Europe in general, as medical wisdom floated among ethno-religious communities.[28] The recommended dates for blood-letting varied even when the same principle — solar calendar, lunar calendar, or zodiac — was used. So, for example, the 'good' and 'bad' dates listed

---

[20] R. A. Simonov, 'Rossiiskie pridvornye "matematiki" XVI–XVII vekov', *Voprosy istorii*, 1986, no. 1, pp. 76–84 (p. 77); Ryan, *The Bathhouse at Midnight*, pp. 392, 399.

[21] A. A. Turilov and A. V. Chernetsov, 'Pskovskii knizhnik XVI veka', *Voprosy istorii*, 1989, no. 11, pp. 139, 143.

[22] Ryan, *The Bathhouse at Midnight*, p. 393.

[23] Ibid., pp. 20, 400.

[24] Mirskii, *Meditsina Rossii*, pp. 16–18.

[25] Arthur Dee, *Fasciculus chemicus, or, Chymical collections*, London, 1650. The introduction closes with the phrase: 'From my Study in Musco, the Calends of March 1629.'

[26] A. P. Bogdanov, 'O rassuzhdenii Samuila Kollinsa', in R. A. Simonov (ed.), *Estestvennonauchnye predstavleniia drevnei Rusi*, Moscow, 1988, pp. 204–08.

[27] Ryan, *The Bathhouse at Midnight*, pp. 381–83.

[28] Justine Isserles, 'Bloodletting and Medical Astrology in Hebrew Manuscripts from Medieval Western Europe', *Sudhoffs Archiv*, 101, 2017, 1, pp. 2–41.

in the calendar text Bodleian 945 and the herbal text in the National Library RGB f. 310 no. 1072 only roughly coincided. The most notable discrepancies concerned the dates 12 November to March, which were 'good' in the Bodleian manuscript and 'bad' in the RGB one.[29]

The users of blood-letting manuals made their own corrections to received wisdom. The user of the herbal RGB f. 310 no. 1072 added sixteen infelicitous days to the list calculated according to the solar calendar and removed two days. The user also emended the list of felicitous and non-felicitous days calculated according to the lunar calendar, marking six days originally designated for blood-letting as 'don't let'. Next to the designation for 'Days 22 and 23, when the sky is clear', the user added the admonition 'Look'. Another user added, 'Let blood of old people when the moon is in the last quarter'.[30]

The lunar calendar presented interpretive difficulties. One compendium warned: 'It was revealed to wise philosophers on which days of the lunar course to let blood and on which not to let it. Calculate the lunar days from that hour in which the new moon appears, that is its birth, and do not look at any notations in the calendar.' However, this manuscript contained two divergent lunar rosters.[31] One compendium included an explanation for the adjustments it made: The 'Russian lunar manuals' (rossiiskie luniki) differed from those of 'Latin medics' (latinski lekari).[32] Combining the lunar cycle with the zodiac created further complications. For example, one healing book recommended:

When the moon stands in the sheep [Aries], then do not let blood from the head or from the face And when the moon is in the calf [Taurus], then do not let blood from the neck or the throat. And when the moon is in the twins [Gemini], then do not let blood from the shoulders or the arms. And when the moon is in the crab [Cancer] — then do not let blood from the stomach.

The copyist seems to have been puzzled by the original. He changed 'crab' to 'calf', and corrected 'stomach' — a foreign word — so many times that the result was almost illegible.[33]

[29] Oxford University, MS Bodl. 945 (SC 9347), fols 623r–623v.; RGB, f. 310, Undol'skogo, no. 1072, l. 48.

[30] RGB, f. 310, Undol'skogo, no. 1072, ll. 42–430b, 480b–490b. The annotations are in different hands.

[31] Moscow, Rossiiskii gosudarstvennyi arkhiv drevnikh aktov (hereafter RGADA), f. 181, Ministerstvo inostrannykh del, no. 1029/1612, ll. 590b–600b, and l. 61; quotation on l. 630b.

[32] Ibid., ll. 63–630b.

[33] RGB, f. 310, Undol'skogo, no. 1072, ll. 59–60.

The twelve signs of the zodiac corresponded not only to times of the year, but also to parts of the body, resulting in auspicious times to bleed from those areas. The inspiration in Russia for associating specific parts of the body with signs of the zodiac for purposes of blood-letting originated in Western Europe. In a printed calendar from 1736, a German block print was inserted into a Russian guide on the seasonality of health.[34] Even sketches labeled in Cyrillic were based on Western European models rather than indigenous drawings of the human figure.[35] However, it was not clear whether the association of a zodiac sign with a particular body part meant that bleeding in that location would be beneficial, or harmful. 'Ptolemy writes in his book', one manuscript warned, 'not to permit blood-letting from that place of the zodiac where the moon stands'.[36]

Blood-letting as Therapy

Compared with the proper times for blood-letting, Russian texts devoted comparatively less attention to its purposes. Blood-letting was presented both as a prophylactic, to maintain health, and as a treatment to alleviate illness. One text touted the salubrious results of regular therapy: 'Cheerfulness and good memory come from it'. In addition to cleansing the various organs: 'it extends life and leads to health. Physicians (*vracheve*) attest that blood-letting is good for all people.'[37] Repeated, regular blood-letting was essential:

> If someone has let blood from the veins, and then stops and time elapses, he will fall into a great illness because the veins fill with blood, and has no exit. And so the excess blood heats up, and from this a fever is born, and a damaging heat causes illness of the head, eyes, and teeth, and the whole body internally. So it is good to let blood from the veins in the proper time.[38]

Blood-letting formed only a part of a complex of diverse treatments.[39] For example, when Drs Hartmann Gramann and Johann Belau were

---

[34] The fragment of the 1736 printed book was combined with a late seventeenth-century astronomical manuscript: Columbus Ohio, Ohio State University, Hilandar Research Library (hereafter HIL), MGU General Slavic Fond, no. 4Gb16.

[35] See the reproduction of a page from a seventeenth-eighteenth-century manuscript in Bogoiavlenskii, *Drevnerusskoe vrachevanie*, p. 67. See also RGB, f. 310 Undol'skogo, no. 1072, l. 44.

[36] RGADA, f. 181, Ministerstvo inostrannykh del, no. 1029/1612, l. 600b.

[37] Ibid., l. 65.

[38] Ibid., l. 570b.

[39] For examples, see Lechebnik, HIL, St Petersburg State University, E-IV-5, dating to the 1630, ll. 250–500b.

asked about how to treat patients with swollen throats and chests, they recommended opening a vein under the tongue, followed by rinsing the mouth with cold vodka. They also prescribed ointments and plasters laid on the affected organs, and medicines if the illness persisted. Tracing the cause of the disease to miasmas arising from the corpses of dead cattle, they recommended burying them fully.[40]

Often instructions directed that blood be taken from the body part that exhibited disease. For example, to alleviate a tic in the eye or headache, blood was to be let from the forehead.[41] Analogously, both Russian folk medicine and Orthodox spiritual healing directed remedies specifically towards the affected body parts, based on the assumption that the disease (or the demon that caused it) had to be expelled from its hiding place.[42] In blood-letting, however, the correct vein to tap could lie quite far from the affected organ; for example: 'Let [blood] from across the arm for disease of the heart or side [and] for prudence.'[43]

Blood-letting could serve not only as a treatment, but as a diagnostic tool. One guide explained how the practitioner (*lekar'*) should examine the veins of the right arm. From the feel of the veins and the pulse, he could then determine which humour was ascendant and which organs were affected. Expecting the terms of humoral medicine to be alien, the author also used the Russian vernacular, and invoked the more familiar hot/cold and wet/dry dichotomies.[44] The blood could be collected in a jar, and left to sit for a time. The colour and consistency of the blood would then reveal whether the patient was ill. For example: 'If the blood is black and a little water floats on the surface, that person is susceptible to a four-day fever.' Another diagnostic method was to take a drop of the blood taken the patient's arm and drop it in a vessel of water. If the drop fell to the bottom, the patient would recover; if it floated, he would not.[45]

[40] N. E. Mamonov, *Materialy dlia istorii meditsiny v Rossii*, 4 vyp., Moscow, 1881–85, vyp. 1, pp. 44–45.

[41] RGADA, f. 181, Ministerstvo inostrannykh del, no. 1029/1612, l. 62.

[42] See Eve Levin, 'Supplicatory Prayers as a Source for Popular Religious Culture in Muscovite Russia', in Samuel H. Baron and Nancy Shields Kollmann (eds), *Religion and Culture in Early Modern Russia and Ukraine*, DeKalb, IL, 1997, pp. 96-114 (p. 107).

[43] RGADA, f. 181, Ministerstvo inostrannykh del, d. 1029/1612, l. 62ob.

[44] HIL, St Petersburg State University, E-IV-5, ll. 263–63ob. The term *lekar'* referred to different kinds of medical practitioners in different contexts. In the Slavonic *Secret of Secrets*, it is used to translate 'physician'; see Ryan and Taube, *The* Secret of Secrets, pp. 310–11. In Muscovite government documents, *lekar'* was used for foreigners who qualified as 'surgeon' in their home country, but also for those medical practitioners, both foreign and Russian, who did not have such certification but performed the same work. Sometimes they carried out doctors' instructions in hands-on treatment, in the manner of medical technicians. *Lekari* were often assigned to military units to provide on-the-spot medical care in the manner of field medics.

[45] RGADA, f. 181, Ministerstvo inostrannykh del, no. 1029/1612, ll. 58–58ob.

The Practice of Blood-letting

While medical manuals described how blood-letting ought to be done, detailed records of actual instances are few. The most complete account comes from 1643, when Tsar Mikhail was the patient.[46] Two doctors attended the Tsar, Hartmann Gramann and Johann Belau, both possessing university education and high rank within the Apothecaries' Chancellery. Wilhelm Cramer performed the actual bleeding; he held the rank of *lekar'* (medical technician) and had been in the employ of the Apothecaries' Chancellery since 1631.[47] In early June, the 'three doctors' (apparently including Cramer) diagnosed the Tsar as suffering from '*rozha*'.[48] They recommended the following treatment: first, an ointment composed of 'wine spirits' and camphor three times a day, along with a medicines, a '*beznaia*' stone to induce sweat, and twelve grains of pepper steeped in vodka:

> [...] in order to separate sharp hot blood so it does not stand in one place. After that, it is necessary to perform blood-letting, in order to withdraw all heat from the head and allow the blood to cool. But if the blood is not allowed to cool, that extremely hot blood will remain to settle in any place at all, wherever nature permits, and from that swellings and sores result. Blood-letting may be performed when a good day has been found.[49]

Later the doctors added a second set of instructions: on the days that the Tsar took the medicine, he should not eat before dinner, and he should take the medicine two hours before the evening meal. The Tsar accepted the advice of the doctors. The actual prescription the doctors wrote differed from the earlier description. It included '*beznaia*' stone, antimony salts, vodka, elder flower, Rhenish vinegar, and sugar. On 3 June, in the 15th hour, the Tsar took this medicine.

[46] The documents concerning this case are published in two places, with slight variations between them: *Akty istoricheskie sobrannye i izdannye Arkheograficheskoiu Kommissieiu*, 5 vols, St Petersburg, 1841–1842, 3, pp. 387–89, and Mamonov, *Materialy*, vyp. 1, pp. 41–43.

[47] On Wilhelm Cramer's status, see Dumschat, *Ausländische Mediziner*, p. 644.

[48] In modern Russian, *rozha* refers to erysipelas, called 'the Rose' popularly in the West. It is caused by a streptococcus infection and manifested by fever and inflamed lesions. See *Taber's Cyclopedic Medical Dictionary*, 16th edn, Philadelphia, PA, 1985, p. 618; *Black's Medical Dictionary*, 38th edn, Lanham, MD, 1995, p. 174. However, a direct connection between modern disease names and premodern diseases cannot be confirmed; see Eve Levin, 'Identifying Diseases in Pre-Modern Russia', *Russian History/Histoire Russe* 35, 2008, 3–4, pp. 321–33.

[49] *Akty istoricheskie*, vol. 3, p. 387. A *beznaia* stone is probably 'bezoar' — a hard mass from the digestive system of animals thought to have curative powers.

The blood-letting itself took place on the following day, 4 June, in the bathhouse (*mylenka*). Wilhelm Cramer opened the Tsar's vein, and Drs Gramann and Belau were present. The blood that was removed was weighed — $3/4$ of a pound. It was then entrusted to two leading boiars: Fedor Sheremetev and Ivan Streshnev. They dug a hole in the garden outside the bathhouse, placed the blood in it, and filled it with earth.

Afterwards, the doctors advised the patient to eat fresh fish — perch, gudgeon, pike, and crab in particular — boiled in broth or fried with lemon juice. Radish and horseradish were prohibited. As a beverage, the doctors recommended high-quality Rhenish wine or sacramental wine, with granulated sugar, or good beer or kvass. Hot wine, vodka, mead, and rum were not recommended. The dietary advice was written down and given to the *okol'nichii* (courtier/official) Vasilii Streshnev, who then presented it to the Tsar.

The next day, on 5 June, the medical personnel involved in the blood-letting — doctors, medics, and interpreters — received a special reward from the Tsar in appreciation of their services. In order to determine an appropriate reward, boiar Fedor Sheremetev consulted the records from previous occasions, in 1641 and in 1630. In 1630, the reward to the doctor (Arthur Dee) consisted of a silver goblet, expensive cloth and sable furs, valued at seventy roubles in total. Wilhelm Cramer had participated in the blood-letting in that year also, but the manuscript breaks off in the midst of listing his bonus.[50]

If we take this account to be typical of blood-letting as practised by specialists of the Apothecaries' Chancellery for the imperial family, then several characteristics emerge. First, the doctors paid attention to auspicious and inauspicious days for blood-letting. However, they seem to have been using a calendar based on the lunar cycle rather than the months, because 4 June was an unlucky day according to the more extensive Russian listing. It was, however, a felicitous day in the lunar cycle — eighteen days after the new moon.[51] Blood-letting was used alongside other therapies including medicinal remedies and diet. However, the explanation of the cause of the illness did not coincide with orthodox humoral theory. It was not a surfeit of blood, a hot substance, that caused the fever, but rather the presence of excessively hot blood, particularly in the patient's head. By removing this hot blood and allowing the rest of the blood to cool, the doctors would prevent further deterioration of the patient's health and enable his recovery. It

[50] *Akty istoricheskie*, vol. 3, p. 388.
[51] For establishment of the lunar cycle in May/June 1643, see http://eclipse.gsfc.nasa.gov/phase/phases1601.html (accessed 24 March 2012).

is also noteworthy how the blood removed from the Tsar was handled: it was entrusted to two of his leading advisers to ascertain that it was disposed of in a manner rendering it safe from magical misuse. The method of disposal — pouring the blood into a specially-dug hole in the garden — recalls ancient rites of blessing fertile ground with blood.[52]

The substantial reward that the medical personnel involved in the Tsar's bleeding received suggests that it was an unusual therapy, and not part of ordinary duties. The bonuses equalled several months' salary, even for the highly-compensated foreign doctors. It was not only because the Tsar himself was the patient, and grateful for his recovery. In 1662, the foreign *lekar'* Sigismund Sommer received two pairs of sables valued at ten roubles total as a bonus for bleeding the Tsar's personal servants.[53] He also received a bonus in 1659, as one of the participants in blood-letting for the Tsaritsa: a silver ladle, cloth, and sables worth twenty roubles, and a similar reward for participating in the blood-letting of the Tsar in 1660, 1661 and 1662.[54] (The regularity — each year in May — suggests a prophylactic blood-letting.) However, at a blood-letting for Tsar Aleksei in 1663, the blood-letting specialist Martyn Mikhailov did not receive a bonus. Feeling mistreated, he petitioned the Tsar to remember his 'little work' (*rabotenka*). Mikhailov's job involved collecting the blood in a cup, perhaps for examination. The Apothecaries' Chancellery staff noted that he had received bonuses for this work in 1659, 1661 and 1662: ten roubles, and in 1661 some good English broadcloth. So his petition was approved, although not at the level he had come to expect: five roubles, and some broadcloth.[55]

Practitioners of Blood-letting at the Apothecaries' Chancellery
The complexity in the instructions about blood-letting meant that practitioners needed to have special knowledge in order to perform it properly. An author warned:

> When someone knowing lets blood, great healing occurs then throughout the insides of that person. However, if he does not know how to let, or he lets too much, or lets too little, or cuts across the vein, either blood will flow to the inside, or it will not flow out of the person

[52] Maria Carlson, personal communication.

[53] N. Novombergskii, *Materialy po istorii meditsiny v Rossii*, 4 vols, St Petersburg, 1905–1910, 1, p. 35. Sommer began his career in Muscovy as a field medic for soldiers, but after he gained the favour of the imperial family, he was promoted to the rank of doctor (*dokhtur*) in 1676. See Dumschat, *Ausländische Meditziner*, p. 677.

[54] Mamonov, *Materialy*, vyp. 2, p. 271; vyp. 3, pp. 767–68.

[55] Ibid., vyp. 2, pp. 271–73.

and that place will swell. From that plague sores develop and the arm is twisted and from this that person experiences death and destruction.[56]

This author echoed the extensive warning in the older *Secret of Secrets* against ignorant physicians (*lekari*): 'But my point in this is that you should not surrender yourself in the hands of those who are not accomplished in the art [of medicine] [...], because there is no treatment among all medical procedures more difficult than blood-letting and giving purgatives.'[57]

Consequently, the Apothecaries' Chancellery employed professionals trained in blood-letting, although none of them had the level of qualification that the *Secret of Secrets* considered to be essential to avoid dire outcomes. Although doctors holding medical degrees supervised blood-letting for the most elite patients, lower-ranking *lekari* performed the actual phlebotomy.

Phillipe Briot practised blood-letting in Muscovy from 1631. Although French by birth, he had immigrated to England with his family, where his family made connections with the royal court. Thus, Briot came with the endorsement of King Charles I to serve the Russian tsar as a pharmacist. However, he actually was assigned to work primarily a *lekar'*, most notably letting blood. In 1644, Briot asked for additional pay for his work as a blood-letter, prompting a reinvestigation of his credentials. Russian administrators of the Apothecaries' Chancellery decided to acknowledge his work as a blood-letter, but not in the manner he had intended. 'Because he opens veins and pharmacists do not open veins', they ruled, he should be officially reassigned to the position of *lekar'*. Briot objected to the loss of rank, but to no avail.[58]

Most blood-letters had less distinguished origins. Ivan and Matvei Taborovskoi, father and son, were ethnic Poles from the border town of Smolensk. Ivan made his living as a barber, and Matvei learned the trade from him. Upon arriving in Moscow in 1678, Matvei petitioned for employment in the Apothecaries' Chancellery, mentioning that his father would also be willing to come in order to keep the family together. Both were hired.[59] Iakov Gladkoi and his son Ivan, Poles from

---

[56] Quoted in N. A. Bogoiavlenskii, *Meditsina u pervoselov russkogo severa*, Leningrad, 1966, p. 108.

[57] Ryan and Taube, *The Secret of Secrets*, p. 321; the translation is theirs. See also the extensive and repeated warnings about unskilled physicians on pp. 310–25.

[58] Mamonov, *Materialy*, vyp. 1, pp. 63–69; quotation on p. 66. See also Maria V. Unkovskaya, *Brief Lives: A Handbook of Medical Practitioners in Muscovy, 1620–1701*, London, 1999, p. 46; Dumschat, *Ausländische Mediziner*, p. 577.

[59] Mamonov, *Materialy*, vyp. 4, pp. 1067–68; 1111–13. See also Unkovskaya, *Brief Lives*, pp. 88–89.

Cracow, both found employment with the Russian army. When Ivan sought a salaried position at the Apothecaries' Chancellery, he testified to experience treating bullet wounds and blood-letting.[60] Martynko Radomskii's story was similar; he came from Kamenets, near Vilnius, the son of a minor nobleman. He learned medicine by working with Iurii Shkinder, a medical technician who had since taken a position as *lekar'* with the Apothecaries' Chancellery. Radomskii himself worked in Lithuania as an army field medic, treating wounds and internal diseases, and blood-letting. He accompanied a Polish nobleman travelling to Moscow, where he reconnected with Shkinder.[61] Stefan von Gaden, who identified himself as 'a Jew of the Lutheran faith', began his career at the Apothecaries' Chancellery as a barber, doing simple bleedings 'with an axe' because he did not have more specialized equipment. He gained the confidence of the imperial family, and was later promoted to the rank of *dokhtur*.[62] Ergar Dliaker, a German oculist from Zwickau, had been captured by the Russian army when he came to the attention of the Apothecaries' Chancellery. Apparently eager to make the best of a bad situation, Dliaker offered to convert to Orthodoxy and serve the Russian tsar instead. He claimed knowledge to treat all kinds of wounds, plague, and internal diseases, as well as blood-letting. He offered to show how to make German blood-letting tools.[63]

Russians, too, performed blood-letting in the employ of the Apothecaries' Chancellery. Mitrofan, Kirill, Artemii, and Timofei — probably brothers as they shared the same patronymic, Petrov — worked as blood-letters in the late 1660s and 1670s. Artemii and Timofei were listed as students; Artemii studying under Mitrofan and Timofei under Kirill. The course of study was apparently quite lengthy; Timofei had been studying with his brother for three years as of 1677. Although both Artemii and Timofei had been assigned for deployment with the army in Putivl', they had not served because of their continuing studies. In 1668, Mitrofan treated a co-worker, the Russian medical technician (*lekar'*) Stepan Alekseev, who was suffering from the 'wet illness (*mokrotnaia*) and the bones in the arms and legs and all joints were swollen greatly'. Apparently Mitrofan bled him repeatedly; Stepan

[60] Mamonov, *Materialy*, vyp. 4, pp. 1088–90. See also Unkovskaya, *Brief Lives*, pp. 69–70.

[61] Mamonov, *Materialy*, vyp. 4, pp. 985–89. See also Unkovskaya, *Brief Lives*, p. 87. On Shkinder, see Dumschat, *Ausländische Mediziner*, p. 672.

[62] Mamonov, *Materialy*, vyp. 2, pp. 454–55. See also Unkovskaya, *Brief Lives*, pp. 34–37.

[63] Mamonov, *Materialy*, vyp. 3, pp. 712–13. See also Unkovskaya, *Brief Lives*, pp. 79–80.

was absent from work from 1 March to 1 September. Kirill accompanied pharmacist Robert Benyon on a trip to England in 1670 to purchase supplies.[64] It is likely that Kirill Petrov's duties in England involved the purchase of blood-letting tools. In 1678–79, the Apothecaries' Chancellery commissioned Vilem Gorsten (Willem Horsten), a foreign merchant living in Moscow, to buy such equipment, among other items. He procured 36 'blood-letting hatchets' purchased in Hamburg: 18 cost 18 schillings apiece, and the other 18 cost 20 schillings apiece. The hatchets, which cost the Chancellery 6 *altyny* and 4 *dengi* apiece in Russian currency, were then offered for sale at the public pharmacy at a price of 16 *altyny* and 4 *dengi* apiece.[65]

Blood-letting outside Government Medical Practice
The sale of blood-letting equipment to the public suggests that there were practitioners of the craft outside of the ranks of Apothecaries' Chancellery personnel. Indeed, many of the foreign blood-letters had practised in Russian territory before their employment in the Chancellery. In addition to Chancellery employees, Russian and non-Russian, some folk healers also included blood-letting among the therapies they offered to patients.

Folk healing of any sort aroused official suspicion. To ward off prosecution as witches, folk healers often identified themselves as 'horse-trainers' — the treatment of horses being acceptable and necessary — even though they ministered to human as well as equine patients.[66] Identifying as a 'blood-letter' (*rudomet*) similarly was safer; there was no prohibition against it.

Ivan Kirillov was one such blood-letter. A native of Pskov, he practised his trade itinerantly. Upon arriving in Ostashkov in 1650, he reported to the local government office, as itinerants were supposed to do. There his bag was searched, revealing forbidden herbs and roots, and Ivan was arrested. He had, however, a wide circle of acquaintances in town, including a palace guard, a musketeer, an artisan, a local horse trainer, and peasants, and they swore surety for him. Two monastery peasants, Ivan Dryzlov and Tikhon Shishkin, testified:

[64] Mamonov, *Materialy*, vyp. 2, pp. 347–48, 395, 473–81, 535–39; vyp. 4, pp. 921–22.

[65] Ibid., vyp. 4, pp. 1182, 1186. For more information about blood-letting tools, see M. B. Mirskii, 'Meditsina v srednie veka na Rusi', *Voprosy istorii*, 2000, no. 11, pp. 106–18 (p. 116).

[66] Eve Levin, 'Healers and Witches in Early Modern Russia', in Yelena Mazour-Matusevich and Alexander S. Koros (eds), *Saluting Aron Gurevich: Essays in History, Literature and Other Related Subjects*, Leiden, 2010, pp. 105–33.

They know this Ivashko Kirillov: This year he has been living in
Ostashkov, supporting himself in the town through horse training and
blood-letting, and working at a tavern, where he indentured himself for
a year. They said that he is by birth from Pskov, and they never saw or
heard anything criminal about him.

Two local artisans gave similar affirmations concerning Ivan Kirillov.
Ivan himself gave the following account about how he entered his
profession:

By birth he is from Pskov. His father Kirilko Ivanov lived in Pskov as
a bondsman. He, Ivashko, left his father and left Pskov because his
stepmother was nasty to him. He lived in Novgorod *uezd* (district), near
Staraia Russa, in the Sovereign's villages, in the parish of Bureg, for a
year, [where] he supported himself as a peasant, reaping pastures. After
that, he travelled the villages with the horse master and horse trainer
Grishka Alekseev, on an indenture, for a year and a half. From that
horse trainer Grishka he acquired the horse and blood-letting craft.
He supported himself that way travelling the villages. In the current
year, 1650, after Christmas he left Borovichi parish in Novgorod
uezd and came to Rzhev *uezd*. From Rzhev *uezd* in Holy Week he
came to Ostashkov. In Ostashkov he came to the Ministry office on
a summons. In the Ministry office, the Ostashkov Ministry official
Fedor Rakhmaninov interrogated him. Seeing that he had blood-letting
horns, and in the bag there were horse and animal herbs and roots, he
turned him over to the guard. He held him for three days, and then
took him from the guard to his house and held him at his house for
six days. He wanted to enslave him by force, but he, Ivashko, did not
become his slave and did not give him servitude [documents]. When
a new Ministry officer, Tikhon Kartsev, arrived in Ostashkov, Fedor
Rakhmaninov turned him [Ivan] over to him with the horse dealer to
Tikhon Kartsev. Tikhon Kartsev sent him to Moscow. There is nothing
criminal about Ivashko; many residents of the Ostashkov region and
town know him, because he previously lived in Ostashkov for a year.
Now traders from Ostashkov are in Moscow at the merchants' court
and the Osip stalls, and the horse and animal herbs and roots were
sent to Moscow with them from Ostashkov. Horse masters know those
herbs and roots.[67]

---

[67] Novombergskii, *Vrachebnoe stroenie*, pp. xxxiii–xxxviii; quotations on pp. xxxv–
xxxvi.

The documents do not reveal Ivan's fate. However, they do provide insight into his practice of blood-letting. Ivan had no formal education, but rather learned individually from a practising horse trainer. Through his craft, whether doctoring horses or people, he acquired a significant number of clients grateful enough to testify on his behalf even though he was suspected of witchcraft, which was a capital offence. The local official also saw him as valuable, trying to coerce him into service to himself. All this suggests a market for blood-letting as a healing therapy, even among people in rural provinces.

Another blood-letter and horse trainer, Dorofei Prokof'ev, had a similar story. Dorofei came from the artisanal class of Nizhnii Novgorod. He learned his trade from another horse trainer, Fedor Bobylev, with whom he had a written agreement and to whom he paid a rouble. In addition to the practice of blood-letting and horse training, he treated internal illnesses of children and adults, using herbs and spells. He also told fortunes, reading palms and casting beans.[68] In 1689, Dorofei was living in the household of the wife of the nobleman Andrei Bezobrazov, where he treated animals. Bezobrazov was denounced for treason, for refusing to appear for service by falsely claiming to be ill and organizing a magical attack on the Tsar (Peter I). Bezobrazov's arrest led to that of Dorofei and then to his teacher Fedor. Under torture, Dorofei and Fedor admitted practising magic, although they denied any intent to cause harm. They were both executed.[69]

The official record of the investigation records the exact words of Dorofei's incantation for blood-letting for horses:

Our God, have mercy upon us! The tsar borrows the borrowed, so borrow blood from the grey (or whatever colour) horse. Two crows fly across the ocean-sea: wave-wave with the wings, yawn-yawn with the wounds, drop-drop blood. Amen to you, blood![70]

Although Dorofei did not admit to using this spell on people, because that would constitute an admission of attempted murder, it could easily be adapted to human patients. The incantation intermingles Christian and folkloric elements in a typical way, combining phrases from

---

[68] On bean divination and palm reading, see Ryan, *The Bathhouse at Midnight*, pp. 113–14, 157–58.

[69] Information about Dorofei, including long quotations from the primary sources, is included in Askalon Truvorov, 'Volkhvy i vorozhei na Rusi, v kontse XVII veka', *Istoricheskii vestnik*, 9, 1889, June, pp. 701–15.

[70] Truvorov, 'Volkhvy i vorozhei na Rusi', p. 709.

Christian prayer with sympathetic magic.[71] The 'tsar' and the 'ocean-sea' are ubiquitous elements in Russian incantations, and interestingly, the crow is one of the figures that appears frequently in popular spells to staunch the flow of blood. However, blood-letting as a therapy contradicted one of the primary uses of curative incantations: stopping the flow of blood.[72] Nonetheless, to Dorofei, blood-letting had become just one more healing ritual, accompanied by its own incantation of a traditional sort.

*   *   *

In conclusion, blood-letting appeared as a therapy in early-modern Muscovy, even though the theory of humours was not well understood. Practitioners of blood-letting included formally-educated doctors in service to the court, although in the few recorded instances, they supervised rather than carried out the mechanics of the treatment. The Muscovite government recruited practically-trained foreign blood-letters to treat members of the court and the army. It arranged for Russian employees of the Apothecaries' Chancellery to learn the techniques and to practise alongside the foreigners. At the same time, ordinary Russians also learned blood-letting, and practised it among their fellow peasants and townspeople.

How can we explain the willingness of Russians to embrace blood-letting as a therapy even though they did not share the understanding of the causes of illness that underlay its use as a therapy? The sources give no direct answer. Russian ideas about the causes and treatment of illness were compatible with a number of aspects of blood-letting. Russians understood that diseases could be classified by symptoms, including the hot/cold and wet/dry dichotomies of humoral theory. They agreed with the notion that certain days were lucky and others unlucky. Because they believed that disease could reside in certain body parts, it made sense to withdraw blood from that place in order to alleviate the symptoms. Furthermore, Russians shared the idea that blood was somehow specially connected with life and health, even though Russian traditional treatment did not include removing it from the body.

---

[71] For more on the style of popular prayers, see Levin, 'Supplicatory Prayers'.
[72] A. L. Toporkov, *Zagovory v russkoi rukopisnoi traditsii XV–XIX vv.: istoriia, simvolika, poetika*, Moscow, 2005, especially part 4, chapter 2: 'Zagovory ot krovotecheniia', pp. 313–33.

Beyond these similarities, though, we should recall how often the extant therapies of the day were ineffective, creating an eagerness to try something new. Blood-letting was exotic — a therapy known to foreigners and available to the tsar and his servitors. The process of removing blood could create in the patient an altered mental state — a lightheadedness and a sense of distance from bodily sensation — that would feel like an improvement to a person who was ailing. Under the circumstances, it is not surprising that Russians were willing to embrace it as an option, even without understanding the principles of ancient science that lay behind it.

The Talitskii File and Its Afterlife: A Revisit

Gary Marker

Stony Brook University, New York

THIS essay concerns the Petrine-era heretic Grigorii Talitskii, who in 1700 prophesied that Peter I was 'the last king', the Antichrist, and that the end of days was at hand. His pronouncements generated considerable chatter at the time and no small measure of apprehension at the highest ranks of Church and state, all of which granted him an enduring visibility — and sometimes outright myth-making — both in lore and in scholarship. I have long been curious about Talitskii, his prophesies about time, degree of scriptural literacy, and way of reading. If one were to search, I wondered, might he turn out to be some sort of Muscovite Menocchio of Friuli whose imaginative vision of heaven and earth Carlo Ginzburg famously reconstructed?[1] If not cheese and worms, was there at least some coherent cosmology lurking beneath the surface just waiting to be decoded? Alas, no, at least not as far as I can discern. Rather, Talitskii's eschatology appears to have been simple and straightforward throughout, with few discursive flourishes. Thus, in place of the bold hermeneutic reading that I had hoped to produce, this essay poses some decidedly more prosaic questions that inquire into specific aspects of what might be termed 'the tale of Talitskii'. If his theologizing truly lacked depth how does one explain the mix of fascination, deep anxiety, and lore that he and his words generated, such that for years thereafter the mere mention of his name could spark unpleasant memories among people in authority, and very occasionally, grudging respect?[2] Similarly, how did 'the tale of Talitskii' take shape in historical memory and why has he maintained such name recognition *vis-à-vis* other eighteenth-century heretics some of whom were more reflective and cerebral?[3] True, some others attract attention — for

---

[1] Carlo Ginzburg, *The Cheese and the Worms: The Cosmos of a Sixteenth–Century Miller*, Baltimore, MD, 1976.

[2] For example, Arsenii Matseevich, the embattled mid-century Metropolitan of Rostov, made a quixotic reference to Talitskii, rejecting his prophesy but expressing respect for being a capable debater: P. P. Pekarskii, *Nauka i literatura v Rossii pri Petre Velikom*, St Petersburg, 1862, vol. 2, p. 82.

[3] In addition to works cited elsewhere in this essay, recent studies that mention Talitskii include Robert Collis, *The Petrine Instauration: Religion, Esotericism, and Science at the Court of Peter the Great*, Leiden, 2012, pp. 229–32; Ernest Zitser, *The Transfigured Kingdom: Sacred Parody and Charismatic Authority at the Court of Peter the Great*, Ithaca, NY, 2004, pp. 74, 170; Nancy Kollmann, *Crime and Punishment in*

example, Samuil Vymorkov, Varlaam Levin, Mikhail Vyshatin.[4] None comes close, however, to matching Talitskii's notoriety. He even has his own Wikipedia page, irrefutable proof these days of cultural resonance.[5] These two inquiries — why then and why later — necessitate revisiting the documents themselves, prefaced by a brief detour into the world of mid-nineteenth-century writers who to a large extent crafted the public persona that endures.

In fact, the Talitskii materials had mouldered undisturbed for over a century until Grigorii Esipov decided to explore them, publish what he found, and write about them.[6] All subsequent research on Talitskii, as well as on eighteenth-century popular religion in general, has benefited immensely from his excavations.[7] Be that as it may, the legacy of Esipov and his ilk (there were quite a few others) constitutes a decidedly two-edged sword. They built their reputations by scouring state archives in search of history's *chudaki*, piquant personalities from a not-so-distant past about whom they could engage their readers with a mix of freshly-published documents and their own retelling of lives and events. The goal was to inform and entertain rather than to moralize or unsettle, even less to engage in scholarly debates. Their audiences resided in the marketplace of the thick journals, and because they wrote for the wider educated public, they focused on readability and a captivating narrative. They generally remained respectful of the sources, but occasionally the allure of larger-than-life personalities, attention-

---

Early Modern Russia, Cambridge, 2015, p. 410; Paul Bushkovitch, *Peter the Great. The Struggle for Power, 1671–1725*, Cambridge, 2001, pp. 222–23; Viktor Zhivov, *Iz tserkovnoi istorii vremen Petra Velikogo. Issledovaniia i materialy*, Moscow, 2004, p. 124; Evgenii Anisimov, *Dyba i knut. Politicheskii sysk i russkoe obshchestvo v XVIII veke*, Moscow, 1999, pp. 36–37.

[4] Vymorkov also has received serious attention. See, for example, S. M. Solov'ev, 'Monakh Samuil (stranitsa iz istorii raskola)', in *Chteniia i rasskazy po istorii Rossii*, Moscow, 1989, pp. 616–20 (the essay originally appeared in *Pravoslavnoe obozrenie* in 1860); M. I. Semevskii, 'Samuil Vymorkov, propovednik iavleniia v Rossii antikhrista, 1722–1725 gg.', in his *Slovo i delo!, 1700–1725*, St Petersburg, 1884, pp. 125–84.

[5] https://ru.wikipedia.org/wiki/Григорий_Талицкий.

[6] G. V. Esipov, 'Posledivateli ucheniia ob antikhriste', in *Raskol'nich'i dela XVIII stoletiia izvlechennyia iz del Preobrazhenskogo Prikaza i Tainoi rozysknykh del Kantseliarii*, St Petersburg, 1861, vol. 1, pp. 1–7, 59–86.

[7] In addition to *Raskol'nich'i dela*, see: Esipov, *Liudi starago veka: Razskazy iz del Preobrazhenskogo Prikaza i Tainoi Kantselarii*, St Petersburg, 1880, especially chapters 2 and 3: 'Slovo i delo', 'Berezka i korablik', pp. 63–125; Semevskii, *Slovo i delo 1700–1725*; *Tainaia Kantseliariia pri Petre Velikom: tainaia sluzhba Petra I. Dokumental'nye povesti*, St Petersburg, 1884. In this context the Soviet scholar N. B. Golikova's 1957 monograph, *Politicheskie protsessy pri Petre I*, deserves special mention for its thoughtful presentation of sources and for identifying some mistakes in the literature: N. B. Golikova, *Politicheskie protsessy pri Petre. Po materialam Preobrazheskogo Prikaza*, Moscow, 1957, pp. 134–37.

grabbing anecdotes, colourful language, or imagined conversations prevailed over documentary clarity or fealty to the evidence. Footnotes tended to be sparse and truncated, and some of the more dramatic or sweeping conclusions were — shall we say — a stretch.[8] Such is the case with several key vectors of the tale of Talitskii. The process of revisiting the file, therefore, unfolds as a running dialogue between master narrative and documents and reveals which parts of it hold up and which endure more through repetition than through fealty to the evidence.

*   *   *

Early modern Russia was famously awash in religious dissent. Old Believers posed the greatest challenge, witness the many who chose self-immolation rather than surrender to satanic earthly rule. There were, however, quite a few others: individual eschatologists, an assortment of seers, numerologists, and preachers, mostly self-taught, not ordained, and for the most part operating outside established religious institutions.[9] The context is well known: Nikon's modifications of Church liturgy and ritual in the 1640s; decades later, Peter's new calendar, new capital, new numbers, new alphabet, forced shaving of beards; a patriarchate in limbo after the death of Patriarch Adrian in 1700; hundreds of imported Europeans in service and the imposition of European dress and mores on serving men and their families. Many Muscovites — servitors, clergy, and peasants alike — experienced all this with a deep sense of cultural and spiritual dislocation. More than a few objected.

Some dissenters, of whom Talitskii was one, embraced a particularly Russian-centred eschatology, deeming the changes to be signifiers of imminent perdition, the end of days, and above all the arrival of the Antichrist. In this scenario Peter I embodied all manner of perfidy: the beast, the son of Lefort, Swedish, a foreign imposter, as well as the Antichrist. The authorities viewed all this talk as damnable, heretical,

---

[8] Sergei Solov'ev, who had his own fascination with Petrine-era heretics, made a similar observation about Esipov, noting that, while his account of the 1750 dossier contained some mistakes, overall these errors were 'insignificant'. Coming from Sergei Mikhailovich this constituted high praise: S. M. Solov'ev, *Istoriia Rossii s drevneishikh vremen*, St Petersburg, 1913, vol. 15, pp. 1371–73.

[9] This roster does not include dissenters such as Dmitrii Tveretinov, who parted company with Orthodoxy in favour of other faiths, in his case Lutheranism. See E. B. Smilianskaia, *Volshebniki, bogokhul'niki, eretiki. Narodnaia religioznost' i 'dukhovnye prestupleniia' v Rossii XVIII v.*, Moscow, 2003, especially pp. 247 ff.

and treasonous, a potpourri of evil doings (*khuly*), false teachings, misreading of Scripture, or plain ignorance; in short, a veritable pot-pourri of popular supernaturalism, or, in the words of Will Ryan, 'magic'.[10]

*   *   *

In the 1740s, and for reasons unknown, Empress Elizabeth commissioned a search for all governmental records pertinent to Talitskii.[11] Thus began his textual resurrection. Duly assembled and presented to her in 1750, the dossier contains most of the relevant investigatory materials, mostly from the Preobrazhenskii *prikaz* or Chancellery (a court in the suburb of Preobrazhenskii; replaced in 1718 by the Secret Chancellery).[12] This is what Esipov published, and, while the archives contain some additional materials pertinent to the investigation, this dossier remains the fundamental source.[13]

'Grishka' Talitskii had worked more or less unnoticed as a copyist and part-time book dealer for perhaps a decade in the employ of monasteries in and around Moscow. We do not know when or where he was born; nor do we know for sure when, where, or how he died. His anonymity came to a spectacular end on 28 June 1700, when Fedor Kazantsev, a church deacon, informed the Preobrazhenskii Chancellery that he had heard Talitskii utter 'abominable words' ('nepristoinye slova'), the formula for an accusation of *slovo i delo* (*lèse majesté*) about the tsar; that Talitskii possessed tablets and wanted to print these and/ or his notebooks in order to circulate his prophesy to the nation.[14] These

[10] In *The Bathhouse at Midnight*, Will Ryan defined 'magic' capaciously, as an open-ended site of unsanctioned supernaturalism. 'When in doubt as to what should be included... I have erred on the side of inclusiveness': W. F. Ryan, *The Bathhouse at Midnight: An Historic Survey of Magic and Divination in Russia*, University Park, PA, 1999, p. 4.

[11] Precisely why Elizabeth became interested in him is not clear, but one possibility is an upsurge at that time in cases of ruler-as-antichrist prophesies.

[12] Moscow, Rossiiskii gosudarstvennyi arkhiv drevnikh aktov (hereafter RGADA), f. 7, op. 3, no. 1348, 'Spravka po delu 1700 goda o knigopistse Grigor'e Talitskom pisavshim ob antikhriste, 1750 g.'.

[13] RGADA's collection of the original hand-written inventories of *Preobrazhenskii prikaz*, *Tainaia ekspeditsiia*, *Tainaia kantseliariia*, and *Sekretnye dela* (now available online) includes several files containing references to Talitskii, most of them brief, that are not a part of the 1750 digest. I was unable to consult the actual files for this paper, but the inventories often describe them in such detail that one can reasonably deduce what they contain: RGADA, f. 141, op. 1, no. 286; f. 371 op. 2, no. 44; f. 371, op. 6, no. 393/1143; f. 371, op. 6, no. 372/1119; no. 325/1058; no. 195/887; f. 7, op. 3, no. 217. My thanks to Robert Collis for alerting me to RGADA's electronic inventory.

[14] Esipov, *Raskol'nich'i dela*, pp. 59–60.

were grave allegations and, in response, the head of the Chancellery, Prince Fedor Romodanovskii, ordered a broad investigation, a sweeping search in multiple locales for the 'blackguard' (*kovarnik*), anyone associated with him, and any and all written material. Although away on campaign, Peter insisted on being kept apprised.[15] Notices went to at least a dozen archbishops commanding that they come to Moscow forthwith as part of the investigation and Romodanovskii offered a reward of 500 roubles to anyone who could identify his whereabouts, a clear sign of concern.

As a state chancellery the Preobrazhenskii Chancellery investigated crimes against the ruler, but *not* heresy, which was the province of the Patriarchate. This brief defines the entire dossier, both in the line of questioning and in the terminology used to describe the accused ('the criminal Talitskii', 'the blackguard', 'defamer', and so on, but never, for example, 'the sinner' or 'the heretic'). It posed questions about who met with whom and when, who said what or showed what to whom (specifically did Talitskii utter defamatory words against the sovereign in their presence), whether other witnesses heard or read defamatory language, and, if so, whether witnesses told anyone, and in particular whether they informed the authorities. The answers determined the degree of criminal guilt and dictated the severity of punishment, but officials did not touch upon blasphemy, offenses to God, excommunication or anathema. When they inquired into the misuse of religious texts, or other offences to the faith, they steered clear of religious doctrine, even when interrogating clergy. That aspect fell to the Patriarchate, in this instance Stefan Iavorskii, who presided over the Church's inquiry and who delivered its verdict.[16]

Nearly two dozen witnesses were brought in: acquaintances, acolytes, relatives, co-workers, at least one boiar, clergy, each subject to torture, often multiple times.[17] All confirmed knowing Talitskii and to one degree or another being aware of his prophecy. Once in custody, Talitskii underwent extensive interrogation, in which he acknowledged what he had done and said, refused to retract them or to seek mercy. Peter himself took note of his defiance, and years later was quoted as

---

[15] In a letter of June 1701 to Peter I, T. N. Streshnev, long a leading overseer of political investigations, offered Peter a quick update on the Talitskii matter ('until all the archbishops arrive there is not much to be done'): in *Pis'ma i bumagi Petra Velikogo*, St Petersburg, 1887, vol. 1, p. 857.

[16] No Talitskii file has been uncovered in church repositories.

[17] The definitive study of eighteenth-century modes of torture is Anisimov, *Dyba i knut*. The records do not clarify the modes of torture employed in the investigation, and simply use the generic пытки.

recalling having said: 'Oh, criminal Talitskii! So, in your eyes I am the antichrist! God knows [the truth].'[18] In short order Talitskii was tried, convicted, and sentenced to death by smoke and fire.[19] Several witnesses related that he had commanded that people should refuse to pay their taxes or obey Peter's decrees, and instead should give their allegiance to Prince Mikhail Cherkasskii, thought to have been a favourite of the *strel'tsy* (musketeers). Talitskii imagined that the *strel'tsy* would descend onto Moscow to choose Prince Michael ('a good man') to rule.[20] In that context, Talitskii was on familiar terms with Prince Ivan Ivanovich Khovanskii, the son of an earlier champion of the *strel'tsy* (during the bloody 'Khovanshchina', *strel'tsy* revolt, of 1682), who confirmed that he had bemoaned to Talitskii about his fallen stature and sought his counsel about how to respond were one of Peter's barbers to attempt to shave off his beard.[21]

Precious little information exists regarding what Talitskii read or how he interpreted what he read. His work as a copyist seems to have afforded him access to monastic repositories, and it appears that he took advantage of that access to acquaint himself with texts, sufficiently so that he could extract passages from them. He somehow used Scripture to calculate the years since Creation, and while his sources, methods, and results are nowhere elaborated,[22] this piece of legerdemain caught the attention of both Iavorskii and Dimitrii Rostovskii, who themselves had wondered privately whether Creation time was arithmetically consistent with the Old Testament.[23] As best as one can determine, the end-of-days prophecy consisted of snippets from the Book of Revelation, and possibly some patristics. He seems to have approached

[18] Semevskii, *Slovo i delo 1700–1725!*, pp. 134–35.

[19] As far as one can discern from descriptions (which are not very explicit), being smoked meant being placed on smoldering pyres but not set aflame, presumably to allow the condemned one final opportunity to confess and seek penance. Once that failed, they would be set to fire.

[20] Esipov, *Raskol'nich'i dela*, p. 61.

[21] Ibid., pp. 68–69; Evgenii V. Akelev, 'The Barber of All Russia: Lawmaking, Resistance, and Mutual Adaptation During Peter the Great's Cultural Reforms', *Kritika*, 17, 2016, 2, p. 251.

[22] The interrogation includes multiple references to this element in Talitskii's work. His words gave the impression that one of his notebooks was devoted explicitly to calculating time since Creation ('ischislenie let ot sotvoreniia sveta'), an explosive topic in 1700 due to the new calendar. But neither he nor his associates elaborated on his calculations, beyond saying that these specific writings did not contain language that was defamatory.

[23] In December 1707 Dimitrii wrote to Iavorskii, 'I remember at some time in the village of Preobrazhenskoe Talitskii debated with your holiness about the years [...]', in M. A. Fedotova (ed.), *Epistoliarnoe nasledie Dimitriia Rostovskogo*, Moscow, 2005, pp. 132–36.

texts not so much to absorb them or learn, but simply to find validation
for what he and others already believed, that Peter was the Antichrist.

Compare, for example, the key passage from Revelation 17:9 with
Talitsii's rendering. The chapter speaks of the fall of Babylon and
the last king — fundamental to Talitskii's preaching — as part of an
angel's declaration in which numbers and the hidden meaning of the
things that surround her, all of which prefigure the impending Last
Judgement, loom large:

> The seven heads are seven hills [...]. They are also seven kings [...].
> 'The beast who once was and now is not is an eighth king. He belongs
> to the seven and is going to his destruction [...]. The woman you saw is
> the great city [that is Babylon] that rules over the kings of the earth.'[24]

Talitskii transposed Babylon to Moscow, but this had already become
a recurrent trope of dissenter discourse, familiar within the monkish
milieu that Talitskii frequented. His own contribution was arithmetic,
stripping the narrative in Revelation down to a formula, and then
grafting it onto Russian rulership:

> [...] the antichrist will be the eighth king [he is quoted as saying]. By our
> count, in this, the third iteration (*slozhenie*) of the Roman monarchy of
> the Greco-Russian tsars, the eighth tsar is Petr Alekseevich. Thus, he is
> the antichrist. The end of time is at hand. The ruling city of Moscow is
> Babylon, its citizens the Babylonians are the servants of antichrist. And
> such a tsar! He is a tormentor. And hence his son the tsarevich is grown
> from a bad root and is but a rotten branch.[25]

Could that have been it? We simply do not know, but only one
witness, a defrocked priest named Grishka Ivanov, said otherwise.
Talitskii, he recounted, had claimed exegetical support for his prophesy
(along with his calculation of time since Creation) from Genesis,
the Gospels, and the Prophets. But Ivanov did not provide a single
quotation or reference, no book or chapter, leading one to surmise
that Talitskii may have verbally alluded to a deeper scriptural base, but
without textual elaboration. No matter: Talitskii was certain, as were
his confederates. He conveyed his convictions verbally and quite freely,
especially to churchmen, whom he repeatedly asked to communicate his

---

[24] Revelation 17:9, *Holy Bible: New International Version*, London, 1998, pp. 1134–35.
[25] S. N. Vvedenskii, 'Neizvestnoe sochinenie Stefana Iavorskogo', *Khristianskoe chtenie*, no. 708, 1912, p. 901.

truths to leading bishops and abbots with whom he was not personally acquainted. He wanted the Church to hear. He knew how to network and cajole, and his manner of speaking came across as authoritative and persuasive, with the result that some men of prominence, including Archbishop Ignatii of Tambov for example, took his spoken words to heart. Herein, I dare say, lay his magnetism.

*   *   *

We come now to those elements of the received narrative whose documentary foundation is less secure, marked by contradictory, unclear, or missing evidence, untraceable quotes, improbable assumptions and occasional mistakes.

1. Death by Fire or Siberian Exile?

Subsequent to his conviction in November 1701, most accounts maintain, Talitskii was quartered, smoked above a pyre, and executed by fire, as prescribed in the verdict.[26] Others, though, describe a very different scenario, one in which he received an eleventh-hour reprieve. The source for this alternative account is a 1722 pastoral epistle, probably composed by Feofan Prokopovich and shortly thereafter published.[27] It spoke of the urgency to protect impressionable lay believers from the seductions of religious dissenters, and in that context the saga of Talitskii received special attention. The epistle stated that he made a last-minute confession, was thenceforth pulled from the fire, and subsequently sent into exile. It describes how his closest confederate, the Moscow icon painter Ivashko Savin, confronted him while both were under guard. Talitskii conceded 'everything that I have said, all that I taught, is false'. The unrepentant Savin — who was indeed soon executed — became overcome with tears, pain and fury, excoriating Talitskii for his betrayal.[28]

---

[26] Esipov, *Raskol'nich'i dela*, pp. 83–84.

[27] *Polnoe sobranie zakonov Rossiiskoi Imperii* (hereafter *PSZ*), vol. 6, no. 3891, 27 January 1722: 'Pastyrskoe Sviateishago Sinoda uveshchanie k obrashcheniiu raskol'nikov v nedra Pravoslavnyia Tserkvi', pp. 493–95. The relevant paragraph is on p. 495. The published text, titled simply *Uveshchanie*, contains the exact language of the version in *PSZ*: T. A. Bykova and M. M. Gurevich, *Opisanie izdanii napechatannykh kirillitsei 1689–ianvar' 1725 g.*, Moscow, 1958, nos. 147 and 156.

[28] Here the pastoral letter employed emotive language so impassioned that it deserves to be quoted: 'О в какую горесть пришел тот Савин! И с какими слезами раскаявался, и пенял на Талицкаго, для чего в такую беду его привел, и что он ни для чего, только вменяя то за истину, страдать рад был.'

This is quite a disparity. According to Synodal records, the initial draft of the epistle did not include any reference to the confession/reprieve scenario, and, that it was Peter himself who added the passage, tears and all, a full two decades after the fact![29] If true, his intervention speaks volumes about the affair's resonance in the memory of the Tsar. But can we believe this dramatic addendum, given that no earlier source mentioned it? I doubt it. One eyewitness, the senior diplomat Ivan Zheliabuzhskii, wrote in his diary that Talitskii was publicly executed in Red Square in 1702.[30] Could Peter have mixed up Talitskii's fate with that of his unwitting apprentice, Ivashko Savel'ev, who, although beaten by the knout, was spared execution at the last minute and sent 'to distant towns in Siberia'?[31] Possibly, but how then does one explain the dramatic pyre scenario? It is indeed curious.

2. Notebooks, Scrolls and Tablets

Fundamental to the case itself and to all subsequent accounts are the engraved tablets and notebooks that Talitskii carried with him and that enumerated his beliefs, arguments, scriptural annotations, and proofs of the end of days. There is no reason to doubt their existence, at least as physical objects, since they are mentioned by nearly everyone who had direct contact with him, including several clergymen. There had been two stone tablets, on which Talitskii had engraved words of the end of days and coming of the Antichrist. The summary further speaks of letters he had given to friends and confederates, but with scant information about what they contained.[32]

The dossier says precious little about what the notebooks and tablets contained. Some deponents acknowledged having held them or looked at them, but without reading. Others had asked to see them but were denied by Talitskii on one pretext or another. One witness described them as being in quarto and written in a formal hand (*polu ustav*), which as a scribe, Talitskii certainly possessed. One or two referred to chapters, implying perhaps that it had some length to it. But the testimony does not elaborate. Bishop Ignatii described hearing them

[29] *Polnoe sobranie postanovlenii i rasporiazhenii po vedomstvu Pravoslavnogo ispovedaniia Rossiiskoi Imperii*, St Petersburg, 1872, vol. 2 (1722), no. 385, pp. 40–42; see Bykova and Gurevich, *Opisanie izdanii*, p. 228.

[30] 'In that year [1702 GM] the criminal Grishka Talitskii was subject to multiple tortures (*muchen raznymi pytkami*) in Red Square on a major state matter and then put to fire (*sozhzhen*). Many people of various ranks both from the parishes and monastic officials were brought in and tortured and there were major investigations.' I. A. Zheliabuzhskii, *Zapiski, 1682–1709 gg.*, St Petersburg, 1840, p. 210.

[31] Esipov, *Raskol'nich'i dela*, pp. 83–84.

[32] Ibid., pp. 6off.

read aloud, to which Talitskii added that the Bishop was so moved that he wept and kissed them (Ignatii did not recall this).[33] A couple of associates did claim to have read the notebooks but failed to recount what they contained. Some testimony implied that there had been additional copies. Talitskii's apprentice Ivashko and his nephew Mishka are perhaps the most helpful witnesses here, since each testified that they had transcribed whole sections of the notebooks involuntarily and under Talitskii's orders.[34] Archbishop Ignatii also confirmed having taken the notebooks from Grishka Talitskii when both were in Moscow, and shortly thereafter burned them himself. And since these notebooks had been burned, Ignatii continued, no one else saw them and he did not tell anyone else about the notebooks and did not give copies of them to anyone.[35]

Neither Ignatii nor Ivashko, however, said anything about the contents other than they were 'about counting the years, the end of days and antichrist, and Peter was the Antichrist'.[36]

What subsequently happened to the notebooks and tablets remains a mystery. Much of the literature, Esipov included, assumes that when investigators apprehended Talitskii they also confiscated the notebook and tablets. Elizabeth's investigators failed to locate them, however, and Esipov surmised that the notebooks must have perished while in the state repositories some time before 1750.[37] This seems unlikely since the notebooks and tablets would have constituted prima facie written proof of guilt and they would have been cited chapter and verse by the inquisitors. This did not happen. In fact, no one in authority ever acknowledged seeing them, let alone reading them. Moreover, the dossier contains no indication that these written materials had once been a part of the original cache.[38]

3. Additional Writings

Esipov and some others maintain that Talitskii penned at least two treatises, 'O prishestvii v mir Antikhrist' ('On the Coming of the Antichrist into the World') and 'Vrata' ('The Gates'), the latter laying out his numerological argument for the end of days.[39] Talitskii's testimony

---

[33] Ibid., p. 64.
[34] Ibid., pp. 71–72, 81.
[35] Ibid., pp. 64–65.
[36] For example, in ibid., p. 66.
[37] Ibid., p. 7.
[38] Some authors have posited an alternative scenario in which Talitskii destroyed the evidence while still on the run. This sounds plausible, but the dossier is silent on the matter.
[39] Esipov, *Raskol'nich'i dela,* vol. 1, p. 5. Esipov suggests that Talitskii may have

did make fleeting reference to these titles, but no one else claimed to have laid eyes on them, or on any works beyond the notebooks and tablets. Possibly the 'texts' and the notebooks were one and the same, or perhaps these were books that Talitskii intended to write as part of a future public campaign to which he aspired (there are one or two opaque allusions to this). But we simply do not know, and, if they did at one point exist (which is unlikely) they have never come to light.

4. Popular Following

Secondary accounts typically speak of Talitskii's broad popular following (he certainly aspired to one), legendary among all ranks of people in his own time and thereafter. Esipov insisted that 'Talitskii was famous 'throughout all corners of Russia' ('...izvesten byl narodu vo vsekh kontsakh Rossii').[40] P. P. Pekarskii referred to Talitskii's 'thunderous renown' ('gromkuiu izvestnost'').[41] M. I. Semevskii ranked him first among the popular preachers whose works 'circulated everywhere'.[42] Acolytes and admirers, we are told, copied and recopied his notebooks, generation after generation. And yet the many archaeographic expeditions and intrepid treks to even remote regions where dissenting communities secreted themselves have to date not uncovered a *single* text, or even a fragment of a text attributed to Talitskii. By contrast, *khulye* prophecies by quite a few other dissenters *have* surfaced, and often in multiple transcriptions and locations. On balance, then, the evidence for popular solidarity seems shaky at best.

5. Old Believers

Esipov further insisted that dissenter communities knew Talitskii's work well and, 'they respected and honoured his memory as a person who sacrificed his life for his beliefs'.[43] This idea has gained traction in the literature,[44] yet it is almost certainly wrong. Over half a century ago N. B. Golikova offered a detailed and careful analysis demonstrating

---

composed still more works, 'O schislenii let', and 'O padenii Vavilona'. They too have never surfaced.

[40] Esipov, *Raskolnich'i dela*, vol. 1, p. 4. For a recent expression of that view see E. I. Konanova, 'Petr I v massovom soznanii naroda Rossii XVIII v.', *Gumanitarnye i sotsial'nye nauki*, 2014, no. 2, pp. 988–89.

[41] Pekarskii, *Nauka i literatura v Rossii pri Petre Velikom*, vol. 2, p. 80.

[42] Semevskii, *Slovo i delo 1700–1725!*, p. 108. See also A. V. Arsen'ev, 'Nepristoinyia rechi: Posledovatel' Talitskago', *Istoricheskii vestnik*, 1897, no. 8, pp. 390–95.

[43] Esipov, *Raskol'nich'i dela*, pp. 4–5.

[44] Filaret Gumilevskii (Chernigovskii), for example, applied the term 'bezpopovets' (priestless Old Believer) to Talitskii, but without any explanation: Filaret Gumilevskii, *Obzor russkoi dukhovnoi literatury*, St Petersburg, 1884, p. 272.

that Talitskii had no known contacts with any Old Believers, and he never expressed even a passing interest in the questions of liturgical and ritual reform that so exercised the adherents of the Old Belief. Their own anxieties about the Age of the Antichrist and the Last Judgement were manifest. However, judging by his total absence from inventories of Old Believer manuscripts, they neither read nor cited Talitskii, either in his own time or later.[45]

6. The Tsarevich

Multiple secondary accounts state that the tsarevich Aleksei Petrovich held Talitskii in high regard. On the surface, this seems plausible and potentially significant (so long as one ignores the 'rotten branch' metaphor, cited above), given Aleksei's engagement with a wide range of religious figures, including some dissenters, and his poisoned relationship with his father. As with so much else, however, the evidence for the tsarevich's regard apparently hangs from a very slender thread, a single he-said-she-said statement of May 1718 from the tsarevich's testimony:

> I had heard from Petr Sudakov that when he was in the *Preobrazhenskii prikaz* he had heard tell that Ivan Suvorov[46] thought that Talitskii was very clever and they would not have caught him had he not chosen not to give himself up. I also saw some sort of paper (*list*). But I do not know in which year that would have been presented.[47]

*   *   *

[45] Golikova, *Politicheskie protsessy pri Petre*, p. 135. For a general survey of Old Believer writings on the Antichrist, see Robert O. Crummey, *The Old Believers and the World of Antichrist: The Vyg Community and the Russian State, 1694–1855*, Madison, WI, 1970, especially p. 63ff. See also, Morin Perri (Maureen Perrie), 'Russkaia narodnaia eskhatologiia i legenda o Petre I – Antikhriste', *Vestnik SPbGU. Istoriia*, 2016, vyp. 4, pp. 77–86. Perrie mentions Talitskii (p. 80) as one of many such prophets, but she does not link him to the Old Believers. A. V. Voznesenskii's annotated inventories of eighteenth-century Old Believer printed books, several of which contain officially-proscribed disquisitions on the Antichrist, make no mention of Talitskii: A. V. Voznesenskii (ed.), *Kirillicheskie izdaniia staroobriadcheskikh tipografii XVIII– nachala XIX veka. Katalog*, Leningrad, 1991; ibid., *Staroobriadcheskie kirillicheskie izdaniia XVIII veka. Predvaritel'nyi spisok*, St Petersburg, 1994. Inventories of Old Believer eighteenth-century manuscripts have a comparable profile, again with no Talitskii.

[46] Both had been senior *pod'iache* (courtiers or officials) there during the Talitskii affair: A. A. Titov (ed.), *Raskhodnaia kniga patriarshago prikaza kushan'am podavshimsia Patriarkhu Adrianu i raznogo china litsam*, St Petersburg, 1890, p. 317.

[47] N. Ustrialov, *Istoriia tsarstvovaniia Petra Velikogo*, St Petersburg, 1859, vol. 7, p. 249.

Taken together, these points form quite a documentary gap in the tale of Talitskii. Moreover, the scholarship has yet to explore adequately the Patriarchate's position, specifically whether Church officials deemed his prophesies particularly worrisome relative to the myriad blasphemers with whom the Church had to cope. Here is where Archbishop Stefan Iavorskii looms large, the one official designated to address the issue of heresy. The proximate cause of Iavorskii's interventions was Peter's command to interrogate Talitskii personally. Iavorskii's anxieties about the potential reach of Talitskii's end-of-days prophesies ran deep, if for no other reason than the allure they had over several clergymen. He went to some lengths to condemn Talitskii's profanation of the faith, first in the face-to-face meetings and subsequently in written statements. Unfortunately, no transcription or digest exists of their confrontation, not even a clarification of whether there was just one meeting or several. Everyone seems to agree that Iavorskii failed to elicit a confession, but beyond that the literature offers nothing more than speculations about the interchange.

We do have Iavorskii's writings, however, specifically his treatise, *The Signs of the Coming of the Antichrist and the End of Days* (*Znameniia prishestviia Antikhristova i konchiny veka*) and his formal denunciation of the accused, *The Condemnation of Grigorii Talitskii* (*Uveshchanie Grigoriiu Talitskomu*) (not to be confused with the previously mentioned 1722 epistle). Written under Peter's orders, both relied heavily on scriptural exegesis, but otherwise they were quite distinct in function, organization, and language. *Znameniia* constitutes a learned, sober, point-by-point, text-by-text disquisition, and is longer and more reflective than *Uveshchanie*, which is focused on Talitskii. Together they reveal a good deal about Iavorskii's own thinking and his concerns about the epidemic of prophesies in those years, as well as giving us a sense of the prophesies in need of refutation.

Znameniia was published around 1703, and it is reasonably well known in the literature.[48] Its hypothetical audience lay in the parishes, but, given its erudition and length, the actual readership would have come almost exclusively from well-educated clergy. Previous scholarship has established its extensive reliance on Thomas Malvenda's *De Antichristo* (Rome, 1604), both as a template and for its commentary. *Znameniia* is much shorter (about 100 pages versus 600 for *De Antichristo*), and Iavorskii likely extracted sections most relevant to Muscovy. Short of undertaking an intensive passage-by-passage comparison, however,

---

[48] See the entries in Pekarskii, *Nauka i literatura*, vol. 2, pp. 77–80, and Bykova, Gurevich, *Opisanie izdaniii*, no. 29, pp. 92–94.

isolating Iavorskii's separate voice is virtually impossible. Both dwelled on issues and interpretation, the spectrum of arguments regarding the coming of the Antichrist, rather than on individuals and without naming specific culprits (hence no mention of Talitskii).[49]

Iavorskii's introduction, like Malvenda's, speaks of widespread curiosity about the coming of the Antichrist and the end of days. This curiosity he deemed unproblematic in itself, since true faith recognized their inevitability.[50] The danger arose when curiosity evolved into a misguided pursuit of hidden secrets, such as 666 and the Seventh Seal, sinful misuses of the Book of Revelation. He offered clarity and guidance to all wishing to remain faithful in the face of those 'slanderous and profane teachings that assault the conscience of troubled believers'.[51]

Relying upon a question-and-answer format, the allegation versus exegetical proof mode that Iavorskii would deploy later in *Kamen' very*, the text walks the reader through a systematic disquisition on the multiple meanings of 'antichrist', its linguistic etymology, its place in Scripture, his true nature, and most importantly the signs of his coming. The overarching argument is two-fold. First, Scripture states repeatedly that no one other than God the Father ('not even the angels or the son')[52] can know when the end of days will arrive, or even what exactly they refer to. Second, the Antichrist will appear in the wake of the end of days and not before. Here the text takes on several mystical and numerological prophesies in order to show their fickleness and the futility of the enterprise.[53]

The insistence that latter days precede the coming of the Antichrist implicitly refutes Talitskii, as does the debunking of secret meanings, but they refute many others as well. Muscovite audiences might have read Talitskii into some other passages, but these too came out of Malvenda. Thus, a chapter on the end of the Roman monarchy and its scriptural meaning briefly mentions Revelation 17, but, following Malvenda, Iavorskii frames the chapter around Paul's epistles (Thessalonians 2:1–3), augmented by Chrysostom's commentaries. It warns believers not to be deceived by false prophesies of the Second Coming, a broad category indeed. It then references the Book of Daniel, where Daniel explains to King Nebuchadnezzar the meaning of his dream about the four kingdoms: 'Your mind turned to things to come [...] The Great God has

---

[49] Collis, *The Petrine Instauration*, p. 230; Pekarskii, *Nauka i literatura*, vol. 2, pp. 79–80. Iavorskii had access to a 1647 edition.

[50] For example, *Znameniia*, pp. 36–39.

[51] Ibid., p. viii.

[52] Ibid., p. 6.

[53] Ibid., pp. 10, 28, 57–62.

shown the king what will take place in the future.'[54] Only God, it says, can reveal the hidden meaning of numbers, signs, and dreams ('No wise man, merchant, magician, or diviner can explain [...] the mystery [...] but there is a God in heaven who reveals mysteries'). Chapter seven of *Znameniia*, 'the throne of Antichrist',[55] turned to Revelation 11 among other texts to show that the Antichrist will appear in Jerusalem in the church of Solomon, on the throne of David (for Russian readers this meant *not* in Moscow or on the Romanov throne).[56] This allusion counters Talitskii, but, once again, its target is much wider, implicitly including Old Believers. Overall, then, extrapolating a specifically anti-Talitskii stream in *Znameniia* (as some have proposed) seems too speculative.

The only text of Iavorskii's devoted explicitly to Talitskii is *Uveshchanie*, yet inexplicably it has received scant attention. Long thought to have been lost, it was rediscovered in 1912 by S. N. Vvedenskii while he was working in the manuscripts of the Russian Society of History and Antiquities.[57] Subsequently only Golikova has discussed it, and in her case without delving into its religious contents (this was, after all, the 1950s). Although relatively brief, *Uveshchanie* mounts a full-fledged, relentless, and furious denunciation of an unrepentant blasphemer. Iavorskii wrote it in monologue, as if speaking directly to Talitskii, for example: 'accursed Grigorii, you [in the singular throughout] thought to read divine scripture for your own purposes [...] substituting your own ignorant reasoning for its exalted essence [...].'[58]

The goal throughout is not to reason with him, not to debate or interpret, but to condemn, and to display Talitskii's ignorance of Scripture: 'Regarding the numbering of years, time, and dating, you pretend to great wisdom, but you forget, accursed one, that Christ says: "It is not for you to know the times or dates the Father has set by his own authority".'[59] The text contains many such quotes, all intended to eviscerate Talitskii's pride and ignorance, and to unmask the sinfulness of his defamation of the Tsar. The rhetorical refrain 'did you not read' is employed repeatedly and to withering effect: 'Did you not read, accursed one, in St Peter's first epistle, chapter two: "Fear God, slaves, honour the king, submit yourselves to your masters with all fervency,

---

[54] Daniel 2:29–45.

[55] *Znameniia*, pp. 25–35, 48ff.

[56] Ibid., pp. 51–55.

[57] MS no. 213, pp. 84–90. S. N. Vvedenskii, 'K biografii mitropolita Stefana Iavorskogo', *Khristianskoe chtenie*, 1912, no. 7–8, pp. 892–919. The text of *Uveshchanie* is on pp. 909–19.

[58] Ibid., p. 910.

[59] Acts 1:7.

not just to those who are good and thoughtful, but also to those who are harsh".' (Peter 1:2, 17–18.). '[...] out of your muddle-headed arrogance in chapter 1 of the book of Baruch the prophet'; '[...] in Titus chapter 2'; '[...] in the first book of Kings [...]'; 'in the Tales of Solomon [...]', and so on.

Towards the middle the *Uveshchanie* shifts focus from denunciation to tutelage, albeit still in the most acerbic language, and specifically sets out how Talitskii ought to set about seeking penance:

> I say to you: give up your prideful honour, o thrice accursed arrogant one, in choosing what you study as the basis of your salvation [...]. O ignorant philosopher [...] you are like a turtle without wings yearning to fly high, and by these secret prophesies and apocalyptic visions of yours you concocted in your own mind these defamations of the holy Church fathers [...].
>
> Repent all your evil deeds if you wish to save your soul. This I bequeath to you in the name of our Lord [...] rejoice in abandoning your thievish ways [...].

The final section of *Uveshchanie* includes an aside to 'Orthodox Christians', simultaneously warning them and beseeching them not to waiver in their faith, to reject Talitskii's 'demonic treacheries, his beastly and seductive efforts at "wisdom", his perversion of the soul'. Then it returns to Talitskii for one final admonition:

> I pray for you, brother Grigorii, and it is my testament to you in the name of our Lord God Jesus Christ, give no thought to earthly matters, and forget your notions of wisdom and your futile debating, I search for your soul [...]. Have no fear of execution and torment, this is temporary and it will soon cease, but do fear eternal torment [...].

This is a blistering piece of writing, an unalloyed, fire-and-brimstone rage whose fulminations figuratively sear the eyes of the reader. Some of the language hints that Talitskii had striven to engage Iavorskii in a personal duel of exegeses (for example, 'you thought to read divine scripture for your own purposes'). Perhaps Iavorskii's tone reflected a frustration that some attribute to him over his failure to prevail against Talitskii in this hypothetical duel (this is what Matseevich thought had happened). If that is so, we never hear Talitskii's side. That Iavorskii chose simply to quote texts — in marked contrast to his other writings — rather than guide Talitskii through their meaning, not even Revelation 19, is striking, and it suggests that he had given up trying to convince him. He alluded to the years and to counting, for example, but he saw no need to show where Talitskii had misunderstood. This structure may also have been part of a deeper rhetorical strategy to deny textual standing to the prophesy's particularities. From that perspective *Uveshchanie's* total silence about the notebooks seems noteworthy.

What about the audience? Since the *Uveshchanie* addresses Talitskii directly one assumes that it must have been presented or read to him. If so, there is no record of his reaction. Iavorskii's reference to Orthodox Christians implies some sort of public circulation, but there is no trace of it, no official order to make it known to the dioceses, or evidence that any parishioners saw it or heard it. It remained in manuscript, and only the one copy has come to light, meaning it almost certainly stayed in-house. No courtiers or chancellery officials mentioned it, and neither did foreign envoys. Peter must have seen it, since it was written on his insistence, and the furious tone likely was meant for his eyes, to assure him that the Church was equally outraged by the profanations against the sovereign. This, I suspect, was its primary, possibly its only purpose, to assuage the Tsar rather than to humble the condemned.

*   *   *

This venture into the Talitskii file began with a long list of questions, and, as we see, more than a few of remain. Still, some conclusions are warranted, particularly about historical memory. Talitskii's post-mortem resilience sprang neither from popular acclaim, of which there is precious little evidence, nor from Old Believer respect, of which there is none. His prophesies and subsequent punishment achieved notoriety to be sure, but almost exclusively among the hierarchs of state and Church, within whose milieux memory of him remained vivid until the mid-eighteenth century. Others may have recalled Talitskii privately, but they left no trace. The purported public visibility, to which he assuredly aspired, came only much later and mostly as a result of Esipov's curiosity. Even then it was constructed entirely on the official record rather than on popular lore. Paradoxically, then, those most responsible for crafting the foundation of Talitskii's memorialization were the two individuals most determined to annihilate him, Peter, the Tsar, and Iavorskii, the Patriarchal locum tenens. Without their words and deeds he might well have rapidly faded from memory. Such are the ironies of history. Magic.

The Adoption of the Swedish Rite in Eighteenth-Century Russia — Acculturation, Power Politics and Mysticism

Yuri Stoyanov

School of Oriental and African Studies

THE liberalization of the study of the history of Freemasonry in Russia and Eastern Europe in the ex-Eastern Bloc countries since the early 1990s has allowed for the increasing accessibility and publication of important archival evidence on the rise, spread and fortunes of Freemasonry in Russia during the eighteenth and early nineteenth centuries. This is all the more significant as the introduction of Freemasonry into Russia and the vicissitudes of its development until its formal ban in 1822 belong to areas of study which have evolved under the influence of religious, ideological and nationalist agendas which still continue to exercise a distorting impact on the historical and current Russian cultural and political discourses on Russian Freemasonry. For several decades after its introduction Freemasonry played a major role in Russian cultural and intellectual life which was largely unparalleled in any other contemporaneous European country.[1] New reassessments of the history and various facets of eighteenth- and early nineteenth-century Russian Freemasonry can also now draw on and benefit from the ongoing progress, findings and inter-disciplinary projects on the study of contemporaneous Freemasonry in Central and Western Europe and North America.

The development of early Freemasonry in Russia[2] was originally conditioned by the activity of foreign Freemasons and lodges: English, Scottish, German and eventually French and Swedish. These lodges were formed by the various foreign colonies of diplomats, merchants

---

[1] Isabel de Madariaga, 'Freemasonry in Eighteenth-Century Russian Society', in eadem, *Politics and Culture in Eighteenth-Century Russia: Collected Essays*, London and New York, 1998, pp. 150–67, especially p. 150.

[2] For an up-to-date discussion of the legends and actual evidence of Masonic presence and influence at the court of Peter the Great, see Robert Collis, 'Freemasonry and the Occult at the Court of Peter the Great', *Aries*, 1, 2006, 6, pp. 1–26; Robert Collis, *The Petrine Instauration: Religion, Esotericism and Science at the Court of Peter the Great, 1689–1725*, Leiden, 2007, pp. 32–35; see also Ernest Zitser, 'A Mason–Tsar?: Freemasonry and Fraternalism at the Court of Peter the Great', in Andreas Önnerfors and Robert Collis (eds), *Freemasonry and Fraternalism in Eighteenth-Century Russia*, Sheffield, 2009, pp. 7–33.

and so on and thus were created by and for foreigners. Russian membership of these early lodges seems to have been largely confined to representatives of the Russian nobility (particularly aristocrats pursuing a military career).[3] Conditions during the reigns of Elizabeth (1741–61) and Peter III (1761–62) allowed for the further spread of Freemasonry and subsequently Russian Masonic systems and lodges expanded and multiplied significantly during the reign of Catherine II (1762–96).

The early prevalence of English Freemasonry found its expression in the appointment by the Grand Lodge of England of Ivan Perfil'evich Elagin (1725–93) — a poet, head of the Imperial Theatre administration and for a time Catherine II's personal secretary — as Grand Master of the Grand Provincial Lodge of Russia. During the heyday of its influence the alliance of lodges presided over by Elagin (the so-called First Elagin Union) comprised fourteen lodges and attracted a number of major figures from the Russian political and cultural elite, active in the upper ranks of the army, the navy, the state administration and the imperial court, including members of Russia's most influential noble families and some Orthodox clergymen.

Operating in accordance with English Craft Masonry, the First Elagin Union coexisted, interacted and on occasions found itself in rivalry with other Masonic systems which had been introducing the newly-created and fashionable Masonic higher degrees rites from Western and Central Europe. The Rite of the Strict Observance was imported into Russia not long after its introduction in Germany by Baron von Hund. With its rich ceremonial and its core legend comprising Templarist and chivalric themes, the Rite of the Strict Observance understandably proved very appealing to various representatives of the Russian aristocratic and military elite who found the whole rite more attractive than the traditional three craft degrees system. The 'clerical' modification of the Rite of the Strict Observance in the system of the so-called 'Clerici Ordinis Templariorum' (or 'Clercs de la Stricte Observance') of Johann August Starck — who spent some time in St Petersburg in the 1760s — also made some inroads in Russia during this period but did not succeed in making a lasting impression on Russian Freemasonry.[4] Finally, in

---

[3] The earlier collection of biographical data on eighteenth-century Russian Freemasons in Tatiana Bakounine, *Le repertoire biographique des franc-maçons russes (XVIII et XIX siècle)*, Paris, 1967, has been now superseded by Andrei Serkov's major work (updated on the basis of much new archival material), the detailed biographical dictionary, *Rossiiskoe masonstvo 1731–2000: Entsiklopedicheskii slovar'*, Moscow, 2001.

[4] On Johann August Starck and his role in Russian Freemasonry, see Boris Telepneff, 'J. A. Starck and his Rite of Spiritual Freemasonry', *Transactions of the*

the mid–1760s there emerged a specific Russian higher grades system, the so-called Melissino Rite which comprised seven grades and was created by General Petr Ivanovich Melissino (1724–92),[5] who was a very active figure in Russian Freemasonry and in the successive alliances of lodges under Elagin. But it was the introduction of the so-called Weak or Relaxed Observance (also known as the Swedish–Berlin) system of Count Zinnendorf (which integrated higher degrees rituals from the Swedish Rite) and was brought into Russia in the early 1770s by Baron Johann G. L. von Reichel (1729–91) which posed the greatest challenge to Elagin's alliance of lodges.

As in Central and Western European Freemasonry, the introduction of higher grades systems in Russia had already led to a growing polemic between the supporters of the traditional craft degrees system and the adherents of the higher degrees concerning the recognition and definition of 'true' and 'false' or 'spurious' Freemasonry. Following Elagin's initial opposition to the Zinnendorf system (which rapidly grew in popularity and membership) a compromise between the Elagin and Reichel alliance of lodges in 1776 entailed the formation of a single union under the Grand Mastership of Elagin but also the adoption of the Zinnendorf Rite in all lodges under the new, reformed, Grand Provincial Lodge. The upper stratum of the hierarchy of the new Elagin–Reichel union included a number of influential Russian political and military figures and its Deputy Grand Master was a no less powerful figure than Count Nikita Panin (1718–93) who as a foreign minister masterminded Russian foreign policy during the early years of Catherine II's reign (including the well-known 'Northern System' of political alliances in northern Europe), while acting also as a tutor for Catherine's son, Grand Duke Paul.[6] Widely seen as a protector of the Grand Duke's interests, Count Nikita Panin had devised ambitious projects to reform the Russian state which, despite her initial interest, Catherine eventually refused to endorse; hence his aspirations to receive monarchical approval and implementation of his programme were re-focused on Grand Duke Paul.

Quatuor Coronati Lodge, 41, 1929, pp. 238–86, *passim.*
    [5] On General Melissino and the background of the Melission Rite, see Robert Collis, 'Illuminism in the Age of Minerva: Pyotr Ivanovich Melissino (1726–1797) and High-Degree Freemasonry in Catherine the Great's Russia', *COLLeGIUM: Studies Across Disciplines in the Humanities and Social Sciences,* 16, 2014, pp. 128–68.
    [6] On the figures of Nikita Panin, his brother Petr Panin, and the political and noble factions associated with their political and social designs, see David L. Ransel, *The Politics of Catherinian Russia: The Panin Party,* New Haven, CT, 1975; Aleksandr Gavriushkin, *Graf Nikita Panin. Iz istorii russkoi diplomatii XVIII veka,* Moscow, 1989.

Despite its ambitions to overcome the internal schisms and divisions among the Russian Masons, the Elagin-Reichel alliance inherited much of the tensions and discords that had plagued Russian Freemasonry before the compromise of 1776. The higher degrees rituals which Zinnendorf had borrowed from the Swedish Rite appeared in his system in an incomplete fashion and in effect did not include much material on the rituals of initiation into the Chapter degrees above the seventh degree. Unsurprisingly some Russian lodges and individual Freemasons were bound to seek a direct contact with Swedish Freemasonry and an unmediated access to the highest degrees of the Swedish Rite.

Soon after the establishment of the Elagin-Reichel union, the young Prince Aleksandr Kurakin (1752–1818), nephew of Count Nikita Panin and childhood friend of Grand Duke Paul, went on an official diplomatic mission to Sweden, accompanied by Prince Gavriil Gagarin (1745–1805). The mission also had a distinct Masonic agenda,[7] as he had been entrusted by the leadership of the newly-expanded version of Russia's Grand Provincial Lodge to make a direct approach to the Grand Lodge of Sweden, asking for his personal initiation into the higher degrees of the Swedish Rite and their introduction into Russian Freemasonry. Initiated a few years earlier into the craft by Count Nikita Panin, he was additionally initiated in Stockholm into the Swedish Rite higher degrees (which the Grand Lodge of Sweden deemed were accessible to him). There are indications that he was also given a charter to open a Chapter in St Petersburg intended to preside over Swedish Rite Freemasonry in Russia.

Reportedly, Duke Karl of Södermanland, brother of the Swedish King Gustavus III and future King Charles XIII, who in 1774 had become Grand Master of both Swedish Rite systems, the Grand Lodge and the Illuminated Chapter, personally conducted Prince Kurakin's initiation into the higher degrees of the Swedish Rite.

The subsequent course of events surrounding the introduction of the Swedish Rite in Russia and its chronology is unclear. Apparently Gustavus III's entourage was expected to bring all the necessary documents needed to open the Swedish Rite Chapter in St Petersburg during his visit to Russia in the summer of 1777.[8] At the same time the negotiations between Elagin's Grand Provincial Lodge and the Swedish Grand Lodge encountered a series of delays and difficulties

---

[7]   On the interlinkage between the political and Masonic agendas of Prince Kurakin's mission, see Ransel, *The Politics of Catherinian Russia*, pp. 256–59.

[8]   On these expectations, see, for example, the material presented in P. P. Pekarskii, *Dopolneniia k istorii masonstva v Rossii XVIII stoletiia*, St Petersburg, 1869, pp. 61ff.

in circumstances which are unclear.[9] For a variety of reasons Elagin eventually declined the offer to head the reformed Russian Grand Provincial Lodge which was expected to practise the Swedish Rite system under the auspices of the Grand Lodge of Sweden.[10]

The Grand Lodge of Sweden and the Russian Freemasons and networks engaged in the establishment of the Swedish Rite in Russia decided to proceed without the participation of Elagin and the lodges and Freemasons who followed his lead. In February 1778, the Phoenix Chapter (Capitulum Petropolitan, Phoenix), headed by Prince Gagarin as a Prefect (Praefectus Magnus), officially opened in St Petersburg, and in May 1779 Gagarin obtained a patent as a Provincial Grand Master from Duke Karl of Södermanland.[11] The formal inauguration of Russia's new Provincial Grand Lodge, practising the Swedish Rite (called also the Russian National Lodge) in May 1779[12] was followed by the formation of another supreme body, the Directorate (or Council) accomplished in the summer of 1780. The Directorate was supposed to coordinate and control the work of the Swedish-system lodges in Russia, act as a judge in disagreements between the lodges, deal with and discipline potential misdeeds in them and act as an important link with the Swedish Rite Illuminated Chapter in Stockholm. Indeed it was envisaged that one of the representatives of the Swedish Chapter would have a permanent place and vote in the Directorate. The creation of the Directorate was legitimized by a French-language *Instruction* forwarded to the Russian National Lodge by Duke Karl of Södermanland.[13]

---

[9]   The evidence of the introduction of the Swedish Rite in Russia upon Prince Kurakin's return to St Petersburg in the spring of 1777 is uneven and sometimes contradictory; cf. the somewhat differing reconstructions of its development and chronology in Aleksandr Pypin. *Russkoe masonstvo. XVIII i pervaia chetvert' XIX v.*, Petrograd, 1916, pp. 140–46; G. V. Vernadskii, *Russkoe masonstvo v tsarstvovanie Ekateriny II*, Petrograd, 1917, pp. 72–82; Tira Sokolovskaia, *Kapitul Feniksa, Vysshee tainoe masonskoe pravlenie v Rossii (1778–1822 gg.)*, Petrograd, 1916; reprint Moscow, 2000, pp. 5–25.

[10]   For assessments of Elagin's motives to decline the offer to head a Russian Grand Provincial Lodge adhering to the Swedish Rite system, cf. Pypin, *Russkoe masonstvo*, pp. 141–43; Vernadskii, *Russkoe masonstvo*, pp. 73–75; Douglas Smith, *Working the Rough Stone: Freemasonry and Society in Eighteenth-Century Russia*, DeKalb, IL, 1999, p. 214 n.138 who (on the basis of his study of Kurakin's correspondence with Stockholm, kept in Moscow, Tsentr khraneniia istoriko-dokumental'nykh kollektsii, f. 1412, op. 1, d. 5300, 1.12) concludes that Elagin's main motive was his increasing concern with the true magnitude of Kurakin's ambitions.

[11]   The text of the patent (based on an eighteenth-century German manuscript) is published in Sokolovskaia, *Kapitul Feniksa*, pp. 107–10.

[12]   The text of the General Laws of the Russian National Lodge, dating from 5 January 1780 (based on an eighteenth-century German manuscript) is published in ibid., pp. 102–07.

[13]   *Instruction pour le Directoire établi á St. Pétersbourg donnée à Stockholm le 9 mai*

The newly-established Russian National Lodge (also known as the Gagarin union) enjoyed a rapid growth and rise to prominence in Russian Freemasonry. Apart from the newly-formed Swedish-system lodges, older lodges also joined the Gagarin union which further gained both individual Freemasons and whole lodges from the Elagin–Reichel alliance. In May 1780 Duke Karl formally legitimized fourteen Russian lodges practising the Swedish Rite in the Gagarin union[14] whose centre of gravity lay in St Petersburg, with four lodges in Moscow and another four in provincial Russian cities.

The expanded Russian Grand National Lodge was soon to encounter serious obstacles caused by both internal and external factors. Duke Karl's declaration in 1780 stated explicitly that Russia constituted a ninth Masonic province directly subordinate to him as a head (Vicarius Salomonis) of the Swedish Rite system. The declaration was seen by some Russian Freemasons, especially in Moscow, as taking too far the Grand National Lodge's dependence on and subordination to the Stockholm Grand Lodge. This perceived subordination led not only to debates and disagreements within the Russian Swedish Rite lodges but also eventually to moves to free the Gagarin union from Swedish control.

Furthermore, along with Elagin's opposition to the Swedish Rite higher degrees, the issue of access to these degrees remained a source of tension and disputes among the Swedish-system Russian lodges. The lodges of the Gagarin union received the higher grades rituals up to and including the Swedish Rite seventh degree from the Grand Lodge in Stockholm but the latter chose to keep the grades above it inaccessible to the Russian lodges. This continuing lack of admittance into the highest chapter degrees of the Swedish Rite led to the re-orientation of some prominent Freemasons from the Gagarin union to other higher degree systems such as the Masonic Rosicrucian Rite of *Der Orden des Gold- und Rosenkreutzes* which since the 1750s had been gaining influence in the German-speaking areas of Europe.

However, what proved truly dangerous for the establishment and existence of Swedish-system Freemasonry in Russia were its high-level links with Sweden which, to an extent encouraged by Catherine herself, came to be viewed in Russian court circles as secret and uncontrollable

---

1780, kept in Moscow, Rossiiskaia gosudarstvennaia biblioteka, f. 147, op. 1, ed. khr. 338, no. 374; published in Pypin, *Russkoe masonstvo*, pp. 441–54.

[14] The formal document with which Duke Karl officially legitimized the fourteen Russian lodges operating the Swedish Rite is published in Sokolovskaia, *Kapitul Feniksa*, pp. 110–12.

channels of communication for potential anti-Russian conspiracies and subversion. Significantly, the Grand Lodge of Sweden adhered to strict and explicit requirements for an old and proven noble lineage as a necessary prerequisite for candidates wishing to join the Swedish Rite. Due to this prerequisite, and the Swedish Rite's evident fashion in Russian society in that period, prominent members of Russia's old and influential houses became a large presence in the Phoenix Chapter and the upper hierarchy of the Grand National Lodge. The entry of so many members of the Russian aristocracy (many of whom played a major political role in the Empire) into a Masonic system formally controlled by and subordinate to an elitist Masonic body in Stockholm, predictably was viewed with alarm and consternation by Catherine. Both Kurakin and Gagarin were not only childhood friends of Grand Duke Paul but had continued to exercise influence at his court as his closest and favourite associates. The leadership of the Gagarin union included other major aristocratic representatives of Paul's 'party'. In a period of intermittent tensions between Russia and Sweden, when also the various strains between the Empress and the heir to the throne were becoming more and more evident (including the issue of foreign policy orientation), Catherine could hardly tolerate the possibility of Swedish influence reaching Paul through Kurakin, Gagarin and their networks.

As the early successes of Swedish-system Freemasonry in Russia were becoming more and more visible and the Gagarin union was expanding through taking over lodges and forming new ones, Catherine and the imperial administration tried to halt this process with swift and well-targeted measures. As early as 1779 the chief of the St Petersburg police, Prince Petr Lopukhin, twice investigated the St Petersburg lodges of the Gagarin union, focusing his inspection on their links and correspondence with their Swedish counterparts and with Duke Karl in particular. Soon after Lopukhin's investigations, Catherine is reported to have ordered the closure of the Swedish-system lodges, while Lopukhin advised the St Petersburg lodges of the Gagarin alliance to discontinue their work.[15] The Empress and her officials then took measures to limit the influence of the major figures who were close to Paul and were also involved in the establishment of the Swedish Rite in Russia. In 1780 the head of the Swedish-system Grand National Lodge,

---

[15] On the circumstances surrounding Lopukhin's investigations and Catherine's first measures against Swedish-system Freemasonry, cf. Mikhail Longinov, *Novikov i moskovskie martinisty*, Moscow, 1867; reprint St Petersburg, 2000, pp. 128–29, Pypin, *Russkoe masonstvo*, pp. 149–51; Vernadskii, *Russkoe masonstvo*, pp. 82–83, 299–301; Sokolovskaia, *Kapitul Feniksa*, pp. 24–25.

Prince Gagarin, was compelled to move to a new government post in Moscow and thus moved away from St Petersburg, then the nerve centre of the Swedish Rite in Russia. In the autumn of the same year Count Nikita Panin retired to his provincial estate and Paul was only allowed to visit his old tutor shortly before his death in 1783. In 1782 Prince Kurakin was also removed from the big political stage – he had to leave St Petersburg and return to his Saratov provincial estate.

In 1780, moreover, Catherine articulated her growing antipathy towards Freemasonry in the publication in French, German and Russian of her first anti-Masonic writing, the anonymous pamphlet, *The Secret of the Anti-Absurd Society, Discovered by Someone Who Isn't a Member*, followed by her three anti-Masonic plays, *The Deceiver, The Deceived* and *The Siberian Shaman*, published and staged anonymously in St Petersburg and Moscow in 1785–87.[16] In addition to her literary onslaught on Freemasonry her police regulations in April 1782 (*Ustav blagochiniia*) contained a clause prescribing measures against illegitimate brotherhoods and societies which could be used against Russian Masonic lodges to order their closure and prohibition.

The beginning of Catherine's campaign against Swedish-system Freemasonry was accompanied by a change of direction in Russia's foreign policy — away from its existing links with Prussia (favoured by diplomats like Count Nikita Panin and indeed by Grand Duke Paul), towards closer links with Austria. Consequently, when in 1782 Paul and his second wife, Mariia Fedorovna, accompanied by Prince Kurakin, embarked on their extended Western European tour, passing through Paris, Vienna and much of the Italian peninsula, and conscious of the Prussophile affinities of her son, Catherine excluded Prussia and Berlin as destinations on the trip. Nevertheless, reports and rumours started to circulate that the Grand Duke took part in the work of Masons or was actually initiated in a Masonic lodge during his stay in Vienna, complementing earlier rumours that he had been initiated into the craft during his earlier trip to Germany in 1776 or that the Swedish king Gustavus III initiated him into the Swedish Rite during his visit to St Petersburg in 1777.[17] The chronology and extent of Prince

---

[16] Published and edited in *Sochineniia Imperatritsy Ekateriny II*, ed. Aleksandr Nikolaevich Pypin, St Petersburg, vol. 1, 1901. On the anti-Masonic nature and satires in the plays, cf. Aleksandr V. Semeka, 'Russkie rozenkreitsery i sochineniia Imperatritsy Ekateriny II', *Zhurnal Ministerstva narodnogo prosveshcheniia*, 39, 1902, 2, pp. 343–401; Pypin, *Russkoe masonstvo*, pp. 262–82; Smith, *Working the Rough Stone*, pp. 145–51.

[17] On the intriguing but scanty and controversial nature of the evidence of the links between Paul and Russian Freemasonry (including some iconographic data), cf.

Kurakin's involvement in the rumoured Masonic episode in Vienna with Paul remain unclear,[18] but if it happened it certainly contributed to Catherine's later decision to remove him from St Petersburg and isolate him on his provincial estate.

Kurakin may have been marginalized on his estate but Gagarin's dispatch to Moscow did not halt the work of Swedish-system Freemasonry in Russia and apparently led to a certain duality in its structure. With the work of the Grand National Lodge and the Phoenix Chapter in St Petersburg being severely curtailed or even ostensibly discontinued, Gagarin ventured to set up another Swedish-system Provincial Lodge and Chapter in Moscow. The mechanisms of secrecy inherent in the hierarchy and structures of communication within Swedish-system Freemasonry (as well as in other related systems) and the work of its chapters clearly were helping its Russian version to sustain its continuity in the new adverse circumstances. However, the conditions for the activity and survival of Swedish-system Freemasonry in Russia were steadily deteriorating. Gagarin tried to create more Swedish-system lodges in Moscow and his new Provincial Lodge there was refashioned into the Sphinx Lodge which became the focal point of the Swedish Rite in Moscow. In this period the Pelican of Charity Lodge in St Petersburg may have assumed some of the functions of the old Phoenix Chapter, including the maintenance of the connections with the Grand Lodge and the Grand Chapter in Stockholm. The other Swedish-system lodges in St Petersburg and elsewhere had to limit greatly the extent and visibility of their work. The increasing prominence of Moscow as the new centre of the Swedish Rite in Russia to a certain extent stemmed from the increasing pressures on its hitherto dominant institutions in St Petersburg. But it was also indicative of the growing influence of a diverse Masonic movement in Moscow which in the next few years overshadowed its counterpart in St Petersburg.

Evgenii Shumigorskii, 'Imperator Pavel I i masonstvo', in Sergei Petrovich Mel'gunov and Nikolai Pavlovich Sidorov, *Masonstvo v ego proshlom i nastoiashchem*, 2 vols, Moscow, 1914–15, 2, pp. 135–52; Tira Ottovna Sokolovskaia, 'Dva portreta Imperatora Pavla I s masonskami emblemami', *Russkaia starina*, 1908, 10, pp. 81–95; Ernst Friedrichs, *Geschichte der einstigen Maurerei in Russland nach dem Quellmaterial der Grossen Landesloge zu Berlin*, Berlin, 1904, pp. 91–97; Vernadskii, *Russkoe masonstvo*, p. 300 (according to Vernadskii the European trip of Paul as a whole had a Masonic agenda); Roderick I. McGrew, *Paul I of Russia, 1754–1801*, New York, 1992, pp. 194–95; Smith, *Working the Rough Stone* p. 175.

[18] For an assessment that Prince Kurakin indeed served as the intermediary through whom Paul was introduced into Freemasonry see Pekarskii, *Dopolneniia*, p. 163.

Towards the end of 1780 or early in 1781 the Moscow Masonic arena witnessed the foundation of a new elitist, self-proclaimed 'secret' and 'scientific' lodge, named Harmony. The lodge founders declared that they aimed to distance themselves from the disagreements and controversies among the various Masonic systems. Instead they intended to focus on the study of the core Masonic doctrines underlying the diverse Masonic rites and on the quest for the higher degrees of true Freemasonry. These founders included very influential figures on the Moscow Masonic scene such as Prince Nikita Trubetskoi, whose lodge Osiris was otherwise involved in the Swedish Rite, hence it made overtures to Prince Gagarin's Sphinx Lodge. This newly founded lodge reflected the growing calls in the Moscow Masonic movement for a general reorientation of Russian Freemasonry and for its release from what was perceived by many as an extreme dependence on Sweden. Among the founders were two enthusiastic supporters of this trend who became a dominant force in Russian Freemasonry in the 1780s — the prominent writer, publisher and educationalist Nikolai Novikov (1744–1816) and Johann-Georg Schwarz (1751–84), lecturer and later professor at Moscow University.

The Harmony Lodge was supposed also to act as a kind of a neutral forum where the leading Masonic figures in Moscow could meet and exchange ideas regardless of the Masonic systems to which they belonged. The lodge was certainly instrumental in the Russian Masonic moves intended to reduce direct Swedish influence and (what was seen as) interference in Russian Masonic affairs which took place in 1781 and 1782. Although Russian Freemasonry comprised various systems, following Duke Karl's proclamation of 1780 declaring that Russia represented the ninth Masonic province subordinate to him, the general perception in Europe at that time was that Russian Freemasonry was on the whole controlled by the Grand Lodge of Sweden.

In view of the forthcoming Masonic convention at Wiesbaden in 1782, in the previous year the Harmony Lodge empowered Schwarz to leave for Germany and present an appeal to Ferdinand, Duke of Brunswick and Grand Master of the Rite of the Strict Observance, pleading for the recognition of Russia as an independent Masonic province. The written appeal deplored the current state of Russian Freemasonry, which it depicted as being inordinately dominated by the high nobility and beset by excessive focus on 'Templarism' and formal ritualism.[19] The appeal also explicitly stated that the links between Russian Freemasonry and

---

[19] The text of the appeal is published in S. V. Eshevskii, *Sochineniia po russkoi istorii*, Moscow, 1900, pp. 214–15.

a Swedish prince of the blood had aroused Catherine II's concern and indignation. Thus the Moscow Freemasons were essentially declaring to the Masonic world that Russian Freemasonry could face political problems because of its close links with the Swedish court and the only way to secure its safety was to disassociate itself from the Swedish *liaison dangereux*.

Duke Ferdinand's reaction to the appeal was positive[20] and he represented Russia at the Wiesbaden convention, which, amid the growing controversies with the Grand Lodge of Sweden over its decisions, granted Russia the status of an independent (the eighth) Masonic province.[21] Leaving the post of the Provincial Grand Master of this newly-established eighth province vacant, early in 1783 the leading Moscow Freemasons began to set up the hierarchy of its Chapter and Directorate in Moscow and its dependent bodies in St Petersburg and the provinces. As the reorganization of the Russian Masonic movement was gathering pace, Gagarin, with his Moscow Sphinx Lodge and most of the lodges dependent on it, began to gravitate closer to, or actually entered the alliance of, the new eighth Masonic province institutions, although some of these lodges continued to maintain close links with Stockholm.

In addition to his contact with Duke Ferdinand during his journeys in Germany Schwarz established close links with some of the leading figures behind the Masonic Rosicrucian Rite of *Der Orden des Gold- und Rosenkreuzes*, concentrated initially around the Berlin Three Globes Lodge. Schwarz was initiated into the German Masonic Rosicrucian Rite and in 1782–83 acted as an energetic intermediary between its Berlin leadership and the elite Moscow Masonic circles around Novikov and Prince Trubetskoi. Relations between the Three Globes Lodge and the Rite of the Strict Observance were complex and in the autumn of 1783 the Berlin lodge declared that it was breaking away from the 'Brunswick' system and alliances established under Duke Ferdinand at the Wiesbaden convention. It notified Schwarz and his Moscow associates that it was sanctioning the creation of a Masonic Rosicrucian offshoot of its order in Russia which was formed by the end of 1783. In another shift in the external alliances of Russian Freemasonry, the leading Masonic figures in Moscow distanced themselves from Duke Ferdinand's Brunswick system and established a Masonic Rosicrucian

---

[20] For an outline of the decisions of Duke Ferdinand, see ibid., pp. 209–10.

[21] On the proceedings and decisions of the Masonic convention at Wiesbaden, see, for example, Ludwig Hammermayer, *Der Wilhelmsbader Freimaurer–Konventvon 1782*, Heidelberg, 1980.

union of four mother-lodges, which significantly included Gagarin's Sphinx Lodge. The realignment of forces in Russian Freemasonry was completed a few months later when this union was reorganized into a new Provincial Lodge in Moscow, with its Chapter, dominated by some of the major figures in Moscow Freemasonry.

In 1784 the growing Russian Masonic Rosicrucian order imported the so-called Theoretical Degree from the Berlin mother-organization and its Russian version was effectively elaborated as another institution with its own separate organization and Directorate. With the introduction of the Theoretical Degree, with its additional secret governing body, the levels of secrecy in the hierarchy and the system of interrelations between the various grades in the Russian Masonic Rosicrucian order reached magnitudes surpassing those hitherto achieved by the Russian version of the Swedish Rite.

However, as in the case of Swedish-system Freemasonry, it was the external alliance of the Masonic Rosicrucian movement in Russia, on this occasion Prussian, which fuelled the suspicions of the Empress and the authorities and proved detrimental to its existence. As Catherine was moving away from previous pro-Prussian policies and alliances, the 1780s saw the intensification of Catherine's suspicions of Freemasonry and potential activation of Paul's Prussian affinities and contacts through any channels, including Masonic networks and lodges. In 1782 rumours and expectations that the post of a Provincial Grand Master of Russia as an eighth Masonic province (within the Prussian-dominated 'Brunswick' system of Duke Ferdinand) was kept vacant to be assumed eventually by Paul did little to endear Freemasonry or the heir to the throne to Catherine. Furthermore, the activities of *Der Orden des Gold- und Rosenkreuzes* in Germany had a characteristic political dimension which was far from negligible, as in the 1780s its membership became socially and politically influential and maintained its political influence in the Prussian court and internal affairs until the death of the Prussian King Frederick William II (reigned 1786–97).

Concurrently, Catherine's imperial administration's suppression of the lodges and the leading figures of the Russian Masonic Rosicrucian order proceeded in successive stages. The first stage of the campaign against the order took place in 1784–87 when Catherine ordered inquiries into their Masonic and Masonic-related public spheres of activities, such as the nature of the books published by Novikov and his circle with the Moscow University Press and the Typographical Company. These inquiries were reportedly followed by explicit or indirect orders to disband Masonic Rosicrucian lodges. Sensing the approaching 'thundercloud' of anti-Masonic repressions, in 1784 Elagin announced that his alliance of lodges was halting its work (although at least some lodges continued their meetings). To counteract the unfolding anti-Masonic campaigns the Russian Masonic Rosicrucian order resorted to the strategy of internal secrecy which it had cultivated in its organizational hierarchy.

The need for secrecy was further highlighted in 1786 and 1787 when the German leaders of *Der Orden des Gold- und Rosenkreuzes* urged their Russian brethren to limit and curb all external and public aspects of their work in view of the growing Illuminati crisis of 1785–86 and its potential to compromise Freemasonry. The Illuminati crisis generated successive waves of rumours and insinuations generally associating the Illuminati with Freemasonry and implicating both in large-scale political subversion throughout Europe. Regardless of the multiplying measures against Masonic and Masonic-related activity in Moscow, two years after the self-imposed closure of his lodges Elagin evidently felt confident enough (or was assured) that the repressive actions were and would be directed primarily against the Masonic Rosicrucian circles and initiated the resumption of the work of his alliance (usually labelled the Second Elagin Union).

At the same time, in the late 1780s, when the Elagin alliance was enjoying its 'Indian summer', the Swedish-system lodges still functioning in St Petersburg and Kronstadt[22] were starting to face a new difficult period in the build-up of political tensions between Russia and Sweden which led to the Russian–Swedish war in 1788–90 and its major Baltic naval battles. The situation was further complicated by the fact that the Swedish fleet was under the command of Duke Karl, while Russian vessels in the Baltic were under the command of Admiral Samuel Greig, who had been for a time a Master of the Swedish-system Neptune Lodge in Kronstadt and also of a naval lodge on the ship *Rostislav*. Greig died in the autumn of 1788; when the Swedish-system lodges tried to institute a commemorative lodge in his name in too public a manner they faced orders to cease their activities and close down.[23]

---

[22] On the activities of these Swedish-system lodges, see, for example, Carl Lissner's testimony, 'K istorii masonstva v Rossii', ed. and trans. N. S. Ivanina, part 1, *Russkaia Starina*, 35, 1882, 9, pp. 533–60 (p. 543); Tira Sokolovskaia, 'O masonstve v prezhnem russkom flote', *More*, 8, 1908, pp. 216–53 (p. 223).

[23] The Swedish-system Pelican of Charity lodge in St Petersburg, however, had by then ostensibly rejoined the Elagin alliance, an act which seems to have secured its survival for some time, as it remained active in the early 1790s — see, for example, Vernadskii, *Russkoe masonstvo*, p. 361 note 232.

The public image of Freemasonry in Russia and in Europe in general had already been gravely affected by the increasingly and popularly-accepted notion of an association between Freemasons and Jacobins which gained massive currency as the French Revolution of 1789 and its reverberations shook the foundations of the European old order. The accusations implicating Freemasonry in anti-monarchical and anti-clerical plots had received a fresh impetus from the Illuminati panic in the mid–1780s. Amid more anticipations of growing instability, revolutions and paranoid fears of large-scale plots and secret societies, courts already hostile to Freemasonry like the Russian one did not need any further incentive to take action against the existing Masonic lodges. Rumours were multiplying alleging that the Freemasons and the Illuminati were responsible for the dramatic murder of the Swedish King Gustavus III in Stockholm in March 1792 or were conspiring to poison the Russian monarch. In 1790 Catherine authorized Prince A. Prozorovskii, the Moscow governor-general, to commence the closure of the Moscow Masonic lodges and in 1792 the campaign against the Moscow Masonic Rosicrucian movement moved into its last stage.

Prozorovskii ordered the arrest of Novikov who was subsequently sentenced to fifteen years' imprisonment. The accusations justifying the heavy sentence strongly emphasized the alleged 'covert' links between the Moscow Freemasons and Prussia, referring both to the Duke of Brunswick and the leading figures from *Der Orden des Gold- und Rosenkreuzes*, who were at the same time high officials in the Prussian state apparatus. Significantly, the Moscow Freemasons stood accused of trying to lure Grand Duke Paul into the 'Masonic sect'. They were further arraigned for publishing illicit forbidden books and performing rituals impermissible in the context of Orthodoxy and contrary to its letter and spirit.

In 1793 Elagin predictably felt compelled to announce the closure of the lodges of his second union, blaming this decision on the violent French Jacobins who had compromised Freemasonry by 'impersonating' Freemasons and thus provoked the consternation of the Russian court and the Empress.[24] Masonic systems that developed varied levels of secrecy in their hierarchy and organization, such as the Russian versions of the Swedish Rite and the Masonic Rosicrucian order, could secure better continuity and the capacity to reorganize in view of the changing adverse circumstances. Some of the Masonic Rosicrucian lodges managed to continue their 'theoretical' and literary activities.[25]

---

[24] See Carl Lissner's testimony published in Ivanina (ed.), 'K istorii masonstva', p. 544.
[25] On the continuation of some activities of certain lodges belonging to the Moscow

Among the earlier Swedish-system lodges it was the Pelican of Charity that apparently managed to continue its activity and links with Sweden, maintaining some of the functions of the old Phoenix Chapter and thus remained best suited for a potential open revival.[26]

Such hopes for a Masonic renaissance were revived in November 1796 when Catherine died amid rumours that she was planning to remove Paul from the line of succession. Now his long wait for the Russian throne was over, Paul began his reign with extensive reforms, some of which altered and reversed Catherine's policies. But such hopes for a Masonic revival proved in vain, although on the orders of Tsar Paul Novikov was pardoned and a number of exiled high-profile Freemasons were promoted in the new imperial administration. Among others, Kurakin was to be awarded with the post of a vice-chancellor, while Gagarin's governmental responsibilities were further increased. Nevertheless Paul envisaged himself as a defender of Europe's old monarchical and aristocratic order threatened by revolutionary Jacobinism in a dramatic period when the widespread rumours and allegations about the links of Jacobinism with Freemasonry had already compromised to a varying degree the Masonic movement in a number of European courts and states. Like Gustavus III before him, Paul aspired to be the leading royal figure in the establishment and direction of a league of European princes against French Jacobinism. Furthermore, for his planned reform of Russian nobility he intended now to use not the Masonic chivalric rites, as some of the high-ranking noble Freemasons in his entourage might have planned and wished, but the actual structures and chivalric traditions of the Order of the Knights of the Hospital of St John of Jerusalem (the Knights of Malta) some of whom found refuge in Russia after Napoleon's takeover of Malta in 1798. With Paul's subsequent controversial election as the Grand Master of the Knights of Malta, his preoccupation with the order and his plans to use it as a major weapon in his battle against the forces of subversion and revolutionary ideas in Europe became even more pronounced. Conversely, he did not display at that stage any visible affinity for Freemasonry and the prohibitions against the movement were not revoked but persisted.[27]

Masonic Rosicrucian movement after the prohibition of 1792, see Andrei Serkov, *Istoriia russkogo masonstva XIX v.*, St Petersburg, 2000, pp. 44–53.

[26] On the continuation of the activities of the Pelican of Charity Lodge in the circumstances of the prohibition of Freemasonry after 1792, see Sokolovskaia, *Kapitul Feniksa*, pp. 26–29.

[27] For documents related to the attempts of Russian Freemasons to circumvent the prohibitions of Freemasonry by proposing to Paul the formation of a new order of the 'Inner Knights' to serve as a disguise for Masonic activities, see Tira Sokolovskaia,

Russian Freemasonry had to wait for a few more years and better conditions to be capable of staging its gradual recovery and the establishment of a new Swedish-system Grand Directorial Lodge in the early years of the reign of Paul's successor, Tsar Alexander I. The cumulative and growing evidence of the adoption of the Swedish Rite in eighteenth-century Russia nevertheless demonstrates its central importance for the study and understanding of the Masonic networks and their influence at the successive eighteenth-century Russian courts, aristocratic and military establishments, the interconnections with the Russian Orthodox Church and Freemasonry's contribution to prominent novel trends in contemporaneous Russian thought, culture and literature. Such a study will undoubtedly further challenge former interpretations that early Russian Freemasonry was dominated by the rationalistic and deistic currents of the Enlightenment, related to the contemporary popularity of Voltaireanism, free-thinking, the ideas of natural law, and so on,[28] with mystical trends starting to gain prominence only with the introduction of the higher degree rites in the 1780s and early 1790s. Early Russian Freemasonry certainly can no longer be sweepingly categorized as the outcome of a simple import of craft Freemasonry, accompanied by the spread of Enlightenment ideas and Voltaireanism. The rise and early evolution of Russian Freemasonry was conditioned by important internal developments in eighteenth-century Russian society such as the gradual development of civil society, the Russian public and private sphere, the proliferation of clubs and societies, the expansion of Russian printing and publishing in the second half of the century, and so on.[29] The aspiration to emulate Western European manners and codes of behaviour which developed in the Russian public were coupled in some Russian Masonic circles, both noble and non-noble, with a growing concern with notions of

'Novye dannye dlia istorii russkogo masonstva po rukopisiam Tverskoi ucheni arkhivnoi komissii', Tver', 1912, reproduced eadem, *Materialy po istorii russkogo masonstva XVIII–XIX vv.*, Moscow, 2000, 132–41 (pp. 137–39). On Paul's designs concerning the Knights of Malta, see the assessments in Norman E. Saul, *Russia and the Mediterranean, 1797–1807*, Chicago, IL, 1970, pp. 32–39, 43–51; Roderick I. McGrew, 'Paul I and the Knights of Malta', in Hugh Ragsdale (ed.), *Paul I: A Reassessment of His Life and Reign*, Pittsburgh, PA, 1979, pp. 44–76; Roderick I. McGrew, *Paul I of Russia, 1754–1801*, New York, 1992, pp. 244–82.

[28] See, for example, Vernadskii, *Russkoe masonstvo*, pp. 140–56; cf. P. Florovskii, 'Puti russkogo bogosloviia', partial reprint in V. I. Novikov (ed.), *Masonstvo i russkaia kultura*, Moscow, 1998, pp. 50–64.

[29] See, for example, Douglas Smith, 'Freemasonry and the Public in Eighteenth-Century Russia', in Jane Burbank and David L. Ransel (eds), *Imperial Russia: New Histories for the Empire*, Bloomington and Indianopolis, IN, 1998, pp. 281–304; Smith, *Working the Rough Stone*, especially chapters 1 and 2.

moral self-improvement, human dignity, social service and action. Indeed due to the social and moral dimensions of its activities Russian Freemasonry could be seen as providing a kind of counterpart to the imperial Table of Ranks in these spheres.[30] Furthermore, the study of the manner in which the Western European Freemasons 'lived' the various ideas of the Enlightenment within the confines of their lodges (including, importantly the principles of constitutional and representative forms of governance),[31] has also been successfully applied to Russian Freemasonry.[32]

Given the aristocratic pedigree requirements of the Russian Swedish-system lodges and the types of governance operating there, it will certainly be worthwhile to explore in the same comparative manner the aristocratic Russian Swedish-system lodges and their Western European counterparts and determine how they relate to the 'practice' of the ideals of the Enlightenment and Counter-Enlightenment.[33] Such exploration will make it possible to test the validity (in the case of Russia) of one of the presumptions in the study of the inter-relations between eighteenth-century European Freemasonry and the Enlightenment, which approaches the craft lodges as proponents of Enlightenment ideologies, while recognizing higher degrees rites as frequently linked with Counter-Enlightenment tendencies and trends.

The model of governance of the Swedish-system Gagarin union, with its elaborate hierarchy, organizational structure and internal order, seemed well-organized and more solid than the looser organization of the First Elagin Union and the Elagin–Reichel alliance. Hence it rapidly could become another unifying body for Russian Freemasonry and also attracted Freemasons who were concerned about the insufficient standardization in the existing rites and grades. The intellectual work in the Russian Swedish-system lodges was also certainly more intense than that in the Elagin's alliances and included orations and discussions on moral, philanthropic and philosophical issues.[34]

---

[30] See the observations of Marc Raeff, *Origins of the Russian Intelligentsia: The Eighteenth-Century Nobility*, New York, 1966, p. 161; cf. Smith, *Working the Rough Stone*, pp. 111–12.

[31] Margaret Jacob, *Living the Enlightenment: Freemasonry and Politics in Eighteenth-Century Europe*, New York, 1991.

[32] Smith, *Working the Rough Stone*, chapters 1 and 2.

[33] For a summary of approaches to this problem, see Yuri Stoyanov, 'Endorsement and Condemnation of Political Radicalism and Reform in 18th-Century Russian Freemasonry', *Lumières*, 7, 2008, pp. 225–45 (especially pp. 235–38).

[34] On the intellectual work in the Swedish-system Russian lodges, see, for example, Vernadskii, *Russkoe masonstvo*, pp. 85–86.

Within Russian internal Masonic polemic, the Swedish Rite is periodically criticized for being too closely entwined with politics and linked to a foreign court which thus could compromise Russian Freemasonry. Given the hegemony of the upper stratum of the Russian Swedish-system Freemasonry through so many high-ranking representatives of the Grand Duke's court and 'party', such charges or perceptions seemed inevitable. The related important question of whether the structure of the Swedish Rite and the Phoenix Chapter in Russia were also related to designs to bring Russian and Swedish nobles closer through Masonic channels in the complex northern European political situation created by Panin's 'Northern System' remains another largely unexplored area.[35] Research is needed to establish whether the Panin brothers intended to make the Masonic movement in Russia 'a rallying point for disaffected groups opposed to the government'[36] or if the Swedish-system Russian lodges 'represented a social extension of the Panin party'.[37] Similarly, the extent to and the manner in which the reformist political agenda of the Panin brothers may have been interrelated socio-politically with Freemasonry (and the Swedish-system Russian Masonic networks in particular) remain an intriguing but difficult territory.[38] The focus of the Panin brothers on Paul as the future monarchical enforcer of their political vision, their manoeuvres between Enlightened absolutism and constitutionalism and the Masonic dimension of their activity need to be explored in the wider context of the changing perceptions of eighteenth-century Russian royal ideology and the political developments in Sweden under Gustavus III's rule before and after 1772.

The formation and expanding influence of the Swedish alliance of the Gagarin union and the Prussian-controlled Russian Masonic Rosicrucian order certainly exacerbated the tensions between native and foreign in Russian culture and society. This process occurred at a sensitive time when the emulation and import of Western ideas and manners were coupled in some sectors of Russian society with intense suspicion and even hostility towards organizations which could be perceived as functioning in alliance with or under the supervision of

---

[35] Sokolovskaia attributes such designs to King Gustavus III in her *Kapitul Feniksa*, p. 10.

[36] Ransel, *The Politics of Catherinian Russia*, p. 4.

[37] Ibid., p. 257.

[38] On the patronage system, family and political networks and designs associated with the Panin 'party', see ibid., pp. 111 ff., 255–62; Smith, *Working the Rough Stone*, pp. 24–27; Stoyanov, 'Endorsement and Condemnation', pp. 241–42.

foreign bodies.[39] The declared universalism of the Masonic movement uneasily encountered emerging re-conceptualizations of the notions of Russia's distinct nature and destiny advanced in some circles of Russian society vis-à-vis the ideological challenges of the Enlightenment. At the same time, Russian Freemasonry, especially its high-degree systems, also strove to develop mechanisms intended to acculturate foreign imports such as the Swedish Rite and to 'domesticate' Masonic universalism and elements of Masonic ideology.

Early Russian Freemasonry undoubtedly contributed to the processes of secularization and the spread of humanism in Russian culture. In the last decades of the eighteenth century some influential Russian Masonic circles, however, came to formulate and elaborate specific Russian versions of Christian mysticism which blended Masonic traditions and imagery with concepts and attitudes inherited from Orthodox Christianity.[40] The Swedish Rite played its role in this process, and the type and ritualization of Christian material present in the grades made available to its Russian offshoot apparently proved particularly attractive to those Russian Freemasons who had intense Christian convictions but were not entirely content with the current state of the Church and the formalism of its ritual. At least for some Freemasons the Swedish Rite thus could provide a near-substitute for Church ritual. Indeed some of the traditional objections raised against Swedish-system Freemasonry in Russia since the days of the Elagin–Reichel union were focused on the perceived 'church-like' character of its ceremonies, viewed by their critics as too ostentatious. This enabled the Swedish Rite to contribute to the formation of a specific and somewhat eclectic Christian religiosity which developed in Masonic circles and outside the spiritual monopoly and control of the Church[41]

---

[39] On these tensions between foreign (especially German) and Russian cultural and intellectual modes and the manner in which they were projected onto Russian Freemasonry, see Smith, *Working the Rough Stone*, pp. 137–38. On the general dichotomy between foreign and native culture in eighteenth-century Russia, see Simon Dixon, *The Modernization of Russia 1670–1825*, Cambridge and New York, 1999, pp. 160–70.

[40] See, for example, the analysis in Raffaella Faggionato, *A Rosicrucian Utopia in Eighteenth-Century Russia: The Masonic Circle of N. I. Novikov*, Dordrecht, 2005, especially pp. 115–83, 239–43; Stoyanov, 'Endorsement and Condemnation', pp. 244–45.

[41] For a discussion of these trends in Russian Masonic Christian mysticism as forms of a kind of 'non-Church' religiosity, see, for example, Nikolai Berdiaev, *Samopoznanie: opyt filosofskoi avtobiografii N. A. Berdiaeva*, Paris, 1949; reprint ed. by A. V. Vadimov, Moscow, 1991, p. 28; V. I. Novikov, 'Masonstvo i russkaia kultura', in Novikov (ed.), *Masonstvo*, pp. 5–50 (p. 7); V. V. Zen'kovskii, 'Istoriia russkoi filosofii', partial reprint in Novikov, *Masonstvo*, pp. 64–69 (pp. 67–68); S. M. Nekrasov, 'Zakliuchenie', in Longinov, *Novikov*, pp. 623–56 (pp. 637–39). Masonic Christian mysticism thrived

(sometimes described in Russian anti-Masonic discourse as leaning towards Protestantism).

These conceptualizations of Russian Masonic Christian religiosity and mysticism occurred in the context of other earlier or contemporaneous developments in the sphere of Russian Christianity such as the earlier Church moves towards religious reforms to 're-Christianize' Russia (with their emphasis on the ideals of moral perfection and spiritual enlightenment),[42] and the eighteenth-century revival of asceticism and mysticism in the Russian monastic tradition. Another notion which played an important role in the Swedish Rite, that of the 'spiritual knight', was also further developed in the Christian mysticism of Russian Masonic Rosicrucian circles; ritual re-enactments of the Last Supper in the Russian version of the Swedish Rite evidently overlapped extensively with this strand of mysticism.[43] Such re-Christianizing and Counter-Enlightenment currents in late eighteenth-century Russian Freemasonry could seek even deeper rapprochement with Orthodoxy and notions of Russianness, including attempts to establish a secret, irregular lodge open to Russian Orthodox nobles,[44] evidently designed to establish purely Russian secret lodges, detached from the European Masonic movement and open only to Russian Orthodox members.[45]

In Russian Masonic utopian discourses, moreover, Christian mystical notions could co-exist with elements drawn from the Panin party's vision of post-Catherinean monarchy with its anticipations of the ultimate advent of the 'true' Tsar Paul, whose rule was expected to bear some of the features of theocracy.[46] Russian Masonic mystical and utopian trends came under the strong impact of Louis Claude de

in the Russian Masonic Rosicrucian movement whose preoccupation with Christian mysticism is evident from the abundance of translations of early and medieval Eastern and Western Christian mystical writings published by Novikov and his circle.

[42] On these developments, see, for example, Gregory Freeze, 'The Re-Christianizing of Russia: The Church and Popular Religion 1750–1850', *Studia Slavica Finlandesia*, 7, 1990, pp. 101–36; Gregory Freeze, 'Institutionalizing Piety: The Church and Popular Religion', in Jane Burbank and David L. Ransel (eds), *Imperial Russia: New Histories for the Empire*, Bloomington and Indianapolis, IN, 1998, pp. 210–49.

[43] For such ritual reenactments of the Last Supper in the Russian version of the Swedish Rite, see Sokolovskaia, *Kapitul feniksa*, pp. 91–92.

[44] Description of the archival evidence in Sokolovskaia, 'Novye dannye', pp. 133–35.

[45] Discussion of the relevant archival data and quotations from primary source material in Nekrasov, 'Zakliuchenie', pp. 650–51.

[46] On these forms of Masonic political and political utopian discourse, see Vernadskii, *Russkoe masonstvo*, pp. 236–65; Serkov, *Istoriia russkogo masonstva*, pp. 110–11; Konstantin Burmistrov and Maria Endel, 'The Place of Kabbalah in the Doctrine of Russian Freemasons', *Aries*, new series, 4, 2004, 1, pp. 27–69 (pp. 8–9).

Saint-Martin's *De Erreurs et de la Vérité*, whether via its original French version (1775) or its Russian translation in 1785, generating utopian speculations about a 'perfect' Masonic monarchical state under the dual guidance of a 'Holy King' and a secret order.

Finally, in contrast to the rationalistic and deistic beliefs shared by many Russian Freemasons (usually belonging to craft Freemasonry), other Russian Masonic circles (mostly associated with the Masonic Rosicrucian and Swedish Rite networks) developed a deep interest in the hidden mystical knowledge (supposedly residing in higher degrees systems) and in the then fashionable quest for the 'wisdom of the ancients'. The conceptual systems elaborated in these circles integrated Kabbalistic, Christian Kabbalistic, alchemical and Hermetic traditions, well represented, for example, in the works published by Novikov and his circle.[47]

Further research in Russian Masonic manuscript collections (and the archival collections of the Grand Lodge of Sweden in Stockholm), which lately have been receiving greater critical attention, will certainly reveal many more aspects and dimensions of the multifaceted impact of the Swedish Rite on elements of Russian religious, mystical, political (and utopian-political thought) from the era of the Enlightenment as well as their later transmutations during the nineteenth and twentieth centuries.

---

[47] On the provenance and re-interpretations of Kabbalistic and Christian Kabbalistic traditions in the teachings of mystically-inclined Russian Masonic circles, see Konstantin Burmistrov and Maria Endel, 'Kabbalah in Russian Masonry: Some Preliminary Observations', *Kabbalah: Journal for the Study of Jewish Mystical Texts*, 4, 1999, pp. 9–59; Burmistrov and Endel, 'The Place of Kabbalah', pp. 27–68.

The Image of *Toska* (Melancholy) in Russian Love Spells

Andrei Toporkov

Academy of Sciences, A. M. Gorky Institute of World Literature,
Moscow

THE word *toska* is defined by dictionaries as 'spiritual longing, anxiety combined with sadness and despondency'. It is a nationally specific word that can cause certain difficulties when translating into other languages. For convenience I shall regularly give the word either in Russian as *toska*, or in English translation as 'melancholy'.

In this article, I analyse the contextual usage of the word *toska* in the Russian love spells which were documented in the seventeenth to the nineteenth centuries. In these texts there are descriptions of how the performer of the magic spell transmits melancholy to the person with whom he wants to enter into an intimate relationship.

For example, one collection of magic spells of the second quarter of the seventeenth century contains the following picturesque text:

> I will get up and bless myself, I will go out and bless myself, I will go to the open field on the sunny side. There stands a wet, sturdy [*kriaknovist*] oak-tree.[1] I, servant of God [name of performer], will worship and submit to the four winds and to the four whirlwinds. You, four winds and four whirlwinds, get up and gather the *strange melancholy and sorrow and sadness* from all four quarters, from the east to the west, from the south to the north, from every person, from a tsar and a tsaritsa, from a monk and a nun, from a man and a woman, from an old person and from a young person to me, servant of God [name of performer], in one place. I, servant of God [name of performer] will worship and submit to four winds and to four whirlwinds. Get up, you four winds and four whirlwinds, carry me, servant of God [name of performer] to the sun and to the moon, to the stars and to the moons, in all directions. Wherever you see her, put *strange melancholy, sorrow and sadness* inside her to make her, servant of God [name of female

This work was supported by the Russian Foundation for Basic Research (grant number 20-012-00117, 'Russian magic folklore from unpublished sources from the 17th to the start of the 20th century; archival searches, preparation of scientific publication, research, and commentary'.

[1] *Kriaknovist* — strong, thick, branching.

addressee], worry about me, servant of God [name of performer] during daytime in the sun, during night-time in the moonlight, on any day, at any hour, at any time, during the old moon, during the full moon, and during the waning moon. May this *melancholy and great sadness* not be swallowed with sugar, not be quenched with water, not go away while [she is] with mother or father, not go away while [she is] with brothers or sisters or neighbours, not be taken away by the wind, not be forgotten while working. For ever and ever. Amen.[2]

In such magic spells *toska* appears in two guises: first, the emotional and sensory state of a person (a performer or an addressee of the magic spell); second, a material substance that can be gathered from different people, transferred from one place to another, and then put into a human body. As the text develops, one meaning of the word *toska* can be changed to the other. For example, in the text quoted above, *toska* first appears as a material substance that can be taken from a tsar and a tsaritsa, from a monk and a nun, and from other people, and later in the text it refers to the emotional state of the addressee of the magic spell.

In some plots the performer appeals to the winds with a request to collect *toska* from the prisoners in jail:

Father-winds, father-whirlwinds! You have been going around all the cities and suburbs, *all the jails and almshouses, around all official unhappy people. There are three lads in these jails and almshouses sitting from youth to old age, from old age to grey beards. They are crying and weeping for their fathers and mothers, young women and girlfriends,*

---

[2] 'Стану благословяс(ь), пэйду благословяс(ь), пойду в чистое поле под с(о)лнечную страну. Там стоит сыр дуб крякновист. Стану аз, раб Б(о)жий имярек, поклонятис(ь) и покорятис(ь) четырем ветром и четырем вехорям: стан(ь)те вы, 4 ветра и 4 вехоря, понесите вы тоску и кручину и печал(ь) необычную со всех четырех сторон, от востока до запада, от юга и до севера, со всякого человека, с царя и царицы, с чернца и черницы, з белца и белиц(ы), стара и млада ко мне, к рабу Б(о)жию имярек, во едино место. Стану яз, раб Б(о)жий имярек, поклонятис(ь) и покарятис(ь) четырем ветром и четырем вехорям: стан(ь)те вы, 4 ветра и 4 вехоря, понесите вы меня, раб(а) Б(о)жия имярек, понесите по солнцу и по месяцу, (по) звездам и по лунам, и по всем сторонам; где еи ни увидите, туто вложите в неи тоску и кручину и печал(ь) необычную, тужила б та раб(а) Б(о)жия имярек по мне, по рабе Б(о)жии имярек, в ден(ь) при солнце, в ноч(ь) при месяцы, по всякой день, по всякой час, по всякое время, месяца ветха и полна и перекроя; тое бы тоски и великие печали сахарем не заесть и пит(ь)ем не запит(ь), ни со отцем, ни с матерью не отседитце, ни з брат(ь)ямы, ни с сестрамы, ни с суседамы не отседетце, ни на ветре не проходитце, ни делом не отделатце. Во век веком. Амин(ь).' A. L. Toporkov, *Russkie zagovory iz rukopisnykh istochnikov XVII–pervoi poloviny XIX v.*, Moscow, 2010, pp. 103–04, no. 28. (Here and henceforth the italics in quotations are mine, to draw attention to these words — A.T.)

for their happy days and festivities. You, take away from them all their yearning melancholy, all shrivelling heart-dryness and bring it to servant of God [name] [...].[3]

In another magic spell, the performer orders a demon to remove the melancholy from him, put it into a cauldron, and then take it to a woman and put it into her heart:

Throw off from me, Basil, servant of God, the melancholy and heart-dryness from my clean white body, from my sugar-sweet mouth, from my pewter eyes, from my one hundred and seventy joints, from my knee tendons, from my heel skin. Put this melancholy and heart-dryness into the copper cauldron, carry them across the fiery rivers, across the fiery lakes, do not spill them, do not get them wet, do not burn them with fire, do not scatter them. Put them in the Akulina's heart, in her soft liver, in her clean, white body, in her sugar-sweet mouth, in her pewter eyes, in her one hundred and seventy joints, in her one hundred and seventy knee tendons, in her heel skin, in her blood under the skin, in her black........ [...].[4]

The earliest manuscript texts of love spells of the seventeenth-eighteenth centuries were found in notebooks or scrolls that had been copied by men and used by them to subordinate a girl or a woman to their will and to enter into an intimate relationship with her. The strategy of a magic spell was to make the woman forget her family, shame and honour, and come to a state where her normal life becomes

---

[3] 'Батюшки ветры, батюшки вихори! вы ходили гуляли по всем городам пригородкам, *по всем тюрьмам, богадельням, по всем начальным несчастливым людям, в тех тюрьмах и богадельнах сидят три молодца от младости и до старости, от старости и до седой бороды, они плачут и рыдают о тятиньках, о мамоньках, о кумушках, о подруженьках и о своем житье гуляньице;* вы и от их отберите всю тоску тоскующую, сухоту сухотующую да понесите к рабице Божьей (имя) ...' : P. Shilkov, 'Zagovor dlia prisukhi', *Zhivaia starina*, St Petersburg, 1892, no. 3, p. 149; undated manuscript.

[4] 'Скиньте с меня, раба Божьего Василья, *тоску и сухоту* с чистого, белого тела, с сахарных устов, с оловянных глаз, со ста семидесяти суставов, с подколенных жил, с подпятной кожи. *Тоску и сухоту* положите в медную котельницу, перенесите через огненные реки, через огненные озера, не рассыпьте, не помочите, на огне не сожгите, никуда не тряхните, — положите в Акулинино сердце, в мягкую печень, в чистое, белое тело, в сахарные уста, в оловянные глаза, во сто семьдесят суставов, во сто семьдесят подколенных жил, в подпятную кожу, в подкожную руду, в черную........ [...]': N. Vinogradov, *Zagovory, oberegi, spasitelnye molitvy i proch. (po starinnym rukopisiam i sovremennym zapisiam)*, St Petersburg, 1908, vyp. 1, p. 45, no. 55, ?19th century. The dotted line is in the manuscript.

impossible: 'May she long for me and grieve for me, servant of God [name], until she becomes obedient in all things.'[5]

This, of course, does not mean that women have not used magic to solve problems in their personal lives, but the female style of magic was fundamentally different from the male. Brides and married women sought to influence their future and current husbands by adding their own sweat, menstrual blood, or breast milk into their food or drink, by giving them their soap, which they used in the bath, and so on. The woman did not do this in order to arouse male passion, but so that her husband would love her, be kind to her, and not use violence on her. Unlike the male love spells, such female actions were accompanied by the utterance of simple magic formulas or did not require verbal elements at all.

It should also be taken into account that the manuscripts which preserved love spells were copied exclusively by men and served mainly male interests (war, relations with judges and authorities, hunting, and herding). The sphere of specific female interests (assistance in childbirth, infant care) was reflected in medical manuscripts and herbals. Women's love magic of the seventeenth–eighteenth centuries is known to us mainly from the questions that priests asked women during their confession, and also from those cases when women gave accounts of their actions during judicial investigations. The situation changed dramatically from the middle of the nineteenth century, when folklorists, ethnographers and local historians started to collect folklore material, and worked mainly with the oral tradition. The collected material of the second half of the nineteenth–twentieth centuries comprised mainly information about the love magic of girls and women, and men's magic associated with the manuscript tradition gradually became less relevant.

Personification of Toska *(Melancholy) in Love Spells*
Special attention should be paid to the fact that the word *toska* in Russian magic spells can refer not only to the emotional state of a person, but also to a personified image that has a certain appearance, a localization in space, and its own attributes. The earliest example of personification of *toska* is in a magic spell recorded in the investigative case of 1688–89 against Captain Semen Vasil'evich Aigustov:

---

[5] 'И чтоб она *московала и горевала* по мне, раб[у] им[ярек] до тех пор, *пока она ко мне послушна будет ео всем*': E. B. Smilianskaia, *Zagovory i gadaniia iz sudebno-sledstvennykh materialov XVIII v.*, in *Otrechennoe chtenie v Rossii XVII–XVIII vekov*, Moscow, 2002, p. 172; 1781.

I shall get up early, I shall go up a high hill, I shall shout, I shall scream with my loud voice: Hey, Satan, with [your] devils, little and big, get out of the ocean-sea, take my burning melancholy, go round the whole world, do not kindle any stumps or logs or wet trees or ground grass, kindle the soul of servant of God [ ] towards me, servant of God [ ]. On the sea-ocean, on the island of Buian there is a bathhouse. In the bathhouse a board is lying. On this board melancholy is lying. I, servant of God [name of performer], have come to you. Why are you, melancholy, longing and grieving? Do not long, melancholy, do not grieve, melancholy. Go, melancholy, enter, melancholy, into servant of God [name of female addressee], make her long for and grieve for me, servant of God [name of performer]. As this fire burns in a year, in a half a year, in the daytime, at noon, in every hour, in every half hour, so may servant of God [female addressee] long for me, servant of God [name of performer] with her white body, ardent heart, black liver, impetuous head and brains, clear eyes, black eyebrows, sugar-sweet mouth. As it is hard and bitter for a fish without water, so may it be hard and bitter for her, servant of God [name of female addressee] without me, servant of God [name of performer].[6]

The main part of the text of the above magic spell is clearly divided into two parts: in the first part the performer summons Satan with his devils to take his fiery melancholy, carry it to the world and kindle the soul of a certain person of the female sex; in the second part the melancholy is represented as a special creature, which is lying on a board in the bathhouse on the island named Buian (Buiagan). A performer addresses it (melancholy) and orders it to go to the same female person and make her long for him, and that her body, heart, liver and so on should be on fire.

In both parts of the text, *toska* is associated with fire and is used by the performer to cause a 'love fire' in the woman's body and soul, but

---

[6] 'Встану ранен(ь)ко, взойду на высок шолом, ускричу, взвоплю своим громким голосом: Ой вы, Сотона со д(ь)яволи со малы, со великими, вылести с окияне моря, возмити огненую тоску мою, пойдити по белу свету, не зожигайти вы не пен(ь)я, не колод(ь)я, ни сырые дерев(ь)я, ни земни тровы, зажгити у рабы по мне рабу душу. На море акияне, на острове на Буяне стоит тут мыл(ь)ня, в той мыл(ь)не лежит доска, на той доске лежит тоска. Пришол я, раб имярек: Что ты, таска, тоскуеш(ь) и гарюеш(ь)? Не таскуй, таска, не гарюй, таска, поди, таска, уступи, таска, рабу имерек, чтоб(ы) она тоскавала и горевала по мне, по робу имерек; как тот огон(ь) горит, в году и в полугоду, днем и полудни, и часу и в получасу, так бы та раба по мне, по робу, горела с белое тело, ретивае серцо, черноя печен(ь), буйная голова з мозгом, ясными очами, черными бровями, сахарными устами. Скол(ь) тошно, скол(ь) гор(ь)ко рыбе без воды и так бы рабу имерек тошно, гор(ь)ко по мне по робу [...]': Toporkov, *Russkie zagovory*, pp. 333–34, no. 2; 1688–89.

in the first case, 'Satan and [his] devils' must inflame the woman, and in the second — the personified *toska* itself. In the first part, the word *toska* is mentioned as an internal experience of the performer of the magic spell, and later it is mentioned as a fiery substance that can be transferred from one place to another; in the second part, *toska* appears as a living creature that is localized in the external world and is capable of independent actions.

In the most detailed variants of this love spell scenario with the image of personified melancholy, there are four formulas. Provisionally they may be categorized as follows:

1. On the sea-ocean, on the island of Buian (or: in the wide field; on the Alatyr' stone; on the white fiery stone; in the iron furnace; under the roots of twelve oaks; on the Terka-river; in a dark forest; on three stones) there are a bathhouse, an *izba* (village house), three coffins; a board is lying; three melancholies are approaching; the melancholy is running, and so on.

2. The melancholy (three or thirty-three melancholies) is lying on a board or under a board, in an *izba*, in a bathhouse, from corner to corner, from one wall to the other; it is grieving, crying, weeping, howling, lashing out, squirming, clinging to the board, rushing from wall to wall (from corner to corner, floor-to-ceiling), throwing itself at the window, beating its 'hands and feet' against the wall and its 'head' against the bench, crouching to the ground, rushing from fire to fire; throwing itself from the board into water, from water to fire, thrashing around like an ermine.

3. Let the melancholy enter the [female] servant of God, let her long for [name of performer]; let a maiden be overcome with melancholy, let the melancholy kindle her [name of female addressee] heart and blood; the melancholy rushes from the bathhouse (*bania*), it flies through the air, it enters the body of the female servant of God, into her blood, into her head, into her face, into her eyes, into her mouth, into her heart, into her lungs, into all her bones, into her tendons, brain and mind, will and wish, let three melancholies take their flame and kindle the female servant of God, her liver, lungs, face, eyes, ideas and thoughts.

4. Let the female servant of God (or male servant of God) grieve and cry, be unable to live without (name of performer) just as a fish

cannot live without water, may she throw herself from window to window, from door to door, from gate to gate, let her run to (name of performer), let her/his womb, heart and blood become inflamed, let her/him suffer from insomnia, be unable to eat enough, to drink enough, to steam herself/himself in the bathhouse, to talk with his/her father and mother.

From the beginning of the nineteenth century magic spells for women begin to appear in manuscripts. This is one of the first love spells, with the help of which a certain maiden (or, perhaps, a married woman or a widow) named Anna planned to charm a certain Mikhail Nikolaevich. Such a magic spell could have been recited by Anna herself, or by some sorcerer or other person to whom Anna had turned for help:

On the sea, on the ocean, on the island of Buiagan is the burning Alatyr' stone; on that stone was built a fire-heated bathhouse; *in that bathhouse there is a board which can burn, there are thirty-three melancholies on this board. And these melancholies rush from wall to wall, from corner to corner, from floor to ceiling, and from there through all the paths, crossroads, and air. Rush, melancholies, throw yourselves, melancholies, into servant of God Mikhailo,* into his impetuous head, into his back, into his face, into his clear eyes, into his sugar-sweet mouth, into his ardent heart; into his brain and mind, will and wish, into his tall white body, and into all his hot blood, and into all his bones, and into all his joints, into his seventy joints, half-joints and sub-joints, and into all his red-and-white tendons, into seventy tendons, tendons, half-tendons and sub-tendons; so that he, Mikhailo Nikolaevich, will *long for, grieve, cry and weep for servant of God Anna* every day, every hour, any time; so that he will not be able to be without her anywhere just as a fish could not live without water; so that he will rush and throw himself from window to window, from door to door, from gate to gate, through all the paths, and roads, and crossroads, trembling and sorrowing, crying and weeping, so that he will quickly go and run to her like a grass-snake, like a toad, like a fierce snake, whenever he hears her voice.[7]

---

[7] 'На море на океане, на острове на Буягане есть горюч камень Алатыр; на том камне устроена огнепалимая баня; в той бане лежит разжигаемая доска, а на той доске 33-ри тоски, и бросаются тоски из стены в стену, из угла в угол, от пола до потолка и оттуда чрез все пути, перепутья и воздухом и аэром. Мечитесь тоски, киньтесь тоски в раба Михайлу, в буйную его голову, в тыл, в лик, в ясныя очи, в сахарныя уста, в ретивое сердце; в его ум и разум, волю и хотение, во все его тело высокое белое и во всю кровь горячую, и во все его кости, и во все составы, в семьдесят составов, полусоставов и подсоставов и во все его жилы

A specific feature of this text is that the formulas that first describe the behavior of *toska*, and then the behaviour of Mikhail Nikolaevich, echo each other, resulting in a looped structure. After the melancholy takes possession of a man, he will behave like thirty-three personified melancholies.

Appearance and Localization of Toska

In magic spells, the personified *toska* usually maintains a visual ambiguity. We do not know what it is 'wearing'; it does not have a 'proper name'. If there is more than one *toska* in the text, but three or even thirty-three *toski*, we are not told whether they differ in any way from each other. Only in one text known to us, of a magic spell for destroying love (*otsushka*), is *toska* called '*krasnaia devitsa*' (beautiful maiden):

> On the sea, on the ocean, on the island of Buian, there is a pillar; and on this pillar there is an oaken tomb; in this tomb there lies a *krasnaia devitsa* [beautiful maiden], a *toska-charovnitsa* [melancholy-the-spellcaster]; her blood does not heat, her legs do not lift, her eyes do not open, her lips do not part, her heart does not grieve. So may the heart of [name of female addressee] not grieve, blood not heat, and she herself not sorrow, not fall into melancholy.[8]

In another magic spell, the beautiful maiden, whom a performer wishes to enchant, is depicted as lying in a coffin; a performer calls her to get up from the coffin and kindle her own heart:

> On the sea, on the *kiian* [for *okean* 'ocean'], on the island of Buian, on the river Iardan [Jordan], there is a coffin, in the coffin lies a maiden.

краснобелыя, в семьдесят жил, жил, полужил и поджилков; чтобы он, Михайло Николаевич, тосковал, горевал, плакал и рыдал по рабе Анне по всяк день, по всяк час, по всякое время; нигде бы без нея пробыть не мог бы, как рыба без воды; кидался бы, бросался бы из окошка во окошко, из дверей в двери, из ворот в вороты на все пути и дороги, и перепутья с трепетом и тужением, плачем и рыданием, зело поспешно шол бы к ней и бежал бы, где ея голос заслышит, ужом и жабою и лютою змеею …': 'Neskol'ko zaklinanii', *Russkii filologicheskii vestnik*, 35, 1896, 1, pp. 21–22; manuscript of the early 19th century.

[8] 'На море на окияне, на острове на Буяне стоит столб; на том столбе стоит дубовая гробница; в ней лежит красная девица, тоска-чаровница; кровь у нея не разгорается, ноженьки не подымаются, глаза не раскрываются, уста не растворяются, сердце не сокрушается. Так бы и у (имярек) сердце бы не сокрушалося, кровь бы не разгоралася, сама бы не убивалася, в тоску не вдавалася': L. N. Maikov, *Velikorusskie zaklinaniia*, Paris, 1992 (St Petersburg, 1869), pp. 22–23, no. 32; mid-19th century.

Servant of God [female name of addressee], get up, wake up, dress up in a coloured dress, take flint and steel, kindle your ardent heart for servant of God [name of performer], and kindle it strongly, and fall into melancholy and sorrow because of me, servant of God [name of performer], like a hanged man in his noose, let [female name of addressee] feel sick because of [name of performer]; as a drowned man in the sea, let [name of female addressee] feel sick for [name of performer], as the soul parts from the body, for ever and ever — Amen.[9]

In a magic spell from a manuscript compiled in 1734, *toska* appears as a strange creature, devoid of arms, legs, and vision: 'There is a board in the filthy sea, and on this board sits *toska*, herself, without hands, without legs, without eyes, and she is crying, sorrowing and grieving for clear eyes and the whole wide world.'[10]

The state of tightness and constriction in which the *toska* finds itself is combined with disorderly, convulsive movements. The *toska* is sorrowing and grieving, dropping to the ground, rushing from fire to fire, mourning, burning in fire, squirming, clinging to the board, rushing from wall to wall (from corner to corner, floor-to-ceiling), 'beating its "hands and feet" against the wall and its "head" against the bench';[11] 'weeping, howling, beating, lashing out'.[12]

In a magic spell from a manuscript of the second quarter of the nineteenth century a unique image of the *toska*-tree appears:

In the dark forest there is a *toska*-tree; the *toska* is sorrowing and grieving, and mourning. I send this *toska* into servant of God [name of female addressee], go into her white body, ardent heart, into her blonde

---

[9] 'На море – на кияне, на острове на Буяне, на реке на Ярдане, стояла гробница; во той гробнице лежала девица. Раба Божия (имрек)! встань-пробудись, в цветное платье нарядись, бери кремень и огниво, зажигай свое сердце ретиво по рабе Божием (имрек), и так зажигай крепко и дайся по мне, рабе Божием (имрек), в тоску – в печаль; как удавшему (удавленнику) в петле, так бы рабе Божией (имрек) было тошно по рабе Божием (имрек); как утопшему в море, так бы рабе Божией (имрек) было тошно по рабе Божием (имрек) – как душа с телом расстается, во веки – аминь': 'Neskol'ko narodnykh zagovorov (soobshcheno A. N. Afanas'evym)', *Letopisi russkoi literatury i drevnosti, izdavaemye N. Tikhonravovym*, Moscow, 1862, vol. 4, section III, pp. 75–76, no. 2b; second quarter of the 19th century.

[10] 'И есть на поганом море доска, а на той доске седит сама тоска, *без рук, без нок, без глас*, а сама плачет, тоскует и горюет по ясных очах и по белому свету': N. N. Pokrovskii, 'Tetrad' zagovorov 1734 goda', *Nauchnyi ateizm. Religiia i sovremennost'*, Novosibirsk, 1987, p. 262.

[11] Vinogradov, *Zagovory*, p. 45, no. 56; 19th century.

[12] P. Pervushin, 'Sueveriia sela Kataiskogo Kamyshlovskogo uezda', *Zapiski Uralskogo obshchestva liubitelei estestvoznaniia*, Ekaterinburg, 1897, vol. 17, vyp. 2, p. 331; late 19th century.

hair, into her hot blood — into her boiling blood, so that she may long for servant of God [name of performer].[13]

Personified *toska* is most often found in the village bathhouse or in the *izba*. The appearance of a bathhouse in love spells is not accidental: on the one hand, a bathhouse was the place where rituals of love magic associated with sweat, water, menstrual blood, hair and so on, were traditionally performed, and on the other — a bathhouse was perceived as a place where evil spirits lurked. Both the bathhouse and the *izba* are sometimes described as a house without windows or doors:

On the sea, on the ocean, on the island of Buian, there is an *izba* without a roof, without a ceiling, without windows, and without doors. In this *izba* there lies a board and on this board lie three melancholy melancholies [*toski*], grieving and weeping.[14]

In the open field, in the wide open country, there is a fiery, hot bathhouse, and *in this bathhouse there are neither doors nor windows, nor brightly-lit benches; there is a board in the middle of the bathhouse, and on this board there is a toska*, it is crying and weeping and falling on the ground.[15]

The words *toska* and *doska* (board), which differ only in one letter, rhyme with each other. In some texts, the board on which melancholy (*toska*) lies is located in a furnace, in a coffin, on a stone, or 'on the filthy sea'.[16] Both the board and the *toska* may stretch from one corner to another in the *izba*, for example:

On the sea, on the *kiian* (ocean) there is an *izba*; there is a *toska* lies, stretching from corner to corner, from wall to wall.[17]

---

[13] 'В темном лесу стоит древо тоски; тоскует и горюет тоска, печалуется (печалится). И посылаю я тоску в рабу Божию (имрек): взойди в ея в белое тело, и в ретивое сердце, и в русы власы, в кровь горячую — в руду кипячую, чтобы она по рабе Божием (имрек) тосковала …': 'Neskol'ko narodnykh zagovorov', p. 76, no. 2c.

[14] 'На море на окиане, на острове Буяне стоит там *изба без верху, без потолка, без окон, без дверей*. В той избе лежит доска, на той доске сидит три тоски тосковыя, горевыя и *плачевныя*': Toporkov, *Russkie zagovory*, p. 695, no. 21; 1810–20.

[15] 'В цистом поли, в шыроком раздольи стоит огненная, горецяя байна, и *в этой байны нету ни двирей, ни окон, ни просветлых лавок*; среди байны лёжыт доска, а на доски тоска, и плацё и рыдаё и г земли припадаё': V. N. Mansikka, 'Zagovory Pudozhskogo uezda Olonetskoi gubernii', *Sborník filologický*. Vydává III Třída České Akademie věd a umění, no. 8, part 1, Prague, 1926, p. 220, no. 168; 1914.

[16] Pokrovskii, 'Tetrad' zagovorov 1734 goda', p. 262; 1734.

[17] 'На море на кияне стоит изба, в той избе лежит таска из угла в угол, из стены в стену …': Smilianskaia, 'Zagovory i gadaniia', p. 134; 1735.

In the wide field there is an *izba*; there is a board stretching from corner to corner; there is *toska* lying on the board.[18]

Sometimes the *toska* is located under the *doska* (the board), resembling a person buried alive:

On the sea, on the *kiyan* (ocean), on the island of Buian, there are twelve oaks, each oak has twelve roots; under these roots lies a cast-iron board, under that board the *toska* of [name of addressee] lies.[19]

In the Russian language and in Russian magic spells, *toska* (melancholy) and *doska* (board) are connected to the semantic field of death. The noun *doska* may refer to the lid of a coffin or one of the boards from which it is made, as well as a metal plate or tombstone. In magic spells, both *doska* and *toska* can be localized in the coffin:

On the sea, on the ocean, on the Buian island there stands a white fiery stone; on this stone three other stones lie; on these stones *three coffins* stand; *in these coffins there are three boards* [*doski*]; *on each board* [*doska*] *there are three melancholies* [*toski*]; the first *toska* was grieving — it was separating from the body; the second *doska* [*sic*] was grieving — it was uniting with the body; the third *toska* was grieving — it had entered the heart.[20]

We may also find the expression '*smertnaia toska*' (mortal melancholy) in magic spells:

Take from me, servant of God, melancholy, and heart-dryness, and black sorrow [...] let servant of God be unable to live without me, servant of God, be unable to exist [without me], and be unable to drink and to eat, but suffer from a *mortal melancholy,* and be unable to swallow this melancholy with bread, be unable to quench this

---

[18] '... в чистом поле стоит изба, в избе из угла в угол лежит *доска, на доске* лежит *тоска*'. P. S. Efimenko, *Materialy po etnografii russkogo naseleniia Arkhangelskoi oblasti*, Moscow, 1878, part 2, p. 141, no. 8; 19th century.

[19] 'На море на кияне, на острове на буяне, там стоят 12 дубов, у каждова дуба 12 корней; под этими корнями лежит чугунная *доска*, под той *доской* лежит имрекова *тоска*: 'Neskol'ko narodnykh zagovorov', pp. 111–12, no. 2; ? 19th century.

[20] 'На море на Окияне, на острове на Буяне стоит бел горюч камень, на том камне лежат три камня, на тех камнях стоят три гроба, в тех гробах три доски, на каждой доски три тоски; первая тоска убивалася, с телом расставалася; вторая доска (так!) убивалася, с телом сопрягалася; третья тоска убивалася, в сердце вошла': Maikov, *Velikorusskie zaklinaniia*, p. 14, no. 15; mid-19th century.

melancholy with drinking, be unable to wash this melancholy away in the bathhouse.[21]

In Russian there is an expression '*do grobovoi doski*' (lit. 'until the coffin board') which means 'until death'; in one of the magic spells, it was found in the reduced form '*do grobnoi doski*':

> ... may she dry up and burn and long for me, the good-looking lad [name of performer], with all her blood and hair till her *grobovoi doski* (deathbed).[22]

There are also other expressions, for example *umirat'* (*propast'*, *udavit'sia*) *ot toski* which mean 'to die' (or 'come to a bad end, 'be strangled') from *toska*, melancholy, and an expression *smertel'naia toska* that means 'mortal anguish'. Consequently, in some magic spells the state of melancholy is compared with death and is depicted as a particular kind of agony:

> let [name of female addressee] always long for me, join her heart to me, *let her dry up but not die*, and be unable to swallow this melancholy with food, be unable to quench *this melancholy by drinking*, be unable to kill herself because of this melancholy but remember me forever, may she shrivel up because of me and grieve for me.[23]

*   *   *

Research by linguists has shown that the word *toska* is one of a rich group of synonyms denoting depressive states (sadness, sorrow, dejection, boredom, mourning, grief, heart-dryness, and so on), but it occupies a distinct position among them. The word portrait of this concept shows that *toska* is active, it attacks a person from outside

---

[21] 'Возьмите от меня, раба Божия, тоску, и сухоту, и черну печаль ... то бы раб Божий не мог бы без меня, рабы Божий, жить и не быть, и не пил бы и не ел бы, *смертной тоской тоскозал бы*, той тоски не мог бы хлебом заись (есть), не питьем запить, не в бани замыть ...': *Pesni, sobrannye P. N. Rybnikovym*, St Petersburg, 1867, part 4, p. 251; undated manuscript.

[22] '... сохнула б и горела и тосковала по мне, по добром молотцы и(мярек), таком-то кровью и волосом, *до гробной доски*': Toporkov, *Russkie zagovory*, p. 371, no. 4; late 17th–early 18th century.

[23] '... по мне бы всегда тосковалася, сердцем со мной сопрягалася, *сохла бы да не умирала*, в еде бы тоски не заедала, в пойле не запивала, *от первыя тоски не положила бы руки*, а век бы меня поминала, сохла бы да тосковала': Maikov, *Velikorusskie zaklinaniia*, pp. 14–15, no. 15; mid-19th century.

and is able to penetrate into his/her body, it behaves like an aggressive living creature: тоска грызет, берет, одолевает, нападает, гложет; it сжимает, давит, теснит сердце, душу и грудь (*toska* gnaws, takes, conquers, attacks, and bites; it squeezes, crushes, grips the heart, soul and chest).[24]

The fact that from a number of synonyms in magic spells the notion of *toska* in particular was personified is largely due to the widespread usage of this word in popular speech and its 'behaviour' in the language. The word *toska* became fixed in magic spells, and this was facilitated by its connection with the noun *doska* (board) and with the predicative adverb *toshno* (wretched), for example:

> Just as *toska* (melancholy) feels sick and bitter on that *doska* (board), as it is not able to see the wide world, so let [name of female addressee] feel sick and bitter the same way about me [a name of a performer] when she does not see me [name of performer].[25]

In love spells, a man seeks to plunge a woman into a state of longing (*toska*), which manifests itself as an anxiety, depression, emotional stress, fixation on the object of his passion, complete detachment from the outside world, inability to lead a normal daily life, communicate with others, or control their condition and behaviour.

A woman who is a 'target' for a *toska* sent in a spell in a sense becomes that *toska*; she rushes in search of the object of her passion, and she may lose her gift of speech. Although *toska* was locked in the *izba* or in the bathhouse and pinned down by the board, and the woman, on the contrary, was surrounded by family and friends, she must feel just as lonely and abandoned by all.

We may say that *toska* as a character in magic spells implements, at the story (plot) and action levels, the hidden semantic potentials that are inherent in the word *toska*. It would appear that the compilers of magic spells followed the logic suggested by language itself. In particular, it is tempting to see the actualization of the archaic root *tъska* 'pressure, constraint, tightness' in the personified image of *toska*, pinned down from above by a board or locked in a coffin.

The connection between words designating emotional depressive states and notions of heaviness, pressure, and tightness is typical

---

[24] V. Glebkin, *Kategorii russkoi kultury XVIII–XX vekov. Skuka*, Moscow, St Petersburg, 2018, p. 189.

[25] 'А коль тошно и горько той тоски на той доске, как она не видит белаго свету, столь бы было тошно и горько той рабе имярек, как она меня, раба имярек, не увидит ...': Pokrovskii, 'Tetrad' zagovorov 1734 goda', p. 262; 1734.

of several languages. For example, the word 'depression' (French *depression* from the verb *presser* — to press, to squeeze, Latin *deprimo* — to press, suppress, squeeze), as well as the Russian words *grust'* (from Old-Russian: *grouzskyi* — heavy, sad, *podavlennyi* (depressed), *ugnetennyi* (oppressed), *ugnetenie* (oppression), *pritesnenie* (repression); compare the Russian expressions: *tiazhelo na dushe* (lit. 'one's soul is heavy'), *gruz zabot* ('burden of care'), *kamen' na serdtse* ('a stone on the heart'), and so on.

The image of love illness that was developed in the magic spells to some extent recalls the interpretation of love passion in the works of Pushkin, Tiutchev, Turgenev, Dostoevskii, Blok, Tsvetaeva and other Russian writers and poets. The common features in the texts of love spells and fiction are the idea of a persistent connection between love and melancholy, love and death; perceptions that love has an irrational character, does not obey the voice of reason and acts on a person like a disease, depriving him/her of sleep, appetite, peace; notions of the spontaneous nature of love which comes suddenly like the wind and destroys like fire, or of the dramatic emotional duel between man and woman. Knowledge of love-magic spells may explain a lot in Russian literary works.

(Translated by Elena Minenok)

Mythographies of the Demonic
(Notes on Slavonic and Balkan Ethnohermeneutics)

Florentina Badalanova Geller

University College London, Royal Anthropological Institute

MYTHOGRAPHIES of the demonic, as attested in Slavonic and Balkan vernacular traditions, contain narratives about the hermetic knowledge and proscribed lore of witchcraft, divination and healing practices. The focal point of analysis in the current discussion will be the portrayal of female representatives of the magical profession in folk oral heritage and iconography. My approach to the subject reflects the stellar contributions of Will Ryan to our understanding of magic and demonology, sorcery and witchcraft, healing and divination lore, as well as other kinds of esoteric knowledge within the Slavonic world, which has paved the way for others to follow.[1]

Ethnographic and Folklore Sources

The Bulgarian ethnographer Dimităr Marinov, one of the most industrious collectors of ethnographic data in the Balkans, thoroughly described the hierarchy of magical practitioners in the first volume of his monumental collection of folk beliefs entitled 'Living Antiquity'.[2] He considered it important to emphasize that the profession of 'magical practitioner' is conventionally designated by the term *veshtitsa* (вещица) 'witch, sorceress', which, strictly speaking, in vernacular tradition denotes exclusively the female representatives of this profession (that is, 'female magician').[3] Marinov duly noted that there exists a cluster of vernacular

---

[1] See W. F. Ryan, 'Magic and Divination: Old Russian Sources', in Bernice Glatzer Rosenthal (ed.), *The Occult in Russian and Soviet Culture*, Ithaca, NY, London, 1997, pp. 35–58; idem, *The Bathhouse at Midnight: An Historical Survey of Magic and Divination in Russia*, University Park, PA, 1999; idem, 'Ancient Demons and Russian Fevers', in Charles Burnett and W. F. Ryan (eds), *Magic in the Classical Tradition*, Warburg Institute Colloquia 7, London, Turin, 2006, pp. 37–58.

[2] Cf. D. Marinov, *Zhiva starina: Etnografichesko (folklorno) izuchavanie na Vidinsko, Kulsko, Belogradchishko, Lomsko, Berkovsko, Oriakhovsko i Vratchansko (Kniga 1: Viarvaniiata ili sueveriiata na naroda)*, Russe, 1891, pp. 45–46; see also the discussion in the seventh volume of Marinov's series *Zhiva starina*, entitled *Narodna viara i religiozni narodni obichai* (published as a monographic issue in the *Sbornik za narodni umotvoreniia i narodopis*, 28), Sofia, 1914, pp. 213–15.

[3] Consult lexicographic data presented by Aleksandr Diuvernua in his *Slovar' bolgarskogo iazyka po pamiatnikam narodnoi slovesnosti i proizvedeniiam noveishei pechati (1885–1888)*, (Dictionary of the Bulgarian Language from Monuments of Folk Verbal Art and Writings Published in the Periodical Literature in the period between

masculine forms, such as *veshternik* (вещерник) and *veshtugiurnik* (вещугюрник),[4] but at the same time confessed that he himself had

1885 and 1888), vol. 1, Moscow, 1889, p. 224; see also G. V. Angelov's ethnographic report, 'Tălkuvanie na prirodni poiavi: ot Bitolsko' ('From the vicinity of Bitolia: Interpretation of natural phenomena'), *Sbornik za narodni umotvoreniia, nauka i knizhnina*, 12, 1895, pp. 123–30 (p. 127). For a concise survey of ethnographic, ethnolinguistic and folkloristic literature on the topic, see the discussion in Tihomir R. Đorđević, *Veštica i vila u našem narodnom verovanju i predanju*, Belgrade, 1953 (*Srpski etnografski zbornik*, knj. 65/*Recueil serbe d'ethnographie*, vol. 66; added title in French: *Sorcière et fée dans la croyance et la tradition populaires*); Svetlana Tolstaia, 'Magicheskie sposoby raspoznavaniia ved'my', *Studia Mythologiva Slavica* 1, 1998, pp. 141–52.

4   The analysis of the cluster of Church Slavonic *nomina agentis* employed to designate 'magician'/'sorcerer'/'witch' (Gr. μάγος/μάγισσα) and 'diviner' (Gr. γνώστης/γνώστρια) brings noteworthy results. The survey of sources indicates that the masc. nouns employed most frequently in such cases are *vesht'ts* (вѣштьцъ), *veshtets* (вѣщѣцъ), *vedatel'* (вѣдатель), *vedetel'* (вѣдѣтель), *ved'ts* (вѣдьць), *vedets'* (вѣдецъ), *vedun* (вѣдунъ), while their feminine counterparts are *veshtitsa* (вѣщица)/ *veshteritsa* (вѣштерица), *ved'ma* (вѣдьма) and so on. To the same semantic cluster belong the nouns *ved'* (вѣдь) (fem.), and *vedenie* (вѣдѣные/вѣдѣнїе) (neut.), denoting 'knowledge' and 'science' (thus rendering Gr. γνῶσις, ἐπιστήμη, δόγμα, τρόπος). All these terms are cognates of the verb *vedeti/vedati* (вѣдѣти/вѣдати), which is a derivative from the Proto-Slavonic form *vede*, the meaning of which is 'to know', 'to understand', 'to be acquainted with'. See Izmail Sreznevskii, *Materialy dlia slovaria drevne-russkogo iazyka po pis'mennym pamiatnikam*, vol. 1, St Petersburg, 1893, pp. 478–82, 502–03; Vladimir Georgiev, Iv. Gălăbov, Iordan Zaimov, Stefan Ilchev, *Bălgarski etimologichen rechnik*, vol. 1, Sofia, 1971, pp. 140–41; A. Bonchev, *Rechnik na tsărkovnoslavanskiia ezik*, vol. 1, Sofia, 2002, pp. 123, 125; Max Vasmer, *Etimologicheskii slovar' russkogo iazyka*, vol. 1, Moscow, 1986, pp. 283, 309; Dora Ivanova-Mircheva (ed.), *Starobălgarski rechnik*, vol. 1, Sofia, 1999, pp. 319–21. In apocryphal tradition, the term *veshitsa* (вѣщица) can also serve as one of the names of the Devil himself, or as an appellation of a wicked child-snatching demon; see the discussion in Moses Gaster, 'Two Thousand Years of the Child-Stealing Witch', *Folklore*, 11, 1900, 2, pp. 129–62; Klimentina Ivanova, 'Za edin răkopis s palimpsest ot Bibliotekata na Ierusalimskata Patriarshiia', *Paleobulgarica*, 18, 1994, 2, pp. 3–31 (pp. 26–27); Vasia Velinova, 'An Itinerant Motif in the South Slavonic Literary Tradition: Amulets Bearing the Name of St Sisinnios', in Elka Bakalova, Margaret Dimitrova, M. A. Johnson (eds), *Medieval Bulgarian Art and Letters in a Byzantine Context*, Sofia, 2017, pp. 479–99 (pp. 494–95). See also the discussion in Ivan Duĭchev, 'Edin răkopisen svităk s apokrifni molitvi i zaklinaniia', *Starobălgarska literatura: Izsledvaniia i materiali*, vol. 1, Sofia, 1971, pp. 157–63; K. Popkonstantinov, V. Konstantinova, 'Apokrifna molitva ot X vek vărkhu olovna plastina', *Die Slawischen Sprachen*, 13, 1987, pp. 45–54; K. Popkonstantinov, 'Kirilitsa i glagolitsa sreshtu diavola, ili oshte edin oloven amulet ot X vek', *Palaeobulgarica*, 18, 2004, 4. pp. 69–75; K. Popkonstantinov, H. Miklas, 'Oloven amulet s glagolicheski tekst', in S. Bărlieva, L. Grasheva, E. Dogramadzhieva, R. Slavova, G. Filipova (eds), *Kirilo-Metodievski studii*, vol. 18, Sofia, 2009, pp. 385–98; M. Pantelić, "Hrvatskoglagoljski amulet tipa Sisin i Mihael', *Slovo*, 23, 1973, pp. 161–203; M. Detelić, 'Saint Sisinnius in the Twilight Zone of Oral Literature', *Studia Mythologica Slavica*, 4, 2001, pp. 225–40; F. Badalanova Geller, 'Between Demonology and Hagiology: Slavonic Rendering of Semitic Magical *Historiola* of the Child-Stealing Witch', in J. Cale Johnson (ed.), *In the Wake of the Compendia: Infrastructural Contexts and the Licensing of Empiricism in Ancient and Medieval Mesopotamia. Science, Technology, and Medicine in Ancient Cultures*, Berlin and Boston, MA, 2015, pp. 177–206. For a

never encountered any male practitioners with these designations. All his interlocutors indicated that the sole representatives of the class of 'professional magicians' were women. The Bulgarian ethnographer further pointed out that the female magicians possess secret knowledge of plants and herbs, and can trigger various meteorological phenomena (for example, wind and rain); they also possess power over strategies of causing (or reversing) erotic attraction. Such women are considered to be acting with the assistance of the Devil, and it is believed that their power stems from the energy of 'the invisible spirits'. This is what Marinov reports on the matter:

> *Veshtitsa* is a woman who is very old; through secret properties of different herbs and plants, and with the assistance of the Devil and evil spirits, she attained supernatural power, talent [lit. gift], and properties [lit. nature]. All the invisible spirits are her permanent retainers and servants. She is constantly in their circle and from them she derives her power and capacity [lit. might] to perform wondrous acts. The *veshtitsa* dwells in a faraway wilderness of forests and mountains, in deep and impenetrable groves, next to a river, spring, or whirlpool. There she lives alone on her own, and she engages in collecting herbs and plants. She has the following supernatural powers: she can heal a man from whatever maladies; she can forecast a man's future; she can reveal a man's secret thoughts. All the elements are under her authority. She can create wind and rain; she can cause floods and deluges; she can transform a man into an animal, into a stone, or into a tree, and she can return one into his primordial form [lit. image]. She is able, if she wishes to do so, to make men happy or unhappy. She has the power to transform herself (*да се префтаря*) into different animals;[5] yet if she wishes, she can become invisible. Snakes are her servants and retainers and help her to collect herbs (*билкіи*), as well as healing and wondrous plants (*буреніе лѣковити и чародѣйни*). A snake's poison does not affect her. Folk concepts cannot define with certainty whether a *veshtitsa* dies like all other people, or what happens to her [if she does or does not]. The *veshtitsa* is an evil spirit and people not only loathe but also fear her. Even today, the epithet '*veshtitsa*' is given to women and maidens as a reproach. There is also a scolding epithet for a man, '*veshternik*' [вещерникъ] or '*veshtugiurnik*' [вещугюрникъ], but a male '*veshtitsa*' I was unable to find.[6]

---

detailed survey of material on the topic see A. L. Toporkov et al., *Sisinieva legenda v fol'klornykh i rukopisnykh traditsiiakh Blizhnego Vostoka, Balkan i Vostochnoĭ Evropy*, Moscow, 2017.

[5] For similar data see Angelov, 'Tălkuvanie na prirodni poiavi', p. 127.

[6] Marinov, *Zhiva starina*, vol. 1, pp. 45–46.

In fact, local chroniclers kept the memories of various environmental misfortunes or weather-related calamities caused by their wrathful local *veshtitsa*. Thus, in 1884 the river Archar in north-western Bulgaria suddenly flooded some of the local settlements, without any previous heavy rainfall that might have triggered it; all of a sudden, the waters rose and engulfed dwellings, wiping away household utensils and agricultural implements; this sudden disaster lasted for one night and shattered the local community. And although it came out of the blue, it was not exactly a total surprise for the inhabitants of the devastated villages; it was believed that the flood was caused by the local *veshtitsa* who was angry with her neighbours. Marinov even quotes the testimony of one of the anonymous witnesses:

Near Lake Rabisha, also known as the Milivsko Marsh, in the cave of Rabishka Magura, there was a *veshtitsa* dwelling there. This *veshtitsa* was occasionally leaving the cave, to go for a walk around the marsh; many villagers saw her there. As it happens, the *veshtitsa* decided to punish people for their sins. She made the lake dance and the flood struck. While the rampant waves were ravaging the place, tossing around haystacks and barrels, livestock and household utensils, people and their possessions, the *veshtitsa* herself, in the image of a duck, was floating on the surface of the waters. When one of the local villagers wanted to shoot her with his gun, his hand shrivelled before he managed to pull the trigger.[7]

Marinov further provides a list of such mighty women with magical powers inhabiting the region in which the disaster took place:

In different villages many such *veshtitsa*-women are remembered; they are: Todora and Mitska from the village of Kriva Bara, Stoïna from the village of Kovachitsa, Tsonka in the village of Komoshtitsa, Pena from the village of Tolovitsa, Duda from the village of Vălchedrăm, Kamena from the village of Vasilovtsi, and many others. There is a whole directory of names of now deceased *veshtitsa*-women who once lived there, performing miracles and causing misfortunes.[8]

According to Marinov and other ethnographers, at the end of the nineteenth century, among the Christian communities in Bulgaria, apart from the designation *veshtitsa*, another term was also in circulation, that of *magiosnitsa* (магиосница)/*magesnitsa* (магесница), meaning

---

[7] Ibid., p. 49.
[8] Ibid.

'witch', 'woman-magician'.[9] The latter class of magical practitioners, as identified by storytellers of folk demonologies, was second in the hierarchy of witchcraft specialists; nevertheless, the term was occasionally used as a synonym for *veshtitsa*. According to Marinov's description, the *magiosnitsa* was believed to be a woman who, like the *veshtitsa,* was in constant communication with evil spirits and possessed the power of herbs and plants. It was maintained that she also could perform miracles, but to a lesser degree than the *veshtitsa*:

The *magiosnitsa* ('woman-magician') is someone who stays in touch with malevolent spirits; with the power of herbs and plants she can perform different miracles, but they are not as great and overwhelming as those of the *veshtitsa*. By the means of her witchcraft, the *magiosnitsa* can perform the following menacing and harmful acts against other people: she can put individuals to death or incapacitate them physically and mentally; she can paralyse and cripple them; she can thus destroy human wholesomeness. Through magic acts, the *magiosnitsa* can play a major role in a love relationship between a husband and wife, or lad and maiden. She can make a husband or lad go mad for a woman or maiden, or make one detest and repulse them. Even when a woman acts in a dishonourable way and her strict husband beats her on account of her misconduct, the witchery of the *magiosnitsa* pacifies him, and he becomes indifferent to the matter. [...] Countless are her deeds.[10]

Marinov further testifies that the supreme forms of the most powerful and grievous witchcraft procedures are performed by virtuosi

---

[9]   While it is true that Diuvernua lists in his *Slovar' bolgarskogo iazyka* the feminine nouns *magiosnitsa* (магйосница)/*magesnitsa* (магесница) along with their masculine counterparts *magiosnik* (магйосник)/*magesnik* (магесник), the lexicographic material presented by him to illustrate the semantic scope of these terms concerns only female practitioners; see idem, *Slovar' bolgarskogo iazyka*, vol. 1, pp. 1156. He finds it important to emphasize that the male magician may be called an *antikrist* (антихрист), that is, 'Antichrist'; see ibid., p. 32. See also Georgiev et al., *Bălgarski etimologichen rechnik*, vol. 3, Sofia, 2012, p. 605. A survey of ethnographic sources from the end of the nineteenth and beginning of the twentieth century shows that data about *măzhe magesnitsi* (мъже магесници) male magicians is rather scarce. When mentioned, such individuals are portrayed as curious exceptions to the general rule. An intriguing account on the matter is presented by V. Angelov in his short essay about male practitioners who allegedly knew how 'to summon the devils'; see idem, 'Svikvane na diavolite', *Sbornik za narodni umotvoreniia, nauka i knizhnina*, 12, 1895, pp. 154–55. As a rule, ethnographers find it important to point out explicitly that male magical practitioners are extremely rare to come across; see, for instance, S. Zlatarov's contribution on magic spells and incantations 'Baianiia' (based on data registered in the vicinity of the city of Nevrokop, now Gotse Delchev, south-western Bulgaria) in the *Sbornik za narodni umotvoreniia, nauka i knizhnina*, 12, 1895, pp. 150–51 (p. 150).
[10] Marinov, *Zhiva starina*, vol. 1, p. 50.

among female magical professionals who possess the secret knowledge of how to draw the moon down from the heavens:

> The most powerful strength and might of the *magiosnitsa* is her ability to force the moon to abandon its domain in the sky, and to come down to earth, descending into her mystical sieve. This 'bringing-down-the-Moon' procedure is surrounded with mystery, allowing folk belief to accumulate numerous anecdotes and vain speculation, to explain the lunar eclipse.[11]

These types of magic rites are performed in utmost secrecy, and if a random passer-by, or uninitiated bystander happened to witness the event, they would become mute, or paralysed.[12]

The annals of witchcraft in every village contain clusters of frightening rumours concerning such unfortunate affairs of tragic encounters with female magicians who were disturbed — deliberately or accidentally — by unwanted observers.

The witchcraft-celebrity Duda from the village of Vălchedrăm, for instance, was involved in one such mysterious incident; when she took down the moon and began interacting with it, a stranger coming from the mountains noticed the luminous shine emanating from her courtyard; what happened after that remained an utter mystery, since the curious beholder-trespasser was found the next morning numb and mute, trying in vain to communicate through the silent language of gestures. A couple of days later he died, the anonymous report concluded soberly.[13]

Clearly Marinov was intrigued by this kind of gossip surrounding the representatives of magical profession, and the hearsay scandalous stories about their power over heavenly luminaries. For more than two decades he continued to investigate the matter and in 1914 published an elaborate description of the hermetic ritual of 'bringing-down-the-Moon', which is considered to be one of the most fascinating pieces of scholarship concerning esoteric knowledge in general and witchcraft in the Balkans

---

[11] Ibid., p. 51; see also idem, *Zhiva starina*, vol. 7, p. 15, p. 34.

[12] Some extremely rare exceptions of lucky escapes were reported, however. If the accidental witnesses vowed before the witches to keep eternal silence about the event beheld, they were not harmed; see in this connection the account, 'How women bring down the moon' ('Kak svaliat zhenite mesetsa'), recorded by D. Vukadinov in the village of Gurmazovo (western Bulgaria) and included in his ethnographic sketch, 'Various beliefs and conceptions from the vicinity of Sofia' ('Ot Sofiĭsko: Razni viarvaniia i predstavi'), published in the *Sbornik za narodni umotvoreniia, nauka i knizhnina*, 13, 1896, pp. 167–71 (pp. 167–68).

[13] Marinov, *Zhiva starina*, vol. 1, p. 52.

in particular. He duly listed the names of some of the interlocutors who provided the necessary information for his report: Stoiana Pavlova (from the village of Knezha, Oriakhovo district), Miariia Ĭovcheva (from the village of Smolianovtsi, Kutlovsko) and Dona Uzun-Nikolova (from the village of Shtipka); all of them are women.

According to their description, the 'bringing-down-the-Moon' ritual may be performed only when the moon is full. The witch undresses until completely naked, just like a new-born infant. Ideally, as the community elders claim, there must be two witches — a mother and daughter. Both of them should have given birth recently, and they both should be breast-feeding their children at the time when the ritual is to be performed.

Having taken off their robes, without any other garments on their bodies, they would mount a *krosno* (кросно) weaving beam and begin riding on it.[14] Then they would put special magic herbs in a white cauldron; next to the cauldron they would leave a sieve;[15] they would start chanting over the cauldron, then over the sieve, while sprinkling themselves with water; thus the moon becomes bewitched, and starts disappearing from the sky, while beginning to shine within the house in which the magic is being performed. The moon then descends from the sky and approaches the witches in the image of a cow,[16] which they milk; and since only the full moon can be milked, according to the general opinion shared by Marinov's interlocutors, the witches perform the ritual when the luminary is in its full phase. After they have finished extracting the milk from the udder of the moon, the witches let their celestial captive go and it, little by little, climbs again skyward and begins to shine, but it is now pale and its light is much diminished. As for the moon milk, it has great magical powers, and the most powerful witchcraft may be performed by those possessing it.[17]

While the act of nursing is one of the ultimate emblems of motherhood, the participation of the representatives of two consecutive generations of one household, each of whom is in her lactation period in the 'bringing-

---

[14] This detail is briefly mentioned also by Angelov, 'Tălkuvanie na prirodni poiavi', p. 124. The negative symbolism of this act is utterly transparent for the storytellers, since placing a *krosno* (кросно) weaving beam between someone's legs is strictly forbidden. It is believed that whoever breaks this taboo and 'mounts a *krosno* will be mounted by the devils in the Beyond' ('Кросно не бива да се іаа, оти коі іаа кросно, на онаі свет кье го іаат гьаволите'); see P. A. Chacharov's report 'Razni viarvaniia, prokobiavaniiia i dr. (Ot Shtip)' in the *Sbornik za narodni umotvoreniia, nauka i knizhnina*, 10, 1894, pp. 121–25 (p. 123, note 32).

[15] For the use of a sieve in magical practices, see Marinov, *Zhiva starina*, vol. 7, p. 123.

[16] See Angelov, 'Tălkuvanie na prirodni poiavi', p. 124.

[17] Cf. Marinov, *Zhiva starina*, vol. 7, p. 183.

down-the-Moon' ceremony, reveals its symbolic dimensions. Encoded in the very poetics of the ritual is the simple principle of *sympathetic magic*: the lactating women — whose breasts are heavy with milk — are terrestrial hypostases of the cosmic cow-moon during its full phase, when its heavenly udder reaches its utmost richness. Moon and women are linked in one and the same web of matrilineal kinship.

At the same time it should be noted that the gender characteristics of the moon, as presented in vernacular Bulgarian tradition, are ambiguous. Indeed, the moon may be portrayed either as a male,[18] or a female celestial creature, but this blend of masculinity and femininity — deeply saturated in its verbal descriptions — does not seem to bother any of the storytellers relating stories about its magical milking. In fact, there exists a cluster of terms designating the 'moon'. The first one is the masculine noun *mesets* (*месец*)[19] that may denote — apart from the notion of the 'moon as a heavenly body' — two other different, but related concepts — 'menstruation' and 'month'. At the same time, the feminine noun *mesechina/meschina* (*месечина/месчина*),[20] is employed predominantly as a term for 'menstruation', but also as an astronym, together with the feminine noun *luna* (*луна*).[21] Surprisingly enough, the gender vagueness attested in moon-related terminology does not seem to have affected in any way the logic of the narratives describing the secret ritual of its milking.

The motif of witches who secretly 'bring-down-the-Moon' in order to acquire omnipotent control over the universe and mankind is also attested in a great number of folk narratives[22] and songs registered throughout the Balkan region by folklorists and ethnographers during the last century and a half. While the vernacular oral prose is engulfed by hearsay lore saturated by elaborate dark rumours concerning the secretive behaviour of the female magical practitioners and scary tales about their unfortunate victims (habitually arranged in a small circle during evening gatherings),[23] the songs about the moon's abduction are

---

[18] It is believed that the Moon is the younger brother of the Sun; see Marinov, *Zhiva starina*, vol. 7, p. 12.

[19] Cf. Georgiev et al., *Bălgarski etimologichen rechnik*, vol. 3, pp. 755–57.

[20] Ibid., pp. 757, 761.

[21] Ibid., pp. 509–10.

[22] See the discussion in Oksana Chokha, 'Novogrătski i bălgarski razkazi za mag'osnitsi, koito svaliat mesechinata', *Bălgarski folklor*, 3, 2017, pp. 287–99; Ljupco S. Risteski, 'The Orgiastic Elements in the Rituals Connected With the Cult of the Moon Among the Balkan Slavs', *Studia Mythologica Slavica*, 5, 2002, pp. 113–29 (pp. 115–19); Petia Hristova, 'How to Call Down the Moon or Cultural Continuity in Southeastern Europe', *Orpheus: Journal of Indo-European and Thracian Studies*, 7, 1997, pp. 101–10.

[23] Storytelling is performed exclusively in the winter-time, during nights (after sunset); see D. Marinov, 'Gradivo za veshtestvenata kultura na Zapadna Bălgariia',

rather laconic. According to them, the moon may be brought down to earth by wicked witches in a *podnitsa* (*подница*)/*chirepnia* (*чирепня*) earthen pot (which is normally used in the mundane process of baking bread, but may also be utilized as a lethal weapon by the malevolent dragons in their cosmic combat with the benevolent ones);[24] along with the moon, *veshtitsa* and *magiosnitsa* women can also fetch from the heavenly vault stars by means of a simple spoon.[25] Songs of this type are presented as the testimony of a young man who confesses to his beloved sweetheart that he had just witnessed how her mother was 'bringing-down-the-Moon' at night-time; as soon as he finishes his confession, the boy, as one would have expected, dies.

The demonological tales about the female witches milking the moon have also iconographic representations (discussed below). As a rule, these types of visual narratives are depicted either in the narthexes, or in the women's compartments of churches, which indicates that the main target of the anti-witchcraft polemics embedded in them are the female members of the congregation.[26]

The ethnographic data regarding the widespread performance of the 'bringing-down-the-Moon' ritual at the end of the nineteenth and the beginning of the twentieth centuries may stimulate further research in at least two major directions.

The first concerns the possible exploration of the attestations of some comparable mythologemes (for example, the idolatrous use of heavenly bodies) that occur both in the text of *3 (Hebrew Apocalypse of) Enoch*[27] 5: 7–9, and in vernacular Slavonic witchcraft narratives (for example, demonological folktales of cosmologically-oriented sorceries enabling witches to bring the moon down to earth to serve their will, and so on). It will be a challenging task to investigate whether these types of

Sbornik za narodni umotvoreniia, nauka i knizhnina, 18, 1901, p. 21.

[24] Ibid., p. 47; idem, *Zhiva starina*, vol. 7, pp. 27, 124–25.

[25] For the use of wooden spoons (made from an elm-tree, ash-tree, hornbeam) in magical practices, see Marinov, *Zhiva starina*, vol. 7, p. 125.

[26] Such scenes are depicted on the frescos of the Church of the Holy Prophet Elijah in the village of Buranovo, Dupnitsa region (painted in 1888), the Church of the Holy Archangel Michael in the village of Leshko, Blagoevgrad region (painted in 1889), to mention just a few among many such cases. See Liubomir Mikov, 'Luna/Krava, Lamia/Viatăr: metamorfoza i tăzhdestvo', in idem, *Izbrani studii*, vol. 3: *Bălgarska folklorna kulturai văzrozhdensko izkustvo*, Sofia, 2018, pp. 211–20 (pp. 211–14).

[27] The corpus of *3 Enoch* is a relatively late text (dated fifth–sixth century). See the general discussion in Philip Alexander, '3 (Apocalypse of) Enoch', in James H. Charlesworth (ed.), *The Old Testament Pseudepigrapha*, vol. 1: *Apocalyptic Literature and Testaments,* Garden City, New York, 1983, pp. 223–315 (pp. 223–53); Peter Schäfer, *The Origins of Jewish Mysticism*, Tübingen, 2009, pp. 33, 315–30; A. Y. Reed, 'From Asael and Šemiḥazah to Uzzah, Azzah, and Azael: *3 Enoch 5* (§§ 7–8) and Jewish Reception-History of *1 Enoch*', *Jewish Studies Quarterly*, 8, 2001, pp. 105–36.

parallel narratives, as related to magical aspects in the *3 Enoch* tradition on the one hand, and Slavonic (and Greek) folklore and iconography on the other, are coincidental, or reflect the criss-crossing of hybrid ideas circulating in clandestinely-related multicultural environments, transmitting traditions stemming from some multifaceted intellectual pedigree.

The second direction of research seems more promising; it concerns the centuries-long transmission of texts and traditions, the earliest attestations of which date back to the period of Classical antiquity. It has been long recognized by specialists in the field that 'drawing down the Moon from the sky' is a familiar trope; it may appear 'either as part of lists of magical acts or as a single act representative of the whole scope of magical possibilities, in sources throughout the ancient Greco-Roman world'.[28] The earliest witness, Aristophanes, referred to the magical ritual of drawing down the moon in his *Clouds* 746–757, and reported that it was performed by Thessalian witches.[29] The data provided by Marinov and his contemporaries shows that the tradition persisted into modern times.[30]

Women as Timekeepers and Memory-Custodians
Some ethnographic sources indicate that female magical practitioners were believed to have been responsible for inserting a cluster of heretical customs into the calendar of 'truly Christian' festivals of 'the New Canon', thus upholding the 'old rules' of 'the Old Canon'. For the origin of these festivals, Marinov quoted a legend which, according to him, was extremely popular among the village clergy; it was narrated by the Priest Tsvetko from the city of Lom:

> When the Council of Nicea took place in 318 [AD], and the Holy Fathers introduced a New Canon, the Old Canon became obsolete. In order to preserve it, three priests and three old women (*babi*) got together: Priest Tornio, Priest Milio, and Priest Kaltsunkio, together with the old woman (*baba*) Petka Gorogleda, the old woman (*baba*) Kandakira, and the old woman (*baba*) Drusna. They were from six villages and gathered together on the hill in the village of Burovan [in north-western

---

[28] See Radcliffe G. Edmonds III, *Drawing Down the Moon: Magic in the Ancient Greco–Roman World*, Princeton, NJ and Oxford, 2019, pp. 1–2.

[29] See further the discussion in ibid., pp. 1–2, 19–34. See also the survey of related data in G. Mishev, *Antichni sledi v magicheski obredi ot Bălgarskite zemi*, Sofia, 2015, pp. 162–71.

[30] The same motif appears in Jewish folklore from Eastern Europe, as documented by B. Serwer-Bernstein, *Let's Steal the Moon: Jewish Tales, Ancient and Recent*, foreword by Dov Noy, New York, 1987, pp. 80–85.

Bulgaria]. They invited the villagers to come along, adults and children, in order to perform idol-worshipping. They slaughtered sheep and rams, ate and drank, and established the following festivals [var. holy days]. The first day of March (the '*Martin den*'),[31] and the first Saturday of March, (the '*Martina săbota*'), to be observed against hailstorms; the Monday of St Theodor's Week (the *Tudorov ponedelnik*), to be observed against flies; the Thursday of the same week (the *Tudorov chetvărtăk*), against crows and ravens; the Thursday of the week before Easter and the following ones (according to the new law) — against hailstorms;[32] the Tuesday of the week after Easter (according to the new law) — against drought; the feast day of Jeremiah — against snakes. Observed during the *Rusalska* Week[33] should be the following festivals: on Wednesday, against insanity; on Friday, against skin diseases; 15th, 16th, 17th of July, against fire; 27th October, against mice;[34] 11th, 12th, 13th of November, are festivals against wolves;[35] 21st November, a rather bad wolf-festival called *Klekutsan*. From 20th to 26th December, a festival that should be observed so that women give birth easily; the Day of St Andrew, to be observed against harm from bears;[36] 8th January — Midwives' Day (*Babinden*);[37] 1st, 2nd, 3rd February, festivals against wolves.[38]

---

[31] See Petko Găbiuv, 'Narodni kalendari ot Tărnovo', *Sbornik za narodni umotvoreniia, nauka i knizhnina*, 16–17, 1900, pp. 19–24 (p. 21); E. Sprostranov, 'Narodni kalendari ot Okhrid', *Sbornik za narodni umotvoreniia, nauka i knizhnina*, 16–17, 1900, pp. 24–40 (pp. 29–30).

[32] See Stefan D. Spasov, 'Tălkuvaniia na prirodni iavleniia, razni narodni viarvaniia i prokobiavaniia ot Sofiĭsko', *Sbornik za narodni umotvoreniia, nauka i knizhnina*, 16–17, 1900, pp. 215–20 (p. 218, note 42).

[33] On folklore beliefs and customs associated with this period, see Liuben Karavelov, *Pamiatniki narodnogo byta bolgar*, vol. 1, Moscow, 1861, pp. 230–32; Sprostranov, 'Narodni kalendari ot Okhrid', pp. 24–40 (p. 32). See also the discussion in Ivan Shishmanov, 'Prinos kăm bălgarskata narodna etimologiia', *Sbornik za narodni umotvoreniia, nauka i knizhnina*, 9, 1863, pp. 443–646 (pp. 544–50), Mikhail Arnaudov, *Studii vărkhu bălgarskite obredi i legendi*, vol. 2, Sofia, 1972, pp. 149–61, 187–201; idem, *Ochertsi po bălgarskiia folklor*, vol. 2, Sofia, 1996, pp. 545–50; Ivanichka Georgieva, *Bălgarska narodna mitologiia*, 1993, Sofia, pp. 150–54, 157, 161–62, 180–84 (notes 38–80).

[34] See Spasov, 'Tălkuvaniia na prirodni iavleniia', p. 216 (note 9); Marinov, *Zhiva starina*, vol. 7, p. 82.

[35] The 'Festivals of the wolves' ('Vălchi praznitsi') are celebrated in the traditional Bulgarian folk calendar twice (in November and February); see Diuvernua, *Slovar' bolgarskogo iazyka*, vol. 1, pp. 254–55; Spasov, 'Tălkuvaniia na prirodni iavleniia', p. 216 (note 10); Marinov, *Zhiva starina*, vol. 7, pp. 77–80.

[36] Ibid., p. 80.

[37] See the data presented by Diuvernua, *Slovar' bolgarskogo iazyka*, vol. 1, pp. 44–45; see also St. D. Spasov, 'Obichai periodicheski ot selo Barievo, Sofiĭsko', *Sbornik za narodni umotvoreniia, nauka i knizhnina*, 16–17, 1900, p. 9; Petko Găbiuv, 'Narodni kalendari ot Tărnovo', *Sbornik za narodni umotvoreniia, nauka i knizhnina*, 16–17, 1900, pp. 19–24 (p. 20).

[38] See Marinov, *Zhiva starina*, vol. 1, pp. 54–55 (footnote a). In fact, the legend

In order to understand the subtext of the legend above, one ought to take into consideration the semantic coverage of the word 'baba'.[39] It has a rather rich range of meanings; it may denote (in a totally neutral manner) an 'old woman', but also a 'midwife' (that is, a female medical practitioner dealing with traditional obstetrics and gynaecology); the same term may likewise be used to designate 'a female healer' who is acquainted not only with matters concerning *materia medica* (herbs and plants, stones and minerals, animals' body parts, and so on), but also with the secret knowledge of curative spells and charms. Then again, the term 'baba' may be used to denote a female 'magician' and 'diviner', as well as 'witch'. Thus, according to the aforementioned legend recorded by Marinov, it was the three old women (*babi*) (that is, 'female agents' practicing magic, divination and healing), together with the three priests, that upheld 'the Old Canon' of religious festivals, thus committing themselves to the idol-worshiping and corrupting the 'true Christian conduct'. The subtle suggestion, encoded in the legend, is that the memory-keepers of 'the Old Canon' are, in fact, the female magical practitioners, who have not only inherited the primordial secrets, but continued to transmit them within the clandestine circle of the initiated; women are thus recognized as the ultimate vessels of esoteric knowledge.

Iconography of the Demonic in Slavia Orthodoxa
The survey of the iconographic heritage in the Balkans shows that magic activities and related healing practices are habitually linked with

narrated by the Priest Tsvetko Bukovets and recorded by Marinov presents a redrafted version of a fragment from an eghteenth-century tract, 'The Womenfolk Feasts, or Against Womenfolk Fables' (*Praznitsi babini ili o babikh basnekh*) composed by the Bulgarian monk Joseph the Bearded (Iosif Bradati). The text was published by V. N. Mochul'skii, *Slova i poucheniia, napravlennye protiv iazycheskikh verovanii i obriadov (k bytovoi istorii bolgar)*, Odessa, 1903, pp. 7–17; D. Petkanova-Toteva, *Narodnoto chetivo prez XVI–XVIII vek*, Sofia, 1990, pp. 335–42. See also the discussion in F. Badalanova, 'Folklorna replika kăm "Praznits babini li o babikh basnekh": Răkopisni kalendari na bălgarskite preselnitsi v Besarabia i Tavriia', *Bălgarski folklor*, 16, 1990, 3, pp. 95–109 (pp. 98, 101–02); *eadem*, 'Clandestine Transparencies: Retrieving *The Book of Jubilees* in *Slavia Orthodoxa* (Iconographic, Apocryphal and Folklore Witnesses)', *Judaïsme ancien/Ancient Judaism*, 5, 2017, pp. 183–279 (pp. 233–34); A. Angusheva-Tikhanova, M. Dimitrova, 'Samokov i borbata na Tsurkvata sreshtu baeneto i gadaeneto', in R. Malchev et al. (eds), *Etnologiia na obshtuvaneto (Godishnik na Asotsiatsiia Ongăl*, vol. 12), Sofia, 2013, pp. 120–34 (pp. 122–23); D. Dimitrova–Marinova, 'Pouchenieto kăm zhenite i momite v răkopisnata traditsiia ot vtorata polovina na XVIII vek', *Starobălgarska literatura*, 33–34, 2005, pp. 380–93. Further on biography and writings of the Bulgarian monk Joseph the Bearded, see D. Marinov, 'Ieromonakh Iosif Bradati: Prinos kăm istoriiata na bălgarskata literatura', *Sbornik za narodni umotvoreniia, nauka i knizhnina*, vol. 18, 1901, pp. 99–131.

[39] See Diuvernua, *Slovar' bolgarskogo iazyka*, vol. 1, pp. 43–45.

demonic agency. As briefly mentioned above, these types of images are depicted either in the narthexes, or in the women's compartments of churches. In some cases they may be painted even on the panels of the iconostasis, next to the altar gates. These types of visual narratives transform the entire discourse of the orally-transmitted demonological tales on which they are based, and turn them into iconographic homilies charged with fierce anti-witchcraft polemics.

One such case is presented by a fresco in the open gallery of the Church of the Holy Archangel Michael near the village of Leshko, south-western Bulgaria, painted in 1889 by the icon-painter Mikhalko Golev (see Fig. 1). It is positioned at the very entrance of the open gallery, and thus is the scene first encountered by villagers when they visit the church to attend the Sunday services or to celebrate other Christian festivals. The image shows the full moon with its human (male) face over a vast figure of the Devil with an extended — long, red dagger-shaped — tongue between his massive white teeth; he is portrayed as a black, hairy, bearded hybrid creature with two horns, a tail, two dragon-like wings, four bird-like feet, and cow's udders, which the witch is milking. She is dressed in a traditional garb with covered head, in a typical milking posture. The eyes of the Devil appear to have been scratched out from the painted surface; local belief holds that a mixture containing this type of substance has curative properties and is recommended to be administered against eye disease. The inscription (positioned between the moon and the Devil) reads: 'And this is a *magesnitsa*-witch who lies to people, that she takes down the Moon to milk it, but milks [in fact] the Devil.'[40]

Next to the image with the witch milking the Devil, in the direction of the church gates, there is a sequence of frescoes depicting other types of sinful behaviour (including a scene presenting women putting make-up on their faces, with a condemnatory inscription above their heads: 'Those who put on [their faces] white and red [colouring matter] have the Devil holding the mirror before them.'[41]

Similar scenes are depicted in other churches (for example, in the open gallery of the Church of St Nicholas in the village of Cherven Breg, Dupnitsa county, south-western Bulgaria, painted in 1882), and usually they are surrounded by an abundance of scattered images of women embraced by winged demons, who are kissing them; all these mini-portraits are included in the bigger panoramic view of female

---

[40] 'А се магесница щото лаже людето ке свале месецо да го мазе въ место месецо даволо мазе.'
[41] 'Който се белатъ и царват даволо имъ держи огледалото.'

Fig. 1. Witch milking the Moon.
Mural painting in the open gallery of the Church of the Holy Archangel
Michael near the village of Leshko, south-western Bulgaria. The fresco was
painted in 1889 by the icon-painter Mikhalko Golev.
Photo F. Badalanova Geller.

misconduct. Certainly, one of the most frequent scenes of 'women's
sinning' deals with depictions of episodes related to healing rituals.

Among the earliest frescoes treating this theme is that painted on
the southern wall of the open gallery of the Church of the Nativity of
the Theotokos, Rila Monastery (Bulgaria) in 1847 by Dimităr Zograf
(possibly with the assistance of his son Zafir) from Samokov (see Fig. 2).[42]

Situated behind the benches on which the pilgrims rest after their
long journey to the monastery, before entering the church itself, the
fresco shows a witch next to the open door of her house, who gives to
a kneeling man — whose face betrays suffering and distress — a magic
potion; he drinks from a vessel above which a red-winged devil with
curled tail defecates; the devil's feet are positioned on the head of the
witch. An inscription in black streams from the devil's mouth towards
the young woman standing behind the sick man; the inscription reads:
'He will recover' — obviously an ironic hint that the entire affair is a
doomed endeavour. On her shoulders kneels another red-winged devil
with his hand around her head. Both the male patient and his female

---

[42] See Angusheva-Tikhanova, Dimitrova, 'Samokov i borbata', pp. 128–31.

companion are dressed in traditional garments. The witch is portrayed as an old woman; her advanced age is betrayed by the white string of hair coming from below her scarf. Like her patients, she is dressed in traditional clothing. Above her head, an inscription tells the viewer that she is a '*samovila*,[43] or *magician*'. A winged-horned devil with curved talons is suspended above her, with his left foot standing on her head and his right leg perched on the roof of her house, while holding hands with the defecating devil; another devil kneels on the shoulders of the woman accompanying the sick man.

Fig. 2. Visiting the healer.
Mural painting on the southern wall of the open gallery of the Church of
the Nativity of the Theotokos, Rila Monastery (Bulgaria).
Photo F. Badalanova Geller.

Behind the kneeling patient and his female companion, a cart with two white oxen harnessed to it is depicted; above them a devil with red wings joyfully dances,[44] holding white handkerchiefs, as required

[43] The term *samovila* is conventionally used to denote a particular type of female demon; see Marinov, *Zhiva starina*, vol. 1, pp. 21–27. In some cases, however, the term *samovila* may be employed to denote 'female magician' and 'witch'; idem, *Zhiva starina*, vol. 7, p. 215.

[44] On 'dance' as a *sui generis* devilish act, see Boris Uspenskii, 'Mifologicheskii aspekt russkoi ekspressivnoi frazeologii', in idem, *Izbrannye trudy*, vol. 2, Moscow,

in a traditional folk dance. In the cart there is a group of people, also dressed in traditional garb. A man is shown in the driving seat, and behind him there is a sick young woman; a worried female relative, possibly her mother, embraces her around her shoulders. Two other devils are shown next to them in the cart. The first, whose wings are black-grey, has his right hand on the maiden's head, while his left hand rests on the shoulder of the accompanying female relative. In the background, behind the maiden and her female companion, the other devil ecstatically dances, with his red wings widely spread. One more demon, with black wings, pushes the wheels of the cart, rushing towards the house of the healer.

Walking after the cart is a young man, pointing towards the distressed family of the ailing maiden; behind him is a horse on which another sick patient rides. A long inscription is placed above the red-winged devil dancing behind the worried female relative and above the patient on the horse; it reads:

The female magicians and *vrazhalitsi*[45] — witches are servants of the Devil; this is why the Devil rejoices a great deal, jumps and dances in front of those who visit them. As for the matter that is administered to drink or to eat, this is devilish faeces. Those who abandon God, the Law, and the Church, and go to visit *vrazhalitsi* witches, they are not servants of God but servants of the Devil.[46]

The inscription quoted above spells out unequivocally the message that the rituals of healing should be considered devilish deeds. This type of polemic generated a series of visual narratives concerned with the axiology of healing practices. Occasionally, the visit of a sick individual to the healer/magician/witch may be situated within the

1996, pp. 67–161 (pp. 73–75).

[45] Traditionally, the terms *vrazhalitsa* (вражалица), *vrazharka* (вражарка) and *vrachka* (врачка) are employed to denote a female 'diviner'; see Diuvernua, *Slovar' bolgarskogo iazyka*, vol. 1, pp. 274–75, and Marinov, *Zhiva starina*, vol. 7, p. 188. The masculine counterpart of the term, *vrazhalets* (вражалец), designates individuals who specialize in treasure-hunting; they are able to perform special divination rituals indicating the place where treasure is located; see ibid., p. 223. The masculine form of the term (sing.) *vrach*/(pl.) *vrachove* (врач/врачове), on the other hand, designates a physician-saint (for example, Saints Cosmas and Damian). See further Georgiev, et al., *Bălgarski etimologichen rechnik*, vol. 1, pp. 179–80, 183. In modern Russian, the lexeme *vrach* denotes 'doctor', 'physician'.

[46] The original Slavonic text reads: 'Магесницыте и вражалицыте са даволски слоуги, за това и даволъ-о многосе радоува, скача и играе, предъ оніа що идаᵀ при ниˣ, и това що запоаваᵀ, и що захраноуваᵀ, оно е даволски гноусотии кои оставаᵀ бꙅ, законъ-а, и церквата, и ходаᵀ при вражалицыте они не са бж҃їи, но даволски слоуги.'

larger framework of the Last Judgement scenario. One such case is the fresco from the Preobrazhenski Monastery in north-eastern Bulgaria, showing the visit of a sick man to the (needless to say, female) witch-doctor; the substance which the healer is administering to the patient is, in fact, nothing other than the Devil's excrement. Depicted in the upper corner of the fresco, on the left-hand side of the composition (from the perspective of the observer), next to the fiery river (at the bottom of which sits the Inferno, personified by the Devil/Satan, holding Judas in his lap), is a scene on which it is shown how the *magesnitsi* ('magicians') are giving a potion to the sick man; he is drinking an allegedly 'healing' substance from a bowl which, in fact, contains the Devil's excrement (see Fig. 3).

Fig. 3. 'The Last Judgement'.
Mural painting on the eastern wall of the narthex of The Preobrazhenski Monastery near the city of Veliko Tărnovo, North-Eastern Bulgaria. The fresco was painted in the period between 1849–1851 by Zakhariĭ Zograf. Photo F. Badalanova Geller.

Occasionally, the 'visit to the female healer' visual narrative can be found depicted even on the panel plinths of the iconostasis. One such case is the altarpiece in the Church of Gorna Ribnitsa, Bulgaria (painted in 1860), which consists of a series of images related to the demonic nature of healing practices (see Fig. 4). Above the scene, an inscription reads: 'These are coming to *vrazhalitsa* so that she gives them a [magic] potion to drink.'[47] Astonishingly, the image of the female healer administering the Devil's excrement to the sick patient is placed below the icon of the Theotokos with the Infant, next to the altar gates.

Fig. 4. Visiting the healer.
Plinth panel from the iconostasis of the church in the village of
Gorna Ribnitsa, south-western Bulgaria (1860).
Photo F. Badalanova Geller.

[47] 'Тїа що идат в на вражалица таи запоюва.'

Next to the plinth panel with the image of the visit to the healer there is another painting (see Fig. 5), showing a *vrazhalitsa*-witch fetching water from a supposedly healing spring; but, as the painting shows, the vessel containing the magic water is full of the Devil's excrement; the inscriptions states: 'This is a *vrazhalitsa*-witch who administers magic water.'[48]

Fig. 5. Witch fetching magic water.
Plinth panel from the iconostasis of the church in the village of
Gorna Ribnitsa, south-western Bulgaria (1860).
Photo F. Badalanova Geller.

[48] 'Таа вражалица що дава вода магишничка.'

Without a single exception, as the visual narratives examined above indicate, the iconographic renditions of the 'visiting the healer' topic depict the medical practitioner as a woman, which is one of the idiosyncratic features of the Balkan demonological mythographies.

*   *   *

The current paper is concerned predominantly with the negative discourse in conceptualizing the image of female magical practitioners. At the same time it should be emphasized that vernacular lore distinguishes witchcraft from magic; these are two different — albeit occasionally overlapping — fields of traditional esoteric knowledge; or, to put it more precisely, while the witchcraft ceremonies belong to the field of magical practices, the magical practices may be totally free of witchcraft characteristics. To sum up, witchcraft is always magic, but magic is not always witchcraft. There is a profound epistemological difference between the two fields.

Following the same line of argument, one should point out that, although healers and diviners are no doubt representatives of magical professions, they are not necessarily outcasts from their communities (unlike witches). In fact, every single village in the Balkans used to have its indigenous physicians and apothecaries who were considered to be a community's ultimate trouble-shooters, to whom people used to turn on an everyday basis for help in various situations (involving all kinds of health problems, family troubles and accidental misfortunes). As a rule, they were charismatic individuals possessing specialized knowledge in the scope of ethnomedicine and ethnopharmacology, the professional secrets of which they have been transmitting from generation to generation, following the rule of either matrilineal or patrilineal kinship. Furthermore, they inhabit the liminal epistemological realm of matters of life and death, health and illness, happiness and misfortune criss-crossing their paths; thus they are between and betwixt purity and pollution, becoming epitomes of their eternal combat in the domain of both the macrocosm and the microcosm. This is why the very existence of healers, their reputation and their daily routine bear the scars from the victories they achieved, or from the defeats they suffer. When they manage to keep the cosmic equilibrium and the human wholesomeness, they are the heroes of the community, but when their actions threaten the balance in the macrocosm and the microcosm, they become its enemy. This is why, perhaps, the axiological borderline between phenomena which the community considers to be acts of benevolent or malevolent magic is often blurred and ambiguous; hence the abundance of overlapping terminology for practitioners of witchcraft, and medical professionals. Still, a tentative hypothesis can be formulated. The terms that tend to be employed in designating harmful professionals are usually feminine nouns (for example *veshtitsa, vrazhalitsa, magiosnitsa, magesnitsa* and so on), although there are rare exceptions of masculine nouns (for example *veshternik, veshtugiurnik*) denoting male witches; in most cases, these are no more than artificial lexicological twins constructed as masculine counterparts of the feminine terms. There are also terms denoting healers who specialize in various ritual curative practices involving both the implementation of *materia medica* and the recitation of particular chants, invocations and prayers (the learning of which involves the performance of hermetic initiation rites transmitted from one generation to the other in the same household). These types of terms are attested in both feminine and masculine gender,[49] with no axiological bias. Finally, there are also terms, for example *basnatarka* (*баснатарка*)[50] denoting practitioners performing exclusively verbal magic, that have only feminine forms. These types of phenomena will be analysed elsewhere.

---

[49] One such case is represented by the fem. *baiachka* (*баячка*) and masc. *baiach* (*баяч*); see the discussion in Iveta Todorova-Pirgova, *Baianiia i magii*, Sofia, 2003, pp. 98–102.

[50] See Georgiev et al., *Bălgarski Etimologichen Rechnik*, vol. 1, p. 38.

TEXTS AND TRANSLATIONS

The Place Where Nobody Went: Where (and What) was Serica?

Ralph Cleminson
University of Oxford

> The question, what is the country described by Ptolemy
> and his contemporaries as Serica, is the most curious
> in the ancient geography of Asia.[1]

THE task that the geographers of the Renaissance set themselves was to reduce to order a body of information perhaps greater than any that had faced their predecessors. Not only did they have before them the works of the geographers of antiquity, now more accessible than ever before, whom they regarded as the originators and prime authorities of the tradition in which they themselves stood, but they lived in an age of exploration which was providing an ever-growing flow of data to be incorporated into the body of knowledge already constituted by the classical writers, which it fell to them to complete, correct or restore. To a large extent this continues the attitude of medieval scholars. Roger Bacon, for example, though professing to rely principally on Pliny, 'like all holy and wise men', is not above pointing out the errors made by him, Ptolemy, and other classical authors.[2] The Renaissance geographers and cartographers were not unanimous in their approach. While some, such as Guillaume Le Testu, believed that since their image of the earth was incomplete, there was a place in it for conjecture as a means of advancing knowledge, others, such as Mercator, eschewed (at least in principle) all speculation in a quest for the recovery (*restitutio*) of the lost truths that had been known to the ancients.[3] Mercator, indeed, aspired to progress to a perfect knowledge of the truth ('ad perfectam veritatis cognitionem progredi') by means of the application of experience and reason to the available data.[4]

---

[1] Hugh Murray, *An Encyclopædia of Geography*, London, 1834, p. 46.
[2] See *The 'Opus Majus' of Roger Bacon*, ed. J. H. Bridges, 2 vols, London, Edinburgh and Oxford, 1903, 1, p. 304.
[3] Marica Milanesi, 'Intentio totius Cosmographiae', in G. Holzer et al. (eds), *A World of Innovation: Cartography in the Time of Gerhard Mercator*, Newcastle, 2015, pp. 131–45 (pp. 133–35). See also the same author's 'Peut-on se fier aux cartes marines?', *Publications [du] Comité français de cartographie*, 216, 1993, pp. 109–18.
[4] Ibid., p. 143.

Among the lands attested by the ancient authors, but as yet by no report from contemporary exploration, was *Serica*, Σηρική, the land of the Seres, which Ptolemy had placed in the extreme north-east of the known world. In modern times there is a widespread and persistent belief that Serica was China, and the Seres the Chinese. Translators render the words thus without comment, as an established fact, following the standard dictionary entries;[5] in the 1930s the Catholic University of Peking established its sinological journal under the title *Monumenta Serica*; and the Bodleian Library has recently placed its catalogue of pre-modern Chinese books on line at the URL http://serica.bodleian.ox.ac.uk/. The reasoning behind this is that *sericum* is silk, silk comes from China, and therefore the Seres must be the Chinese. Any reasonably attentive reading of the primary sources, however, will suffice to show that this cannot possibly be the case.

The first mention of the Seres by a European writer is in Strabo's *Geography*, 11.11.1, in a passage relating to Bactria and quoting the authority of the earlier historian Apollodorus of Artamita:

> The Greeks who rebelled, through the excellence of the country conquered both Ariana and the Indians, as Apollodorus of Artamita says, and overcame more peoples than Alexander, especially Menander — if indeed he crossed the Hypasis to the east and went as far as the Isamus — he conquered some, and Demetrius son of Euthydemus king of Bactria conquered others: not only did they take Patalene, but also the other coastal areas, that which is called Saraostus and the kingdom of Sigerdis; and they extended their rule as far as the Seres and the Phauni.[6]

This describes the expansion of the Hellenistic kingdom of Bactria towards the south-east: Patalene is identified as in the Indus delta region, Saraostus as Saurashtra (Kathiawar) and Sigerdis more tentatively as the region between it and Bombay. The Hypanis (Hypasis, Hyphasis

---

[5] For example, Henry George Liddell, Robert Scott, *A Greek-English Lexicon*, revised and augmented throughout by Sir Henry Stuart Jones with the assistance of Roderick McKenzie, Oxford, 1940, s.v. Σήρ.

[6] οἱ ἀποστήσαντες Ἕλληνες αὐτὴν διὰ τὴν ἀρετὴν τῆς χώρας ὥστε τῆς τε Ἀριανῆς ἐπεκράτουν καὶ τῶν Ἰνδῶν, ὥς φησιν Ἀπολλόδωρος ὁ Ἀρταμιτηνός, καὶ πλείω ἔθνη κατεστρέψαντο ἢ Ἀλέξανδρος, καὶ μάλιστα Μένανδρος — εἴ γε καὶ τὸν Ὕπανιν διέβη πρὸς ἔω καὶ μέχρι τοῦ Ἰσάμου προῆλθε — τὰ μὲν αὐτός, τὰ δὲ Δημήτριος ὁ Εὐθυδήμου υἱὸς τοῦ Βακτρίων βασιλέως· οὐ μόνον δὲ τὴν Παταληνὴν κατέσχον ἀλλὰ καὶ τῆς ἄλλης παραλίας, τήν τε Σαραόστου καλουμένην καὶ τὴν Σιγέρδιδος βασιλείαν· καὶ δὴ καὶ μέχρι Σηρῶν καὶ Φαύνων ἐξέτεινον τὴν ἀρχήν. Quoted according to the latest edition: *Strabons Geographika*, trans., commentary, ed. Stefan Radt, 10 vols, Göttingen, 2002–2011.

— different authors use different variants of the name) is the Sutlej or perhaps rather its tributary the Beas. From this it is clear that Strabo regards the Seres as an Indian people, inhabiting an area at the limit of Indo-Greek influence, and thus probably in the present-day Punjab or Gujarat.

No clue as to their more precise whereabouts can be gained from their evident proximity to the Phauni. These an even more obscure people than the Seres, apparently mentioned nowhere else. Most modern authors read Φρυνῶν, but, as Radt points out,[7] this is entirely unsupported by the manuscript evidence, and is an editorial emendation based on the supposed identity of this people with the Φρῦνοι of Dionysius Periegetes (*Periegesis*, l. 752). They, however, are not to be found in the text of that work in the most recent critical edition,[8] which reads Φροῦροι, consigning Φρῦνοι, along with Φροῦνοι, to the apparatus. Other editors have identified the Φρῦνοι (further emended to Φοῦνοι) with the Thuni of Pliny, and accordingly spoonerized Pliny's 'Thuni et Focari'[9] into 'Phuni et Tochari'. 'So much,' as Sir Ellis Minns says, 'for arguments founded on the supposed etymology of tribal names.'[10]

Strabo, moreover, warns his readers about the reliability of his information concerning the lands east of the Hypanis (*Geography*, 15.1.37):

> All the land beyond the Hypanis is agreed to be very good, yet it is not described with accuracy, but because of ignorance and distance everything is told as being greater or more marvellous, such as the gold-digging ants and other beasts and men of strange appearance and exceptional powers (as they say that the Seres are long-lived, attaining to over two hundred years).[11]

---

[7]   Ibid., vol. 7, p. 295.

[8]   Dionysius Periegetes, *Description of the Known World*, with Introduction, Text, Translation and Commentary, ed. J. L. Lightfoot, Oxford, 2014.

[9]   *Historia Naturalis*, 6.55.

[10]   E. H. Minns, *Scythians and Greeks: a Survey of Ancient History and Archaeology on the North Coast of the Euxine from the Danube to the Caucasus*, Cambridge, 1913, p. 122 n.4.

[11]   ἀρίστη δ' ὁμολογεῖται πᾶσα ἡ τοῦ Ὑπάνιος πέραν, οὐκ ἀκριβοῦται δέ, ἀλλὰ διὰ τὴν ἄγνοιαν καὶ τὸν ἐκτοπισμὸν λέγεται πάντ' ἐπὶ τὸ μεῖζον ἢ τὸ τερατωδέστερον, οἷα τὰ τῶν χρυσωρύχων μυρμήκων καὶ ἄλλων θηρίων τε καὶ ἀνθρώπων ἰδιομόρφων καὶ δυνάμεσί τισιν ἐξηλλαγμένων (ἃς τοὺς Σῆρας μακροβίους φασὶ πέρα καὶ διακοσίων ἐτῶν παρατείνοντας).

This should put us on our guard against trying to deduce anything about the Seres from travellers' tales that are not anchored in some genuine geographical feature or historical event, and particularly those that describe them as in some way extraordinary. There is an almost universal tendency to look for marvels at the edge of the known world, and one of the few consistently reliable facts known about the Seres to classical authors was the extreme distance of their habitation, for which they seem to have become a byword — 'ultimi Seres', as Seneca calls them twice.[12] This was to reach its ultimate conclusion in the chronicle of George Hamartolus, for whom the Seres are the noblest of noble savages:

> For in each country and people, among some there is a written law, and among others custom. For tradition seems to be law to the lawless. Of whom first the Seres, who inhabit the furthest part of the earth, have as a law the inherited custom not to fornicate or to commit adultery or to steal or to slander or to murder or to do any kind of evil at all.[13]

This is quoted in the Russian *Primary Chronicle*:

ИБО КОМУЖДО ІАЗЫКУ. ѠВѢМЪ ИСПИСАНЪ ЗАКОНЪ | ЕСТЬ. ДРУГИМЪ ЖЕ ОБЫЧАИ. ЗАНЕ БЕЗАКОНЬНИ|КОМЪ ѠТЕЧЬСТВИЕ МНИТСА. Ѿ НИХ ЖЕ ПЕРВИЕ СИ|РИИ ЖИОУЩЕ НА КОНЕЦЬ ЗЕМЛА. ЗАКОНЪ ИМУТЬ | Ѿ СВОИХ ѠБЫЧАИ. НЕ ЛЮБОДѢІАТИ И ПРЕЛЮБОДѢІАТ͠И. | НИ КРАСТИ НИ ѠКЛЕВЕТАТИ ЛИ ОУБИТИ ЛИ ЗЛО ДѢ|ІАТИ ВЕСЬМА.[14]

The Seres thus have a presence from an early period in the literature of old Rus', where they have been overlooked by lexicographers.

Strabo wrote in the second and third decades of the first century AD, though the events that he describes here took place in the third and second centuries BC, after which there seems to have been little direct contact with the Seres — or at least none that found a place in the record — until around the turn of the millennium. Florus (*Epitome*, 2.34), again writing some time after the event, describes the embassies

---

[12] *Hercules Oetaeus*, l. 414, and *Phaedra*, l. 389; the disputed authorship of the former play is irrelevant in the present context.

[13] ἐν γὰρ ἑκάστῃ χώρᾳ καὶ ἔθνεσιν ἐν τοῖς μὲν ἔγγραφος νόμος ἐσήν, ἐν τοῖς δὲ ἡ συνήθεια. νόμος γὰρ ἀνόμοις τὰ πάτρια δοκεῖ. ὧν πρῶτοι Σῆρες οἱ τὸ ἄκρον τῆς γῆς οἰκοῦντες νόμον ἔχουσι τὸ πατρῷον ἔθος μὴ πορνεύειν ἢ μοιχεύειν ἢ κλέπτειν ἢ λοιδορεῖν ἢ φονεύειν ἢ κακουργεῖν τὸ σύνολον.

[14] *Повѣсть временныхъ лѣтъ*, 14,15–22, quoted according to the Laurentian text as edited by Donald Ostrowski and David Birnbaum, http://pvl.obdurodon.org/pvl.html (accessed 25 November 2019).

sent to Augustus from the various ends of the earth, and among them one including the Seres:

> For even the Scythians and Sarmatians sent envoys seeking friendship. Even the Seres and the Indians, who dwell beneath the very sun, though they brought also elephants with gems and pearls among their goods, esteemed nothing [of this] greater than the length of the journey, for they took four years over it, and the very complexion of the men declared that they came from under a different sky.[15]

Here again, when mentioned in the context of a historical event, the Seres are linked with the Indians both in their origins and in their skin colour, which was also noted in passing by Ovid ('colorati Seres', *Amores*, 1.14.6). This only tends to confirm the implications of the first mention of them by Strabo.

The next writer on geography to mention the Seres is Pomponius Mela (*De Chorographia*, 1.11 and 3.60), who wrote about the middle of the century. He locates them between the Scythians and the Indians, in the middle of the easternmost parts of Asia. This might suggest China to the modern reader, who should however recall that East Asia, in present-day terms, was a foreign concept to antiquity, and that anything beyond what might be thought of today as a broad arc from the mouth of the Ob' to the mouth of the Ganges was for the ancients either ocean or *terra incognita*. Mela's location of the Seres arises, moreover, not from any information, but for purely formal considerations. Having constructed his work in the form of a periplus, and conducted his readers along a fictional north coast of Asia (thus encouraging later generations in their fruitless search for a Northeast Passage), he is then forced to say something about its eastern coast, where he encounters an acute lack of data. The resulting text is a compound of ignorance, conjecture and the more sensational passages of Herodotus (the giant ants are even bigger this time). All that can be securely deduced from all this is an awareness of the existence of the Seres as a people who lived even further away than the Scythians and Indians.

Mela is, however, the main source for the homeland of the Seres in Pliny (unless they were both working from a common source now lost), as is clear from a comparison of the two relevant passages (*De Chorographia*, 3.59–60 and *Historia naturalis*, 6.20):

---

[15] Nam et Scythae misere legatos et Sarmatae amicitiam petentes. Seres etiam habitantesque sub ipso sole Indi, cum gemmis et margaritis elephantos quoque inter munera trahentes, nihil magis quam longinquitatem viae inputabant — quadriennium inpleverant; et iam ipse hominum color ab alio venire caelo fatebatur.

Thence our course turns into the Eastern Sea, and to the shore of the land that looks towards the East. This, from the Scythian promontory to Colis is at first impassable because of the snows, and then uncultivated because of the primitive nature of the inhabitants. The Scythians are Cannibals and Sacae, separated by a region which is uninhabitable because it is full of wild beasts. Then vast expanses are infested by monsters, as far as the mountain called Tabis that rises above the sea. The Taurus[16] rises a long way from it. Between them are the Seres, a people full of justice, and famous for their trade, which they conduct without being present, leaving their things in the wilderness.[17]

From the Caspian Sea and the Scythian Ocean the course turns to the East, the aspect of the coasts being towards the East. The first part of it, from the Scythian promontory, is uninhabitable because of the snows, the next uncultivated because of the savageness of the people. Cannibal Scythians inhabit it, feeding upon human bodies; for alongside them are vast deserts and a multitude of wild beasts, surrounding a not dissimilar savagery of men. Then there are more Scythians and more deserts, with monsters, as far as the mountain range called Tabis that runs down to the sea. Nor is that region inhabited until almost half-way down its coast, which faces north-east. The Seres are the first people who are known […].[18]

This is as much as Pliny has to say about the location of the Seres, though he does provide more information about them as suppliers of textiles, which will be discussed below. It is, however, worth noting that he more than once refers to the Seres and the Indians in the same breath (12.39 and 14.5), and that he praises the quality of 'sericum

---

[16] In ancient usage, the Taurus is conceived not only as the range that bears that name today but extending from it to the east along the southern shore of the Caspian Sea as far as the Hindu Kush and beyond.

[17] Ab his in Eoum mare cursus inflectitur, inque oram terrae spectantis orientem. pertinet haec a Scythico promunturio ad Colida primum ob nives invia, deinde ob inmanitatem habitantium inculta. Scythae sunt Androphagoe et Sacae, distincti regione, quia feris scatet, inhabitabili. vasta deinde iterum loca beluae infestant, usque ad montem mari inminentem nomine Tabim. longe ab eo Taurus adtollitur. Seres intersunt, genus plenum iustitiae, et commercio quod rebus in solitudine relictis absens peragit notissimum.

[18] A Caspio mari Scythicoque oceano in eoum cursus inflectitur, ad orientem conversa litorum fronte. inhabitabilis eius prima pars a Scythico promunturio ob nives; proxima inculta saevitia gentium. anthropophagi Scythae insident humanis corporibus vescentes; ideo iuxta vastae solitudines ferarumque multitudo, haut dissimilem hominum inmanitatem obsidens. iterum deinde Scythae iterumque deserta cum beluis usque ad iugum incubans mari quod vocant Tabim. nec ante dimidiam ferme longitudinem eius orae, quae spectat aestivum orientem, inhabitatur illa regio. primi sunt hominum qui noscantur Seres.

ferrum', which has been convincingly demonstrated to be Indian steel.[19] No inference whatsoever should be drawn from the much discussed red-haired, blue-eyed Seres of *Historia naturalis*, 6.32, since, according to the same passage, they are also giants ('narravere [...] ipsos vero excedere hominum magnitudinem'), and manifestly belong to the category of τὸ μεῖζον ἢ τὸ τερατωδέστερον.

Pausanias, by contrast, writing in the second century AD, makes no attempt at the geography of the Far East, but he does mention the Seres in the course of a long and quite gratuitous digression at the end of his description of Elis, apropos of the flax and hemp that grows there, from which, he says, the clothes of the Seres are quite different (*Graeciae descriptio*, 6.26.6–9):

> They have in that land a little creature that the Greeks call sēr, though by the Seres themselves it is called something else, and not sēr. Its size is twice that of the largest of dung-beetles, but otherwise it resembles the spiders that spin their webs beneath the trees, and indeed it has feet eight in number as spiders have. The Seres rear these creatures, providing them with houses adapted to the wintertime and the summertime; and the work of the creatures turns out to be a skein wound about their feet. They rear them for four years, feeding them millet, but in the fifth (for they know that they will not live any longer) they give them green reeds to eat. This is the food that the creature likes above all, and having gorged itself upon the reeds it bursts from fulness, and when it has died in this way they find the greater part of the thread inside it.
>
> Seria is known to be an island lying in an inlet of the Erythraean Sea. But I have also heard that it is not the Erythraean Sea, but a river that they call the Ser that makes it an island, just as the Delta of Egypt is surrounded by the Nile and not by any sea, and that the isle of Seria is just such another. Some say that the Seres themselves are of the Ethiopian race, and that the inhabitants of the neighbouring islands, Sacaea and Abasa, are like them; but others say that they are not Ethiopians, but Scythians mixed with Indians.[20]

---

[19] Wilfred H. Schoff, 'The Eastern Iron Trade of the Roman Empire', *Journal of the American Oriental Society*, 35, 1915, pp. 224–39.

[20] ἔστιν ἐν τῇ γῇ ζωύφιόν σφισιν, ὃν σῆρα καλοῦσιν Ἕλληνες, ὑπὸ δὲ αὐτῶν Σηρῶν ἄλλο πού τι καὶ οὐ σὴρ ὀνομάζεται· μέγεθος μέν ἐστιν αὐτοῦ διπλάσιον ἢ κανθάρων ὁ μέγιστος, τὰ δὲ ἄλλα εἴκασται τοῖς ἀράχναις, οἳ ὑπὸ τοῖς δένδρεσιν ὑφαίνουσι, καὶ δὴ καὶ πόδας ἀριθμὸν ὀκτὼ κατα ταὐτὰ ἔχει τοῖς ἀράχναις. ταῦτα τὰ ζῷα τρέφουσιν οἱ Σῆρες οἴκους κατασκευασάμενοι χειμῶνός τε καὶ θέρους ὥρᾳ ἐπιτηδείους· τὸ δὲ ἔργον τῶν ζῴων κλῶσμα εὑρίσκεται λεπτὸν τοῖς ποσὶν αὐτῶν περιειλιγμένον. τρέφουσι δὲ αὐτὰ ἐπὶ μὲν τέσσαρα ἔτη παρέχοντες τροφήν σφισιν ἔλυμον, πέμπτῳ δὲ — οὐ γὰρ πρόσω βιωσόμενα ἴσασι — κάλαμον διδόασιν ἐσθίειν χλωρόν· ἡ δέ ἐστιν ἡδίστη

Thoroughly garbled as this is, it is nevertheless recognizable as a description of the rearing of the domesticated silkworm, *Bombyx mori*, the first in European literature.[21] It is also important in that, unusually, it explicitly associates the Seres with thread produced by this insect: for the most part, those ancient authors who describe the production of textiles do not name the fabrics in question, while those who refer to them by name do not say how they were produced, which complicates the task of the researcher who is determined to approach the sources without preconceptions. Pausanias' evidence is also important not only as the first recorded use of σήρ in the sense of 'silkworm', but also as proving that this is a Greek word, and not the native name for the creature. It is an instance of the use of an ethnic designation for a characteristic product of the country, a common enough phenomenon, exemplified also by such words as the Italian *sarda* or the English *swede*. This is worth emphasizing, in view of the totally unwarranted assumption that the name of the Seres is somehow connected with the Chinese word for silk (in modern Mandarin *sī*). This remarkable exercise in reverse logic (for *sericum* takes its name from the Seres, as the ancients were already well aware,[22] and not the other way round) seems to have originated with the seventeenth-century Jesuit Michał Boym[23] and to have persisted virtually unchallenged in the literature to the present day. It is rejected only by Janvier,[24] Dihle[25] and Malinowski,[26] though Malinowski's own hypothesis, identifying the Seres with the Chera, can hardly be valid in respect of the people bordering on the expanded Bactrian kingdom, as no Indo-Bactrian king ever penetrated

τροφὴ πασῶν τῷ ζῴῳ, καὶ ἐμφορηθὲν τοῦ καλάμου ῥήγνυταί τε ὑπὸ πλησμονῆς καὶ ἀποθανόντος οὕτω τὸ πολὺ τῆς ἀρπεδόνης εὑρίσκουσιν ἔνδον.

γινώσκεται δὲ ἡ Σηρία νῆσος ἐν μυχῷ θαλάσσης κειμένη τῆς Ἐρυθρᾶς. ἤκουσα δὲ καὶ ὡς οὐχ ἡ Ἐρυθρά, ποταμὸς δὲ ὃν Σῆρα ὀνομάζουσιν, οὗτός ἐστιν ὁ ποιῶν νῆσον αὐτήν, ὥσπερ καὶ Αἰγύπτου τὸ Δέλτα ὑπὸ τοῦ Νείλου καὶ οὐχ ὑπὸ μιᾶς περιέχεσθαι θαλάσσης· τοιαύτην ἑτέραν καὶ τὴν Σηρίαν νῆσον εἶναι. οὗτοι μὲν δὴ τοῦ Αἰθιόπων γένους αὐτοί τέ εἰσιν οἱ Σῆρες καὶ ὅσοι τὰς προσεχεῖς αὐτῇ νέμονται νήσους, Ἄβασαν καὶ Σακαίαν· οἱ δὲ αὐτοὺς οὐκ Αἰθίοπας, Σκύθας δὲ ἀναμεμιγμένους Ἰνδοῖς φασιν εἶναι.

[21] For the celebrated description of silk in Aristotle, see below.

[22] 'Sericum dictum quia id Seres primi miserunt', Isidore of Seville, *Etymologies*, 19.27.5.

[23] Gościwit Malinowski, 'Origin of the name Seres', in G. Malinowski, A. Paroń, B. Sz. Szmoniewski (eds), *Serica – Da Qin. Studies in Archaeology, Philology and History of Sino-Western Relations (Selected Problems)*, Wrocław, 2012, pp. 13–25 (p. 15).

[24] Y. Janvier, 'Rome et l'Orient lointain: le problème des Sères. Réexamen d'une question de géographie antique', *Ktèma*, 9, 1984, pp. 261–303, by far the best account of the Seres in ancient sources, on p. 283.

[25] Albrecht Dihle, *Antike und Orient: gesammelte Aufsätze*, eds V. Pöschl, H. Petersmann, Heidelberg, 1984, pp. 201–15 (p. 213).

[26] Malinowski, 'Origin', which is largely devoted to the examination of this notion and its refutation.

as far south as Kerala. Malinowski appears unaware that the derivation from Chera had already been proposed by Kennedy[27] and Schoff,[28] though the latter considered these Seres 'a totally different people' from the silk traders, with whom, he believed, they had been confused by Latin authors.

In view of the considerable inaccuracies in Pausanias' description of the silkworm, we cannot place too much reliance on what he says about the Seres. He has, understandably, confused silk traders with silk producers, having no knowledge of the latter (silk was not yet produced in India in his time). However, his description fits the Indus Delta very well, and this, as an area where incoming 'Scythian' peoples (Sakas, Bactrians and Parthians) lived alongside an older 'Indian' population, is a place where racial intermingling would be very likely (even though, according to Strabo, the Seres were already there when the Bactrians arrived four centuries earlier). As for 'Ethiopians', the word has a wide variety of meanings in ancient authors and may mean no more than that the Seres were a dark-skinned people. Moreover, the Indus Delta was the location of one of the two main ports on the west coast of India, 'Barbarikē', the other being Barygaza (present-day Bharuch, on the Gulf of Khambhat), the former being in the territory of the Indo-Scythian kingdom and the latter in the Saka kingdom, the beginning of India proper. These two ports are described in the *Periplus of the Erythraean Sea*, written between AD 40 and 70 by a Greek merchant from Egypt,[29] which deals with the sea trade from the Red Sea ports along the northern coast of the Indian Ocean to India, with much information about commodities and other matters of interest to those engaged in maritime commerce. Barbarikē exported, *inter alia*, 'Σιρικὰ δέρματα καὶ ὀθόνιον καὶ νῆμα Σιρικόν'[30] (Seric skins[31] and cloth and Seric thread), so it was natural for merchants from among the Seres, even if their proper homeland was further inland, to be present there. At this time silk production was still almost entirely confined to China,[32] and

[27] J. Kennedy, 'Seres or Cheras?', *Journal of the Royal Asiatic Society*, 36, 1904, 2, pp. 359–61.

[28] Schoff, 'The Eastern Iron Trade', p. 236.

[29] *The Periplus Maris Erythraei: Text with Introduction, Translation and Commentary* by Lionel Casson, Princeton, NJ, 1989. The 'Erythraean Sea', ἡ Ἐρυθρὰ θάλασσα, included not only the Red Sea but the entire Indian Ocean, to the extent that it was then known.

[30] Ibid., p. 74.

[31] These were evidently a particularly fine sort of fur or leather: Pliny (*Historia naturalis*, 37.77) says that the skins (pelles) obtained from the Seres were the best sort of pelt (tergus).

[32] 'There are sufficient grounds for asserting that that silk technology probably arrived in Khotan sometime in the first half of the 1st century CE,' according to John

the author of the *Periplus*, the first among European writers, is aware of its export thence along those branches of the Silk Road that led to India, even though his 'Thina'[33] is described as a city rather than a country:

> Beyond this country, already beneath the very north, going out into a certain place where the sea ends, there lies a very big inland city called Thina, from which silk floss and thread and cloth are brought overland to Barygaza through Bactria, and again to Limyrikē[34] through the River Ganges. It is not possible to go to this Thina easily, for only occasionally some few people come from it. The place lies right under Ursa Minor, but it is said to border on the outward-facing parts of the Pontus and of the Caspian Sea, down which the nearby Lake Maeotis debouches together with it into the ocean.[35]

This involves the paradox of the import of Seric goods into Serica (though in point of fact the *Periplus* mentions neither Serica nor the Seres, only applying the adjective σηρικός to certain wares). However, the Greeks applied the word σηρικός to silk because they obtained it from the Seres, just as they had called it μηδικός[36] at the period when

E. Hill, *The Western Regions according to the Hou Hanshu*, 2nd edn, 2003, Appendix A. Electronic edition, https://depts.washington.edu/silkroad/texts/hhshu/appendices. html#a (accessed 9 December 2019), but no evidence of it anywhere else outside China.

[33] It has been repeatedly asserted in the secondary literature (almost invariably without reference to sources) that 'Thinae' was known to Eratosthenes, as cited by Strabo. However, editors ever since Kramer have rejected the reading διὰ Θινῶν in favour of δι' Ἀθηνῶν. See G. Kramer, *Strabonis Geographica*, Berlin, 3 vols, 1844, 1, pp. 100, 105, and Radt, *Strabons Geographika*, vol. 1, pp. 162, 170, 214.

[34] The Malabar Coast.

[35] Μετὰ δὲ ταύτην τὴν χώραν ὑπ' αὐτὸν ἤδη τὸν βορέαν, ἔξωθεν εἴς τινα τόπον ἀπολληγούσης τῆς θαλάσσης, παράκειται δὲ ἐν αὐτῇ πόλις μεσόγειος μεγίστη, λεγομένη Θῖνα, ἀφ' ἧς τό τε ἔριον καὶ τὸ νῆμα καὶ τὸ ὀθόνιον τὸ σηρικὸν εἰς τὴν Βαρύγαζαν διὰ Βάκτρων πεζῇ φέρεται καὶ εἰς τὴν Λιμυρικὴν πάλιν διὰ τοῦ Γάγγου ποταμοῦ. Εἰς δὲ τὴν Θῖνα ταύτην οὐκ ἔστιν εὐχερῶς ἀπελθεῖν· σπανίως γὰρ ἀπ' αὐτῆς τινὲς οὐ πόλλοι ἔρχονται. Κεῖται δὲ ὁ τόπος ὑπ' αὐτὴν τὴν μικρὰν ἄρκτον, λέγεται δὲ συνορίζειν τοῖς ἀπεστραμμένοις μέρεσιν τοῦ Πόντου καὶ τῆς Κασπίας θαλάσσης, καθ' ἣν ἡ παρακειμένη λίμνι Μαιῶτις εἰς τὸν ὠκεανὸν συναναστομοῦσα. Classical geographers greatly underestimated the extent of Inner Asia, so it is understandable that China should be thought of both as occupying the northern part of the Asiatic land mass and as bordering upon the Black and Caspian Seas. The Caspian was believed to be connected to the Northern Ocean, and Pliny (*Historia naturalis*, 2.67) reports a disagreement whether the Sea of Azov ('Palus Maeotis'), was simply a bay of the Black Sea or 'a narrow overflow of a different sea' (angusto discreti situ restagnatio), which must necessarily be the Caspian. The author of the *Periplus* evidently takes the latter view.

[36] 'ἡ μέταξα [...] ἣν πάλαι μὲν Ἕλληνες μηδικὴν ἐκάλουν, τανῦν δὲ σηρικὴν ὀνομάζουσιν' (Procopius, *De bello Persico*, 1.20, written in the sixth century AD).

their commercial activity did not extend so far to the east. The inference that the word indicates the original producers is fallacious.

A very different approach was taken by Pausanias' contemporary Ptolemy, who attempted an accurate description of the surface of the known world, which was much more strictly geographical, even to the extent of providing co-ordinates for the places he describes. Unfortunately, the further east one goes, the less reliable these become,[37] so that at this distance from his native Alexandria they are of no value at all in determining locations. Ptolemy too is aware of the existence of the Chinese (οἱ Σῖναι), and that they are a different people from the Seres, though that does not necessarily mean that he has an accurate notion of the position of China. According to him (*Geography*, 7.3.1), the lands of the Sinae are bounded on the west by 'India beyond the Ganges', on the south and east by *terra incognita*, and on the north by part of Serica. Of Serica itself he says (6.16.1):

> Serica is bounded on the west by Scythia beyond Mount Imaon, along the line already defined, on the north by terra incognita at the same latitude as Thule, on the east also by terra incognita along a meridian whose end-points are 180° 63° and 180° 35°, on the south by the remaining part of India beyond the Ganges along the same latitude as far as the end whose position is at 173° 33° and again by the Sinae along the line continued until the boundary of terra incognita already defined.[38]

This is a vast area: twenty-eight degrees of longitude, as calculated by Ptolemy, would amount to about 1,400 miles, which means that in Ptolemy's view of Asia, Serica is comparable to India or Scythia in its extent and diversity. He lists a number of geographical features (mountains, rivers and so on) within it, none of which can be reliably identified, if indeed they can be identified at all. He also lists the peoples who inhabit it (who do not, surprisingly, include the Seres), beginning with the remotest:

---

[37] D. A. Shcheglov, 'Oshibka po dolgote v Geografii Ptolemeia', Σχολή, 9.1, 2015, pp. 9–23.

[38] Ἡ Σηρικὴ περιορίζεται ἀπὸ μὲν δύσεως τῇ ἐκτὸς Ἰμάου ὄρους Σκυθίᾳ, κατὰ τὴν ἐκτεθειμένην γραμμήν, ἀπὸ δὲ ἄρκτων ἀγνώστῳ γῇ παρὰ τὸν αὐτὸν τῷ διὰ Θούλης παράλληλον, ὁμοίως δὲ καὶ ἀπὸ ἀνατολῶν ἀγνώστῳ γῇ κατὰ μεσημβρινὴν γραμμήν, ἧς τὰ πέρατα ἐπέχει μοίρας ρπ° ξγ° καὶ ρπ° λε° ἀπὸ δὲ μεσημβρίας τῷ λοιπῷ μέρει τῆς ἐκτὸς Γάγγου Ἰνδικῆς διὰ τῆς αὐτῆς παραλλήλου μέχρι πέρατος οὗ ἡ θέσις ἐπέχε μοίρας ρογ° λε° καὶ ἔτι Σίναις διὰ τῆς προσεκβαλλομένης γραμμῆς μέχρι τοῦ ἐκτεθειμένου πρὸς τῇ ἀγνώστῳ γῇ πέρατος.

The northernmost parts of Serica are inhabited by tribes of cannibals, and before them the people of the Annibi dwell upon the mountains of the same name. Between them and the Auxacia are the people of the Sizyges, and before them the Damnae, and then, as far as the River Oechardes the Pialae (or Piaddae), and before them the Oechardae. Then, furthest to the east from the Annibi are the Garinaei and Rhabannae or Rhabbanaei, and before them the land of Asmiraea beneath the mountains of the same name, before these as far as the Casia are the Issedones, a great people, and further east than them the Throani, then, before these, the Ithaguri, to the east of the mountain of the same name, before the Issedones the Aspacarae, and again before them the Batae, and furthest south, along the Emoda and Seric mountains are the Ottorocorrhae.[39]

Most of these are similarly unidentifiable. However, the Ottorocorrhae are the Uttarakuru of Indian legend, another of those blameless tribes said to inhabit the furthest reaches of the earth, in this case the uttermost North.[40] There is therefore a certain logic in placing them in the very south of Serica, which, according to Ptolemy, is just beyond the northernmost confines of India. The Issedones are also mentioned by Herodotus (*Histories*, 4.13–28), as the furthest people about whom first-hand information is available; beyond them, to the north, there are only rumours of legendary creatures such as one-eyed men and griffins. Herodotus' known world certainly does not extend as far as Ptolemy's: his Issedones inhabit a land east of the Don with a very cold climate, perhaps part of present-day Russia. In both authors, however, they figure as the people who dwell at the ends of the earth. The cannibal tribes may also be a reminiscence of Herodotus (4.18.3).

The extraordinary difference between Ptolemy's account and Strabo's is no doubt largely to be explained by the difference in both their sources and their methods. Strabo, in this instance, essentially repeats the information given by historians, while Ptolemy is reliant on the accounts

---

[39] Τὰ μὲν οὖν ἀρκτικώτατα τῆς Σηρικῆς κατανέμονται ἔθνη ἀνθρωποφάγων, ὑφ' οὓς Ἄννιβοι ἔθνος ὑπέρκεινται τῶν ὁμωνύμων ὀρῶν, μεταξὺ δὲ τούτων καὶ τῶν Αὐξακίων Σίζυγες ἔθνος, ὑφ' οὓς Δᾶμναι, εἶτα μέχρι τοῦ Οἰχάρδου ποταμοῦ, Πίαλαι (ἢ Πιάδδαι) καὶ ὑπ' αὐτὸν ὁμώνυμοι Οἰχάρδαι. Πάλιν δὲ ἀνατολικώτεροι μὲν τῶν Ἀννίβων Γαριναῖοι καὶ Ῥαβάνναι ἢ Ῥαββαναῖοι, ὑπὸ δὲ τούτους ἡ Ἀσμιραία χώρα ὑπὲρ τὰ ὁμώνυμα ὄρη, ὑπὸ δὲ ταῦτα μέχρι τῶν Κασίων Ἰσσηδόνες μέγα ἔθνος, καὶ ἀνατολικώτεροι αὐτῶν Θρόανοι, εἶτα ὑπὸ μὲν τούτους οἱ Ἰθάγουροι, ἀπὸ ἀνατολῶν τοῦ ὁμωνύμου ὄρους, ὑπὸ τοὺς Ἰσσηδόνας Ἀσπακάραι, καὶ ἔτι ὑπὸ τούτους Βάται, καὶ μεσημβρινώτατοι παρὰ τὰ Ἠμωδὰ καὶ Σηρικὰ ὄρη Ὀττοροκόρραι.

[40] They are supposed to be the same people as the Attacori of Pliny (*Historia naturalis*, 4.26, 6.23), who says that they occupy a similar position in Asia to that of the Hyperboreans in Europe.

of travellers (that is, merchants), who by his own admission had not actually been there (1.11.6) and encountered the people in question,[41] but retailed second-hand information in which they themselves were not always entirely confident. Moreover, while Strabo was content to describe, Ptolemy's enterprise was cartographic, which forced him to locate the places he referred to at specific points on the surface of the earth. As the modern reader who compares Ptolemy's maps with our present-day knowledge of the globe will immediately observe, he had considerably more success nearer to home, where he had more extensive and better information, than in the Orient. Serica was at the limit of his knowledge; though convinced that it was a real place, 'beyond' those of which he had more precise reports, he could not relate it to them more exactly, and consigned it to the empty space in the north-east corner of his map, peopling it accordingly with races traditionally inhabiting the ends of the earth. It is also possible that, in the shifting geopolitics of northern India, the Seres had by Ptolemy's time begun to lose their ethnic and geographical identity, and that their persistence beyond that date in Latin literature is at least partly due to later writers' practice of imitating the poets of the Augustan age. While not going as far as some modern authors who have denied that there ever was such a place as Serica or such a people as the Seres,[42] it must be admitted that some of the later writers of antiquity seem to have had no clear idea of who or where the Seres were, and to have applied the name generically to any people either fitting the traditional notion of the inhabitants of the far north-east, or engaged in the production or supply of silk.[43]

This was the situation inherited by the geographers of the Renaissance. Medieval Europe had been aware and respectful of the classical authors, and as their works became more readily available in the course of the fifteenth century, they were intently studied by humanist scholars, among whom Pomponius Mela, Pliny, Solinus (who in the present context is entirely derivative), Strabo and Ptolemy enjoyed particular prestige.[44] Scholars were of course aware of the problems of reconciling the different classical geographers' accounts with each other, and with recent discoveries, and their aim was essentially to achieve a synthesis of the best information they could obtain, from whatever source, so that

---

[41] 'Dieser Männer wußten von einem Volk der Serer nichts.': Dihle, *Antike und Orient*, p. 210.

[42] J. R. Köne, *Ueber die Sprache der Römischen Epiker*, Münster, 1840, p. 224.

[43] Cf. Dihle, *Antike und Orient*, where this is discussed at length.

[44] Patrick Gautier Dalché, 'The Reception of Ptolemy's *Geography* (End of the Fourteenth to the Beginning of the Sixteenth Century)', in David Woodward et al. (eds), *The History of Cartography*, Chicago, IL, and London, 1987–2015, pp. 285–364.

the classical and medieval heritage was 'in a state of revision — but not rejection'.[45] Among these sources Ptolemy enjoyed a practical advantage as the only one to have prepared actual maps on mathematical principles, so that his maps and concomitant writings were almost inevitably the actual starting point for Renaissance cartography. In north-east Asia, from which no contemporary data was yet available, the classical geographers remained the only source, and so Serica continued to be indicated on maps more or less where Ptolemy had located it throughout the sixteenth century.

Serica was thus, still, a place where no one had actually been, but to which one could in principle go. Mercator, in a letter written in 1580,[46] declared that:

> The voyage to Cathaio[47] by the East, is doutlesse very easie and short, and I have oftentimes marveiled, that being so happily begun, it hath bene left of, and the course changed into the West, after that more then halfe of your voiage was discovered. For beyond the Island of Vaigats and Nova Zembla, there foloweth presently a great Baie, which on the left side is inclosed with the mightie promontorie Tabin.[48] Into the mids hereof there fall great rivers, which passing through the whole countrey of Serica, and being as I thinke navigable with great vessels into the heart of the continent, may be an easie means whereby to traffique for all maner of merchandize, and transport them out of Cathaio, Mangi, Mien,[49] and other kingdoms thereabouts into England.

John Dee, who identified Serica with Cathay,[50] confidently expected ships to be able to sail up the Oechardes (named by Ptolemy as one of the rivers of Serica) as far as Beijing.[51] Such firmly-held beliefs did much

---

[45] Alfred Hyatt, *Terra Incognita*, London, 2008, p. 167.

[46] Richard Hakluyt, *The Principal Navigations, Voyages, Traffiques and Discoveries of the English Nation*, London, 1599, p. 444.

[47] Mercator follows a tradition in European geography going back to Marco Polo in distinguishing between Cathay (northern China, including Beijing) and Mangi (southern China, according to his 1569 world map, a province which is also called Cin and China — 'provincia quę & Cin & China').

[48] Although Pomponius Mela and Pliny give the name Tabis to a mountain or mountain range on the eastern coast of Asia (see above), sixteenth-century geographers interpreted it as a promontory extending into the Arctic Ocean on its northern coast.

[49] Mien: a kingdom described by Marco Polo, generally identified with Burma.

[50] E. G. R. Taylor, 'John Dee and the Map of North-East Asia', *Imago Mundi*, 12, 1955, pp. 103–06 (p. 104).

[51] Hakluyt, *Principal Navigations*, p. 437. Even to his contemporaries Dee could seem over-enthusiastic in his navigational projects: see D. S. Smith, M. Payne, M. Marshall 'Rediscovering John Donne's *Catalogus librorum satyricus*', *The Review of English Studies*, 69, 2018, pp. 455–87, and specifically no. 20 on p. 480.

to encourage the search for a Northeast Passage, but, since that did not exist, Serica remained undiscovered. It fell to Hakluyt's successor, Samuel Purchas, to uncover a text that appeared to recount an actual visit to the country:

> Musæus Bishop of the Dolens related to the Authour of the Tractate *De Moribus Brachmanorum* (supposed to be Saint Ambrose) that hee intending to goe into India to see the Brachmans, had travelled thorow almost all the Region Serica, in which hee said there were Trees (which brought fourth not only leaves, but very fine wooll also, of which they make Garments called Serica; and that there was a memorable Pillar of stone thus inscribed: *I Alexander came hitherto*; and that having passed thorow many Countreyes, he came at last to Ariana neere the River Indus, and by the intolerable heat was inforced to returne into Europe, not having seene the Brachmans.[52]

Purchas is wisely cautious about this, saying, in a marginal note: 'Edit. Paris. 1614. This Tractate is in the Vatican, Florentine and Millan Libraries attributed to Saint Ambrose. Others doubt whether that Father bee the author, or Palladius, &c.' Rightly so: the pseudo-Ambrosian tractate is in fact an expanded Latin paraphrase of a Greek work *De gentibus Indiae et Bragmanibus* attributed to one Palladius, who is probably not to be identified with the author of the *Historia Lausiaca*. The corresponding passages in this read:

> For [the Brahmins] are settled far from India and Serica, dwelling by the River Ganges; but I only got as far as the further limits of India a few years previously with the blessed Moses, Bishop of Adule [...] For he [Alexander], as I believe, never crossed the Ganges, but getting as far as Serica, where the Seres produce silk, he erected there a stone column and wrote upon it: Alexander the Macedonian came as far as this place.[53]

---

[52] Samuel Purchas, *Hakluytus Posthumus, or Purchas his Pilgrimes*, 4 vols, London, 1625, 1, p. 89. The failure to close the brackets is in the original.

[53] *Palladius de Gentibus Indiae et Bragmanibus*, hrsg. von Wilhelm Berghoff, Meisenheim am Glan, 1967, p. 2 πόρρω γάρ εἰσιν ἀπῳκισμένοι καὶ τῆς Ἰνδικῆς, καὶ τῆς Σηρικῆς, τῷ Γάγγῃ παροικοῦντες ποταμῷ· ἐγὼ δὲ εἰς τὰ ἀκροτήρια μόνον ἔφθασα τῆς Ἰνδικῆς πρὸ ἐτῶν ὀλίγων, μετὰ τοῦ μακαρίου Μωυσέως, τοῦ ἐπισκόπου τῶν Ἀδουληνῶν· [...] οὔτε γὰρ αὐτός [sc. ὁ Ἀλέξανδρος], ὡς οἶμαι, τὸν Γάγγην ἐπεραιώθη, ἀλλ' ἄχρι τῆς Σηρικῆς φθάσας, ἔνθα τὸν μέταξον οἱ Σῆρες τίκτουσιν, κἀκεῖ λιθίνην στήλην στήσας, ἐπέγραψεν· Ἀλέξανδρος ὁ Μακεδὼν ἔφθασε μέχρι τοῦ τόπου τούτου.

Even the writer of this text, therefore, does not in fact claim that he or his companion actually reached Serica, but that they abandoned their projected visit to the Brahmins[54] having traversed an 'Indian' realm which was evidently distinct from it. It is notable once again that Serica is identified as the limit of Alexander's expedition into the East, that is, the banks of the Hypanis, or the present-day Punjab. As for the Seres producing silk, this may once again be a confusion of producers and purveyors, but by this period — the end of the third century — it may be a reality, as sericulture had reached northern India by the beginning of the century,[55] and it is entirely likely that it followed the same route as silk and was first practised by people who had previously dealt in the commodity.

The last chapter in the history of silk in European antiquity, which concerns the introduction of sericulture to Constantinople in the reign of Justinian, still does nothing to solve the mystery of where it came from, though it is important in establishing beyond doubt that ἡ μέταξα is the thread produced by the larva of *Bombyx mori*. The best-known version is that of Procopius (*De bello Gothico* 4.17.1–8), according to whom 'some monks from among the Indians' (τῶν τινὲς μοναχῶν ἐξ Ἰνδῶν), who, given the vagueness with which the word was used in Late Antiquity, may not have been Indians at all,[56] approached the Emperor and offered to reveal how silk could be produced in the empire, thereby circumventing the Persians, saying that they 'had spent a length of time in a country beyond the many peoples of the Indians, which is called Serinda' (χρόνου γὰρ κατατρῖψαι μῆκος ἐν χώρᾳ ὑπὲρ Ἰνδῶν ἔθνη τὰ πολλὰ οὔσῃ, ἥπερ Σηρίνδα ὀνομάζεται). The Emperor accepts the offer, and they then bring back silkworm eggs from Serinda and establish the industry in Constantinople. 'Serinda' is mentioned by no other author. Modern scholars are understandably dubious of the identification with Sirhind, a typical eighteenth-century conjecture based on phonetic

---

[54] By 'βραγμάνοι' the Greeks do not mean the Brahmin caste as such, but Hindu philosophers and ascetics; their absence from this part of the subcontinent at this period, if it has a historical basis, may reflect the Indo-Scythians' embrace of Buddhism.

[55] Heleanor B. Feltham, 'Justinian and the International Silk Trade', *Sino-Platonic Papers*, 194, 2009, p. 12, http://sino-platonic.org/complete/spp194_justinian_silk.pdf (accessed 9 December 2019).

[56] It can mean anything from India to South Arabia to Axum. See Philip Mayerson, 'A Confusion of Indias: Asian India and African India in the Byzantine Sources', *Journal of the American Oriental Society*, 113, 1993, pp. 169–74. It is also worth noting that although the monks are widely assumed in the literature to have been Nestorians, Procopius says nothing of this.

coincidence[57] (though it is not *a priori* implausible, since Sirhind is in the Punjab), and have proposed various other hypotheses, but it is hard to avoid the suspicion that Procopius had simply invented the name on the basis of the roots *sēr-* and *ind-*, and that he did not really know where they had come from.[58] Caution is also indicated from the fact that Photius, though he summarizes Procopius' histories in his *Myriobiblion* (§ 63), does not mention this story, preferring (in the very next section) the version by Theophanes of Byzantium (whose history is now known only through Photius' epitome of it). There are no monks in this version, only 'a Persian' who brought the 'seed', that is, eggs, of the insect from the Seres to Byzantium.[59]

The situation remains the same: the Seres are a real people, from whom real goods are obtained, but with whom there is no direct contact, and no first-hand information about their homeland. It is little wonder that Isidore (*Etymologies*, 9.2.40) quotes what appears to be a proverbial expression: 'Ignoti facie, sed noti vellere Seres' — the Seres are known by their fleeces, not by their faces.

It is therefore worth considering the evidence of the textiles obtained from the Seres as they are described by the ancient authors,[60] which must be done against the background of their ideas about exotic stuffs. The first European writer to describe silk is, famously, Aristotle (*Historia animalium*, 5.19.6):

From a certain great worm, which has something like horns and is different from others, there arises first, when the worm changes, a caterpillar, then a cocoon, and from that a moth: in six months it changes all these forms. From this creature certain women undo the cocoons and wind them up, and then weave them; and it is said that the first to have woven them was Pamphile, daughter of Plates, in Cos.[61]

---

[57] It appears to originate with J.-B. d'Anville, *Antiquité géographique de l'Inde*, Paris, 1775, p. 63. D'Anville also found 'Serindis' in Ammianus Marcellinus, but the correct reading is 'Serendivis'.

[58] The name has been — and by French writers still is — used, on the assumption that the Seres were the Chinese, by modern scholars to embrace the whole territory from the Pamirs to the Pacific watershed: see Sir Aurel Stein, *Serindia*, 5 vols, Oxford, 1921, who discusses it in vol. 1, p. viii.

[59] 'Οὗτος δὲ ἐκ Σηρῶν ὁρμηθεὶς ὁ Πέρσης τὸ σπέρμα τῶν σκωλήκων ἐν νάρθηκι λαβὼν μέχρι Βυζαντίου διεσώσατο.'

[60] References to various types of fabric in classical literature have been comprehensively collected and discussed by James Yates, *Textrinum Antiquorum: an Account of the Art of Weaving among the Ancients*, London, 1843, which saves later authors from multiplying examples.

[61] Ἐκ δέ τινος σκώληκος μεγάλου, ὃς ἔχει οἷον κέρατα καὶ διαφέρει τῶν ἄλλων, γίγνεται πρῶτον μὲν μεταβαλόντος τοῦ σκώληκος κάμπη, ἔπειτα βομβύλιος, ἐκ δὲ

One should not scrutinize this too closely — it occurs in the context of a longer passage on 'worms' in which the modern biologist would find little or nothing of scientific value — but it is accepted that Aristotle is referring to wild silk,[62] most probably that obtained from *Pachypasa otus*, which is endemic to areas of the eastern Mediterranean including Cos. This provided the 'Coae vestes' of the ancient authors,[63] and was evidently something that had been known to the Greeks from time immemorial, since the invention of the art is ascribed to a legendary figure.

Cotton was described even earlier, though more briefly, by Herodotus (*Histories*, 3.106): 'τὰ δὲ δένδρεα τὰ ἄγρια αὐτόθι φέρει καρπὸν εἴρια καλλονῇ τε προφέροντα καὶ ἀρετῇ τῶν ἀπὸ τῶν οἴων· καὶ ἐσθῆτι Ἰνδοὶ ἀπὸ τούτων τῶν δενδρέων χρέωνται' (the wild trees there bear as fruit wool that in beauty and excellence surpasses that of sheep, and the Indians make clothes from those trees). This may appear strange to the modern reader, who is accustomed to think of cotton as derived from the annual herb *Gossypium hirsutum*; but this is a New World species that was unknown to antiquity. The cotton of ancient India was *G. arboreum*, which is indeed a small tree. It originated in India and/or South-East Asia and has been in cultivation for so long that no true wild forms are known: it was grown in the Indus Valley over seven thousand years ago. It is still grown on a small scale in India and Pakistan. Also known in the ancient world was *G. herbaceum*, an African species.[64]

It is against these facts that we must interpret the references to Seric fabrics in classical literature, which begin in the Augustan age with Propertius and, most notably, Virgil (*Georgics*, 2.120–121), as part of a passage enumerating the diverse products yielded by different climes:

> With Ethiops hoary Trees and woolly Wood,
> Let others tell: and how the Seres spin
> Their fleecy Forests in a slender Twine.[65]

τούτου νεκύδαλος· ἐν ἓξ δὲ μησὶ μεταβάλλει ταύτας τὰς μορφὰς πάσας. Ἐκ δὲ τούτου τοῦ ζῴου καὶ τὰ βομβύκια ἀναλύουσι τῶν γυναικῶν τινες ἀναπηνιζόμεναι, κἄπειτα ὑφαίνουσιν· πρώτη δὲ λέγεται ὑφῆναι ἐν Κῷ Παμφίλη Πλάτεω θυγάτηρ.

[62] For an explanation of this passage and Aristotle's terminology, see William T. M. Forbes, 'The Silkworm of Aristotle', *Classical Philology*, 25, 1930, pp. 22–26.

[63] Yates, *Textrinum Antiquorum*, pp. 176–78.

[64] See 'Section 1 – Cotton (Gossypium spp.)', in *Safety Assessment of Transgenic Organisms*, vol. 4: OECD Consensus Documents, Paris, 2010, and the literature cited therein.

[65] Dryden's translation of 'quid nemora Aethiopum molli canentia lana, | velleraque ut foliis depectant tenuia Seres?'.

This has consistently been taken to refer to silk, at least since the commentary of Servius (written at the end of the fourth or beginning of the fifth century):

> Among the Ethiopians, Indians and Seres there are certain worms in the trees, and they are called *bombyces*, which after the manner of spiders spin very fine threads, from which *sericum* [silk] comes; for we cannot accept arboreal wool [cotton], which is produced everywhere.[66]

This is valuable in proving that at that time there was an opinion that the passage referred to cotton (otherwise Servius would not have needed to refute it). One cannot fault Servius' understanding of Virgil's intention, nor his reasoning; his error is to assume that the cultivation of cotton had been as widespread in Virgil's time as it was in his own. With that objection disposed of, the passage may be reconsidered, and it is noticeable firstly that Virgil mentions the Seres together with the Ethiopians, who did at that time grow cotton but who certainly did not produce silk, and, secondly, that while cotton does grow on trees, silk does not: the silkworms are kept in special houses, and the mulberry leaves are picked and fed to them there. The details given by Virgil are too tenuous to allow a definitive answer to the question, but it certainly cannot be excluded that the *vellera* of the Seres are for him cotton. The very word is much more appropriate for raw cotton than for domesticated silk, which is unwound from the cocoons as thread (*fila*, νῆμα), and it occurs repeatedly in the ancient writers in combination with the adjective *serica*. They are no less persistent in ascribing a vegetable origin to it; this is commonly dismissed as ignorance by modern authors, who would, perhaps, be less ready to impute it to the ancients if they were more willing to admit it in themselves. It should not be forgotten that the Greeks and Romans had known about cotton, even if they did not wear it, since the late fourth or early third century BC:

> In the island of Tylos [Bahrain] (it lies in the Arabian gulf) they say that there is such a great number of trees on the eastern side that when the tide goes out they form a wall [...] and that the island also bears many wool-bearing trees. These have leaves like those of the vine, but small, and bear no fruit: that in which the wool is enclosed is the size of a

---

[66] apud Aethiopiam, Indos et Seras sunt quidam in arboribus vermes et bombyces appellantur, qui in aranearum morem tenuissima fila deducunt, unde est sericum: nam lanam arboream non possumus accipere, quae ubique procreatur.

spring apple, and when it is ripe it opens and lets out the wool, out of which they weave garments, both ordinary and luxurious. This grows both in the Indies (as has been said) and in Arabia.[67]

Pliny, who draws heavily on this passage (*Historia naturalis*, 12.21), adds the detail that these trees produce wool 'in a different way from those of the Seres' (*alio modo quam Serum*), in that 'their leaves are barren' (*folia infecunda*). This evidently refers to what he has previously said of the Seres, in the words that follow on immediately from the passage quoted above (*Historia naturalis*, 6.20):

The first men who are known are the Seres, famed for the wool of their woods, who comb off the whiteness of the leaves, sprinkled with water, whence our women have the double labour of setting up the threads and weaving them again: by such complex work, and over such a long distance is it obtained, so that a lady may expose herself in public![68]

This passage is problematic, and, in particular, the expression 'redordiendi fila rursusque texendi' has given rise to the ludicrous notion, still current even today, that 'The workers [in Greece and Rome] used some raw silk from East Asia, but they derived most of their yarn by unravelling silk fabrics from the East.'[69] This depends on an understanding of *redordior* as 'unweave'; however, the word is peculiar to Pliny, so that dictionary definitions depend on the compilers' preconceptions about this very passage, resulting in circular reasoning. However, this is not the only place where Pliny uses it: it is also found at *Historia naturalis*, 11.26:

From a larger worm which bears twin horns of a peculiar sort there develops first a cocoon, then what is called a *bombylis*, and from that a

---

[67] Theophrastus, *Historia plantarum*, 4.7.7: Ἐν Τύλῳ δὲ τῇ νήσῳ, κεῖται δ᾽ αὕτη ἐν τῷ Ἀραβίῳ κόλπῳ, τὰ μὲν πρὸς ἕω τοσοῦτο πλῆθος εἶναί φασι δένδρων ὅτ᾽ ἐκβαίνει ἡ πλημμυρὶς ὥστ᾽ ἀπηχυρῶσθαι. [...] φέρειν δὲ τὴν νῆσον καὶ τὰ δένδρα τὰ ἐριοφόρα πολλά. Ταῦτα δὲ φύλλον μὲν ἔχειν παρόμοιον τῇ ἀμπέλῳ πλὴν μικρόν, καρπὸν δὲ οὐδένα φέρειν· ἐν ᾧ δὲ τὸ ἔριον ἡλίκον μῆλον ἐαρινὸν συμμεμυκός· ὅταν δὲ ὡραῖον ᾖ ἐκπετάννυσθαι καὶ ἐξείρειν τὸ ἔριον, ἐξ οὗ τὰς σινδόνας ὑφαίνουσι, τὰς μὲν εὐτελεῖς τὰς δὲ πολυτελεστάτας. Γίνεται δὲ τοῦτο καὶ ἐν Ἰνδοῖς ὥσπερ ἐλέχθη καὶ ἐν Ἀραβίᾳ.
[68] primi sunt hominum qui noscantur Seres, lanicio silvarum nobiles, perfusam aqua depectentes frondium canitiem, unde geminus feminis nostris labos redordiendi fila rursusque texendi: tam multiplici opere, tam longinquo orbe petitur ut in publico matrona traluceat.
[69] *Encyclopædia Britannica*, online edition, s.v. *silk*, https://www.britannica.com/topic/silk (accessed 19 February 2020).

necydallus, and from that, in six months, a *bombyx*. They weave webs like spiders which serve for women's clothes and luxury, which are called *bombycina*. The first to discover how to set them up and weave them again was the woman Pamphile, daughter of Platea, in Cos, who is not to be deprived of the glory of having devised a means whereby clothing can leave women naked.[70]

This passage is manifestly derived from Aristotle, with whose terminology Pliny struggles somewhat. There can be no question here of the unravelling of an existing fabric. *Redordior* means essentially the same as *ordior*, 'set up the warp on a loom', and the prefix conveys little more than perfectivity (compare *solvo/resolvo*). As for 'weaving again', according to Pliny the worms 'weave' (*texunt*) their threads, so when they were made into cloth, they were woven again.[71]

Considering the above, it is hard to avoid the conclusion that Pliny, lacking any solid information about the Seres, simply synthesized an account from Aristotle and Virgil (note the use again of the word *depecto* — which Pliny also uses for combing out flax, *Historia naturalis*, 19.3, not a process appropriate for silk); his text links *sericum* both to the wild silk of Cos and to the cotton of Tylos, perhaps seeing a similarity between the two fabrics, so that he could have been referring to silk, or to cotton, or to both. Perhaps the most informative point in this passage is Pliny's reference to 'our women' weaving the cloth, implying that yarn was imported and woven in the Roman world. This accords with the testimony of the *Periplus Maris Erythraei*, according to which both cloth and thread were exported from India.[72]

In both passages Pliny remarks on the translucence of the fabric, and he is not the only Roman author to do so, for example Seneca, *De beneficiis* 7.9.5:

I see Seric garments, if garments they can be called, in which there is nothing to protect the body, or even modesty, wearing which a woman can hardly truthfully swear that she is not naked. These are acquired

[70] ex grandiore vermiculo gemina protendens sui generis cornua primum urica fit, dein quod vocatur bombylis, ex ea necydallus, ex hoc in sex mensibus bombyx. telas araneorum modo texunt ad vestem luxumque feminarum, quae bombycina appellatur. prima eas redordiri rursusque texere invenit in Coo mulier Pamphile, Plateae filia, non fraudanda gloria excogitatae rationis ut denudet feminas vestis.

[71] Yates, *Textrinum Antiquorum*, p. 442, comes to a similar conclusion.

[72] As noted above, from Barbarikē 'Σιρικὰ δέρματα καὶ ὀθόνιον καὶ νῆμα Σιρικόν', and from Barygaza 'ὀθόνιον παντοῖον καὶ σηρικὸν καὶ μολόχινον καὶ νῆμα', Casson, *The Periplus*, pp. 74, 80.

at vast expense from peoples unknown even to commerce, so that our ladies may show no less of themselves in public than they do to their paramours in their chambers.[73]

This may indeed suggest silk, wild or domesticated, although fine cotton fabrics are no less revealing, and the reports of travellers to India (albeit of a later period, but Indian weaving techniques remained constant over centuries) are strikingly reminiscent of these classical descriptions:

> Il se fait aussi à Séronge une sorte de toile, qui est si fine que quand elle est sur le corps on voit toute la chair comme si elle estoit à nû. [...] C'est de quoy les Sultanes & les femmes des Grands Seigneurs se font des chemises & les robes pour la chaleur, & le Roy & les Grands se plaisent à les voir au travers de ces chemises fines & à les faire danser.[74]

The only real difference is the contrast between the travellers' orientalist enjoyment and the Roman writers' note of moral outrage, directed not so much at the fabrics themselves as at their ladies' adoption of a style of dress suitable only for courtesans, to use no grosser term. (Of a woman of the latter sort Horace remarks almost approvingly 'Cois tibi paene videre est | ut nudam'.)[75] It is not safe to conclude, therefore, that at this early period the adjective *sericus* was applied to a particular material, but rather to all fabrics obtained from the Seres, whatever their composition; it was only later that it came to be used exclusively for silk.[76]

This is most likely because cotton enjoyed only a brief vogue during the Augustan age; presumably silk was preferred as a luxury material as it became more widely available, while cotton could not compete with the native linen for everyday use. It is hardly mentioned in Greek

---

[73] Video sericas vestes, si vestes vocandae sunt, in quibus nihil est, quo defendi corpus, aut denique pudor possit: quibus sumptis, mulier parum liquido nudam se non esse jurabit: haec ingenti summa ab ignotis etiam ad commercium gentibus accersuntur, ut matronae nostrae ne adulteris quidem plus sui in cubiculo, quam in publico ostendant.

[74] *Les six Voyages de Jean Baptiste Tavernier, Ecuyer Baron d'Aubonne, Qu'il a fait en Turquie, en Perse, et aux Indes [...] Seconde partie, où il est parlé des Indes, & des Isles voisines*, Paris, 1697, p. 38. For other similar accounts see Sir Edward Baines, *History of the Cotton Manufacture in Great Britain*, London, n.d. [1835], pp. 57–59.

[75] 'You can see her in her wild silks almost as if she were naked', *Satires*, 1.2.101.

[76] The point is worth stressing, though it was already made by Janvier, 'Rome et l'Orient', p. 301: 'Certes, il n'est pas question de nier que le monde romain se soit procuré de la soie blanche de Chine. Mais il n'est pas absolument certain que le mot *sericum* désigne toujours ce textile-là, surtout dans les plus anciens de nos textes.' Cf. also Yates, *Textrinum Antiquorum*, p. 180.

or Roman sources, or even in those from Egypt,[77] and the word that should properly denote it, κάρπασος/carbasus actually normally refers to flax.[78] Indeed, in the vast majority of cases *carbasus* means 'sailcloth', and in the rest, where the material can be established, it is linen. Even Yates, who takes the ancient writers to mean cotton whenever there is no evidence to the contrary, admits that, 'considering *Carbasus* as a poetical term, they often by a *catachresis* employ it where they mean to speak of linen'.[79] In fact we can exonerate the poets even of this licence: they were merely following normal usage in the Latin of their day. This evolution of meaning is understandable, considering that the mariners engaged in the Indian Ocean trade must inevitably have needed on occasion to equip their vessels in foreign ports, thus acquiring sails of *kārpāsa*, and the word, once it had entered the sailors' jargon, would easily spread to the Mediterranean, where sails were made of linen.

Thus, although in the beginning σηρικός/*sericus* simply referred to the Seres and to the goods obtained from them, it soon — probably by the end of the first century AD — came to denote a specific commodity, namely domesticated silk. Moreover, the classical writers distinguish this from wild silk,[80] already designated by Pliny as *bombycina*; so for example Ulpian: 'Vestimentorum sunt omnia lanea, lineaque, vel serica, vel bombycina, quae induendi [...] causa parata sunt'[81] — clothes are all things of wool, and linen, or silk, or wild silk, which are made in order to be worn: it is noticeable that he does not mention cotton. The more learned writers, such as St Clement of Alexandria,[82] also distinguish the Oriental silkworm, σὴρ ἰνδικός, from the βόμβυξ, the 'hairy caterpillar', δασεῖα κάμπη (which the larva of *Pachypasa otus* certainly is, but the silkworm is not), at the same time displaying their erudition by adapting Aristotle's account of its metamorphosis. St Basil does the same, this time applying it to the Oriental silkworm, the metamorphosis of which he uses as an allegory of the general resurrection.[83] This displays the combination of contemporary knowledge with classical authority

---

[77] Allan C. Johnson, Louis C. West, *Byzantine Egypt: Economic Studies*, Princeton, NJ, 1949, p. 122.

[78] See the article (by F. T. Olck) in *Paulys Realencyclopädie der classischen Altertumswissenschaft*, ed. G. Wissowa, Stuttgart, 1899, vol. 3, s.v. *carbasus*. The modern Greek word for cotton βάμβαξ or πάμβαξ, of Persian origin, may have entered the language as early as the first century BC, see B. Hemmerdinger 'De la méconnaissance de quelques étymologies grecques', *Glotta*, 48, 1970, pp. 40–66 (p.64)).

[79] Yates, *Textrinum Antiquorum*, p. 342.

[80] Ibid., pp. 189–92.

[81] Justinian, *Digesta*, 34.2.23, generally considered an accurate record of the text of Ulpian, who lived c.170–223.

[82] *Paedagogus*, 2.10.

[83] *Hexaemeron*, hom. 8.

which was to characterize scholarship from Late Antiquity through the Middle Ages and into the Renaissance. It also shows that a certain stability of usage had been attained: that silk, obtained from *Bombyx mori*, was *sericum* in Latin (as it is to this day) and σηρικόν in Greek (until the word was replaced by μέταξα in the early Byzantine period). The Seres, the suppliers (and, as generally supposed, producers) of silk, were a people dwelling in the east, but so far away that no Europeans had ever visited them in their homeland. This led to their being thought of either purely in terms of the product with which they were chiefly associated, or else in largely mythical terms as one of the peoples inhabiting the furthest reaches of the known world. Thanks, largely, to the influence of Pliny and Ptolemy, it was the 'literary' rather than the 'historical' view of the Seres that came to predominate in the early modern world, placing them in north-east Asia and, in combination with their association with silk, leading early on to an identification with the Chinese which, although occasionally contested, from Purchas's objections in 1625[84] to the devastating critique by Janvier,[85] persists to this day. It is a remarkable example of the inertia of received ideas.

---

[84] Purchas, *Hakluytus Posthumus*, vol. 1, p. 89, marginal note.
[85] Janvier, 'Rome et l'Orient', pp. 282, 289.

The Legend of the Golden Belt:
Revisiting the Sources

Sergei Bogatyrev
University College London, School of Slavonic and
East European Studies

In his seminal work on Russian magic, Will Ryan examines the cultural role of belts. In many respects, belts were as important as baptismal crosses: a belt defended its owner from evil spirits and illness; one had to remove his or her belt before performing magic or divination; removing a belt also had sexual connotations; in folk tales, negative personages often did not wear a cross or a belt.[1] In this paper I will re-examine the most famous story about a belt to be found in the East Slavic chronicles: the legend of the golden belt. The story unfolded in the context of a conflict among the descendants of Grand Prince Dmitrii Donskoi (1350–89). After the death of Dmitrii's son and successor Vasilii I in 1425, the title of grand prince went to his son Vasilii II. However, Vasilii II was challenged by his uncle and Dmitrii Donskoi's son Iurii of Galich, who claimed the title for himself. The legend tells us that Iurii's sons, Vasilii Kosoi and Dmitrii Shemiaka, attended Vasilii II's wedding on 8 February 1433. Vasilii Kosoi was wearing a golden belt which was allegedly stolen from Dmitrii Donskoi. At the banquet, Vasilii II's mother, the dowager Grand Princess Sofiia Vitovtovna, stripped Vasilii Kosoi of the belt. Furious, Vasilii Kosoi and Dmitrii Shemiaka left the wedding. According to the legend, the result of the incident was an interfamilial war.

Vasilii II was to a large extent responsible for brutalizing the war of succession. Princely conflicts had always been violent, but that one was exceptionally cruel. Vasilii II did not invent blinding as a political tool, but he was the first prince of Moscow repeatedly to use it against his opponents, including Vasilii Kosoi. Dmitrii Shemiaka retaliated by blinding Vasilii II. Despite his injury, Vasilii II defeated Shemiaka by poisoning him and secured the succession for his heir, the future Ivan III, Grand Prince of Moscow. What was the role of the golden belt legend in that war?

The first scholar to examine the legend was N. M. Karamzin. Modern scholars usually see Karamzin as a good storyteller, but he

---

[1] W. F. Ryan, *The Bathhouse at Midnight: An Historical Survey of Magic and Divination in Russia*, University Park, PA, 1999, pp. 51, 65 note 171; 222–23.

did more than this through his study of the legend. In his *Istoriia gosudarstva Rossiiskogo* (*History of the Russian State*, 1818), Karamzin established that the chronicles contain two versions of the incident. The main text of Karamzin's work follows an expanded version, which he took from the *Nikon* (*Nikonovskaia*) *Chronicle*. According to that chronicle, it was one of the banquet attendees, Petr Konstantinovich Dobrynskii who recognized the belt; then Sofiia Vitovtovna removed it from Kosoi.[2] But in his notes (*primechaniia*), Karamzin also quoted a short version from the *Arkhangel'sk Little Chronicle* (*Arkhangel'skii letopisets*), which modern scholarship sees as the second redaction of the *Ustiug* (*Ustiuzhskaia*) *Chronicle*. That variant says nothing about Sofiia or Dobrynskii but insists that the belt was identified by Zakharii Ivanovich Koshkin, who claimed that the item had been stolen from his treasury (no connection with Dmitrii Donskoi is mentioned).[3]

Karamzin was perfectly aware that the *Nikon Chronicle* is late and often unreliable. Nevertheless, he preferred its expanded variant of the golden belt episode noting the chronicle's entry about Vasilii Kosoi and Dmitrii Shemiaka robbing the treasuries of various princes on their way from Moscow. Karamzin did not, however, explain how the pillaging of treasuries in 1433 could be relevant to the theft that allegedly happened under Dmitrii Donskoi. Karamzin returned to the legend after the publication of his *History*, adding to his own copy of the edition a note about the pedigree of Vasilii II's wife, Mariia, on the basis of the *Second Sofian* (*Vtoraia Sofiiskaia*) *Chronicle*.[4]

It is surprising that later historians have not examined the relationship between the various accounts of Vasilii II's wedding. In his multivolume *Istoriia Rossii s drevneishikh vremen* (*History of Russia from the Earliest Times*), S. M. Solov'ev mentioned the two chronicle

---

[2] N. M. Karamzin, *Istoriia gosudarstva Rossiiskago*, 5th edn, St Petersburg, 1842, book 2, vol. 5, column 151; *Primechaniia k V tomu*, column 116 note 270; *Polnoe sobranie russkikh letopisei* (hereafter PSRL), vol. 12, Moscow, 2000, p. 17. In his discussion of the sources of the legend, Karamzin did not acknowledge the *Nikon Chronicle* directly, but he referred to its compiler as a Muscovite chronicler. The part of Karamzin's work which contains the golden belt legend is generally based on two Muscovite chronicles, the *Nikon* and *Resurrection* (*Voskresenskaia*) ones. A textual analysis shows that Karamzin followed the former in his treatment of the legend. On Karamzin's use of chronicles, see L. L. Murav'eva, 'Letopisnye istochniki *Istorii gosudarstva Rossiiskogo* N. M. Karamzina (t. IV–V), [chast' 1]', in *Issledovaniia po istochnikovedeniiu istorii SSSR dooktiabr'skogo perioda: Sbornik statei*, ed. V. I. Buganov, Moscow, 1982, pp. 4–36; Murav'eva, 'Letopisnye istochniki [...], [chast' 2]', in *Issledovaniia po istochnikovedeniiu [...]*, Moscow, 1983, pp. 4–34.

[3] PSRL, vol. 37, Leningrad, 1982, pp. 4–6 (introduction), 85 (text).

[4] Karamzin, *Istoriia*, book 2, vol. 5, *Primechaniia k V tomu*, column 116 note (*); PSRL, vol. 6, 2, Moscow, 2001, column 64.

versions, but accepted the expanded variant, as is apparent from his conclusion that the incident served as a pretext for war among the princes.[5] In the 1930s, S. B. Veselovskii boldly and carelessly combined the two chronicle versions, assuming that Petr Dobrynskii recognized the belt and Zakharii Koshkin seized it. Veselovskii called the story about the origin of the belt a fable, but did not question the chronicle account of the incident at the wedding, drawing on Karamzin's reading of it.[6] Subsequent studies heavily relied on the analyses of Karamzin, Solov'ev and Veselovskii, using the legend of the golden belt for various explanations of the war of succession, the centralization of the Russian state, the history of royal regalia, marriage politics and the role of women in the Muscovite political system. Without a source analysis, all these interpretations remain entirely speculative.[7]

A textual study of fifteenth-century chronicles inevitably involves hypothetical reconstructed texts known as compilations (*svody*). While such compilations help us contextualize the legend of the golden belt, the main conclusions of this paper are based on existing chronicles and documents. The earliest account of Vasilii II's wedding appears in the *Younger Redaction of the First Sofian Chronicle* (*Mladshaia redaktsiia Sofiiskoi Pervoi letopisi*, hereafter *SofiY*, see Table 1, section 1 and Appendix). Ia. S. Lur'e believed that *SofiY* was based on the hypothetical *Compilation of 1448*, more precisely, its later version extended through 1476 (6964). However, modern studies date that *Compilation* to 1418, not to 1448. Still, Lur'e was correct that *SofiY* was compiled during the dramatic and dynamic period of the inter-princely war; as a result, its content became rapidly outdated and required reworking depending on

---

[5] S. M. Solov'ev, *Istoriia Rossii s drevneishikh vremen*, 2nd edn, St Petersburg, [1895], book 1, vol. 4, columns 1055–56 (orig. 1851).

[6] S. B. Veselovskii, *Issledovaniia po istorii klassa sluzhilykh zemlevladel'tsev*, Moscow, 1969, pp. 251, 308, 342–46, 511–12, 525–26.

[7] Gustave Alef, 'A History of the Muscovite Civil War: The Reign of Vasili II, 1425–62', unpublished PhD dissertation, Princeton University, 1956, pp. 125–26; L. V. Cherepnin, *Obrazovanie Russkogo tsentralizovannogo gosudarstva v XIV–XV vekakh*, Moscow, 1960, pp. 756–57; Nancy Shields Kollmann, *Kinship and Politics: The Making of the Muscovite Political System, 1345–1547*, Stanford, CA, 1987, pp. 134–35; A. A. Zimin, *Vitiaz' na rasput'e. Feodal'naia voina v Rossii XV v.*, Moscow, 1991, pp. 52–54; Isolde Thyrêt, 'The Cultural Politics of the Grand Princesses of Moscow and the Emergence of the Muscovite Dynasty', *Russian History*, 33, 2006, 2–4, pp. 333–52 (pp. 339–40); A. B. Mazurov, A. Iu. Nikandrov, *Russkii udel epokhi sozdaniia eginogo gosudarstva: Serpukhovskoe kniazhenie v seredine XIV–pervoi polovine XV vv.*, Moscow, 2008, p. 154; C. K. Woodworth, 'Sophia and the Golden Belt: What Caused Moscow's Civil Wars of 1425–50', *Russian Review*, 68, 2009, 2, pp. 187–98; V. A. Kuchkin, 'Moskovskie Riurikovichi: Genealogiia i demografiia', *Istoricheskii vestnik*, 4 (151), 2013, pp. 6–73 (p. 35); Nikolai Borisov, *Vasilii Temnyi*, Moscow, 2020, pp. 167–68.

the changing political situation.[8] *Sofiỹ*'s short and factual account of Vasilii II's wedding gives us the name and pedigree of the bride, Mariia, daughter of Prince Iaroslav Vladimirovich of Iaroslavets (later known as Maloiaroslavets). The chronicle calls him 'Lithuanian' because his mother was Elena, daughter of Algirdas (Ol'gerd) of Lithuania and first cousin once removed of Vasilii II's mother Sofiia Vitovtovna.[9]

Table 1. *Chronicle Accounts of Vasilii II's Wedding*

> **1. Original Account**
> ***Sofian 1st Chronicle, Younger Redaction* (*PSRL*, 5, St Petersburg, 1851, pp. 264–65, left column)**
> Въ лѣто 6941 [...]. Тое же зимы женися князь великій Василей Васильевичь, и поя дщерь княжю Ярославлю Володимеровича Литовьского княжну именемъ Марью. Тое же весны князь Юрьи Дмитреевичь възлютився за то, что ему не далъ царь княженія великаго, поиде ратью къ Москвѣ на великого князя Василья Васильевича; то же слышавъ князь великій Василей Васильевичь, поиде противу его ратію, и срѣтошася на рѣцѣ на Клязмѣ и бысть имъ бой [...].

> **2. Expanded Account**
> ***Vologda-Perm' Chronicle* (*PSRL*, 26, Moscow, 2006, pp. 188–89)**
> В лѣто 6941. Побежал от великого князя боярин его Иван Дмитреевич ко князю Костянтину на Углечь, а оттоле во Тферь. Тое же зимы женился князь великии Василеи Васильевич на Москвѣ, февраля в 8, понял княжну Марью, Ярославлю дщерь Володимеровича. Тое же зимы Иван Дмитреевич отъѣхал изо Тфери в Галич ко князю Юрью Дмитреевичю и начатъ подговаривати его на великое княжение. И князь Юрьи, по его думе, посла по дѣти свои, по князя Василья и по князя Дмитрея Шемяку, на Москву. А они тогды были на свадьбе великого князя, и тогда познал Петръ Костянтинович на князе на Василье *поясъ золотъ на чепех с камениемъ, что был приданои князя великого Дмитрея Ивановича от князя Дмитрея Костянтиновича Суздальского. Се же пишем того ради, поне же много зла от того сотворися. Тот бо поясъ о свадьбе великого князя Дмитрея Ивановича подменил Василеи тысяцкои, князю великому дал меншии, а тот дал сыну своему*

---

[8] Ia. S. Lur'e, *Obshcherusskie letopisi XIV–XV vv.*, Leningrad, 1976, pp. 116–21; Ia. S. Lur'e, *Dve istorii Rusi XV veka: Rannie i pozdnie, nezavisimye i ofitsial'nye letopisi ob obrazovanii Moskovskogo gosudarstva*, St Petersburg, 1994, pp. 71–72; A. G. Bobrov, *Novgorodskie letopisi XV veka*, St Petersburg, 2001, pp. 130–60.

[9] Mazurov, Nikandrov, *Russkii udel*, pp. 78, 149–50; Kuchkin, 'Moskovskie Riurikovichi', pp. 20–21.

Микуле. А за Микулою была того же князя Дмитрея Суздальского дочи Мария большая, и Микула тот поясъ дал в приданые же Ивану Дмитреевичю, а Иван дал его за своею дочерью князю Ондрью Володимеровичю. Потом же по смерти княж Ондрьеве и по Ордынскомъ приходе Иван Дмитреевич княж Ондрьеву дочерь, а свою внуку обручал за князя Василья Юрьевича и тот поясъ дал ему, и на свадбе великого князя был на нем, княгини же великая Софиа снят с него тогды. И с того князь Василеи и князь Дмитреи роззлобившися, побегоша с Москвы ко отцю в Галич и пограбиша Ярославль, и казны всѣх князеи розграбиша. Пришедшим же им ко отцу в Галич, а онъ уже собрася со всѣми людьми своими, хотя итти на великого князя. Сим же к ним пришедшим, и поиде с ними со многою силою на великого князя, **а Иван Дмитреевич с ним же**, а великому князю не ведущу того. Прибеже же тогда из Ростова к великому князю намѣстник его Петръ Костянтинович, поведая ему, что идеть на него дядя его князь Юрьи и з дѣтми и со многою силою, а уже тогда бяху в Переславле.

[Details of Vasilii II's attempts to make peace with Iurii and **Ivan Dmitrievich's opposition to it**]

Князь же велиеии, что было тогда около его людеи, собра тѣх да и Москвич, гостеи и прочих поим с собою, поиде противу и стрѣтился со князем съ Юрьем на Клязьмѣ за 20 верстъ от Москвы […]. Бои же сеи бысть в суботу, канун мироносицъ, апрѣля 25.

3. **Short Account**
Abridged Compilation (Letopisi i khroniki, Novye issledovaniia, 2013–2014, Moscow and St Petersburg, 2015, p. 224)

В лѣто 6940 […]. Того же лѣта во осенинѣ князь велики обручал за себѣ княжну Марью дщерь Ярославлю, а вънуку Марьи Голтяевы […].

В лѣто 941 князь Василеи Васильевич женился на Москвѣ по Крещении з мясоѣдъ великои. И на тои свадбѣ Захариа Иванович Кошкин имался за поясъ у князя у Василья Юрьевича у Косово, и с тое свадьбы князи и бояре разъѣхашася восвояси. И совокупися князь Василеи да князь Димитреи Шемяка и поидоша ко отцу своему в Галич. Тое же весны князь Юрии Дмитреевич съ своими дѣтми да **Иван Дмитреевич с ними же** и съ своими дѣтми и совокупиша силы много, и поидоша к Москве на великого князя, и приидоша на рѣку на Клязму без вести за 20 поприщ от Москвы в субботу, канун Мироносицам, апрѣля 5.

SofıY also gives us the main reason for the outbreak of violence in 1433. Contrary to Solov'ev and many modern scholars, the war started not because of the golden belt incident, which is not even mentioned in *SofıY*, but because Iurii of Galich failed to secure support for his claim on the title of grand prince at the court of the Mongol khan. Indeed, tension between Vasilii II and Iurii had been building up since the death of Vasilii II's father, Vasilii I, in 1425. The period between 1425 and 1433 saw repeated demonstrations of military force and short-lived agreements between Vasilii II and Iurii. The deaths of major political actors, Vasilii II's maternal grandfather Vytautas (Vitovt) of Lithuania (1430) and Metropolitan Fotii (1431) paved the way for the intensification of the conflict. In 1432 Vasilii II used force to expel Iurii from Dmitrov. After the breakdown of his negotiations with the khan, Iurii mobilized his troops. He was already marching with his army towards Moscow when, according to later chronicles, the belt incident happened.[10]

The history of Vasilii II's wedding is radically expanded in the *Vologda-Perm' Chronicle* (*Vologodsko-Permskaia letopis'*, hereafter *Vol-Perm*), including its early variant which can be found in the *Museum Little Chronicle* (*Muzeinyi letopisets*, hereafter *Mus*, see Appendix).[11] Both *Mus* and *Vol-Perm* contain identical accounts of the royal wedding (Table 1, section 2). This dramatized variant has contaminated many later chronicles, including the *Nikon Chronicle*, which has informed, via Karamzin's work, all modern interpretations of the incident. Lur'e has tentatively suggested that *Mus* derives from the hypothetical *Compilation of 1453* (*Svod 1453 g.*). As for *Vol-Perm*, he thought that it stemmed from another hypothetical compilation of the early 1470s. However, B. M. Kloss has recently rejected this assertion and argued that *Vol-Perm* originates from the hypothetical *Compilation of 1477* (*Svod 1477 g.*).[12] The following analysis confirms Lur'e's suggestion about the *Compilation of 1453* and Kloss's opinion of the *Compilation of 1477*.

---

[10] Veselovskii, *Issledovaniia*, p. 510; Gustave Alef, 'The Battle of Suzdal' in 1445. An Episode in the Muscovite War of Succession', in Alef, *Rulers and Nobles in Fifteenth-Century Muscovy*, London, 1983, article II, pp. 11–20 (p. 18); Zimin, *Vitiaz'*, pp. 34–48; V. D. Nazarov, 'Dinasticheskaia voina moskovskikh Riurikovichei. Preliudiia 1432 g.', in *Kompleksnyi podkhod v izuchenii Drevnei Rusi*, ed. E. L. Koniavskaia, Moscow, 2019, pp. 139–40.

[11] *PSRL*, vol. 26, Moscow, 2006, pp. 188–89; I. M. Kudriavtsev, 'Sbornik poslednei chetverti XV–nachala XVI v. iz Muzeinogo sobraniia', *Zapiski Otdela rukopisei Gosudarstvennoi biblioteki im. V. I. Lenina*, 25, Moscow, 1962, pp. 220–88 (p. 230), http://drevlit.ru/docs/russia/XV/1400-1420/Kratk_letop/pred1.php (accessed 11 July 2020).

[12] Lur'e, *Obshcherusskie letopisi*, pp. 131, 144, 145–47; Lur'e, *Dve istorii*, p. 16; B. M. Kloss, 'Predislovie k izdaniiu 2006 g.' in *PSRL*, vol. 26, pp. v–xv (pp. vi–ix).

The expanded account of Vasilii II's wedding draws on the original account of *SofiY*, as is apparent from their common details (Table 1, sections 1 and 2, single underline). New added facts include the exact date of the wedding and that of a battle between Vasilii II and Iurii on the river Kliaz'ma as well as the distance from the place of the battle to Moscow (Table 1, section 2, dashed underline). Most importantly, the expanded version reports that at the wedding Vasilii Kosoi was challenged by Petr Konstantinovich (Dobrynskii). What is interesting is that he appears in the expanded account twice (Table 1, section 2, squiggly underline). First, he recognized the belt worn by Kosoi at the banquet in Moscow. But then, according to the chronicle, he came to Moscow from Rostov to inform Vasilii II about the advancement of Iurii of Galich and his sons, who joined their father after the incident at the royal wedding.

The logistics of Petr Dobrynskii's movements remains suspiciously murky because the chronicle suggests that he appeared in Moscow twice within a short period. Furthermore, the chronicler correctly introduces Petr Dobrynskii as the vicegerent of Rostov at the second mentioning, but not in the preceding account of Vasilii II's wedding, where Petr Dobrynskii allegedly played such an important part. To explain all these oddities, we should remember that the chronicle is a compilation of various bits of text produced at different times. Clearly, the second entry about Petr Dobrynskii coming to Moscow from Rostov and alerting the Grand Prince is original. Apparently, Petr Dobrynskii did travel to Moscow to inform Vasilii II. The creator of the golden belt legend used this episode to construct the literary image of Petr Dobrynskii as a loyal informant of the Grand Prince at his wedding.

The image of Petr Dobrynskii in the expanded account serves the purpose of exposing the treason of boiar Ivan Dmitrievich Vsevolozhskii, who provoked Iurii of Galich to challenge Vasilii II. The theme of Ivan Vsevolozhskii's betrayal dominates the entire yearly entry for 1433 (6941) (Table 1, section 2, bold). The literary story of Ivan Vsevolozhskii's intrigues is intertwined with the most famous part of the expanded account, a legend about the provenance of Vasilii Kosoi's belt which was removed by Sofiia Vitovtovna at the wedding (Table 1, section 2, italics). Made of gold and decorated with chains and precious stones, the belt was a dowry for the wedding of Dmitrii Donskoi in 1366, but it was stolen from Dmitrii. Subsequent owners also used the item as a dowry which, through Ivan Vsevolozhskii's machinations, ended up in Kosoi's possession. The invented 'biography' of the item is introduced with a note about the golden belt episode causing much evil (Table 1, section 2, bold italics). This commentary has no historical significance whatsoever because even the expanded account itself admits that Iurii, urged on by Ivan Vsevolozhskii, had already called his sons back from Moscow before the incident.

Other parts of the story about the belt are also fabricated. In particular, the legend insists that Mikula, son of the Muscovite thousandman (*tysiatskii*) Vasilii Vel'iaminov, gave the item to Ivan Vsevolozhskii as a dowry. However, Mikula was killed, without issue, in 1380 when Ivan Vsevolozhskii was hardly over ten years old.[13] But, like any sophisticated lie, the legend of the golden belt contains an element of truth. Golden belts indeed served as dowries.[14] What historians have overlooked is that the legend has many parallels with documents from the Grand Prince's chancery. Kosoi did have a golden belt with chains and stones (*poias zolot s kamen'em, na chepekh, bez remeni*). However, contrary to the legend, he received it not as a dowry from Ivan Vsevolozhskii but as an inheritance from his father Iurii of Galich. Kosoi's belt is mentioned in Iurii's will, which V. D. Nazarov dates to the first half of July 1433. Furthermore, Iurii's will also indicates that Kosoi's brother Dmitrii Shemiaka inherited from Iurii a belt that had originally belonged to Dmitrii Donskoi (that belt is also registered in one of Donskoi's wills).[15] During his lifetime, Kosoi was also implicated in stealing a dowry. Again, such accusations were levelled not by Sofiia Vitovtovna or a boiar, as the legend would have us believe, but by his own brother Dmitrii Shemiaka, who was married to Sofiia, daughter of Dmitrii Vasil'evich Zaozerskii. In his agreement with Vasilii II from 13 June 1436, Shemiaka demanded restitution of his dowry seized by Kosoi should Vasilii II come into possession of that dowry.[16] Shemiaka addressed his request to Vasilii II because the Grand Prince had kept Kosoi in custody after blinding him on 21 May 1436.

During his conflict with the princes of Galich, Vasilii II released documents from his chancery to loyal bookmen. In particular, on 29 December 1447, the synod of the Russian Church issued a letter to Shemiaka, quoting his agreement with Vasilii II and encouraging

---

[13] Zimin, *Vitiaz'*, p. 52; *Redkie istochniki po istorii Rossii*, 2, Moscow, 1977, p. 65.

[14] L. V. Cherepnin (ed.), *Dukhovnye i dogovornye gramoty velikikh i udel'nykh kniazei XIV–XVI vv.* (hereafter *DDG*), Moscow, Leningrad, 1950, p. 16.

[15] *DDG*, p. 75, cf. p. 36; Nazarov, 'Dinasticheskaia voina,' p. 139. M. M. Rudkovskaia lists belts from the princely wills with no attempt at analysis in her 'Dragotsennye poiasa v sisteme regalii kniazheskoi vlasti v srednevekovoi Rusi', *Vestnik RGGU*, 4 (84), 2012, pp. 11–19.

[16] *DDG*, pp. 91, 94, 96, 99; Zimin, *Vitiaz'*, p. 74; Kuchkin, 'Moskovskie Riurikovichi', pp. 36, 37; V. D. Nazarov, 'O vkliuchenii Iaroslavskogo kniazheniia v sostav Rossiiskogo Gosudarstva', in *Rus', Rossiia: Srednevekov'e i Novoe vremia*, 4, Moscow, 2015, pp. 51–80 (p. 60).

Shemiaka to observe that agreement and surrender to Vasilii II.[17] Among these trusted literati was the creator of the golden belt legend. He borrowed from the above-mentioned documents the fact that Iurii of Galich's sons possessed a belt that belonged to their grandfather Dmitrii Donskoi. Verbatim description of Kosoi's belt and the theme of Kosoi stealing a dowry also came from the chancery documents. The latest of these documents, the 13 June 1436 agreement, which mentions the plundering of Shemiaka's dowry by Kosoi, defines the *terminus post quem* of the expanded account, which contains the legend of the golden belt.

To determine the *terminus ante quem* of the legend, we should return to the prominent part of Petr Dobrynskii in it. His relations with Vasilii II changed dramatically in early February 1446, when Shemiaka seized Moscow while Vasilii II was on pilgrimage at the St Sergius-Trinity monastery. On behalf of Shemiaka, one of Petr Dobrynskii's numerous brothers, Nikita Konstantinovich Dobrynskii, arrested Vasilii II and escorted him to Moscow, where Vasilii II was blinded. After the mutilation of Vasilii II, the two Dobrynskii brothers moved to the court of Shemiaka's ally Ivan Andreevich of Mozhaisk. Disability did not prevent Vasilii II from reclaiming Moscow and counter-attacking first Dmitrii Shemiaka and then, in 1454, Ivan Andreevich. Threatened by Vasilii II, Ivan Andreevich and Nikita Dobrynskii escaped to Lithuania, while Petr Dobrynskii made a donation to the metropolitan see, apparently, in anticipation of punishment from Vasilii II.[18] The legend of the golden belt obviously appeared prior to Petr Dobrynskii's break with Vasilii II in early February 1446, something which narrows down the dating of the legend to the period from the second half of 1436 to early 1446. This period brings us back to Lur'e assertion that *Mus*, which includes the expanded account with the legend, stems from the *Compilation of 1453*. The expanded account made its way to the *Compilation of 1453* which transmitted it directly to *Mus* and, via the *Compilation of 1477*, to other chronicles, including *Vol-Perm* and the *Nikon Chronicle* (see Appendix).[19]

In his struggle with Shemiaka, Vasilii II combined military pressure with what we would now call a memory war. The legend of the golden

[17] *Russkii feodal'nyi arkhiv XIV–pervoi treti XVI veka*, [issue 1], Moscow, 1986, pp. 107, 111.

[18] Veselovskii, *Issledovaniia*, pp. 310–13; Zimin, *Vitiaz'*, pp. 110, 161–62; I. G. Ponomareva, 'Okruzhenie moskovskogo velikogo kniazia Vasiliia II v nachale ego pravleniia', *Drevniaia Rus', Voprosy medievistiki*, 1 (75), 2019, pp. 100–04 (pp. 101–02).

[19] For the expanded account of Vasilii II's wedding in the *Compilation of 1477*, see *PSRL*, vol. 28, Moscow, Leningrad, 1963, pp. 265–66.

belt implicated Shemiaka indirectly by questioning the provenance of movables inherited by the princes of Galich from Dmitrii Donskoi (Shemiaka, we recall, owned Donskoi's golden belt). The compiler of the legend avoided a direct attack on Shemiaka as he still possessed considerable military power. Vasilii II preferred to make a deal with Shemiaka, as evidenced by the above-mentioned synod letter from 1447. Rather, the legend harrased the vulnerable blinded Kosoi, who remained in custody until his death in 1447/48.

Sofiia Vitovtovna's gesture as recounted in the legend of the golden belt is particularly dramatic in the context of Ryan's observations about the cultural connotation of removing a belt. By pulling out the golden belt Sofiia not only exposed Kosoi as possessor of a stolen item but also deprived him of the symbolical protection provided by his belt. The legend presents the whole episode as a conflict of two familial memories: in her capacity as the dowager Grand Princess, Sofiia restored the broken memory of the Muscovite ruling family and exposed the (allegedly) false claims of the Galich princely family to the inheritance of Dmitrii Donskoi, despite the fact that he was a common ancestor of both families.

The expanded account of the 1433 wedding also legitimizes Vasilii II's demands for restitution. The war of succession was accompanied by plundering princely treasuries. Inter-princely agreements reveal that the princes of Galich pillaged the treasuries of Vasilii II and his mother Sofiia Vitovtovna on several occasions.[20] The scene with Sofiia removing the belt is a literary device which reinforced Vasilii II's attempts to reclaim his family's property stolen not during the reign of Dmitrii Donskoi, but during the war with the princes of Galich.

We can now turn to the short account of Vasilii II's wedding which, as was mentioned above, connects the belt incident with Zakharii Koshkin. The earliest existing version of that short account can be found in the *Abridged Compilation* (*Sokrashchennyi svod*, hereafter *AbrC*), especially its early variant in the Solovki (Solovetskii) copy, whose antigraph dates to the second half of the 1470s–early 1480s (Table 1, section 3).[21] A similar short account appears in the *Ermolin* (*Ermolinskaia*) *Chronicle* (hereafter *Erm*, antigraph after autumn 1480, the extant manuscript from the late 1480s–early 1490s). *AbrC* and *Erm* originate from a common source, the hypothetical *Compilation of 1472* (hereafter *Com1472*, the year in the title refers to the latest

---

[20] *DDG*, pp. 77, 79, 80, 88, 91, 93–94, 96, 99, 102, 104, 109, 111, 141.
[21] O. L. Novikova, '"Sokrashchennyi svod" v 70–90-kh gg. XV veka i ego Solovetskii vid', in *Letopisi i khroniki: Novye issledovaniia, 2013-2014*, Moscow, St Petersburg, 2015, pp. 162–234 (p. 183).

entry in the compilation). According to Kloss, *Com1472* was prepared in 1473. A study of the relationship among *Com1472*, *AbrC*, and *Erm* is complicated by the fact that the compilers of *AbrC* and *Erm* often altered the text of *Com1472* in their respective chronicles. Fortunately, the common source of *AbrC* and *Erm* has also contaminated (via intermediate compilations) two later chronicles, the *L'vov* (*L'vovskaia*, *Lv*) and above-mentioned *Second Sofian* (*Sof2*) chronicles.[22] When *AbrC* and *Erm* offer alternative readings, those that are supported by *Lv* and *Sof2* should be attributed to *Com1472*.

The short account of Vasilii II's wedding also made its way to the *Ustiug Chronicle* (hereafter *Ust*), which, as we remember, was used by Karamzin (see Appendix). Unlike *AbrC* and *Erm*, *Ust* attributes to Zakharii Koshkin a statement about the belt being stolen from his treasury (Table 2, italics). There is no reason to assume that *Ust* utilizes some unknown sources on Koshkin because generally *Ust* derives from *AbrC*. Rather, *Ust* has been probably affected here by the golden belt legend with its central theme of theft. Koshkin's direct speech is a late fictional addition typical of *Ust*.[23]

Table 2. *Short Account of Vasilii II's Wedding in Various Chronicles*

Abridged Compilation, (*Letopisi i khroniki, Novye issledovaniia*, 2013–2014, p. 224)	Ermolin chronicle, (*PSRL*, 23, p. 147)	Ustiug chronicle, (*PSRL*, 37, p. 41)
Захариа Иванович Кошкин имался за поясъ у князя у Василья Юрьевича у Косово, и с тое свадьбы князи и бояре разъѣхашася восвояси.	Захарья Ивановичь Кошкынъ имался за поясъ у князя Василья у Юрьевича у Косого, и князи и бояре разъѣхашася по домомъ,	Захарья Иванович Кошкин имался за пояс у князя Василья Юрьевича у Косово, *а сказал: «Тогда у меня пояс пропал из моеи казны, коли казну мою крали».*

[22] Lur'e, *Dve istorii*, p. 85. Lur'e believed that *AbrC* and *Erm* were based on a compilation prepared at the Kirillo-Belozerskii monastery, but modern studies reject this conjecture. *AbrC*: Novikova, 'Sokrashchennyi svod', p. 190. *Erm*: B. M. Kloss, 'Predislovie k izdaniiu 2004 g.', in *PSRL*, vol. 23, Moscow, 2004, pp. iv–vi; O. L. Novikova, 'Ob antigrafe Ermolinskoi letopisi i ee redaktore', *Vestnik 'Al'ians-Arkheo'*, 30, Moscow, St Petersburg, 2019, pp. 3–34 (pp. 8, 30). On *Com1472*, see B. M. Kloss, 'K kharakteristike Svoda 1472 goda', in *Letopisi i khroniki: Novye issledovaniia, 2017–2018*, Moscow, St Petersburg, 2019, pp. 59–64.

[23] Novikova, 'Sokrashchennyi svod', p. 179; Lur'e, *Dve istorii*, pp. 44, 82, 206.

In his study of alternative chronicle narratives, Lur'e has noted that the short description of Vasilii II's wedding draws on the expanded account. However, he did not include the golden belt episode in his reconstruction of historical facts, leaving open the question about the reliability of various accounts of the golden belt incident.[24] Kloss has detected a number of features of *Com1472* which are essential for our understanding of the short account. The compiler of *Com1472* has a keen interest in the activities of various boiars, especially their military exploits and failures.[25] Indeed, *Com1472* gives unique personal characteristics to various boiars. In particular, speaking of Fedor Konstantinovich Dobrynskii and Prince Fedor Davydovich Pestryi Paletskii, *Com1472* proclaims 'honour to these military commanders during their lifetime and eternal memory after their death'.[26]

The chronicler's attention to boiars helps us understand his approach to the history of Vasilii II's wedding. The compiler of *Com1472* focuses on the role of individual boiars in the key events of 1433, the royal wedding and the battle on the Kliaz'ma. *Com1472* has apparently borrowed some details of these events from the expanded account, like their dates (some of them are garbled in the existing copies of the short account), the distance from the river Kliaz'ma to Moscow (Table 1, section 3, dashed underline), and the name of Ivan Dmitrievich Vsevolozhskii participating in Iurii of Galich's campaign against Moscow (Table 1, section 3, bold). At the same time, *Com1472* has resolutely dropped the fanciful parts of the expanded account of Vasilii's wedding: the falsified 'biography' of the golden belt, Sofiia Vitovtovna's intervention and the claim that the golden belt episode caused a war.

Lur'e was thus correct in assuming that the short account derives from the expanded version, but there are important factual differences between these two accounts. According to the short variant, the incident was caused not by Petr Dobrynskii, but Zakharii Koshkin. Contrary to the expanded account's claim that Sofiia Vitovtona stripped (*sniat*) Vasilii Kosoi of his golden belt, *Com1472* insists that Koshkin just grabbed (*imalsia za*) it. Why does the compiler of *Com1472* leave out the name of Petr Dobrynskii? There is no need to assume animosity against the Dobrynskii clan behind this editing. We have seen that *Com1472* praises Fedor Konstantinovich Dobrynskii who was one of Petr Dobrynskii's brothers.

---

[24] Lur'e, *Dve istorii*, pp. 79, 81.
[25] Kloss, 'K kharakteristike', pp. 62–63.
[26] Novikova, 'Sokrashchennyi svod', p. 223; *PSRL*, vol. 20, 1, St Petersburg, 1910, p. 233; *PSRL*, vol. 6, 2, column 53.

Rather, *Com1472* has substituted Petr Dobrynskii with Zakharii Koshkin for two reasons. First, the chronicler has a natural interest in a good drunken brawl, especially when it involves high-profile courtiers. For example, the chronicler spares no effort to describe a fight with participation of the prominent Muscovite commander F. V. Basenok. He accompanied Vasilii II during his visit to Novgorod in 1460. After drinking with the local major, Basenok was on his way to the royal residence in Novgorod when he was attacked by mobsters, who killed his servant. The result was a commotion which Novgorodians misinterpreted as a Muscovite military assault. It is typical that other chronicles seek to reinterpret this episode as the Novgorodians' intention to kill the Grand Prince and his children. A. A. Zimin has correctly dismissed these politicized accusations as a fantasy.[27] Similarly, in contrast to the partisan expanded account of Vasilii II's wedding, *Com1472* provides a factual no-nonsense report about the incident of Kosoi's belt as it happened, including Koshkin's stunt. The chronicle has not included Petr Dobrynskii's name because his role in the incident is a literary invention, as apparent from the textual analysis provided above.

There is another and more important reason to trust the account of Vasilii II's wedding in *Com1472*. The patron of that chronicle knew what happened at the banquet better than anybody else. Kloss has persuasively argued that *Com1472* was produced under the patronage of Mariia Iaroslavna during her stay as the dowager Grand Princess in Rostov.[28] *Com1472* reveals a special interest in Mariia, who was of course the bride at the 1433 wedding. In addition to the account of the wedding, *Com1472* provides a unique entry about Mariia, including Vasilii II's engagement with her and the name of her maternal grandmother Mariia Goltiaeva, who was married to Fedor Goltiai Koshkin (Table 1, section 3, double underline). Mariia was thus the daughter of Zakharii Koshkin's female cousin.[29] The iconic image of Sofiia Vitovtovna pulling out the golden belt has completely overshadowed Mariia Iaroslavna's contribution to the success of her troublesome husband Vasilii II. Born probably in late 1420 or early 1421, Mariia was still a teenager at the time of her marriage to Vasilii II. However, in her capacity as the bride, she obviously performed a more important ceremonial role than Sofiia

---

[27] *PSRL*, vol. 23, p. 156; cf. *PSRL*, vol. 20, 1, p. 264; *PSRL*, vol. 6, 2, column 131; Zimin, *Vitiaz'*, pp. 181, 182.

[28] Kloss, 'K kharakteristike', pp. 63, 64.

[29] Novikova, 'Sokrashchennyi svod', p. 224; *PSRL*, vol. 20, 1, p. 238; *PSRL*, 6, 2, columns 64–65. On Mariia Iaroslavna's maternal ancestors, see Zimin, *Vitiaz'*, p. 53; Kuchkin, 'Moskovskie Riurikovichi', p. 28.

at the wedding. Mariia's father Iaroslav Vladimirovich died in 1426, apparently, leaving her a significant dowry. Mariia's later transactions with immovable and movable property indicate that she was a woman of considerable means, undoubtedly a factor in choosing her as the bride for Vasilii II. Other reasons for Vasilii II marrying Mariia included securing the loyalty of her brother Vasilii Iaroslavich of Serpukhov, who was to become an important political actor, as well as strengthening Vasilii II's connections with the Koshkins and also with Lithuania (see above about Mariia's genealogy).

During the war of succession, Mariia accompanied Vasilii II in refuge and exile. She bore Vasilii II nine or ten children, including the would-be heir Ivan III. She was pregnant at the time of the traumatic blinding of her husband in 1446. Once the exiled Vasilii II was ready to reclaim the Muscovite throne, Mariia went to Moscow prior to her husband to ensure the loyalty of the citizens and prepare for his return. When Vasilii became ill in 1462, Mariia resisted his attempts at self-treatment. Nevertheless, Vasilii insisted with a stubbornness which, according to the chronicle, eventually caused his death. In her capacity as the dowager Grand Princess, Mariia was instrumental in securing the succession from Vasilii II to his son Ivan III. She mediated between Ivan III and his brothers, facilitated dynastic marriages in the family, sat on a war council and participated in court and Church ceremonies.[30] Mariia sponsored projects commemorating members of the ruling family, including the renovation of the Cathedral of the Ascension convent in the Kremlin, which became a mausoleum for royal women. She became a nun at the convent in 1478 and was buried there after her death in 1485.[31] Mariia is also credited for shaping the posthumous memory of her husband. The *Compilation of 1479* reports a miracle associated with the birth of Vasilii II. The chronicler received information about that miracle from a secretary and a seal keeper who, in their turn, heard it from Mariia. The textual history of this entry is

---

[30] On Mariia Iaroslavna, see Mazurov, Nikandrov, *Russkii udel*, pp. 149–50; Kuchkin, 'Moskovskie Riurikovichi', pp. 28, 34–35; Nazarov, 'O vkliuchenii', pp. 66–67; S. N. Bogatyrev, 'Kovsh tsaritsy Marii, zheny Ivana Groznogo: Proiskhozhdenie i funktsii kovshei v kniazheskikh sokrovishchnitsakh XIV–XVI vekov', *Istorik i istochnik: Sbornik statei k iubileiu Sergeia Nikolaevicha Kistereva*, St Petersburg, 2018, pp. 199–218 (pp. 202–203); Borisov, *Vasilii*, pp. 167, 170, 231, 257, 302. J. L. I. Fennell, *Ivan the Great of Moscow*, London, New York, 1961, index; E. V. Pchelov, *Riurikovichi: Istoriia dinastii*, Moscow, 2003, pp. 396–97; D. V. Donskoi, *Riurikovichi: Istoricheskii slovar'*, Moscow, 2008, pp. 446–49.

[31] Thyrêt, 'Cultural Politics', pp. 342, 347; *PSRL*, vol. 23, pp. 178, 185, 193.

unclear.[32] But, whatever its origin, the entry appeared during Mariia's lifetime, corroborating her role as keeper of the memory of Vasilii II.

Kloss's assertion about the involvement of Mariia's Rostov court in the preparation of *Com1472* is highly plausible in light of her role in transmitting family memory and her long-term affiliation with Rostov. Vasilii II and Mariia cultivated connections with Rostov, which was then still an independent principality, from 1439, when the Grand Prince moved there after the devastation of Moscow by the Tatars. Rostov became the place of refuge for Mariia and Sofiia Vitovtovna after the Tatars captured Vasilii in 1445. After his blinding, Vasilii spent the Easter of 1448 in Rostov. In 1458, Mariia successfully interceded for Archbishop Feodosii of Rostov to Metropolitan Iona, receiving in return for her mediation one of Feodosii's hamlets, a striking example of Mariia's close ties with the Rostov clergy and also of her business aptitude. In his will, Vasilii granted Mariia control over Rostov. She relocated there in 1472, possibly for safety's sake to escape an invasion of Khan Ahmed of the Great Horde. Mariia bequeathed her possessions in Rostov to her son Ivan III.[33]

Mariia's patronage was a strong stimulus for setting the record straight about the role of her relative Zakharii Koshkin at her wedding in *Com1472*. That chronicle also reveals a very specific attitude to the memory of Dmitrii Shemiaka, openly stating that he was poisoned in Novgorod in 1453 and even providing the names of perpetrators who acted on order of Vasilii II, secretary Stefan Borodatyi and under-secretary Vasilii Beda.[34] According to Lur'e, the chronicler was so open because he was independent from the official grand-princely chronicle writing. In his turn, Kloss treats *Com1472* from the perspective of the traditional and problematic classification of chronicles as princely and Church ones. In his view, *Com1472* was prepared by Mariia's secretaries, among whom we find the above-mentioned Stefan Borodatyi and Vasilii Beda. Kloss also insists that despite its compilation in Rostov, *Com1472* had nothing to do with the Rostov see.[35]

---

[32] *PSRL*, vol. 25, Moscow, 2004, p. 242; Lur'e, *Obshcherusskie letopisi*, p. 161.

[33] Borisov, *Vasilii*, pp. 197, 213, 247; Fennell, *Ivan*, pp. xiii, xiv, 68 note 2; A. A. Zimin, *Rossiia na rubezhe XV–XVI stoletii*, Moscow, 1982, p. 58; *PSRL*, vol. 6, 2, column 129.

[34] *PSRL*, vol. 23, p. 155; cf. Novikova, 'Sokrashchennyi svod', p. 230; *PSRL*, vol. 20, 1, p. 262; *PSRL*, vol. 6, 2, column 126.

[35] Lur'e, *Dve istorii*, pp. 18, 81, 82; Kloss, 'K kharakteristike', p. 64. According to A. A. Shakhmatov and A. N. Nasonov, *Erm* derived from a compilation prepared in the archbishopric of Rostov: A. A. Shakhmatov, *Istoriia russkogo letopisaniia*, vol. 2, St Petersburg, 2011, p. 176; A. N. Nasonov, *Istoriia russkogo letopisaniia XI–nachala XVIII veka*, Moscow, 1969, pp. 322–36, 351.

It is hard to see how a chronicle sponsored by Mariia Iaroslavna could be completely independent from the grand princely court. Mariia herself was a prominent figure at Vasilii II's court; after Vasilii II's death, his trusted secretaries, as we saw, moved to Mariia's court in Rostov. It is equally difficult to imagine that Mariia and the compiler of *Com1472* would ignore the authority and cultural resources of the Orthodox Church. Rather, the peculiarities of *Com1472* should be attributed not to the institutional affiliation of its compiler, but to Mariia's patronage. Mariia was of course Vasilii II's widow, but she also had close connections with people who had either suffered from her late husband or had cherished the memory of his victims. Mariia was heavily influenced by the prominent cleric Pafnutii of Borovsk. A contemporary tale of Pafnutii's death in 1477 tells us that the leading members of the Muscovite royal family, including Ivan III, Mariia Iaroslavna and Sofiia Palaiologina, sent their envoys to bid farewell to the dying monk. The tale singles out Mariia as the only member of the royalty who developed special relations with Pafnutii, calling him 'her intercessor' (*svoi bogomolets*). Pafnutii had long-standing connections with Dmitrii Shemiaka, as the monk had established a monastery on the Prince's land. Pafnutii continued to commemorate Shemiaka after his assassination, resolutely ignoring Metropolitan Iona's order to stop venerating the enemy of Vasilii II. Despite pressure from Iona, who even temporarily imprisoned Pafnutii, the monk persevered in his determination to preserve Shemiaka's memory. The land where Pafnutii's monastery was located eventually went to Mariia's brother Vasilii Iaroslavich of Serpukhov, who was a close ally of Vasilii II. However, Vasilii II arrested Vasilii Iaroslavich for no obvious reasons in 1456. The Grand Prince suppressed with extreme brutality an attempt of Vasilii Iaroslavich's loyalists to free him in 1462.[36]

All these factors affected recollections of Vasilii II's reign in *Com1472*, which was produced under Mariia's patronage during Pafnutii's lifetime and when her brother Vasilii Iaroslavich was still in custody (he died in chains in 1483). It is hardly surprising that the chronicler was quite sympathetic to the victims of Vasilii II, including Shemiaka and the 1462 conspirators.[37] Obviously, there was no place for the golden belt legend, which insulted Shemiaka's familial memory, in *Com1472*.

---

[36] *Pamiatniki literatury Drevnei Rusi: Vtoraia polovina XV veka*, Moscow, 1982, p. 492; Zimin, *Vitiaz'*, pp. 155–56; Mazurov, Nikandrov, *Russkii udel*, pp. 169–82, 205.
[37] Novikova, 'Sokrashchennyi svod', p. 232; PSRL, vol. 23, p. 157; PSRL, vol. 20, 1, p. 276; PSRL, vol. 6, 2, column 158; Kloss, 'K kharakteristike', p. 63.

*   *   *

We may conclude that there was an incident at Vasilii II's wedding in 1433: Zakharii Koshkin grabbed Vasilii Kosoi's belt. The sources do not explain why, but it is safe to assume the influence of alcohol. Excessive drinking was common at Vasilii II's court and even affected his military performance in 1433 and 1445.[38] Alcohol also played a part in the above-mentioned incident with another member of Vasilii II's court, Fedor Basenok in Novgorod in 1460. Taking into account the cultural status of belts studied by Ryan, it is obvious that Koshkin's escapade was offensive. But the episode with Kosoi's belt had no serious political consequences, and so it was omitted in the original account of the royal wedding.

However, during the war of succession, Vasilii II's bookmen turned the drunken incident into the golden belt legend to castigate the princes of Galich. Part of the expanded account of the 1433 wedding, the legend ignores Zakharii Koshkin, probably because the Koshkins did not participate actively in the military conflict. Zimin asserts that they might be biding their time to see the outcome of the war.[39] Rather, the legend attributes initiative in 'exposing' Vasilii Kosoi's corruption to Petr Dobrynskii, who was already known as a loyal informant of the Grand Prince. The expanded version weaves themes borrowed from the royal chancery documents into the twisted legend by mispresenting Kosoi's (and by extension Shemiaka's) familial inheritance as stolen property. Compiled between 1436 and 1446, the legend adds insult to injury, and quite literally. For Muscovite authorities, it was not enough to blind Vasilii Kosoi. The legend of the golden belt is a calculated assault on the familial memory of the descendants of Iurii of Galich. The story of Kosoi's belt as reported in the expanded account of Vasilii II's wedding is a blatant fabrication. It would be reckless to use this legend as a source on regalia, kinship or marriage politics. Rather, the legend demonstrates how Muscovite ideologists weaponized familial memory during the war of succession.

Furthermore, the legend of the golden belt misrepresents the roles of individual women in Vasilii II's family. The legend has created a powerful image of Sofiia Vitovtovna who was in fact a victim of theft. For many years, she desperately tried to reclaim her property pillaged

[38] Zimin, *Vitiaz'*, pp. 57, 104.
[39] A. A. Zimin, *Formirovanie boiarskoi aristokratii v Rossii vo vtoroi polovine XV–pervoi treti XVI v.*, Moscow, 1988, p. 183.

during the inter-princely war. On the contrary, Mariia Iaroslavna, who is only briefly mentioned in the legend, was a strong and resilient person: a mother and a wife, who took care of her children and disabled husband amidst a grim war; a shrewd financier, who augmented her property and passed it on to her children; and the patron of a chronicle that rejected Muscovite falsifications of the memories of the Galich princes.

Mariia's court generated a revised history of Vasilii II's wedding which lacked mesmerizing theatrical gestures like Sofiia Vitovtovna publicly stripping Kosoi of his golden belt. Still, Mariia's cultural activities reveal much more important issues associated with familial memory and female royal patronage. Elite women played an essential part in preserving and shaping familial memories. The Muscovite war of succession was accompanied with proclamations and fabrications of familial memories which were often transmitted through expensive objects, like golden belts.[40] The chronicle sponsored by Mariia undertook the task of reconciling these conflicting memories in the aftermath of the succession war.

---

[40] On the role of elite women in keeping familial memory, see Matthew Innes, 'Keeping It in the Family: Women and Aristocratic Memory, 700–1200', in Elisabeth van Houts (ed.), *Medieval Memories: Men, Women and the Past, 700–1300*, Harlow, 2001, pp. 17–35. On objects as carriers of memory, see Elisabeth van Houts, *Memory and Gender in Medieval Europe, 900–1200*, Basingstoke, 1999, pp. 93–120.

Appendix. *Relationship of Accounts of Vasilii II's Wedding*

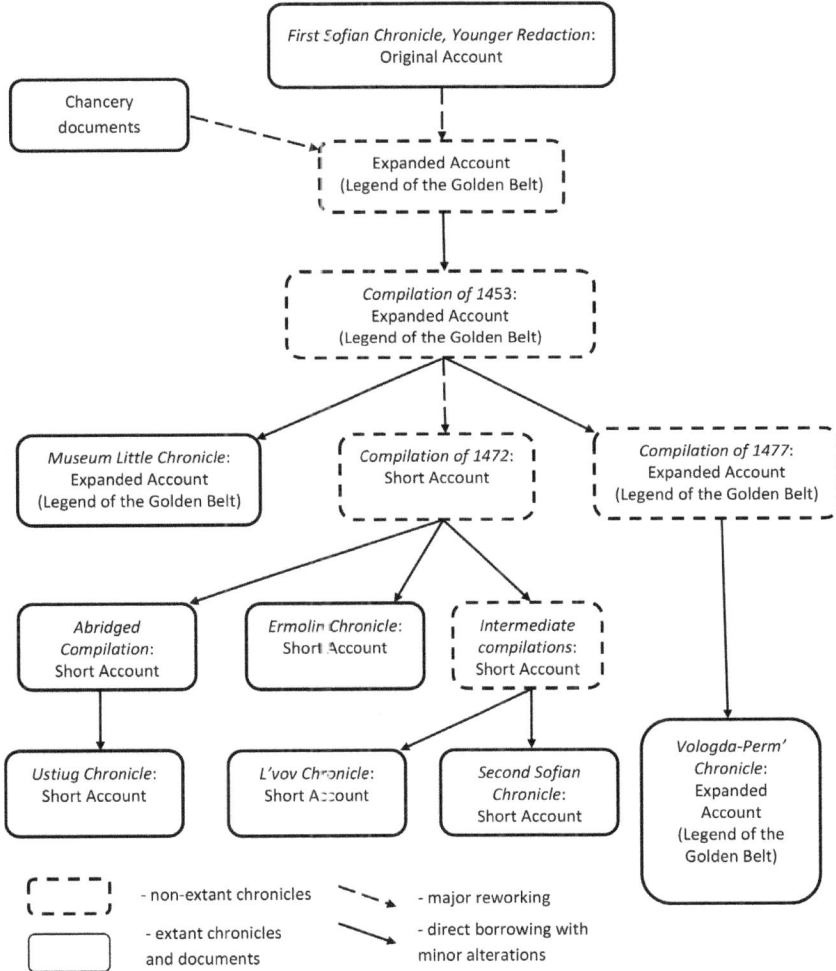

First Sofian Chronicle, Younger Redaction:
Original Account

Chancery
documents

Expanded Account
(Legend of the Golden Belt)

Compilation of 1453:
Expanded Account
(Legend of the Golden Belt)

Museum Little Chronicle:
Expanded Account
(Legend of the Golden Belt)

Compilation of 1472:
Short Account

Compilation of 1477:
Expanded Account
(Legend of the Golden Belt)

*Abridged
Compilation*:
Short Account

Ermolin Chronicle:
Short Account

*Intermediate
compilations*:
Short Account

Ustiug Chronicle:
Short Account

L'vov Chronicle:
Short Account

*Second Sofian
Chronicle*:
Short Account

*Vologda-Perm'
Chronicle*:
Expanded
Account
(Legend of the
Golden Belt)

- non-extant chronicles
- extant chronicles
and documents

- major reworking
- direct borrowing with
minor alterations

On the Rendering of some Philosophical Terms in the Fifteenth-Century Slavic Translations from Hebrew

Moshe Taube

The Hebrew University of Jerusalem

THE unexpected emergence of translations of scientific texts from Hebrew into Slavic in the second half of the fifteenth century has been one of my major fields of interest since the 1970s. One of these translations, the *Secret of Secrets*, has become since the early 1990s the topic of a prolonged collaboration with Will Ryan who had begun investigating this text some thirty years earlier, a collaboration leading to close friendship and resulting in the publication of the critical edition of the *Secret of Secrets* in 2019 by the Warburg Institute.[1]

The translations are preserved mostly in Russian copies, though some of the earliest are in Ruthenian. Ruthenian is a neutral name in English for the language of the Grand Duchy of Lithuania, a language that the Russians prefer to call *zapadno-russkii*, or 'West-Russian', while the Ukrainians and the Belarusians, who claim it as ancestor, call it, respectively, Old Ukrainian and Old Belarusian. Another Slavic self-qualifying term is *prosta mova* or 'simple speech'.

Since the historical circumstances which gave rise to this corpus of translations have been amply discussed in our 2019 edition of the *Secret of Secrets*[2] as well as in some of my earlier work, I will not repeat here all the evidence identifying the Jewish translator, nor the indices pointing to the translations being the fruit of collaboration between a Jewish translator and a Christian scribe who wrote them down in Cyrillic letters.[3] I will instead try to focus on illustrating the skills and knowledge of the Jewish translator of these texts, as well as his cultural frame of mind and his biases, by analysing some details of the translations in terms of additions, omissions and modifications.

[1] W. F. Ryan, Moshe Taube, *The* Secret of Secrets: *The East Slavic Version. Introduction, Text, Annotated Translation, and Slavic Index*, London, 2019.
[2] Ibid., pp. 16–30.
[3] Moshe Taube, *The Logika of the Judaizers: A Fifteenth-Century Ruthenian Translation from Hebrew. Critical Edition of the Slavic Texts presented alongside their Hebrew Sources, with Introduction, English Translation, and Commentary*, Jerusalem, 2016, p. 50.

The translations were carried out in the second half of the fifteenth century (c.1450–80), probably all of them by a single man, a learned Jew from Kiev named Zechariah ben Aharon ha-Kohen,[4] with the help of an anonymous Christian Slav who wrote them down. Written down in Cyrillic script, they were clearly intended for a Christian audience.[5] The translations display several instances of modifications by the translator that should be seen as a conscious attempt to adapt the text for its intended Christian readership. Formulae that might raise questions about the differences between the understanding of God's unity in Judaism (as well as in Islam) and in Christianity are omitted, and Aristotle's pagan teaching is legitimized by naming some of the Jewish prophets as sources of his thinking — indeed as his mentors.[6] Most of the translations ended up in Russified copies preserved in Russian monastic libraries.

The Hebrew texts translated into Slavic include:

a. An astronomical work, written originally in Hebrew by the fourteenth-century Jewish mathematician from Provence Emmanuel Ben Jacob Bonfils, titled *Six Wings* שש כנפים.

b. A cosmography, written originally in Latin by the thirteenth-century English mathematician who taught at the Sorbonne, Johannes de Sacrobosco, titled *De Sphaera* and translated anonymously into Hebrew as ספר האשפירא הקטן 'The small book of the sphere'.

c. An exposition in Arabic of philosophy, logic, and metaphysics by the eleventh-century Persian theologian Abu Ḥāmid Muḥammad Al-Ghazālī titled *Maqāṣid al-falāsifah*, translated anonymously into Hebrew as כוונות הפילוסופים 'the intentions of the philosophers'.

d. A short exposition of Logic written in Judeo-Arabic (Arabic in Hebrew script) and traditionally ascribed to Maimonides, titled *Logical Terminology* — מילות היגיון lit. 'Vocables of Logic'.

Items **c** and **d** in this list were combined in Slavic to form a philosophical miscellany called *Logika*.[7]

e. A tenth-century Arabic 'mirror of princes' stemming from the circle of the 'Brethren of Purity' and pretending to be a work written by Aristotle for his disciple Alexander the Great, titled *Sirr al-asrār*, in

---

[4] Ryan and Taube, *The Secret of Secrets*, pp. 16–18.
[5] Further details can be found in Taube, *The Logika*, pp. 57–58.
[6] Ibid., pp. 60–61.
[7] See Taube, *The Logika*.

Hebrew סוד הסודות 'the secret of secrets'.[8] It includes in Slavic four major interpolations, three of them from works by Maimonides:

Maimonides' *fī-l-jimāʿ* — 'On Coitus' — מאמר המשגל in its entirety.[9]
Maimonides' *Kitāb al-sumūm w-al-taḥarruz min al-ʾadwiya al-qattāla* — 'On Poisons and the Protection against Lethal Drugs' — על סמי המוות והרפואות נגדם — only the second part dealing with mineral poisons.
Maimonides' *Maqāla fī-l-rabw* — 'Treatise on Asthma' — ספר הקצרת — only chapter 13.
Rhazes' chapter on Physiognomy from his *Kitāb Almanṣūrī fī-l-ṭibb* — 'Book on medicine for Mansur' חכמת הפרצוף מתוך אלמנצורי לאל-ראזי על.

f. An eight-line sorites (cyclical maxim) 'on the soul', that may have been originally part of the previous item, but is now preserved in Slavic as part of a miscellany (wrongly) named 'The Laodicean Epistle'.[10]
g. A collection of nine Old Testament *hagiographa* preserved in a unique sixteenth-century Codex (F-10-262) now in Vilnius. With the exception of the Psalms, which were adapted from the extant Russian Church Slavonic version (based on the Septuagint) by comparing it with the Latin Vulgate, the books were translated directly from the Hebrew Masoretic Text, either exclusively (Proverbs, Job, Ecclesiastes, Esther, Ruth, Lamentations) or partly on the basis of earlier translations (Song of Songs, Daniel).[11]

Given that the translations show common traits of lexicon and grammar, and since for one of them we have an almost contemporary

---

[8] See Ryan and Taube, *The* Secret of Secrets.
[9] W. F. Ryan, Moshe Taube, 'The Slavonic version of Maimonides' *De Coitu* in Maimonides', in *On Coitus: A New Parallel Arabic-English Edition and Translation*, trans. by Gerrit Bos, with editions of medieval Hebrew translations by Gerrit Bos, medieval Latin translations by Charles Burnett and a Slavonic translation by W. F. Ryan and Moshe Taube, Leiden and Boston, MA, 2018, pp. 129–51.
[10] See Moshe Taube, 'The "Poem on the Soul" in the *Laodicean Epistle* and the Literature of the Judaizers', *Harvard Ukrainian Studies*, 19, 1995, pp. 671–85, and Moshe Taube, 'The Spiritual Circle in the *Secret of Secrets* and the *Poem on the Soul*', *Harvard Ukrainian Studies*, 18, December 1994, 3/4 [appeared 1998], pp. 342–55.
[11] Discussed further in: Moshe Taube, 'On Two Related Slavic Translations of the Song of Songs', *Slavica Hierosolymitana*, 7, 1985, pp. 203–10; Moshe Taube, 'The Vilnius 262 Psalter: A Jewish Translation?', in W. Moskovich et al. (eds), *Jews And Slavs*, 1, 2004, pp. 36–45; Moshe Taube, 'The Book of Job in Vilnius', in W. Moskovich et al. (eds), *Jews and Slavs*, 15, 2005, pp. 281–96; Moshe Taube, 'The Book of Proverbs in Codex Vilnius 262', in Alexander Kulik, Mary MacRobert, Svetlina Nikolova, Moshe Taube, Cynthia Vakareliyska (eds), *The Bible in the Slavic Tradition*, Leiden and Boston, MA, 2015, pp. 179–94.

Slavic testimony ascribing דֹ to Cxapia — [Scharia] — 'Zechariah',[12] we are led to posit, with a high degree of probability, a single translator for the whole corpus. The obvious candidate for that task is the copyist and annotator of Hebrew manuscripts of scientific and philosophical texts Zechariah ben Aharon ha-Kohen. Zechariah was a learned Jew from Kiev, with a Byzantine handwriting. Consequently, he was in all likelihood part of the Romaniote community that lived in Kiev at least from the mid-tenth century onward, that is, from the time when pagan Kiev had a Khazar governor, half a century before the Christianization of Russia by Vladimir, Prince of Kiev, and several centuries before Ashkenazic Jews began their migration into Eastern Europe.

Zechariah's name came down to us in a series of colophons in Hebrew manuscripts which he copied and annotated with glosses.[13] These are:

— Johannes de Sacrobosco's (c.1195–1256) cosmography *De Sphaera*, *On the Sphere*, written originally in Latin, and translated into Hebrew as קיצור ספר הגלגל. The anonymous fourteenth-century translation was copied by Zechariah in Kiev in 1454.

— Qalonymos of Provence's משרת משה — *Moses' Servant*, a commentary on Maimonides' *Guide of the Perplexed*, copied in 1455.

— Anonymous thirteenth-century Hebrew philosophic encyclopaedia in the Maimonidean vein (variously ascribed to Samuel Ibn Tibbon, Jacob Anatoli and others), called רוח חן — *Spirit of Grace*, copied in 1456.

— Abu-l-Abbas Ahmad al-Farghānī, *Elements of Astronomy*, translated by Jacob Anatoli from both the Arabic and the Latin as קיצור אלמגיסטי 'abridgment of the Almagest', copied in Kiev in 1468.

— Averrroes' *On the Substance of the Orbs*, translated by Solomon Ibn Ayyub as מאמר בעצם הגלגל-. The last two pages were copied by Zechariah in Damascus in 1485.

In this last item, Zechariah calls himself איש ירושלים, 'man of Jerusalem', which signifies that he had made a pilgrimage to the Holy Land at some point between 1471, when he is mentioned as arriving in Novgorod in the retinue of Prince Mikhailo Olelkovich of Kiev, and 1485.

Zechariah in all likelihood did not know Arabic, but he had a broad enough knowledge of other philosophical texts in Hebrew for him not only to come up with learned guesses about the meaning of

---

[12] Ryan and Taube, *The Secret of Secrets*, p. 23.
[13] For details see ibid., pp. 17–18.

philosophical terms, but even to add explanations for the benefit of the non-initiated Christian readers.

Thus, in the second chapter of the section on Logic in Al-Ghazālī's *Intentions of the Philosophers,* in the discussion of the difference between definition and description, bringing as example the necessary components for the definition of 'man', we find:[14]

2.4.9 ומחובר החי והמדבר גדר אמתי, כי הגדר מליצה ממה שיצייר אמתת מהות הדבר
בנפש השואל. 2.4.10 ואם המרת המדבר במקרה, יבדילהו משאר הבעלי חיים, 2.4.11
כאמרך חי נצב הקומה רחב החזה מביט למעלה פנים צוחק בטבע, הנה זה יבדילהו משאר
הבייח, 2.4.12 אבל הוא יקרא רושם, ותועלתו ההכרה לבד. 2.4.13 ואולם הגדר הנה ידרש בו
אמתת עצמות הדבר, ולא הגיע אלא בזכר ההבדלים העצמותיים כולם.

In Slavic, the translator adds the phrase (marked by italics) *but you will not express his quiddity*, which shows his good understanding of the philosophical point under discussion, namely the difference between essential and accidental properties:

2.4.9 сложенїе же жива и словесна съо르ꙋженье истин'но чл҃кꙋ, [...]
им'же образꙋется ч'товьство [...] пытаное пытателеви: 2.4.10 а
аще ѿмѣниши словесно⸀ прикл{юче}нїамъ, въвсоби꙼ е⸀ ѿ ины҄
живы҄. но и не исповѣси что⸀ства е⸀. 2.4.9

2.4.9 And the combination of 'animal' and 'rational' is the true definition *of 'man,'* [for definition is the term for that] whereby the [true] quiddity of what was asked about is conceived (represented) by the asker. 2.4.10 But if you replace 'rational' with accidents, you may differentiate him from other animals, *but you will not express his quiddity.*

Another example showing the translator's mastery of philosophical material on the one hand, and of his awareness of what is appropriate for the non-Jewish readership on the other hand, comes from the introduction to Al-Ghazālī's Theological section of the *Intentions of the Philosophers* dealing with the division of Sciences:[15]

0.1.2 והדברים הנמצאים אשר אפשר שיהיה מעויין בם בחכמות יחלקו אל שני חלקים:
0.1.3 אחד מהם מה שממציאותם בפעולותינו, כשאר המעשים האנושיים מהחקים וההנהגות
והעבודות וההרגלים וההשתדלויות וזולתם. 0.1.4 ואל מה שאין מציאותם בפעולותינו,
כשמים והארץ והצמח והחי והמתכות ועצמי המלאכים והשדים והשטנים וזולתם. 0.1.5 ואין
ספק שתחלק החכמה ההקשית אל שני חלקים: 0.1.6 אחד מהם מה שיודיע עניני מעשינו,

---

[14] Taube, *The* Logika, pp. 370–71.
[15] Ibid., pp. 264–65.

ותקרא חכמה מעשית, ותועלתה שיגלה בה מציאות המעשׂים אשר בם יסודר תקוננו בעולם,
ויאמן בעבורם תקותנו באחרית. ^{0.1.7} והשני יודע בו הגלוי מעניני הנמצאות כלם, כדי שתגיע
בנפשותינו תכונת המציאות כלו על סדורו, כמו שיגיעו הצורות הנראות במראה, ^{0.1.8} ותהיה
הגעת זה שלימות לנפשותינו. כי הכנת הנפש לקבלתם היא סגולה לה, ותהיה בעת ההיא
מעלה, ובאחרית סבת ההצלחה, כמו שיבא.

In the enumeration of entities not accomplished through our deeds
in 0.1.4, the Slavic is rather different from the Hebrew. First, it omits
some of the more dangerous items from the list of examples found in
the Hebrew, which has: 'heaven and earth and plants and animals and
metals and the essence of angels and demons and devils and others.'
Second, the translator added the two phrases. (1): *and by which human
corporeality is perfected* of unknown source; and (2): *Associating the
intellect and the intelligent (subject) and the intelligible into one.*

This last maxim appears in Maimonides' *Guide of the Perplexed*, I, 68:
המאמר אשר אמרוהו הפלוסופים בשם יתעלה, והוא אמ־ו שהוא השכל והמשכיל והמושכל
— 'The dictum which the philosophers said about God, may He be
exalted, namely that He is the intellect as well as the intellectually
cognizing subject and the intellectually cognized object.'[16]

In Slavic:

^{0.1.2} єстєства оубо о ни^х жє смышлаєтса в прємꙋдростѣхъ
разнатса на двоє. ^{0.1.3} а̃. ижє совєршєны дѣлы нашими яко бы
дѣиства человѣческа и законы и повѣданїа и работы и наоуки.
^{0.1.4} в̃. єжє нє совєршєны дѣлы нашими. яко бы нбо и зємла.
и цвѣ^т. и аггли. [...] и иныи. ^{0.1.5} прємꙋдрость жє ровналнаа
дѣлитса на двоє. ^{0.1.6} а̃. [...] имжє оправатса дѣла наша зємскїа.
и совєршится тєлєствїє чл̃чїє. и оувѣритс ихъ ради надєжа
наша пачєишаа. ^{0.1.7} в̃. ижє ими изяснатса єстєства вса дш̃а^м
нашимъ по радꙋ яко прообразованїє в зєрцалѣ. ^{0.1.8} симжє
исполни^тса дш̃а наша [...] да бꙋдє^т тꙋто чєсть. а тамо жизнь
вѣчнаа. [...] *свє^д оумъ и оумны и оумѣты во єдиность.*

^{0.1.2} The entities to which consideration is given in the sciences are
divided into two (parts): ^{0.1.3} One. Those which are accomplished
through our deeds, as, for example (through) man's actions, laws,
(social) customs, (religious) observances and (learning-) practices [...]
etc. ^{0.1.4} Two. Those which are not accomplished through our deeds,
as, for example, heaven and earth, vegetation, angels, etc. ^{0.1.5} As for
the syllogistic science, it is divided into two (parts): ^{0.1.6} One. [...] That

[16] Maimonides, *The Guide of the Perplexed*, ed. and trans. S. Pines, Chicago, IL,
1963, p. 163.

by which our earthly deeds are put in order, *and by which human corporeality is perfected*, and thanks to which our ultimate hope (sc. eternal life) is secured. [0.1.7] Two. That by which all entities are elucidated for our souls in an orderly manner, like a reflection in a mirror. [0.1.8] By that, our soul is perfected, [...] so as to have here (sc. in this world) — honour; and there (in the next) — eternal life [...]. *Associating the intellect and the intelligent (subject) and the intelligible into one.*

A third example of the translator's departure from the Hebrew is found in the discussion of the figures of syllogisms in Chapter 7 of Maimonides' *Logical Terminology*:

[7.6.1] השנית והשלישית הפכיות בכמות ובאיכות, [7.6.2] רצוני בזה כי השנית תשמר סדר הכוללת ולא תשמר סדר המחייבת ותוליד ולא תוליד כוללת ולא תוליד מחייבת, [7.6.3] והשלישית בהפך זו, כי היא שומרת סדר המחייבת ולא תשמר סדר הכוללת ולכן תוליד מחייבת ולא תוליד כוללת. ובכלל שהשנית לא תשמר סדר חיוב ולא תולידהו, והשלישית לא תשמר סדר כולל ולא תולידהו.

Here the translator into Slavic adds a reference, certainly lost on the Slavic readers, to a '*Long Logic*', showing once again his broad knowledge of philosophical literature.[17] He displays his skills, first, by adding into the text the relevant explanation from Al-Ghazālī's Logical section,[18] and second, by adding a reference to a *Long Logic*, which is surely a reference to Averroes' *Intermediate Commentary* on the logical books of the *Organon* (*Categories, Prior and Posterior Analytics, Topics*), containing the longest discussion of valid and invalid syllogisms and of demonstrative proof available in Hebrew to readers at that time.

[7.6.1] алє дрȢгаа и трєтиа прєвращєны сȢть количєствомъ и качєство^{м}. [7.6.2] рєкомо ижє дрȢгїи хранитъ ра^{д} всачєства. а нє хранитъ чинȢ приложєнїа. а родитъ всачєство. а нє приложєнїє. [7.6.3] а трєтїи прєвращєнъ сємȢ. занєжє храни^{т} ра^{д} приложєнїа. но оставлаєтъ ра^{д} всачєства. а родитъ приложєнїє. а нє родитъ всачєскои. [...] [7.6.4] *а вси образы дрȢгїи и трєтїи наврататса к пєрвомȢ образȢ. а пєрвыи нє навратитса до нихъ. а роди^{т} оклады чєтыри прєдрєчєнныхъ.* [7.6.5] *а ровны жє сȢ^{т} образы три си^{м} ижє нѣ^{т} ровнанїа з двȢ прєдковъ частны^{х}. ни з двȢ оуємны^{х}. ни малыи оуємныи, а вєликїи частныи.* [7.6.6] *а болє сєго ищи в долгои логицє.*

[17] Taube, *The* Logika, pp. 186–87.
[18] See also ibid., pp. 504–06.

7.6.1 But the second and the third (figures) are opposed to each other in quantity and quality. 7.5.2 That is, the second preserves the order of universality but not the order of affirmation, and yields universality but not affirmation, 7.6.3 whereas the third is the opposite thereof, for it preserves the order of affirmation but renounces the order of universality, and yields affirmation, but does not yield universality. [...] *7.6.4 And both these figures, the second and the third, revert to the first (that is, in order to yield a conclusion), while the first (need) not revert to them, and it yields the four aforementioned quantifiers. 7.6.5 And the three figures are equal in that there is no syllogism from two particular premises, nor from two negative ones, nor from a negative minor and a particular major. 7.6.6 And for more (details) look in the Long Logic.*

This whole section comes from the explanation interpolated into the Tibbonian Hebrew translation of the *Logical Terminology* — ביאור שלא מן המאמר 'an explanation not from the treatise' — ascribed to the thirteenth-century physician from Naples, Jacob Anatoli, and attested in four manuscripts of Ibn Tibbon's translation. In the passage marked by italics in the English translation, we read the additions in Slavic by the Jewish translator, showing his mastery of logic. A similar added reference to a *Long Logic* is found also in the Slavic version of the parallel section of Al-Ghazālī.[19] No wonder Zechariah knew the parallel text from Al-Ghazālī, since it was he who translated that text as well, although Al-Ghazālī's *Logic* did not make it to Muscovy and did not become part of the *Logika*, where it is replaced by Maimonides' *Logical Terminology*, probably on account of it being shorter and clearer. The Kievan manuscript of Al-Ghazālī's *Logic* in Slavic has not survived, having disappeared during the Second World War. Luckily it was published in 1909 in the University of Kiev journal by Sergei Neverov, a student who was not even in a position to identify the text but managed nevertheless to put the folios of the manuscript in order (they were badly disordered, with several folios missing), and to guess the meaning of many of the terms. In the 2016 edition of the *Logika*, Neverov's text is reproduced at the end, after the *Logika* itself, together with the corresponding Hebrew.[20]

In contradistinction to his knowledge of Hebrew philosophic literature, Zechariah shows no acquaintance with the, albeit limited, philosophical terminology current in Slavic. Unlike in the West Slavic regions, where Catholic Christianity was adopted and Aristotle was being taught (in Latin) at the Universities of Prague and Cracow, in

---

[19] See ibid. p. 506.
[20] Ibid., pp. 426–573.

the East Slavic regions, where Orthodox Christianity was adopted, there were no universities and no knowledge of Aristotle's works. Consequently no philosophical terminology was to be found, with the exception of some terms in St John of Damascus' Πηγή γνώσεως (*Source of Knowledge*), the philosophical chapters of which circulated in Russian translation in a very small number of manuscripts under the title *Dialektika*.[21] Our Jewish translator apparently knew nothing about this and had to invent a brand new terminology. His approach was simple — translate literally, if possible. Sometimes, though, when deemed necessary, we witness an attempt of interpretation. Some examples of this literality are the following:

Slavic	literal tr. of Sl	Arabic	Hebrew	English term
прилѣпенїе	gluing, sticking	مُلازمة	דבקות	inalienability
ударенїе	hitting	ضَرْب	הכאה	multiplication
пожичєныи	borrowed	مُسْتَعَار	מושאל	metaphorical
поновлєнъ	renewed	مُحَدَّث	מחודש	temporaneous
заблудшїи	misleading	سُفِسطائى	מטעה	sophistic
попущєныи	released	مُطْلَق	משולח	absolute
погнаныи	pursued	مُرادف	נרדף	synonym
рєчєныѧ	the said (pl.)	مَقولات	מאמרות	the Categories
обрѣтєныи	found	مَوْجود	נמצא	existent

In all the examples above the Slavic renders literally the Hebrew which, in its turn, is mostly a literal translation of the Arabic. The Slavic term for 'sophistic', namely *zabludshii* 'misleading', is the result of interpretation by the translator into Hebrew of Arabic *sufisṭāʔī* (a calque of the Greek) as *maṭʕeh* 'misleading'. All the Slavic terms are everyday words, but in their scholarly sense they are semantic neologisms, not found anywhere else in Slavic in this sense.

As for the terms which result from interpretation by the translator into Slavic, I wish to focus on the rendering of the term צורה (*tsura*) 'form', a central concept in medieval thought, whether Muslim, Jewish or Christian, adopting the Aristotelian doctrine of hylomorphism, according to which all substances (except God) are composed of form

---

[21] See Eckhard Weiher, 'Studien zur philosophischen Terminologie des Kirchenslavischen', *Die Welt der Slaven*, 9, 1964, pp. 47–175.

and matter. The term 'form' in this context does not refer to a thing's 'shape', but to:

> its definition or essence — what it is to be a human being, for example. A statue may be human-shaped, but it is not a human, because it cannot perform the functions characteristic of humans: thinking, perceiving, moving, desiring, eating and growing, etc.[22]

In the Slavic translations the Hebrew term *tsura* 'form', when employed in its Aristotelian meaning of εἶδος 'form', as opposed to ὕλη 'matter', is rendered by a Slavic word containing the semantic component 'soul'. This is so, since within Aristotle's hylomorphic framework, the rational soul is the form (=essence) of man.

This view is echoed in Maimonides' writings. Thus in the first chapter of the *Guide of the Perplexed*, dealing with Hebrew words appearing in the Bible that risk being interpreted as instances of anthropomorphism which Maimonides utterly rejects, the Biblical word צלם [*tselem*] 'image' is characterized as follows (Hebrew in Samuel Ibn Tibbon's translation):

> אמנם צלם הוא הצורה הטבעית, ר״ל על העניין אשר בו נתעצם הדבר והיה מה שהוא, והוא. אמתתו, מאשר הוא הנמצא ההוא אשר העניין ההוא העניין באדם, הוא אשר בעבורו תהיה ההשגה האנושית. ומפני ההשגה הזאת השכלית נאמר בו, בצלם אלהים ברא אותו, ולכן נאמר צלמם תבזה, כי הבזיון דבק בנפש אשר היא הצורה המינית, לא לתכונת האברים ותארם.

The term *image*, (צלם), on the other hand, is applied to the natural form, meaning to the notion in virtue of which a thing is constituted as a substance and becomes what it is. It is the true reality of the thing in so far as the latter is the particular being. In man that notion is that from which human apprehension derives. It is on account of this intellectual apprehension that it is said of man: *In the image of God created He him*. For this reason also, it is said: *Thou contemptest their image*. For *contempt* has for its object the **soul**, which **is the specific form**, not the shape and configuration of the body.[23] Man's specific form then, is his soul.

An explanation equating 'rational soul', man's constitutive characteristic, with 'form of man' appears in the *Guide of the Perplexed* I, Chapter 41 (Hebrew in Samuel Ibn Tibbon's translation):

---

[22] See *Stanford Encyclopedia of Philosophy*, sub Matter vs. Form, https://plato. stanford.edu/entries/form-matter/.

[23] English translation by Pines, Maimonides, *The Guide of the Perplexed*, vol. 1, p. 22.

נפש שם משותף, הוא שם הנפש החיה הכוללת לכל מרגיש אשר בו נפש חיה, והוא גם שם הדם, לא תאכל הנפש עם הבשר, והוא גם הנפש המדברת כלומר צורת האדם.

Soul (nephesh) is an equivocal term. It is a term denoting the animal soul common to every sentient being. Thus (Gen. 1:30): *Wherein there is a living soul.* It is also a term denoting blood. Thus (Deut. 12:23): *Thou shalt not eat the soul* (i.e. *the blood*) *with the flesh.* It is also a term denoting the rational soul, I mean the form of man (English translation by S. Pines 1963, vol. 1, p. 91).

In the Slavic *Logika*, the instances of 'form' in the Aristotelian sense are therefore rendered by a noun derived from 'soul' — душєвєнъство, literally 'animacy'.

Thus, in the portion of the *Logika* deriving from Maimonides' *Logical Terminology*, in a sentence only partially rendering the Hebrew, we read (Hebrew translation by Moshe b. Judah Ibn Tibbon):

9.1.5 דמיון זה האדם מן העניינים הטבעיים חמרו הוא החיות, וצורתו הוא הכח המדבר, ותכליתו הוא השגת המושכלות, ופועלו הוא אשר נתן לו הצורה ר״ל הכח ההוא המדבר. כי ענין הפועל אצלנו ממציא הצורות בחמרים, והוא האל ית׳ ואפילו לפי דעת הפלוסופים, זולת שהם יאמרו כי הוא הפועל הרחוק ויבקשו לכל נמצא מחודש פועלו הקרוב.

For example, man, belongs to the natural order, his matter is living, his form is the rational faculty, his purpose [telos] is the attaining of ideas, and his agent is the one who gave him his form, that is, his rational faculty, because by 'agent' we mean the creator of form in matter, and this is God, blessed be He, even according to the philosophers; albeit they maintain that He is the remote cause, and for every created thing they seek its proximate agent.[24]

In the Slavic translation we read:[25]

яко^Ж рече^М о чл҃цѣ [...], ижє тѣлєство єго животъ. а дш҃євєнъство єго слово. а дѣлатєль єго дш҃єдавєць. а статокъ єго доставати разⷹмо^М истинны [...].

We say, e.g., of Man [...] that his matter is life, his form (lit. 'animacy') is rationality (lit. 'word'), his agent is the Giver of form (lit. 'giver of soul'), and his purpose is the attainment of truth by the intellect. [...].

[24] Translation based on Israel Efros, *Maimonides' Treatise on Logic: The Original Arabic and Three Hebrew Translations*, New York, 1938, p. 50.
[25] Taube, *The Logika*, pp. 204–06.

A similar usage is attested in the other component of the Slavic *Logika*, Al-Ghazālī's *Intentions of the Philosophers*, section on Theology:[26]

מאמר בדבקות ההיולי והצורה ^{1.9.1} ההיולי אין לה מציאות בפעל בעצמה בלתי הצורה כלל, אבל יהיה לעולם מציאותה עם הצורה, ^{1.9.2} וכן הצורה לא תעמוד בעצמה בלתי ההיולי.

In Slavic:

1.9.0 слово о прилѣпенїи гїюла и душевенства
1.9.1 Гїюли же не имаⷮ естества в дѣле сама беⷥ дш҃евенства. но естество ее [...] съ дш҃евенствоⷨ 1.9.2 и такеⷤ дш҃евенство не стоиⷮ беⷥ нее.1.9.0

1.9.0 Discourse on the Inalienability of Hyle and Form (lit. 'animacy')
1.9.1 Hyle has no actual existence by itself without form (lit. 'animacy'), but its existence is [always] with form (lit. 'animacy').1.9.2 Likewise, form (lit. 'animacy') does not stand [by itself] without it (sc. hyle).

The lengths to which the translator went in preserving this use of Aristotelian 'form' in the translation can be exemplified by another passage from the Theological part of Al-Ghazālī's *Intentions of the Philosophers*,[27] where Hebrew צורה (*tsura*) 'form' is rendered not by a lexeme, but by forming an abstract notion using morphological derivation.

Anonymous Hebrew translation:

ואשר יצטרך אל משכן יחלק אל ... ואל מה שישכון במשכן, ותעמוד אמתת המשכן בו, ותומר בסבת כניסתו האמתות ותשובת המהות, כצורת האדם בשכבת זרע וצורת העכבר בעפר. ... והטפה, כאשר השתנתה אדם, אי אפשר שיאמר טפה בתשובת מה הוא, ולא העפר כאשר שב עכבר, וישאל ממנו, אי אפשר שיאמר שהוא עפה. ... והעפר לא ישאר עפר עם צורת העכבר, ולא הטפה תשאר טפה עם הצורה האנושית.

[...] дѣлитса... TA1.2.4 в҃. иже пребываеⷮ во одержители да исполняетъ истиннꙋ его. да измѣняется входоⷨ его истинна, и ѿвѣⷮ чтовьственыи. ꙗко бы чл҃чество в насѣнїи своемъ. и мышество в перст꙯и. [...] TA1.2.7 а насѣнїе премѣнившеса в чл҃чество, не наречетса насѣнїе ани персть мышествомъ.

[26] See ibid., pp. 314–15.
[27] See ibid., pp. 280–81.

[entities requiring a residence, ...] '...divides into... 2. (Those) wherein (the accident) resides in a subject and implements its truth, and with its (sc. the accident's) advent, the truth and the answer (to the question) of quiddity changes, such as human form (lit. 'humanness') in semen, and the form of a mouse (lit. 'mouseness') in dirt. [...] Whereas semen transformed into human form (lit. 'humanness') is not to be called semen, nor dirt (transformed into) mouse form (lit. 'mouseness').'

The neologism мышество, literally 'mouseness', that is, 'being a mouse' stands here for Hebrew צורת העכבר, literally 'the form of mouse' in the Aristotelian sense, and likewise чл̃чество, literally 'humanness' for הצורה האנושית 'the human form'.

As we can see from the examples given, translating these texts into a Slavic vernacular without a philosophical tradition was a very demanding task, especially for a Jew. The result was a text sometimes obscure and sometimes totally incomprehensible to medieval Christian readers in Muscovite Russia, since the language of the translations is close enough to Russian yet different in many details in grammar and especially in the lexicon, thus yielding many false friends.

Given what we know about the translator, his willingness to undertake this rather difficult task looks rather bold, since, despite his knowledge of Hebrew philosophy, he did not have adequate mastery of either the source language of his translations, the Arabicized Hebrew, or the target language, the Slavic vernacular used in the Grand Duchy of Lithuania. The only plausible motivation for his drive to undertake such a task must therefore be an ideological agenda lying behind the whole enterprise of translations. I have proposed in several previous publications[28] a scenario linking these translations to the 'Heresy of the Judaizers' that started in Novgorod in the 1470s and then expanded to Moscow, in the context of the eschatological fervour around the year 7000 from creation (1492 CE), date of the expected Second Coming, till its eradication in 1504. As motive for the translations on the Jewish side, I brought evidence[29] about the views of Rabbi Moses the Exile, a contemporary scholar residing in Kiev, who not only was making calculations predicting the End of Times to arrive around the same time, but also emphasized the importance of proselytes for the expected Redemption (coming of the Messiah).

---

[28] See Moshe Taube, 'Transmission of Scientific Texts in 15th-Century Eastern Knaan', *Aleph: Historical Studies in Science and Judaism*, 10, 2010, 2, pp. 315–53; Moshe Taube, *The Logika*, pp. 67–69; Ryan and Taube, *The Secret of Secrets*, pp. 16–30.

[29] For example, ibid., pp. 28–29.

Be that as it may, it remains that our ideologically-motivated Kievan translator Zechariah ben Aharon, disregarding the difficulties and obstacles, produced a body of translations that was copied and recopied, and of which some parts, like the *Secret of Secrets*,[30] had a lasting impact both in Russia and beyond.

---

[30] See ibid., pp. 59–69.

Diplomacy and Language
(a Russian Embassy to Italy in 1659)

Boris Uspenskij

National Research University, Higher School of Economics Moscow

AFTER his accession to the throne in 1645, Tsar Aleksei Mikhailovich adopted a new title. He started self-styling not in the manner of his immediate predecessors on the throne, but rather in that of Ivan IV, the first crowned Russian tsar. Like Ivan IV, Aleksei Mikhailovich would refer to himself as *otchich* ('paternal heir'), *dedich* ('ancestral heir') and *naslednik* ('successor'), thus putting emphasis on his hereditary right to the throne of the Russian tsars. In his case, unlike that of Ivan, this right looked somewhat dubious: Aleksei Mikhailovich was not related by blood to the dynasty of Rurikids. He began to engage more zealously in international affairs, wanting his new status to be recognized. He sent embassies with friendly letters (*liubitel'nye poslaniia,* literally 'loving epistles') and valuable gifts to various European countries with which Russia had not had earlier diplomatic relations. The main objective of these embassies was not so much establishing friendly relations as receiving any sort of return document where, according to the etiquette of diplomacy, the Tsar's complete title would be reproduced precisely in the way it was written in the letter sent with the embassy. In this way, the new title of Aleksei Mikhailovich that had raised considerable doubt in Western Europe would be confirmed and recognized. The process was not always smooth, however. The very persistence of the Russians in demanding that the title be reproduced accurately would inadvertently raise suspicions that the issue of the title was not merely formal and that political ambitions were involved.[1]

---

[1]   Thus, in 1667 Aleksei Mikhailovich and Louis XIV of France ('Le Roi Soleil') exchanged messages of friendship. The letter from Aleksei Mikhailovich had his complete title, including the words *samoderzhets, otchich, i dedich, i naslednik, i gosudar', i obladatel'* ('autocrat, paternal heir, and ancestral heir, and successor, and Sovereign, and dominator'). According to the diplomatic protocol, the exact title was expected to be fully reproduced in the return letter from the King to the Tsar. However, the King's response omitted the words 'autocrat, paternal heir, and ancestral heir, and successor, and Sovereign, and dominator': or rather, the original Latin letter of the King did not contain them, although they were present in the Russian copy given to the Russian ambassadors. This discrepancy did not go unnoticed, and the ambassadors, the *stol'nik* (an honorary court title) Petr Ivanovich Potemkin and the *d'iak* (a senior official) Semen Rumiantsev, protested to the French authorities by pointing out that the original letter from the King had omitted 'the highest titles':

These suspicions were in fact not totally groundless, since Aleksei Mikhailovich saw himself as an heir or successor of the Byzantine emperors which meant that he, like a Byzantine emperor, would consider the other Christian monarchs to be his potential vassals.[2] At his coronation, Aleksei Mikhailovich received the following words in blessing from the head of Russian Orthodox Church, Patriarch Iosif: '[...] may you be the Sovereign of the Universe, Tsar and Autocrat of Christians, and may you co-shine like the sun among stars.'[3] It was at the same ceremony that the Patriarch, referring to the wish that the father of the new Tsar (Mikhail Fedorovich) had expressed on his deathbed, stated that henceforth Aleksei Mikhailovich should be styled as 'paternal heir, and ancestral heir, and successor, and dominator'.[4] This wording was perceived as a formula asserting the hierarchical superiority of the Russian tsar over other Christian monarchs.

In 1666–67 Grigorii Kotoshikhin was asked in Sweden why the Russian tsar addressed other Christian monarchs as his vassals, styling himself the 'paternal heir, and ancestral heir, and successor, and Sovereign, and dominator':

> Why does the Tsar of Muscovy write to Christian states [styling himself] in the full long titles of an overlord [...] 'paternal heir, and ancestral heir, and successor, and Sovereign, and dominator', and never uses these titles when writing to heathen countries. What is the reason for it?

Puteshestviia russkikh poslov XVI–XVII vv: Stateinye spiski, Moscow, 1954, p. 288; see also *Drevniaia rossiiskaia vivliofika … izdannaia Nikolaem Novikovym* (hereafter DRV), 2nd edition, 20 vols, Moscow, 1788–91, 4, pp. 529–33. A similar episode took place earlier the same year involving the same two ambassadors during their mission in Spain: the royal document in Spanish handed to them had the Tsar's title shortened: *DRV*, vol. 4, pp. 422–32. When the ambassadors protested, the comment they received was: 'His Royal Majesty had a session with his councillors on this matter, so His Royal Majesty instructed us to tell you that there was no better way of wording in Spanish. And the ambassadors told the officer appointed to look after them: if His Royal Majesty is not going to have this letter of his corrected and re-written, we shall not take such a letter to our Great Sovereign His Majesty the Tsar, — and they returned him the letter. And the officer did not take the letter back but said he would inform His Royal Majesty'. Ibid., p. 431.

[2] See B. Uspenskij, V. Zhivov, 'Tsar and God: Semiotic Aspects of the Sacralization of the Monarch in Russia', in Boris Uspenskij and Victor Zhivov, *'Tsar and God' and Other Essays in Russian Cultural Semiotics*, Boston, MA, 2012, pp. 13–17.

[3] *DRV*, vol. 7, p. 266.

[4] On the meaning and perception of the word *obladatel'* 'dominator' present in the titles of all Russian tsars from Ivan IV to Peter I, see B. A. Uspenskij, 'Zagadochnaia forma v titule russkikh tsarei', *Slověne: International Journal of Slavic Studies*, 8, 1, 2020, pp. 163–84.

Kotoshikhin's response was that the Tsar did it just for his glory without any reason and that it was the custom in some countries to address the monarch this way for the sake of courtesy, due to the general custom of calling the addressee 'lord' and oneself 'servant', while these countries are not actually his vassal states:

> [...] To some states, the Tsar writes [in this manner] for his own glory, not for any reason, and there is a custom in these states to address the Tsar by belittling themselves and praising his person, calling themselves his serfs (*kholopy*), just as some states have a custom of writing 'your humble servant' by a lord to another lord. And they [the Russians], from these self-belittling letters, assume that they [these states] are actually their vassals, which is not true.[5]

Kotoshikhin's explanation can be illuminated by a case which is the subject of the present contribution.

*   *   *

In 1658, an embassy of the nobleman Vasilii Bogdanovich Likhachev and the *d'iak* Ivan Fomin was sent to Florence.[6] Shortly before that,

---

[5] *Grigorij Kotošixin. O Rossii v carstvovanie Alekseja Mixajloviča. Text and Commentary*, ed. A. E. Pennington, Oxford, 1980, p. 53 [fols 56v–57r].

[6] Sources disagree as to when the ambassadors were sent and when they actually arrived in Italy. According to the Russian ambassadorial reports (*stateinie spiski*), the Tsar's order to send the ambassadors was issued on 23 June 7167 (= AD 1659), they were in Arkhangel'sk by 9 September 7168 (= 1659), left Arkhangel'sk on 20 September 7168 (= 1659), arrived in Livorno on 5 January (1660), left Florence on 15 February (1660) and were back in Arkhangel'sk by early June (1660): *DRV*, vol. 4, pp. 339, 340, 342, 355, 359; *Pamiatniki diplomaticheskikh snoshenii Drevnei Rusi s derzhavami inostrannymi* (hereafter *PDS*), 10 vols, St Petersburg, 1851–71, 10, columns 509, 514, 516, 532, 612, 664. However, the contemporary Italian documents on this embassy consistently have the year 1659 rather than 1660: thus, the letters from Livorno reporting the arrival of the embassy date from 19 and 20 January 1659, the letter from the Grand Duke of Tuscany handed to the ambassadors at their departure from Florence was issued on 24 February 1659 etc.: *Documenti che si conservano nel R. Archivio di Stato in Firenze, sezione Medicea, riguardanti l'antica Moscovia (Russia)*, trans. and compiled Michele Boutourlin, 2 vols, Moscow, 1871, 1, pp. 236, 248, 273. (The difference in days is due to the difference between the Gregorian and Julian calendars.) Upon their return to Moscow, the Ambassadorial Chancellery (*Posol'skii prikaz*) provided a translation of the letter from Ferdinand II delivered with the embassy. The translation bears the date presumably referring to when it was undertaken, and it is 2 August 7167 (= 1659): A. [D.] Chertkov, 'Opisanie posol'stva, otpravlennogo v 1659 godu pri tsare Aleksee Mikhailoviche k Ferdinandu II-mu, Velikomu gertsogu Toskanskomu', *Russkii istoricheskii sbornik, izdavaemyi Obshchestvom istorii i drevnostei Rossiiskikh*, vol. 3, book 4, Moscow, 1840, p. 365. Ivan Fomin, the second ambassador, in his letter of application to the Tsar specifies that he was on the mission in 1658–59: *Akty*

Likhachev was granted the title of viceroy of Borovsk. Viceroyalties were in fact defunct by that time,[7] and Likhachev's title was hardly more than nominal, being merely a token intended to impress foreigners (which it did). The embassy was sent to thank the Grand Duke of Tuscany for his earlier (1656) reception of other Russian ambassadors, the *stol'nik* Ivan Ivanovich Chemodanov and the *d'iak* Aleksei Postnikov, who were passing through his domain on their way to Venice.[8] The Likhachev mission is well documented: there are two reports from the ambassador himself and a number of Italian documents related to this event. A juxtaposition of these sources allows us to reconstruct much of the actual course of events.

The mission was remarkably successful: the ambassadors were received with appropriate ceremony and much grandeur,[9] and,

Moskovskogo gosudarstva, izdanye imp. Akademiei nauk, 3 vols, St Petersburg, 1890–1901, 3, nos. 167, 150; S. B. Veselovskii, *D'iaki i pod'iachie XV–XVII vv.*, Moscow, 1975, p. 559. One has to assume that it is the ambassadorial reports that have the wrong date: all other data indicate that the Likhachev–Fomin embassy sailed from Arkhangel'sk on 20 September 1658 and had been in the Duchy of Tuscany between 5 January and 15 February 1659 according to the Julian Calendar.

[7]   Viceroyalties had been abolished under Ivan IV, but some survived locally until the early seventeenth century: see, for example, R. V. Fomenko, 'Namestnich'e upravlenie i ego al'ternativa: problema effetivnosti mestnogo upravleniia v Russkom gosudarstve v kontse XV–XVI vv.', *Iuridicheskii vestnik Samarskogo universiteta*, 5, 2019, 3, pp. 30–31.

[8]   V. Korsakova, 'Likhachev Vasilii Bogdanovich'in *Russkii biograficheskii slovar'*, vol. *Labzina–Liashenko*, St Petersburg, 1914, p. 485; see also *PDS*, vol. 10, column 558. An Italian agent who met the ambassadors in Livorno (where they had arrived from Arkhangel'sk by sea) reported the rumour that the 'first ambassador' (Likhachev) was 'the governor of some large city unknown to me and that he is generally a more important person than the previous first ambassador [Chemodanov], and that the previous ambassador allegedly never speaks to this first ambassador [of the present mission] with his hat on. Then I asked the interpreter about the purpose of the present embassy, but he told that he heard nothing about it from the ambassadors, save for the fact that they were carrying gifts of much value from the Tsar to His Highness [the Grand Duke of Tuscany], but the interpreter himself believed there was no purpose other than reporting the great respect with which Muscovy received the news of the friendly reception extended by His Highness on their previous mission sent to Venice: Boutourlin, *Documenti che si conservano nel R. Archivio di Stato in Firenze*, vol. 1, pp. 56, 233. Before his departure for Venice, Chemodanov was made viceroy of Pereslavl'–Zalesskii. Again, his appointment must have been purely token: ambassadors seem to have been made viceroys just for the sake of looking important abroad. Chemodanov's position in Russia was actually much higher than Likhachev's, and the rumours of their inequality were apparently spread on purpose, that is, merely for show. The next person after Likhachev who was given the title of viceroy of Borovsk would be P. I. Potemkin, the ambassador to Spain and France in 1667–68; later on (in 1680), Potemkin was made viceroy of Uglich, on the occasion of a new mission to the same countries: N. V-n-v" (N. Voinov?), 'Potemkin Petr Ivanovich', in *Russkii biograficheskii slovar'*, vol. *Plavil'shchikov–Primo*, St Petersburg, 1905, pp. 583–84. After the mid-seventeenth century 'viceroy' seems to have become a token title reserved for ambassadors.

[9]   One reads in the correspondence between the hosts of the event: 'We are dealing

moreover, Ferdinand II, the Grand Duke of Tuscany, when receiving the Tsar's letter, declared himself and his family to be *serfs* of the Russian tsar. The ambassadorial report has the following account of the meeting between the Grand Duke and the ambassadors in Pisa:

> And the Duke received the Sovereign's letter from the Ambassadors, and kissed it, and started weeping, and spoke in Italian through the interpreter thus: for what [virtue] is it that your Grand Duke Aleksei Mikhailovich, renowned in all States and Hordes, Autocrat of all the Russias, Great and Little and White, sought me, *his serf* (*kholopa svoego*), from his faraway great and most glorious city of Moscow, and sent me his letter of love and gifts? And he the Great Sovereign is as high as heaven above earth, so great he is, glorious and most glorious from one end of the universe to the other; and his name is most glorious and awful [that is, awe-inspiring] in all the States, from the old Rome to the new one and to Jerusalem; and how can I, a poor man, pay tribute to the Great Sovereign for his great and abundant favour? And I, and my brothers Mattias, and Leopoldo, and Gian Graziano, and my son Cosimo, are the Great Sovereign's slaves and serfs (*rabi i kholopi*); and the Tsar's heart is in God's hand; that being God's will. [10]

A similar wording was used then by the wife of Ferdinand II, the Great Duchess Victoria della Rovere,[11] who invited the ambassadors to her Florentine palace:

> Your Great Sovereign, the most glorious and valiant Tsar, paid us a visit from his faraway great state, sent to my husband, son and brothers

with such a strange and significant mission [...], that His Highness [the Grand Duke of Tuscany] is even deigning to abandon the conventional protocol that is the custom at his court; I consider whether it would be proper, instead of the Lord Senior Majordomo, to have at the city gates Duke [*sic*, actually, Marquis] Salviati himself who at the time of his mission to the German Emperor was granted by His Highness the title of cousin of his Most Illustrious House [...]'; see Boutourlin, *Documenti che si conservano nel R. Archivio di Stato in Firenze*, vol. 1, pp. 242–43.

[10] *DRV*, vol. 4, pp. 345–46; Chertkov, 'Opisanie posol'stva', p. 328. The interpreter in question was Lieutenant Ivan (Giovanni) Sacx in service at the court of the Grand Duke. Initially, the embassy had their own interpreter from Italian, Timofei Toporovskii, who previously had been in Venice with the mission of Chemodanov and Postnikov, but he died suddenly shortly after the departure from Arkhangel'sk, so that 'we were left without any interpreter from the Italian tongue at all', as Likhachev wrote in his report: *DRV*, vol. 4, pp. 339–41. When the Likhachev–Fomin embassy arrived in Livorno, the Grand Duke sent them an interpreter of his own: see *DRV*, vol. 4, pp. 339–41, 348; Chertkov, 'Opisanie posol'stva', p. 328; *PDS*, vol. 10, column 518.

[11] In the embassy's reports she is referred to as *kniaginia Anna* 'Princess Anna': *DRV*, vol. 4, p. 349; *PDS*, vol. 10, column 601.

his gifts of love and a letter of his, the Great Sovereign; by which great favour of his he put *us his serfs* (*nas kholopei svoikh*) into great amazement and delight, since from the beginning of the world such things were unheard of. And we from you, the ambassadors of His Royal Majesty, are pleading for mercy and humbly begging you, may you not blame us in our folly and simplicity if we have not pleased or gratified you, and if anything would have been done not by your custom, because we do not know how to make you pleased; have mercy on us and bestow us with your benevolence and mercy, and tell your Great Sovereign of our diligence, care and love, and ask him the Great Sovereign to have mercy on us, so that he the Great Sovereign will henceforth favour my husband, son and brothers; and my husband, son and brothers are *his slaves and serfs forever* (*vechnye ego raby i kholopi*); this is what I beg of you.[12]

There are two surviving recensions of Likhachev's report. The full text recension is a detailed formal account after the standard template, registered in the Chancellery of Secret Affairs (*Prikaz tainykh del*);[13] the second version cited above[14] was written by Likhachev himself.[15] In the full text version, the Grand Duke of Tuscany calls himself also a *rabotnik* ('servant, worker') of the Russian tsar and asks for his patronage, and on one single occasion even refers to himself as the tsar's *rab* ('slave'):

And he, the Grand Duke of Tuscany, with his issue, is pleased to serve the Great Sovereign, His Royal Majesty, and to work for him as his *slave* (*rab*).[16]

[12] *DRV*, vol. 4, column 354; Chertkov, 'Opisanie posol'stva', pp. 340–41.
[13] See *PDS*, vol. 10, columns 515–666. The manuscript contains 180 sheets in quarto. Each sheet has a registration signature by *d'iak* Artemii Stepanov: Chertkov, 'Opisanie posol'stva', p. 365. Artemii Stepanov had been a clerk of the Chancellery of Secret Affairs from 1660 and was promoted to the position of *d'iak* in 1674; see Veselovskii, *D'iaki i pod'iachie XV–XVII vv.*, p. 490. The Chancellery of Secret Affairs was abolished in 1676 after the death of Aleksei Mikhailovich. The full-text recension of Likhachev's report must therefore have been registered in 1674–76.
[14] *DRV*, vol. 4, columns 339–55.
[15] Korsakova, 'Likhachev Vasilii Bogdanovich', pp. 485–86.
[16] *PDS*, vol. 10, column 571. According to the full text version, when meeting the ambassadors in Pisa, Ferdinand II said: 'Delighted with so much favour from your Great Sovereign, Tsar and Grand Duke Aleksei Mikhailovich, Autocrat of all the Russias, Great and Little and White, His Royal Majesty, that he, your Great Sovereign, His Royal Majesty, from such a [faraway] state of his has honoured me, *his servant* (*rabotnika svoego*) with his lordly favour, for which lordly favour I do not know what to pay in tribute. But I am pleased to serve the Great Sovereign and work for him forever, as much as he the Great Sovereign pleases and I am able to:' *PDS*, vol. 10, column 550, see also columns 557, 580, 581, 591, 593. Ferdinand's valedictory speech in the full text

Likhachev apparently prized his report very much. On the way back across the Gotthard Pass 'the state treasury and baggage [...] were carried by oxen, but the letter of the Florentine Duke and the report were carried by the clerks, for horses with packs, if the wind is strong, are thrown into deep abysses [...] And Ambassador Vasilii Likhachev and all the others were walking on foot'.[17] Obviously, the document contained exactly what the Russian Tsar wanted to hear.

One can safely assume that Ferdinand II Medici, the Grand Duke of Tuscany, never saw himself and his family as serfs of Tsar Aleksei Mikhailovich. Does this suggest that the whole episode was invented by the ambassador? Historians have favoured this interpretation: for example, V. D. Korsakova wrote that, in Likhachev's view, 'there was no person more illustrious than Tsar Aleksei Mikhailovich, so he was just putting into the mouth of the Grand Duke of Tuscany the words [normally] heard in the Kremlin.'[18]

However, this is unlikely to have been the case. More probably the report of the Russian ambassador was based on the actual words pronounced by the Grand Duke but understood by Likhachev in his own way. The whole story seems to have arisen from the phenomenon described by Kotoshikhin, namely, the Duke's declaration that he and his family are the serfs (*kholopi*) of Tsar Aleksei Mikhailovich, derives from a common Western formula of courtesy, misinterpreted by the Russians in a too literal sense, cf.: 'And they [the Russians], from these self-belittling letters, assume that they [these countries] are actually

version closely matches what his wife says in the shorter one (her words have been cited above): 'As you with God's help arrive to the reigning city of Moscow and you see your Great Sovereign, His Royal Majesty, in his most illustrious person, then if I pleased not him the Great Sovereign, His Royal Majesty, in any way or committed any indiscretion against him the Great Sovereign, His Royal Majesty, may you address the Great Sovereign, His Royal Majesty, and intercede for me, and plead his mercy so that your Great Sovereign, His Royal Majesty, spread his lordly mercy over my simplicity and henceforth me, *his eternal servant* (*vechnago rabotnika svoego*), and my son, and my brothers be honoured with his great lordly favour; and to him the Great Sovereign, His Royal Majesty, for his great lordly favour and honour, we are to serve forever and to work for him now and henceforth, as well as our successors, for the rest of our lives, and as best we can.' *PDS*, vol. 10, column 611.

[17] *DRV*, vol. 4, p. 356. The Likhachev-Fomin embassy, as mentioned above, arrived in Italy by sea, from Arkhangel'sk to Livorno. They had no ships chartered for their return journey (see Boutourlin, *Documenti che si conservano nel R. Archivio di Stato in Firenze*, vol. 1, p. 244), so that the whole embassy had to cross the Alps in order to get to Amsterdam, from where they would sail to Arkhangel'sk.

[18] Korsakova, 'Likhachev Vasilii Bogdanovich', p. 487. According to Chertkov, 'One does not know who translated the speech of Ferdinand II [...], but it seems to be different in wording from what the Duke presumably must have said': Chertkov, 'Opisanie posol'stva', p. 328.

their vassals, which is not true.'[19] Indeed, Ferdinand II in his response to the Tsar refers to himself as his 'most humble servant' and uses a number of other formulas of courteous self-deprecation.[20] Likhachev clearly misunderstood the conventions of courtesy and was inclined to interpret the rhetoric quite literally, since it was consistent with his idea of how foreign monarchs should address the Russian tsar.

The Grand Duke of Tuscany's declarations of servant-like devotion and loyalty must have attracted attention in Moscow. It is hardly a coincidence that the fuller version of Likhachev's report was brought not to the Ambassadorial Chancellery (as it should have been) but to the Chancellery of Secret Affairs: there must have been a special request for the manuscript. Ferdinand's words did not only gratify the vanity of Aleksei Mikhailovich, but were in line with his self-perception, reinforcing his notion of the Muscovite tsar as the true successor of the Byzantine emperors. At the same time, for the more experienced clerks at the Ambassadorial Chancellery, such as Kotoshikhin, the mechanisms that created such texts were apparently no secret.

[19] Pennington, *Grigorij Kotošixin*, p. 53 [fol. 56v–57r].
[20] See the letter from Ferdinand II sent with the Russian embassy: Boutourlin, *Documenti che si conservano nel R. Archivio di Stato in Firenze*, vol. 1, pp. 273–74, no. XLVIII (a draft in Italian: ibid., pp. 77–78, no. XLII). The translation of the document from Latin into the Russian officialese (see Chertkov, 'Opisanie posol'stva', pp, 365–67) fails to convey the refined style of the original.

Toll House 'Magicians' in the *Vita of Basil the Younger* from St Dimitrii of Rostov's *Menaion* and Late Balkan Sources[1]

Adelina Angusheva-Tihanov

University of Manchester

THE *Vita of Basil the Younger*,[2] a saint celebrated in the Orthodox Christian calendar on 26 March, is not only one of the most peculiar texts which the Byzantine literary culture has left to us, but also a work with a complex and convoluted textual history. I would like to revisit an episode in the *Vita* which tells of the journey of Theodora's soul through the aerial 'toll house' (Greek τελώνιον, Slavonic мытарство) where the souls of those dealing with magic are tried for their sins. I shall concentrate on Slavonic renditions of the text, and especially on its late seventeenth- to early eighteenth-century reworking by Dimitrii of Rostov (1651–1709) and some later Balkan versions. My starting point is an insightful observation by W. F. Ryan on Slavonic words relating to magic and divination that:

> [I]t is usually impossible to know with any degree of clarity what lies behind the various terms used for magical practices and their devotees, especially when words surviving from a pre-Christian belief-system are used in a later Christian context, for example to translate Greek words in Patristic literature.[3]

The *Vita of St Basil the Younger* is no exception: practitioners of magic and supernatural activities of all sorts appear in many episodes of the texts, and the translation of Greek terms related to magic demonstrates an attempt to use extant Slavonic linguistic resources to present adequately the content of the Greek original. What was then the place in this process of Dimitrii's version and those of the later compilers and translators?

The *Vita of St Basil the Younger* has a distinctive hagiographic composition, a mixture of ascetic narratives, dream visions,

---

[1] This text is dedicated to Will Ryan, a man of exceptional wisdom, wit and generosity. The piece is short and modest, but to express my gratitude to him neither the length of St Basil's *Vita*, nor that of St Dimitrii's *Menaia* will be enough.

[2] Henceforth the *Vita*.

[3] W. F. Ryan, *The Bathhouse at Midnight: An Historical Survey of Magic and Divination in Russia*, University Park, Pennsylvania, PA, 1999, p. 68.

eschatological and didactic discourses, all presented in the political context of late ninth- and early tenth-century Constantinople. The story oscillates between the Byzantine provinces and the capital, the city and the country estate, between power games in Constantinople and personal grievances in a medieval village, not to mention heavenly realms and 'afterlife' experiences. Although it is impossible to claim with certainty that Basil was a real historical figure, on the grounds of the events, emperors and dignitaries mentioned in the text, it has been calculated that the death of Basil, which the narrative places in mid-Lent period, could have happened either in 944 or 952.[4] According to the text, St Basil was captured in Asia Minor and brought to the Byzantine capital, wrongly accused of spying, tried and tortured until he proved his holiness through miracles, predictions and spiritual guidance which he offered even to the emperors. E. Patlagean remarks that the origin and identity of the saint remains unknown in the narrative: 'Basile apparaît, et disparaît à la fin, sans que personne ait su son identité.'[5] The presentation of the saint in the *Vita* also falls between the categories of a specific hagiographic type, as the classical elements of a martyr's narrative (the trial, the physical torments and miraculously resolved impossible ordeals) are combined with visions, interpretations and admonitions, characteristic of hermits' *Lives*. A number of scholars point at the similarities between this text and the *vita* of St Andreas Salos, and even regard the *Vita* as a life of a holy fool,[6] although, as Patlagean acknowledges, this particular type is indicated but not

---

[4] Henry Grégoire and P. Orgels, 'L'invasion hongroise dans la "Vie de Saint Basile le Jeune"', *Byzantion*, 24, 1954, 1, pp. 147–54 (p. 147); Lennart Rydén, 'The Life of St Basil the Younger and the Date of the Life of St Andreas Salos', *Harvard Ukrainian Studies*, 7, 1983, pp. 568–86 (p. 572); Andrei Timotin, 'Byzantine Visionary Accounts of the Other World: A Reconsideration', in John Burke (ed.), *Byzantine Narrative: Papers in Honour of Roger Scott*, Leiden, 2006, pp. 404–20 (pp. 406–08). See also Paul Magdalino, review of *The Life of Saint Basil the Younger. Critical Edition and Annotated Translation of the Moscow Version*, ed. and trans. Denis F. Sullivan, Alice-Mary Talbot, and Stamatina McGrath (Dumbarton Oaks Studies XLV), *The Catholic Historical Review*, 2015, 101.4, pp. 903–04.

[5] Evelyne Patlagean, 'Byzance et son outre monde. Observation sur quelques récits', in *Faire croire. Modalités de la diffusion et de la réception des messages religieux du XIIe au XVe siècle. Collection de l'École française de Rome*, 51, 1981, pp. 201–21 (p. 207).

[6] Rydén 'The Life of St. Basil the Younger', p. 577. Different Greek versions of the *Vita* describe St Basil the Younger as being wise and skilful in his speech, but simulating foolishness to visitors who were inclined to praise him. The passage exists in the South Slavic versions (though missing from MS Sinai 20 N), presenting Basil as being 'idiotic in [his] words' (въюдный в словесе), that is, talking nonsense, and also pretending to be unreasonable, and insane (несмисливъ). The Slavonic text is quoted here from the edition of Sergei Vilinskii, *Zhitie sv. Vasiliia Novago v russkoi literature*, Odessa, vol. 2, 1911, p. 630.

completely or consistently developed throughout the texts.[7] Comparing the *vitae* of the two saints, P. Magdalino claims that 'their very differences are complementary to a degree which makes it impossible to understand either text and its place in Byzantine hagiography without reference to the other'.[8] The work was also compared to the *Vision of Kosmas* and other similar texts all of which present a 'mixture of genre and unusual length'.[9] It is commonly accepted that the *Vita* was written in the late tenth century by the saint's disciple, Gregory. The narrative deviates from the traditional hagiographic composition; in a large part of it Gregory acts as the main protagonist while St Basil appears only in his dreams to consult and console him, or sometimes to condemn his actions. Two very long episodes of the text present Gregory's dream visions granted through the prayers of St Basil — the afterlife journey of the soul of Theodora, the servant of the saint, and the vision of the Last Judgement. Relatively early on, these two parts began to appear in the manuscript tradition as separate works. Their importance cannot be overstated — they are regarded as sources of the Orthodox iconography of Hell's toll houses and the Last Judgement.[10]

It was the exceptionally rich content of the *Vita* that made it extremely popular in the Byzantino-Slavic context and ensured its uninterrupted distribution long after the medieval period, up to the end of the nineteenth century. The text is known in different Greek versions. In the long and extensive history of the study of the *Vita* scholars disagree on the textual delineations and the classification of the extant versions, but A. N. Veselovskii's suggestion, expressed at the end of the nineteenth century, that the copy in Codex Mosquensis Synodalis 249 (from the sixteenth century) reflects the oldest and most complete version of the text seems to be commonly accepted.[11]

---

[7] Patlagean, 'Byzance et son outre monde', p. 207.

[8] P. Magdalino, '"What we heard in the Lives of the saints we have seen with our own eyes": The Holy Man as Literary Text in Tenth-Century Constantinople', in J. Howard-Johnston, P. A. Hayward (eds), *The Cult of Saints in Late Antiquity and the Middle Ages: Essays on the Contribution of Peter Brown*, Oxford, 1999, pp. 83–112.

[9] Denis F. Sullivan, Alice-Mary Talbot and Stamatina McGrath, *The Life of Saint Basil the Younger. Critical Edition and Annotated Translation of the Moscow Version* (Dumbarton Oaks Studies XLV), Washington, DC, Cambridge, MA, 2014, p. 49.

[10] See Irina V. Dergacheva, 'Toposy inogo mira v "Zhitii Vasiliia Novogo"', in *Iazyk i tekst*, 3, 2016, 4, http://psyjournals.ru/langpsy/2016/n4/Dergacheva.shtml (accessed 10 January 2020); Aleksei Gudkov, 'Litsa' sudnogo dnia: illiustrovannye rukopisi "Zhitiia Vasiliia Novogo"', 2018, https://zen.yandex.ru/media/ruvera/lica-sudnogo-dnia-illiustrirovannye-rukopisi-jitiia-vasiliia-novogo-5ae8305cad0f2291ff292ea8 (accessed 1 June 2020).

[11] Aleksandr Veselovskii. 'Razyskaniia v oblasti russkogo dukhovnogo stikha', vyp. 5, XI–XVII, *Sbornik Otdeleniia russkogo iazyka i slovesnosti Imperatorskoi*

While parts of this copy were previously edited by Veselovskii and Vilinskii,[12] the text from this codex has only recently been published in its entirety.[13] Another Greek witness (from MS Athous Dionysiou 107), which apparently stands closer to the earliest Slavonic translation, has been edited and analysed by L. Shchegoleva and S. A. Ivanov.[14]

The *Vita* was translated in the Slavic milieu at least twice during the medieval period, and from two distinct Greek versions.[15] While the earlier translation was probably produced among the Eastern Slavs in the eleventh century,[16] the second, fourteenth-century rendition based on a different Greek text, appeared in the Balkans. The earliest extant South Slavonic version comes from a manuscript (Codex Sinai 20 N) compiled between 1369 and 1370 at the time of Bulgarian Tsar Ivan Alexander (1331–70).[17] According to Pentkovskaia, the scarcity of copies of the earliest translation could be explained by the arrival of the fourteenth-century South Slavonic translation which gained popularity in medieval Rus' and served as the basis for a version which spread mainly in Russian manuscripts from the late sixteenth, seventeenth and eighteenth centuries.[18] Vilinskii appropriately named it the 'second Russian redaction'.[19]

At the end of the seventeenth century, St Dimitrii of Rostov reworked the *Vita* as part of his *Reading Menaia,* using, according to Vilinskii, the first Slavonic translation of the text, an edition of

Akademii nauk, 46, 1889, no. 6, pp. 117–72 and the appendix pp. 4–102; see also Tat'iana Pentkovskaia in T. V. Pentkovskaia, L. I. Shchegoleva, S. A. Ivanov, *Zhitie Vasiliia Novogo v drevneishem slavianskom perevode po rukopisi GRB sobranie E. E. Egorova 162 s parallel'nym grecheskim tekstom po rukopisi Athous Dionysiou 107*, 2nd edn, Moscow, 2019, pp. 15–16.

[12] Veselovskii, 'Razyskaniia', Appendix pp. 4–102; Vilinskii, *Zhitie sv. Vasiliia*, vol. 1, pp. 1–128. Vilinskii further outlined four distinct groups of the Greek texts and edited witnesses of the second and third groups: ibid., vol. 2, pp. 5–142, and 143–283, http://books.e-heritage.ru/book/10071407.

[13] Sullivan, Talbot, McGrath. *The Life*, with a palaeographic note by Nadezhda Kavrus-Hoffmann.

[14] Pentkovskaia, Shchegoleva, Ivanov, *Zhitie.*

[15] Vilinskii, *Zhitie sv. Vasiliia*, vol. 1, p. 232; Tat'iana Pentkovskaia, 'Drevneishii russkii perevod zhitiia Vasiliia Novogo i ego grecheskii original', *Vizantiiskii vremennik*, 63 (88), 2004, pp. 114–28.

[16] See the recent, authoritative, edition by Pentkovskaia, in Pentkovskaia, Shchegoleva, Ivanov, *Zhitie.* Previously Vilinskii published a witness of the same version from the March *Reading Menaion* of Metropolitan Makarii, *Zhitie sv. Vasiliia*, vol. 2, pp. 350–623.

[17] The text is edited and commented by Ilias Evangelou, 'The Bulgarian Translation of the Vita of St Basil the New According to Manuscript 20 N in the Monastery of Sinai', in *Scripta & e-Scripta*, 7, 2009, pp. 181–251.

[18] Pentkovskaia, in Pentkovskaia, Shchegoleva, Ivanov, *Zhitie*, p. 32.

[19] Vilinskii, *Zhitie sv. Vasiliia,* vol. 2, p. 743.

the Greek version, and the editorial preface in Latin from the *Acta Sanctorum* as its basis.[20] Tereshkina claims that *Acta Sanctorum* were the key source for St Dimitrii's *Menaia* in general.[21] In this case, however, the preface to the text in the *Acta* served Dimitrii as a way to add specific historical details and to gloss places in the topography of Constantinople, mentioned in the work — that is, to recreate (no matter how partially) Byzantine reality for his readers. The introduction to the *Vita* in his version follows the simplicity and matter-of-factness of a typical Synaxarion *vita* and differs from the earlier version. Involved in the delicate task of choosing between the different versions available to him, Dimitrii of Rostov shortened passages, elaborated phrases, simplified the narrative line, but most importantly tried to preserve the authenticity of the spiritual world of St Basil and his followers by underlying the didactic aspects of the text. Dimitrii of Rostov turned this medieval hagiographical classic into a crucial vehicle for expressing both Baroque spirituality and Enlightenment moralism. The cutting of some episodes, the compression of others, and updating the language made the version even more accessible to the broader (growing) eighteenth-century audience, but paradoxically also sharpened the text's animadversions against immoral acts and enhanced its eschatological overtones. Vilinskii accepts A. V. Rystenko's opinion that the 'the *Reading Menaia* of St Dimitrii, immediately on its appearance became "popular consciousness"',[22] but one should add that it was a 'consciousness' suitably imposed, reinvented and promulgated through a new channel — the printed book. The compilation of the full collection of the *Menaia* took St Dimitrii about twenty years (1684–1705), but the volumes were reprinted up to the beginning of the twentieth century,[23] and became widely known not only among the Eastern Slavs, but also in the Balkans.[24]

In the wake of Balkan national revivals in the late eighteenth century, Bulgarian priest Sofronii of Vratsa (1739-1813) produced a version of the *Vita* following very closely Dimitrii of Rostov's text. What

---

[20] Vilinskii, *Zhitie sv. Vasiliia*, vol. 1, pp. 269–70. I have also used the third volume of the 1764 edition of the *Menaia*: Svt. Dimitrii Rostovskii, *Zhitia Sviatykh. Kniga tret'ia. Mart, Aprel', Mai*, 1764 (reprint St Petersburg, 2009) pp. 142–58.

[21] Dar'ia B. Tereshkina, *Chet'i Minei i russkaia slovestnost' novogo vremeni*, Velikii Novgorod, 2015, p. 10.

[22] Rystenko quoted in Vilinskii, *Zhitie sv. Vasiliia*, vol. 1, p. 264. The translation is mine.

[23] Andrei A. Kruming, 'Chet'i Minei sviatogo Dimitriia Rostovskogo: ocherk istorii izdaniia', in *Sviatoi Dimitrii, mitropolit Rostovskii. Filevskie chteniia*, Moscow, 1994, vol. 9, pp. 5–52.

[24] N. Dylevskii, 'Dmitrii Rostovskii i bolgarskoe Vozrozhdenie', in *Issledovaniia po drevnei i novoi literarature*, Leningrad, 1987, pp. 85–90.

Sofronii updated, however, was not just the language of the text. His reworking further indicates a changing attitude to the miracles retold in the narrative: in all versions of the *Vita*, Dimitrii's included, St Basil was thrown into the deep sea by his tormentors, but was safely brought to the shore by two dolphins. There is no mention of the sea creatures in Sofronii's text — St Basil comes back from the sea unaccompanied. Sofronii's adaptation limited the episodes of the *Vita of Basil the Younger* to only a few, thus giving prominence to the part which contained the *Peregrination of Theodora's Soul* through the aerial toll houses. It was precisely this part of the *Vita* that acquired a popularity in the Balkans. Ioakim K"rchovski (Yoakim Karchovski) (*c*.1750–*c*.1820) translated this text into his Western Bulgarian dialect under the title *The Book Named Toll Houses* (*Книга нарыцаемаа Мытарства*). The work was printed in a number of editions between 1814 and 1860.[25] A different early nineteenth-century version of the text is preserved in MS Gaster 1572 in the John Rylands Library, Manchester.[26] It is difficult to establish with certainty whether the work presents a new translation whose author, however, was aware of the existences of at least K"rchovski's and other versions, be they Greek or Slavonic, or whether it is a short compilation retold in the language of its producer. The lexis, and the rendition of specific expressions, however, undoubtedly show a degree of closeness between St Dimitrii's text and the three post-medieval Bulgarian versions.[27]

Some of the substantial changes which St Dimitrii introduced concerned specifically the part of the *Vita* in which saint's disciple, Gregory, met the soul of the recently-deceased servant Theodora, who

[25] There are differences between K"rchovski's editions. In this text the 1860 edition is used: Ioakim K"rchovski, *Kniga narycaemaia Mytarstva*, Belgrade, 1860 >http://www.strumski.com/books/Krchovski_Mitarstva_Belgrad.pdf>. On the 1843 edition see Liubka Nenova, 'Edno izdanie na "Mitarstvata" ot epokhata na B"lgarskoto v"zrazhdane', *B"lgarski ezik i literatura*, 61, 2019, 3, pp. 282–94.

[26] Ralph Cleminson, *The Anne Pennington Catalogue: A Union Catalogue of Cyrillic Manuscripts in British and Irish Collections*, ed. V. Du Feu and W. F. Ryan, London, 1988, p. 204. See the study and edition of the text in A. Angusheva, M. Dimitrova, M. A. Johnson, 'Evergreen Texts and Ever-Changing Language: The Journey of Theodora's Soul in Gaster 1572 from the John Rylands Library, Manchester', *Annual of Saint Kliment Ohridski University of Sofia. Faculty of Slavic Studies*, vol. 105, 2020, pp. 5–42. Eastern Bulgarian dialect features are prevalent in the language of the text. The author expresses her gratitude to the John Rylands Research Institute, University of Manchester, for the Collaboration grant 2019/20 on which the study is based.

[27] I will briefly illustrate this with the following example: The phrase Пріиде гла(с) ѿ велелѣпныѧ славы in Dimitrii is the same in Sofronii, but rendered in K"rchovski as и дойде гласъ ѿ велелѣпïа славы and only orthographically 'updated' in MS Gaster 1571: и дойде гласъ ѿ велелѣшіе славы, while MS Sinai 20N presents a different rendition: приде гла съвыше гла.

disclosed (or rather graphically described) to him the secrets of death, and her journey through the toll houses where the souls were tried for their unconfessed or forgotten sins. The passage through these toll houses (operated by infernal spirits) decides the fate of the souls, either sending them down to Hell, or elevating them to Heaven.[28] The sins are presented in a rising sequence topped not by 'murder' or any other wrongdoing, but by 'heartlessness'. The fourteenth-century South Slavonic translation describes the prince of this toll house as 'entirely cruel and arid and dejected'.[29] In the versions of the *Vita* that predated St Dimitrii's *Menaia* the *telonia* are usually twenty-one in number. Dimitrii reduced them to twenty, and rearranged the sequence of the sins, while still preserving 'heartlessness' at the top.[30]

The story of the peregrination of Theodora's soul substantially differs from other medieval narratives of 'netherworld' journeys and discourses on the spiritual ladder, although it shares with them the conceptualization of the sins and outer space. Unlike the apocryphal visits to Hell, it does not take place in the Inferno, but in the aerial space leading to Heaven. Like the apocryphal journeys of St Peter, St Paul and the Virgin Mary, and beyond Judeo-Christian tradition, the journey of Mohamed, Theodora's *Peregrination* is a descriptive revelatory narrative in which the traveller (in this case her soul) is always accompanied by a supernatural guide. Theodora's soul is supported by angels, and she and her companions move up and up from one *telonion* to another. Illuminated Russian manuscripts from the sixteenth century onwards visually translated this path into a climbing ladder.[31] This should not be confused with the *Scala* of St John Climacus (died *c.*649) which describes the thirty steps of virtue and grace that lead to Heaven. It is a chain of trials, which the soul undergoes, and any of them may doom the soul's path to Paradise. Thus, unlike St Peter, St Paul and

---

[28] The images of the outer world have been discussed at length in studies of Byzantine and Slavonic eschatology. See for instance Veselovskii, 'Razyskaniia', pp. 117–72; V. A. *Sakharov, Eskhatologicheskie sochineniia i skazaniia v drevne-russkoi pis'mennosti i vliianie ikh na narodnye dukhovnye stikhi*, Tula, 1879; Vasileios Marinis, *Death and the Afterlife in Byzantium: The Fate of the Soul in Theology, Liturgy, and Art*, Cambridge, 2017, especially chapter 8.

[29] See the original in Evangelou, 'The Bulgarian Translation', p. 202. The English translation here is mine.

[30] For example excessive drinking and eating, which were tried in different toll houses in earlier versions, were combined by him in one.

[31] See Oleg Iu. Tarasov, *Ikona i blagochestie. Ocherki ikonnogo dela v imperatorskoi Rossii*, Moscow, 1995, p. 115; Aleksei Gudkov, '"Litsa" sudnogo dnia: illiustrovannye rukopisi "Zhitiia Vasiliia Novogo", 2018, https://zen.yandex.ru/media/ruvera/lica-sudnogo-dnia-illiustrirovannye-rukopisi-jitiia-vasiliia-novogo-5ae8305cadof2291ff292ea8 (accessed 1 June 2020).

the Virgin Mary, Theodora's soul is not simply a sympathetic observer, but an active participant, whose fear, horror, anxieties, and reliefs are presented at each step of the journey. It is important to mention that Theodora's soul preserves her gender identity, and in both the Greek and Slavonic versions the grammatical feminine is consistently used to designate it. At the same time — quite typical for the Christian conceptualization of the relationship between the body and the soul — the latter describes its departure from the physical body with both pity and detachment.

Like the apocryphal *Journey of the Virgin in Hell*,[32] yet another Byzantine text that gained popularity in the Slavic context, very few of the sins mentioned in the texts are punishable by civil legal codes (for example, murder and theft); most of them (slander, idleness, envy, vanity) reflect Christian ethics and are subject to punishments prescribed in penitentials. However, the *Journey of the Virgin in Hell* demonstrates more archaic layers than the *Peregrination of Theodora's Soul*, since cannibals, those involved in incestual relations, and people cursed by their parents are among the punished. The *Journey of the Virgin* also focuses on the morals of the clergy (depicting the torments of a priest who sold the church utensils, monks who indulged in bodily temptations, and even priests' widows who remarried). No specific social group is noted in the *Peregrination of Theodora's Soul*, though Theodora is clearly socially profiled in the text — the soul comments that she cannot be reproached for avarice or usury as she possessed no wealth. One could conclude that the *Journey of the Virgin* has not been used by the Byzantine compiler of the *Pergrination of the Theodora's Soul*, and whatever similarities could be established between the two texts, they only reflect the Christian conceptualization of sins and virtues and a common Christian cultural frame.

In my view, the 'inventory' of sins in St Paul's Epistle to the Galatians 5:19–21,[33] served as a canvas for the author of the *Vita* to construct the image of toll houses of sins, although he did not follow the order in which they are listed in the Epistle. Some wrongdoings that appear in the *Peregrination* but are absent in any of the versions of

[32] Milena V. Rozhdestvenska.a, *Khozhdenie Bogoroditsy po mukam. Podgotovka teksta perevod i komentarii. Biblioteka literatury Drevnei Rusi*, Moscow, 1980, vol. 3, http://lib.pushkinskijdom.ru/default.aspx?tabid=4930 (accessed August 2020).

[33] Erwin Nestle, Kurt Aland, *Novum Testamentum Graece*, Stuttgart, 1898 and 1993, p. 501, Gal.5:19–21: φανερὰ δέ ἐστιν τὰ ἔργα τῆς σαρκός, ἅτινά ἐστιν (μοιχεία cf. the variations), πορνεία, ἀκαθαρσία, ἀσέλγεια, εἰδωλολατρεία, φαρμακεία, ἔχθραι, ἔρις, ζῆλος, θυμοί, ἐριθεῖαι, διχοστασίαι, αἱρέσεις, φθόνοι (and also φόνοι – cf the variations on the same page), μέθαι, κῶμοι και τὰ ὅμοια τούτοις.

Galatians 5 could have been added from already-established Christian penitentials. In some instances, the Byzantine writer kept similar sins separately, as they are mentioned in the Epistle, thus indicating their specific meaning and place in Christian perception: for instance, in the Greek text of the *Vita* and in the Slavonic translations from the eleventh and from the fourteenth century there are three toll houses in which sexual indiscretions are tried — the one of adultery (прѣлюбодѣаниѥ[34] — μοιχεία), the second of fornication (блѫдъ/блоудъ — πορνεία), and a third, unlisted in the Epistle, of sodomy. In the oldest preserved Slavonic manuscripts such as the Codices Marianus and Zographensis, and Euchologium Sinaiticum μοιχεία translates прѣлюбодѣаниѥ; in Euchologium блѫдъ also translates πορνεία.[35] I. Khristova-Shomova, who discussed the Slavonic translations of Galatians 5:19, posits that the earliest Slavonic translation rendered the two words (μοιχεία and πορνεία) very similarly прѣлюбодѣаниѥ and любодѣаниѥ, and only from the translations done in Preslav (very late nineth/early tenth centuries) onwards are they differentiated as прѣлюбодѣаниѥ (μοιχεία) and блѫждениѥ, блѫдъ (πορνεία), but as often in the Greek copies of the New Testament texts only one of the two words is retained, and it is difficult to assert which of them was in fact translated.[36] No such confusion could be detected in the early versions of the *Vita*, where блоудъ is consistently rendered πορνεία, and прѣлюбодѣаниѥ (любодѣаниѥ) as μοιχεία. However, their specific connotations might not have been entirely clear, for Dimitrii of Rostov not only put the three sexual sins next to one another in the *Peregrination* narrative, but, unlike other versions, he also presented мытарство блоудьное before прѣлюбодѣаниѥ and described it as любодѣаниѥ [*sic*] which according to him includes all sexual fantasies, inappropriate sexual acts, touching, and so on. The long list of sexual transgressions in his text broaden even further the potential audience of his reworking and make it relevant for lay and monastic communities alike. It is followed by the next toll house, мытарство прѣлюбодѣиное, which penalizes only extra-marital affairs.

The interchanges between the two words/concepts obviously puzzled the copyist of the early nineteenth-century reworking of the text, preserved in MS Gaster 1572, who followed the sequence of the sins

---

[34]   In some copies of the first version, любодѣаниѥ.

[35]   Ralia Tseitlin, R. Vecherka, E. Blagova, *Staroslavianskii slovar' (po rukopisiam X–XI vekov)*, Moscow, 1994, pp. 545 and 93.

[36]   Iskra Khristova-Shomova, 'Nazvaniiata na grekhovete', in *Bog be slovo. Etiudi v"rhu Khristianstvoto prez prizmata na ezika*, Sofia, 2015, pp. 267–79. The *Vita of St Basil the Younger* is not among the texts discussed there.

from the old versions of the *Vita*, and not Dimitrii's order, although, judging from his text, he clearly knew if not Dimitrii's *Menaia* at least its reworking by Sofronii. He felt the need to eschew these terms and to describe one of these sins as an extra-marital affair without using the lexeme прѣлюбодѣіании, and to present the other toll house (possibly of πορνεία, fornication) as a place where the non-wedded lovers are tried, again without applying either of the Slavonic words.

St Dimitrii acted as both admonishing preacher and conceptualizing interpreter when he used the words блоудъ and любодѣіани in Slavonic texts to designate a number of sexual activities and desires, while at the same time giving a narrower, specific meaning to прѣлюбодѣіании. The copyist of MS Gaster 1572 avoided the terminology, but kept the distinction between adultery and fornication, associating each with the status of the individual (married or not). The revisions of Dimitrii of Rostov, of Sofronii (who very closely follows him), and of K"rchovski are the only ones to establish a different hierarchy of sins, and to present adultery as less forgivable than fornication. In his reworking the toll house of 'heresy' (in earlier copies combined with that of idolatry) is moved up on the scale from the fifteenth to the nineteenth toll house, making it the second worse sin, while the station 'magic', traditionally located on the thirteenth place, is moved to the fifteenth toll booth. Perhaps this descending hierarchy of less serious to more serious sins mirrors more closely the Nomocanon, the manual of Church law whose various versions prescribed more severe punishment for sexual transgressions and magic than for other sins, for example usury, and even theft.

The word used to designate magic activities in the *Peregrination* does not add anything new to the repertoire of known Slavic terms, but gives insight into the ways in which the translators accommodated the Byzantine concepts of supernatural practices into the Slavonic linguistic milieu. Thus, the list of the magic activities in the *Peregrination*, no matter how short, offers an opportunity to see how Slavonic translators 'negotiate' the specificity of these terms. According to Pentkovskaia, the oldest East Slavonic translation of the *Vita* stands closer to the Greek version preserved in MS Athous Dionysiou 107, but still differs from it in some places.[37] Therefore it could not have been entirely indicative for the choices or abridgements that the translator and the later copyists might have made, but is still important for understanding how Byzantine concepts were reflected and even reimagined within the new cultural milieu. In MS Athous Dionysiou 107, at the thirteenth toll

---

[37] See Pentkovskaia, Shchegoleva, Ivanov. *Zhitie*, p. 19.

house the following magical agents and activities were listed:[38] ἐπαοιδός — using songs to charm and heal; (as noun) enchanter,[39] φάρμακον — medicine, drug (or φαρμακός — sorcerer, poisoner), μάγος — magician, μαντεῖον — divination, κληδονισμός[40] — omen reading, reception of an omen.[41] According to the early Slavonic translation this toll house is called чародѣиство и̇ потвори, вълхвованї̇е и̇ ѡбавникъ.[42] The word чародѣиство might have been used to render 'charming through singing' (incantation?), as in the extant witnesses from the early period of Slavonic written culture, to which this text belongs; the word чародѣи (spell-caster), related to чародѣиство, translates ἐπαοιδός.[43] In other instances, however, the word translates φαρμακός.[44] The word потвори (pl.) is less frequently used, and is known mainly from Russian sources. It means 'potion', and 'malefic magic'[45] and thus may translate φάρμακον. Other early Slavonic sources translate φαρμακός also as ѡбавникъ,[46] and as чародѣи.[47] The text of the *Peregrination*, however, shows that, although ѡбавникъ most often translates φαρμακός in Slavonic tradition, it may also be used to designate other types of magical agents, as this example suggests. One may wonder whether 'чародѣиство' is used for ἐπαοιδός, or whether the translator was not entirely sure whether the genitive plural φαρμάκων referred to φαρμακός or to φάρμακον and translated it twice as both 'чародѣиство и̇ потвори'. What is, however, clear in both cases, is that the translator associated φάρμακον with poisoning and saw it as an act of magic. In an episode of the *Vita*, preserved in the medieval translations of the *Vita*, but disregarded by Dimitrii, St Basil exposes the abbess who used magic to conjure two monks to satisfy her bodily desires. The text describes her as чародѣица (sorceress).

---

[38] Ibid., *Zhitie*, p. 352: τελῶνιον εὐθύς ὅπερ ἔφασκον εἶναι ἐπαοιδῶν καὶ φαρμάκων, μάγων καὶ μάντ[ε]ων και κληδωνιστῶν.

[39] H. G. Liddell and R. Scott, *Greek–English Lexicon,* Oxford, 1983, pp. 242, 267.

[40] Pentkovskaia, Shchegoleva, Ivanov, *Zhitie,* p. 352: κληδωνιστῶν.

[41] Cf. also κληδόνισμα — omen.

[42] Pentkovskaia, Shchegoleva, Ivanov, *Zhitie,* p. 353.

[43] Cf. the instances from *Codex Supraslienis* given in Tseitlin, Vecherka, Blagova, *Staroslavianskii slovar',* p. 776.

[44] Atanasii Bonchev, *Rechnik na c"rkovnoslavianskiia ezik,* 1966 (reprint 2012), Sofia, vol. 2, p. 329.

[45] Vladimir I. Dal', *Tolkovyi slovar' zhivogo velikorusskogo iazyka,* St Petersburg, 1883, 2nd edn, vol. 3, p. 365, https://dal.slovaronline.com/; Cf. also A. Bonchev, *Rechnik,* p. 49: потворникъ – μάγος, φαρμακεύς.

[46] Tseitlin, Vecherka, Blagova, *Staroslavianskii slovar',* p. 390, point to the rendition of Psalm 57:6. On its visual representation see Ryan, *The Bathhouse at Midnight,* p. 84.

[47] Khristova-Shomova, 'Nazvaniiata na grekhovete', pp. 205, 207, Liljana Makarijoska, *Leksikata od oblasta na istorijata na medicinata.* Skopije, 2011, p. 116. These two studies, however, do not mention the passage in the *Vita*.

St Basil performed a silent pantomime in front of the nuns putting breadcrumbs in a glass to demonstrate how she enchanted the monks.

The word вълхвование translates both μαγεία and φαρμακεία in the early sources such as the *Codex Supraslienis*, and designates magic activities in general, with вльхвъ (often translating Greek μάγος), being one of the most frequently applied Slavonic terms for sorcerer and wizard,[48] and attested in early translations of the Gospel text.[49] In an episode of the *Vita*, St Basil himself is seen as a wizard (вльхвъ) by the ignorant soldiers, who were surprised to see no trace on him of the torture he had undergone in prison the day before. The text exploits a cliché of the early Christian martyrdoms but resolves it somewhat differently. While in the earlier texts the miraculous healing of the martyrs usually prompts the soldiers to convert to Christianity, which would be somewhat anachronistic for the tenth-century Byzantine context, the miracle in the *Vita* contributes to the first perception of the saint as an enemy and the Other.

Unlike the earlier Slavonic translation of the text, in the second, South Slavonic rendition of the *Vita*, which is based on a different Greek text, only two terms are attested: обаіанїе и отравленїе' (enchanting and poisoning) which possibly render ἐπαοιδός and φάρμακον.[50]

The rework of Dimitrii presents the most extensive account of the toll house of 'wБaанïе и чьродъанïе' (spell-casting and enchantment) where 'wБaанïе магïи wтравленïе, шепотwвь и призованïе демонwвъ' (spell-casting, magic, poisoning, whispers, and conjuration of demons)[51] are dealt with. The bishop of Rostov updated the terminology using the Greek word магïа, following the South Slavonic rendition of poisoning with отравленïе, but his version is far from a direct translation of the text. The presence of шепоты (whispers) is not surprising: whispers were broadly used as signs in predictions in Antiquity and in later periods. It suffices to mention the rustling of the oak leaves at the oracle of Dodona, or post-medieval Russian and Balkan folk tradition of guessing the name of a future spouse according to a voice heard in dream or at the moment of awakening, or most importantly the long list

---

[48] See Ryan, *The Bathhouse at Midnight*, pp. 70–72.

[49] Iskra Khristova-Shomova, *Sluzhebniiat Apostol v slavianskata traditsiia*, Sofia, 2004, p. 496 posits that both коренитьць and влъхвъ are known from the early Slavonic translation of the New Testament, with коренитьць probably indicating the Cyrillo-Methodian translation, and being replaced as less known with влъхвъ already in the early period of Slavonic written tradition.

[50] Evangelou, 'The Bulgarian Translation'. p. 199: обааниıа и wтравленïıа; Vilinskii, *Zhitie sv. Vasiliia*, vol. 1, p. 644: wзаания и wтравленïıа.

[51] Vilinskii, *Zhitie sv. Vasilija*, vol. 1, p. 965.

of divinatory practices mentioned in the East Slavic indices of forbidden books, expanded in the sixteenth century.[52] They include divinations by noises of birds and animals, house and fire creaks. Dimitrii might have had in mind not only κληδόνισμα (an omen), but also a word related to it — κληδών (an omen, a rumour, a calling) in his rendition. It is unclear whether the 'conjuring of demons' was mentioned in a possible Greek source used by Dimitrii, or whether he tried to bring to the attention of his readers a magic strongly condemned by the Church — a practice, which became more popular from the fifteenth century onwards.[53] Thus, he did not simply translate the Greek text, but renewed its content and addressed the growing concerns of the Christian authorities.

This tendency to revamp the tenth-century hagiographic text in order to approach contemporary issues is even more pronounced in the two early nineteenth-century texts of the *Peregrination of Theodora's Soul*. According to MS Gaster 1572 in this toll house are tried 'those who visited the diviners (local healers) and engage in divining (healing) and enchanting, and were calling the devil for help'.[54] The text employs the word врачь (and the related verb врачувам), attested in the medieval sources, which initially meant 'a healer, a physician'. In modern Bulgarian it obtained a specific (negative) connotation of a wiseman, a local healer engaged in pagan practices, divining and healing through incantation and magic. Dimitrii, K"rchovski and MS Gaster 1572 mention the evocation of the evil powers (devil in the later cases). K"rchovski further reiterates 'poisoning' and 'whispers' attested in Dimitrii, but presents even the whispers as generated by the devil. According to his version, the toll house of magicians is a place 'where the fairies (sorceresses) and witches and [the one] who visit them and who divine, and call devils and the poisoning and the whispering of the devil are tried'.[55] Unlike all

---

[52] Ryan, *The Bathhouse at Midnight*, pp. 139–44.

[53] See for instance the growing number of manuscripts containing instructions for evocation and conjuring evil spirits in Europe from the fifteenth century onwards: Samuel Liddell MacGregor Mathers, *The Key of Solomon the King (Clavicula Salomonis): Now First Translated and Edited from Ancient MS in the British Museum*, London, 1889; Chester Charlton McCown, *The Testament of Solomon Edited from Manuscripts at Mount Athos, Bologna, Holkham Hall, Jerusalem, London, Milan, Paris and Vienna*, Leipzig, 1922; Richard Kieckhefer, *Forbidden Rites. A Necromancer's Manual of the Fifteenth Century*, Stroud, 1998; *The Magical Treatise of Solomon or Hygromanteia*, ed. and trans. Ioannis Marathakis, Singapore, 2011.

[54] MS Gaster 1572, p. 20: Тамо испытваха които ходили по врачовы, и си врачували, и баели, и викали діавола на помощъ. (The translations from Gaster and K"rchovski are mine.)

[55] K"rchovski, *Kniga narycaemaia Mytarstva*, 1860, p. 33: 'дека тражатъ самовили [in the original самоволи] и баснарицы и кой вражалъ и викалъ діаволи и тровенѣ и шепотенѣ на діавола.'

other compilers, K"rchovski talks about women-sorceresses, using local designations for them ('самовили и баснарицы'). The two words are also attested in the number of sermons against witches and sorceresses, produced by a monk from Rila Monastery, Iosif Bradati (*c.*1714–died sometime after 1758). No term used in the Byzantine texts of the *Vita* and the Slavonic translations specifically indicates magic activities done by women, which may further prove the influence of the Iosif's sermons on K"rchovski's reworking of the *Peregrination*.

One further detail, missing in the earlier medieval copies and in Dimitrii, is that both K"rchovski's text and MS Gaster 1572 speak of the practitioners of magic, as well as of those who seek their help. This directly relates the texts to a post-medieval image, 'The visit to the witch', known from a number of Bulgarian churches from the eighteenth and nineteenth centuries. Based on ideas expressed in Iosif's sermons, these images vividly admonished those who asked the local witches for a cure about the eternal condemnations that awaited them. Through translations of a sort, K"rchovski's text and MS Gaster 1572 engaged in more complex intertextual, intermedial relations with works produced in their cultural milieu.

Starting with St Dimitrii's reworking of the *Peregrination of Theodora's Soul*, the later works demonstrate a clear attempt to follow less the Byzantine versions, and to interact more with contemporary texts, images and ideas. The medieval Slavonic translators of the text might have struggled to find the precise parallels of the Greek terms for magic agents and activities but were still able to convey to their readers its admonitions. Compared with them, the works of the later compilers showed a long and intricate process of cultural shifts and linguistic changes. In this process, however, St Dimitrii of Rostov has a special place — both continuer of the old and inventor of the new tradition.

Peter the Great as a Comparative Lawyer

William E. Butler

Pennsylvania State University; University College London

RULERS, especially monarchs, may be given less than their due as original legislators; that is, as the actual draughters of legislative acts. The historical image is that of a monarch served by countless advisers and specialists who comply with every whim and produce legislative texts for general discussion or merely signature and promulgation. The actual involvement of the monarch in the legislative process is rarely explored in its own right, the more so from the perspective of legislative history — the sources consulted for inspiration, ideas, precedents, examples, norms or formulations to avoid as well as to emulate.

Rare is the legislator who wants or needs to 're-invent the wheel' — to prepare draft legislation, especially fundamental enactments or large codes, without learning from the lessons of the past. Even rarer is the monarch who was intellectually inclined to become personally engaged in law-creative activity from beginning to final product. Lessons from the past are to be gleaned not only from the experience of one's own realm, but from the experience of others — historical and contemporary. Catherine the Great (reigned 1762–96) was an unusual example, for she early in her rule undertook to prepare her celebrated *Nakaz* — one of the few cases of a ruler who earned the encomium 'Great' for her contributions to law and personally produced the primary text of the draft enactment. Civilian historians tend to deprecate the originality of her contribution in the belief that she 'copied' or 'compiled' her text from the works and ideas of others. Catherine's interest in foreign law extended to Sir William Blackstone (1723–80),[1] the first volume of whose *Commentaries* she had Semen Efimovich Desnitskii (c.1740–89) translate and whose entire work in its French translation she acquired, read, and annotated.[2]

Anyone who has undertaken to prepare draft legislation quickly apprehends that the originality of the enactment lies in the symmetry and restructuring of earlier endeavours complemented by new and

---

[1] Marc Raeff, 'The Empress and the Vinerian Professor: Catherine II's Projects of Government Reforms and Blackstone's *Commentaries*', *Oxford Slavonic Papers*, new series, 7, 1974, p. 39.
[2] W. E. Butler, 'Catherine the Great, William Blackstone, and Comparative Law', in Eric Bylander, Anna J. Cornell and Jakob Ragnwaldh (eds), *Forward! Bnepeð! Formåt!: Essays in Honour of Prof Dr Kaj Hobér*, Uppsala, 2019, pp. 43–56.

sometimes highly technical adjustments. What is omitted can be as revealing as what is included. The sequence of draft provisions may fundamentally alter their meaning or the underlying concept. Words matter, but so do punctuation, paragraphing, division into sections, chapters, articles, and the like. 'Legislative technique' (*zakonodatel'naia tekhnika*) is a world of its own.

Although the intellectual process of 'comparison' inheres in any legislative drafting exercise, that term most commonly means recourse to 'foreign' and 'international' law — the legislation of foreign jurisdictions, judicial practice, doctrinal writings, or international treaties and customs. The recent publication of the candidate dissertation written but not completed by Nikolai Alekseevich Voskresenskii (1889–1948),[3] coupled with his collection (also uncompleted) of early Petrine legislation,[4] offers a view of the role of Peter the Great, under-appreciated in legal circles, as a comparative lawyer.

To categorize Tsar Peter as a comparative jurist requires a brief explanation. It has long been known that Russia in the person of the Emperor was interested in foreign legislation and collected or consulted the same. Missing from this scenario of Russian law-making has been a full understanding of how extensive and systematic this activity was and how the fruits of collecting such material contributed to the development of Russian law. These were not exceptional examples; they were routine, an integral part of the Russian legislative process. Peter the Great played an active role, indeed initiated, directed, evaluated, encouraged, and insisted upon that process.

There are no professional requirements to be satisfied in order to become a comparative or international lawyer: no Bar, no obligatory professional association, no legal education. Comparative law is not a body of substantive law — it is the application of the comparative method to the study of law and legal institutions; in its practical or applied dimension, it is the study of law and legal institutions for the purpose of drafting new law or reforming existing law by looking to other legal systems for experience, models, and/or lessons. The law of nations is a separate legal system whose principal subjects are states. Peter the Great will have learned something of natural law and Russian

---

[3] N. A. Voskresenskii, *Petr Velikii kak zakonodatel': issledovanie zakonodatel'nogo protsessa v Rossii v epokhu reform pervoi chetverti XVIII veka*, ed. D. O. Serov, Moscow, 2017. Also see the thoughtful review by M. G. Murav'eva in *Vivliofika: E-Journal of Eighteenth-Century Russian Studies*, 7, 2019, pp. 128–33.

[4] N. A. Voskresenskii, *Zakonodatel'nye akty Petra I: redaktsii i proekty zakonov, zametki, doklady, donosheniia, chelobit'ia i inostrannye istochniki*, Leningrad, 1945, vol. 1. Volumes 2 and 3 appeared in 2020 under the editorship of E. V. Anisimov and D. O. Serov; volume four was unfinished by Voskresenskii.

law, including the law of nations, from his tutors. He brought to that field an intellect, an openness to comparison, a curiosity and interest, and a common sense rarely encountered among rulers.

The archives confirm that Peter the Great was not a passive lawmaker who signed that which his associates produced by way of legislative text. Often he was the initiator of edicts which he issued, supervised their drafting or undertook to draft himself, sometimes being the sole author.[5] His role as supreme legislator he appreciated and esteemed; later in life he wrote of his role in drafting legislation, noting with respect to the 1722 Naval Statute that he 'began in 1720' and completed his work in '1722, working twice a day, in the morning and the evening at various times'.[6]

Assembling Comparative Legal Material
Peter I had an intense, one might say insatiable, interest in collecting the raw materials for comparative legal work. Although studies existed, and had done for centuries, comparing the laws of different jurisdictions, not least comparisons of national or local law (English, Germanic, Italian, Hebraic, and others) with Roman law, the emergence of comparative law as a discipline lay decades ahead. Whatever Russia was to do along these lines would have to be improvised without the benefit of guidance from the science of comparative law.

Procuring examples of foreign legislation was a first step. Several approaches were pursued simultaneously: (a) the purchase or acquisition otherwise of foreign legislative acts or collections of legislation; (b) the translation into Russian or other accessible language (mainly German) of foreign legislative acts; (c) the recollection from memory by foreign personnel recruited to work in Russia of the texts of foreign legislation with which they had reason to be familiar; (d) the preparation of diplomatic reports by Russian ministers or residents abroad that incorporated information on customs, practices, or administrative regulations; (e) the knowledge of foreign diplomatic personnel or other foreigners in Russia; (f) using foreign legislation when preparing Russian draft legislation. These were not passing interests or methods, although some fields of legislation at certain times received more attention than others. The acquisition of material was systematic, comprehensive, constant, apparently reasonably well-financed, and undertaken with future as well as present needs in mind:

[5] Voskresenskii, *Petr Velikii kak zakonodatel'*, p. 113.
[6] Cited in ibid., p. 113, from the Cabinet of Peter the Great, otd. 1, kniga 62, l. 830. Peter similarly claimed authorship in 1716 of the Military Statute.

(a) *The Purchase or Acquisition otherwise of Foreign Legislative Acts or Collections of Legislation*

Peter's reforms, whatever may have generated reformist ideas in his mind, the legislative materials suggest, were contemplated in advance rather than merely visceral reactions to events. If the assembly of relevant legislative materials is a legitimate guide, Peter often thought five or more years ahead. Voskresenskii suggests that once Peter had an idea for some sort of transformation, he began to collect relevant materials. His diplomats abroad would be so instructed, and on occasion he would send agents especially for this purpose.

Sweden was at the forefront of administrative reforms in Europe during the Petrine era. When Peter thought that the Great Northern War might be coming to a close, he wrote in 1715 to Ivan Iur'evich Trubetskoi (1667–1750), a Russian prisoner of war in Sweden who enjoyed considerable freedom, to send books dealing with laws, rights, and reforms at all levels in Sweden, preferably in Latin but, if not, then in whatever language they happened to be published.[7]

A similar request was made to the Russian ambassador in Denmark, Vasilii Lukich Dolgorukov (1670–1739), on 12 September 1715, to send to St Petersburg a list of Danish laws, including civil and military legislation and statutes on the state colleges (central government departments).[8] This request and follow-up queries give evidence of a comparative instinct for primary sources. Not one book would suffice because no single book addressed everything; Peter the Great was interested in all that was germane to his inquiry.

Some requests were secret instructions to his agents, who were not merely to acquire printed material but to gather information on how legislative enactments operated in practice or were supplemented by local customs, practices, and rules. In comparative legal terms, Peter was interested in both the 'law in books' and in the 'law in action'.

(b) *The Translation into Russian or other accessible Language (mainly German) of Foreign Legislative Acts*

Acquiring legislative texts was merely the first step. As they were in foreign languages, Peter instructed that they were to be translated

---

[7] Voskresenskii, *Zakonodatel'nye akty Petra I*, vol. 1, p. 50, 'Edict of Peter I to Prince Trubetskoi on Sending the Complete Collection of Laws of the Swedish State, and also Notes of Practice Based on Customs', undated, in Peter's own hand, without signature and date.

[8] Ibid., vol. 1, p. 44. Written and dated in Peter's own hand, without signature. Although the Tsar preferred printed texts of the Danish materials, he was prepared to accept manuscript versions; the Danish legislation was of interest because Peter I had heard that the Swedes had borrowed some of their reforms from it.

into Russian or, if that was too arduous, then into Latin or German. He issued an edict to this effect in 1717, directing that the legislative acts of the strongest naval powers be acquired and translated into Russian, especially English, Dutch, and French. The task of translation, he said, should be undertaken by 'Russian officers who had a command of English'.[9]

French maritime legislation was instructed by the Tsar to be translated from 1713 onwards. Konon Nikitich Zotov (1690–1742) was assigned the task to translate first the *Ordonnance de Louis XIV, Roy de France et de Navarre. Donné à Fontainebleau au mois d'Août 1681. Touchant la Marine.* A year later Peter directed Zotov to translate the *Ordonnance de Louis XIV pour les Armées Navales et Arsenaux de Marine* (Paris, 1689). Zotov's journal noted the day on which the translation was undertaken: 11 September 1714.[10]

Other foreign legislation known to have been translated under Peter and at his direction included the 1683 Swedish Military Statute (which was among the sources used for the 1716 Russian Military Statute); Swedish legislation on local self-government (also used when preparing Russian local governmental reforms); the 1700 Danish Instruction on the Law of War; the 1672 Dutch Instruction on Shipping; the Swedish Naval Statute.[11]

(c) *The Recollection from Memory by Foreign Personnel Recruited to Work in Russia of the Texts of Foreign Legislation with which they had Reason to be Familiar*

The origins of the 1720 Naval Statute date to 1669, when Captain D. Butler, a Dutchman in Russian service, wrote down from memory and had translated into Russian key articles from the Dutch naval disciplinary regulations of 17 September 1662. His version was retained in the Ambassadorial Chancellery (*Posol'skii prikaz*) together with Russian translations of the 1688 Dutch regulations and English regulations of 1692. Peter the Great drew upon these virtually verbatim when crafting his regulations of 1706, 1710 and, finally, 1720.[12]

---

[9] Voskresenskii, *Petr Velikii kak zakonodatel'*, p. 114.

[10] The attribution of the translation of the *Ordonnance* to Zotov was first noted in P. P. Pekarskii, *Nauka i literatura v Rossii pri Petre Velikom*, 2 vols, St Petersburg, 1862, 2, p. 351.

[11] Voskresenskii, *Petr Velikii kak zakonodatel'*, p. 123.

[12] See P. A. Krotov, 'Ob ispol'zovanii gollandskogo voenno-morskogo zakondatel'stva pri razrabotke ustavnykh polozhenii rossiiskogo flota vo vtoroi polovine XVII – pervoi chetverti XVIII veka', in *Istochnikovedenie: poiski i nakhodki*, Voronezh, 2000, pp. 120–30.

(d) *The Preparation of Diplomatic Reports by Russian Ministers or Residents abroad that incorporated Information on Customs, Practices, or Administrative Regulations*

In his instructions to Prince Trubetskoi in Stockholm during 1715, Peter asked for data on the entire administrative structure, the system of ranks and titles, and the like — 'in a word, the entire establishment of the Swedish State' from the lowly peasant and soldier up to the Senate, including local customs. This type of instruction became routine for Russian diplomats abroad and was a 'targeted' instruction — the Tsar wanted this data for immediate needs, not mere curiosity.

In the case of Denmark, Peter directed his diplomats to report on the state administrative offices, personnel structure, salaries, ranks, and the like — details which he required 'without delay'. When written laws were not available, manuscript versions (copies) were requested, and accounts of customs as reflective of administrative practices, including local government.

(e) *The Knowledge of Foreign Diplomatic Personnel or other Foreigners in Russia*

Foreign envoys in Moscow or St Petersburg were a source of help in obtaining and/or explaining foreign legislation. Danish legislation on the 'right of salute', as explained by a Danish vice-admiral sent to Russia, Just Juel (1664–1715), influenced the drafting of naval regulations in Russia.[13] The French ambassador to Russia from 1721 to 1726, Jacques de Campredon (1672–1749), was asked to explain the functions of a 'state secretary' — a rank and title included in the Table of Ranks.

(f) *Using Foreign Legislation when preparing Russian Draft Legislation*

Systematization and codification were among the objectives Peter pursued as part of his legislative reforms, including a possible revision of the 1649 *Ulozhenie* (Law Code). To this end he appointed law reform commissions, which produced little of consequence. Nonetheless, the Tsar directed them to have regard to foreign legislation. On 9 December 1719 Peter issued an edict to the commission for the composition of a new *ulozhenie* to be guided by translations of laws on estates from Estland and Lifland 'because they are similar' and have the same manner of possession as in Russia.[14]

---

[13] See W. E. Butler, 'Imperial Russian Maritime Legislation: 1803/1817', *Jus Gentium: Journal of International Legal History*, 4, 2019, pp. 179–90.

[14] Voskresenskii, *Zakonodatel'nye akty Petra I*, vol. 1, p. 74.

Because the Russian members of the Commission were not able to
read German, the estate laws of Estland and Lifland were translated
into Russian and circulated to Commission members.[15]

When Peter I considered Russian legislation on orphans, he drew
upon Swedish laws but also gave attention to Estland and Lifland
enactments.[16] If Peter did not have foreign legislative texts available or
was uncertain whether they existed, orders would be given to search
for the relevant item. Manuscript sources indicate, for example,
that Peter wondered whether foreign laws existed on the subject of
whaling and instructed that a search be undertaken.[17]

It would appear that Peter the Great's interest in foreign law was
long-standing in duration and catholic in subject matter. Civil, family,
administrative, criminal, maritime, and military law were significant
domains of interest, but so too was religion. On 16 January 1723 Feofan
Prokopovich (1681–1736) informed the Senate that Peter the Great
had issued an oral edict to collect Roman, Lutheran, and Calvinist
catechisms and other church books and translate and print them in the
Slavic dialect. On the same day it was reported to the Senate that much
of the translation had already been completed.[18]

The earliest indication of Peter's interest in foreign law dates to 3 July
1699, when General Adam van der Weyde (1667–1720) sent to Peter the
Great a draft military statute for consideration.[19] Ten days later Count
James David Miles Bruce (1669–1735), in Russian service, sent to Peter I
at his prior request a concise description of Scottish, English, and French
laws on heirs and English legislative materials on ranks and titles used
in England during wartime and peacetime. Some years later Peter I
returned to the issue of inheritance and drew upon the Bruce materials,
but wished to update them. For this purpose he sought the original texts
of 'French, English, and Venetian rules', the Venetian rules having been
supplied by Petr Vasil'evich Postnikov (1676–1716) from Italy. If the texts
could not be found in the Ambassadorial Chancellery, foreigners in
Moscow were to be asked if they could supply the texts. The texts were
to be immediately translated into Russian. Episodic interest in foreign
inheritance law on the part of the Tsar continued until 1714, when Peter
the Great himself drafted a law on the issue.[20]

---

[15] Ibid., p. 84.
[16] Voskresenskii, *Petr Velikii kak zakonodatel'*, p. 120.
[17] Ibid.
[18] Ibid., p. 121.
[19] See *Voinskii ustav, sostavlennyi i posviashchennyi Petru Velikomu Generalom Veide,
v 1698 godu*, St Petersburg, 1841.
[20] Lindsey Hughes, *Russia in the Age of Peter the Great*, New Haven, CT, and

When the Emperor and Russian administrative institutions prepared the draft Table of Ranks, the archives disclose that they had numerous foreign examples in translation at their disposal: the Danish enactment of 11 February 1717; the Swedish enactment of 21 February 1696; the Prussian enactment of 15 April 1705; and relevant enactments from England, France, Saxony, Venice and Poland — all held in the Archive of the Russian Ministry of Foreign Affairs together with the tables based on them.[21]

Organization of Translations
Given how directly involved Peter the Great was in commissioning, supervising, editing, and arranging the publication of translations, we dwell briefly on how this task was organized. The initiator of translations was the Tsar himself. He relied upon Aleksei Vasil'evich Makarov (c.1675–1740), the Cabinet Secretary, to oversee the execution of orders to produce translations. Most clerical work and correspondence relating to translations flowed through Makarov. For translations Peter the Great appears initially to have relied upon Adam Weyde and James Bruce, as noted above, that is upon foreigners. Bruce first translated English ranks in the artillery and then in the armed forces in general. When he became head of the Artillery Chancellery, it became a major centre of translation operations. Bruce purchased foreign laws and supervised their translation, usually into Russian, but sometimes into German. The flow of books was so substantial that Bruce's chancellery and the cabinet secretary could not cope.

Andrei Andreevich Vinius (1641–1716) was involved either in supervising legal translations and/or undertaking some himself. Peter the Great wrote to the Senate in 1712: 'When the bearer of this letter, Iakov Veselovskii, appears, then direct him to be with Andrei Vinius to assist in the translation of the laws of other states.'[22] Ivan Tamesz (Tamesh), a Dutch merchant, on 4 August 1720 sent to Peter the Great his completed translation of a book on the British Admiralty, noting his tardiness in completing the work by reason of the difficult terminology.[23]

London, 1998, pp. 176–77.
   [21] These are reproduced as an Annex in Voskresenskii, *Zakonodatel'nye akty Petra I*, vols 2–3, pp. 89–118.
   [22] Quoted in Voskresenskii, *Petr Velikii kak zakonodatel'*, p. 127. On Vinius, see I. N. Iurkin, *Andrei Andreevich Vinius (1641–1716)*, Moscow, 2007, pp. 427–28, for details of his translation of a work on military justice.
   [23] Tamesh had a bookplate, probably engraved in Europe but conceivably in Russia. See W. E. Butler, 'Portrait of a Bookplate: "John James" or "Ivan Temesh"', *Bookplate International*, 2, 1995, pp. 222–24.

Peter the Great recruited Heinrich Claus von Fick (1678–1750) to assist with his administrative reforms and the introduction of colleges to replace the former *prikazy*.[24] Translations of relevant foreign legislation which he obtained from Sweden were among Fick's tasks. Some translators found the legal terminology too daunting and were unable to complete translations commissioned by the Tsar, particularly from the Swedish. Fick proposed an acceptable, albeit temporary, solution: translate from Swedish into German, and then find individuals in Russia who were capable of working from German into Russian — an easier task. In 1718 Fick was appointed by the Tsar to 'watch over translations from foreign sources', assisting Weyde and Bruce in this undertaking.

Fick had administrative experience and some knowledge of Swedish and other European legislation, but little if any knowledge of the Russian language. He could administer the translation activity generally and offer advice, which he undertook; the translations themselves were referred to the state colleges by instruction of the Senate on behalf of the Tsar. Once the colleges were formed, the posts of translators were established and qualified individuals sought more systematically. If a lengthy law needed to be translated, it was divided into parts, circulated to colleges, and several translators became involved. Among those involved was Sigismund Adam Wolf, originally of Swedish origin; he had served in the Dorpat Landgericht as a judge, became a Russian subject in 1704, and from 1718 translated Swedish normative legal acts in the chancery of the Senate, later becoming a counsellor in and vice-president of the College of Justice.

Given that several translators worked on a single large text, often they signed the parts which they undertook. Differences in terminology and style were discussed and corrections made. An editor would sometimes be appointed to resolve issues that arose. Often college assessors or vice presidents took on this role. Ernst Friedrich Krompein (1670–1734), for example, who read law at the Universities of Jena and Leipzig, worked as an *advokat* in Reval, entered Russian service in 1710, and from 1720 to 1723 was an assessor in the College of Justice; he acted as 'editor' of a translation of Swedish revenue legislation.

Usefulness of Comparative Legal Material
The evidence is overwhelming that Peter the Great in his capacity as legislator found the foreign legal materials generally of immense use, although to be sure some will have been more germane than others

---

[24] Hughes, *Russia in the Age of Peter the Great*, 1998, p. 117.

to preparing draft edicts or to shaping his thinking about legislative change. There is no evidence that he was troubled about inspiration from common law or other continental jurisdictions. Both legal families seem to have been regarded as appropriate sources of investigation, adaptation, borrowing, or inspiration. Peter seems to have relied upon positive written foreign laws. He did not appoint outside foreign legal advisers as such, although he did consult from time to time with foreigners in his service, foreign diplomatic personnel, merchants, and others about specific legal matters, whether to ask for assistance in supplying foreign legal texts or seeking a point of clarification on legal customs or behaviour. But obtaining legal advice from others appears to have been uncommon, and so far as the record discloses, for information rather than how to act in a particular situation.

The translations were mostly full texts, not excerpts or abstracts, of foreign enactments. Peter was interested in doctrinal writings, but it remains unclear to what extent these may have influenced him or those who served him. Accessions to his own library and to the private libraries of senior officials such as James Bruce, Robert Erskine, P. P. Shafirov, A. A. Vinius, and others contain titles of doctrinal works, some of which were translated (for example, Samuel von Pufendorf, Abraham de Wicquefort) and published; others remained in manuscript (Hugo Grotius). Above all, however, Peter was interested in primary sources, the written law in its statutory forms — not summaries, abstracts, excerpts, copies and the like. He was not overly dependent on the perceptions of others as to what was important in the text of a law; he had complete freedom of choice about what might be best suited to his ideas. It was he who determined what would be useful in foreign legislation.

One outcome was that the translation of a law on a specific topic, such as the law of the sea, might influence other legislation unrelated to that topic. The *Ordonnance* of Louis XIV, for example, in its Russian translation influenced Petrine approaches to organizing state control over administrative and management of affairs, including military hospitals, the syllabus for theological institutions, and others.

Of greater import, however, was the impact of foreign legislation on the Tsar from the standpoint of forming a comparative legal consciousness. He was deeply, not casually, involved in all aspects of 'research' on foreign law precisely because this was central to his thinking about societal reform and modernization. Can it be said that Peter the Great was among those who thought conceptually, or theoretically, however crudely, about the elements of comparison as such? This is not something to be exaggerated. But assuming no formal training in matters legal (which seems to be the case except for whatever his tutors may have taught him) and little reading among foreign works that might have inclined him in this direction, we are left with the proposition that close attention to the content of foreign law contributed to Peter's world-view, his intellectual horizons, his command of legislative drafting, and his perceptions of what course his country should be following. As Voskresenskii observed: 'With the study of foreign laws, Peter matured, became more independent, more profoundly perceptive, and more skilful in lawmaking.'[25]

*   *   *

Although recourse to foreign law in Petrine Russia has its place in Petrine studies, there are larger implications for the field of comparative law. The origins of the discipline of comparative law have traditionally been dated from the 1830s and developments in France,[26] although a recent convincing analysis moves those origins to the 1750s.[27] Petrine Russia may be an early, if not the earliest, example of the ruler of a European jurisdiction employing the comparative method on a massive scale, at his initiative and under his personal direction, to use foreign law as the principal catalyst and vehicle for modernizing the statute book and undertaking fundamental legal reforms.

The principal elements of the comparative method are in evidence: description, generalization, analysis.[28] Peter the Great devoted immense energy and resources to collecting the primary sources of foreign law and arranged for their translation into Russian, either directly or through an intermediate language. He commenced that process at least as early as 1699 and it continued until his death. It may be no exaggeration to say that the investigation and translation of foreign legislation was a primary vehicle of the transformations of the Russian Empire.

The Tsar was clever in using diplomatic, commercial, academic, and other channels to amass the texts of legislation for consideration. Sometimes he instructed the acquisition of specific texts; on other occasions he gave a standing instruction for any relevant material. His diplomats and agents, sometimes incognito and sometimes specially

[25] Voskresenskii, *Petr Velikii kak zakonodatel'*, p. 124.

[26] H. C. Gutteridge, *Comparative Law*, rev. edn, Cambridge, 1949.

[27] O. V. Kresin, *Comparative Legal Studies: 1750 to 1835: Approaches to Conceptualization*, ed. and trans. W. E. Butler, 2 vols, London, 2019.

[28] See G. Samuel, *An Introduction to Comparative Law Theory and Method*, London, 2014; M. Siems, *Comparative Law*, 2nd edn, Cambridge, 2018; Uwe Kischel, *Comparative Law*, Oxford, 2019.

sent for this purpose, would have haunted the bookshops and printing houses seeking new material or rumours of materials in process. Antiquarian books were required, as were new publications. Of the agents assigned to acquire items, the names Konon Zotov among Russians and Heinrich Fick among foreigners appear in the archives with frequency. Zotov purchased primarily naval items, and Fick civil legislation broadly understood.

The Petrine archives indicate that land and naval military materials were sought in quantity, including: enactments from all the leading powers; rich materials relevant to the Table of Ranks; civil legislation, especially on inheritance, family, property, and commercial relations; enactments regulating religious matters — legislation determining the legal status of rival or foreign professions of faith.

Although sometimes legislation was sought with urgency, most seems to have been assembled over a lengthy period, indicating that the Tsar was thinking ahead about possible reforms and, insofar as military campaigns permitted, reflecting on what might and should be undertaken. Comparative legal thinking, in other words, was not visceral and reactive, as a rule. It was based not on individual examples of foreign jurisdictions, but a substantial selection of continental and common law countries. Periods of assembling materials for five years or more in advance of reforms were not uncommon.

Peter the Great played the dominant role in commanding the acquisition of items, initiating or commissioning their translation into Russian or another language, supervising, editing, revising, criticizing, and determining whether to publish a translation, sometimes with his own preface, introduction, or annotation. He chose the translators and the supervisors thereof, determined the deadlines for completion of the work, watched over progress made, and could be suitably annoyed when deadlines were not met. He would comment on choice of terminology, was known to translate a chapter or so himself as guidance, improve style of exposition, and, when ordering publication, took an interest in the physical appearance of the publication — illustration, type design, binding, and print run.

In the absence of qualified Russians, he first turned to unqualified foreigners whose knowledge of Russian was rudimentary to produce translations. Strenuous efforts were made to train young Russians of promise and ability to translate — which in principle should have resulted in better Russian texts. It would be an exaggeration to say no expense was spared, but the resources expended on legal and other translation were substantial. The management of translations usually came from the Cabinet of Peter the Great in the person of A. V. Makarov and/or prior to the introduction of state colleges, from the Artillery Chancellery under the direction of A. A. Vinius and James Bruce. Once the state colleges had been formed, most legal enactments were translated by translators employed therein, sometimes on a shared basis, under the direction of the college vice presidents, who were foreigners. The Holy Synod undertook some translation assignments.

The Tsar did not appear to play favourites among the European jurisdictions whose legislation was of potential interest to him. Large powers or small, modernizing or not, Peter the Great's quests for legal information were comprehensive rather than selective. Once he had settled on a topic of interest, he wanted to acquire all available materials. The Russians became knowledgeable about the structures, procedures, and legal rules in their European neighbours and will have enhanced the continuing formation of a Russian legal consciousness. The translation and publication of legislative acts transformed the vocabulary of Russian law as substantial numbers of calques found their way into the Russian legal vocabulary.

The Petrine reception of European legal concepts, rules, and terminology occurred at two levels. The discourse above emphasizes the active borrowing and adaptation of domestic legal models from the internal legal systems of European countries. But simultaneously Russia was coming to be recognized as a fully-fledged European power subject to the law of nations; Russia absorbed more actively and comprehensively the concepts, rules, and terminology of the international legal system — a system of which Russia was a constituent part and whose terminology began to be absorbed in its eighteenth-century manifestations.[29]

The evidence would appear to support the proposition that in the world of comparative law Peter the Great is among the rarefied group of rulers (another does not come to mind) who took a leading personal role in the adaptation and transplantation of foreign legal rules in his own country, that he did so by design and with considerable skill over a quarter century, and that his comparative legal ventures embodied much of the essence of transformation that he brought to Russia. Peter the Great may legitimately be called an early Russian comparatist in the field of law.

---

[29] W. E. Butler, 'Vklad P. P. Shafirova v nauku mezhdunarodnogo prava', in P. P. Shafirov, *Rassuzhdenie, kakie zakonnye prichiny Petr I, tsar' i povelitel' vserossiiskii, k nachatiiu voiny protiv Karla XII, korolia shvedskogo, v 1700 imel: Adaptirovannyi tekst. Fragmenty originaly. Kommentarii*, Moscow, 2016, pp. 203–45.

TRAVEL, TECHNOLOGY AND EXPLORATION

The Transition to 'Enlightenment Exploration': Russian Expeditions to Siberia and the Far East in the Late Seventeenth and Early Eighteenth Centuries

Denis J. B. Shaw
University of Birmingham

'I have often heard the Czar say, that he intends to send people on purpose to take a true map of his country, as soon as he has peace and leisure to apply his mind to it.'
John Perry, 1716

PETER THE GREAT never did in fact manage 'to take a true map of his country'. But the range of his geographical endeavours was considerable, extending well beyond mapping into surveying, navigation, regional survey, statistics, geographical education, the translation and publishing of geographical literature and exploration.[1] Since Will Ryan is a distinguished vice-president and former president of the Hakluyt Society, a body devoted to the scholarly publication of 'records of voyages, travels and other geographical materials', it is entirely appropriate that a Festschrift in his honour should include a consideration of the question of how far the process of exploration in Russia changed during Peter's reign.

Peter's interest in geography stemmed not only from curiosity about the extent of his realm and the place it occupied in the world. Like other European rulers of his day, he was keen to construct an inventory of his country's territories, survey and defend its frontiers, assess its wealth including its natural resources, determine its overland, riverine and maritime routes, and achieve a series of similar practical objectives. In the spirit of the Hakluyt Society, this paper focuses on geographical exploration as one method he employed to achieve such goals.

Peter was of course by no means the first Russian ruler to launch exploratory journeys. Surveying the numerous accounts of Russian travels in the sixteenth and seventeenth centuries, N. I. Prokof'ev divided them into four types.[2] Firstly there was the literature associated

---

[1] Denis J. B. Shaw, 'Geographical Practice and its Significance in Peter the Great's Russia', *Journal of Historical Geography*, 22, 1996, pp. 160–76.
[2] N. I. Prokof'ev, 'Vvedenie' in *Zapiski russkikh puteshestvennikov XVI–XVII vekov*, Moscow, 1988, pp. 5–20.

228   *Denis J. B. Shaw*

with pilgrimage which was the only kind of travel literature between the twelfth and fourteenth centuries. Then, in the first half of the fifteenth century, there began the literature of secular journeys (principally concerned with commercially-oriented journeys into foreign lands), of which *The Journey beyond Three Seas* (1466–72) by Afanasii Nikitin is regarded as exemplary.[3] In the sixteenth century appeared the first official reports and accounts of ambassadors, primarily concerned with diplomatic relations and discussions but often containing descriptions of journeys undertaken and of the landscapes and peoples encountered. Finally came the official reports of travellers and explorers. It is with the latter two types of travel account that the present paper is concerned.

That Peter was a modernizer, keen to introduce to his realm the scientific, technical and cultural advances he had witnessed in the Western European countries to which he journeyed, requires no emphasis. Pre-Petrine Russia knew little or nothing of modern science and education, lacked universities, had few schools and the population was largely illiterate. Peter began the long process of rectifying this process, establishing schools and some institutions of a mainly technical and naval orientation, hiring foreign scholars, and translating and publishing text books.[4] The Tsar's educational and scientific policies culminated in his founding of the Academy of Sciences in 1725.[5]

Peter's modernizing policies extended into the realm of geography. The travels and expeditions which took place before Peter were of a traditional kind, lacking in precision in either observation or reporting, with a reliance on serendipity and usually small in scale. In Western Europe expeditions of this kind had long been the norm, Christopher Columbus' celebrated voyage to the Americas in 1492 being perhaps the most memorable.[6]

Over time, however, new approaches to the process of exploration were adopted. Such approaches, which Charles Withers has termed 'Enlightenment exploration', were gradually introduced to European

---

[3] For a recent edition see A. N. Nikitin, *Khozhdenie za tri moria: 1466–1472*, Kaliningrad, 2004.

[4] See, for example, the account of the Mathematical and Navigation School in W. F. Ryan, 'Peter the Great and English Maritime Technology', in Lindsey Hughes (ed.), *Peter the Great and the West: New Perspectives*, London, 2001, pp. 130–58.

[5] Lindsey Hughes, *Russia in the Age of Peter the Great*, New Haven, CT, and London, 1998, pp. 298–331.

[6] For more on early modern European exploration and territorial expansion, see Klaus A. Vogel, 'Cosmography', in Katharine Park and Lorraine Daston (eds), *The Cambridge History of Science*, vol. 3, *Early Modern Science*, Cambridge, 2006, pp. 469–96; and Klaus A. Vogel, 'European Expansion and Self-Definition', in ibid., pp. 818–39.

expeditions from the late seventeenth century.[7] For Withers, the European Enlightenment was the period 'when the world was made modern'[8] — conventionally coinciding with the 'long' eighteenth century (c.1685–c.1815).[9] Scientifically and geographically, Enlightenment exploration 'sought to bring the globe under the sovereignty of science'.[10] In other words, unlike earlier expeditions, those which occurred in this period moved towards reliance on stricter and what we might call scientific methods of observation and recording. Often this involved accurate measurement and calculation using scientific instruments, the collection of samples and specimens in the field, systematic sorting and analysis of what was discovered, and ultimately attempts at theoretical explanation. Withers' description of Enlightenment exploration also includes other features relating to the size, composition and organization of Enlightenment expeditions. These are matters, however, that will be given only brief consideration here.

The central question for this paper is to consider to what extent the Petrine period in Russia witnessed the introduction of Enlightenment exploration practices. Three expeditions conducted shortly before and during the reign will be examined. The three are those of Nikolai Spafarii (1675–78) which took place just before the reign, Vladimir Atlasov (1697–99) which occurred soon after its beginning, and Daniel Messerschmidt (1720–27) which happened at its end. All were directed towards Siberia, the Russian Far East and China, the main direction of Russian exploratory activity in the period. The expeditions will be examined chronologically to assess how far they appear to conform to the notion of 'Enlightenment exploration'.

The Spafarii Expedition (1675–78)

The Spafarii expedition took place just a few years prior to the official beginning of Peter's reign. Essentially an ambassadorial journey, it seems a typical, if sophisticated, example of pre-Petrine exploration.

Nikolai Milesku Spafarii (Spafarius, Spathari) (1636–1708) was born into a noble family in Moldavia.[11] He received a broad education in languages, philosophy and humanities at the Greek Patriarchal School in Constantinople before embarking on a career as an administrator,

---

[7] Charles W. J. Withers, *Placing the Enlightenment: Thinking Geographically about the Age of Reason*, Chicago, IL, 2007, p. 88.

[8] Ibid., p. 1.

[9] Ibid.

[10] Ibid., p. 88.

[11] A. Kizel' and V. Solov'ev, 'Vvedenie: Nikolai Milesku Spafarii (1636–1708)', in *Nikolai Milesku Spafarii: Sibir' i Kitai*, Kishinev, 1960, pp. 3–18.

soldier and diplomat and travelling to several European countries in consequence. In 1671 Spafarii was sent by Patriarch Dositheos of Jerusalem to Moscow in connection with the Russian Church schism and to strengthen ties between the Eastern churches generally. In Moscow, under the protection of Artamon Matveev, head of the Ambassadorsial Chancellery,[12] Spafarii was appointed translator in that department, no doubt a reflection of his learning and linguistic abilities.

It was in connection with Moscow's wish to strengthen trade relations with China, and with armed clashes between Russian Cossacks and the Chinese which had occurred along the as yet ill-defined Russo–Chinese border, that Spafarii was ordered to lead an embassy to China in 1675. As was usual in such cases, Spafarii was issued by the Ambassadorial Chancellery with a set of instructions prior to his departure. The major aim was clearly to establish friendly relations with the Chinese emperor which presumably included the settlement of frontier disputes and the securing of trade relations.[13] Spafarii was also instructed to compose a detailed account of the Chinese state. More germane to our enquiry, however, is the fact that the ambassador was commanded to discover the best route to China, whether by river or overland, and to provide a full description of his journey to the Chinese border. The latter was to include all towns and settlements along the route, including the distances between them, details about the indigenous peoples living there, whether they were peaceful and whether they served the tsar,[14] and also information about Russia's new domains beyond Lake Baikal and along the Amur. Furthermore, he was to provide a comprehensive map of the region. All this is testimony to the Russian government's limited knowledge of Siberia's geography and concern to verify earlier accounts.

In order to ease his task, the ambassador was provided with various aids, including copies or summaries of earlier travel accounts including that of Fedor Baikov (1654–58),[15] and various scientific equipment including astronomical instruments and a compass.[16] He may also have

---

[12] *Posol'skii prikaz*, the department of state responsible for foreign affairs.

[13] *Nikolai Milesku Spafarii*, pp. 134–35.

[14] In other words, whether they paid the fur tribute (*iasak*), a tax imposed upon many of the Siberian native peoples, or served him in some other capacity.

[15] Baikov travelled to China in the role of ambassador, composing a detailed account of his journey. See N. F. Demidova and V. S. Miasnikov (eds), *Pervye russkie diplomaty v Kitae*, Moscow, 1966, pp. 113–45.

[16] N. M. Spafarii, *Opisanie pervyia chasti vselennyia imenuemoi Azii, v nei zhe sostoit Kitaiskoe gosudarstvo s prochimi ego gorody i provintsii*, Kazan', 1910, p. xii; D. M. Lebedev, *Geografiia v Rossii v XVII veke (dopetrovskoi epokhi)*, Moscow and

had access to some Russian and foreign sources, including the Godunov map of Siberia (1667). It has been suggested that, during his month-long stay in Tobol'sk, the chief city of Siberia, in April 1675, Spafarii sought the advice of Iurii Krizhanich.[17] Krizhanich, a Croatian Catholic who was living in exile in Tobol'sk at the time, was author of an important geographical account of Siberia written in Latin.[18]

Spafarii left Moscow in early spring, 1675, arriving in Tobol'sk on 30 March. He left the latter on 2 May, accompanied by an entourage of 150 people, including a military escort. He reached Nerchinsk, close to the disputed border with China, on 4 December, subsequently proceeding to Peking (now Beijing), the Chinese capital. He returned to Moscow on 5 January 1678. Among the texts he submitted to the government on his return were a detailed description of the Chinese state, and a journal of his journey from Tobol'sk to the Chinese border. The latter was published by the Russian Geographical Society in 1882.[19] In addition he submitted an official ambassador's report (*stateinii spisok*) on the course of his diplomatic mission.[20]

Spafarii's journal is often referred to as a road or route book (*dorozhnik*), but in fact it is far more than that. It does give an account of the route he took and the dates he arrived at and left significant points. Other than the fact that he carried details of the routes taken by earlier travellers and no doubt acted on the advice of others, including perhaps that of Krizhanich, we cannot know why he took the particular route he did. On the road between Lake Baikal and Nerchinsk, moreover, he tells us that he passed through places 'where formerly no-one had been' — his exact route is uncertain.[21] In fulfilment of the instructions he had received, Spafarii gives many topographical and ethnographical details of the phenomena he encountered including the mountains, rivers, tributaries, lakes, forests, the populated places and peoples he saw or met with, and details of the precise distances (in either *versty*

Leningrad, 1949, p. 129. For Russian scientific instruments in this period, see W. F. Ryan, 'Scientific Instruments in Russia from the Middle Ages to Peter the Great', *Annals of Science*, 48, 1991, pp. 367–84.

[17] Kizel' and Solov'ev, 'Vvedenie', p. 10.

[18] This is known as *Historia de Sibiria*. See A. A. Titov, *Sibir' v XVII veke: sbornik starinnykh russkikh statei o Sibiri i prilezhashchikh k nei zemliakh*, Moscow, 1890 pp. 161–216. The term 'historia' or 'history' here means 'survey' or 'account'.

[19] 'Puteshestvie chrez Sibir' ot Tobol'ska do Nerchinska i granits Kitaia, russkogo poslannika Nikolaia Spafariia v 1675g. Dorozhnyi dnevnik s vvediem i primechaniiami Iu. V. Arsen'eva', *Zapiski IRGO po otdeleniiu etnografii*, vol. 10, vyp. 1, St Petersburg, 1882.

[20] *Nikolai Milesku Spafarii*, pp. 289–506.

[21] Kizel' and Solov'ev, 'Vvedenie', p. 11.

or travel days) between points along his route. Furthermore, his account is interspersed with detailed discussions of some of Siberia's major geographical features such as the 'celebrated' river Irtysh, with a discussion of its course, the origins of its name, its major tributaries and the distances between confluences, together with other particulars. Somewhat similar treatment is accorded the river Ob' and Lake Baikal, with less detailed discussions of other geographical features. A striking point is that Spafarii's account ranges far beyond the regions which he himself had visited, drawing on earlier accounts, material taken from European geographies, and probably information provided by other intermediaries. According to Arsen'ev, Spafarii's report was used by the Russian authorities to correct the Godunov map of Siberia and formed a basis for the later cartographic work of Semen Remezov.[22]

Spafarii's journal provides a vivid description of his journey across Siberia and added considerably to geographical knowledge. But it displays little evidence of the disciplined, systematic approach discussed by Withers. His journey was essentially an ambassadorial one in which science played at best a secondary role. It had few if any of the characteristics of 'Enlightenment exploration'.

The Atlasov Expedition (1697–99)[23]

Unlike Spafarii, Atlasov seems unlikely to have had any kind of higher education and was almost certainly without any European experience. He was born in the early 1660s but his birthplace is uncertain.[24] He appears to have served for many years as a *iasak* collector in Siberia and was then appointed commander of the fort of Anadyr' (*Anadyrskii ostrog*) close to the Pacific coast in 1695. Two years later Atlasov was sent with a large party of servitors and hunters on the tsar's service 'for the finding of new lands and for the bringing of new, non-*iasak*-paying peoples under the high hand of the great autocratic sovereign'.[25] Having some knowledge of the existence of the Kamchatka peninsula brought by earlier explorers, he proceeded down its full length along

---

[22] 'Puteshestvie chrez Sibir', pp. 3–4. S. U. Remezov, the Siberian cartographer, produced what Valerie Kivelson calls 'a dazzling corpus of cartographic material' relating to Siberia from the 1690s onwards. See Valerie Kivelson, *Cartographies of Tsardom*, Ithaca, NY, 2006, p. 21.

[23] I am grateful to Professor James R. Gibson for his advice on this section.

[24] Some sources suggest Velikii Ustiug in north European Russia.

[25] 'Skaski Vladimira Atlasova o puteshestvii na Kamchatku', in *Zapiski russkikh puteshestvennikov XVI–XVII vekov*, Moscow, 1988, pp. 415–28 and 506–09 (p. 415). See also L. S. Berg, *Otkrytie Kamchatki i Kamchatskie ekspeditsii Beringa*, Moscow and Petrograd, 1924.

its west coast but with diversions to the Pacific side and to the valley of the river Kamchatka which runs south–north through the peninsula's south–central part before entering the ocean. In the course of his adventures, Atlasov met local Koriak, Kamchadal (Itel'meny) and Kuril' (Ainu) peoples, imposing the *iasak* and engaging in armed clashes, even extending to the occasional massacre. He returned to Anadyr' in 1699, proceeding to Iakutsk along with his booty where he gave his first oral report, written down in 1700. He was then ordered to Moscow where he gave a second oral report in the Siberian Chancellery (*Sibirskii prikaz*)[26] in February 1701. The latter formed the basis of the written report examined here.

Atlasov's report is rather unsystematic, which is perhaps what one might expect of an oral account. As far as we know, unlike Spafarii and other ambassadors, he was issued with no list of instructions prior to his departure but his report, which is quite comprehensive, does suggest that it is based on the answers he gave to quite specific questions. The report focuses on people rather than on the physical geography, though in one or two places he discusses aspects of the latter. With reference to Kamchatka's celebrated volcanoes, for example, he tells us that:

> [...] travelling up along the Kamchatka river for a week, there is a mountain, shaped like a stack of grain, exceedingly great and high, and another nearby, like a haystack and also very high; and from it by day smoke can be seen, and by night sparks and a fiery glow, and the Kamchadals say that if a man ascends half way up that mountain and hears a great noise and thunder, he can hardly endure it. And whoever ascends higher does not return, and what becomes of him is unknown.[27]

Likewise Atlasov comments on the climate: he tells us that in winter it is warmer in Kamchatka than in Moscow, and there is less snow in the Kurils. Kamchatka has twice as much sunshine in the winter than Iakutsk whilst in the Kurils in summer, he claims, the sun is directly overhead and casts no shadow. Equally, however, the summers are rainy and there are many storms. He also speaks of the freezing of the ocean in winter: in the Bering Sea, for example, in the Aleutian Strait northeast of the coast of Kamchatka there is ice in winter though the ocean as a whole does not freeze. Ice may come and go close to the coast, but there is no ice in the open ocean. On the river Penzhina side (that is, on

[26] The Siberian Chancellery was the department of state overseeing Siberian affairs.
[27] *Zapiski russkikh puteshestvennikov*, p. 425.

the Sea of Okhotsk side) of the peninsula, the sea freezes in winter but to no great depth.

In talking of the natives, Atlasov has much to say about the animals and plants upon which they depended. Naturally, much is said of the sable, the most valuable of the fur-bearing animals. Kamchatka was particularly rich in sables.[28] Atlasov, however, tells us that, though the native peoples have bows, spears, knives and axes (their iron being acquired through trade), they do not catch sables[29] but live on fish and clothe themselves with fox furs. Moreover, according to our informant, between the river Kolyma and Anadyr' is an 'unavoidable' or 'impassable' (*neobkhodimoi*) cape (*nos*) and the Chukchi people who live near this cape and at the mouth of the Anadyr' river say that opposite this cape is an 'island' from where, in winter as the sea freezes, come 'foreigners' (*inozemtsy*) speaking their own language and bringing poor-quality sable 'like polecats'. It seems possible that the cape referred to is Cape Dezhnev and the 'island' a part of Alaska, populated by Eskimos.[30] In another reference to the sable, we are told that far beyond the Kamchadals live the Kuril' (Ainu) people whose lands are warmer than Kamchatka and, as a result, their sables are of poorer quality.

Marine fauna, including fish, naturally formed a very important part of the diet and domestic resources of the indigenous peoples. Whales and pinnipeds (seals) are referred to, the whales commonly killed on the beaches where they were often stranded at high tide.[31] Many marine fish are said by Atlasov to enter Kamchatka's rivers including various types of salmon unfamiliar to the Russians. Kamchatka's rivers were also rich in riverine fish and numerous mammals came to catch them, including sables, foxes and otters. Other animals mentioned include beavers, bears and wolves. In Kamchatka Atlasov and his men ate venison, whilst reindeer were also used for transportation, either saddled and ridden, or attached to sledges in winter. Seabirds including ducks, gulls and swans were also to be seen. Among the flora listed are various berries (whortleberry, honeysuckle), wild garlic, an edible sweet grass and nuts. Trees noted, some of which were used for food, include

---

[28] See James R. Gibson, *Feeding the Russian Fur Trade: Provisionment of the Okhotsk Seaboard and the Kamchatka Peninsula*, Madison, WI, 1969, pp. 9–10.

[29] This seems to have been true of some parts of Kamchatka: see D. M. Lebedev, *Geografiia v Rossii Petrovskogo vremeni*, Moscow and Leningrad, 1950, pp. 43–44.

[30] The island might also have been St Lawrence Island. The editor suggests the Alaska Peninsula, but this seems too far to the south-east.

[31] The stranded animals may also have included Steller's sea cow, a sirenian which seems to have become extinct by about 1768.

cedar, birch, larch and fir on the Pacific coast and birch and aspen on the west coast.

Atlasov's rich ethnographic descriptions cover many facets of the lives and cultures of the indigenes: their appearance and clothing, their tools, equipment and weapons, their livelihoods including their modes of hunting and gathering, their ways of travelling (overland, principally using reindeer but also by sea — using large often two-masted wooden boats (*busy*) or umiaks (*baidary*) made from sealskins sewn together on wooden frames — and their religions (time and again Atlasov tells us that the indigenes have no religion but do have shamans). Other matters discussed included the indigenes' means of warfare, their housing — the winter quarters of the Kamchadals were called *yurtas* (timbered and thatched dugouts) and the summer residences *balagans* (thatched pyramidal huts elevated on piles),[32] — cooking methods and trade (trade between the Ainu and the Japanese, we are told, furnished the former with valuable crockery and garments made from Chinese fabrics such as cotton and silk). In summary, despite its many inaccuracies and incomplete descriptions,[33] Atlasov's is a remarkably interesting discussion for its time.

For neither Spafarii nor Atlasov was regional description their primary task. The former had diplomatic duties to attend to; the latter was primarily engaged in bringing the indigenes under the tsar's 'high hand'. Both greatly extended geographical understanding but lacked the 'reliance on stricter methods of observation and recording' and the other practices which characterize Withers' definition of 'Enlightenment exploration'. This began to change during the course of Peter's reign.

The Messerschmidt Expedition (1720–27)
Whilst other eastern expeditions of Peter's reign, such as those of Evert Ysbrant Ides to China (1692–95) and the geodesic expedition of F. Luzhin and I. Evreinov to the Kurils (1719–22) displayed growing evidence of mathematical and instrumental precision,[34] arguably the most significant expedition of Peter the Great's reign was that of

---

[32] Gibson, *Feeding the Russian Fur Trade*, p. 39.
[33] Compare Atlasov's discussion, for example, with that in Gibson, *Feeding the Russian Fur Trade*, pp. 50–56, though the latter mainly concerns a later period.
[34] For example, the Luzhin-Evreinov expedition was commissioned to find out whether there was a land connection between Asia and America and undertook a precise astronomically-based survey of parts of the Pacific coast. See O. A. Aleksandrovskaia, *Stanovlenie geograficheskoi nauki v Rossii v XVIII veke*, Moscow, 1989, p. 40.

the German naturalist and scholar, Daniel Gottlieb Messerschmidt
(1720–27). Lebedev describes this as a 'genuinely scientific expedition'
whilst Novlianskaia states that Messerschmidt 'was the first scholar
to undertake a scientific study of Siberia'.[35] Such assertions, of course,
assume that the term 'scientific' has a clear and uncontentious meaning
when applied to the eighteenth century. However, this is far from being
the case. John Pickstone has broken down the concept of science into a
series of elements, or 'ways of knowing'.[36] According to him, the period
considered by this chapter was dominated in science by the 'way of
knowing' which he terms 'natural history'. Natural history 'is about
knowing the world, about describing and collecting, identifying and
classifying, utilising and displaying; it is about the "notebook" cultures
of men and women who love to "take note" of their surroundings'.[37] In
other words, it is about knowing what is in the world and is the kind
of science which predominated prior to the rise of the more specialized
analytical sciences from the early nineteenth century. This section
will argue that this is the realm to which Messerschmidt's endeavours
belong and that they can therefore be justly labelled 'scientific', meeting
many if not all of the criteria specified by Withers.

Messerschmidt was born in September 1685 in the Polish city of
Danzig (Gdańsk) where his father was in Polish service. He began
studying medicine at university in Jena in 1706.[38] Two years later he
moved to Halle where he continued his studies of medicine together
with zoology, botany and eastern languages. At this time the University
of Halle was well known for its interests in natural history and linguistic
specialisms and was a centre for Russian and other eastern studies.[39] It
was also noted for Protestant pietism,[40] propounded by such influential
scholar theologians as A. H. Francke who was ambitious to proselytize

---

[35] Lebedev, *Geografiia v Rossii petrovskogo vremeni*, p. 77; M. G. Novlianskaia,
Daniil Gotlib Messershmidt i ego raboty po issledovaniiu Sibiri, Leningrad, 1970, p. 5.

[36] John V. Pickstone, *Ways of Knowing: A New History of Science, Technology and
Medicine*, Manchester, 2000.

[37] Ibid., p. 60.

[38] For details of Messerschmidt's life and activities, see W. Steinitz and A. V. Topčiev,
'Einleitung', in E. Winter and N. A. Figurovskii (eds), *Daniil Gotlib Messersmidt,
Forschungsreise durch Sibirien (1720–1727)*, Berlin, part 1, 1962; part 2, 1964 (part 1, pp.
1–20); Novlianskaia, *Daniil Gotlib Messershmidt*; and E. Winter, *Nauchnoe issledovanie
Sibiri v petrovskoe vremia. Semiletniaia nauchnaia ekspeditsiia D. G. Messershmidta v
Sibir' (1720–1727)*, Moscow, 1971, pp. 3–14.

[39] E. Winter, 'Halle als Ausgangspunkt der deutschen Russlandkunde im 18.
Jahrhundert', *Veröffentlichungen des Instituts für Slawistik*, no. 2, Berlin, 1953.

[40] Pietism was a religious reform movement which took root among German
Lutherans in the seventeenth century in protest against the perceived formalism of the
official Church.

the east. Messerschmidt came under pietistic influence whilst at Halle, a fact which was to colour the rest of his life. Graduating doctor of medicine in 1713, he returned to his home city of Danzig where he practised as a physician but also continued his studies in natural history and classical languages, including Hebrew.

In 1716, on his way to visit Western Europe for the second time, Tsar Peter stayed in Danzig where he met the naturalist J. P. Breyne, an acquaintance of Messerschmidt. As always Peter was keen to recruit local specialists to work in Russia and it seems likely that Breyne recommended Messerschmidt as someone well qualified to study the resources and environment of Siberia. Messerschmidt entered Russian service from the beginning of 1718 and arrived in St Petersburg later in the same year where he signed a contract with the Apothecaries' Chancellery[41] to undertake a scientific expedition to Siberia. The Tsar's decree of November 1718 specified that the expedition, now overseen by the Apothecaries' Chancellery, was to be principally concerned with the collection of medicinal herbs, seeds and similar medical resources.[42] It soon became clear that Messerschmidt's own ambitions encompassed an even wider spectrum of interests, including extending his studies into China. But the latter proposal was refused by the Tsar on the grounds that Messerschmidt's task was to research Russian territory and resources rather than those of other realms. Contrary to the assertions of some scholars, it seems unlikely that Messerschmidt was provided with exact instructions. Even his route across Siberia and his timetable seem to have been left to his discretion.[43]

Foreign visitors to Russia have long been aware of the bureaucratic difficulties which are likely to beset their endeavours. The same was true in the eighteenth century. Thus Messerschmidt's departure for Russia was delayed by problems in securing the necessary documentation and his initial pay, and he was met by similar problems in St Petersburg. Hence he arrived in Moscow only in March 1719, and here he was further delayed by tortuous negotiations with the Siberian Chancellery which lasted until September. He arrived in Tobol'sk towards the end

[41] The Apothecaries' or Pharmacy Chancellery (*Aptekarskii prikaz*) was the department of state responsible for medical matters.

[42] Novlianskaia, *Daniil Gotlib Messershmidt*, p. 10. In typical eighteenth-century encyclopaedic style, he was also instructed to study the land, natural history and its components, the Siberian nation and its philology, monuments and other antiquities and other 'strange and interesting items'. See A. te Heesen, 'Boxes in Nature', *Studies in the History and Philosophy of Science*, 31, 2000, 3, pp. 381–403 (p. 381); P. S. Pallas, 'Nachricht von D. Gottlieb Messerschmidts siebenjährige Reise nach Sibirien', *Neue Nordische Beyträge*, 3, 1782, pp. 97–107.

[43] Novlianskaia, *Daniil Gotlib Messerschmidt*, pp. 13–14.

of December only to suffer a further hold-up until March 1721. The problems here seem to have included securing the necessary supplies, equipment and men, and also the documentation needed to ensure that his journey across Siberia would be facilitated rather than hindered by local officials. A bonus for Messerschmidt, however, was the presence in Tobol'sk of a group of Swedish prisoners of war,[44] most notably Philipp Johann von Strahlenberg (also known as Tabbert), an educated soldier who had spent his captivity studying the environment of the local area. He was able to advise Messerschmidt about Siberian nature, accompanied him for the first part of his expedition, and eventually played a key role in publicising his scientific work.

Leaving Tobol'sk at the beginning of March 1721, and eventually accompanied by only a handful of servants and a cook, Messerschmidt proceeded to Tomsk just east of the river Ob' and then to Krasnoiarsk on the river Enisei. His journey then took him on a somewhat circuitous route through the Saian mountains and then north down the Enisei to Turukhansk and from there up the lower Tunguska and across the watershed to the upper Lena, eventually reaching Irkutsk near Lake Baikal. Crossing the lake, the expedition continued to Chita and eventually arrived at Nerchinsk near the Chinese border in July 1724. Messerschmidt's return journey began almost immediately (he had been ordered to return in 1723) but, having accidentally strayed into Chinese territory, he was detained a short while (meanwhile making a study of the Mongolian language) before being allowed to resume his itinerary. The return journey took a somewhat more direct route across Siberia. Messerschmidt finally arrived back in St Petersburg towards the end of March 1727.

Driven no doubt by his pietistic ethic, Messerschmidt fulfilled an enormous programme of study during his seven-year expedition. This encompassed not only the collection of 'rarities and medicinal herbs' envisaged in Peter's original 1718 decree, but also many other things: collections and descriptions of many types of plant, classified according to the then current systems (notably that of the French botanist J. P. de Tournefort), descriptions and classifications of fauna, collections and an attempted classification of minerals, reports on weather, the locations of places and routes, many drawings of flora, fauna, antiquities, indigenous peoples and their habitations, many maps, histories and archives relating to local peoples, accounts and discussions of their languages and ways of life, incidences of disease, and much else. During the journey, Messerschmidt sent regular reports to St Petersburg and

---

[44] The Great Northern War against Sweden lasted from 1700 until 1721.

collections of materials were boxed up and sent back to the authorities. St Petersburg thus acquired an enormous amount of both written and material evidence on the geography of its eastern territories, more than could easily be processed at the time. Unfortunately, much was lost during a fire in the Academy of Sciences in 1747. Part of the written archive survived, however, and is housed in the Russian Academy of Sciences archive in St Petersburg.

One of the most important artefacts of the Messerschmidt expedition is his travel journal, a daily diary which he kept religiously throughout his journey recording his activities and his observations of nature and of the people he encountered. This has been published only relatively recently.[45] A few extracts will give an impression of the rich contents of this work, so much more informative than the accounts of Spafarii and Atlasov discussed earlier. Thus on the road between Tobol'sk and Tara, on the first day of March 1721, Messerschmidt met a Tatar hunter who described the eagles to be found locally:

This hunter also named three types of eagle to be found in these parts: the first and biggest is called the Burkut, which is bigger than a Calicut cock, pitch-black except that on the wings and tail it is somewhat grey; but when it is old it is mainly grey behind; the beak is also pitch-black, round and crooked, the skin over the nostrils lemon yellow as are also the feet; the eyes are brilliant and black. It stays mainly in high mountains or very dark forests; at times some are seen and found hereabouts near the town of Tara.[46]

Over a year later on 4 May 1722 in Krasnoiarsk, Messerschmidt reported on the fish to be found in the vicinity:

Because fish are quite rare hereabouts, I can only report that we have eaten two kinds which are caught in the Enisei (though not often), namely the Kusch and the Kargus. The first is quite like herring and is delicate enough; the other, however, is at least two or three times as big and fat and not as pointed in the head, yet its flesh is very tasty and sweet. There is also said to be a type of very big fish caught in the Enisei, which the Tatars and Russians call Taiming which is said to be like salmon but not as red. However, because, I myself have not yet seen one, and they are seldom to be had, I can report on it in the future.[47]

[45] Winter and Figurovskii (eds), *Daniil Gotlib Messersmidt*.
[46] Ibid., part 1, p. 41.
[47] Ibid., part 1, p. 213.

As well as reporting on plants and animals, the doctor frequently commented on the landscapes through which he passed. Thus, on 16 March 1721, he wrote:

> We thus went from here at 11 o'clock midday. The road went now south-east, now somewhat more to the south, and we saw along the way to the side some small fir or spruce bushes, which are very rare in this steppe for during a three- or four-day journey one can see only birch trees thinly scattered here and there and very seldom thick and dense birch forest. Along this road we passed many bogs and small lakes.[48]

A fascinating study of Messerschmidt's working methods has been provided by Anke te Heesen through a detailed analysis of his travel journal and also of the reports and other materials he sent back to the capital.[49] In the journal Messerschmidt described not only the principal events of each day with observations and comments concerning both people and nature, but also minutiae such as his detailed activities in recording, analysing, storing and conserving his materials. A painstaking examination of this source thus enables a reconstruction of his scientific activity, 'a precise reconstruction of his daily routines, practices and collection activities'.[50] According to te Heesen, Messerschmidt used two main instruments for collecting data and physical objects which she terms 'organizing material principles for his fieldwork':[51] firstly written lists and notes, and secondly boxes and cases. He followed the empirical and systematic methods which were typical for the period, recording everything 'worthy of mention' and then arranging his notes in a systematic way (for example, according to discipline — geography, philology, archaeology, mineralogy, botany, zoology, medicine and so on) and gradually working towards systematic catalogues, classifications and indices. The chronological nature of his fieldwork meant that his note-taking and recording had to be done in an open-ended way, so that addenda, modifications and corrections could be made as he went along. The collection of material objects and samples proceeded in a similar manner, with initial collection in the field followed by careful systematic sorting and organization and then storage using elaborate containers and cases, with recording and cataloguing as this proceeded. All the materials collected also needed to be conserved, often involving resorting, cleaning and careful repacking.

[48] Ibid., p. 62.
[49] A. te Heesen, 'Boxes in Nature'.
[50] Ibid., p. 382.
[51] Ibid., p. 381.

In summary, the overall goal was to provide an 'account book of nature' accompanied by a systematic set of collected samples taken from the field.[52] In this way the German doctor tried to make sense of the vast amount of data he collected and to enable its further analysis into the future.

Messerschmidt, having been educated at the University of Halle, imported European research methods into Russia. His was Russia's first expedition to have an avowedly scientific (or, to use Pickstone's term, 'natural-historical') and ethnographic purpose, to study Siberia's environment and peoples, rather than science being merely an adjunct to some other principal goal, be this diplomatic, commercial or other. That said, many European expeditions at this time were characterized by a multiplicity of purposes.[53] Although 'science' was clearly Messerschmidt's main purpose, the apparent absence of clearly-specified instructions to guide him, even regarding the route to be taken, may strike the modern reader as oddly deficient, signifying a 'pre-scientific' rather than a scientific character to the expedition. However, as Carey has argued, this is because of our modern conception of science as a strictly-planned activity. In an earlier period, when there were inevitable problems in identifying and classifying objects, it was problematic to issue strict scientific instructions since what was there to be studied or collected was partly unknown. In principle everything 'of note', including human beings as natural-historical objects in their own right, was of interest to the traveller, and the character of science itself changed in response to new discoveries made in the field rather than the field merely serving as a place where scientific hypotheses might be confirmed or disproved.[54] Furthermore the rigorous way in which Messerschmidt listed and catalogued the data and objects he collected suggest a disciplined, scientific approach to his studies rather than that of a mere dilettante. The contention that Messerschmidt's expedition was Russia's first scientific expedition therefore has much to commend it.

The collections which Messerschmidt made during his expedition were an important feature which distinguished his work from that

[52] Ibid., p. 392.

[53] D. Carey, 'Compiling Nature's History: Travellers and Travel Narratives in the Early Royal Society', *Annals of Science*, 54, 1997, 3, pp. 269–92; Katharine Anderson, 'Natural History and the Scientific Voyage', in H. A. Curry, N. Jardine, J. A. Secord and E. C. Spary (eds), *Worlds of Natural History*, Cambridge, 2018, pp. 304–18 (pp. 304–05).

[54] For more on the historical relationship between the field and science, see the essays in Jeremy Vetter (ed.), *Knowing Global Environments: New Historical Perspectives on the Field Sciences*, New Brunswick, NJ, 2011.

of his predecessors. Those scholars who have investigated earlier Russian expeditions disagree about whether they included ancillary assistants such as cartographers, or medical personnel able to make collections of herbs and medicinal plants, but it is certain that nothing on the scale of Messerschmidt's endeavours was attempted. Much of the material Messerschmidt sent back to St Petersburg ended up in the Tsar's Kunstkammer, originally 'His Majesty's Cabinet' of curiosities, established by Peter on the basis of collections begun under Ivan IV and then by Peter's father Aleksei Mikhailovich.[55] Transferred to St Petersburg by Peter and with new acquisitions added (including gifts from foreign rulers and collections purchased from abroad), and opened to the public in 1719, the Kunstkammer became a major museum of scientific knowledge eventually classified into *naturalia*, artefacts and antiquities. It was greatly enriched by the objects acquired by Messerschmidt.

Messerschmidt's life's work ended in tragedy. Peter the Great had died early in 1725 and there subsequently developed a dispute over access to Messerschmidt's written accounts and collections which were retained by the Apothecaries' (now renamed Medical) Chancellery and the new Academy of Sciences. In 1729 Messerschmidt returned to Danzig but lost further notes and materials in a shipwreck on the way. Only in 1731, after the accession of Empress Anna and through the good graces of several scholars and officials (such as V. N. Tatishchev, G. F. Müller and Archbishop Feofan Prokopovich) was he allowed to return but even then he was denied full access to his collections. He died in 1735 and it was almost certainly because of the dispute that the greater part of his work remained unpublished. That said, his written and material collections continued to be used throughout much of the rest of the eighteenth century, laying the foundation for the First Kamchatka Expedition (1727–30) led by Vitus Bering and for subsequent expeditions. In 1730, furthermore, Strahlenberg published his celebrated account of the geography of the northern and eastern part of Europe and Asia, citing the work of Messerschmidt by name and calling it to public and even international attention.[56] As Aleksandrovskaia writes: 'the results of [Messerschmidt's] journey were

---

[55] See Oleg Neverov, '"His Majesty's Cabinet" and Peter I's Kunstkammer', in Oliver Impey and Arthur MacGregor (eds), *The Origins of Museums: The Cabinet of Curiosities in Sixteenth and Seventeenth-Century Europe*, London, 2001, pp. 71–80. See also Brigitte Buberl and Michael Dückershoff (eds), *Palast des Wissens: Die Kunst und Wunderkammer Zar Peters des Grossen*, Munich, 2003.

[56] P. J. von Strahlenberg, *Das Nord- und Östliche Teil von Europa und Asia*, Stockholm, 1730. See Novlianskaia, *Daniil Gotlib Messerschmidt*, p. 171.

well known in the eighteenth century and had no small influence on the development of reliable conceptions of the geography of Siberia.'[57] In other words, Messerschmidt's achievement represented a major advance on the earlier exploits of Spafarii, Atlasov and others.

*   *   *

In comparing the expeditions of Spafarii and Atlasov on the one hand with that of Messerschmidt on the other, one is immediately aware of a step change. Only Messerschmidt's expedition was centrally focused on what might be called 'science': the collection of medicinal herbs and plants in the first instance, a focus which evidently broadened as time went on. The expedition was administered by the Apothecaries' Chancellery, the department of state with a medical focus (the Academy of Sciences was established only in 1725). The expeditions of Spafarii and Atlasov, by contrast, had other priorities: diplomacy and trade relations (overseen by the Ambassadorial Chancellery) and the expansion and enforcement of the *iasak* (under the supervision of the Siberian Chancellery) respectively. In neither of the latter two cases was science (the expansion of geographical knowledge) a central concern.

These differences are underlined by the personalities concerned. Spafarii was clearly an educated man but his education was apparently a humanistic one, including languages, and as a product of the Orthodox world he was unlikely to have had a good understanding of the latest ideas in the study of nature. Atlasov, by contrast, may have had little education (he was perhaps illiterate) but, as testified by his oral reports, he seems to have been a keen observer. He was essentially a hunter, *iasak* collector and soldier rather than a naturalist and impresses through his ethnographic observations rather than through those on the natural environment. Only Messerschmidt was a university educated naturalist and linguist with the skills necessary to undertake a scientific study of Siberia. It was probably these facts which commended him to J. P. Breyne and ultimately to Peter.

The shift from Spafarii and Atlasov to Messerschmidt represents a shift from an expeditionary focus on general albeit sometimes vivid description and fact gathering to systematic and disciplined observation, recording and the gathering of specimens, samples and materials. Te Heesen's studies demonstrate the exhaustive and strictly controlled methodology employed by the German doctor. Whilst Messerschmidt may not have been a 'scientist' in the modern sense, his

[57] Aleksandrovskaia, *Stanovlenie geograficheskoi nauki*, p. 41.

accomplishments were a harbinger of what was to come. Comparison with the First and Second Kamchatka expeditions (1727–30 and 1733–43 respectively) indicates the much bigger scale and allocation of resources which characterized those enterprises.[58] Those expeditions foreshadow the larger, planned European and Russian expeditions which featured in the second half of the eighteenth century. To suggest that Messerschmidt's expedition was an example of Enlightenment exploration may be premature. But it was certainly a big step in that direction, a step which would have been impossible without Peter the Great's resolute policy of modernization.

[58] The decree for the First Kamchatka expedition was signed by Peter shortly before his death. For these expeditions, see V. I. Grekov, *Ocherki iz istorii russkikh geograficheskikh issledovanii v 1725–65 gg.*, Moscow, 1960; E. G. Kushnarev, *Bering's Search for the Strait: The First Kamchatka Expedition, 1725–30*, ed. and trans. E. A. P. Crownhart-Vaughan, Portland, OR, 1990; *Under Vitus Bering's Command: New Perspectives on the Russian Kamchatka Expeditions*, eds Peter Ulf Møller and Natasha Okhotina Lind, Aarhus, 2003; Georg Wilhelm Steller, *Eastbound through Siberia: Observations from the Great Northern Expedition*, trans. and annotated by Margritt A. Engel and Karen E. Willmore, Bloomington, IN, 2020.

From Northern Europe to the Aegean Archipelago: Lord Effingham's Military Tour with the Russian Navy in 1770

Elena B. Smilianskaia

Higher School of Economics, Moscow

and

Julia Leikin

University of Exeter

Of the five best-known portraits of Thomas Howard, the third Earl of Effingham (1746–91), one anonymous engraving stands out. The portrait portrays Lord Effingham as a young warrior, armed to the teeth (with a rifle, a pistol, sword and dagger), standing at full height on a jagged rock. On top of his high-collared linen shirt he wears the traditional dress of Balkan and Levantine warriors: Vraka trousers and a cloth scarf worn as a belt around his waist.[1] Just a few decades later Lord Byron would appear in a similar 'Albanian dress' in a famous 1813 portrait by Thomas Phillips.[2] Although dated to 1790, the Effingham portrayed might be the twenty-four-year-old volunteer with the Russian forces during the siege on the island of Lemnos in September 1770. The Russian Archipelago Expedition (1769–74), in which the third Earl of Effingham fought under the command of Count Aleksei Orlov alongside Balkan, Greek, and Slavonian rebels, just might have been his own Eastern Mediterranean grand tour, infused with romantic notes of philhellenism that permeated British writing just a few decades later.

A notable personality of his time, Effingham made waves in late eighteenth-century British society with his eccentric flourishes and unconventional politics. An Etonian, a mason, and a Whig of great conviction, Effingham held the post of Master of the Royal Mint, and was invited to serve in government when his party took power. Effingham was a peer of the House of Lords, a position he inherited along with his title in 1763 at the age of sixteen; however, like his

[1] Anonymous, *Portrait of Thomas Howard, 3rd Earl of Effingham*, engraving, 1790. London, The British Museum. Available at https://www.britishmuseum.org/collection/object/P_1870-1008-2548 (accessed 12 September 2020).
[2] *Thomas Phillips, Portrait of George Gordon, 6th Baron Byron of Rochdale in Albanian Dress, oil on canvas, c. 1835.* London, National Portrait Gallery. Available at https://www.npg.org.uk/collections/search/portrait/mw00991/Lord-Byron?LinkID=mp00691&role=sit&rNo=2 (accessed 17 September 2020).

ancestors, he was eager to fight and pursued a military career. As a youth, he fought in the Seven Years' War and by the age of nineteen was made captain in the infantry. In 1774–75, Effingham gained notoriety with his uncompromising position on what became the American War of Independence. In 1775, to protest 'fratricide' in America, he traded military service for parliamentary battles, resigning his commission and becoming a vocal opponent of the war on the floor of the House of Lords.[3] In his own way, he commented on the topical issues of the day, from his essay on public finance[4] to an oblique reference to the Boston Tea Party in the naming of his hunting lodge, Boston Castle.[5] In 1789, William Pitt appointed Effingham as governor of Jamaica, where he died two years later, in 1791.

Effingham's life and career took many directions, leaving behind a scattered and not entirely cohesive legacy. His name lives on in his former estate, Thundercliffe Grange, near the town of Rotherham, which was built in 1777 by the architect John Platt and, after several transformations, operates as a co-operative housing project to this day.[6] His stated support for the rebel American colonists made him important in the history of the United States as well. Two counties — one in Illinois and the other in Georgia — bear his name, monuments have been dedicated to him, and two US war ships were named in his

---

[3] On 24 February 1775 he delivered what one newspaper described as a 'very spirited and manly Speech' to the House of Lords in an ongoing effort to stem the conflict with the colonies. His contemporary, the famous politician and intellectual Horace Walpole, expressed what must have been a common sentiment about Effingham's speech following his persistent protests about the war: 'Was there ever any thing, ancient or modern, better, either in sentiment or language, than his late speech! [...] is it not a pity that a man of such integrity and ability should be what he is.' *The Correspondence of Horace Walpole, Earl of Orford, and the Rev. William Mason; now first published from the original mss.*, ed., with notes by the Rev. J. Mitford. London, 1851, vol. 1, pp. 194–95.

[4] *An Essay on the Nature of a Loan: being an introduction to the knowledge of the public accounts. [by the Earl of Effingham]*, York, 1782.

[5] Walpole explained to his correspondent that Boston Castle was '[a] room which [Effingham] built [...] on a fine brow of a hill [...]. He christened it Boston Castle, because no tea was ever to be drank in it. The statute is religiously observed': *The Correspondence of Horace Walpole*, vol. 1, p. 195.

[6] Julia Leikin, 'Seeking Thomas Howard in Rotherham: Local Groundings for a Global Life', *Historical Transactions: The blog of the Royal Historical Society*, 13 May 2019, https://blog.royalhistsoc.org/2019/05/13/thomas-howard-rotherham/ (accessed 12 September 2020); 'History', https://thundercliffegrange.co.uk/history (accessed 12 September 2020). See also Peter Feek, *Thundercliffe Grange: An Eclectic History of a House and Its People*, Rotherham, 2019. In 2019, the authors visited Thundercliffe Grange, Boston Castle, and the surrounding areas. We are very grateful to Janet Worrall, Peter Feek, Julia Brammer, Jeremy Blundell and David Christopher, who generously shared their knowledge about Thomas Howard during this visit.

honour. His hunting lodge in South Yorkshire, the whimsically-named Boston Castle, has been turned into a museum commemorating his life, passions, and projects. While it combines his interests under one roof, it also commemorates the diversity of his interests without presupposing that there might be a thread running through them. This essay proposes that his travels around Europe in the late 1760s and early 1770s, and particularly his journey to the Aegean Archipelago with the imperial Russian navy, had a transformative effect that might have shaped his political interests and loyalties across the Atlantic a few years later.

Effingham's journey to the Eastern Mediterranean and participation in the Russian–Ottoman War of 1768–74 is one of the least-documented episodes of his life.[7] Few of his own letters and notes describing how he fought alongside Russian forces in support of the Greek uprising (often referred to as the 'Orlov rebellion') against the Ottoman Empire in 1770 have survived. However, through the memoirs of his contemporary and compatriot, John Elphinstone, we learn that Effingham kept a journal during the Russian Archipelago expedition (which has not been located and is likely lost forever). In fact, Effingham not only shared the journal with Elphinstone, but allowed the latter to copy substantial excerpts into his own memoirs. And while his first-person recollections are largely lost to us, Effingham plays a prominent role in Elphinstone's narrative of the Russian navy's expedition to the Mediterranean.[8] It is through Elphinstone that some details of Effingham's mysterious journey to the Eastern Mediterranean can be recovered. This expedition, we argue, was a pivotal event in which his political sympathies for revolts and rebellions crystallized. Our essay follows his journey through northern Europe to the Court of St Petersburg and then around the continent to the Eastern Mediterranean, through the Russian campaigns in the Archipelago, before returning as a transformed man to Britain.

---

[7] Hilda Engbring Feldhake, *The Lords Effingham and the American Colonies*, Effingham, IL, 1976. The authors would like to thank Janet Worrall, secretary of the Friends of Boston Castle and Parklands Society, for sharing her unpublished manuscript about Thomas Howard.

[8] Princeton University Library, Special Collections, John Elphinstone Papers Relating to the Russo-Turkish War, *Russian Faith, Honour & Courage, Displayed in a Faithful Narrative of the Russian Expedition by Sea in the Years 1769 & 1770* (hereafter JEP), Box 3, vols 1–4. The Russian translation of this text was published as: '*Russkaia vernost', chest', i otvaga'. Dzhona Elfinstona. Povestvovanie o sluzhbe Ekaterine II i ob Arkhipelagskoi ekspeditsii Rossiiskogo flota*, ed. and trans. Elena Smilianskaia and Julia Leikin, Moscow, 2020. The English text is in preparation for the Hakluyt Society. We are grateful to Will Ryan for his enthusiastic support of this publication, which this essay on Lord Effingham's travels to the Aegean Archipelago recognizes and echoes.

From Northern Europe to the Aegean Archipelago
The events that inspired Effingham to head to the Aegean Sea can only be surmised from the circumstances preceding the decision. In 1768, as a captain on half-pay and newly married to Catherine Proctor, Effingham departed for a long tour around Europe. One year later, the couple found themselves in northern Europe, where upon arriving in Sweden they were introduced to the royal family by the British ambassador, Sir John Goodricke, on 22 April 1769.[9] Later, Effingham expressed his gratitude to Sir John, who gave him 'little knowledge of ye state and interest in ye Northern Part of Europe', and stressed that 'without his assistance I had travelled through a considerable part of these countries in vain'.[10] From Sweden, Effingham and his wife, now also joined by his brother, headed to Russia. The British ambassador in St Petersburg, Lord Charles Cathcart, related in his diplomatic correspondence that the Effinghams appeared in the Russian capital on 12 August 1769,[11] and the next day, the three 'were presented on Sunday to the Empress and received with particular distinction'.[12] The ambassador's wife, Lady Jane Cathcart, noted in her diary that *'après la Cour'* she had dinner with Lady Effingham and the day was *'tout à fait raisonable'*.[13]

The northern capital made an impression on the Effinghams. Catherine Effingham described the Russian court and Empress Catherine II enthusiastically in her letter to Lady Delaval:

> I am quite charm'd with this place; it is a superb Capital & I have spent my time very agreeably [...] the magnificence of this Court is not to be gues'd at; & the Empress the most extraordinary Princess I ever saw, Gracious to a degree & Eligant [*sic*] in her person with a most superior understanding: I was at a Ball at Court [...] the Empress [was] so gracious it is a pleasure to see her.[14]

The Effinghams' stay in St Petersburg overlapped with the hectic preparations of Russian naval squadrons for an unprecedented journey

---

[9] *Salisbury and Winchester Journal*, 15 May 1769; *The Ipswich Journal*, 20 May 1769.
[10] Moscow, Arkhiv vneshnei politiki Rossiiskoi Imperii (hereafter AVPRI), f. 6, op. 2 (Sekretneishie dela – Perliustratsii), d. 532 (1765–1771), l. 150b.
[11] Unless otherwise indicated, all the dates are in New Style.
[12] London, The National Archives (hereafter TNA), State Papers (hereafter SP) 91/82, fols 24, 26v.
[13] Edinburgh, National Library of Scotland, Acc. 12686/5, Journal 21 of Lady Cathcart, 1769.
[14] Northumberland Record Office (hereafter NRO), 429/20/1, Seaton Delaval MSS, K. Effingham to Lady Delaval, n.d. We are grateful to Janet Worrall for sharing this archival document with us.

to the Mediterranean.[15] Although neither Cathcart nor any of the Russian sources mention it, it was during this visit that Effingham decided to take part in the Russian expedition to the Aegean Sea. Catherine Effingham informed her correspondent in England that Lord Effingham was planning to travel with the fleet, for which she had 'sum'd up great Courage' to bear his departure as she saw him off with wishes of success 'relative to this great undertaking'.[16] It is odd that John Elphinstone, who described these hasty preparations in great detail, just as he faithfully relayed his encounters with members of the British Factory in St Petersburg, makes no mention of Effingham in these weeks. Nor does he relay any mention of any member of Catherine's inner circle. As far as Elphinstone knew, no trusted adviser of the Russian court approached the young British aristocrat to extend an invitation to fight in the Russian–Ottoman war. When Effingham did leave St Petersburg, it was to make preparations for the journey ahead; his wife reported: 'I am now very dull as you may imagine having lost my dear Lord; I should not like living in England during his absence therefore having met with so gracious a reception from the Empress, I propose staying a couple of months longer, & then going to Moscow; to indulge my eyes with their manafactorys [sic], which are all further up in the Country.'[17]

Effingham's determination to join the Russian–Ottoman war with the Russian fleet was a topic of discussion in the highest government circles. On 22 October 1769, the Russian ambassador to London, Count I. G. Chernyshev, informed the head of the Russian College of Foreign Affairs, N. I. Panin:

> Rochford [the British secretary of state] told me that Lord Effingham, who had only recently returned to Britain a few days ago, called on him to discuss asking His Majesty permission to join the campaign with our squadron under the command of Rear-Admiral Elphinstone who, they say, has her Imperial Majesty's permission to take him onboard and give him a captain's duties.[18]

Information about this controversial decision leaked through to the press. In November 1769 British newspapers reported:

---

[15] On the Russian Archipelago Expedition, see Elena B. Smilianskaia, *Grecheskie ostrova Ekateriny II: opyt imperskoi politiki Rossii v Sredizemnomor'e*, Moscow, 2015; I. M. Smilianskaia, M. B. Velizhev, and E. B. Smilianskaia, *Rossiia v Sredizemnomor'e: Arkhipelagskaia ekspeditsiia Ekateriny Velikoi*, Moscow, 2011.

[16] NRO, 429/20/1.

[17] NRO, 429/20/1.

[18] AVPRI, f. 35/6, d. 211, l. 950b, 22 October 1769.

The Earl of Effingham, who returned in the Russian fleet from a tour that he had been making in the north was in high esteem with Her Imperial Majesty, and in an audience which he lately demanded acquainted His Majesty with a message from her Imperial Majesty, that he should have the command of a corps of picked veterans as soon as he had gained his Sovereign's permission to enter into her service; on which His Majesty was graciously pleased to give him leave; and these troops being in Admiral Elphinston's fleet, his Lordship will go on board to take his command as soon as Admiral enters the Humber or Spithead.[19]

These reports evidently exaggerated both the future role and the nature of the King's permission for Effingham's journey. The fact was that British subjects' presence alongside the Russians, especially that of a notable English aristocrat in Ottoman territory in time of war, raised serious concerns for the British ambassador in Constantinople and for representatives of the Levant Company. In October 1769, several dispatches were presented to the King, reporting concerns about British subjects fighting alongside the Russians against the Ottoman Empire, warning that it might impede trade and put Europeans living in Ottoman territories in danger.[20] To address these concerns, Effingham received royal assent to join the Russian–Ottoman war as a *volunteer*, the role in which he set foot on one of the ships of Elphinstone's squadron.[21]

Effingham was only one of several British subjects who found themselves sailing with the Russian fleet to the theatre of war in the Mediterranean. He sailed for the Archipelago with a Scot, a captain of the Royal Navy and Russian Rear-Admiral, John Elphinstone, who himself had struggled to get the King's permission to serve in Russia.[22] Others included seamen of various ranks, pilots, surgeons, and two other named volunteers who appeared at Effingham's side: Mssrs

[19] *Caledonian Mercury*, 22 November 1769; *Kentish Gazette*, 18 November 1769.

[20] TNA, SP 91/82, fols 166–68. Letters dated from 24–25 October 1769 from representatives of the Levant Company requested that British subjects be denied permission to serve in the Russian army and navy. The *Derby Mercury* reported that the Levant Company feared that the 'spirited young man' — Effingham's — appearance among the Russians would complicate its relationship with the Ottomans (22 December 1769). The British ambassador to Constantinople, John Murray, shared these concerns.

[21] *Newcastle Courant*, 25 November 1769.

[22] For a broader discussion of the role of British subjects in this expedition, see *Russkaia vernost', chest' i otvaga*, pp. 78–89; on British subjects in the Russian navy in general, Anthony Cross, '*By the Banks of the Neva*': *Chapters from the Lives and Careers of the British in Eighteenth-Century Russia*, Cambridge, 1997, pp. 159–223.

Stapleton and McQuinsley and their servants.[23] A few months later, to reassure British subjects with business interests in the Ottoman Empire, the British secretary of state informed the ambassador in Constantinople, John Murray, that Effingham had not received the King's permission to join the war and, if he did join the Russian forces in the war against the Ottomans, he would not be able to count on the King's protection as a British subject.[24]

In January 1770 Effingham was formally introduced to Elphinstone by the Russian envoy in England, A. I. Musin-Pushkin, as a participant in the expedition, personally invited by the Empress.[25] While it is possible that Elphinstone and Effingham might have encountered one another during Effingham's short stay in St Petersburg, during which time Elphinstone was hastily preparing his squadron for departure, it is unlikely that Elphinstone would have omitted such a memorable acquaintance with a respected figure from his recollections of those months. Whether it was because of his high standing in British society or his keen interest in naval technology,[26] Effingham earned Elphinstone's highest praise: 'His Lordship altho' being bred a Soldier was a very good judge of Sea Maneuvers — as He took great delight in them.'[27] Elphinstone's reverential attitude towards Effingham continued throughout the journey, and is ultimately the reason why we know so much about Effingham's participation in the expedition.

We can only speculate as to why Effingham, while touring northern Europe, suddenly chose to head south to join the war. British newspapers conjectured, that *Captain* Effingham may return from this assignment a colonel.[28] When he himself applied to King George III for permission, he stated: 'I went by your Majesty's Permission for some Years into foreign parts with a view to improve myself in the study of my profession.'[29] But perhaps in her allusion to Effingham's 'great undertaking', Lady Effingham meant other, loftier goals, for

[23] For brief biographies, see *Russkaia vernost', chest' i otvaga*, pp. 418–19.

[24] TNA, SP 97/46, fol. 127v.

[25] *Leeds Intelligencer*, 23 January 1770.

[26] Keen to procure a new British pump, Elphinstone wrote: 'The Earl of Effingham attended the trial, & gave me the Extract of the tryals. Those pumps will discharge with only 14 men two tons of water in one minute, which will parhaps [sic] in future be of great utility in emptying the canals at Cronstadt, & also the camells used at St Petersburg for conveying the Ships from thence into Deep Water': JEP Box 3, vol. 1, fol. 66.

[27] JEP, Box 3, vol. 2, fol. 126.

[28] *Leeds Intelligencer*, 2 January 1770.

[29] *The Correspondence of King George the Third from 1760 to December 1783, Printed from the Original Papers in the Royal Archives at Windsor Castle: July 1773–December 1777*, ed. John William Fortescue. London, vol. 3, 1927-28, p. 108.

which her husband might choose to fight. The Russian Empress's stated aims for the war in the Archipelago might have made a persuasive case for Effingham to join the Russian war effort against the Ottoman Empire, particularly the desire to liberate the Christian denizens of the Archipelago and Balkans from the Ottoman yoke. Certainly, by the time Effingham returned to Britain in October 1769 to prepare for the journey ahead, the British press had begun alluding to the 'Greek factor' in his future service and on the significance of reports from Russia that he brought to England.[30] By this time, Russia's military intervention in the Mediterranean Sea and Catherine II's plans to use the revolt of Ottoman Orthodox Christian subjects to weaken the Ottoman Empire and perhaps even secure a Mediterranean base for Russia in the process — planned in secret from at least the middle of 1769 — was no longer secret, but became a topic of much discussion throughout Western Europe.

From the Eastern Mediterranean to Disillusionment
In mid-May 1770, the squadron carrying Effingham aboard the ship *Sviatoslav* approached the Peloponnese. Whether he was recruited or volunteered, Effingham's presence among the Russian troops was a symbolic victory for the Russian war effort. The level of responsibility in the operation which would be entrusted to the twenty-four-year-old English volunteer remained unclear. No clear orders to give Effingham a commanding role had travelled to the Mediterranean with him. Instead, it was the commander of his squadron, John Elphinstone, who wrote to the head of the Archipelago expedition, Aleksei Orlov, to inform him that the English officer Effingham was now in his service and that he (Elphinstone) had already ordered the commanders of the land forces to place *all Greek volunteers* under Effingham's command:

> By Her Imperial Majesty's permission, I brought with me the Earl of Effingham of the first family in England as a volunteer [...] to serve under Your Excellence. I have orderd the commanding officer of the land forces to put His Lordship at the head of all the Greek volunteers. I have also with me two volunteers, who will remain with the Earl of Effingham untill they receive Your Excellency [*sic*] commands.[31]

The Russian land forces transported by the first two squadrons to the Eastern Mediterranean were hardly enough to sustain the fighting in the Morea and across the islands of the Archipelago. In Catherine II's

---

[30] *Kentish Gazette*, 21 October 1769; *Leeds Intelligencer*, 24 October 1769.
[31] JEP, Box 3, vol. 1, fol. 100.

conception, the navy was intended to support the Ottoman Christians, who would themselves have to fight for their freedom.[32] However, there was no clear candidate among the Russian officers who would have been able to organize the local troops and the volunteers from the rebelling communities. Whereas Aleksei Orlov had turned to natural leaders from the local communities to serve as intermediaries and to lead the local forces — these leaders included Antonio Psaro, Alexander Policutti, Count Ivan Voinovich — Elphinstone wanted to entrust the British aristocrat with this responsibility.[33]

Elphinstone's suggestion to place Effingham in charge of Balkan volunteers highlighted the differences that existed between the two men. Throughout the war and after, the Russian government struggled to fit the Greek, Balkan, and Slavonian recruits neatly into the Russian army and naval hierarchy, unable — for legal and fiscal reasons — to enlist them as regular troops. In practice, these troops were organized into ethnic battalions with a unique organizational structure.[34] Effingham's youthful military experience nearly a decade earlier ran orthogonal to that of combatants with knowledge of the region's terrain, local power dynamics, and a personal stake in the outcome of the battle.[35] Elphinstone's suggestion that Effingham be placed at the head of these troops, in addition to reiterating his own contemptuous attitude towards foreign military experience, ran counter to normal Russian practice of keeping discrete groups of troops separate and in supporting the local rebellion rather than leading it.

By the time that Effingham disembarked from the *Sviatoslav* with a small regiment of Russian cuirassiers and artillery troops on the shores of Laconia Bay in the south of the Peloponnese, the uprising in the Morea had been subdued and was soon entirely suppressed. The Russian land forces once again embarked on their ships and the squadron set off

---

[32] Smilianskaia, *Grecheskie ostrova*, p. 26.

[33] On Voinovich, see Smilianskaia, *Grecheskie ostrova*, pp. 40–48, 83, and G. L. Arsh, *Rossiia i bor'ba Gretsii za osvobozhdenie: ot Ekateriny II do Nikolaia I*, Moscow, 2013, pp. 55–63.

[34] On this problem see: Julia Leikin, 'Greeks into Privateers: Law and Language of Commerce Raiding Under the Imperial Russian Flag, 1760s–1790s', in *Ideologies of Western Naval Power, c. 1500–1815*, eds J. D. Davies, Alan James and Gijs Rommelse, London, 2019, pp. 209–25; Radi Boev, 'Voenno-politicheskoe sotrudnichestvo mezhdu balkanskimi narodami i Rossiiei v khode russko-turetskoi voiny 1768–1774 godov', *Études Balkaniques*, 1975, no. 2, pp. 118–27.

[35] The local knowledge of these fighters and the significance of power struggles between regional clans in this theatre of war is not to be overlooked. See John C. Alexander, *Brigandage and Public Order in the Morea 1685–1806*, Athens, 1985; John Vasdravellis, *Klephts, Armatoles and Pirates in Macedonia During the Rule of the Turks (1627–1821)*, Thessaloniki, 1975.

in pursuit of the Ottoman warships. By this time Effingham had no one left to command, even if he had intended to carry out these orders.

With an undefined status in the Russian army and lack of a clear role in the military operations, Effingham appeared to choose the military operations in which he and his two companions, Stapleton and McQuinsley, would take part.[36] The first operation in which Effingham took part was the capture of a small fortress on the island of Negroponte (Euboea) on 11 June 1770. Admiral Samuel Greig, Effingham's compatriot, reported on this operation in his own memoirs:

> Lord Effingham and several armed galleys descended on Negropont and brought a few old metal armaments from the ancient fortress, evacuated by the Turks before the arrival of the Russians. Lord Effingham served as a volunteer on Admiral Elphinstone's ship. He joined that expedition with the permission of the king solely out of his love for warcraft.[37]

The action was so notable that even Catherine II knew about the capture of the cannons on Negroponte, seeking to reward the capture with a bounty.[38] However, no rewards were ever bestowed on Effingham.

Soon Effingham became a witness to the biggest Russian naval success: the destruction of the Ottoman fleet at Chesme (Çeşme) (5–7 July 1770) and Elphinstone's effort to force his way through the Dardanelles to reach Constantinople (July–August). Here it seemed that Effingham's great hopes for taking part in a heroic battle were realized; Elphinstone observed: 'His Lordship was enjoying himself with the pleasing hopes of the attack.'[39] But Elphinstone's squadron could not break through the Dardanelles. Effingham, together with Stapleton and McQuinsley, decided to leave Elphinstone, who continued the blockade of the Dardanelles, to join Count Aleksei Orlov at the siege of the Fortress Litodi (now in Myrina) on the island of Lemnos.

The siege of Lemnos offered the English volunteers an opportunity to act alongside their Balkan counterparts and regular Russian troops.

---

[36] McQuinsley's full name could not be established. He appears as Kingsley in Elphinstone's copy of Effingham's journal, but as McQuinsley in other parts of the text.

[37] 'Sobstvennoruchnyi zhurnal kapitana-komandora (vposledstvii admirala) S. K. Greiga', in *Morskie srazheniia russkogo flota: Vospominaniia, dnevniki, pis'ma*, compiled V. G. Oppokov, Moscow, 1994, pp. 107–08.

[38] 'Reskripty i pis'ma imperatritsy Ekateriny II na imia grafa A. G. Orlova-Chesmenskogo', *Sbornik Imperatorskogo Russkogo istoricheskogo obshchestva*, St Petersburg, vol. 1, 1867, p. 53.

[39] JEP, Box 3, vol. 2, fol. 175.

The siege began in July 177c and drew the majority of Russian resources — artillery, infantry, and marine troops — to the island. Greek and Slavonian volunteers from the Balkan peninsula arrived there to fight. These were the troops that Effingham was intended to command, but never did; and here he had a chance to fight alongside them. Its proximity to the Dardanelles made Lemnos an ideal location for a Russian base in the Mediterranean, which required taking the one remaining stronghold on the south-west corner of the island. After shelling the fortress for a few days, Orlov chose to pull back and wait for the fortress to surrender. On 5 October, just as the fortress agreed to surrender, Ottoman reinforcements arrived on the other side of the island and the Russian forces retreated.

Our source for Effingham's role in the siege is an excerpt from his journal that John Elphinstone copied directly into his memoirs. We cannot be sure what Elphinstone omitted, but for the sake of authenticity he kept Effingham's daily reflections, the rhythm and pacing of his days, and his sympathies and judgements — at least as far as they matched his own. Like Elphinstone himself, Effingham was forthright about his disappointment with the Russian actions. 'The siege was not carried on with any great vigour from the Beginning and was afterwards turn'd into a blockade',[40] he wrote. Both seemed disappointed that after two weeks the island had still not been taken. Effingham's passing judgements on Aleksei Orlov's inaction and infrequent appearances at the site of the siege were likely another point of agreement between the two.

The (in)action at the siege of Lemnos appeared to escalate the tension around Effingham's uncertain position in Russian military operations. As a British aristocrat, a ranking officer in the British army, and a figure of some authority, he commanded the respect and reverence of compatriots with high ranks in the Russian navy. In addition to his collegiality with Elphinstone, he was also on good terms with Samuel Greig, with whom he both dined socially, but also discussed operational tactics.[41] Although his own proposals for operations were seemingly dismissed by senior members of the Russian military, Russian officials relied on Effingham as a figure of authority with the English sailors who crewed several ships. He was called on to smooth relations with the seamen, who expressed discontent with being asked to serve under Russian command. More than that, he wrote in his journal that the English sailors in the fleet 'desired [...] that I should lead them into

---

[40] JEP, Box 3, vol. 3, fol. 233.
[41] Ibid., fol. 234.

either of the breaches' — a plan of attack he intended to present to both Samuel Greig and Aleksei Orlov but which they both subsequently dismissed.

Effingham's disappointment in Russian operations began to set in before the spectacular success at Chesme. From the island of Paros, which housed the Russian naval base of operations in the Eastern Mediterranean, he dispatched a letter to the British ambassador, Cathcart, in St Petersburg. Amidst pleasantries, thanking Cathcart for his reception and hospitality in St Petersburg (and obliquely understanding that the letter will be read by others than the intended recipient), Effingham expressed disappointment in the development of events around him: 'We are this afternoon got under way to attack ye enemys fleet. I hope the next accounts may be satisfactory to that extraordinary princess of whose court you reside. I so admire her uncommon talents that regret more than she does herself the weak condition or want of ardour in those who are intrusted by her.'[42] However, his plans to 'winter at Mahon' and to take part in the campaign the following year[43] suggest that he had not yet begun contemplating a departure from the region. The events surrounding the siege on the island of Lemnos in late August 1770 more likely precipitated his return to Britain.

Effingham's greatest disillusionment stemmed from Russian reluctance to act. Unwilling to risk Russian lives, Aleksei Orlov and Grigorii Spiridov chose not to deploy Russian land troops to storm the fortress. Elphinstone recounts Effingham's reaction to seeing fleeing families, women and children, evacuating the island with the imminent arrival of Ottoman reinforcements:

> The Earl of Effingham — who now was with me since the Day the Count came into the Harbour [Porto Mudro] equip'd himself on the first hearing of the firing not doubting but every one that could carry a Musquet would be Order'd to Land. His Lordship earnestly desired I would suffer him to go on shore to assist the Greeks — but as I saw the Danger was too Great & no Honour [in margin: Could be got without a sufficient Force]. I would not permit his Lordship to go unless any of the Regulars were Order'd [...] As I thought every moment an age till something was done to relieve those distress'd people [...].[44]

---

[42] A copy of the perlustrated letter dated 19/30 June 1770 is located in AVPRI, f. 6, op. 2 (Sekretneishie dela – Perliustratsii), d. 532 (1765–1771), l. 15a.
[43] Ibid.
[44] JEP, Box 3, vol. 3, fol. 247.

Effingham's own account notes that he had approached Orlov 'to beg for arms' in order to 'go to meet the enemy in the mountains'.[45] Later Orlov tried to justify his miscalculations at Lemnos by citing his ailing health, and more importantly — after the unsuccessful joint operations with the Greeks on the Peloponnese — that he no longer trusted the Balkan volunteers to participate in joint actions with him. Orlov's order for a hasty retreat after news of a small descent of Ottoman troops on the island seemed incomprehensible to Effingham. The Englishman evidently expected more: more strategy, better tactics. Even more, he seemed disillusioned with the events at Porto Mudro, on a different part of the island, where Greek and Slavonian volunteers, who arrived on the island with their wives and children, were left undefended upon the arrival of the Ottoman troops.

Soon after these events Effingham decided to leave the Archipelago and return to his homeland. He left the Archipelago on the *Hazard*, an English vessel in Russian service. Together with some English surgeons and pilots, who likewise wanted to withdraw from Russian service, he travelled to Leghorn (Livorno).[46] Newspapers reported that Effingham was seen together with Count Fedor Orlov in Pisa in April, and that in June he arrived in London.[47] His participation in the Russian–Ottoman war and efforts to assist in the liberation of the Greeks from Ottoman control ended there.

But the war in the Archipelago was not forgotten by the eccentric aristocrat. In 1772, the first complete account of the Russian expedition to the Archipelago, including the events of 1770, was published anonymously in London.[48] The Earl of Effingham's name appears only on the first page, as part of the dedication, and there is little concrete evidence in the text itself to point to the actual author of the account. As its title page states, it is likely that *An Authentic Narrative* drew on the notes of several members of the expedition, including

---

[45] JEP, Box 3, vol. 3, fol. 238.

[46] Spiridov's order to dismiss 33 English sailors from service, who left aboard the *Hazard*, is dated 23 December 1769 (OS). He ordered to allocate them provisions for six weeks, recognizing that they would need more for the quarantine in Livorno. For the 'volunteer Lord' Effingham, Spiridov ordered comfortable quarters. St Petersburg, Rossiiskii gosudarstvennyi arkhiv voenno-morskogo flota, f. 190, op. 1, d. 42, ll. 190–91. The brig, delayed on Paros, only departed on 3 February 1771: Moscow, Rossiiskii gosudarstvennyi voenno istoricheskii arkhiv, f. 846, op. 16, d. 1860, l. 1330b. A month later the Englishmen arrived in Livorno: *Caledonian Mercury*, 4 May 1771; *Leeds Intelligencer*, 16 April 1771, p. 3.

[47] *Gazette d'Amsterdam*, 1771, № 34; *Leeds Intelligencer*, 4 June 1771.

[48] *An Authentic Narrative of the Russian Expedition against the Turks by Sea and Land*, London, 1772.

the journals kept by Effingham. Several passages that are attributed to Effingham in Elphinstone's copy appear in *An Authentic Narrative* almost verbatim, or with light editing. With the stringent permissions and the delicate international situation surrounding his presence and participation in the war, Effingham would have every reason to try to minimize and obscure the extent of his participation in Russian military operations. But one can almost imagine, confronted with earlier examples of Effingham's sense of humour, that he just might take a poke at conventions of patronage by publishing an anonymous account dedicated to himself.

The year 1770, which Thomas Howard, the third Earl of Effingham spent in the Archipelago, coincided with a cultural rediscovery of the classical civilization in southern Europe. Alongside the Greek Enlightenment, an intellectual and cultural revival coupled with a rediscovery of ancient Greek cultural heritage, the British elite were rediscovering Greek civilization.[49] British philhellenism, which found its romantic apex in Lord Byron's verses, was finding its footing. The uprising in the Morea in 1770, which was readily covered by the European press, cast a light on the struggles and commenced a new European philhellenic discourse. In their own way, the English volunteers who set out to the Archipelago to fight for Greek liberation were at the forefront of a new kind of movement. Although Effingham did not become a full-fledged philhellene, his journey to the Archipelago might have clarified his understanding of 'freedom' and 'liberation' — sentiments which he later applied to the rebel American colonies.

---

[49] Brian Dolan, *Exploring European Frontiers: British Travellers in the Age of Enlightenment*, Basingstoke, 2000, pp. 118–21.

'A Delicious Country': The British in Crimea from the Treaty of Kuchuk-Kainarji to the Treaty of Paris, 1774–1856

Anthony Cross
University of Cambridge

PERHAPS the most famous 'progress' of Catherine the Great's reign took the Empress in 1787 to her recently-acquired territories in the south and gave rise to the phrase 'Potemkin villages' to describe the arrangements that Prince Grigorii Potemkin, her viceroy of New Russia, allegedly made to present a picture of flourishing villages and well-fed peasants along her route. In her suite of Russian and foreign dignitaries was the British ambassador Alleyne FitzHerbert, later first Baron St Helens (1753–1839), reporting back to London in his official dispatches, but there were two other Englishmen whose activities are perhaps more worthy of recognition. The 'instant' gardens that greeted the Empress at several places chosen for overnight stays during her journey were laid out by Potemkin's gardener, William Gould (1735–1812) and may well have contributed to the myth of the 'Potemkin villages', while places and events along the way were captured in a series of watercolours by the talented but little-known artist William Hadfield (b.1761) and were subsequently presented to the Empress in a green morocco folder that lay in the Hermitage in obscurity for some two centuries.[1]

Accorded an audience with the Empress and well aware of her planned journey, an Englishwoman had left St Petersburg for Crimea a year earlier in February 1786, firstly for Moscow, from where she was to pen a potted history of 'that peninsula called the Tauride, which, from the climate and situation, I look upon to be a delicious country', adding words that for readers in the twenty-first century have an ominous ring, 'an acquisition to Russia which she should never relinquish'.[2] Although

---

[1] On Gould, see Anthony Cross, *By the Banks of the Neva: Chapters from the Lives and Careers of the British in Eighteenth-Century Russia*, Cambridge, 1997, pp. 274–76; on Hadfield, Anthony Cross, 'Which Hadfield?', *Study Group on Eighteenth-Century Russia Newsletter*, 25, 1997, pp. 24–26. It is also likely that Samuel Bentham, who was in Potemkin's service, also followed the Empress into Crimea. See Ian R. Christie, *The Benthams in Russia 1780–1791*, Oxford and Providence, RI,, 1993, p. 188.
[2] Elizabeth, Lady Craven, *A Journey through the Crimea to Constantinople. In a Series of Letters from the Right Honourable Elizabeth Lady Craven to His Serene Highness the Margrave of Brandenburg, Anspach, and Bareith. Written in the Year MDCCLXXXVI*, Dublin, 1789, p. 191. Such an opinion was also conveyed by Sir John

there were those at Catherine's court who had opined that in Crimea 'the air is unwholesome, the waters poisonous, and that I shall certainly die if I go there',[3] the intrepid Elizabeth, Lady Craven (1750–1826) arrived in Crimea by the beginning of April and for the next two weeks she travelled through the peninsula, from Perekop down the western side and as far along its southern coast as Sudak, noting the preparations that were being made for the Empress's arrival, particularly at the khan's palace at Bakhchisarai.[4] There is, in truth, little of substance in her letters, although her exhilaration at the natural beauty of the area is everywhere apparent as is her interest in the local inhabitants and their way of life. Her belief in Crimea's unrealized potential even led her to express the 'wish to see a colony of honest English families here; establishing manufactures, such as England produces, and returning the produce of this country to ours [...]',[5] unaware that Potemkin precisely at this period was considering a somewhat different colony for deported British convicts.[6] Craven's *Journey through the Crimea to Constantinople* was published in London in 1789, pirated in Dublin in the same year, and enjoyed German and French translations, from the latter of which was taken a Russian version appearing in 1795 and obviously containing nothing that the Empress would consider offensive. Craven's work was the first by a British Grand Tourist of either sex to describe Crimea, although she was neither the first British visitor to Crimea since its annexation in 1783, nor, strictly speaking, the first into print with a description of it.

The year of her journey, 1786, saw the publication of an 'Account of the Krimea' in *The Gentleman's Magazine*.[7] It was included in a series of letters describing a journey to the Russian south allegedly undertaken in 1785 by a correspondent signing himself M.M.M., who met in Azov a Captain P*, a British officer who supplied him with a succinct account of the history and geography of Crimea that was far more informative than Craven's offering. Although the whole account, including the

Sinclair (1754–1837), visiting Russia during a Parliamentary recess in 1786 and writing in a special memorandum that 'the country is very unhealthy to those who are not accustomed to the climate, and the water and the springs in the plains are particularly unwholesome' (*General Observations Regarding the Present State of the Russian Empire*, privately printed, 1787, p. 18).

[3] Craven, *A Journey through the Crimea*, p. 184.

[4] Ibid., pp. 213–58.

[5] Ibid., p. 249.

[6] See Roger P. Bartlett, *Human Capital: The Settlement of Foreigners in Russia 1762–1804*, Cambridge, 1979, p. 128.

[7] *The Gentleman's Magazine*, 56, 1786, 2, pp. 644–48, 847–51. This was the title given when it was reprinted two years later in the *Annual Register for the Year 1786*, 1788, Miscellaneous Essays, pp. 129–34.

Crimean section, was in fact the production of an armchair traveller, the Rev. William Tooke (1744–1820), at that time chaplain to the English congregation in St Petersburg, where he was friendly with many of the German professors at the Academy of Sciences from whose works he largely extracted his information, the assertion that it was 'the only account of the Krimea ever given to the [English] public' was essentially valid.[8] The choice of a British officer as its putative author was equally appropriate. Craven writes of the British 'captains or lieutenants' serving with the Russian Black Sea fleet when she was at Sevastopol', where she had stayed in the house of the recently deceased Admiral Thomas Mackenzie, who had been largely responsible for the construction of the harbour.[9] Following the Treaty of Kuchuk-Kainarji in July 1774 that had brought to an end the Russo–Turkish War of 1768–74 and, importantly, gave Russia the port of Kherson to the west of Crimea and, within Crimea, the town of Kerch', commanding the strait between the Black Sea and the Sea of Azov, many of the British naval officers recruited in particularly large numbers at the beginning of Catherine's reign and again in 1783 sailed the Black Sea and were soon to see action in the new conflict that began in 1787. It was a war that also brought to an end the presence of British travellers visiting the peninsula on the way to and from Moscow and Odessa (and thence to Constantinople).

Two further British travellers visiting Crimea before 1787 deserve, however, brief mention, although their personal records of their visits remain unpublished. Enjoying the hospitality of Potemkin both in St Petersburg and in the south was Reginald Pole Carew (1753–1835), owner of the Antony estate in Cornwall and later an influential MP, who left the Russian capital in July 1781 and, delighted with a brief excursion to Crimea, extolled 'une Souveraine aussi sage, aussi bénévole qu'Elle est magnanime'.[10] Travelling the opposite direction to Moscow from Constantinople, where he had met a homeward-bound Lady Craven, Sir Richard Worsley (1751–1805), the noted antiquarian, was kept in quarantine for two weeks at Sevastopol' before spending a further two weeks exploring the usual sites. He makes mention of a Logan Henderson employed by Potemkin to set up a botanical garden and two young Englishwomen to run a dairy, as well as of an architect named Robinson building a palace 'partly European & partly Asiatic' in style.[11]

---

[8] Ibid., p. 648. M[ilitia] M[ea] M[ultiplex] was the family motto of the Tooke family. For Tooke's mystification, see John H. Appleby, 'Tooke, William', *ODNB*.

[9] Craven, *A Journey through the Crimea*, p. 246.

[10] Torpoint, Cornwall, Antony House, Carew-Pole MSS, CO/R/3/175.

[11] Lincoln, Lincolnshire Archives Office, Yarborough Collection, Worsley MS, no. 24, ff. 164, 171. Henderson and the two women, one of whom was his mistress, had

With the cessation of hostilities in 1792 Crimea was again open to the traveller and among the first to venture into the peninsula was the Oxford don John Parkinson (1754–1840) who was accompanying as travelling tutor or, more picturesquely, as bear-leader, the young aristocrat Edward Wilbraham-Bootle (1771–1853), later first Lord Skelmersdale, on an impressively extensive Grand Tour, the itinerary of which was to a large extent dictated by events in Europe. Parkinson was a meticulous diarist, but seems never to have had the wish to become a publishing traveller to rival his near contemporary the Rev. William Coxe (1747–1828). The excerpts published in 1971 give a far too streamlined version of the days they spent in Crimea in August–September 1794, after a long and hazardous journey through Siberia to Astrakhan' and from there to the peninsula via Georgia: we read only of their stay at Bakhchisarai, the inevitable object of both visit and description for foreign visitors, but are given a glimpse of yet another Englishman in Russian service, Major Thomas Cobley (1761–after 1827), distinguished in the storming of the fortress of Ochakov in 1788 and later governor of Odessa under Alexander I, who was staying with his sister, the beautiful Henrietta (1764-1843), wife of Admiral Nikolai Mordvinov (1754–1845), who had served in the British navy in the 1770s and was an important figure in the development of Catherine's New Russia.[12] It was the Empress's promise of land and estates in the south for noble refugees from the French Revolution that brought another Englishwoman, Mary Kynnersley (d. 1812), Baroness de Bode, married to a nobleman from Alsace, to St Petersburg in August 1794. A year later, travelling with her eldest son, she went first to Ekaterinoslav, where the Bodes had been given a town house, and then made an excursion into Crimea in the autumn of 1795 to see further tracts of land that the Empress had promised them. She was overwhelmed by 'the beauty of the southern part of the Crimée. ''Tis like the beautiful dales of Derbyshire', visited the vineyards of Sudak, and stayed with the Mordvinovs at Bakhchisarai.[13] Her wish to return to Crimea was thwarted firstly by the death of the Empress and soon afterwards by that of her husband.

---

travelled from England with Jeremy Bentham, whom Worsley was subsequently to meet with his brother Samuel at Potemkin's estate of Krichev (Krychaw) in present-day Belarus. For the Benthams' dismay at Henderson's character and conduct see Christie, *The Benthams in Russia*, pp. 137–40, 155–57.

[12] John Parkinson, *A Tour of Russia, Siberia and the Crimea 1792–1794*, ed. William Collier, London, 1971, pp. 193–98.

[13] William S. Childe-Pemberton, *The Baroness de Bode 1775–1803*, London, 1900, p. 222.

In St Petersburg Mary Kynnersley had become close to members of the Zubov clan, particularly Olga Zherebtsova, mistress of the British ambassador, and her all-powerful brother Platon Aleksandrovich Zubov, Catherine's very young and last favourite, who had succeeded Potemkin as viceroy of Ekaterinoslav and Taurida regions. It was Zubov who, a few months before Mary left for the south, appointed William Hastie (1755–1832), a Scottish stonemason who had arrived in Russia in 1784 to work for Charles Cameron at Tsarskoe Selo, as his chief architect and sent him in July 1795 to work on the restoration of the khan's palace at Bakhchisarai. Hastie was to stay for four years in Crimea, unremarked by any British visitors and, unlike his patron, was not dismissed by the new Tsar. He produced as a lasting evidence of his excellence as draughtsman an album of measured and coloured drawings of the palace as an aid to its restoration and repair, as well as a number of panoramic views of Crimean towns such as Kozlov and Kaffa (Theodosia/Feodosiia), which he presented to Paul I.[14]

Anglo-Russian relations during the short reign of Paul (1796–1801) were marked by changes as violent as the Tsar's mood swings. All seemed set fair in 1799, when a coalition was formed against France and the commercial agreement was extended, but the situation deteriorated rapidly to such an extent that by the following year Paul had moved to renew the League of Armed Neutrality (established by Catherine in 1780 to protect neutral shipping against inspection by the British royal navy), place an embargo on British shipping, and break off diplomatic relations. There were British travellers in Paul's Russia and there were those who reached Crimea, but none who published at that time. It was in 1802 that there appeared two works that provided the British public and the British traveller with the detailed description of Crimea that had hitherto been missing but both had their origins in Catherine's reign. *Travels through the Southern Provinces of the Russian Empire, in the Years 1793 and 1794* appeared in English dress in two sumptuous volumes, illustrated by the Leipzig artist C. G. H. Geissler, and was soon followed by other and cheaper editions. Its author was the German naturalist and explorer Peter Simon Pallas (1741–1811). English-speaking and Fellow of the Royal Society since 1764, he had been professor of natural history at the Academy of Sciences in St Petersburg since 1767 and took part in expeditions across Siberia to the frontiers of China in

[14] *Plans and Elevations of the Antient Khans Palace at Bakshisarai and Other Buildings in Crim Tartary MDCCXCVIII.* See the reproductions in C. E. B. Brett, *Towers of Crim Tartary: English and Scottish Architects in the Crimea, 1762–1853,* Donington, 2005, pp. 44, 46–48.

1768–74 and to Astrakhan' and the Caucasus and Crimea in 1793–94. In 1795, given a large estate near Simferopol' by the Empress, he and his wife travelled to Crimea, where they lived until her death and his return to Berlin in 1810. Pallas provided a very detailed account of his first visit to Crimea, commenting on every aspect of its history, archaeology, geology, scenery and inhabitants. So too did the putative author of the second work, Mrs Maria Guthrie (née Romaud-Survesnes, d.1800), who in 1795–96 sent some ninety-three letters to her husband, Matthew Guthrie (1743–1807), a Scottish doctor who had served with the Russian army in the south of Russia in the 1770s before practising in the capital. It was he who not only translated his late wife's letters from the French but edited and amplified them to include all manner of archaeological and historical material and a large number of engravings of coins and inscriptions, producing a mighty tome with the title *A Tour, Performed in the Years 1795-6, through the Taurida, or Crimea....*[15]

Pallas and Guthrie were long-standing St Petersburg friends and it occasions no surprise that Mrs Guthrie spent much time with the Pallases in Crimea. She was but one of numerous travellers, such as Parkinson and Mary de Bode, who benefited from an acquaintance with the hospitable German scholar. During Paul's reign two further such travellers were John Tweddell (1769–99) and Edward Daniel Clarke (1769–1821), both fellows of Cambridge colleges, coevals but destined for very different fates. Tweddell was to die in Athens of a fever after four years of travel that included a long stay with the Pallases during two months in Crimea, where, using key descriptive words of the epoch, he enthused that the Crimean landscape 'offered some points of view more romantic and picturesque than the most romantic and most picturesque part of Switzerland'.[16] Pallas was Clarke's 'exemplary friend', who 'provided him with drawings, charts, maps, books, antiquities, minerals, and whatsoever else might serve to gratify his curiosity, or to promote the object of his travels; accompanying him upon the most wearisome excursions, in search, not only of the insects and plants of the country, but also of every document likely to illustrate its antient or modern history'.[17] He also agreed to sell his herbarium to

---

[15] There is a considerable literature on Guthrie. See, for instance, Anthony Cross, 'Articus and the *The Bee* (1790–4): An Episode in Anglo-Russian Cultural Relations', *Oxford Slavonic Papers*, new series, 2, 1969, pp. 62–76, and K. A. Papmehl, 'Matthew Guthrie: the Forgotten Student of 18th Century Russia', *Canadian Slavonic Papers*, 11, 1969, pp. 172–81.

[16] Robert Tweddell (ed.), *Remains of John Tweddell*, 2nd edn, London, 1816, pp. 201–02. Tweddell's diaries and drawings made during his stay in Crimea and said to be virtually ready for publication disappeared in somewhat controversial circumstances.

[17] E. D. Clarke, *Travels in Various Countries of Europe Asia and Africa*, 2 vols, 4th

John Marten Cripps (1780–1853), a Jesus College student whom Clarke accompanied as travelling tutor.[18] Clarke's debt to Pallas is everywhere openly acknowledged as he explored the peninsula, where he found so much of interest from the Crimean past and so much to condemn in its Russian present. His antipathy towards Paul and his Russia permeates his judgments on all aspects of post-annexation Crimea:

> They have laid waste the country; cut down the trees; pulled down the houses; overthrown the sacred edifices of the natives, with all their public buildings; destroyed the public aqueducts; robbed the inhabitants; insulted the Tahtars [*sic*] in their acts of public worship; torn up from their tombs the bodies of their ancestors, casting their relics upon dunghills, and feeding swine out of their coffins; annihilated all the monuments of antiquity; breaking up alike the sepulchres of Saints and Pagans, and scattering their ashes in the air.[19]

His Russophobic sentiments notwithstanding, Clarke, who was later to become professor of mineralogy at Cambridge University, made a serious contribution to the study of the peninsula's archaeology and history. He produced many drawings of buildings, historical sites and other objects of historical interest as well as of flora and fauna that were engraved for his influential work that was published, however, only in 1810.[20]

During the period between Clarke's journey through Crimea and the publication of his account Anglo-Russian relations continued to fluctuate: following the accession of Alexander I after Paul I's assassination British tourists were again much in evidence, some drawn initially to attend the Tsar's coronation in Moscow but many travelling much further afield before Alexander's reconciliation with Napoleon at Tilsit in July 1807 again halted the flow. Almost all of these young travellers, predominantly aristocratic or monied gentry, did not seek to publish accounts of their journeys, but in several cases there followed much delayed or posthumous publication of letters or diaries in what were often termed their 'literary remains'.[21] In his prefaces to

edn, London, 1, p. 162.

[18] Ibid., vol. 1, p. v. By 1810 the herbarium was in the possession of the botanist Aylmer Bourke Lambert (1761–1842), founder member of the Linnaean Society.

[19] Ibid., vol. 2, pp. 179–80.

[20] For a recent study of Clarke's illustrations, see V. M. Chekhmarev, *Rossiia v angliiskoi grafike: evropeiskaia, aziatskaia i amerikanskaia chasti v tsarstvovanie Ekateriny II i Pavla I (1762–1801 gg.)*, Moscow, 2020, pp. 97–108.

[21] See in detail in Anthony Cross, 'From the Assassination to Tilsit: The British in Russia and Their Travel Writings (1801–1807)', *Journal of European Studies*, 42, 2012, 1, pp. 1–17.

the first and second editions of his own travelogue Clarke mentions three such 'sources', to which he was in some measure indebted. Philip Yorke, Viscount Royston (1784–1808) and Charles Kelsall (1782–1857), recently down from Cambridge, and Reginald Heber (1783–1826), a fellow of All Souls, Oxford, all travelled through Russia independently of each other in 1805–07, including visits to Crimea in their itineraries. It was Heber's detailed diary of his journey, undertaken with his best friend John Thornton of Cambridge in 1806, that Clarke used in numerous footnotes, extensively but selectively, perhaps not sharing his valedictory enthusiasm of 'we, with great regret, quitted the Crimea and its pleasing inhabitants; it was really like being turned out of paradise.'[22] Crimea became a sort of surrogate Greece, which was of course the true paradise for the Oxbridge Hellenists at the beginning of the nineteenth century: for some it was the extreme point of their travels, where they could study the different cultures that had left rich archaeological remains in the peninsula; for others it was a staging post on the journey from Moscow to Constantinople via Odessa (founded in 1793) and then to Greece itself, at that time part of the Ottoman Empire.

Distinctly uninterested in the history of Crimea but undoubtedly attracted by its agricultural prospects was the Rev. Arthur Young (1767–1827), son of Arthur Young (1741–1820) the famed advocate of 'speeding the plough' who had in the previous century instructed young Russian students in the wonders of English agriculture on his Suffolk farm. Rev. Mr Young had arrived in Russia in June 1805 to undertake an agricultural survey of the Moscow region and on its completion in 1809 journeyed to Crimea, where he was to purchase a sizeable estate of some 9,000 acres at Karagoz, a few miles inland from the coastal town of Kaffa. It was a property belonging to a by then aged General Schütz and described enthusiastically by Pallas over a decade earlier but since fallen into deep neglect. Young enthused about the suitability of his property for sheep and cattle and for all manner of cultivation including a kitchen garden: 'as water from the river flows in this hot summer through & over every bed, & every channel & funnel in every part of the garden, & the soil very fine, yielding great crops, tho' never

[22] *The Life of Reginald Heber, D.D. Lord Bishop of Calcutta, by His Widow, with Selections from his Correspondence, Unpublished Poems, and Private Papers; together with a Journal of his Tour in Norway, Sweden, Russia, Hungary and Germany, and a History of the Cossaks*, ed. Amelia Heber, 2 vols, London, 1830, 1, 274. For Royston, see *The Remains of the Late Viscount Royston (with a Memoir of His Life)*, ed. Henry Pepys, London, 1838; for Kelsall, Mêla Britannicus [pseud.], *Esquisses de mes travaux, de mes voyages, et de mes opinions: dans une lettre à son ami Agathomerus*, London, 1830.

manured in the memory of man.'[23] His ambitious plans, however, never really came to fruition. Thwarted in his attempts to gain a Russian 'rank' and the right to buy 'slaves' (serfs), Young returned to England in the spring of 1814 and the following year advertised in local Suffolk papers for farmers wishing to avoid English taxes and willing to join him in 'the most beautiful province in the Russian Empire', on parcels of land they could rent or buy.[24] In the event he returned to Russia in late 1815 with a Mr and Mrs Holderness and their four children who were to remain until 1820 at Karagoz, where Young himself was to die in 1827 after unsuccessful attempts to sell his estate.

During his visit to London in 1814, a few months before the visit of Alexander I, signalling a new highpoint in Anglo-Russian relations, Young had discussed with the publisher Longman his wish to publish an account of his Russian experiences but in the event it was the long-suffering, pious, resourceful, and talented Mary Holderness who met success with the account she published soon after her return, *Notes relating to the Manners and Customs of the Crim Tartars, Written during a Four Years' Residence among that People* (1821). Two years later she incorporated these 'notes' (some 168 pages) into her *New Russia: Journey from Riga to the Crimea, by way of Kiev...*, re-titled for a second edition in 1827 *A Journey from Riga*, in the Preface to which she alludes to materials put at her disposal by a 'friend', although it is regrettable that she includes nothing about their life at Karagoz. Mention has earlier been made of the disreputable English gardener Henderson and his 'milkmaids' that Jeremy Bentham escorted to Crimea, and Young and the Holdernesses are examples of English 'colonists' from a later reign. Young himself in his letters mentions visiting a Mr Woodrow from Norfolk who had taken a ten-year lease on a farm at Chorgona near Balaklava as well as a Mr Woodcock, an acquaintance of the Holdernesses, who came to purchase the estate but drank himself to death.[25] He also mentions a visitor of quite a different complexion, the Rev. Lewis Way (1772–1840) of Stansted Park in Sussex, a leading figure in the London Society for the Promotion of Christianity among the Jews, who visited Karagoz in May 1818, seeking initially to buy Karagoz and establish there a settlement of converted Jews.[26]

---

[23] John G. Gazley, 'The Reverend Arthur Young, 1769–1827: Traveller in Russia and Farmer in the Crimea', *Bulletin of the John Rylands Library Manchester*, 38, 1956, p. 390.
[24] *The Times* carried the story on 8 May 1815 (Gazley, 'The Reverend Arthur Young', p. 394).
[25] Gazley 'The Reverend Arthur Young', pp. 387, 404.
[26] Ibid., pp. 398–401. See Geoffrey Henderson, *Lewis Way: A Biography*, London, 2014.

The Rev. Mr Way, however, was an example, albeit a very eccentric one, of an increasing number of British subjects who were very keen to preach and spread God's word in many parts of the Russian Empire, including Crimea. British missionaries had been active in Russia since the beginning of Alexander I's reign when the Edinburgh Bible Society established a colony at Karass in the Caucasus but it was only a few years after the foundation in 1813 of the Russian Bible Society, encouraged by the British and Foreign Bible Society, that the first missionaries travelled through Crimea. Among the most prominent of them and leaving published records of their journeys were the Reverends John Paterson (1776–1855) and Robert Pinkerton (d.1855) in 1816 and later, in 1821, the Rev. Ebenezer Henderson.[27] However, the most remarkable among them was not a Scot but a Tatar noble, Katti Geray (Qattı Giray) (1789–1847), the son of Selim III, the last Khan of Crimea, baptized in 1807 and thereafter utterly dedicated to spreading Christianity among his fellow countrymen. After years of study in Edinburgh, where he also acquired a Scottish wife, Anne Neilson (d. 1855), and interrupted only by a visit to Odessa in 1817 in the company of the Rev. Mr Way, he finally made his home in 1821 in Crimea, where he attempted to establish with the support of the Tsar a Christian seminary for Muslims at Bakhchisarai.[28] His attempts to evangelize the local Muslim population, for which Mrs Holderness had such high hopes, met only with hostility and a British traveller, seeking to meet the Gerays in 1837, commented wryly that: 'notwithstanding the influence he must possess over his compatriots, it is said he has not succeeded in prevailing upon a single Tartar to abjure Mahometanism, — perhaps because he could not ensure them a paradise inhabited by *houris*.'[29] Although professing a faith that did not encourage evangelical activities, there were also Quakers preaching to the local communities in Crimea in 1819, seeking the 'opportunity of proclaiming the salvation that comes by Jesus Christ to Tartars, Mahometans, Jews, Greeks and Armenians', distributing religious texts in translations into various languages, and visiting everywhere prisons

[27] Robert Pinkerton, *Extracts of Letters from the Rev. Robert Pinkerton, on His Late Tour in Russia, Poland, and Germany to Promote the Object of the British and Foreign Bible Society*, London, 1817; Ebenezer Henderson, *Biblical Researches and Travels in Russia; including a Tour in the Crimea; and the Passage of the Caucasus*, London, 1826.
[28] Hakan Kirimli and Hazan Kirimli, 'Crimean Tatars, Nogays, and Scottish Missionaries: The Story of Katti Geray and Other Baptised Descendants of the Crimean Khansı', *Cahiers du monde russe et soviétique*, 40, 2004, pp. 61–107.
[29] Mary Holderness, *New Russia: Journey from Riga to the Crimea, by Way of Kiev*, London, 1823, p. 128; Edmund Spencer, *Travels in Circassian, Krim-Tartary, &c. including a Steam Voyage down the Danube, from Vienna to Constantinople, and Round the Black Sea in 1836*, 2 vols, 3rd edn, London, 1839, 2, pp. 48–49.

and schools, as recorded in the diaries of Stephen Grellet (1773–1855), who accompanied William Allen (1770–1843) from St Petersburg, where a group of Quakers had recently arrived at the Tsar's invitation to effect agricultural improvements.[30]

In 1823 there began what might be termed the Vorontsov period in British presence in Crimea. It was in that year that the son of a long-serving Russian ambassador to the Court of St James's, educated in England and strongly Anglophile, and whose sister was married to the Earl of Pembroke and was mother of the future British secretary of state for war during the Crimean War, Sidney Herbert, Count Mikhail Semenovich Vorontsov (1781–1856) became governor-general of New Russia that included Crimea. Although his official residence was to be in Odessa, which flourished during his tenure, his home was to be in Crimea and specifically at Alupka where he was to employ British architects in the construction of his palace and the laying-out of its gardens. Ironically, neither Thomas Harrison (1744–1829) nor Edward Blore (1787–1879), who was appointed after Harrison's death, set foot in Crimea and saw the actual setting for what they envisaged and designed. Little of what Harrison planned was accomplished, and it was to be Blore, whom Vorontsov engaged on a visit to England in 1831, who was to be the true architect of a palace that was to astonish visitors by a north-facing facade that was reminiscent (more or less) of Tudor England and its southern side overlooking the Black Sea, redolent of the Moorish style of the Alhambra. Its interior contained a library modelled on Sir Walter Scott's at Abbotsford (with, of course, an English librarian) and the house boasted the very latest in English hygiene and plumbing, with no fewer than ten lavatories! In the absence of the architects, two highly competent clerks of works were sent out from England: Francis Heiton (d.1833), but briefly, followed by William Hunt, who was exemplary not only in carrying out Blore's and the Count's wishes but added features of his own devising: the forty-mile macadamized road leading to the palace that he had constructed was much admired. There were also a number of British master craftsmen, such as the carpenter Charles Williams and the furniture maker Edwin Rice, employed to guide and instruct a multinational workforce.[31] Visits to Alupka were inevitably to feature prominently in the travelogues of

[30] *Memoirs of the Life and Gospel Labours of Stephen Grellet*, ed. Benjamin Seebohm, 2 vols, 3rd edn, London, 1862, 2, pp. 411–22; *Life of William Allen, with Selections from his Correspondence*, 2 vols, London, 1846, 2, pp. 1–93.
[31] For a detailed discussion of the palace, see Brett, *Towers of Crime Tartary*, pp. 55–114.

British visitors to Crimea during the reign of Nicholas I: their reactions were far from uniform, although most were impressed by the setting — the mountain Ai-Petri (St Peter) that loomed behind the palace and the magnificent vistas from the terraces towards the sea — and almost all were the recipients of Vorontsov's lavish hospitality.

Vorontsov's vast investment in Alupka was the incentive for other wealthy Russians to buy properties and estates along the southern littoral of Crimea and for the first time there was mention of villages and beauty spots that had hitherto been largely ignored by travellers. Such was Yalta (Ialta), perhaps now the most famous of all Crimea's towns but only receiving that status in 1838: Charles Scott, visiting in 1850, wrote that 'an attempt is being made to turn Yalta into a watering-place, a humble kind of Brighton', but conceded that the setting was 'delightful', the climate 'delicious', and it was a 'charming' place for the invalid.[32] Laurence Oliphant (1829–88), touring two years later, opined that 'it is not long since the Crimea became a fashionable resort among Russian nobility', following the example of Vorontsov and the Tsar, Nicholas I, who after a visit to Alupka was inspired to build a palace for the Empress Aleksandra Fedorovna at Oreanda and employ on Vorontsov's recommendation a Scottish gardener by the name of Ross to lay out the grounds.[33] William Hunt, who supervised the building of Oreanda, was himself soon to design and build the Gaspra palace, a few miles from Alupka, for Prince Aleksandr Golitsyn in the 1840s.

It was, however, Sevastopol' that commanded most attention from British travellers and increasingly so throughout the 1840s and '50s up to the outbreak of war. Although it was the ruins of nearby Chersonesos, a sixth-century BC Greek settlement, that had excited Clarke and his fellow Hellenists, Catherine's 'venerable city', founded in 1783, grew into a naval and military stronghold. Its harbour was hailed by a British visitor as 'perhaps the finest in the world. It has so great a depth of water in some of the bay's inlets that line-of-battle ships of the largest size lay close to the shore'.[34]

The first major figure in its development was a Scot and it awaited only the expertise of an Englishman to realise its full potential. Neither

[32] Charles Henry Scott, *The Baltic, the Black Sea, and the Crimea: comprising Travels in Russia, a Voyage down the Volga to Astrachan, and a Tour through Crim Tartary*, 2nd edn, London, 1854, p. 240.
[33] Laurence Oliphant, *The Russian Shores of the Black Sea in the Autumn of 1852, with a Voyage down the Volga, and a Tour through the Country of the Don Cossacks*, 2nd edn, Edinburgh and London, 1854, p. 240–41.
[34] William Jesse, *Notes of a Half-pay in Search of Health; or, Russia, Circassia, and the Crimea, in 1839–40*, 2 vols, London, 1841, 1, pp. 142–43.

has the monument he deserves in the city nor due recognition in Russian historiography. Thomas Mackenzie (1740–86), who entered Russian service in 1765 and gained fame as the commander of one of the fireships that destroyed the Turkish fleet at the battle of Chesme bay in 1770, rose to the rank of rear-admiral and was responsible for the initial development of the city and its harbour for some two and a half years before his untimely death.[35] It was, however, John Upton (1774?–1851), a half century later, who possessed the engineering skills to turn Sevastopol' into a fortress-city and a major military port. Escaping trial for embezzlement in England, Upton entered Russian service in 1826 and for the next twenty-five years helped to transform Sevastopol'.[36] Numerous British travellers enjoyed his hospitality and marvelled at the feats of construction and engineering he was achieving, together with one of his four sons, William (1811–93). William Jesse (1809–71), a half-pay officer who visited Sevastopol' in late 1838, noted that Upton was 'a pupil of the great [Thomas] Telford' and praised and described in detail the dry docks 'erecting here under the Colonel's superintendence, and from his own plans; they are unique of their kind'.[37]

The aqueducts that brought fresh water to the city aroused particular admiration: one stretched for some six miles from Inkerman, requiring tunnelling through solid rock: 'I am told, though it seems scarcely credible, that it was a question here of whether *magic* was not employed in the construction of the tunnel.'[38] The purveyor of this information was Lt-Colonel William De Ros (1797–1874), who, together with a naval colleague, was dispatched to Crimea by the British government in late 1835 to check on 'unusual preparations' for war — with the full knowledge of the Russians.

The British maintained a keen interest in events in Crimea and the Black Sea area during Nicholas I's reign, beginning with the Russo-Turkish conflict of 1828–29, as reflected in the titles of at least two travel accounts — T. B. Armstrong's *Journal of Travels in the Seat of War, during the Last Two Campaigns of Russia and Turkey* (1831) and James Edward Alexander's *Travels to the Seat of War in the East,*

[35] For the championing of Mackenzie's role, see Mungo Melvin, *Sevastopol's Wars: Crimea from Potemkin to Putin*, Oxford, 2017, pp. 75–78.

[36] On John Upton and his sons, see Capt. Y. Kulikov, E. Kulikova and Major C. D. Robins, 'The Sevastopol Docks, and Upton: Traitor or an Honourable Man?', *The War Correspondent*, 28, April 2010, pp. 28–34; Michael Vanden Bosch and Roger Bartlett, 'More Light on the Upton Family in Russia and in the Crimean War', ibid., 29, July 2011, p. 9; 30, April 2012, pp. 26–32, and 30, October 2012, pp. 10–19.

[37] Jesse, *Notes of a Half-pay*, vol. 1, p. 136.

[38] William De Ros, *Journal of a Tour in the Principalities, Crimea, and Countries adjacent to the Black Sea in the Years 1835-36*, London, 1855, pp. 113–14.

through Russia and the Crimea, in 1829 (1830). Captain, later General, Sir James Alexander (1803–85) sailed with the Russian fleet, but was arrested as a spy, although later exonerated after a personal interview with the Tsar. Admiral Adolphus Slade's (1804–77) *Records of Travels in Turkey, Greece, etc., and of a Cruise on the Black Sea with the Captain Pasha* (1832) reflected his Turcophile sympathies that more widely were sustained by the pro-Ottoman, Russophobic campaign conducted by David Urquhart (1805–77), secretary at the British embassy in Constantinople. Britain came near to war in 1836 with the seizure by the Russians of the gun-running British schooner *Vixen* in the Black Sea, but tension was temporarily diffused in the 1840s with Nicholas I's state visit to London in 1844.[39] The Tsar, who produced such a favourable impression on Queen Victoria, was paradoxically in many respects an Anglophile; indeed, according to an Englishman who met him a few years earlier in Alupka:

> [...] he spoke of England and the English in the most flattering manner; said how pleased he was to see them at all times in Russia, and hoped, on our return, that we would tell them of the beautiful scenery of the Crimea, in order that they might come in numbers and make it their summer tour, now that there was such facility of travelling by steam.[40]

By a supreme irony these words appeared in print virtually at the same time that Britain and France declared war against Russia on 28 March 1854.

Following the landing of the Allied forces at Kalamita Bay on 14 September 1854 literally thousands of British subjects were indeed to set foot on Crimean soil, but they were for the most part men in uniform, often engaged in long and bloody battles at places on the Crimean peninsula that became in Britain virtually household words — the Alma, Balaklava, Inkerman, Sevastopol' — and they had little time or inclination to comment on the scenery or places of historical interest other than to detail the extremes of the weather, bitter cold to intense heat, and the minutiae of hardly bearable day-to-day existence.[41] Many accounts by participants in the conflict, usually based on letters and diaries, were subsequently published, some surprisingly quickly, others,

---

[39] See Harold N. Ingle, *Nesselrode and the Russian Rapprochement with Britain, 1836–1844*, Berkeley, Los Angeles, CA, and London, 1976.

[40] Capt [Edmund] Spencer, *Turkey, Russia, the Black Sea, and Circassia*, London, 1855, p. 284.

[41] For the most recent and comprehensive account, see Orlando Figes, *Crimea: The Last Crusade*, London, 2010.

decades later, while more remain in family and public archives: together they provide a moving testament to the horrors of warfare. Some, however, reveal, that, come the cease-fire, and, indeed, even before, there was an almost irresistible urge to restore what was had been the normality of everyday life, at least for the officer classes. There are over a dozen accounts of the organizing of horse racing and of other sporting and recreational events and of officers making excursions to see, for example, the palace of Bakhchisarai and the imposing natural sights of the Baidar Pass and the caves at Balaklava.[42] There was some fraternization and one officer describes, for example, how he and a companion went to Simferopol' and sat among Russian counterparts at the Café Odessa, while expressing surprise at the high cost of champagne and porter.[43]

With the outbreak of war between Britain and Russia the British public turned to newspapers and journals and hastily compiled books to be informed not only about the progress of the war itself but also about the theatre in which it was taking place, about precisely where and what was Crimea. James Wyld (1812–87), geographer to the Queen, soon published a detailed map of 'The Town & Harbour of Sevastopol with the Batteries & Approaches' and was responsible for creating the model of Sevastopol' at the Great Globe in Leicester Square.[44] *A Description of some of the Principal Harbours and Towns of the Krimea*, compiled by Montague Gore, went through three editions in a matter of weeks. There were a number of historical works, such as the Rev. Thomas Milner's *The Crimea, its Ancient and Modern History* (1855) and W. Burckhardt's *Short Historical Account of the Crimea: from the Earliest Ages and during the Russian Occupation* (1855) with its sting in the final word of the title. Travellers who had been in Crimea in earlier times rushed into print — such were De Ros, now back in Crimea as the British army's quartermaster-general, who disinterred his diary from eighteen years earlier for publication in 1855, or the MP Henry Seymour, amplifying his own impressions of travels in 1844 with material from other works in order 'to satisfy public curiosity'. Laurence Oliphant, the

---

[42] See, for instance, William Jervis-Waldy, *From Eight to Eighty: The Life of a Crimean and Indian Mutiny Veteran*, London, 1914; Daniel Lysons, *The Crimean War from First to Last*, London, 1895; Nathaniel Steevens, *The Crimean Campaign with the Connaught Rangers 1854–56*, London, 1878; Frederic Wraxall, *Camp Life; or Passages from the Story of a Continent*, London, 1860.

[43] John Alexander Ewart, *The Story of a Soldier's Life; or, Peace, War, and Mutiny*, 2 vols, London, 1881, 1, p. 425. General Sir John (1821–1904) was then a major in the Sutherland Highlanders.

[44] See generally en.wikipedia.org › wiki › Wyld's_Great_Globe.

most recent of travellers in the region in 1852, responding to the great response to his book published the following year, was soon adding a final chapter to update three more editions in 1855.

The year 1855 saw also the publication of Mrs Frances Isabella Duberly's *Journal*. Fanny Duberly was still at that time in Crimea, where she had accompanied her husband, the regimental paymaster of the 8th Hussars, from the beginning of the campaign. A formidable horsewoman, who witnessed the battle of Balaklava and the charge of the Light Brigade, she was the only officer's wife remaining throughout the campaign, although there were other wives there periodically, as well as countless unsung regimental wives.[45] There were, however, books that reveal a less appealing aspect of the tragic conflict, the phenomenon of war tourism, which may not have had its origins in the Crimean War but undoubtedly gained unfortunate momentum during and for long after the war.[46] 'Travelling Gents' and 'Lady Amateurs', as they were called, were soon in evidence, some prompted by proper concerns for loved ones, others for the thrill or intrusive curiosity. Helen Rappaport suggests that the first representative of the female variety was Ellen Palmer (1830–63), daughter of an Irish baronet, whom she accompanied to Crimea at the end of 1854 and spent a month, displaying foolhardy bravery and fluttering officers' hearts.[47] At least she did not speed to publish her impressions as did some of her male counterparts. Henry Bushby was among the first tourists in the war zone, arriving at Evpatoriia Bay on 3 October 1854, witnessing the initial bombardment of Sevastopol' and something of the battles at the Alma and Inkerman, before leaving after an 'enjoyable trip' on 10 November to publish his letters, albeit anonymously, the following year.[48] Others examples were the brothers A. and George Money, publishing in 1856 *Sevastopol: Our Tent in the Crimea; and Wanderings in Sevastopol by Two Brothers* (1856) and Edward Sullivan's, *A Trip to the Trenches in February and March, 1855. By an Amateur* (London, 1855), although

---

[45] For these and others, including, of course Florence Nightingale and Mary Seacole, see Helen Rappaport, *No Place for Ladies: The Untold Story of Women in the Crimean War*, London, 2007.

[46] War Tourism has become the subject of academic study, now frequently and often confusingly called Dark Tourism or even Thanatotourism, and is associated with the Institute for Dark Tourism Research of the University of Central Lancashire and with the work of Professors Richard Sharpley and A. V. Seaton (credited with introducing the word 'thanatotourism' in 1996).

[47] Rappaport, *No Place for Ladies*, pp. 146–48. See Ellen Palmer, *Crimean Courtship*, ed. by Betty Askwith, Wilton, 1985, pp. 63–91.

[48] [Henry Jeffreys Bushby], *A Month in the Camp before Sebastopol. By a Non-Combatant*, London, 1855.

the Flashman-like exploits of the Rev. William Wickenden (1795–1864), allegedly borrowing a soldier's greatcoat to experience trench life, beggars belief.[49]

The Treaty of Paris on 30 March 1856 brought the war to its official end and the evacuation of the British forces began. Crimea was to be left to the tourists who came over the coming years, at times in large numbers, to visit the battle sites, gather mementoes, and to pay homage at the several war cemeteries and memorials hastily created by the departing British forces.[50] A mere seventy-five years had elapsed since Admiral Mackenzie had sailed into Akhtiar Bay to begin the construction of Sevastopol' that had grown impressively through the engineering skills of Colonel Upton but now lay in ruins. A 'delicious country' had been ravaged.

[49] William S. Wickenden, *Adventures before Sebastopol*, London, 1855.
[50] See, for example, John Pulling, *A Tour in Southern Europe and the Crimea*, London, 1858; Edwin Galt, *The Camp and the Cutter: or, A Cruise to the Crimea*, London, 1856; John Gadsby, *A Trip to Sebastopol, Out and Home, by way of Vienna, the Danube, Odessa, Constantinople, and Athens*, London, 1858.

Samuel Bentham, Inventor

Roger Bartlett
University College London, School of Slavonic and
East European Studies

SAMUEL BENTHAM (1757–1831) is not a name to conjure with among the general public. Overshadowed by his philosopher and jurist brother Jeremy, Samuel was also eclipsed by others of his generation in his own field of engineering, at a time of extraordinary progress and achievement in Britain's industrial development. Thus a recent popular work on *Pioneers of the Industrial Age* celebrates Robert Stevenson (lighthouses), George and Robert Stephenson (railways), Richard Trevithick, Thomas Telford, John Rennie, Marc and Isambard Kingdom Brunel: men whose engineering creations were 'expressions of the nation's industrial might that the engineers had themselves made possible'.[1] Among aficionados and historians of the British navy, however, Bentham's name is immediately recognizable and held in high regard as a naval reformer who played a major role in 'shift[ing] thinking in the royal dockyards to a new level of technological performance' at the height of the Napoleonic wars.[2] He is also becoming better known to historians of the Napoleonic conflict.[3] After a successful career (1780–91) in Catherine the Great's Russia, during which he reached the Russian rank of brigadier-general, and spent long periods in Siberia, Samuel Bentham's technical skills and insights sufficiently impressed the Lords of the British Admiralty that they appointed him to the novel post of inspector-general of naval works, which he held from 1795 to 1808 and continued under diminished circumstances as civil architect and engineer to the navy until 1812. His inventions, innovations and determination to inculcate new working patterns and mental habits marked the beginning of the industrial revolution in the royal navy;[4]

---

[1] Martin Worth, *Sweat and Inspiration: Pioneers of the Industrial Age*, Stroud, 1999.
[2] Roger Morriss, 'The Office of the Inspector General of Naval Works and Technological Innovation in the Royal Dockyards', *Transactions of the Naval Dockyards Society*, 1, 2006, pp. 21–29 (p. 28).
[3] Roger Knight, *Britain Against Napoleon: The Organization of Victory 1793–1815*, London, 2013, especially pp. 377–81. I am indebted to Simon Dixon for this reference and other help.
[4] Bentham's career and innovations are documented in several writings of his widow and biographer Mary Sophia Bentham: notably 'Memoir of the late Brigadier-General Sir Samuel Bentham, with an Account of His Inventions', in *Papers and Practical Illustrations of Public Works of Recent Construction both*

but as this paper will show, his contributions were by no means confined only to naval matters.

Samuel Bentham's fascination with things nautical began early, to the extent that his wealthy lawyer father gave up the idea of a liberal professional career for him and bound him as a naval apprentice at the age of fourteen. His superior apprenticeship allowed him to combine systematic study of the sciences with hands-on dockyard work and, later, enabled experience at sea: a combination of the theoretical and the practical which was fundamental to his later career. He also benefited from closeness to his elder brother Jeremy: the brothers had a particularly strong relationship. 'Both had exceptionally fertile and inventive minds, and a passion for reform and improvement in their several fields of endeavour; many projects were shared and there was a constant exchange of ideas throughout their lives;'[5] moreover their thinking was informed by an education and a mind-set which drew upon the great thinkers and the new ideas and 'natural philosophy' of the Enlightenment and took in questions of public good and social progress as well as their own interests and personal career. Both brothers sought to apply logic, blue-skies thinking and rational analysis to problems of contemporary life, whether ship-building and engineering or law, constitutions and penal reform: Jeremy later observed to a correspondent, 'To the objects of his pursuits [Samuel] bears much the same relation that I do. You will read me in his manner of stating and reasoning.'[6]

Already during his apprenticeship Samuel approached his field critically and creatively; and already he came up against problems

British and American, London, 1856, reprint 2017, pp. 41–79; *The Life of Brigadier-General Sir Samuel Bentham KSG, formerly Inspector-General of Naval Works, lately a Commissioner of His Majesty's Navy with the distinct duty of Civil Architect and Engineer of the Navy. By his Widow M. S. Bentham*, London, 1862. The story of Samuel and Jeremy Bentham's relations with Russia under Catherine II is told by M. S. Anderson, 'Samuel Bentham in Russia 1779–91', *American Slavonic and East European Review*, 15, 1956, 2, pp. 157–72; I. R. Christie, *The Benthams in Russia 1780–1791*, Oxford and Providence, RI, 1993; Anthony Cross, *By the Banks of the Neva: Chapters from the Lives and Careers of the British in Eighteenth-Century Russia*, Cambridge, 1997, *passim*; Roger Morriss, *Science, Utility and Maritime Power: Samuel Bentham in Russia, 1779–91*, London, 2016. For Samuel's later career see publications by Mary Bentham; J. Coad, *The Portsmouth Block Mills. Bentham, Brunel and the Start of the Royal Navy's Industrial Revolution*, Swindon, 2005; Morriss, 'The Office'; R. Morriss, *Science, Utility and British Naval Technology 1793–1815: Samuel Bentham and the Royal Dockyards*, London, 2020.

[5]   C. Pease-Watkin, *ODNB* on-line, s.v. 'Samuel Bentham'.

[6]   *The Correspondence of Jeremy Bentham*, ed. T. Sprigge et al., 12 vols to date, Oxford 1968–2006 (hereafter *Correspondence*), 10, p. 156, no. 2713, Jeremy Bentham to J. Joaquin de Mora, 15–17 November 1820.

of private versus public interest and of merit versus patronage which would dog and shape his career throughout his life. In 1772, aged fifteen, he designed improvements to a ship's pump which he offered to the Navy Board. The Board commended the invention, but declined to order a trial; Bentham later discovered that they considered his pump superior to the existing one but had refused it for reasons of convenience and private expediency.[7] Throughout his career Bentham continually formulated new ideas and mechanical inventions — the list published by his widow, champion and biographer Mary Bentham runs to three closely-printed pages.[8] He was also driven by the broader desire to achieve 'utility' — scientific, economic or social improvement — in all situations, whether new Russian trade in the Far East, the development of Russian and British industry, or the rational and economic organization of Britain's dockyards. A third motivation was his own self-interest, whether a preoccupation with potential lucrative openings during his explorations in northern Europe and Russia, or his (quite justified) concern with salary and remuneration offered for the various official posts he held. Telling a correspondent in 1791 of his doings in 'my ever-beloved Siberia', which offered boundless opportunities to develop shipping, trade and industry and where he had 'projects of discovery and improvement, some executed, others, I hope, executing, and many more to execute', he added: 'the inquiry, how utility is to come of it, is what must forever occupy me. It makes but little difference to me, what be the country.'[9] Equally continual was his concern or struggle with the human or managerial dimension of his ambitions: the necessity of mobilizing the patronage, support and funding which could enable the realization of his inventions and projects, the need to conciliate or overcome opposition, and the need to provide means for his workers to produce the right result.

Russia in the eighteenth and early nineteenth centuries was widely seen as a land of opportunity. Samuel, on the point of setting off to seek his fortune in 1779, reminded Jeremy: 'I need not recall to you the feasts we have so often heated our imaginations with, when we have been contemplating the progress of improvement in that rising country.'[10] He went out to Russia in 1779 with excellent letters of introduction, and

[7] Pease-Watkin, *ODNB on-line*, s.v. 'Samuel Bentham'; Mary Bentham, 'Memoir', p. 77; Morriss, *Science, Utility and Maritime Power*, pp. 87–89.

[8] Mary Bentham, 'Memoir', pp. 77–79.

[9] *Correspondence*, vol. 4, p. 319, 8 July 1791. Russia had been alluring because of the opportunities it offered; later, on the prospect of an equally rewarding career, Samuel was happy to stay in England. After 1812 possibilities in France were also attractive.

[10] Quoted by Anderson, 'Samuel Bentham in Russia', p. 158.

the protection of the British ambassador Sir James Harris introduced him to influential figures at Court. Initially he declined a post offered in the state service, wishing to maintain his independence and to discover the lie of the land regarding technology and the economy, as well as investigating potentially lucrative economic and technical projects. But experience soon taught him that for social and economic success in that country state rank and a post in the service were essential: not only did they give noble status, privilege and access to higher society, as well as lucrative employment; they also gave standing essential to negotiating agreements with private Russian industrialists. Therefore on the prospect of an advantageous post (and also because at that point he was contemplating a Russian marriage) in 1783 he entered state service, receiving the rank of court counsellor (rank 7 in the Table of Ranks). He travelled widely: in 1781–82 he had toured Siberia with official support — an epic twenty-month exploration which could rank with the Academy expeditions of the eighteenth century; after entering state service and a year supervising the Fontanka canal in St Petersburg, he worked for four years in the south in the employ of the favourite, Grigorii Potemkin, managing one of the Prince's estates and taking part in the second Turkish war, before returning to command a regiment in Siberia in 1789–91.

During his two tours in Siberia, Bentham's inventive character came to the fore in his practical response when faced with immediate deficiencies and difficulties. The soldiers of his Siberian regiment were in need of education: so he established a regimental school for them.[11] At one point, travelling in Kirghiz territory, he wished to establish survey data. 'Their rulers would not have permitted any visible measurement of their country, he therefore invented a new description of way-metre; it was a kind of spring projection on the felloe of a wheel, which on pressure against the ground gave motion to a recording mechanism of the distance passed over.'[12] During his first tour he stayed for six months at Nizhnii Tagil, a Urals metallurgical centre built up by the Demidov family, where he studied the nature and efficiency of the Demidov works; he also addressed himself to his personal problem, as a traveller, of journeys in different seasonal conditions and across wide and unbridged Siberian rivers. He imagined an amphibious coach, a boat-shaped 'ship-carriage', which the Demidov facilities enabled

[11] K. A. Papmehl, 'The Regimental School Established in Siberia by Samuel Bentham', *Canadian Slavonic Papers*, 8, 1966, pp. 153–68.

[12] Mary Bentham, 'Memoir', p. 48.

SKETCH OF A SHIP-CARRIAGE.

THE SHIP-CARRIAGE REPRESENTED IN ITS SEVERAL FORMS.

Fig 1. Sketches of a ship-carriage, constructed and used in Siberia
(see footnote 13).

him to build, at once boat, carriage and sledge.[13] His ship-carriage was successful: consequently, on his second Siberian tour he built ship-carriages both for himself and his assistants. He improved on his initial design, now using diagonal planking and additional water-proofing with hides which were smoked after being fixed.[14] The ship-carriage had a long life — it was subsequently experimented with for military purposes by both the Russian and the British authorities, the British version being built unprecedentedly of metal. Later it was claimed that Potemkin had equipped an army corps with such vessels; and a model of it was immortalized in the St Petersburg Naval Museum.[15] At Nizhnii Tagil Samuel found the Russian carpenters unable to produce wooden parts to the required precision, so took a hand himself; his longer-term solution to this difficulty, and at the same time a contribution to his hosts' industrial works, was to invent a mechanical means of producing precision parts, a machine for planing wood and cutting mouldings, which he would subsequently develop and patent on his return to Britain.[16] Bentham's proclivity for inventing solutions to current problems remained with him throughout his life. Travelling in France in 1816 and disgusted by the state of French inns, he constructed conveyances which accommodated all the family's chattels, including a piano, and enabled the company to be independent of nightly accommodation and to sleep wherever a halting place offered. The conveyances did not always live up to ideal expectations, to the increasing discontent of his daughters. Mary Bentham however claimed that these vehicles 'were the first of the kind, but served as a model for the omnibuses in Paris, which were afterwards introduced into this country.'[17]

On his return from his first Siberian expedition in 1782 Bentham presented a formal report on his experiences and on Siberian potential and problems, to which both Potemkin and the Empress Catherine (reigned 1762–96) personally paid considerable attention and which led on to his service appointment. Later, at Potemkin's instigation, Samuel switched from the civilian to the military service, receiving the rank

---

[13] 'Sketch of a ship-carriage, constructed and used in Siberia', *United Service Journal and Naval and Military Magazine*, 2, 1829, pp. 579–98; Mary Bentham, *Life*, pp. 26–29, 116–17; Morriss, *Science, Utility and Maritime Power*, pp. 66–68.

[14] Mary Bentham, 'Memoir', p. 48.

[15] Ibid., pp. 44, 78; Morriss, *Science, Utility and Maritime Power*, p. 182; A. B. Granville, *St Petersburgh. A Journal of Travels to and from that Capital.* [...], 2 vols, London, 1829, 2, pp. 59–63.

[16] Mary Bentham, 'Memoir', pp. 44, 77; Morriss, *Science, Utility and Maritime Power*, pp. 68–70.

[17] George Bentham, *Autobiography 1800–1834*, ed. M. Filipiuk, Toronto, London, 1997, pp. 30–32, 37; Mary Bentham, 'Memoir', pp. 71–72.

of lieutenant-colonel (also rank 7, in the military Table of Ranks). He travelled south to Potemkin's huge estate of Krichev on the Dnieper (now in Belarus), to take command of a battalion which he was to train in ship-building and naval skills; but he soon found himself in managerial control of the whole estate, which included a complex of industrial enterprises. He remained at Krichev for over two years, 1786–87, during which time Jeremy came out to visit him. To improve the output of the enterprises, Bentham undertook various experiments. Mary Bentham later summarized some of them: 'he reduced the cost of glass materially, though of improved quality; he effected the improvement of steel; made a variety of Reaumur's porcelain so insensible to variations of temperature, as to bear, when red-hot, to be plunged into cold water, and so impervious as to form crucibles for melting brass.'[18]

One of Samuel's most notable Krichev inventions was his 'vermicular'.[19] Potemkin wished to construct vessels capable of carrying timber and freight on the shallow, winding and unpredictable Dnieper; for the Empress's celebrated southern tour of inspection in 1787 he also wanted a 'fast galley' to carry her down the lower stretches of the river to Kherson. Samuel was commissioned to design and construct a suitable vessel. His solution was a series of linked articulated barges, able to swivel and bend, drawing no more than six inches when laden, driven swiftly by numerous oarsmen and providing ample stowage or accommodation. This concept answered to the river conditions admirably, and the imperial version, consisting of six barges duly arrayed for Catherine's use, was a great success with the Empress and especially with Potemkin. 'The Empress at several different times and to different persons spoke in praise of Verm.' When the vermicular with Potemkin on board reached Ekaterinoslav:

> He was so pleased with Verm that, although it was such windy weather, and he had a house of his own in the place, he would not go ashore. It was about 4 o'clock but as the Emperor [Joseph II of Austria] was come there to surprise the Empress, the Prince went to pay him his visit at his lodgings and the Emperor came and returned it on board Verm. As the Prince chose to sleep on board, there is no doubt but the Emperor as well as everybody favoured the invention.[20]

---

[18] Ibid., p. 46; Morriss, *Science, Utility and Maritime Power*, pp. 124–57, gives more details.

[19] Ibid., pp. 169–82.

[20] London, British Library (hereafter BL), Add. MSS 33540, fols 365–67, quoted by Morriss, *Science, Utility and Maritime Power*, pp. 180–81.

However, the ultimately best known of Samuel's Krichev innovations was not produced to order, but as in other cases mentioned was a direct response to practical problems encountered on the ground: a means to organize, control and improve the productivity of his labour force — the Inspection House or Panopticon. Drawing on memories of the French École Militaire, which he had visited in Paris in the 1770s, Bentham envisaged a circular building with a central inspection chamber enabling an inspector to survey the entire space. Persons outside the inspection chamber would be unable to see in, and so must assume that they were under inspection at all times.[21] At Krichev, with Potemkin's consent, Samuel was uniquely placed to build this remarkable conception. But before he could do so, Potemkin sold the estate, and war broke out with the Ottoman Empire. The Krichev Panopticon remained on paper. However, Jeremy took up the idea with enthusiasm, and it has since had a long history as a controversial template for prison architecture.[22] It has also emerged as an icon of the new social science of surveillance studies, which has evolved since the 1950s, given particular impetus by Michel Foucault ('the grandfather of surveillance studies')[23] in the 1970s, to such works as Simone Browne's 2015 combination of libertarian criticism with black feminism and other disciplines in *Dark Matters: On the Surveillance of Blackness*, and no doubt beyond; the Panopticon also continues to fascinate other scholars and observers.[24] The point to be emphasized here is that the original Panopticon plan, only distantly connected to the topography of the École Militaire, is a product of abstract logic, a theoretically rational approach to a pressing local problem, as utopian and untested as Jeremy Bentham's codification template.[25] In 1806–07, sent by the Admiralty to

[21] Philip Steadman, 'Samuel Bentham's Panopticon', *J. Bentham Studies* 14, 2012, pp. 1–30 (p. 29); Haroldo A. Guizar, '"Make a Hard Push for It": The Benthams, Foucault, and the Panopticons' Roots in the Paris École Militaire', *Lumen*, 37, 2018, pp. 151–73.

[22] R. Evans, *The Fabrication of Virtue: English Prison Architecture 1750–1840*, Cambridge, 1982; N. Johnston, *Forms of Constraint: A History of Prison Architecture*, Champaign, IL, 2000.

[23] https://web.mit.edu/gtmarx.www/surv_studies.pdf (accessed 2 August 2020).

[24] See for instance *The Routledge Handbook of Surveillance Studies*, ed. K. Ball, K. Haggerty, D. Lyon, Abingdon, New York, 2014; D. Lyon, *The Culture of Surveillance*, Cambridge, 2018. Other recent treatments: https://blog.digitalpanopticon.org/building-benthams-panopticon/ (accessed 23 July 2020); J. Crawford, 'Little Brother's Big Brother House', *Fallen Glory. The Lives and Deaths of Twenty Lost Buildings from the Tower of Babel to the Twin Towers*, London, 2015, chapter 15; F. Cottell and M. Mueller, 'From Pain to Pleasure: Panopticon Dreams and Pentagon Petal', in *Bentham and the Arts*, ed. A. Julius, M. Quinn, P. Schofield, London, 2020, pp. 244–69.

[25] In 1824 Jeremy, by now disillusioned with Tsar Alexander I, nevertheless wrote to his friend Admiral Nikolai Mordvinov, 'I should now absolutely despair, but that here and there, in my Constitutional Code, an arrangement might be found applicable with

Russia on an abortive mission to build ships for the British navy, Samuel did succeed in building one Panopticon, the College of Arts at Okhta in St Petersburg (1806–18), and he continued to advocate the principle as a dockyard panacea.[26] The short-lived College of Arts seems to have functioned adequately as a training institution, though its success in supervision is unclear; subsequent attempts to build panoptical prisons have been at best problematic.

On the outbreak of Catherine's second Turkish war (1787–92) Bentham was posted to Kherson, where his brief, although he was an army officer, was to prepare Russia's Black Sea defences against the Turkish fleet. The ships at his disposal were a motley collection of small boats and pleasure craft. Making a virtue of necessity, he adapted and reinforced the vessels to take heavy guns, an unconventional and potentially dangerous measure, and minimized recoil. In the Liman (mouth of the Dnieper) his highly-mobile heavy guns did great damage to the Turkish fleet, including ships of the line which struggled to manoeuvre in the shallow waters. He was rewarded for the victory with an advance in rank, a ceremonial sword, and the prestigious Cross of the Order of St George. But army rank was not formally or socially acceptable in the navy, so Potemkin reassigned him at his own wish to the command of a regiment, which in 1789 he exchanged for another in Siberia.[27]

In 1791 Bentham took leave to visit Britain. He intended to return to Russia, but events conspired against it: the Russian reaction to the French Revolution, then the death of Potemkin in October 1791, that of Samuel's and Jeremy's father in 1792 by which the brothers inherited substantial resources, and his involvement in Jeremy's plans for a panopticon prison, convinced him otherwise. He built machines for the new prison for which he took out patents in 1791 and 1793; these attracted the attention of parliamentarians and Lords of the Admiralty, so that he was able officially to visit dockyards and, to demonstrate his ship-building ideas, was authorized to construct seven experimental vessels of his own advanced design. Mary Bentham lists 25 'principal

no less advantage in your monarchy than in my Utopia.' *Correspondence*, vol. 12, pp. 12–16.

[26] Steadman, 'Samuel Bentham's Panopticon'; Roger Bartlett, 'Samuel Bentham's Mission to Russia 1805–07 and the St Petersburg Panopticon', forthcoming in the proceedings of the Study Group on Eighteenth-Century Russia conference at Strasbourg in 2018; C. Pease-Watkin, 'Jeremy and Samuel Bentham — the Public and the Private', *J. Bentham Studies*, 5, 2002, pp. 1–27 (pp. 24–26).

[27] Mary Bentham, 'Memoir', pp. 47–48; Mary Bentham, *Life*, pp. 78–91; Morriss, *Science, Utility and Maritime Power*, pp. 166–67, 183–203.

innovations' in these ships, and their performance on active service demonstrated their worth.[28]

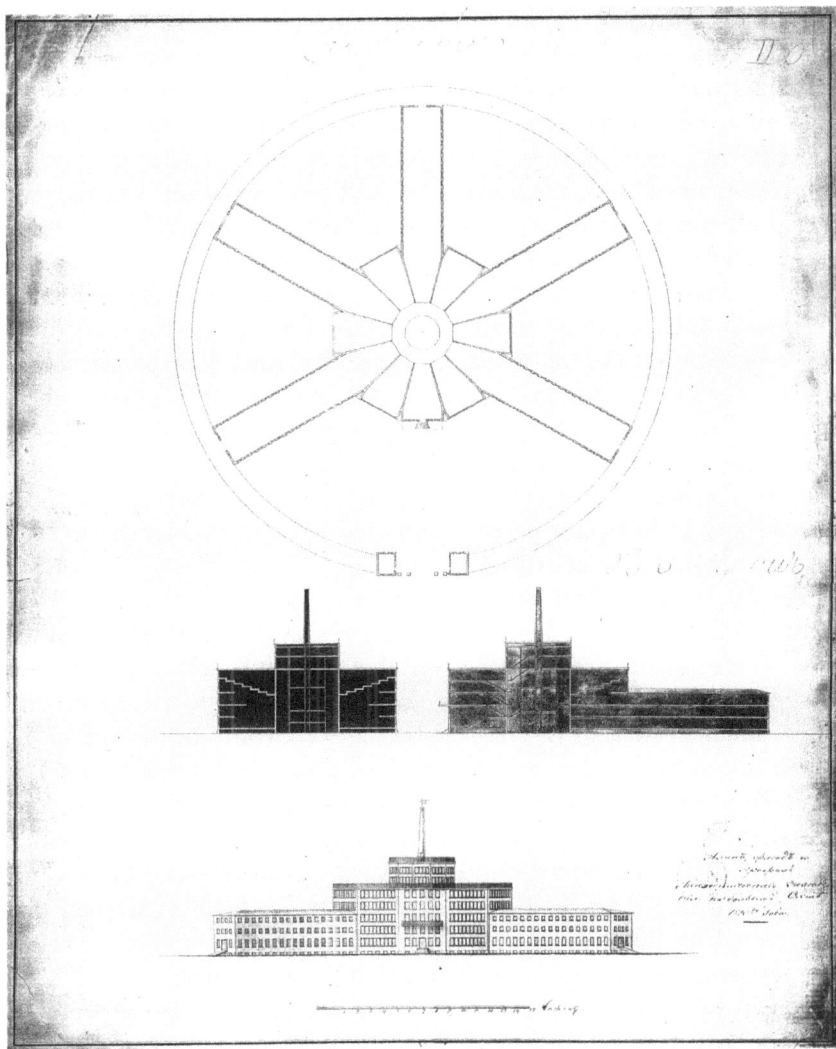

Fig 2. Ground plan, section and façade of the Okhta Panopticon (1810)
(Russian State Archive of the Navy, St Petersburg)[29]

[28] Mary Bentham, *Life*, pp. 106–14, 151–54, 163–69, 313–15; Mary Bentham, 'Memoir', p. 52; Granville, *St Petersburgh*, vol. 2, pp. 59–63.
[29] St Petersburg, Rossiiskii gosudarstvennyi arkhiv voenno-morskogo flota, f. 326, op. 1, d. 10043; https://www.ucl.ac.uk/bentham-project/who-was-jeremy-bentham/panopticon/st-petersburg-panopticon-image (accessed 17 January 2019). Reproduced by kind permission of the Director of the Russian State Archive of the Navy.

Finally, in 1795, he was appointed to the new post of inspector-general of naval works. The job description required him to concern himself with improvement of the building, arming and operating of ships, the best construction of docks and other naval infrastructure, and the economical provision of naval supplies and stores. His remit was thus very wide-ranging, and he had a large number of specialist assistants. Bentham's appointment was an indication of widespread concern over the efficiency of the royal navy. In 1791 a Society for the Improvement of Naval Architecture had been formed; it was alarmed that the French had appointed a special inspector-general to improve their dockyards.[30] His new post, an Admiralty appointment, reflected the Admiralty's desire for modernization and reform in naval affairs, but was an intrusion into the domain of the Navy Board, which put up constant resistance to his measures. From 1795 until 1805 Bentham was able to introduce major change; in 1805 he was sent off to Russia, where he stayed until 1807. His post was meanwhile abolished and he was made a junior commissioner of the navy with the rank of civil architect, his ability to act and to influence much reduced: he was retired in 1812.[31] His activity as inspector-general and commissioner has recently been closely studied by Jonathan Coad and Roger Morriss.[32]

As inspector-general Bentham was in a position to pursue both utility and invention. The evolution of the steam engine had by now made steam power very suitable to application for various purposes within the dockyards, and this was one of Bentham's achievements. He also re-planned the entire layout and use of space, enabling complementary activities to take place on restricted sites. The increasing size of warships had made existing dry docks problematic, and Bentham introduced methods of design and construction which enabled their modernization. He ensured a local water supply for the dockyards, which had never had one before, and combined this with new fire-fighting capacity. Over time he also produced a variety of mechanical inventions, both small and great: from augers with universal joints which could be used in confined spaces, and newly-adapted instruments for making bolts, screws and fixings, to a steam

---

[30] Coad, *The Portsmouth Block Mills*, p. 21.

[31] In 1813 Bentham published *Services rendered in the Civil Department of the Navy [...]*, which gives an extensive apologetic account of his work. The British Library copy at 1414.d.3. has preliminary hand-written material by Mary Bentham.

[32] Coad, *The Portsmouth Block Mills*; Morris, 'The Office'; also Jonathan Coad, *Support for the Fleet: Architecture and Engineering of the Royal Navy's Bases 1700–1914*, Swindon, 2013; R. Morriss, *Naval Power and British Culture 1760–1850. Public Trust and Government Ideology*, Abingdon, New York, 2016, part 2, chapter 7; R. Morriss, *Science, Utility and British Naval Technology 1793–1815*. See also Mary Bentham, *Life*, pp. 115–305.

dredger,[33] cement mill and timber-seasoning houses. At the same time he was equally concerned to modernize working practices and to counter or conciliate the opposition of the workmen involved.

The innovations which drew the greatest attention were the Wood Mills, a development of wood-processing machinery he had invented in Siberia and had improved in Krichev and after returning to London; the Metal Mills, which introduced machinery to smelt, cast and roll metal; and the Block Mills. The Portsmouth Block Mills revolutionized the manufacture of pulley blocks, which the navy used in huge numbers for working rigging and guns — annual requirement around 1800 was about 10,000, purchased essentially from outside private suppliers. The mills became 'the first full-scale factory in the world to use machine tools for mass production'.[34] The machinery was the brain-child of the French émigré Marc Brunel, but Bentham enthusiastically supported both his initial proposals and the process of building the necessary structures and machines at Portsmouth. Bentham's concern extended beyond the immediate technical and logistical challenges. He was aware of the public impact which the new installation could have, and 'considered it highly conducive to the hastening of the introduction of a general system of machinery, that public opinion should be obtained in its favour'; he therefore determined that the block-making machines should have 'a pleasing arrangement to point of appearance as well as use'.[35] This concern was well founded: conservative and dockyard opposition to the Block Mills rubbished their capacity and decried them as 'an idle fantasy of the projector's brain'.[36] But their ultimate success was enormous, and they proved right Bentham's wish to engage public opinion: the Block Mills became and remained a leading industrial site and a great tourist attraction.[37]

[33] T. G. Chesnel, 'The Steam Dredging Machine – Narrative of the Claims of Sir Samuel Bentham to its Invention', *Mechanics' Magazine*, 45, 1845, pp. 113–20, cited by A. W. Skempton, 'A History of the Steam Dredger, 1797–1830', *Transactions of the Newcomen Society*, 47, 1977, pp. 97–116. I am indebted for this reference to Hugh Torrens. The first steam dredger in Britain operated in Sunderland harbour 1798–1804, evidently not very successfully: the equipment was sold off in 1804. The Admiralty approved Bentham's new plan for Portsmouth in 1800, improved 1801; the machinery may have been worked up by his assistant Goodrich. The Portsmouth dredger began trials in 1802 and regular service in 1803; its success led Bentham to propose another which worked at Woolwich from 1807. A controversy over priority brought a vindication of Bentham by Chesnel, evidently Samuel's grandson: https://gw.geneanet.org/pierfit?lang=fr&p=louis+pierre+francois+adolphe&n=de+chesnel (accessed 30 August 2020).

[34] Coad, *The Portsmouth Block Mills*, p. 49.

[35] Ibid., p. 55.

[36] Mary Bentham, *Life*, p. 62.

[37] Coad, *The Portsmouth Block Mills*, p. 102.

Bentham's time at the Admiralty and Navy Board was not entirely happy, and he had to struggle to implement his vision against determined conservative opposition and the vagaries of contemporary politics. Nevertheless his contribution to the modernization and industrialization of the royal navy's dockyard infrastructure was revolutionary. Bentham used his imagination to reconcile contemporary technology and dockyard opportunities. He dealt in ideas, systems and general desiderata as much as in concrete structures such as docks and dams. He regarded himself as a facilitator as well as administrator, fully aware of the political and ideological dimensions of his work, and sought consciously to undermine resistance to, and encourage acceptance of, new ways of working. His approach privileged individual responsibility and accountability, and he had a keen eye to value for money. He used his scientific knowledge and mind-set to improve both materials and working practices; and he made a critical contribution to the functionality of the royal navy in the Napoleonic period and beyond.[38]

*   *   *

In the first, Russian, period of his active career, Bentham's position was such as to give him full rein to indulge his creative energies and flair for innovation. In a letter drafted to send to William Pitt the Younger from Krichev in 1787 he declared that:

> Inventions in the mechanical line, of which, such as they are, I have some stock, are my chief amusements here; and the opportunities, which my situation affords me, of carrying them into practice, form one of the principal ties which attach me to this country.

At the same time he offered Pitt his personal involvement, 'the zeal of the projector himself' as an earnest of his commitment, if Pitt should wish to adopt one of his inventions in Britain.[39] With this self-identification as 'projector' Bentham associated himself with a mind-set and a social type which was to be found universally across eighteenth-century Europe and which had a high profile. The term 'projector' has now gone out of use except in a different meaning, but this was a pursuer or purveyor of 'projects': what would now be termed an entrepreneur. Projectors at the time had a dubious reputation, since many of their projects failed or were dishonest, and in eighteenth-

---

[38] Morriss, 'The Office', p. 28.
[39] *Correspondence*, vol. 3, p. 535, no. 590, to William Pitt, draft, late April 1787. This letter was docketed as written by Jeremy; the content is in the voice of Samuel.

century circumstances due diligence and corroborative research and development were in short supply. Samuel Johnson in his *Dictionary* of 1755 gave two definitions of this social type: a neutral, general one, '[some]one who forms schemes and designs', and a pejorative one: 'one who forms wild impracticable schemes.' Jeremy Bentham in his *Defence of Usury*, written in Russia in 1787, undertook to make the case for honest and useful projectors against Adam Smith's condemnation of 'undertakers' in *The Wealth of Nations*.[40]

Samuel Bentham shared many of the features of the classic projector. His fertile mind produced proposals and solutions for any situation, and particularly any mechanical contrivance. His inventions naturally worked within the contemporary bounds of technology, but he was abreast of contemporary scientific knowledge and constantly sought to push the boundaries and think 'outside the box' — he wanted for instance to make steam engines with cheap wooden boilers and mount them on wheels. He had the projector's propensity to move from one good idea to another and leave projects unfinished. Thus the British experiments with his ship-carriage, conducted under the prestigious aegis of the Duke of York, promised widespread application in the army but were abandoned when Samuel was appointed inspector-general. Jeremy was similarly inclined: much of his work remained incomplete. A friend upset by his absence from London during his Russian visit of 1787–88 complained of both brothers: 'With one-tenth of your genius, both Sam and you would long since have risen to great eminence. But your history since I have known you has been to be always running from a good scheme to a better. In the meantime life passes away, and nothing is completed.'[41]

Samuel also shared the frequent projector combination of real ardour for change and reform with equally real concern for his own social and financial advantage. He was not inclined to the mere capitalist accumulation of vast wealth from his enterprises — he wished to improve for the common good rather than to exploit for

[40] *Defence of Usury*, Letter XIII, 'To Dr Smith, on Projects in Arts & c.', republished in: *Jeremy Bentham's Economic Writings*, ed. W. Stark, London, 1952, pp. 167–87; see further E. Pesciarelli, 'Smith, Bentham, and the Development of Contrasting Ideas on Entrepreneurship', *History of Political Economy*, 21, 1989, pp. 521–36; J. Crimmins, 'Political Economy and Projectors: Bentham's *Defence of Usury*', in T. A. Artem'eva (ed.), *The Science of Morality: Jeremy Bentham and Russia*, St Petersburg, 1999 (*Filosofskii Vek* 9), pp. 58–72. See, in general, R. Bartlett, 'Utopians and Projectors in Eighteenth-Century Russia', in R. Bartlett, L. Hughes (eds), *Russian Society and Culture and the Long Eighteenth Century: Essays in Honour of Anthony G. Cross*, Münster, 2004, pp. 98–115; M. Novak (ed.), *The Age of Projects*, Toronto, 2008.

[41] G. Wilson to Jeremy Bentham, 26 February NS 1787, *Correspondence*, vol. 3, p. 526, also quoted by Anderson, 'Samuel Bentham in Russia 1779–91', p. 158.

his own enrichment; but especially in his early years he had an eye for profitability and resolutely pursued personal interest. In 1782 after his first trip to Siberia he was undecided whether or not to return home: but the choice would depend solely on who made him the best offer. His initial report to Potemkin stated:

> Attached from infancy to the study of natural philosophy, it was impossible for me to perceive imperfections in matters of such importance without employing my thoughts in search of the means of remedying them [...].
>
> Some of these methods are inventions of my own in a finished state; [other] inventions [...] stand in need of some preparatory experiments [...].
>
> If ideas such as these should appear to deserve the attention of her Majesty, and she were to condescend to let me know to whom it is her pleasure I should give in a more particular description of them, I should esteem myself but too happy to have rendered myself, in the least degree, contributary to her exalted views.[42]

His final application to Catherine, in best projector fashion, asked for a major industrial facility where he could prove his claims of improvement, which relied entirely on his unsupported word and promised gold mines of increased revenues:

> Your Majesty being willing once to employ me would have only to trust to me the direction of an establishment of every kind where my different inventions might be introduced as for example the salt works upon the Kama, an iron mine and another of brass, which are not far from those salt works. These establishments might furnish examples enough to prove the utility of all the alterations I have proposed, and I have no doubt but that the increase of revenues which might be made from them, even in the first year, would be sufficient to defray the expenses occasioned by those innovations.

And his report to the Empress naturally stressed the advantages to be gained by following his recommendations, disregarding any possible disadvantageous side-effects.[43] Catherine, who understood perfectly the discourse and the dangers of project-making, took him into service; but instead of the industrial test site first mooted for him he was initially given subordinate charge of a canal.

---

[42] Morriss, *Science, Utility and Maritime Power*, p. 236.
[43] Ibid., pp. 251, 94–95.

Bentham was also fully alive to the value of patronage, the lifeblood of the projector: he collected dozens of letters of recommendation before going to Russia, and in the Empire his good personal relations during Catherine's reign with Potemkin and with the Empress, and later with her grandson, Alexander I (reigned 1801–25), were of crucial benefit, enabling much of his activity. In 1805, besides building warships, he was also instructed to make himself agreeable to the new Tsar, which he did by offering his services. His letter of 1806 to the Tsar drew upon previous imperial expressions of benevolence and offered his talents in classic projector mode:

> […] as Your Imperial Majesty has been pleased not only by a letter which I had the honour to receive while in England, but by the verbal messages I have received through General Hitroff as well as Admiral Tchichagoff, to express Your approbation and disposition to put into execution some plans of mine, […] I am induced to take the liberty of soliciting Your Imperial Majesty that You would be graciously pleased to signify to me whether there be any particular object to which it may be Your Imperial Majesty's pleasure that I should direct my attention during this excursion, and whether I may be permitted from time to time to submit to Your Imperial Majesty any plans or proposals which may appear likely to contribute to the prosperity of Your Majesty's Empire.[44]

Patronage was equally important in Georgian England. From the beginning of his career, and especially during his time as inspector-general of naval works, Bentham was engaged in and benefited from the mesh of politics and patronage relationships which shaped the course of national and naval internal affairs: as Ann Coats observed, 'family networks and political patronage were embedded in the new [dockyard] structures Samuel Bentham's pivotal place within dockyard and parliamentary networks enabled his ideals of individual responsibility, classification of labour and central financial control to become enshrined within nineteenth-century naval administration.'[45] Thus Samuel Bentham's talents, integrity and circumstances combined to make him a successful entrepreneur, in the sense not so much of wealth accumulation as of realizing his technical and organizational goals — one of those projectors defended by Jeremy in *Defence of Usury*.

[44] BL, Add. MSS 33544, fols 162–62v., Samuel Bentham to Alexander I, 18 March 1806 (OS).
[45] Ann Coats, 'The Block Mills: New Labour Practices for New Machines?', *Transactions of the Naval Dockyards Society*, 1, 2006, p. 80.

In Russia in 1805–07 Bentham also profited from the new Tsar's eagerness to discover and remedy Russia's ills and to enlist the support of reformers. In his early years on the throne Alexander created a small circle of reliable friends, the so-called 'Unofficial Committee', with whom he could discuss anything, no holds barred, and also actively encouraged a variety of people around him to speak their truth to him frankly, something which courtiers and ordinary citizens could normally do only with great caution.[46] And at the start of the reign he appointed his secretary and personal assistant Nikolai Novosil'tsev to a quite new post of what can only be called 'receiver of projects'.[47] This was a clear step beyond the traditional Russian practice of humble petitions addressed to the sovereign. Novosil'tsev apparently found his new duties more entertaining than burdensome, but saw them as clearly contributing to the Tsar's reforming agenda. In August 1801 he wrote to S. R. Vorontsov, the ambassador in London, describing a cloud of typical projectors which had engulfed him:

> I don't know if you have been informed, Count, that I have a position just newly created by the Emperor, which is the one to which all those must address themselves who have something useful to propose to the government, in whatever field it might be; and I am the person charged with presenting the proposal to the Emperor, after having gathered all the necessary information and explanations and having sought the opinion of the various departments which it may concern.
>
> You could not imagine how the decree in which I was nominated to receive everything anyone wanted to propose has set people's minds working: my morning is nothing but a continual series of visits, and I believe that no other remit or employment has ever brought anything so comic or so agreeable. One person brings me a machine or a model, another a project, a discovery, a proposal to the government; that one talks to you about commerce and industry, this one about finances, currency, the national debt; here you have a clever man, a man of intelligence, there — a lunatic, an ignoramus, and bringing up the rear a charlatan or a wretch who is out to deceive you.
>
> However troublesome it is to pass all that through the crucible to obtain pure metal, it must be admitted that it is quite amusing and also not without utility; because it cannot be assumed that these projects

[46] For example, V. Karazin, G. Parrot, T. von Bock; see P. O'Meara, *The Russian Nobility in the Age of Alexander I*, London, 2019.

[47] *Polnoe sobranie zakonov Rossiiskoi Imperii, sobranie pervoe*, 47 vols, St Petersburg 1830, 26, no. 19965, 7 August 1801 (OS), 'Concerning the encouragement of those making inventions and discoveries tending to perfection of agriculture, commerce and business.'

will all be up to the standards of precision and perfection which every measure must have to be adopted by the government, but it is nevertheless indubitable that they offer and will offer valuable pointers, and they are so many means of gaining leverage against the inertia of raw matter. On the other hand you could say that this process puts the different departments of the administration in some degree under public scrutiny.[48]

Four years later, as Bentham set off on his 1805 Admiralty mission, Vorontsov sent with him a letter to Novosil'tsev couched in a similar vocabulary: enthusiastically endorsing the mission, he described Samuel as 'a mathematician of great genius and who applies his knowledge to useful inventions. In his own field he's another Ramsden'.[49] The comparison with the late Jesse Ramsden, FRS (1735–1800),[50] leading London maker of scientific, navigational and astronomical instruments, member of the Imperial Russian Academy of Sciences, with whom Vorontsov had been on friendly terms and whom he greatly admired, was intended as a compliment and recommendation; it bears further scrutiny.

Ramsden had a greater public and international scientific reputation than his younger contemporary Bentham, as his memberships of the Royal Society and the Russian Academy of Sciences show; Vorontsov's friends referred to him, both before and after his death, as 'l'immortel Ramsden'.[51] The two were in some respects very different; but there were also parallels in both their careers and their mentalities. Chronologically Ramsden spanned the divide between the individual hand-craftsman and the mechanization of instrument-making: he 'turned the scientific instrument [...] into a cost-effective industrial artefact, but where high quality was made to cost less in real terms than ever before'.[52] He worked at the time of the great debates about longitude, and his

---

[48] *Arkhiv Kniazia Vorontsova* (hereafter *AKV*), 40 vols, Moscow, 1870–95, 30, pp. 296–97, 28 August 1801 (OS). My (RB) translation from the French.

[49] *AKV*, vol. 11, pp. 418–19, 18/30 July 1805.

[50] On Ramsden see Anita McConnell, *Jesse Ramsden (1735–1800): London's Leading Scientific Instrument Maker*, London, New York, 2016; Allan Chapman, 'Scientific Instruments and Industrial Innovation: The Achievement of Jesse Ramsden', in *Making Instruments Count. Essays on Historical Scientific Instruments presented to Gerard L'Estrange Turner*, ed. R. G. W. Anderson, J. A. Bennett, W. F. Ryan, Aldershot, 1993, pp. 418–30. Will Ryan worked with Gerard Turner in Oxford. The distinguished Professor Turner was also noted for establishing the Equinoctial Club, a twice-yearly dining society, 'to provide a forum for instrumental gossip' (p. x). Will was a staunch member and participant.

[51] *AKV*, vol. 29, pp. 33–34; vol. 27, p. 271.

[52] Chapman, 'Scientific Instruments', p. 418.

achievements were made possible by the development of reliable lunar tables in the 1750s and 1760s. In the same way Bentham's subsequent application of steam power in the dockyards was enabled by Boulton and Watt's development and improvement of the steam engine. Ramsden's reputation rested firstly on the dividing engine which he invented, the improved 1774 version of which the Admiralty was pleased to purchase from him and which enabled the mass production of sextants and other instruments; secondly, on the unrivalled quality of the instruments produced in his workshop, and especially on his astronomical circles. In mechanizing the calibration of instruments, Ramsden made it possible for an unskilled labourer to achieve the results of a skilled craftsman in a fraction of the time — something Bentham also achieved with the machines in Portsmouth dockyard. Ramsden used new combinations of existing components to innovate, which Bentham also did in his experimental ships. But like the Panopticon, the astronomical circles on which his scientific reputation rested had no established precedent; they also presented a variety of technical puzzles which could take years or even decades to solve.

Unlike Bentham, Ramsden was able to fund his commercial business and also the far less lucrative astronomical circles from the sale of his common instruments such as sextants; he had little need of patronage or outside funding to finance his circles. Ramsden spent his whole career based at London workshops, and worked on commercial contracts in the defined sphere of scientific instruments, whereas Bentham ranged across Europe, wishing to engage major patrons or governments with his plans in a variety of fields — Jeremy confidently offered his (Samuel's) services to Spain, and in his last years his hopes turned to France.[53] Like Bentham Ramsden was not motivated by wealth-seeking — he was in fact much more indifferent to money than the former. For him 'the challenge of invention was consistently more appealing than the financial exploitation of the ensuing machine',[54] whereas Bentham's primary goal was the efficiency and utility offered by his innovations. But Ramsden and Bentham, in their separate spheres, were alike in using scientific knowledge combined with independent thinking and technical inventiveness to bring about transformational change in the technological practices of their time. Bentham and Ramsden both belong among the 'pioneers of the industrial age'.[55]

---

[53] *Correspondence*, vol. 10, p. 156, no. 2713, 15–17 November 1820; BL Add MSS 33546, fols 454–55, 15 August 1830.

[54] Chapman, 'Scientific Instruments', p. 429.

[55] See note 1.

The 'Amur Question': The Problem of Russian Access to the Pacific from Siberia in the Eighteenth and Nineteenth Centuries

James R. Gibson

York University, Toronto

By the end of the eighteenth century imperial Russia's *modus operandi* of eastward expansion — by boat and on foot from one interlocking river system to the next, founding forts at strategic crossings and junctions, hunting out the sables and foxes, and subduing the indigenous peoples by both taking hostages and exacting tribute in sables and foxes in each basin before advancing to the next — had taken the Cossacks, *promyshlenniki* (fur hunters/traders), merchants, and explorers across the Siberian vastness of the Old World from the Urals to the uncharted North Pacific and beyond to the Northwest Coast of the New World. The process had taken two centuries, facilitated not only by nature but also by the disinterest of isolationist Qing (Manchu) China (1644–1912) and Tokugawa (Shogunate) Japan (1603–1867) to the immediate south. No other imperial power coveted the Asian north because at that time there was little or nothing to covet, so it became synonymous with wilderness and remoteness.

The settlements that were spawned by this imperial outreach necessitated the delivery of personnel, *matériel*, and dispatches from and to the Russian government and the shipment of sea otter, furs and fur seal skins to market. Within Siberia this task was not too difficult, given the rivers and plains, although the 'tyranny of distance' protracted movement. In the North Pacific, however, supply was rendered problematic by mountain barriers abutting the Siberian seaboard from the Bering Sea to the Sea of Japan. The requisite officials and workers, provisions and commodities, and orders and reports had to be hauled in riverboats from Irkutsk along the river Lena as far as Iakutsk, the hub of Iakutia on the river's great bend, and from there at enormous difficulty and huge cost on riverboats and pack-horses over the Iakutsk–Okhotsk Track for 700 gruelling miles (1,126 kilometres) to the shallow and exposed harbour of Okhotsk, which became Russia's main Pacific port for want of a better.[1]

---

[1] See James R. Gibson, *Feeding the Russian Fur Trade: Provisionment of the Okhotsk Seaboard and the Kamchatka Peninsula, 1639–1856*, Madison, WI, 1969, part 2.

The logistical problems led to attempts to find an easier, faster, and
cheaper way of supplying Russian settlements and enterprises around
the North Pacific rim. The river Amur appeared to be the sole alternative
— indeed, a godsend, for it was the only river that offered a convenient
route from the continental interior to the Pacific Ocean by breaching
the mountain barrier between Eastern Siberia and the Russian Far
East. And it was long (2,800 miles [4,500 kilometres]), wide (3.5 miles
at its mouth at low water), and voluminous (primarily in summer,
opportunely for transport) with an enormous watershed (the world's
tenth largest). Russians also still regarded the river and its valley — its
left bank at the very least — as rightfully theirs, for they had occupied
it for almost all of the second half of the seventeenth century, whereas
Chinese control had been merely suzerain, with little occupation and
exploitation. However, by the terms of the Treaty of Nerchinsk of 1689,
the outmanned and outgunned Russians had been forced to withdraw
to Transbaikalia on the northern side of the Stanovoi–Iablonovyi
mountain chains by China's Qing (Manchu) emperors, who, despite
their autarkic isolationism, would not abide foreign encroachment upon
their northern and ancestral (Manchurian) frontier abutting the Amur,
or the 'River of the Black Dragon'.

This situation occasionally prompted proposals from various Russian
figures to regain the Amur. The eminent historian and geographer
Gerhard Friedrich Müller, for example, who had experienced first-hand
the logistical nightmares of the Second Kamchatka Expedition (1733–43)
of Vitus Bering and Aleksei Il'ich Chirikov on the Iakutsk–Okhotsk–
Petropavlovsk route, believed that the reacquisition of the waterway
was even worth the risk of war with China.[2] Peter I, while discussing
the future development of his Empire with one of his favourites, Fedor
Matveevich Apraksin, the first president of the Admiralty Board, is
supposed to have asserted that three points were vital to Russia: the
mouths of the rivers Don, Neva, and Amur.[3]

Despite the significance of the Amur for its North Pacific interests,
however, Russia took no action on the various schemes for securing
the river as a supply line — and for good reasons. Firstly, the remote
Amur was much less important to the Empire than the Neva and the
Don rivers, whose mouths opened towards nearby powerful neighbours

[2] See Lothar Maier, 'Gerhard Friedrich Müller's Memoranda on Russian Relations
with China and the Reconquest of the Amur', *Slavonic and East European Review*, 59,
1981, 2, p. 231.
[3] D. Romanov, 'Prisoedinenie Amura k Rossii. Period II. Poteria Amura. (1689–
1847 g.)', *Russkoe slovo*, 6 June 1859, pp. 332–33; A. Sgibnev, 'Amurskaia ekspeditsiia
1854 g. (razskaz ochevidtsa)', *Drevniaia i novaia Rossiia*, 3, 1878, no. 11, p. 217.

(such as Charles XII's Sweden and the Ottoman Empire) that posed the chief threats to Russia's security. Asia did not loom large in Russia's foreign policy because Asia did not pose much of a threat, thanks to the ending of steppe invasions from the east and to the advent of both Chinese and Japanese isolationism. Russia was in any event no match in Amuria for the neighbouring Celestial Empire.

Secondly, Russia feared that if it pressured China on the Amur question, Peking might retaliate by decreasing or suspending Sino-Russian trade at Kiakhta on the Mongolian frontier to the south of Lake Baikal. This trade, involving mainly Russian furs (as well as sea otter skins to those residents of north China who could afford this luxury fur) and Chinese teas and cottons, yielded handsome profits and sizeable duties to Russian merchants and revenuers respectively. It was because of the existence of this port of entry that China refused to allow Russian ships access to Canton, where European and American firms had trading factories.

Thirdly, and most importantly, explorations by reputable navigators — the Frenchman Jean-François de Galaup, Comte de La Pérouse in 1785–88, the Englishman William Broughton in 1795–98, and the Russian Ivan Fedorovich Kruzenshtern (Adam Johann von Krusenstern) in 1803–06 — had shown that the Amur was not accessible to seagoing vessels, its mouth being too shallow, and that, moreover, Sakhalin was not an island but a peninsula connected to the mainland by a narrow isthmus just south of the Amur's mouth — thereby blocking entry into the river from the Sea of Japan via Tatar Strait.[4] Consequently,

---

[4] See [J. F. G. de La Pérouse]. *A Voyage Round the World, Performed in the Years 1785, 1786, 1787, and 1788, by the Boussole and Astrolabe ...*, ed. L. A. Milet-Mureau, London, 1799, vol. 2; William Robert Broughton, *A Voyage of Discovery to the North Pacific Ocean ... in the Years 1795, 1796, 1797, 1798*, London, 1804; and [Captain A. J. von Krusenstern], *Voyage Round the World, in the Years 1803, 1804, 1805, & 1806 ... on Board the Ships Nadeshda and Neva ...*, trans. Richard Belgrave Hoppner, London, 1813, vol. 2. La Pérouse's expedition was intended to rival the three great voyages of James Cook and bring scientific glory and naval prestige to France, just as Alejandro Malaspina's was intended to accomplish the same for Spain (coincidentally, both expeditions ended tragically — the French venture in the loss of both ships and all hands in the Coral Sea on the homeward leg, and the Spanish voyage in the long-time imprisonment in Galicia of the Tuscan commander, a victim of court intrigue; fortunately, one of La Pérouse's officers, Jean Baptiste de Lesseps, had disembarked at Petropavlovsk to return to Paris overland with most of the papers of the doomed vessels). Lieutenant Broughton was fresh from his command of the *Chatham*, Captain George Vancouver's tender during his survey of the Northwest Coast on the precisely opposite side of the North Pacific. Captain (and future Admiral) Ivan Kruzenshtern, one of several of the Russian Empire's notable Baltic German mariners, was homeward-bound on his country's first round-the-world voyage with Captain-Lieutenant Iurii Fedorovich Lisianskii in the flagship *Nadezhda* and the consort *Neva*, respectively.

there was no point in risking both military hostilities and commercial disruptions with China over an inaccessible river.

Circumstances, however, gradually changed in favour of a Russian resolution of the 'Amur question'. For one thing, from the 1820s the colonial fur trade in the North Pacific region declined steadily. The depletion of the most desirable (and hence most lucrative) furs (sea otter, fur seal, beaver) by improvident hunting and expanding farming, a change in fickle fashion away from wearing fur (especially from felt to silk hats), and the disruption of traditional markets (particularly in China) by invasion and rebellion were the primary culprits. The fur trade's decline meant that the Kiakhta trade lost most of its importance for Russia, so that China could no longer use it as leverage for safeguarding the Amur against Russian encroachment.

Additionally, by the second quarter of the nineteenth century, Russia was a more powerful and a more confident state. It boasted the largest standing army in Europe, as well as a navy, and had been instrumental in the defeat of Napoleon Bonaparte. Russia was not only a fully-fledged member of the European concert of nations but also an aspiring Asian power with extensive territorial acquisitions in Transcaucasia and Central Asia. So Russia was able to flex more muscle in the Far East, where there were incursions on its borderlands from American and British whalers in the Bering and Okhotsk Seas, including hunting unchecked in Russian waters, landing uninvited on Russian soil, and trading illicitly at Russian ports.

Furthermore, the Amur question had not been definitively resolved by La Pérouse, Broughton, or even Kruzenshtern, whose attempt had been the most thorough. The Russian mariner, however, had not navigated the entire channel between Sakhalin and Tatary, had not actually seen the supposed isthmus joining the two, and had not even seen the mouth of the Amur, let alone entered it. That is why he was only 'quite' convinced and could conclude with only 'considerable' confidence that the river was inaccessible. And subsequently his confidence would have been even more qualified if he had known of the explorations of Mamiya Rinzō, a Japanese cartographer, who in 1808–09 surveyed and mapped Karafuto, or Kita Ezo, that is, Sakhalin, and demonstrated that it was an island by sailing though Tatar Strait and into the river Amur.[5]

Meanwhile, British power and capital were bullying navy-less China, which was forced to allow the opium trade that was so profitable

---

[5] See Brett L. Walker, 'Mamiya Rinzō and the Japanese Exploration of Sakhalin Island: Cartography and Empire', *Journal of Historical Geography*, 33, 2007, pp. 283–313.

to private 'country traders' in the wake of the 1834 termination of the British East India Company's monopoly on the Canton trade. The First Opium War of 1839–42 was ended by the Treaty of Nanking, the first of the so-called 'unequal treaties' forced upon a weak China, with the Middle Kingdom agreeing to open five ports to British trade, pay Britain $21,000,000 in reparations, and cede Hong Kong to the British Empire. China's Manchu rulers, enfeebled by internal division as well as by foreign aggression, were unable to resist. They kowtowed again in 1843 by granting Britain extra-territorial rights — epitomized by Shanghai's International Settlement — and in 1844 they were forced to grant the same privileges to France and the United States. Russia was not included among the European countries given access to the new treaty ports because it already had a port of entry at Kiakhta, although that trade, however, began to be undermined by British mercantile penetration of China. Obviously there was a mounting need for Russia to protect its interests in the Far East, and the Amur still represented the best route for the movement of soldiers and supplies.

Thus, by the 1840s Russia had more need of the Amurian waterway and had less to fear from its Chinese owners. The Russians who shaped, made, and implemented policy reacted accordingly. Two of them — Eastern Siberia's governor general V. Ia. Rupert in 1842 and the naturalist Aleksandr Fedorovich Middendorf (Alexander Theodor von Middendorff) in 1845 — urged St Petersburg to recognize the necessity of Russian navigation of the Amur and to this end open talks with Peking.[6] This proposal, however, was opposed by the long-serving and conservative minister of foreign affairs (1816–56), Karl Nesselrode, who 'did not want to hear about the Amur', fearing that any Russian advance towards the river would antagonize both the Chinese and the British.[7] Nevertheless, the Tsar himself, Nicholas I, was sympathetic. He hoped to fulfil his predecessors' dream of regaining the Amur, referring to it as the 'Russian river Amur'.[3]

Meanwhile, in 1843 the Russian-American Company's factory at the woeful port of Okhotsk had been transferred nearly three hundred miles south to Aian, and the even more woeful Iakutsk–Okhotsk track had been replaced by a shorter and easier Iakutsk–Aian route at the insistence of Lieutenant (later Admiral) Vasilii Stepanovich Zavoiko, at the time the Okhotsk factory's manager. The relocating and rerouting

[6] Sgibnev, 'Amurskaia ekspeditsiia', p. 217.
[7] Ivan Barsukov, *Graf Nikolai Nikolaevich Murav'ev-Amurskii po ego pis'mam, offitsial'nym dokumentam, razskazam sovremennikov i pechatnym istochnikam (materialy dlia biografii)*, 2 vols, Moscow, 1891, 1, pp. 201–02.
[8] B. V. Struve, *Vospominaniia o Sibiri, 1848–1854 g.*, St Petersburg, 1889, p. 3.

of the Iakutsk–Pacific link incurred great expense on the part of both the Company and the government, and neither the new port nor the new route proved significantly better than their predecessors. This predicament came to the attention of the new governor-general of Eastern Siberia, Nikolai Nikolaevich Murav'ev, one of the two men who were to be most instrumental in resolving the Amur question in Russia's favour, an accomplishment that was to gain him fame as 'the conqueror of the Amur'[9] and, for that feat, the honorific title of 'Murav'ev-Amurskii' (that is, 'Murav'ev of the Amur' or, loosely, 'Count of the Amur').[10] Murav'ev was determined to verify the Amur's utility once and for all to Russia's advantage. The matter was raised even before he took office, when his audience with Nicholas I about his Siberian posting ended with the royal words: 'As regards the Russian river of the Amur, that is a question for the future.'[11] Although their views on the Amur were similar, and the time was opportune, the Tsar was restrained by the advice of his cautious foreign minister Nesselrode, an adherent of the principle of legitimism in international relations and an advocate of the maintenance of the status quo.

Before going to Irkutsk to begin his governor-generalship, Murav'ev went to St Petersburg for briefings. There he met the other resolver of the Amur question, the navigator Gennadii Ivanovich Nevel'skoi (1813–76),[12] who had just been appointed commander of the naval transport *Baikal*, which was under construction in Helsingfors (Helsinki) and was slated to deliver supplies to Petropavlovsk and Okhotsk upon its completion in September 1848. Upon Murav'ev's arrival in the capital, Nevel'skoi was ordered by Admiral Prince Aleksandr Sergeevich Menshikov, the head of the Naval Ministry, to present himself to the governor-general because he would be taking the *Baikal* to ports under

[9] Peter Kropotkin, *Memoirs of a Revolutionist*, ed. James Allen Rogers, Garden City, NY, 1962, pp. 142–43.
[10] On Murav'ev see N. P. Matkhanova, *General-gubernatory Vostochnoi Sibiri serediny XIX veka: V. Ia. Rupert, N. N. Murav'ev-Amurskii, M. S. Korsakov*, Novosibirsk, 1998, pp. 101–243, and ibid., *Graf N. N. Murav'ev-Amurskii v vospominaniiakh sovremennikov*, Novosibirsk, 1998.
[11] Barsukov, *Graf*, vol. 1, p. 171.
[12] On Nevel'skoi see A. I. Alekseev, *Gennadii Ivanovich Nevel'skoi, 1813–1876*, Moscow, 1984. For additional documentation see: M. V. Gridiaeva, *Rossiia na dal'nevostochnykh rubezhakh (k 200-letniu so dnia rozhdeniia G. G. Nevel'skogo): Materialy vserossiiskoi nauchno-prakticheskoi konferentsii 21–22 noiabria 2013 goda*, Iuzhno-Sakhalinsk, 2014, especially the papers of the conference's second session; T. S. Federova (comp.), *G. I. Nevel'skoi: Dokumenty i materialy (1813–1876)*, St Petersburg, 2017; M. S. Vysokov and M. I. Ishchenko, *Kommentarii k knige G. I. Nevel'skogo Podvigi russkikh morskikh ofitserov na krainem vostoke Rossii 1849–55 gg. Pri-Amurskii-Ussuriiskii krai*, Vladivostok and Iuzhno-Sakhalinsk, 2013.

the jurisdiction of Irkutsk.[3] Nevel'skoi recollected that they discussed 'the supply of our Siberian ports' and 'the vital significance' of the river Amur, and Murav'ev agreed that 'not only the return of this river to our possession but also the opening to us of unrestricted navigation on it were of enormous significance to Siberia'. However, added the governor-general, everyone (including the Tsar) was convinced that the river was 'unenterable by ships from the sea' — to which Nevel'skoi replied that 'this really widespread conclusion [...] seemed very doubtful to me' after having 'studied carefully [...] all of the published information and surveys', so 'I believe that a thorough exploration of the mouth and the estuary [liman] is an urgent necessity.' Whereupon Murav'ev, 'having listened attentively to my arguments [...] expressed his complete sympathy with my proposal and said that for his part he would try to use every means to realize it.'[14]

Afterwards Nevel'skoi reported this conversation to Prince Menshikov and asked him if it would be possible to use the *Baikal* to survey the estuary and the mouth of the river Amur and the southernmost coast of the Okhotsk Sea. The Prince replied that Nevel'skoi would have neither the time nor the money to do so, for the transport would not reach Kamchatka until the autumn of 1849 and had been underwritten for only one year. Besides, he added, it had already been 'fully demonstrated' that the Amur's mouth was blocked by sandbars. Moreover, such a venture would displease the Chinese, and Nesselrode would neither consent to it nor present it to the Tsar. Consequently, Nevel'skoi was to forget the 'impossible' and strive instead to relieve under-supplied Petropavlovsk and Okhotsk 'as opportunely as possible'.[15]

Nevel'skoi concluded from this response that the 'main reason' for Menshikov's rejection of his proposal was the lack of time. So he decided that he would have to make Petropavlovsk by May and unload his cargo by June in order to have the summer free to probe the Amur's estuary and mouth. He also reckoned that he would have to make the probe appear to be accidental in order to avoid antagonizing China.[16]

The *Baikal*'s keel was laid in January 1848 and planking was scheduled for the spring. Nevel'skoi told the private shipyard that

[13] G. I. Nevel'skoi, *Podvigi russkikh morskikh ofitserov na krainem Vostoke Rossii 1849–1855*, ed. A. I. Alekseev, Khabarovsk, 1969, pp. 77–78. Nevel'skoi's account has been re-published many times; the latest edition is the tenth, edited by N. A. Beliaeva and published in Moscow in Vladivostok and Iuzhno-Sakhalinsk in 2013.
[14] Nevel'skoi, *Podvigi*, pp. 78–79.
[15] Ibid., p. 79.
[16] Ibid., pp. 79–80.

Prince Menshikov would be pleased if the transport were ready by July, and he asked them to accelerate construction, for he reckoned that only by leaving Kronstadt, Russia's chief naval base situated in the Gulf of Finland, early could he hope to reach Kamchatka safely and promptly. Menshikov had served as governor-general of Finland, and as a result the builders promised to launch the ship by July, more than a month and half before the contracted date.[17]

Pleased by the prospect of an earlier completion of the *Baikal* and its haulage of as much cargo as much larger transports, Menshikov agreed to Nevel'skoi's plan. He reminded Nevel'skoi, however, that although he fully concurred with the necessity of charting the southernmost stretch of the shoreline of the Okhotsk Sea, that stretch was considered by Nesselrode to be Chinese. However, governor-general Murav'ev had submitted a petition against that view.[18]

From this conversation Nevel'skoi anticipated that permission to explore the south-western shoreline of the Okhotsk Sea would be forthcoming, provided the *Baikal* left Kronstadt early and provided Murav'ev's petition was successful, so in the middle of February 1848 he wrote to Murav'ev that he intended to embark at the beginning of August and to reach Kamchatka at the beginning of May 1849, that he needed only two and a half weeks to unload at Petropavlovsk, and that he could use the rest of the spring and summer to, firstly, survey the southernmost coast of the Okhotsk Sea, secondly, explore the river Amur's mouth and estuary, and, thirdly, examine the western coast of Sakhalin. Nevel'skoi assured Murav'ev that 'I would use all of my energy and ability to make a conscientious map of the places that have heretofore been closed to us by darkness'. The 'chief questions' that he would try to answer were 'firstly, the degree to which the river and estuary of the Amur are accessible to seagoing vessels and, secondly, whether there are harbours on the coast of this territory at which a port could be conveniently established.'[19]

Thanks to Menshikov's intervention, all of the *Baikal*'s cargo (217 tons) was packed properly and delivered to Kronstadt by the beginning of July. The transport itself (250 tons, 8½ knots) was launched in mid-July, and by the end of August it was ready to sail.[20] Outfitted

---

[17] Ibid., pp. 80–81.

[18] Ibid., pp. 83–84.

[19] Ibid., pp. 84–85.

[20] Ibid., pp. 85–86. Before embarking Nevel'skoi was told by Menshikov that he would have to make his exploration of the Amur's estuary and mouth appear to be 'accidental', and the Prince also said that he did not believe that the estuary was inaccessible and that he was 'completely in sympathy with the necessity of exploring it' (pp. 87–88).

as a brig-type schooner, the *Baikal* left Kronstadt at the beginning of September 1848 with nine officers, twenty-eight sailors and fourteen craftsmen. It made Petropavlovsk via Cape Horn in late May 1849 after a speedy passage of eight months and twenty-three days with nobody on the sick list.[21] Kamchatka's commandant subsequently reported to Prince Menshikov that never before had such a full measure and such a superior grade of supplies been delivered to the peninsula, so much so that Siberia's Pacific ports would have enough prime supplies for at least four years.[22]

In the meantime, governor-general Murav'ev was becoming apprehensive to the point of paranoia that Britain would pre-empt Russia on the Amur, and he began to play a Far Eastern version of the 'great game' between the Russians and the British over Afghanistan. His Anglophobia was shared by his assistant, Berngard Vasil'evich Struve (Bernhard Wilhelm von Struve), who even condemned as a spy the English traveller Samuel Hill, who spent several months as a tourist in Irkutsk and, in Struve's words, 'managed to worm his way into all layers of society'. He warned: 'The English penetrate everywhere, trace everything, and learn everything to achieve very definitely-created and persistently-pursued aims.' 'The English', he added, 'are not fools.'[23] Another Englishman, the engineer Charles Austin, who had lived in Russia for several years, arrived to undertake geological exploration. Intending to raft down the Amur, he was prevented on Murav'ev's orders. The governor-general then wrote to minister of the interior, Lev Alekseevich Perovskii, to warn of the danger to Russia's Amurian interests posed by uninvited foreign guests masquerading as tourists or scientists and 'learning everything that the English government needs to know'.[24]

---

[21] Not that the passage was smooth sailing, with contrary or variable winds, calms, squalls, repairs — all of which were normal, however. Most of the *Baikal*'s predecessors had fared worse, particularly the naval transport *America* (600 tons, 10 knots), Captain Johann Eberhard von Schanz, which had taken ten months and twenty-five days in 1834–36 and had arrived with ten of its fifty-three men sick; the *Abö* (600 tons, 10+ knots), Captain Iunker, which had taken twelve months and fifteen days in 1838–41 and had arrived with twenty-two of its seventy-three men sick; and the naval transport *Irtysh* (450 tons), Captain Ivan Vonliarliarskii, which had taken fourteen months in 1843–45 and had arrived with eight of its fifty-three men sick. The navy ship to have made the fastest Kronstadt–Petropavolovsk run was the sloop *Kamchatka*, under Captain Vasilii Mikhailovich Golovnin, which did it in eight months and eight days in 1817–19, but it was a sloop of 900 tons and could travel at more than 11 knots (Nevel'skoi, *Podvigi*, p. 93n.).

[22] Nevel'skoi, *Podvigi*, pp. 92, 93–94.

[23] Struve, *Vospominaniia*, pp. 32, 33. Hill wrote an account of his Siberian adventures (S. S. Hill, *Travels in Siberia*, London, 1854, 2 vols. in 1).

[24] Struve, *Vospominaniia*, p. 34.

Murav'ev was determined to seize the Amur Country before Britain. In late September of 1848, barely a month after Nevel'skoi's departure from Kronstadt, he wrote to Perovskii 'about the necessity and possibility of our occupation of the left bank of the Amur and part of Sakhalin island with a view to forestalling the seizure of these places by some foreign power', namely, Britain.[25] He also argued that if Russia were to acquire the Amur, it would have to possess its headwaters as well as its outlet in order to exert control.[26] Moreover, he believed that the fear of undermining the Kiakhta trade by regaining the river — a fear that had long hamstrung Russia's Pacific aspirations — was baseless. After all, that trade had lost much of its lustre; besides, it was not unknown for countries to be on unfriendly terms but still trade with each other.[27]

Illness prevented Perovskii from replying to Murav'ev until early February of 1849, and his answer did not reach the governor-general until the middle of March.[28] The interior minister wrote that Murav'ev's misgivings had been relayed to Count Nesselrode, who responded that, firstly, the natives of northern Sakhalin paid tribute to China and the Chinese regarded all of the left bank of the river Amur as their territory, so that any attempt to acquire it would inevitably alarm Peking and might provoke a conflict, and, secondly, the occupation of Sakhalin by the British was unlikely.[29]

Undaunted, and supported increasingly in court circles by influential sympathizers to the reformist/nationalist cause in general and the Amur mission in particular as Grand Duke Konstantin Nikolaevich, the Tsar's second son, Murav'ev continued to press St Petersburg for action on Amuria. In a report to Nicholas I in early March of 1849 he expressed his conviction that 'the entire future prosperity of Eastern Siberia consists in a reliable and convenient communication with the Eastern [Pacific] Ocean [...] via the Amur.'[30] He cautioned that the British intended to occupy the mouth of the Amur and navigate it as far upstream as Chita in Transbaikalia in order, firstly, to consolidate their intervention in China by means of the river's right-bank tributaries that flowed from Manchuria and Mongolia and, secondly, to outcompete Russian entrepreneurs in gold mining in Eastern Siberia and in trading

[25] Ibid., p. 48.
[26] Ibid., p. 4.
[27] Ibid.
[28] In the middle of the century it took the post under the best conditions eight weeks to go from St Petersburg to Irkutsk and back (ibid., pp. 83–84).
[29] Ibid., pp. 49–50.
[30] Barsukov, *Graf*, vol. l, p. 206.

at Kiakhta. If they were successful in the latter object, he predicted, then Eastern Siberia might even separate from Russia, for its economy was dominated by private traders and miners who were motivated more by profit than by patriotism.[31]

In another report to the Tsar in late May Murav'ev reiterated his concerns, stressing that it was necessary to tap the gold-bearing rivers flowing down the southern slopes of the Iablonovyi and Stanovoi mountain ranges into the Amur by settling the river's left bank, as well as to overcome the difficulty of communication with Kamchatka via Iakutsk and Okhotsk by plying the Amur with steamboats.[32] He wrote (with a touch of Halford Mackinder's 'Heartland thesis'):

It is indisputable that the English need the mouth of the Amur and the navigation of the river in order completely to possess all the trade in China. If the Amur were not the only river flowing from Siberia to the Eastern Ocean, then we could still tolerate their enterprises, but the navigation of the Amur, as the sole convenient route to the Orient, is an age-old dream of the inhabitants here [Irkutsk, that is, Eastern Siberia] of all classes, perhaps instinctively for some but nevertheless justifiably, and I, by reason of my knowledge of all of the circumstances here, dare to say that whoever possesses the mouth of the Amur will possess Siberia at least as far as [Lake] Baikal, and possess it firmly, for it is sufficient to have the mouth of this river and navigation of it under lock and key in order for Siberia to become more populated and more flourishing both agriculturally and industrially [...].[33]

The governor-general's concern for the Russian Far East did not, incidentally, extend to Russian America. He disliked monopolies, and he even questioned the continued existence of the financially-straitened Russian-American Company in the face of the decline of the fur trade and hence the Kiakhta trade (and its failure to undertake whaling as a profitable alternative), as well as the high cost of imported foods and goods from gold-rush California.[34] Later he would urge St Petersburg to abandon its overextended foothold in North America and consolidate its more promising position in eastern Asia, arguing that just as it was 'natural' — that is, ordained — for the United States to possess all of the North American continent, so was it 'natural' for Russia to possess

---

[31] Struve, *Vospominaniia*, pp. 52–55.
[32] Ibid., p. 63.
[33] Ibid., pp. 62–63.
[34] Ibid., pp. 92–93.

all of Siberian Asia (including the Amurian watershed).[35] But, in the meantime, the Company could serve as a useful cover for Russian expansion into Amuria and Sakhalin (especially as all of the Company's colonial governors after 1821 were naval officers).

In order to test his belief that Kamchatka could not be effectively linked to the 'mainland' by the long-standing Iakutsk–Okhotsk route, Murav'ev decided to see for himself. In the summer of 1849 the governor-general, accompanied by his wife, became the first Siberian governor to undertake an inspection of the Okhotsk seaboard and Kamchatka peninsula.[36] They travelled from Irkutsk by land to Kachuga Landing on the uppermost river Lena, by riverboat down the Lena to Iakutsk, on horseback over the Iakutsk–Okhotsk Track to Okhotsk, by ship over the Okhotsk Sea to Petropavlovsk, by ship across the Okhotsk Sea again to Aian, by horse and boat to Iakutsk, and by river and land back to Irkutsk. Murav'ev was appalled and exhausted by the journey, particularly the Iakutsk–Okhotsk leg. Upon reaching Okhotsk in early July he wrote to Count Perovskii that he had just completed 'one of the most difficult of journeys, that is, from Iakutsk to here', adding that 'Okhotsk should not have already existed [for] one hundred years'.[37] Certainly his experience reinforced his belief in the logistical necessity of the Amur route.

In the meantime, in early February the Tsar had appointed a special committee on the Amur question. It recommended that the Russian-American Company send a land party from Aian to the mouth of the Amur in order to open trade with the Gilyaks (the Nivkh) and that Captain Nevel'skoi, after unloading at Petropavlovsk, should also sail there to explore 'thoroughly' the waters between Sakhalin and the mainland, particularly the estuary and mouth of the Amur and the river itself (in rowing boats flying no flag), in order to determine their navigability, possible sites for ports and forts, and the insularity or peninsularity of Sakhalin.[38] Nevel'skoi was not to publicize either his orders or his findings, which were to be couriered secretly to Murav'ev and to Menshikov (for submission to the Tsar).[39]

[35] Ibid., pp. 154–56.
[36] Although the incoming governor of Russian America, Baron Ferdinand von Vrangel' (Wrangel), had closely inspected the Iakutsk–Okhotsk route in 1829 with his wife and infant daughter *en route* to Novoarkhangel'sk (Sitka), the colony's capital.
[37] Barsukov, *Graf*, vol. 1, p. 217.
[38] Ibid., vol. 1, pp. 195–96; Nevel'skoi, *Podvigi*, pp. 94–95.
[39] Ibid., p. 95. However, because the winter post to Kamchatka from Okhotsk had already left, Nevel'skoi's instructions were sent express via Irkutsk by staff captain Mikhail Korsakov, who commanded Eastern Siberia's military (he was a first cousin of Murav'ev and would succeed him as governor-general in 1862). Korsakov reached

Upon his arrival in May at Petropavlovsk Nevel'skoi had received Murav'ev's letter advising him that in all likelihood imperial permission to survey Tatar Strait would soon arrive from St Petersburg.[40] Undaunted and impatient Nevel'skoi decided to proceed without the Tsar's sanction in hand.[41] To save time he exhorted his officers to unload as quickly as possible, and he 'forewarned' them of the 'essence' of the Amur question and of the 'importance' of their mission. Within two weeks captain and crew were ready to proceed, and on 12/24 June Nevel'skoi's expedition departed in the *Baikal* for Sakhalin, carrying a kayak sent expressly from the Aleutian Islands and a small sloop with rowboats, both for navigating shallow waters.[42]

Nevel'skoi's historic survey lasted three months — from late June until the middle of September. To him the 'primary question' that he had to answer was: 'is the mouth of the Amur and its estuary accessible to seagoing vessels?'[43] To find the answer he examined all of Tatar Strait between Sakhalin and the mainland in the *Baikal*, the southern and northern approaches to the Amur's estuary in the transport and the sloop, and the Amur's estuary and mouth in the sloop and the kayak, as well as possible harbours on the mainland between Tatar Strait and the Okhotsk Sea.[44] Subsequently he reported his findings in a secret report to Prince Menshikov: 'the *approach* to the estuary of the river Amur from the sea to the north is very distinct, superior, and generally safe' and 'it is possible to enter the estuary of the river Amur from the north and from the south — the Amur and its estuary are open to large-class ships.' He had demonstrated conclusively that Sakhalin was not a peninsula but an island, separated from the mainland by a channel with a width of four miles and a minimum depth of thirty-five feet — and not connected by an isthmus, as surmised by La Pérouse, Broughton,

---

Irkutsk in April, whereupon he was directed by Murav'ev to deliver the instructions to Nevel'skoi in Petropavlovsk before his mid-June departure to explore Tatar Strait. Korsakov, however, was delayed by ice at Okhotsk until June, so he sailed directly to northern Sakhalin in order to try to intercept the *Baikal*, but he failed to find Nevel'skoi and so proceeded to Aian to await Murav'ev there upon his return from his tour of inspection (Barsukov, *Graf*, vol. 1, p. 197; Struve, *Vospomininaiia*, pp. 47–48).

[40] Barsukov, *Graf*, vol. 1, pp. 197–98.

[41] In his account of his voyage, however, Nevel'skoi dissembles (presumably in order to protect his supporters, notably Murav'ev) by saying that the Tsar's confirmation was already awaiting him upon his arrival at Petropavlovsk (Nevel'skoi, *Podvigi*, p. 94). For the instructions (from Perovskii) see N. A. Ivashintsov, *Russian Round-the-World Voyages, 1803–1809 with a Summary of Later Voyages to 1867*, trans. Glynn R. Barratt, Kingston, ON, 1980, pp. 132–33, citing Sgibnev.

[42] Nevel'skoi, *Podvigi*, pp. 95–96.

[43] Ibid., p. 103.

[44] He describes his survey in detail in ibid., pp. 97–108.

and Kruzenshtern. He had also proved that the Amur's estuary was enterable from Tatar Strait via a southern channel for ships of all sizes and via a northern channel for ships drawing no more than twenty-three feet of water. The river proper had proven enterable, too, from the estuary for shallow-draught seagoing vessels (those drawing no more than fifteen feet of water).[45] So the river Amur was indeed accessible to seagoing vessels, albeit only to those of shallow draught, such as sloops and barques.

Meanwhile, governor-general Murav'ev had finished his inspection of Petropavlovsk and proceeded to Aian, where with the courier Mikhail Semenovich Korsakov he was awaiting Nevel'skoi. The *Baikal* arrived on 15/27 September, but before Nevel'skoi had time to lighter ashore the impatient governor-general boarded a cutter and hurried to meet him. Approaching the transport, Murav'ev hailed Nevel'skoi and asked where he had been, whereupon the captain megaphoned his famous eureka reply:

> Sakhalin is an island, and it is possible for seagoing vessels to enter the estuary and the river of the Amur from the north and the south. An age-old delusion has been completely dispelled and the truth has been revealed! I will report on this now to Your Excellency and then to Prince Menshikov for submission to the Tsar.[46]

Nevel'skoi was confident that his voyage was historic. He wrote:

> The results of our explorations are the basis of the vital significance of the Maritime Territory [Russian Far East] to Russia, for they demonstrate that the river Amur, with the aid of Tatar Strait, communicates directly with the Sea of Japan. Moreover, our discoveries show the vital significance of the Amur as an artery connecting the ocean with Eastern Siberia, which has hitherto been regarded as cut off from it by barrens, mountains, and vast empty spaces.[47]

Nevel'skoi immediately couriered a report on his voyage to Prince Menshikov via Korsakov.[48] With Korsakov went another report to Menshikov by Murav'ev, who boasted that none of the expeditions of Nevel'skoi's predecessors had had such important consequences for Russia as did his. And he noted that it had been accomplished with only

---

[45] Ibid., pp. 106–07.
[46] Ibid., p. 111; Struve, *Vospominaniia*, p. 79.
[47] Nevel'skoi, *Podvigi*, p. 112.
[48] Ibid., pp. 107, 108–09.

the negligible resources allotted for the regular delivery of supplies to Siberia's ports (Okhotsk, Aian, Petropavlovsk) and without any special expense to the treasury.[49] A week later on his way to Iakutsk over the new track from Aian the governor-general wrote to Count Perovskii that 'I met Nevel'skoi, who had fulfilled his commission superbly and so completely, expeditiously, conscientiously, and intelligently that even the immortal Kruzenshtern and the omniscient Middendorf could envy him.'[50]

An obvious question remains: why did Nevel'skoi succeed where other navigators of equal or more skill had failed? One possible answer is that he was more determined and/or more focused. The attempts of La Pérouse, Broughton, and Kruzenshtern were, after all, mere sideshows of grander ventures. Certainly, Nevel'skoi had more time, and he was better prepared in terms of craft for navigating shallow waters. Nevel'skoi was also luckier with the weather.[51] His predecessors encountered stronger winds and thicker fogs, which were the norm even in summer. The latter astounded the writer Ivan Goncharov aboard the frigate *Pallada* in 1854:

But what sorry sailing it is in these parts! What a climate! There is practically no summer; in the morning it is neither cold nor hot, in the evenings definitely cold. The fog is so thick you can't see your own nose. Yesterday they [the crew] shot off the cannon and beat the drums, to help the launches with our officers find the way to the frigate. The winds are mostly fresh and cold, there is practically no calm at any time, and this is mid-July.[52]

[49] Ibid., pp. 111–12.
[50] Barsukov, *Graf*, vol. 1, p. 225. The exultant confidence of both Nevel'skoi and Murav'ev notwithstanding, the former's findings were received politely but negatively in St Petersburg, such was the repute of Nevel'skoi's illustrious predecessors and the opposition of the conservative Nesselrode, who headed a special committee on the Amur question (which feared a conflict with China and even doubted Nevel'skoi's findings). Within a year, however, in the face of the almost total disintegration of Peking's central authority under further internal rebellion and foreign intrusion, Russia advanced into the 'power vacuum' of the Amur Country along the lines urged by Nevel'skoi and Murav'ev and with their active participation (still under the guise of the Russian-American Company), founding two posts and planting the Russian flag on the river. It was then that Nicholas I, who had come to scold the special committee (and even replace its head with the tsarevich) and praise Nevel'skoi, uttered the stirring phrase, 'where once the Russian flag has been raised, it must never be lowered'.
[51] Just as the Cossack headman Semen Dezhnev had been in 1648, when an abnormally warm polar summer allowed him to sail from the East Siberian Sea around the Chukchi Peninsula into the Bering Sea and thereby prove the separation of Asia and North America three-quarters of a century before the Bering–Chirikov expedition did so from the opposite direction.
[52] Ivan Aleksandrovich Goncharov, *The Frigate Pallada*, trans. Klaus Goetze, New

Furthermore, the findings of earlier navigators were not necessarily mistaken. During the nearly half century between Kruzenshtern's and Nevel'skoi's voyages unnavigable shallows may well have been deepened and impassable sandbars may well have been reduced — and even peninsulas destroyed — by wind or water erosion or tremors. Tatar Strait is, after all, a part of the unstable Pacific 'rim of fire' of active faults and plates. The Amur's mouth, in particular, was subject to annual changes wrought by spring ice floes and summer freshets. These also impressed Goncharov:

> The mouth of the river Amur, hardly yet charted and not yet indicated on the map, has a mass of sandbanks. If these were constant, one would have known them precisely. But they are shifting, forming themselves anew every year. Entry and exit in these waters can therefore not be guided by navigation, and we often stood still near some cape or cliff. Thank goodness there was no current in the estuary, but once we really ran into a sandbank [...]. Once the schooner was sticking so fast in the sand that it had to be propped up on the side, to keep it from keeling over.[53]

Little wonder that a combination of meteorological good fortune and nautical acumen was required to determine the usefulness of the Amur.[54]

Following Nevel'skoi's dramatic discoveries, subsequent Amurian events appear somewhat anticlimactic. The locus of Russia's Far Eastern and North Pacific interests shifted rapidly and firmly southwards during the 1850s in the wake of not only the discovery of the navigability of Tatar Strait and the river Amur but also of the continuing enfeeblement of China, the growing probability of war with Britain and France, and in St Petersburg the decreasing influence of foreign minister Nesselrode and the increasing influence of the *konstantinovtsy* ('Constantinians',

---

York, 1987, p. 548. Incidentally, the 'tiny, kind, obliging purveyor of the officers' table' (p. 15) aboard the ship was Lieutenant Petr A. Tikhmenev, who was later to write a valuable two-volume official history of the Russian-American Company.

[53] Ibid., p. 550.

[54] Incidentally, Tatar Strait still bears witness toponymically to its pre-Nevel'skoi perception. All of the strait — from Sakhalin Bay at its northern entrance to its narrowest point (Nevel'skoi Strait) between Capes Lazarev and Murav'ev seventy-five miles to the south — is still denoted the Amur estuary on maps as a result of the former belief that Sakhalin and the mainland were connected just to the south of the river's mouth by an isthmus, even though it has been known for 170 years that this expanse is simply the northernmost part of the strait and not, in fact, an estuary at all. The Amur does have an estuary, but it stretches only twenty-five miles east-west from the river's mouth to that Strait.

after Grand Duke Konstantin Nikolaevich), a coterie of upper and lower ranks at the Naval Ministry who believed in the crucial importance of naval power and the positioning of naval bases on the world ocean rather than in enclosed seas. In the spring of 1853, the Russian-American Company was paid by the state to occupy Sakhalin on its behalf. At the outset of 1854, following the outbreak of the Crimean War (1853–56),[55] Nicholas I authorized Murav'ev 'to sail on the river Amur'[56] in the first of four consecutive spring expeditions down the river intended to bolster Russian defences at its mouth and to settle and supply its valley. By the end of the spring of 1855, when the Tsar ordered Murav'ev to strengthen Russia's grip on the river by occupying its left bank, there were up to 4,000 Russian personnel (mostly military) along the Amur, half of them at Nikolaevsk-on-Amur.[57] The Empire's main Pacific port shifted from Okhotsk to Petropavlovsk to Nikolaevsk-on-Amur to — eventually (1871) — Vladivostok ('ruler of the East'), whose founding in 1860 on the Sea of Japan's Peter the Great Bay, abutting both China and Korea and athwart Japan, was authorized by Murav'ev the year before he resigned his governor-generalship and shortly thereafter retired to Paris, presumably secure and content in the knowledge that he and Nevel'skoi had regained the river Amur for their country.[58] Unfortunately, the vaunted waterway and its valley were not quite to live up to their billing — but that is another story.[59]

---

[55] What the Russians called the 'Eastern War' took place in several theatres (the Balkans and the Caucasus and the Black, Baltic, White, and Bering Seas). In the North Pacific the smaller size of the Russian fleet put it on the defensive, and Russian warships took advantage of their knowledge of the Amur's fairway and eluded Allied warships by entering the river, while Petropavlovsk withstood an Allied bombardment. In Russian America the Russian-American and Hudson's Bay companies avoided the hostilities (and shielded their profits) by securing a neutrality agreement. On the Crimean War in the North Pacific, see John Stephan, 'The Crimean War in the Far East', *Modern Asian Studies*, 3, 1969, 3, pp. 257–77.

[56] Struve, *Vospominaniia*, p. 170.

[57] Iu. Zavoiko, 'Vospominaniia o Kamchatke i Amure (1854–1855)', *Russkii vestnik*, 123, 1876, no. 6, p. 493.

[58] Officially acknowledged in the Treaty of Aigun of 1858 and the Treaty of Peking of 1860, two more of the unforgotten 'unequal treaties' that were forced upon an impotent China by predatory Western powers.

[59] Partly told in James R. Gibson, 'Russia on the Pacific: The Role of the Amur', *Canadian Geographer*, 12, 1968, 1, pp. 15–27.

The Search for Mythical Lands and Straits in the Arctic and Northern Pacific Oceans: Exploration and Mapping of these Regions, 1800–1845

Alexey Vladimirovich Postnikov
Russian Academy of Sciences, S. I. Vavilov Institute for
the History of Science and Technology

PROFESSOR WILL RYAN, Fellow of the British Academy, is one of the leading world experts on Russian language and history. He has been a member of the Council of the Hakluyt Society for many years and was the president of the Society from 2008 to 2011. He was always very supportive of the publication of Russian sources, including those which concerned expeditions to explore and map the Northern Pacific which are the topic of this paper. The Hakluyt Society has a particular interest in the subjects which are the focus of this paper, namely descriptions of indigenous people and the development of mapping. In the first half of the nineteenth century the Russians made great advances in knowledge in both areas, as this paper will demonstrate, and credit for this lies primarily with prominent individuals whose contributions to scholarship are discussed below.

Before the nineteenth century, the Russians had explored the waters and coasts of the northern Pacific between the Kamchatka peninsula and Alaska with some success, but maps of regions to the north and the south of the main maritime routes connecting the Kamchatka peninsula or the port of Okhotsk (on the Sea of Okhotsk) with Alaska continued to show islands and coasts (and straits) which were based on mythical travels of the sixteenth century. They also, however, drew on the work of Joseph-Nicolas Delisle, a Frenchman in Russian service, who had played a significant part in the publication of the first complete atlas of Russia, the *Atlas Rossicus*, published in 1745 by the Academy of Sciences in St Petersburg. By the late eighteenth century, the Russians had established a formal presence in coastal settlements on the west coast of North America, in what is now Alaska and California in the United States of America. The Russian-American Company was granted a monopoly over Russian colonies in North America in 1799 and the Russian Orthodox Church established a missionary presence at the same time.

Delisle had also published an ethnographic account of the peoples of Siberia following his expedition there in 1740 to observe the transit of Mercury across the sun. Most ethnographical studies in the eighteenth century had been by foreign specialists in Russian service (such as Johann Gottlieb Georgi and Peter Simon Pallas). In the early nineteenth century, however, missionaries of the Orthodox Church also conducted serious ethnographical studies of indigenous peoples and their customs in both Kamchatka and Russian America.[1]

Hieromonk Gideon (Gavriil Fedotov, born 1770) had been sent in 1804 to investigate the activities of Orthodox clergy in Kamchatka and Russian America and collected substantial and detailed material, based on oral evidence, of the history, origins and cosmic beliefs of the Kodiaks who inhabited Kodiak island (now part of Alaska). His assessment of the origins of the people of Kodiak island was as follows:

> [...] the people of Kodiak, according to folk legend, came to Kodiak from Alaska. Their ancestors lived previously on the northern side of Alaska near the big River Kwignat [Yukon]. A person named Atliuvatu was their anayugak [leader — angayqaq]. He had an only daughter who disappeared without trace. To find her he collected his party together with another anayugak by the name of Iakunak; they travelled for a long time through different places, reaching the southern side of Alaska, where they beheld a land and named it Kigikhtak [Qikertaq], which means an island in their language. Kodiak had thus been known prior to the Russian arrival by this name. Then Atliuvatu and Iakunak became curious about the island, and finding opportunities for profit, persuaded others to settle in Kigikhtak with all their families.

The affinity between the Alaskan and Kodiak languages supports this interpretation. It also demonstrates that the Kodiak people had an awareness of their geographical position vis-à-vis the North American mainland. Possibly this is also the first reference in a Russian source to the river Yukon, which is referred to as the 'big River Kwignat'. This geographical name was very close to the name (Kwikpak and Kwikhpak) that would be used for the Yukon in subsequent Russian sources.

---

[1]   The section on missionaries is drawn from A. V. Postnikov, 'Learning from Each Other: On a History of Russian-Native Contacts in the Exploration and Mapping of Alaska and the Aleutian Islands (Late Eighteenth- Early Nineteenth Centuries)', http://www.loc.gov/rr/european/mofc/postnikov.html. See also Postnikov, Marvin Falk, *Exploring and Mapping Alaska: The Russian America Era 1741–1867*, trans. Lydia Black, Fairbanks, AK, 2015.

Gideon also wrote that the Kodiaks had the following belief about the creation of the world:

> There had lived a Kishshiakhiliuk [a wise man or cunning person], and at that time there was neither day nor night. He began to blow into a straw, which resulted in an imperceptible but gradual increase in the dry land from the water. While he continued to blow, the sky opened, the sun began to shine, and then, after the night had come, the stars appeared and the moon rose; at last they saw animals and men.

This vivid description of the creation of the world was closely connected in my view with the lifestyle of the Kodiak people who were sailors and hunters of sea animals, for whom the image of a land gradually rising from the sea and widening on the horizon was an everyday experience. Father Gideon noted that the experience of sea voyages had led the Kodiaks to the conclusion that the earth was round. He illustrated this through the following story: 'Their forefathers had sent two kayaks with youngsters, who returned as old men but could not find an end of the earth.' The story showed that the earth had no end, and therefore must be round. Father Gideon also demonstrated that the Kodiaks had passed down from generation to generation a unique knowledge about local conditions which affected sailing through the coastal waters of Alaska. The art of weather forecasting was one of the most important elements of this knowledge, about which the Russian monk remarked that: '[...] a diligent hunter would often go out in the night to look at clouds to ascertain the weather, and he would plan his hunt depending on his observations.'

Father Ioann Veniaminov (Ivan Evseevich Popov, 1797–1879) was a missionary and then Bishop and Archbishop in Alaska, and later became the Metropolitan of Moscow and St Innokentii (Innocent). He is known for his scholarship on the peoples and languages of Alaska; he mastered six dialects spoken in Alaska and translated parts of the Bible and other religious works into those dialects. Veniaminov recorded in detail the geographical knowledge and navigational skills of the indigenous peoples of Russian America.

In the search for possible new islands, Veniaminov quoted tales by Aleuts (people who lived on the Aleutian islands off the coast of Alaska and on the Kamchatka peninsula) about an island which they called Akliun (Haklyun), which was rumoured to be situated to the south of Samalga island (in the Fox islands group of the eastern Aleutian islands). Although later explorations would prove that there was no such island in this location, Veniaminov's description of the methods of orientation used by the Aleuts to reach this or other islands is of much interest in demonstrating their navigation techniques when sailing in open sea beyond the sight of land. The Russian clergyman described their methods in the following way:

> First they steered while guided by the positions of the islands Samalga and Four Mountains, in such a way that the first island should remain behind their stern, and the second island should remain over their right shoulder. They sailed in this direction until the Four Islands disappeared from view; then the Aleuts would leave behind some buoy or beacons, using for the purpose an ordinary inflated seal bladder with stones as anchors. From the first mark, and taking into consideration the direction of waves, they would sail until this buoy began to disappear at which time they dropped the second buoy; after the third buoy the Akliun island [Haklyun] would be seen.

From this passage we can see that as a basis for orientation during their sea voyages the Aleuts made use of their knowledge of the relative positions of islands to each other, as well as the turbulence of the sea near the coast of these islands. This included the direction of waves, as well as their refraction and interference when they hit the shore. Such methods (or variations of these methods) were known to be used by many other peoples who dwelled on coasts and who lived by hunting sea animals and by fishing (for example, sea charts made by the inhabitants of the Marshall Islands from palm branches, which have become very well known in the history of world cartography).

Scholars have not found any evidence of maps used by the Aleuts during the period of the first Aleutian contacts with the Russians. Nevertheless, it is clear that the Aleuts had a thorough knowledge of the geography of their native lands and had mental images of these regions. Veniaminov often stressed that the Aleuts were very well aware of the natural features of the waters surrounding their islands, with which they had an inseparable connection throughout their lives. He wrote, for example, that when at sea they would always know the height and speed of a wave, and they would compare simple waves with large breakers in the open sea and with waves in the shallows or on rocks. Veniaminov was also impressed with the extraordinary physical prowess of the Aleuts, who could row for fourteen to twenty hours a day in the open sea without any rest, as well as with their unusually good eyesight, which the Aleuts themselves attributed to the lack of salt in their diet.

Veniaminov pointed out, as had Father Gideon, the ability of the Aleuts to study methods of navigation scientifically, and he commented that those Aleuts who had had an opportunity to study navigation were highly regarded by the Russians as well as by their fellow Aleuts. For instance, Andrei Ustiugov, who was an Aleut, was recognized as very skilled and his chart of the river Nushagak in Alaska (which was the first of its kind) continues to be regarded as accurate. The Aleuts navigated not only by using the coastlines and the direction of the waves but also established their position from observations of the movements of the sun and moon. Veniaminov observed that, in regard to the sun, the Aleuts understood that during the solstices it remained static for two and a half days, and before and after the solstice it moved slowly. The Aleuts said that the moon could be seen on the third day in its first phase and their astronomers could show a point on the horizon or in the sky where each new moon would set during a whole year.

The Aleuts also understood the connections between the phases of the moon and the ocean tides, a knowledge which was reflected in their characterization of the seasons of the year: as well as dividing the year into four main seasons, they used more discrete division by months, beginning the year with March. New moons and full moons in March and other months were ascertained through the observation of the tides and the changes in the strength of ocean currents. Their whole calendar, which included twelve months, was conditioned by natural phenomena; each month received its name from the hunting of different kinds of animals and their prevalence, or from some other local circumstances, so that the names of the months varied by region.

Veniaminov gave particular credit to the Aleuts for their knowledge of local hydrological and meteorological conditions, and their proficiency in forecasting the weather. He noted that:

> The Aleuts could forecast weather and especially the wind. The key signs which they used to forecast weather for the next day were primarily the sunset and the following sunrise, which were sufficient for an expert to say accurately what the coming day would be like. They watched the changes in colour of the first light so meticulously that they called this process as 'speaking' with the sun and the dawn.

*　　　*　　　*

The exploration of the sea coast and islands off northern Siberia in the early nineteenth century was prompted to a large extent by the discovery by Russian fur traders of the islands comprising the New

Siberian archipelago (the island of Faddeev in 1805, the New Siberian islands in 1806, the islands of Vasil'ev and Semenov in 1815, and others). There were also 'mythical' islands which were rumoured to be in the north but which never in fact existed. One such mythical island was the so-called 'Sannikov land', which the cartographer Iakov Sannikov claimed to have sighted north of Kotel'nyi island in 1811 (and which was fictionalized in the novel *Sannikov Land* by the science fiction writer Vladimir Obruchev in 1926). Another mythical island was the so-called 'Andreev land', supposedly north-east of the Bear islands.

In 1803–10, during an expedition led by Matvei Matveevich Gedenshtrom (Mathias Hedenström) and Petr Pshenitsyn, who were exploring New Siberian island and the islands of Faddeev and Kotel'nyi and the straits between them, the first chart was compiled depicting the New Siberian archipelago as a whole and also of the coastline between the mouths of the rivers Iana and Kolyma. This expedition also produced the first detailed geographical description of the islands. In the 1820s these same regions were visited by the Iana expedition (1820–24) headed by Petr Anzhou (Pierre Anjou), and the Kolyma expedition (1821–24), headed by Ferdinand Petrovich Vrangel' (Ferdinand Friedrich Georg Ludwig Freiherr von Wrangel, 1796–1870), which continued the work of the Gedenshtrom expedition. They were instructed to survey the coast from the river Lena to the Bering Strait and conclude the search for the mythical 'Andreev land' and 'Sannikov land'.

As before, it proved impossible to find these mysterious lands, and the expedition discovered only a few more small islands in the New Siberian archipelago and off the mainland coast. The main achievement of the expedition was the compilation of a more accurate chart of the entire mainland coast of the Arctic Ocean from the river Olenek to Koliuchin Bay, and also charts of the New Siberian, Liakhov (names after Ivan Liakhov) and Bear islands. These charts were based on 115 points with astronomically-defined geographical co-ordinates. In the eastern section of Vrangel''s chart there is an island indicated on the basis of information supplied by the local inhabitants, with the inscription: *Mountains are visible from the Cape of Iakan in the summer-time.* This island was also depicted on charts in the atlases of Ivan Fedorovich Kruzenshtern (Adam Johann von Krusenstern) (1826) and Gavriil Andreevich Sarychev (1826). In 1867, this island was discovered by the American whaler and explorer Thomas Long and named 'Wrangel' in honour of the remarkable Russian polar explorer. The work of the Anzhou and Vrangel' expeditions resulted in twenty-six manuscript charts and plans, as well as scientific reports and publications.

This was a period in which Russian mapping became far more scientific and professional. New instructions were issued for the compilation and use of symbols on large-scale charts and maps. The uniform use of symbols on land maps (military-topographical maps) and sea charts (navigational charts) was a matter of particular concern. This issue was resolved quite effectively largely due to the fact that between 1827 and 1837 the Military Topographical Department and the Hydrographic Department of the General Staff of the Navy were under the unified command of the remarkable Russian cartographer and geodesist Fedor Fedorovich Shubert (Theodor Friedrich von Schubert, 1789–1865).[2] This was reflected in the demand by the Hydrographic Department that ocean surveys and the compilation of navigational charts in Russian North America should also be unified. In order to achieve this, the head office of the Russian-American Company sent Vrangel' a copy of Sarychev's *Rules of Ocean Geodesy* (*Pravila morskoi geodezii*), first published in 1804 but republished in 1833 by the Naval Cadet Corps. Vrangel' was instructed that all officers of the navigational corps must have this book in their possession:

> The head office of the [Russian-American] Company, has appended a copy of the book, and asks that you forward the latter to surveyor Dingel'shtet [Konstantin Fedorovich Dingelstedt] for his guidance so that he can follow the rules laid down in this publication when conducting surveys and taking soundings.[3]

Uniform symbols for military topographical maps and hydrographic charts and plans were issued in 1833, compiled by the Hydrographic Department. This guide was sent to Russian America the following year. Vrangel', as an outstanding governor (or chief manager) of the Russian-American Company and a leading scholar of hydrography, also made strenuous efforts to improve the hydrographic knowledge and the navigational charts of Russia's North American possessions. Almost every skipper of the Russian-American Company's ships received instructions from Vrangel' to search for new lands off the Alaskan coast and to improve the existing navigational charts.

Indigenous peoples played an important role as guides in the hydrographic work in this period in Russian America. For instance, we know the names of the crew who participated in the expedition under

---

[2] For more details see A. V. Postnikov, *Razvitie krupnomasshtabnoi kartografii v Rossii*, Moscow, 1989, pp. 118–43.

[3] Moscow, Arkhiv vneshnei politiki Rossiiskoi Imperii (hereafter AVPRI), f. 404, op. 888, rulon [roll] 8, d. 970, ll. 432–33, papers of the Russian-American Company.

Ivan Filipovich Vasil'ev (1775–1812) of the corps of navigators, to whom this important work has been entrusted. Along with the name of the cabin boy [*iunga*] Fedor Beliaev, there are sometimes Russified names (indicating that they had probably converted to Russian Orthodoxy) of five Aleuts — Andrei Agiza, Vasilii Tunulikhna, Matvei Nigilitknak, Ivan Mordvinov, Ivan Amikhkak — and the pilot and interpreter who was a Tlingit called Pavel (the name Tinglit mean the 'peoples of the tides').[4] It should be noted that Tlingit Pavel had, beside Vasil'ev himself, great experience in expeditionary explorations and enjoyed a well-deserved and excellent reputation in the Russian North American colonies. On the eve of Vasil'ev's expedition, Vrangel' wrote as follows:

> The Tlingit Pavel, who had served on the *Chichagov* during her last voyage has proved himself to be, according to the testimony of Captain-Lieutenant Arvid Adol'f Etolin, an excellent pilot for the straits; he behaved diligently and deserved encouragement [...].[5]

Adol'f Karlovich Etolin (Arvid Adolf Etholén, 1799–1876, born in Finland) played a prominent role in the exploration of Russian America. He is mentioned in Khlebnikov's history of Baranov, (published in 1835), including the following comment made to Khlebnikov concerning Etolin:

> In one friendly and frank conversation which was, so to speak, conducted in the manner of good-natured seafarers, with the host of the meeting Mr Iankovskii, Baranov stated in tears that: 'If only the Head Office [of the Russian-American Company] could have sent me men like yourself earlier, then I would very likely have had more success, and I would have found it pleasant to pass the time in their company!'[6]

Etolin served as a ship's master from 1818 to 1825. He was part of a group that surveyed the Bering Sea from 1822 to 1824. He was the adjutant for the governor of Russian America in 1834, and became the governor from 1840 to 1845. He was a member of the board of the Russian-American Company in St Petersburg from 1847 to 1859.

The hydrographic work which had been actively pursued as a result of Vrangel''s instructions in the years 1830–33 brought substantial

[4] AVPRI, f. 404, op. 888, rulon 35, d. 997, ll. 146–46 ob.
[5] Ibid., l. 139.
[6] K. T. Khlebnikov, *Zhizneopisanie Aleksandra Andreevicha Baranova glavnogo pravitel'ia rosiiskikh kolonii v Amerike*, St Petersburg, 1835, p. 207.

results. One of these was the evidence of the non-existence in the northern part of the Pacific Ocean of the mythical islands sought by many mariners, cited above, such as 'Sannikov land' and 'Andreev land'. Vrangel' reported this to the head office of the Russian-American Company in his dispatch number 75, dated 10 April 1834, headed 'On Zarembo's voyage with the brig *Chichagov* on a search for islands and the failure to find such [islands]'. Dionysius Zarembo was a Polish employee of the Russian-American Company. Along with Zarembo's chart, Vrangel' appended to his dispatch a 'Chart indicating the routes of vessels which have searched for land in the Northern Sea to the west of the Pribilov islands [now called Pribilof islands, but named after Gavriil Pribilov] in the years 1831, 1832, and 1833'. This chart, as well as the collected testimonies by navigators of the Russian-American Company demonstrated, in Vrangel''s opinion, the pointlessness of any future searches for the mythical islands. He wrote the following:

> As far as renewing the search for new lands throughout the entire expanse of the Northern part of the Great Ocean to the south of the Aleutian Chain, guided by the possibility and the likelihood [of finding them], I find any future enterprise [of this sort] superfluous. Should it be the will of the Head Office to determine with mathematical precision each point in the ocean, this would demand centuries of uninterrupted searches.[7]

Vrangel' believed, and justifiably so, that the perfection of cartographic knowledge about the coasts and seas of Russian America was of greater significance than the search for mythical lands and expressed satisfaction that work of this nature was conducted successfully under his watch as governor. Responding to instructions from the head office in 1832 with regard to the type of information to be supplied for a coastal survey for the Russian colonies, Vrangel' instructed all captains of the Russian-American Company vessels to describe all the seas known to them and put at their disposal all the old journals and charts then present in the Novo-Arkhangel'sk (now Sitka) archive.

Lieutenant Mikhail Dimitrevich Teben'kov (1802–72, later vice-admiral and then governor of Russian America from 1845 to 1850) was most active in carrying out this assignment. It was at this time that Teben'kov began his remarkable cartographic activity, the results of which were compiled in 1852 as the *Atlas of the North-West Coasts*

---

[7] AVPRI, f. 404, op. 888, rulon 36, d. 997, ll. 98–99.

of America. In 1834, Vrangel' wrote about the young cartographer as
follows:

> Lieutenant Teben'kov presented me with nine charts of all our
> possessions in America, compiled by him from surveys already
> known to the public: of Captains Beechey, Litke and Staniukovich and
> those not yet known: by Messrs Vasil'ev (a navigator who is presently
> departing), Ingstrem, Chernov, Zarembo, Khramchenko, Arvid Adol'f
> Etolin, with analysis of the same and remarks about the voyage
> from Novoarkhangel'sk to Unalaska Island and to the North, to the
> Bering Strait. These nine charts, analysis, and comments, compiled
> by Lieutenant Teben'kov, I am forwarding to the Head Office for
> transmittal to the Office of the Hydrographer-General, as a very useful
> and not unimportant work of Mr Teben'kov [...].

On 28 April 1834, Vrangel' dispatched to the head office of the
Russian-American Company, with the memorandum number 199,
twenty-three charts and one plan described in the *Register of Charts
and Plans*, including two summary charts by Ivan Vasil'ev showing
the area from Cape Douglas along the southern coast of the Alaska
peninsula.[8] The charts dispatched to the head office of the Russian-
American Company demonstrate the attention devoted by Vrangel' to
questions of geographical exploration and cartography of the North
American Russian colonies. As the documents of the period attest,
Vrangel' came to count more and more on using regular commercial
journeys by parties of the Russian-American Company's employees,
on information collected from outposts and from individuals and on
information from indigenous peoples.

On 29 October 1835, Vrangel' left the post of governor of the North
American Russian colonies for Russia and the post was taken by the
captain of the first rank of the guards, in the Naval Department,
Ivan Antonovich Kupreianov (1794–1857). In June of 1840, captain of
the second rank Etolin replaced Kupreianov as governor of Russia's
colonies in North America. Etolin had enormous first-hand experience
of working in Russian America. In his person the Russian-American
Company acquired another scholar of the natural history and of the
peoples of Alaska.

Lieutenant Lavrentii Alekseevich Zagoskin (1808–90) became one
of the most outstanding executors of Etolin's plans.[9] The cartographical

---

[8] AVPRI, f. 404, op. 888, rulo 36, d. 997, ll. 187–89.
[9] A. V. Postnikov, 'Ekspeditsiia L. A. Zagoskina 1842–1844 gg.: ee znachenie i

results of Zagoskin's expeditions were remarkable, and this was due
not only to the fact that he personally conducted precise surveys on
the march and made astronomical determinations of coordinates,
but because he also summarized the work of his Russian and foreign
predecessors with great care, checking their data against information
provided by the local inhabitants and by experienced Company
employees. The Zagoskin Expedition in 1842–44 also showed the
exceptional importance of local knowledge to Russian explorers.
Information from indigenous people had a prominent, and sometimes
even the dominant place in the contents of Zagoskin's field diary,
largely because Zagoskin found this information to be trustworthy and
accurate. This was clear in the early stages of the expedition in relation
to the Mikhailov redoubt on the Norton sound (now called St Michael),
as Zagoskin noted:

> [...] in the period when the redoubt was founded, one native woman
> from a nearby settlement advised the Russians not to settle on that
> location, telling them that she remembered two occasions when the
> spot had flooded. Her words had been disregarded as a fantasy, but we
> could confirm her story by finding huge half-decayed trees that floated
> to the relatively high spots of the island situated at a distance more than
> a mile from the shore.

Zagoskin's experience showed that local geographical information
was, on the whole, reliable. Its scientific usage, however, required a
thorough analysis and an appreciation of the notions held by indigenous
people about the terrain. In addition, it was important to appreciate the
particular style which was employed when local people spoke about
their travels. Zagoskin stressed that a local man talking about his
journeys would not omit anything (including, for example, the places
where he smoked his pipe, drank water, saw some animal, and so on),
and for each of these episodes he would crook his finger, counting in
this way the number of his rests or stops. Even those who understood
this way of narration had to be very careful about how to use it, and
even Zagoskin questioned whether it was possible with any authority
to determine, for example, from the number of crooked fingers that
it would take a certain number of days for the journey. Nevertheless,
evidence of this type of calculation can be found in many published
travel descriptions, and not exclusively in Russian ones. Zagoskin also

posledstviia', in *Russkii puteshestvennik i obshchestvennyi deiatel': Lavrentii Zagoskin
(k 299-letiiu so dnia rozhdeniia). Issledovaniia i materialy,* Riazan', 2008, pp. 82–119.

found that Kolmakov (named after Fedor Kolmakov) redoubt was not defended with any walls or towers, which he explained by the fact that Semeon Ivanovich Lukin, the manager of the Kolmakov redoubt, and all his relatives had become completely immersed in their natural and ethnic environment. The following extract from the expedition's travel log explained this as follows: 'Did Lukin himself, being married to a native woman from Ugavik [or Uknavik] settlement, or all of his party being themselves or through their wives connected with natives of the five settlements, need to be afraid of being killed by their relatives?'[10]

Zagoskin compiled a manuscript *Mercator Chart of Part of the North-West Coast of America*, which summarized the results of his expeditions in the years 1842, 1843 and 1844 and is now preserved in the State Archive of the Navy of Russia in St Petersburg.[11] According to the official report of Etolin, the governor of the North American colonies, this chart was sent as part of a set together with other surveys of the Russian-American Company's possessions, attached to the dispatch number 382 dated 15 May 1845. This chart was of outstanding quality and is testimony to Zagoskin's achievement in determining the hydrographic schema of the lower and middle courses of the rivers Yukon and Kuskokwim. His ability to do this and to map accurately the relative size of the basins of these great Alaskan rivers was due to his use during his expedition of portage routes which had been used by local tribes since time immemorial.

In Zagoskin's work, the geographic descriptions of the territory were considerably enhanced through the inclusion of information, maps, reports and narratives by his predecessors, be they Russian or the indigenous people who were the original explorers of the rivers discharging into the Bering Sea and Arctic Ocean. Russian and English charts and maps also served as materials for compilation of the map published in Zagoskin's book, the *Mercator General Map of a Part of Russia's Possessions in America, compiled by Lieutenant Zagoskin in the course of the Expeditions in the Years 1842, 1843 and 1844.* Thus, the coastline of Alaska is reproduced from the original charts by John Franklin (1825–26), Peter Dease and Thomas Simpson (1837), Frederick Beechey (1827), the survey by James Cook, the chart and survey by Vasilii Khromchenko (or Khramchenko) (1822), from the original chart

---

[10] For more details see A. V. Postnikov, 'Learning from Each Other: A History of Russian-Native Contacts in Late Eighteenth – Early Nineteenth Century Exploration and Mapping of Alaska and the Aleutian Islands', *International Hydrographic Review*, 6, 2005, 2, pp. 6–19; http://www.loc.gov/rr/european/mofc/postnikov.html.

[11] St Petersburg, Rossiiskii gosudarstvennyi arkhiv voennogo morskogo flota, f. 1331, op. 4, d. 255.

of the apprentice navigator and Aleut Andrei Ustiugov (1819), and the chart of Fedor Petrovich Litke (Friedrich Graf von Lütke) (1828) and others. To represent the interior territories, as well as his own surveys Zagoskin used journals and surveys by Ivan Vasil'ev and maps by Fedor Kolmakov and Semeon Lukin.

Etolin, the governor of the North American colonies, used Zagoskin's data, together with his own data, to devise new instructions for local Russian officials in the colonies. These instructions were aimed primarily at continuing the exploration of the interior of Alaska and its coastlines and at creating a data source which could be continually updated. Specifically, Etolin ordered Lukin to follow these 'Particular instructions',[12] that is, he was required to sail down to the Mikhailov redoubt by 10 July by which time the vessel from Novo-Arkhangel'sk was expected to arrive. In his reports, Lukin had to write his own notes about the number of inhabitants, the localities and the potential of the region for the fur trade.

The manager of the Kolmakov redoubt (on the Kuskokwim river, named after the trader Fedor Kolmakov), Semeon Lukin, had been extremely helpful during Zagoskin's expedition and was highly valued by Zagoskin. This resulted in a satisfactory outcome for Lukin and for some of Lieutenant Zagoskin's local assistants, as conveyed to Lukin in a letter from governor Etolin dated 14 May 1845 (number 272):

> In accordance with your wish conveyed to me by Lieutenant Zagoskin, your son Konstantin is admitted into the [Russian-American] Company service with a salary of 250 roubles per year. Your son Ivan is appointed as your deputy and the creole Aleksei Matrozov as travelling starosta [leader] with salaries as specified in the budget, effective 1 January of this year of 1845. After representations by Mr Lieutenant Zagoskin, I award to the Severnov *toion* [chief] Kantel'nuk for his loyalty to the Russians and the aid rendered to Mr Zagoskin's expedition, the silver medal 'Allies of Russia'.[13]

Beside this instruction to Lukin, the governor sent a circular instruction, which came from the head office of the Russian-American Company, dated 10 February 1845, addressed to all district and redoubt managers (beginning with the Mikhailov redoubt) specifying that volcanoes had to be identified and described. The managers were to do the following:

---

[12] AVPRI, f. 404, op. 888, rulon 50, d. 1012, ll. 68–70ob.
[13] Ibid., rulon 49, d. 1011, ll. 317–180b.

[...] you are instructed to collect all possible information from the savages about presently flaming [erupting] and extinct volcanoes (or peaks) in the North should there be such and if possible to learn when and under what conditions they began, continued, and stopped to erupt. This kind of information you are to continue collecting in the future and deliver to the Chief Manager [governor] for presentation to the Head Office should the savages report that a peak was beginning to emit flames, smoke or to stop erupting. However, such information is to be accurate and not an invention by the savages as has happened often before.[14]

The governor instructed that there should be a particular investigation of the region in the interior of Alaska near the settlement of Nulato outpost (*odinochka*). The entire basin of the Kvikhpak (the Yukon), from the Tutago-Igudov settlement upstream to its very source, was included with particular reference to the possibility of the procurement of furs. In the 'Instruction for the Management and the Productivity of the Nulato outpost' compiled by Etolin in 1845, much attention was devoted to regulations on the hunting of animals for fur and measures for their preservation from complete extinction. To achieve this, the following limits were set on hunting:

Shooting beaver and land otters with firearms is forbidden and the manager will be held strictly accountable; he also is to take care that the destructive habit of taking beaver by breaking up their lodges, especially in the spring when only pregnant females remain there [in the lodges], is stopped; explain to the natives that taking [beaver] this way they only deprive themselves of future income.[15]

The governor of Russia's North American colonies demanded that implementation of his instructions was to be achieved only through friendly persuasion and under no circumstances was force to be used against indigenous people as he made clear: 'Gentleness is necessary in dealing with the natives, and as their chief shortcomings are laziness and lack of foresight it is the manager's responsibility, through example, to demonstrate the benefit of work and thrift.' In contrast, Etolin demanded that the strictest discipline be observed among the Russians and creoles who were official employees of the Russian-American Company. To maintain this discipline, especially in their dealings

---

[14] Ibid., rulon 50, d. 1012, l. 250b.
[15] Ibid., l. 73.

with the local people, he was prepared to use corporal punishment.[16] Etolin sent out a detailed instruction for the assessment of the value for commerce and the fur trade of the Nulato outpost.[17]

Further to explore and control the lower Yukon region the same instruction directed that a new outpost should be established called the Andreev outpost. A special directive gave this outpost authority over the entire region of the lower Kvikhpak (Yukon) from the Chinak mark to the shore:

> [...] including all the branches of the river. Moreover, the settlement of Andreev outpost is to be placed on the right shore of the Kvikhpak [Yukon], where the river Nypyklaik [Nychiglik] enters into it, because this is the most convenient place for travel on all the branches of the Kvikhpak delta and especially for communication with the Akalmuit [Akulmiut].

Localities with useful resources such as forests with high-quality trees, meadows, hunting grounds and so on were to be specifically indicated.

Because of the imperfect knowledge of the lowest reaches of the Yukon delta, the Etolin directive stated that because:

> [...] the first trips into Kvikhpak branches are poorly known to us; the manager has to undertake [the trips] himself, leaving the outpost in charge of his assistant. Journals of trips are to be presented to the Chief Manager [governor] of the Colonies. In them should be noted the names of settlements, the number of inhabitants of both sexes, the appearance of the country, its natural resources, the direction of water communications, and in general anything that is worthy of mention in regard to trade in that region. Sketches (maps) based on reconnaissance survey are to be appended to them.[18]

In the very same year, 1845, the Kvikhpak mission (named the Russian mission after the sale of Alaska to the United States) was established in the settlement of Ikogmuit (Iqugmiut), about 200 *versty* distant from the Mikhailov redoubt upstream along the river Yukon. It was headed by priest Iakov Netsvetov (later St Jacob Netsvetov), a creole whose father was a Russian and whose mother was an Aleut. The mission was to bring the word of God to the inhabitants of the Kvikhpak and Kuskokwim

[16] Ibid., ll. 74–75ob.
[17] Ibid., ll. 78ob.–79.
[18] Ibid., ll. 80ob.–81, 88.

basins and their tributaries.[19] The Andreev outpost was destroyed by the local indigenous people in 1855.

On 18 January 1845, captain of the second rank, Mikhail Dmitrievich Teben'kov (1802–72) was appointed governor of Russia's colonies in North America and in April of the same year, in Okhotsk, he accepted the office from governor Etolin. The governors who predated Teben'kov had put matters of geographical exploration and the cartography of the inland and island possessions of Russia in North America on a firm scientific, technical and organizational footing. This guaranteed the uninterrupted production of new navigational charts and surveys for the colonial management and for the Hydrographic Department. The last 'portion' of such materials was dispatched to St Petersburg by Etolin prior to his departure from the colonies. His final *Report* demonstrated that by this time due to his efforts and those of his predecessors the compilation of charts and collections in Novo-Arkhangel'sk was properly organized.[20]

The materials sent from the colonies were received in St Petersburg with approval, but in the letter of 8 March 1846 (number 493) the head office of the Russian-American Company instructed Teben'kov, in accordance with the request by the Hydrographic Department, in the future to send appropriate journals and surveys with the charts so that corrections could made.[21] It was also confirmed that Teben'kov was to continue geo-magnetic and meteorological observations at the observatory in Novo-Arkhangel'sk.

*   *   *

The paper about Zagoskin's travels was read at the meeting of the Imperial Russian Geographical Society, which had been founded in 1845 in St Petersburg, and is one of the oldest geographical societies in the world. Furthermore, the publication of Zagoskin's memoirs in 1847 aroused tremendous interest in Russian scholarly circles. It is no coincidence that the interest of Russian scholars shown in the overseas possessions of the Russian Empire was aroused at that particular time by the arrival in St Petersburg of the natural science and ethnographic collections of Etolin and also of Il'ia Gavrilovich Voznesenskii (1816–71), who had also explored Alaska and collected many specimens (and

[19] S. G. Fedorova, *Russkoe naselenie Aliaski i Kalifornii: konets XVIII veka – 1867 g.,* Moscow, 1971, pp. 130–31.
[20] AVPRI, f. 404, op. 888, rulon 59, d. 1012, ll. 99–100.
[21] Ibid., rulon 16, d. 878, ll. 116–160b.

was then made curator of the Zoological Museum in St Petersburg in recognition of his achievements). Both men had left the North American colonies in 1845.[22] The collections of Voznesenskii and Etolin to this day remain some of the most valuable sources for scientific study. The value of Etolin's ethnographic materials was clearly demonstrated in the publication, supported by the National Administration of Antiquities of Finland, by the Finnish scholar Pirjo Varjola, with the participation of the Russian ethnographers the late Iuliia Pavlovna Averkieva and the late Roza Gavrilovna Liapunova.[23] The collections of Etolin and Voznesenskii, together with Zagoskin's reports, attracted the attention of the leading scholars in the Imperial Russian Geographical Society. The Society resolved to undertake a study of Russia's natural environment and economy by means of a questionnaire, and it is no coincidence that they began this project with Russia's North American territory,[24] given the expertise which had been acquired there both in mapping and in ethnographic studies by the remarkable missionaries and explorers who have been the subject of this chapter. One consequence, however, of the achievements of these men was that the 'mythical' islands had been exposed as a fantasy.

[22] Ibid., rulon 49, d. 1011, ll. 370–710b.
[23] Varjola Pirjo (with contributions by Iu. P. Averkieva and R. G. Liapunova), *The Etholén Collection: The Ethnographic Alaskan Collection of Adolf Etholén and his Contemporaries in the National Museum of Finland*, Helsinki, 1990.
[24] The details of the first steps of this project can be found in St Petersburg, Russkoe Geograficheskoe obshchestvo, f. 1–1846, op. 1, d. 9: On the compilation of a statistical programme.

Pilgrimage and Politics:
Two 'Sailor Princes' in Jerusalem, 1859

Simon Dixon

University College London, School of Slavonic and
East European Studies

FEW scholars combine Will Ryan's expertise in the history of both pilgrimage and naval technology.[1] No less exclusive is the company of significant historical actors who shared these apparently disparate interests. One such was the Grand Duke Konstantin Nikolaevich (1827–92), second son of Nicholas I, whose efforts to convert part of the Black Sea fleet into a commercial carrier for Russian pilgrims to Jerusalem first attracted scholarly attention more than fifty years ago.[2] A later generation of historians portrayed the Grand Duke mainly as the patron of a group of like-minded reformist technocrats.[3] Recently, however, the spotlight has swung back to his promotion of Russian Orthodoxy in the East in a campaign managed by one of his young *konstantinovtsy*, B. P. Mansurov (1826–1910).[4] This essay compares a

Jonathan Parry and Alexa von Winning generously helped to improve this essay. Dates in the text are given in New Style according to the Gregorian calendar, twelve days ahead of the Old Style Julian Calendar used in nineteenth-century Russia. Footnotes referring to Old Style sources give both dates. Punctuation has been modernized throughout.

[1] 'The Life and Journey of Daniel Abbot of the Russian Land', trans. W. F. Ryan, in John Wilkinson, with Joyce Hill and W. F. Ryan (eds), *Jerusalem Pilgrimage 1099–1185*, Hakluyt Society, second series, 167, London, 1988; W. F. Ryan, 'Peter the Great and English Maritime Technology', in Lindsey Hughes (ed.), *Peter the Great and the West: New Perspectives*, Basingstoke, 2001, pp. 130–58.

[2] W. E. Mosse, 'Russia and the Levant, 1856–1862: Grand Duke Constantine Nicolaevich and the Russian Steam Navigation Company', *Journal of Modern History*, 26, 1954, 1, pp. 39–48; Derek Hopwood, *The Russian Presence in Syria and Palestine 1843–1914: Church and Politics in the Near East*, Oxford, 1969, pp. 55–61, 70–74.

[3] W. Bruce Lincoln, *In the Vanguard of Reform: Russia's 'Enlightened' Bureaucrats, 1825–1861*, DeKalb, IL, 1982, pp. 141–48; Jacob W. Kipp and Maia A. Kipp, 'The Grand Duke Konstantin Nikolaevič: The Making of a Tsarist Reformer, 1827–1853', *Jahrbücher für Geschichte Osteuropas*, 34, 1986, 1, pp. 3–18; A. P. Shevyrev, *Russkii flot posle Krymskoi voiny: Liberal'naia biurokratiia i morskaia reforma*, Moscow, 1990.

[4] K. A. Vakh (ed.), *Velikii kniaz' Konstantin Nikolaevich i russkoe palomnichestvo v Sviatuiu Zemliu*, Moscow, 2011; K. A. Vakh (ed.), *Velikii kniaz' Konstantin Nikolaevich i Russkii Ierusalim*, Moscow, 2012; *Pis'ma B. P. Mansurova iz puteshestviia po Pravoslavnomu Vostoku v 1857 g.*, eds Kirill Vakh and Alexa von Winning, Moscow, 2014 (hereafter *Pis'ma B. P. Mansurova*); Vsevolod Voronin, 'Velikii kniaz' Konstantin Nikolaevich na pravoslavnom Vostoke i arabskom Zapade v seredine 1840-kh gg.',

pivotal episode — Constantine's own pilgrimage to the Holy Land in May 1859 — with the visit to Palestine two months earlier by another 'sailor prince': Alfred (1844–1900), the second son of Queen Victoria.[5] Setting both royal tours in the context of the unstable international politics of their time, I argue that the year 1859 marked a turning point not only in the status of Russian Orthodoxy in Jerusalem, but also in the relative prestige there of Britain and Russia.

War and Peace in Italy and the Mediterranean
No-one could have anticipated in 1859 that Alfred would marry into the Russian imperial family.[6] Indeed, the two princes had little in common. By the time he reached Jerusalem, Constantine had led the Naval Ministry in St Petersburg for six years. 'Affie', by contrast, was but a callow fourteen-year-old midshipman, attached to HMS *Euryalus*, under the command of Captain John Tarleton, in a widely-derided attempt by the Prince Consort to convert his son's boyish enthusiasm for the navy into a modern professional commitment. So, while both sovereigns had cause to lament the two princes' absence on protracted Mediterranean tours, the Tsar suffered a greater political loss than the Queen.[7] Whereas Victoria characteristically struggled to balance the pain of separation against the irritation caused by Affie's presence — 'it is such a contrary feeling!' she confessed when he finally reappeared — Alexander II was deprived of his 'right hand man in the most serious affairs'.[8] Engaged in tense preparations for the emancipation of the serfs, and diverted by a financial crisis leading to the collapse of the state banks in September 1859, the Tsar unsurprisingly longed for Constantine's return.[9] Britain, too, faced a period of political uncertainty after Lord Derby's minority Conservative administration was defeated on the issue of parliamentary reform on 31 March. Though the government limped on until 11 June, its authority was weakened,

Rossiiskaia istoriia, 2019, no. 2, pp. 78–97.

[5] Since some of the sources I quote are British, it is convenient hereafter to refer to Konstantin Nikolaevich as Constantine.

[6] See my 'The Russian Royal Wedding of 1874', forthcoming.

[7] Alfred sailed from Spithead on 27 October 1858 and returned to Osborne on leave on 21 July 1859; Constantine left St Petersburg on 8/20 October 1858 and reached Tsarskoe Selo via Odessa on 12/24 June 1859.

[8] Roger Fulford (ed.), *Dearest Child: Private Correspondence of Queen Victoria and the Crown Princess of Prussia, 1858–1861*, London, 1964, p. 235, 29 February 1860; *Pis'ma B. P. Mansurova*, p. 190, Mansurov to his father, 17/29 December 1857.

[9] See L. G. Zakharova and L. I. Tiutiunnik (eds), *1857–1861: Perepiska Imperatora Aleksandra II s Velikim Kniazem Konstantinom Nikolaevichem; Dnevnik Velikogo Kniazia Konstantina Nikolaevicha*, Moscow, 1994 (hereafter *1857–1861*).

and the foreign secretary, Lord Malmesbury, already so 'worn out' by early March that he would have been 'glad to resign', proved ill-equipped to navigate the international crisis over the Italian question that loomed ominously behind both royal tours.[10]

Austria's declaration of war on Piedmont-Sardinia on 29 April exposed Malmesbury's misplaced trust in the pacific intentions of Napoleon III, who had conspired with Cavour to provoke a conflict intended to evict the Habsburgs from Lombardy and destroy the settlement of 1815.[11] Though the fighting proved short — peace was concluded at Villafranca on 11 July after heavy Austrian defeats at Magenta (4 June) and Solferino (24 June) — such an outcome was scarcely predictable in the spring, when fears of a general conflict were widespread. 'Who can foresee where it will end?' wondered Constantine, in Athens when war broke out.[12] 'I can remember no period of equal confusion and danger', the Prince Consort declared on 16 April. 'Suspicion, Hatred, Pride, Cunning, Intrigue, Covetousness, Dissimulation dictate the despatches.'[13] Victoria's anxiety for Affie — 'poor dear boy he may see fire before long' — was outweighed by her embarrassment as a supporter of the Court of Vienna.[14] The Tsar, by contrast, determined to punish Austria for remaining neutral in the Crimean War, had concluded a secret defensive treaty with France on 3 March.[15] When *The Times* revealed this compact on the day before war was declared, falsely alleging the existence of a separate offensive alliance, fears of a Napoleonic invasion spread across England and panic gripped the Foreign Office, unconvinced by the repeated denials of any hostile intent by the Russian minister of foreign affairs, Prince Aleksandr Gorchakov.[16] In fact, the spectre of concerted Franco-

[10] Earl of Malmesbury, *Memoirs of an Ex-Minister: An Autobiography*, London, 1885, p. 468.

[11] Nick Carter, 'Hudson, Malmesbury, and Cavour: British Diplomacy and the Italian Question, February 1858 to June 1859', *Historical Journal*, 40, 1997, 2, pp. 389–413, is more critical than Geoffrey Hicks, *Peace, War and Party Politics: The Conservatives and Europe, 1846–59*, Manchester, 2007.

[12] *1857–1861*, p. 104, Konstantin Nikolaevich to Alexander II, 22 April/4 May 1859.

[13] Theodore Martin, *The Life of the Prince Consort*, 5 vols, London, 1875–80, 4, p. 425, to the Dowager Duchess of Coburg.

[14] Fulford (ed.), *Dearest Child*, p. 188, 27 April 1859.

[15] M. A. Chepelkin, 'Diplomatiia Rossii nakanune avstro-italo-frantsuzskoi voiny 1859 g.', *Vestnik Moskovskogo universiteta, Seriia 8: Istoriia*, 1987, no. 5, pp. 61–72, revised a literature stretching back to B. H. Sumner, 'The Secret Franco-Russian Treaty of 3 March 1859', *English Historical Review*, 189, 1933, pp. 65–83.

[16] *The Times*, 28 April 1859, p. 7; Jonathan Parry, *The Politics of Patriotism: English Liberalism, National Identity and Europe, 1830–1886*, Cambridge, 2006, pp. 226–27. Malmesbury's correspondence with Sir John Crampton in St Petersburg is at The

Russian aggression was illusory because the two powers' aims were incompatible. As A. J. P. Taylor long ago observed, the Russians had no interest in a general European war that offered them scant reward in the Near East: 'They wanted the opposite: a revision of the Treaty of Paris without a serious revision of the settlement of 1815.'[17] Unable to achieve this goal alone, Russia remained preoccupied with domestic reform and keen to localize the Italian war.

While Europe's attention was focused on Italy, parallel royal tours of the Mediterranean were bound to expose tensions between Britain and Russia, still uneasily seeking a *modus vivendi* three years after the truce in the Crimea. Since British power in the Mediterranean was secure, there was no risk in showing off Malta's defences to Constantine, who sailed into Valletta in February 1859, two months after Affie. However, according to the Grand Duke, the faces of the younger British officers were full of 'hatred for us'.[18] And the more cordial reception accorded to him by the authorities — 'the first real interchange of courtesies between England and Russia since the termination of the great war' — in turn prompted a sarcastic reaction in the British press. One blunt Lancastrian wanted to send 'thirty sail of our first-class steamers' to assist Constantine in his inspection: 'Probably he is only looking out for a harbour of refuge, in case he should have to run away; be that as it may, surely we can afford to send a fleet on a voyage of dissembled pleasure as well as the Emperor of Russia.'[19] When the Italian conflict began, diplomats were even more suspicious. To the British ambassador at Constantinople, it seemed hardly coincidental that the Grand Duke should reach the Ottoman Empire, via Paris and Turin, 'just at the time when he must have been certain that war was likely to break out'. And Sir Henry Bulwer felt bound to notice that Constantine was attended by other admirals, 'which, looking at it as simply a pilgrimage, was not precisely necessary'.[20]

Among those reminded of Russian naval adventures in the Mediterranean between 1770 and 1829, a frisson of alarm was understandable. Even so, their jibes were misplaced. Though Constantine clearly revelled in his confidential tête-à-têtes at the courts of Europe, the Tsar had no intention of establishing a *secret du roi*. Russian diplomacy was conducted through official channels and the Grand

National Archives, London (hereafter TNA), FO 65/535, 65/536.
[17] A. J. P. Taylor, *The Struggle for Mastery in Europe 1848–1918*, Oxford, 1954, p. 105.
[18] *1857–1861*, p. 92, Konstantin Nikolaevich to Alexander II, 24 February/8 March 1859.
[19] *Evening Mail*, 7–9 March 1859, p. 4; *Wigan Observer*, 4 March 1859.
[20] TNA, FO 78/1431, Bulwer to Malmesbury, no. 302, 3 May 1859.

Duke learned about the Franco-Russian treaty only after the event. In any case, he regarded the war in Italy primarily as a smokescreen for his own priority: the Russian cause in Palestine. Here, too, he was nervous lest Gorchakov take him for a meddler.[21] His schemes must not be allowed to aggravate matters in the Holy City, where the first Russian consul, appointed in 1858, was already at loggerheads with the first bishop at the head of the Russian Ecclesiastical Mission. Gorchakov courted Arab Orthodox Christians, in whom Constantine expressed little interest. However, while they might differ over tactics, their strategy was entirely compatible. In 1857 Gorchakov had portrayed Jerusalem to the Tsar as 'the centre of the world' and promoted a new, post-Crimean policy designed to establish Russia's 'presence' there, 'not politically but through the church': 'While our influence was strong we could afford to conceal our activities and thus avoid envy, but now that our influence in the East has weakened we, on the contrary, must try to display ourselves so that we do not sink in the estimation of the Orthodox population who still believe in us as of old.'[22]

As a prominent feature of Russian display, Constantine's pilgrimage naturally fascinated rival powers. So what follows draws on the despatches of the British consul, James Finn, who less than a month before the Grand Duke's arrival had paid host to Prince Alfred at the peak of his own bitter dispute with the Anglican bishop of Jerusalem.

Prince Alfred in Jerusalem 23–28 March 1859
Whereas the Russian press printed but a single article on Constantine's pilgrimage, written by a member of his own suite,[23] the British monarchy faced more searching scrutiny. By no means confined to the radical papers, which predictably dismissed Affie's 'sham apprenticeship' as a 'lying farce', criticism intensified in the face of the special treatment he received on tour.[24] The Queen was particularly offended by reports from Malta, where the whole squadron manned the yards every time her son left his ship. After even 'the impudent *Times* thought fit to disapprove his being properly loyally received', the floodgates were open.[25] One newspaper complained that there

[21] K. A. Vakh, 'Kak nachinalas' Russkaia Palestina: Ierusalim v pis'makh B. P. Mansurova i V. I. Dorgobuzhinova. 1858–1860 gg.', in *Pravoslavnyi Palestinskii sbornik*, Moscow, 2017, pp. 175–78, Mansurov to Gorchakov, 15/27 January 1859.

[22] Hopwood, *Russian Presence*, p. 51.

[23] [A. V. Golovnin], 'Ierusalim: Pis'mo s eskadry Sredizemnogo moria', *Sankt Peterburgskie vedomosti*, 1859, no. 180.

[24] *Reynolds's Newspaper*, 14 November 1858, p. 7.

[25] TNA, ADM 53/6897, HMS *Euryalus*, ship's log, 20 December 1858; *The Times*, 30

had been no 'more absurd and foolish specimen' in the 'whole history of flunkeyism'. Another wondered why the circus entrepreneur P. T. Barnum had not been placed in charge: 'If the Prince is to go about for a show, to be gazed at and cheered, saluted and adulated, surely the thing would be best done by a professional manager of such clap-trap exhibitions.'[26] Since the potential for embarrassment lingered when Affie contributed his 'mite' to the officers' ball in honour of the Maltese people — 'I think it was 3s 6d', reported a mordant correspondent for the *Evening Standard* — the Prince was henceforth ordered to travel incognito.[27] Even then, it proved impossible to prevent a succession of Ottoman potentates from lavishing praise and gifts on their royal guest. The bey of Tunis proclaimed him as 'the adopted son of Africa'.[28] The viceroy of Egypt treated the crew of the *Euryalus* to gargantuan quantities of bread and fruit, a breach of regulations which the Foreign Office asked the Admiralty to tolerate 'because the Turks could not be made to understand a refusal in any other light than as an affront'.[29]

No such anxieties emanated from Jerusalem, where the British were relieved to see Affie accorded due courtesy by a governor unsympathetic to European influence. While Süreyya Pasha sent fine horses to Jaffa for the Prince, a different challenge faced the British consul and his wife, who surrendered the bedrooms of their children and nanny to Affie and his governor, Major John Cowell. Friends later told the foreign secretary that Finn had been 'compelled to borrow money, at 28 per cent interest, to purchase linen, glass (his own family drinking out of tin mugs) & other needful things: & now he is living in hourly dread of proceedings for this debt'.[30] In fact, the consul was already in financial straits, thanks partly to his wife's ill-fated schemes to stimulate Jewish agricultural labour, and Mrs Finn's subsequent recollections betray little sense of self-sacrifice. On the contrary, they bristle with the excitement she experienced while racing to fill her small rented home with opulent soft furnishings. In the event, the expense

December 1858; Fulford (ed.), *Dearest Child*, p. 155, 1 January 1859.

[26] *Bell's Weekly Messenger*, 1 January 1859, p. 4; *Examiner*, 1 January 1859, p. 3.

[27] *Evening Standard*, 11 February 1859, p. 5.

[28] TNA, FO 335/114/2, 'Memorandum on the reception of HRH Prince Alfred by the Bey'.

[29] Captain Tarleton calculated the average daily value of Said Pasha's 'presents' at just under £55, a figure inflated by the press to £200: see TNA, FO 78/1478, Admiralty to Hammond, 2 March 1859; 'List of Articles received daily on board HMS Euryalus, with the average cost'; Hammond to Admiralty, 5 March 1859, draft; *John Bull*, 28 March 1859, p. 204.

[30] *The Collected Letters of Harriet Martineau*, ed. Deborah Anna Logan, 5 vols, London, 2007, 4, pp. 239–40, to Lord John Russell, 22 September 1860.

was unnecessary. Affie turned out to be 'very friendly' and responded with 'unaffected simplicity' to her motherly attentions. When she helped him to fit his sunglasses, it seemed 'strange enough to feel his silky hair under my hand'.[31]

Determined to exploit the Prince's visit in the rivalry between European powers in Jerusalem, Finn was keen to scotch any attempt by the French to capitalize on Affie's tour of the Holy Sepulchre. Although the Franciscan Father Vicar had encouraged him to try on the sword and spurs of the crusader, Godfrey de Bouillon, Finn insisted that the Prince had 'in no sense' been invested as a Knight of the Sepulchre: 'there were no preparatory ceremonies observed, such as fasting, watch &c.; the Latin oath was not administered; His Royal Highness is not a member of the Roman Catholic Church; and his name is not recorded in the register of the Knights.'[32] At the mosque of Omar, Affie could be accurately acclaimed as the first Christian to gain access since the end of the Crimean War, even if the template had been set in 1855 by the Duke of Brabant (later Leopold II of Belgium).[33] However, the prospect of an unprecedented inspection of the mosque at Hebron turned out to be a mirage when armed Arab tribesmen blocked the entrance in defiance of the Ottoman authorities. 'The offer of admission to a place of such solemn veneration was extremely alluring', Finn confessed, 'and I cannot but think that the opportunity of that privilege, thus lost to us through the Pasha's weakness, is now reserved for other illustrious visitors who may follow Prince Alfred in Palestine'.[34]

Any disappointment on this score was compensated by an excursion to the valley of Artas, where Mrs Finn employed Jewish labourers in collaboration with the London-born convert, John Meshullam. Many European visitors to Palestine shared her conviction that the land was fertile enough if only it could be rescued from lazy and incompetent Orientals.[35] However, as a pre-millenarian committed to a literal belief in Old Testament prophecy, Mrs Finn took a distinctive view of the question, striving not only to instil Jewish paupers with a Christian work ethic, but also to defray her mounting debts by selling allotments to Evangelical friends keen to own a patch of the Land of Promise. 'All the way to Bethlehem', she later recalled, 'there was chat with Major Cowell and the Captain (both of whom knew their Bible very well) on

---

[31] Elizabeth Finn, *Reminiscences*, London, 1929, pp. 187–207 (pp. 191, 195).
[32] TNA, FO 195/604, fols 317–17v, Finn to Malmesbury, no. 8, 20 April 1859.
[33] See James Finn, *Stirring Times*, 2 vols, London, 1878, 2, chapter 25.
[34] TNA, FO 195/604, fols 324v–25, Finn to Malmesbury, no. 9, 20 April 1859. Constantine did not visit this mosque.
[35] See, for example, *Pis'ma B. F. Mansurova*, p. 145, to his father, 17/29 March 1857.

the prospects of this land and the Jews'.[36] Though the Artas experiment was notoriously troubled — Meshullam had joined forces with the Finns only after quarrelling with an American investor, Clorinda Minor, and was soon to denounce the consul and his wife as swindlers[37] — all was sweetness and light during the Prince's visit. The union jack fluttered over Meshullam's farmstead; Affie regaled the company with stories of the Queen's fondness for pig-sticking at Osborne; and Captain Tarleton speculated playfully on how many warships would fit into the Pools of Solomon.[38] Indeed, the picnic went so well that Major Cowell bought a hillside terrace on the Prince's behalf.[39] Before he left Jerusalem, each of the Finns' children presented him with a grain of Palestinian wheat, skewered on the point of a needle, with a Hebrew inscription of Deuteronomy 8:8: 'a land of wheat and barley, of vines and fig trees and pomegranates, a land of olive trees and honey'.[40]

To the chagrin of the Foreign Office, the Finns' schemes brought them into conflict with an equally obstinate set of personalities working for the London Society for Promoting Christianity amongst the Jews under the aegis of the Anglican bishop of Jerusalem. Since this rivalry had long since spilled over into the British press, Prince Alfred's visit offered fresh opportunities for an unseemly exchange of insults. The consul's main mouthpiece was the *Daily News*, to which Mrs Finn's father had sent a stream of polemical letters in 1858.[41] One focus of the dispute was the Society's hostility towards the convert, Simeon Rosenthal. So the Finns were delighted to trumpet the fact that Affie's entourage had lodged at Mrs Rosenthal's hotel, an establishment 'almost unvisited during the past year, a circumstance which cannot be attributed to accident'.[42] Worse soon followed after Finn used Affie's incognito as an excuse to prevent Bishop Gobat from bringing his missionaries to pay their respects at the consulate. Gobat took his

---

[36] Finn, *Reminiscences*, p. 196.

[37] [Clorinda S. Minor], *Meshullam! or, Tidings from Jerusalem*, 2nd edn, Philadelphia, 1851; Barbara Kreiger, *Divine Expectations: An American Woman in 19th-Century Palestine*, Athens, OH, 1999, chs 1 and 2.

[38] *Daily News*, 19 April 1859, p. 5; Finn, *Reminiscences*, pp. 198, 203.

[39] For a hand-drawn map by Mrs Finn, see Ruth Kark, 'Land Purchase and Mapping in a Mid-nineteenth-century Palestinian Village', *Palestine Exploration Quarterly*, 129, 1997, p. 157.

[40] Finn, *Reminiscences*, p. 208: there was one gift each for Affie, the Queen, Prince Albert and the Prince of Wales.

[41] These were later collected for equally polemical purposes by Mrs Finn's brother, Samuel McCaul (ed.), *Jerusalem: Its Bishop, its Missionaries, and its Converts: A Series of Letters addressed to the Editor of the 'Daily News' in the Year 1858, by the Late Rev. Alexander McCaul, D.D.*, London, 1866.

[42] *Daily News*, 19 April 1859, p. 5.

revenge by praying to preserve the Prince from 'contamination', a barely concealed reference to the Finns, who were snidely associated by the Bishop's supporters with Tractarian opposition to his campaign to proselytize Arab Orthodox Christians. When this slur was repeated in the Calvinist *Record*, the Finn camp responded by condemning 'the excessive vulgarity' displayed by 'the worst-mannered bishop in or out of Jerusalem':

> Could not Bishop Gobat let the young Prince alone, even whilst at his devotions? Could he not allow him for one short minute to forget the accompaniments of rank and station, during the few hallowed moments that were allowed him to worship in Jerusalem, perhaps for the only time in his life? But we have said enough. Bishop Gobat will be Bishop Gobat still. [...] We trust however that no future authorities in Church or State will venture upon so dangerous an experiment, as catching a foreign and semi-Oriental backwoodsman and making him a bishop![43]

In Jerusalem itself, such backbiting was temporarily eclipsed by celebrations which brought the city's European residents welcome relief from their customary claustrophobia. Noting the 'atmosphere of youthful life, at once fresh and delightful', a visiting Swedish Evangelical appreciated the accompanying spiritual uplift: 'During the swelling of this springtide, thought has flowed with greater inwardness — has sought to advance to the primal sources of mind: blessed be its power to raise and to calm the too weak heart!'[44] Though markedly less exalted, Affie's feelings were just as positive. 'The most interesting of all the expedition', he confided to his Coburg aunt Alexandrine on reaching Rhodes, 'was that to Jerusalem and all through Palestine which Journey was entirely performed on horseback and sleeping in tents being sometimes 16 hours in the saddle'.[45]

Grand Duke Constantine in Athens 26 April–6 May 1859
On the day Affie wrote this letter, Constantine reached Athens, his final destination before the Holy Land. Until the last moment, he had planned to be in Greece for Easter. However, less than an hour before

---

[43] *Bell's Weekly Messenger*, 23 April 1859, p. 4. Gobat was a French-speaking Swiss with strong Prussian leanings.

[44] Fredrika Bremer, *Travels in the Holy Land*, trans. Mary Howitt, 2 vols, London, 1862, 2, p. 223.

[45] John van der Kiste, *Alfred: Queen Victoria's Second Son*, London, 2013, p. 27, 26 April 1859.

he was due to sail from Naples, he received a telegram from Gorchakov insisting on delay. It would not do to embarrass King Otto, a Bavarian Catholic, with a display of Orthodox piety. Delay created hazards of its own. When the Russian squadron finally anchored off Piraeus, the public reception was subdued. 'The Greeks are not on these occasions very demonstrative', reported the British minister at Athens, Sir Thomas Wyse, 'unless particular pains be taken with them beforehand, and what disposition they might have had to mark their sentiments towards Russia and its dynasty was considerably damped by the disappointment experienced in not having seen the Grand Duke earlier.'[46]

No-one had been more anxiously anticipating his arrival than Archimandrite Antonin (Kapustin), sardonic chaplain of the Russian embassy church in Athens since 1850.[47] Training his telescope on the island of Aegina in search of the first puff of Russian smoke, Antonin settled down to rehearse his welcome speech 'like a schoolboy'.[48] When they eventually met, following reconnaissance by 'a certain Mansurov', the chaplain admired Constantine's cultured intelligence. He sighed deeply when speaking of the 'twilight' descending on Russia; chided his son for running about ('Kolia, surely you know that *we* are not allowed in front of the altar'); and talked frankly about the relative states of the Greek and Russian Churches (though both were governed by *faux-conciliar* synods, neither Constantine nor Antonin yearned to restore the Russian Patriarchate). Such stimulating exchanges helped Antonin to swallow with good grace the ritual amendments imposed upon him. He was surprised to be told to kiss the royal couple's hands when they kissed his after prayers. He also had to alter his choir, since the Grand Duke, one of many Russians to whom the nasal Greek chant sounded as offensive as it did to most British Protestants, had brought his own precentor to train a performance approximating to St Petersburg's court cappella ('with military drums', Antonin was tempted to add until discretion proved the better part of valour).

An avid reader of the newspapers, Antonin had long been keeping a characteristically irreverent eye on the peregrinations of 'the great (?) admiral Romanov' and his royal British rival. By January 1859, rumours of Affie's planned visit to Athens had drowned out those about

[46] TNA, FO 32/268, fols 177v–78, Wyse to Malmesbury, no. 53, 28 April 1859. Wyse himself was an Irish Roman Catholic.

[47] See L. A. Gerd, 'Atticheskie nochi arkhimandrita Antonina Kapustina', in Arkhimandrit Antonin (Kapustin), *Dnevnik god 1850*, eds L. A. Gerd and K. A. Vakh, Moscow, 2013, pp. 135–72.

[48] This paragraph draws on Arkhimandrit Antonin (Kapustin), *Dnevnik gody 1856–1860*, eds L. A. Gerd and K. A. Vakh, Moscow, 2017, pp. 371–80, 14/26 April – 24 April/6 May 1859.

Constantine.[49] Affie, however, came only in December, when he made a better impression on the Greeks than had the Grand Duke.[50] Meanwhile, Antonin was left with memories of 'the great Philhellene' W. E. Gladstone, then a controversial high commissioner of the Ionian Islands, who attended his church in December 1858. According to Antonin, Gladstone 'did not *pray*', but he declared the liturgy 'very solemn, & the music most beautiful & devout'.[51] Less sympathetic British commentators had long regarded the petite Byzantine church as a symbol of tsarist designs on Constantinople. Critical of the largesse distributed to labourers employed on its restoration, the Palmerstonian *Morning Post* thought the danger more insidious still: 'The Russian system is to make even its humblest supporter feel that *his* exertions and devotion *are not overlooked* by the Emperor; and *this* is Russian influence in the East.'[52]

If that was so, then it was a mistake for Constantine to neglect the far from humble egos of the 'Russian party' at Athens. Looking back, his closest adviser blamed the Grand Duke's 'highly superficial and one-sided' grasp of Greek politics on the suffocating influence of King Otto's 'small German court'. Anxious to isolate the growing opposition to his regime, the King persuaded Constantine not to grant private audiences to leading politicians.[53] Instead, his free time was spent clambering over the Acropolis with a young photographer in his entourage. Gabriel de Rumine, a Parisian *émigré* keen to foster Franco-Russian co-operation, portrayed the Parthenon as a backdrop to the modern city, helping to set a trend blurring distinctions between East and West and highlighting continuities between the classical and contemporary worlds.[54] Meanwhile, palace ceremonial did little to compensate for the Grand Duke's lack of confidential contacts. Haughty by nature, he was rarely impressive in public, and the result was a series of mutual

[49] Ibid., p. 346, 20 January/1 February 1859.

[50] Robert Holland and Diana Markides, *The British and the Hellenes: Struggles for Mastery in the Eastern Mediterranean 1850–1960*, Oxford, 2006, pp. 54–55, inadvertently describes Constantine as the brother of Nicholas I.

[51] Antonin (Kapustin), *Dnevnik gody 1856–60*, p. 333, 7/19 December 1858, original emphasis; *The Gladstone Diaries*, ed. H. C. G. Matthew, 14 vols, Oxford, 1968–94, 5, p. 349, 19 December 1858.

[52] *Morning Post*, 10 December 1855, p. 6, original emphasis. On the restoration, see I. L. Zhalnina-Vasil'kioti and M. V. Shkarovskii, *Russkaia sviato-troitskaia tserkov' v Afinakh: Proshloe i nastoiashchee*, Moscow, 2017.

[53] A. V. Golovnin, *Velikii Kniaz' Konstantin Nikolaevich*, ed. B. D. Gal'perina, St Petersburg, 2006, pp. 173–74.

[54] Peter J. Holliday, 'Early Photography and the Reception of Classical Antiquity: The Case of the Temple of Athena Nike', in Judith M. Barringer and Jeffrey M. Hurwit (eds), *Periklean Athens and its Legacy: Problems and Perspectives*, Austin, TX, 2005, p. 246.

disappointments: Constantine received a less effusive welcome than
he had expected; Russia's leading Greek supporters felt snubbed. 'No
hopes of a Byzantine empire held out', Wyse assured London, 'nor aid
or encouragement to a fresh aggression on the frontier of Turkey. In a
word, his conduct is a perfect enigma to the regular Russian party here,
whose idea of a Russian Grand Duke destined to lead them to St Sophia
was in every respect a perfect contrast.'[55]

For Constantine, however, Athens was merely a prelude to the Holy
Land. Writing from Palermo during the first week of the Great Fast, a
time of intense spiritual reflection 'when we take our confession', he
had implored the Tsar to grant his 'heartfelt wish' to worship at the
Holy Sepulchre. Three previous requests — in 1845, 1846 and 1852 —
had been refused. 'But then our policy was directed by Nesselrode, who
feared anything to do with the East like the plague.' Now times had
changed, and his appearance in the Holy City should provoke no more
rumours than that of any other royal prince, especially since 'Europe's
attention [was] currently directed much more towards Italy than to
the East.' To bypass Palestine would signal 'a coldness and neglect of
Orthodox affairs on the part of Russia'. There was no risk of 'turmoil'
because Jerusalem would be 'almost empty' after Easter. Instead, the
first Russian royal visit to the Holy City would mark 'the beginning of
a new era', just as his voyage to Mount Athos had done in 1845, granting
the Orthodox Church 'new strength and new authority'.[56]

Fortunately for Constantine, this plea caught the Tsar at a favourable
moment. The Great Powers had accepted his proposal for a congress on
Italy; the emancipation legislation seemed to be proceeding smoothly;
above all, a long conversation with Mansurov had convinced him of the
possibility of a favourable outcome for Russian interests in Jerusalem.[57]
At Naples, Constantine received his brother's consent to the pilgrimage,
and Mansurov awaited him in Athens, ready to accompany him to the
Holy Land.

Grand Duke Constantine in Jerusalem 12–21 May 1859
So barren was Judea that many European travellers, reared on
Romantic images of Palestine, were shocked by their first glimpse of
Jerusalem. Constantine, by contrast, seems to have experienced only
an overwhelming sense of emotion. Tears recurred throughout his
pilgrimage. They flowed liberally at the tomb of the Virgin, and again

[55] TNA, FO 32/268, fols 208v–09, Wyse to Malmesbury, no. 59, 12 May 1859,
confidential.
[56] *1857–1861*, p. 97, Konstantin Nikolaevich to Alexander II, 25 February/9 March 1859.
[57] Ibid., p. 99, Alexander II to Konstantin Nikolaevich, 17/29 March 1859.

at the farewell liturgy when it proved 'impossible to tear oneself away'. Only during services conducted by the Greek Patriarch of Jerusalem, at the Holy Sepulchre and the Cathedral of the Resurrection, did the 'appalling singing' prevent the Grand Duke from praying. The contrast with the Russian communion service at Golgotha was marked. There, in the absence of an iconostasis, the clergy were open to view. To hear the words 'Drink from this, this is my *blood*' at the very site of the Saviour's sacrifice produced 'such a dreadful and deep impression' that Constantine's emotions froze. He did not weep, he later told the Tsar, because the tears simply melted away: 'I shall not forget that service for the whole of my life!'[58]

If Bishop Kirill (Naumov) deserved praise as a celebrant, his conduct as head of the Russian Ecclesiastical Mission was more questionable. Since the Tsar had instructed his brother to try to moderate the 'excessive fervency' of Kirill's critical reports on the Greeks, Constantine's relations with the Mission cannot have been straightforward. The most he could promise in the short term was that Kirill would not openly oppose the consul.[59] Nevertheless, at his best in the company of Russians whom he trusted, the Grand Duke established the same sort of rapport with the ascetic Ieromonakh Leonid (Kavelin) as he had in Athens with Archimandrite Antonin. Impressed by the calibre of the royal entourage, Leonid had every reason to curry favour since his imminent return to Russia was already confirmed.[60] 'So, we are old acquaintances!' Constantine exclaimed on learning that Leonid had served as an officer in the guards. Later, the Grand Duke gave him a signed portrait and enjoyed a joke about schismatic self-immolation when discussing the Greek monks' smoking habits. Coffee was permissible, Leonid suggested, but not pipes, as the Old Believers had proved by burning down their monasteries.[61]

Like Prince Alfred, Constantine followed a typical traveller's itinerary, visiting not only the dilapidated shrines of Jerusalem, but also Bethlehem and Hebron.[62] All passed without controversy until

[58] Ibid., p. 111, Konstantin Nikolaevich to Alexander II, 13/25 May 1859, original emphasis; see also, diary, ibid., pp. 164–67, entries for 30 April/12 May – 9/21 May 1859.

[59] Ibid., p. 100, Alexander II to Konstantin Nikolaevich, 31 March/12 April 1859; p. 112, Konstantin Nikolaevich to Alexander II, 13/25 May 1859.

[60] See G. V. Bedzhanidze (ed.), *Perepiska Konstantina Zedergol'ma so startsem Makariem Optinskim (1857–1859)*, Moscow, 2013, p. 199, Zedergol'm to Makarii, 16/28 March 1859. Leonid was released from Jerusalem on grounds of health on 20 May/1 June.

[61] A. A. Kashcheev, 'Zapiski o prebyvanii velikogo kniazia Konstantina Nikolaevicha na Sviatoi Zemle: Materialy iz arkhiva arkhimandrita Leonida (Kavelina)', *Observatoriia kul'tury*, 1, 2016, 1, pp. 112–21 (pp. 117–18).

[62] The fullest chronicle, Constantin Tischendorf, *Aus dem heiligen Lande*, Leipzig,

violence, never far beneath the surface of life in the Holy City, erupted
at the mosque of Omar. At the Grand Duke's behest, the Pasha granted
open admission, allowing what Finn described as 'a multitude of the
lowest and most ignorant Russian and Wallachian pilgrims' to join
respectable residents and travellers, while 'the lowest class of Jerusalem
Christians also took their opportunity of screaming, laughing and
running about'. Chaos ensued:

> One of the great gates of the most sacred building was broken off its
> hinges by a rush of the tumultuous crowd — the Moslems, chiefly
> youths, threw stones, and uttered curses freely. An English clergyman
> was assailed by a fanatic youth, and bit with his teeth in the shoulder
> — the soldiers were enraged and attacked every body indiscriminately
> — the Honorable Mr Roden Noel was thrown violently to the ground
> by one of them. Inside the Mosque of Aska, the Moslems ascended
> the pulpit of the Kad, and cursed and spat on the crowd below them.
> At the same time the Greek clergy uttered enthusiastic cries in praise
> of their deliverer Constantine [...] Altogether the scene was one of
> irrecoverable confusion, which many contrasted with the reverential
> behaviour of the English and others preceding on such occasions.[63]

Having thought twice about this lurid despatch, Finn added a rider
stressing that the Russian party had 'behaved with the greatest decorum'.
But he did not exaggerate much since the Grand Duchess wrote that one
of her husband's adjutants had been injured in the scrum.[64]

Unlike Prince Alfred, whose time in Jerusalem was confined to
tourism, the Grand Duke took the opportunity for some serious
business. While staying with his wife's cousin, Prince Moritz of Saxe-
Altenburg, an earlier traveller in the East, he had met the biblical scholar
Constantin Tischendorf, whose manuscript studies were sponsored by
the Russian government and who now joined the royal entourage in
the Holy Land. In September 1859, the *Codex Sinaiticus* went to St
Petersburg in a controversial coup for the tsarist regime.[65] Discussions

---

1862, pp. 156–287, stresses the Grand Duke's familiarity with the burgeoning scholarly
literature, some of it studied on the voyage from Athens.

[63] TNA, FO 195/604, fols 347–47v, Finn to Malmesbury, no. 13, 23 May 1859. Scion
of a prominent Evangelical family, the poet Roden Noel (1834–94) travelled in the East
after taking his Cambridge MA in 1858.

[64] Ibid., fol. 343, Finn to Malmesbury, no. 15, 25 May 1859; Velikaia kniaginia
Aleksandra Iosifovna, *Pis'ma s Vostoka k moim rodnym*, ed. K. A. Vakh, Moscow,
2009, p. 38, 12/25 [*sic*] May.

[65] *1857–1861*, pp. 143, 166, diary, 31 October/11 November 1858, 4/16 May 1859; Stanley
E. Porter, *Constantine Tischendorf: The Life and Work of a 19th Century Bible Hunter*,

with the French consul marked an early stage in the protracted process that led to the restoration of the dome of the Holy Sepulchre between 1867 and 1869.[66] Echoes of the Italian war were faint, though Finn reported that 'the most remarkable feature' of the banquet for the European consuls 'was the silence with which the Austrian Consul was treated'. The Grand Duke paid most attention to Prussia's Dr Rosen — not, as Finn supposed, 'on account of the family alliance between Russia and Prussia', but because Constantine found Rosen 'very interesting'.[67]

The most important feature of the pilgrimage was the boost it gave to Russia's profile in Palestine. 'Jerusalem', Finn reported, 'seemed to have become a Russian city'. The Patriarchate and the Russian consulate overflowed with the imperial suite; officers crowded the hotels; sailors and white-uniformed marines filled the streets and monasteries. No less 'astonishing' was 'the influx of money' they brought with them — 'the hucksters, shopkeepers, and money change[r]s picked up as many Russian words for use as possible'. 'In sum', the consul warned, 'the Russians are far more influential, and really powerful in Jerusalem, than they were at any period preceding the late war'.[68] The *Daily News* drove the point home in a version of Finn's despatch presumably filed by his publicity-conscious wife. Since Constantine was preoccupied less with the past than 'with the business of present actual life, and in sowing seeds for the future', the 'religious associations of the Jordan and Dead Sea' mattered less to him than 'an inspection of the ground purchased for buildings outside the city'.[69] And indeed the Grand Duke was delighted with the 'very well chosen' plot recently acquired through the agency of Finn's dragoman, Moosa Tanoos, in a sale which fuelled rampant inflation in the price of property near the former parade-ground.[70] Over the following five years, stylish new churches, decorated

London, 2014, pp. 40–44.

[66] N. N. Lisovoi et al., 'Proekt dvukh imperatorov: Rossiia i Frantsiia v Sviatoi Zemle', *Rossiiskaia istoriia*, 2013, no. 6, p. 74; O. V. Anisimov, 'Nikolai Pavlovich Ignat'ev, arkhimandrit Antonin (Kapustin) i franko-russkoe soglashenie o restavratsii kupola Sviatogo Groba', in *Perepiska Antonina (Kapustina) s grafom N. P. Ignat'evym 1865–1893*, eds K. A. Vakh and O. V. Anisimov, Moscow, 2014, pp. 23–37.

[67] TNA, FO 195/604, fol. 348v. Finn to Malmesbury, no. 13, 23 May 1859; *1857–1861*, p. 167, diary, 8/20 May 1859. Gobat also attended, but Constantine was amused that the Roman Catholic Patriarch Valerga declined his invitation on the grounds that it was a fast day.

[68] TNA, FO 195/604, fols 349v–51v, Finn to Malmesbury, no. 13, 23 May 1859.

[69] *Daily News*, 14 June 1859, p. 6.

[70] *1857–1861*, p. 164, diary, 2/14 May 1859. See also, Vakh, 'Kak nachinalas' Russkaia Palestina', pp. 178–85, Dorgobuzhinov to Mansurov, 22 January/3 February 1859. The deed of sale, dated 2 February 1859 N.S., is in N. N. Lisovoi (ed.), *Rossiia v Sviatoi Zemle: Dokumenty i materialy*, 2 vols, Moscow, 2015, 1, pp. 221–23.

with furniture personally approved by Alexander II and transported by sea via England and Malta, sprang up alongside the castellated consulate and pilgrim barracks that gave the mushrooming Russian 'compound' its distinctive and dominant appearance.[71]

Any doubts that Russia was the coming European power in the Holy Land were dispelled by the reactions to Constantine's visit. Shortly before his arrival, the Russian consul reported that the Greek monks were 'putting on a display in earnest'.[72] This was no exaggeration. Mrs Finn never forgot 'the little coffee cup holders of gold filagree [sic] set with diamonds', shown off to the European consuls in the palatial new accommodation built adjoining the Patriarchate.[73] On his journey home, the Grand Duke reported that Patriarch Kirill, who had returned from Constantinople expressly for the occasion, had 'done his utmost to oblige'.[74] Such efforts were wholly self-interested. At Bethlehem, the Patriarch waylaid Constantine to urge his support over the Dedicated Monasteries in Wallachia and Moldavia, whose revenues, vital to the income of the Brotherhood of the Holy Sepulchre, were threatened with sequestration by Prince Cuza.[75] The Brotherhood's finances were also squeezed by Russia's growing influence in Jerusalem. According to Finn, the only Greek cleric not 'silently champing the hard curb already felt' in 1858 was Metropolitan Meletios, who, 'still cherishing his disappointment at not having been elected Patriarch', had joined forces with the Russians. Just as he had guided Mansurov in 1857, Meletios was Constantine's chaperone from the moment he landed at Jaffa.[76] A still more significant index of Russia's rising stock was the behaviour of the Arab chieftain, Abu Ghosh, whose armed supporters had until recently terrorized the Judean countryside. Now, his power emasculated by an encroaching Ottoman bureaucracy, he courted Russia by offering the Grand Duke a banquet for 300 guests (the invitation was flourished, but declined).[77] Most importantly of all, Constantine's travels through Palestine prompted precisely the sort of popular reaction to the Russian

[71] Iana Zelenina and Zhanna Belik, *Pervye russkie khramy v Ierusalime: Troitskii sobor i tserkov' v muchenitsy Aleksandry*, Moscow, 2011.

[72] Vakh, 'Kak nachinalas' Russkaia Palestina', p. 219, Dorgobuzhinov to Golovnin, 3/15 April 1859.

[73] Finn, *Reminiscences*, p. 207.

[74] *1857–1861*, p. 112, Konstantin Nikolaevich to Alexander II, 13/25 May 1859.

[75] K. A. Vakh (ed.), *Velikii kniaz' Konstantin Nikolaevich na Sviatoi Zemle v 1859 godu*, Moscow, 2009, pp. 50–54.

[76] TNA, FO 195/604, fols 21–21v, Finn to Clarendon, no. 3, 13 March 1858.

[77] *1857–1861*, p. 164, diary, 29 April/10 May and 30 April/11 May 1859; Kashcheev, 'Zapiski o prebyvanii velikogo kniazia Konstantina Nikolaevicha na Sviatoi Zemle', p. 114.

clergy that he wanted to see: 'as the bishop passed through the kneeling crowd, the pilgrims pressed the hem of his robe to their lips, and looked up to him as if they regarded him as an angel from heaven.'[78]

*   *   *

Returning to Russia via Constantinople, the Grand Duke was pleased to see 'our old acquaintance the patriarch of Jerusalem', who had followed him to Smyrna too The Patriarch of Antioch also sought a bite of the financial cherry, along with the Ecumenical Patriarch, Kirillos VII (1855–60), to whom Constantine took an instant dislike. By then, he and his wife had spent two months in the East and were ready for home. The weather was thundery, the Sultan's conversation vacuous. However, since Sultan Abdulmejid I (ruled 1839–61) was 'reliably said to have spent more than *two million* silver roubles' on their reception, to stay for less than a week 'would be to answer incredible hospitality with rudeness'. While the Grand Duchess visited the harem, her husband saw more of the foreign minister, Fuad Pasha and his colleagues, sceptical of the Sultan's generosity. Britain's ambassador, Constantine told the Tsar, was also 'badly out of sorts'.[79]

That was putting it mildly. Incandescent at the lavish reception planned for the Russians, Bulwer had remained unimpressed by reassurances that equivalent courtesies would in future be extended to British royalty. 'Thank the Grand Vizier for me', ran the lofty instruction to his dragoman, 'and you may point out to His Highness at the same time that the Sultan did not pay the compliment to HRH the Duke of Cambridge of going down to Tophana to receive him, which he is now about to pay to the Grand Duke Constantine':

> These things are remarked, they increase the pretensions of the Greek population, they dispel the spirit of the Sultan's Turkish subjects, and they are not uncalculated to disgust or displease His Imperial Majesty's allies without in the least gaining the sincere good will of the power they mean to conciliate.[80]

In fact, the Tsar was delighted with the reception planned for his brother, taking it as a sign of improved relations with the Porte that

---

[78] Mary Eliza Rogers, *Domestic Life in Palestine*, London, 1862, p. 399.

[79] *1857–1861*, pp. 113–14, Konstantin Nikolaevich to Alexander II, 19 May/10 June [*sic*], original emphasis; pp. 169–70, diary, 22 May/3 June, 30 May/11 June 1859.

[80] TNA, FO 78/1432, Bulwer to Etienne Pisani, 31 May 1859.

would help to prevent 'a new war with England'.[81] As further insurance, he allowed Constantine to inspect British naval dockyards in August 1859 on a private visit that proved unexpectedly successful. Even the Queen and Prince Albert were 'extremely nice, talkative and polite, very different from the welcome I received in 1857'.[82]

In one sense, Bulwer's irritation reflected no more than an ambassador's natural obsession with ceremonial precedence. At a deeper level, the episode symbolized the growing frustration Britain experienced in its attempts to preserve the Ottoman Empire. Lacking the swagger of his predecessor, Lord Stratford de Redcliffe, Bulwer found the Sultan quixotic and his government resistant to European pretensions. As Europe focused increasingly on Italy and Germany, Jerusalem, briefly the centre of international attention between 1847 and 1853, again became a diplomatic backwater. As before, Russia protected the Orthodox Christians and France the Roman Catholics. But the two powers' hesitant post-Crimean *rapprochement* placed Britain at an increased disadvantage. Ignoring an arch French invitation to solicit subscriptions from English, Irish and Maltese Catholics, the British government disdained the Franco-Russian project to restore the dome of the Holy Sepulchre.[83] Meanwhile, Britain's self-appointed role as protector of the Jews had been hampered by the controversial activities of James and Elizabeth Finn. The visit of the Prince of Wales, who followed Affie to Jerusalem in 1862, allowed the consul's enemies to hasten his removal. While Britain's prestige was diminished by his ignominious departure, Russia's, by contrast, blossomed in spite of internal divisions. After a stormy interval under Leonid (Kavelin), the Russian Ecclesiastical Mission passed in 1865 into the gentler hands of Antonin (Kapustin), more sympathetic to the Greeks and still resident in Jerusalem in 1882 when another 'new era' dawned under the umbrella of the Imperial Orthodox Palestine Society that was to realize many of the ambitions expressed by Grand Duke Constantine in 1859.

---

[81] *1857–1861*, p. 112, Alexander II to Konstantin Nikolaevich, 17/29 May 1859.
[82] Ibid., p. 117, Konstantin Nikolaevich to Alexander II, 3/15 August 1859.
[83] TNA, FO 78/1521, fol. 33, Finn to Russell, no. 5, 23 February 1860.

Scottish Missionaries in Manchuria and the Arrival of the Russian Railway, 1894–1900

Paul Dukes
University of Aberdeen

IN 1864, the Russian foreign minister Prince Aleksandr Gorchakov wrote to tsarist representatives abroad: 'The United States in America, France in Algeria, Holland in her Colonies, England in India — all have been irresistibly forced, less by ambition than imperious necessity, into this onward march, where the greatest difficulty is to know when to stop.'[1] In particular, the British and Russian onward marches clashed in Central Asia in the 'Great Game', and threatened to spread to the Far East. There was no shortage of Russians pressing for 'forward policies' in the Far East in addition to those in Central Asia. An outstanding example was Nikolai M. Przheval'skii, best known in the West for his identification of a species of wild horse on the Mongolian steppe, but also stating in 1888 that he was 'convinced of the rotten state of China', and finding that: 'The Chinese people are a nation long past its prime.' For Chekhov: 'People like Przheval'skii I loved without end.' The great writer compared him to the 'discoverer' David Livingstone, declaring: 'One Przhevalskii or one Stanley is worth ten institutes or a hundred good books.'[2]

The race for empire had speeded up with the arrival of the 'iron horse' or steam locomotive. Count E. F. Kankrin, Nicholas I's minister of finance, had told the Scottish geologist Sir Roderick Murchison in 1840:

> Railroads can never answer here for the next century, because there are no great commercial or manufacturing *entrepôts*, and especially because they would, in charging the country with enormous cost, throw out of employment thousands of peasants, whose sole subsistence in winter is derived from transporting commodities from Moscow and the south to the north.[3]

---

[1] *Correspondence Respecting Central Asia*, C. 704, Parliamentary Papers, London, 1873, p. 73.

[2] David Schimmelpenninck van de Oye, *Towards the Rising Sun: Russian Ideologies of Empire and the Path to War with Japan*, DeKalb, IL, 2001, pp. 35–36, 39–40.

[3] Michael Collie and John Diemer (eds), *Murchison's Wanderings in Russia: His Geological Exploration of Russia in Europe and the Ural Mountains, 1840 and 1841*, British Geological Survey Occasional Publication no. 2, London, 2004, pp. 154–55.

However, a railway across the continent soon became a gleam in the eye for several tsarist bureaucrats until in 1892, in a full report submitted to Tsar Alexander III, Sergei Witte, minister of finance, emphasized that the great project of the Trans-Siberian Railway 'ranks it as one of those *world events* that usher in *new epochs in the history of nations* and not infrequently bring about the radical upheaval of established economic relations between states.' He hoped that it might prove to be a rival in world communication comparable to the Suez Canal, while constituting a weapon that would enable the Russian navy to exert 'control over the entire movement of international commerce in Pacific waters'. Witte feared that: 'European policy might attempt to arouse against us the aggressive tendencies of China for seizure of the poorly-defended eastern section of the Siberian railway and all adjoining territory, the maritime strip and Vladivostok not excepted.' However, under the influence of the Buriat-Slavophile P. A. Badmaev, Witte declared that '*from the shores of the Pacific and the heights of the Himalayas Russia would dominate not only the affairs of Asia but those of Europe as well.*'[4]

As far as the jewel in the crown of the British empire on the other side of the Himalayas, India, was concerned, Karl Marx had already written mid-century of sea as well as land: 'The day is not far distant when, by a combination of railways and steam vessels, the distance between England, measured by time, will be shortened to eight days, and when that once fabulous country [India] will thus be actually annexed to the Western world.'[5] Major-General Sir Charles MacGregor was among those writing on the implications of this development in a work entitled *The Defence of India* and published in 1884.[6] In 1885, a young army officer Francis Younghusband who had read a number of books on Manchuria, Mongolia and North China and compiled itineraries from them succeeded in convincing his superiors, including Sir Charles Macgregor, that 'if the Indian Empire were to be saved, I must at once be sent on duty to Manchuria' under the leadership of a member of the Indian Civil Service, Sir Henry Evan Murchison James.[7]

---

[4] B. A. Romanov, *Russia in Manchuria, 1892–1906*, trans. Susan Wilbur Jones, Ann Arbor, MI, 1952, pp. 41–42, 46–47. The italics are by Witte. The work was originally published in Leningrad in 1928.

[5] From dispatches published in the *New York Daily Tribune*, no. 856, 8 August 1853 (written London, 22 July 1853).

[6] In particular in Major-General Sir C. M. MacGregor, *The Defence of India: A Strategical Study*, Simla, 1884, a work full of military statistics, marked 'Confidential' on the title page.

[7] George Seaver, *Francis Younghusband: Explorer and Mystic*, London, 1952, p. 8.

Younghusband wrote later of Manchuria's many interests as 'the cradle of the present ruling dynasty of China' and 'its lovely scenery'. Moreover, Younghusband observed, 'as its proximity to Russian territory on the one hand and Japan on the other gave it military and political interests also, we felt that time spent in such a country would not be wasted.'[8] After a few months of military exercises in India, Younghusband and his companions set off for Manchuria in March 1886. In Newchang (Yingkow), the main treaty port, the party was lucky enough to recruit Henry Fulford of the Chinese consular service as interpreter and adviser.

Moving out into the country after a brief stay in Mukden (formerly also known as Fengtian, now Shenyang), the crowded capital, the expedition was able to scrutinize 'John Chinaman' at leisure. Younghusband considered that the Chinese immigrants, who had largely replaced the original Manchus, 'were, in fact, doing here exactly what our colonists have been doing for so many years in Canada'.[9] Crossing the river Yalu (also called river Amrok), although short of supplies and bothered by midges, the British travellers went on to climb 'The Long White Mountain' (see below), where the intrepid Younghusband braved treacherous rocks and bitter cold to make scientific, especially topographical, observations.

After several weeks of further arduous travel, the expedition reached the central Manchurian town of Kirin (Jilin), where Younghusband did what he could to find out about the local production of field guns and rifles. He and his companions were given warm hospitality by the local Chinese, who were extremely polite and good in conversation, if disparaging about Europeans: 'they [the Chinese] are lamentably ignorant of geography, for instance, and they generally annoy the stranger by asking if his country is tributary to China.' But Younghusband also realized that from 'such a lofty standpoint' as he occupied, the Chinaman was 'not all simple self-conceit' since 'he had in him the pride of belonging to an empire which has stood intact for thousands of years, and which was approaching civilization when we ourselves were steeped in barbarism.'[10] Later, en route for the frontier, he observed that villages were of considerable size and that small hamlets or separate farmhouses were rare 'probably on account of the

[8]   Captain Frank E. Younghusband, C.I.E., Indian Staff Corps, Gold Medallist, Royal Geographical Society, The Heart of a Continent: A Narrative of Travels in Manchuria, Across the Gobi Desert, through the Himalayas, the Pamirs, and Chitral, 1884–1894, 4th edn, London, 1904, pp. 3–5.
[9]   Ibid., p. 10.
[10]   Ibid., pp. 19, 20.

brigandage, which was very rife all over North Manchuria'.[11] He and his companions dropped by a French Roman Catholic mission where they received 'that warm, heartfelt greeting which one European will give to another, of whatever nationality'.[12] Younghusband was able to inspect a fort at Sansung on the river Sungari, a major tributary of the Amur, equipped with Krupp guns transported there with enormous difficulty but allowed to go to rust and ruin.

The British party crossed the frontier with Russia without difficulty via the town of Hunchun and soon encountered a band of Cossacks, 'hard, strong-looking men, fair in complexion, with cheery good-natured faces'. Although in barracks inferior to the Chinese if rough and clean, the Cossacks were careless in dress, simply fed and poorly paid, but apparently 'ready to buckle to and fight there and then'.[13] After lavish local entertainment, Younghusband and his colleagues proceeded to the Russian port of Novokievsk, south of Vladivostok. As well as dispensing more generous hospitality, the commandant said that his government was anxious to colonize eastern Siberia with Russians. Younghusband imagined that, 'with a railway to aid in its development, all those regions about the Amur and its tributaries ought to equal the most thriving parts of Canada'.[14] At the same time, a remark about a development on the sea: a British fleet had recently appeared in the nearby bay and aroused the apprehension that it was about to seize the port since Port Hamilton consisting of a group of small islands about ten miles to the south of Korea had just been occupied. In his own account of the expedition, James recorded the comments of the commandant, Colonel Sokolovskii: 'Ma foi, said he, what is it that you'd get if you did take the place? A few old mud and log barracks, some ponies and harness, and these barren hills. I wish you joy of them.'[15]

The long, difficult winter journey back to Peking (Beijing) was relieved in Mukden at the Scottish mission. Younghusband wrote:

Messrs. Ross and Webster and Dr. Christie came running out of the house as they saw us driving up in the cart, and it was only as we were shown into a cosy drawing-room, where the ladies were having tea, that we realised how rough we had grown on the journey. We had each of us developed a beard, which, as well as our hair, now, in the light of

---

[11] Ibid., p. 22.
[12] Ibid., p. 24.
[13] Ibid., p. 33.
[14] Ibid., p. 38.
[15] H. E. M. James, of Her Majesty's Bombay Civil Service, *The Long White Mountain or A Journey in Manchuria: With Some Account of the History, People, Administration, and Religion of that Country*, London, 1888, p. 356.

civilization, seemed very unkempt. Our faces were burning red from the exposure, and our clothes — especially our boots — were worn out and torn with the rough wear they had undergone. We had many trials on our journey, but this facing a ladies' tea-party in a drawing-room in our disreputable condition was the hardest of them all.[16]

Then, while Mr Webster provided clean white shirts and socks, Mrs Webster produced 'every kind of clothing', made up a cosy room for each of the travellers, and brought out 'the most astonishing variety of Scottish cakes and scones and muffins'.[17]

Younghusband was given to understand that the Scottish mission differed from its fellows, not neglecting the lower orders but concentrating on the Chinese officials and gentry. With this aim in mind, highly-trained men were sent out and adopted a higher style of living and dress that would meet with easier acceptance from their intended converts. They were encouraged to take their wives and helpmates, and to include doctors. Younghusband and his companions saw something of the work of Dr Dugald Christie, saving souls as he cured bodies and striving to understand the outlook of both educated Chinese and their 'ignorant inferiors'. We shall meet Dr Christie as well as Messrs Ross and Webster again later.

At Newchang, James left for Port Arthur, where, he considered, Englishmen would soon be followed by Americans and Russians. James commented with some evident irony: 'It is, indeed, impossible not to admire the imperturbable calmness with which the Chinese, looking — and I do not want to blame them — absolutely and entirely to their own interests, play off against one another the disinterested European nations who only want to benefit the poor dear Chinese.' Giving up Port Hamilton to the Chinese, James considered, could help to make them friendly to the British.[18] Indeed, Britain soon gave up Port Hamilton, partly owing to international pressure.

Crossing the Great Wall, the Younghusband and Fulford encountered two English navvies walking along the road, one enquiring of the other about them 'I wonder who he — that is, Bill?' They themselves were miners in a colliery owned by Chinese but managed by an Englishman, a Mr Kinder. At first afraid of a steam engine imported from Hong Kong by a 'foreign devil', the Chinese were now accepting the beginning of a railway from Peking to Tientsin (Tianjin), with an extension to the east and another projected into Manchuria.[19]

[16] Younghusband, *The Heart of a Continent*, p. 44.
[17] Ibid., p. 44.
[18] James, *The Long White Mountain*, p. 407.
[19] Younghusband, *The Heart of a Continent*, pp. 50–51.

More hospitality ensued in Tientsin, where the British consul introduced Younghusband to a Russian counterpart and Russian merchants, and in Peking at the British Legation, where he met Europeans of every nationality, remarking that 'it is only in the last thirty of the three thousand years during which the Chinese Empire has existed that such a thing has been possible'.[20] James, who had played such an important part in the expedition, having left for Japan, Younghusband now met up with Colonel M. S. Bell, VC, of the Royal Engineers, whom he had previously encountered in the Intelligence Department in India. He managed to arrange to travel back with Bell to India overland, setting off in spring 1887, about a year after arriving in Manchuria.

At this point, we are to take our leave of Younghusband, but not before summarizing some of his conclusions about his travels. While recognizing that all religions 'shared the feeling that there was some Great Spirit or Influence guiding and ruling all things', he also believed that there was 'something in the Christian religion vastly superior to others'. And, while he indicated that Christianity had been a huge influence on European civilization in general, he also believed in the special qualities of the English people.[21] More particularly, in his official report on the Manchurian expedition compiled in Peking with the help of the British envoy, Sir John Walsham, Younghusband came to the conclusion that there was no sign of an immediate Russian threat to Manchuria.[22]

The situation was about to change radically with the coming of the railway. The distinguished American historian G. A. Lensen wrote that by the end of the nineteenth century:

> [...] the flood of allegations ascribing aggressive designs to the tsarist government continued unabated, even though it was privately conceded that Russia was too weak in the Far East to expand by force. The reason was the lack of trust in what the Russians said, another was the usefulness of the Russian 'menace'. Repeatedly the Russian bear was used as a bugbear by the various powers to intimidate and contain their rivals or to justify their own moves in the international balance of intrigue.[23]

---

[20] Ibid., p. 54.

[21] Ibid., pp. 304–10. In the usage of the time, 'English' probably included 'Scottish'.

[22] Patrick French, *Younghusband: The Last Great Imperial Adventurer*, London, 1955, p. 42.

[23] G. A. Lensen, *Balance of Intrigue: International Rivalry in Korea and Manchuria*, Tallahassee, FL, 1982, pp. 853–54.

John Ross and the Manchus

John Ross had been born in 1842 at Rarichie, Easter Ross, and spoke Gaelic as a boy. But he learned English as well, excelled at school and moved to Edinburgh where he graduated at Theological Hall before going out as a missionary to Manchuria. As part of his calling, he translated the New Testament into Korean, among other publications, but here we will concentrate on just two of them.

First, in 1891, John Ross brought out a book with the title *The Manchus: The Reigning Dynasty of China: Their Rule and Progress.* In the preface, he declared: 'We have long inferred that China must from her nature, assume an attitude of suspicion and defiance towards Russia; and she has long succumbed under the humiliation of taxes levied on opium at the dictation, and under the compulsion, of the British Government.'[24] But China was stirring from inertness, and in her own manner.

In a 'Preliminary Dissertation on the Political Principles of China' which followed, Ross observed: 'It is to the commanding influence of thought that China owes her continuous history. It is because mental power is, and always has been more highly esteemed than physical force.' Therefore, he declared: 'China will not, therefore, merely append Western forms of civilization, but is sure to gradually assimilate them to her own constitution.' China was modernizing her army, but 'Chinese opposition to the laying of railways [...] is like that to Christian missions, wholly and only political.' Thus, he continued, 'Until the Chinese government is convinced that western nations have no serious designs upon her freedom, we do not expect to see railways and their mechanical and steam-powered largely employed.' Ross suggested: 'We ourselves are subjected to by designing or timid men to a periodical Russian scare, and surely the Chinese have much more reason to believe in the ability and the desire of western powers to injure her than we in that of Russia to maim us.'[25]

It should not be forgotten, Ross averred, that 'the Chinese were a cultured people more than twenty centuries before Scott opened our eyes to the grand moods and the gentle soothing voice of nature, and before the lake poets sang its praises to an all but sullen audience.' Moreover, they had developed printing, gunpowder (if only for fireworks) and the compass or 'needle-fix-the-south', as well as spectacles and playing cards. They had taken embroidery with silk and the carving of ivory to a high level. Their agriculture was advanced, as well as their codification of

[24] John Ross, *The Manchus or The Reigning Dynasty of China: Their Rise and Progress*, London, 1891, p. 8.
[25] Ibid., pp. xii, xv, xvi.

laws. Their government was *'absolute only for the wellbeing of the people'*, Ross emphasized, adding later that *'absolute government, founded on and governed by democratical principles'* made 'the Chinese people one of the most democratic in the world' even if the government was based on divine right'.[26]

Therefore, Ross considered, 'We do not believe that Russia will now be ever able to conquer China, and we are certain that the Chinese people would suffer in most things and benefit in nothing by transference to the Russian rule.' The Chinese peasants, in his view, were happier and more cultured than their Russian counterparts. Nevertheless, Chinese dynasties became corrupt and rebels based their action on justice: 'better the storm of revolution than quietude under the blighting cancer'. The Chinese were more Whig than conservative in other words.[27]

Ross concluded his 'Preliminary Dissertation on the Political Principles of China' with the assertion: 'Whether we will or no, China is rapidly becoming a great and powerful nation; but the reception of Christianity alone can make the Chinese a moral people, who will benefit the whole world.'[28]

The Rev. Ross next begins the introduction to his monumental work with the observation:

As soon might we expect the water oozing from a mossy rock to become a mighty river, bearing on its bosom the peaceful fleets of all nations as the few ignorant descendants of the Tartar Aisin Gioro to become, by their own despicably insignificant resources, the legislators of a fourth of mankind, and the rulers of a fourth of mankind, and the rulers of the most populous empire under the sun.

If it was necessary that the movements of the Manchus should have been regulated by wise bravery, it was even more essential that reckless folly should misguide their no less brave opponents [...][29]

(Ross rejected the comparison of the Manchu conquest of China with the British conquest of India because British troops in India were conscious of their own superiority, in weaponry in particular, and their opponents equally conscious of their own inferiority.)

The Manchus were also inspired by their sacred bird, the magpie, as Ross pointed out in the following account. One fine day, two centuries

[26] Ibid., pp. xvii, xix, xxiii.
[27] Ibid., pp. xxiv–xxvii.
[28] Ibid, p. xxxii.
[29] Ibid., p. 1

before, three heaven-descended maidens were bathing in a lake below
the White Mountains when a magpie dropped a red fruit on the skirt
of the youngest who ate it before dressing and, as a consequence, bore
a son who could speak from birth and was remarkable in a number
of other ways. When he was full-grown, his mother told him that he
was born of heaven, to set to rights the troubled nations', and having
given him the name Aisin Gioro or 'Gold Dynasty', she ascended into
heaven.[30] The remarkable nature of the young man was recognized
by three local contending peoples, who elected him their joint ruler,
whereupon he gave them the name 'Manchu' which means 'pure'.

Myth was accompanied by history from the middle of the sixteenth
century when an obscure chieftain named Nurhaci extended his power
over most of what was to become known as Manchuria, then turned
his attention from 1618 to the conquest of China. Nurhaci died in 1626,
but is usually credited with the founding of the Qing or 'Pure' (as
in Manchu so in Chinese according to Ross) dynasty even if his son
actually established it in 1644.

After a survey of several versions of the consequences of eating
the red fruit recorded from 1635 to 1739, the historian Lin Sun has
commented:

> Through analysis of the Manchu origin myth, the history of the
> Manchus can be traced as they moved from being conquerors to rulers
> of a vast empire. The myth that had originally served to underpin the
> unity of the ruling elite and to legitimate a dominant clan in order to
> prevent future divisions from the 1640s, disseminated among the wider
> group of Manchu, Mongol, and Han bannermen [Chinese clansmen],
> all of whom were invited to claim a Manchu identity based on the
> original myth.[31]

As he moved to begin the conquest of China, Nurhaci did not leave his
native land completely behind him. Both he and his successors made
formal visits for reasons varying from the mystical to the practical,
and maintained much of Manchuria (although they did not call it that)
as a frontier region of their empire beyond the Great Wall. For several
centuries, this included the Wild East, bandit country, a refuge for
runaways, known in the West as Tartary.

---

[30] Ibid., p. 4.
[31] Lin Sun, 'Writing an Empire: An Analysis of the Manchu Origin Myth and the
Dynamics of Manchu Identity', *Journal of Chinese History*, 1, 2017, 1, p. 25. There were
versions of the myth in Japanese and Korean as well.

The myth of the birth of 'Manchuria' was not unlike that of many other societies throughout the world, providing for them, too, a source of inspiration. Some would say that all humankind originated in the story of another young woman eating fruit, that we are all the children of Eve. But the Rev. Ross was almost certainly not among those who considered the Garden of Eden to be mythical. In any case, the sequel to the gift of the magpie, the story of the Manchus need not detain us here, since the book of Ross is a detailed narrative running to some seven hundred pages describing the manner in which their dynasty extended its hold throughout China. Suffice it to say that a major role is played by a series of individual leaders triumphing with what Ross called 'wise bravery' over the 'reckless folly' of their opponents.

John Ross and 'Manchuria'

To turn to a second publication, in an article published in 1895, John Ross began by pointing out: 'The name Manchuria is a purely geographical term, and is unknown to both Chinese and Manchus.' But, he continues: 'There was a kingdom of Manchu established three centuries ago [...], which gradually extended its sway over its smaller neighbours [...] [and] also included what is now known as the Russian Maritime Province to the north of Korea.'[32]

In his article, Ross described the geography of what was known to the Chinese as the 'Three Eastern Provinces' (from south to north Fungtien, also known as Mukden, Kirin and Heilungkiang) just before they were transformed by the arrival of the railway. From the port of Newchang by the adjoining Liaotung (Liadong) Peninsula, Ross observed, a magnificent, virtually unbroken plain stretched north-east to the river Amur with just an occasional hill. Higher ground could be found towards Mongolia to the west and adjacent to Korea to the east, where the Changbai Shan or Ever White Mountain, which appeared to be continually covered in snow because of the colour of its stone, rose to about 8,000 feet. This height had been calculated by two recent travellers, Messrs James and Younghusband. The double range south of the town of Liaoyang called the Chienshan (Qianshan) or the Thousand Peaks contained many Buddhist and even more Taoist monasteries.

The Ever White Mountain was a watershed for the river Ussuri which flowed directly north to form the boundary between Manchuria and the Russian Maritime Province and for the river Sungari which was a tributary of the mighty river Amur, which formed another boundary

---

[32] The Rev. John Ross, 'Manchuria', *The Scottish Geographical Magazine*, 11, 1895, 5, p. 217.

between Manchuria and China. The Russians had excluded the Chinese from the Amur, but for some years a small Russian steamer had plied the Sungari as far as Kirin, the middle of the three provinces. The river Yalu separated Manchuria from Korea, while the river Liao flowed through the great plain of Manchuria to enter the sea about twenty miles from Newchang.[33]

April could be said to be the only spring month, for May quickly became summer. 'So rapid is the growth under the bright sunshine and the penetrating power of the daily increasing heat', Ross remarked, 'that wheat sown in the beginning of April is cut down in the end of June or the beginning of July.' Up to the end of July, rain was rare and light, so clouds were regarded with special favour 'not only as containing the promise of needed rain, but as a feature of beauty in the usually cloudless sky'.[34] Towards the beginning of August, when the heat was greatest, the heaviest rains came. Floods could cause great havoc, with farmers sinking to their knees as they tried in vain to save some of their crops.

September was the normal harvest month, and then, a finer month than October in Manchuria would be difficult to find anywhere. But frost crept in at night towards the end of October, and then applied its iron grip from November until March. Thus, after one month of spring, there were four and a half months of summer, one and a half of autumn and five of winter. At least ten months of the year were very dry.

The main crop was sorghum, a variety of millet. It resembled barley, and, boiled whole to be eaten often with beans or other vegetables, was far more nutritious than rice. Sorghum could be used for making spirit, as was almost all the barley grown. Wheat was widely cultivated. There were many kinds of beans, one of which (this was soy, although Ross does not name it) was valuable as the main item of export. Tobacco and opium were largely exported, as was indigo. Vegetables, in particular a large cabbage and a bitter turnip, were consumed locally, often soaked in brine, for the Chinese never used salt in its pure state. Root crops were plentiful, but never fed to cattle. Fruit was grown according to prevailing conditions, while mushrooms could be found in the mountains. There was plentiful game, too — deer, wild boar, goats and hare — while fish from the rivers and the sea were also readily available. The Scotsman Ross was no doubt surprised to learn that the Chinese did not appreciate the flavour of salmon.

[33] Ibid., pp. 218–22.
[34] Ibid., pp. 222–23.

There was gold in the Manchurian hills running from the river Sungari to the sea. However, with the exception of a famous mine in Kirin, 'where the miners have for generations made a little kingdom of their own and defied the Government', the present dynasty had forbidden the extraction of the precious metal, and for two reasons. One was superstitious, 'based on the belief that it is unlucky to interfere with the configuration of the earth'. The other was to do with law and order since, when the supply of gold ran short, unsuccessful miners 'went with their matchlocks to the nearest highway and helped themselves to the goods of travellers'. Silver and copper abounded in many localities, but were bound by the same laws as gold. Manchuria was 'particularly rich in good coal and excellent iron', but the working of them was barely tolerated: 'In many places coal crops out above the ground, but the people dare not touch it.'[35] Nevertheless, Manchurian iron attained a price higher than European, and a German officer had declared that swords made in Mukden were as good as any. However, Ross noted, the smelting processes were so crude and primitive that it cost more to put this iron on the local market than to introduce the metal from Glasgow or Belgium.

The most noteworthy tradesmen were furriers and tanners. Mukden, the city at the centre of the most southerly of the three eastern provinces comprising 'Manchuria', Fengtian, was probably a world leader in quantities of furs cured, while tanners produced vast numbers of skins from horses, mules, donkeys, deer and sheep.

The size of the population was impossible to calculate in such a great territory. Of the three provinces, Fengtian had accommodated over the previous twenty years hundreds of thousands of diligent farmers and produced new cities. Kirin was already possessed by the ploughman, but Tsitsikar (Qiqihar) or Heilungkiang to the north was still waiting for husbandmen to exploit its huge resources. Overall, Ross calculated that the population could not be less than 25 million, and could be as much as that of England.[36]

Although the country was named after the Manchus, many of them had emigrated as soldiers to China when the new dynasty was established, while there had been a great influx of Chinese, who formed

---

[35] Ibid., p. 224.

[36] Ian Nish, *The History of Manchuria, 1840–1948: A Sino-Russo-Japanese Triangle*, vol. 1, *Historical Narrative*, Folkestone, 2016, p. 4, writes that the population is estimated as 15 million in 1900, 18 million in 1911 and 30 million, of which 28 million were Chinese, in 1931. The further north, the sparser the population. According to the census of 1901, the population of England and Wales was 32,527,843, of Scotland 4,472,103. It is possible that by 'England' Ross meant Britain.

at least three quarters of the population. Only in Mukden were the Manchus still able to assert their cultural personality, although their language held out in some remote valleys against the Peking dialect of Chinese. Ross declared: 'Competent judges have pronounced the inhabitants of Manchuria to be possessed of an amount of comfort greater than that of any other Asiatic people', with light taxation and abundant if coarse food, fuel and clothing.[37]

In his article, the Rev. Ross moved on from his description of Manchuria at the end of the nineteenth century to note: 'In the voluminous history of China the affairs of other nations are noted only when these nations come into friendly relations or hostile conflict with the Celestial Empire.' He proceeded to give a survey of successive dynasties before concluding: 'The lessons of the numerous changes in Manchuria throughout the past two thousand years are an emphatic protest against much of the sentimental teaching of the present day.' For Ross, 'the amelioration of the savage is due to the individual, not to the race.' Thus, 'the most valuable product of this earth is [...] the man who can dare and who can do, the man who can be the leader of men into a life nobler than they have hitherto led.'[38] No doubt the Scottish missionary would have agreed with his fellow-countryman Thomas Carlyle that the history of the world was but the biography of great men. He probably had in mind empire builders among others although he gave no examples. And he probably had more than an inkling that the greatest change in the history of Manchuria was about to occur with the coming of the railway. But Harbin, soon to be a considerable city as a railway junction, does not appear on the map that he attached to his article because it as well as the railway were yet to be founded, and Manchuria as a whole was evidently awaiting modernization.

Dugald Christie and the Boxers

Published in 1895, Ross's article on 'Manchuria' must have been written some time before since, although he showed considerable knowledge of the region, his only reference to Russian incursion was of a steamboat on the river Sungari rather than of a construction of the railway. Later disturbances and changes were evocatively described by Dugald Christie, a colleague of his born like him in Gaelic-speaking Scotland, in Glencoe in 1855. The ninth to arrive in a large family, Christie had been driven by poverty to move to Glasgow where his faith was excited by attendance at a Moody and Sankey revival meeting. He completed

---

[37] Ross, 'Manchuria', p. 227.
[38] Ibid., pp. 230–31.

his medical education in Edinburgh before moving to Manchuria as a medical missionary in 1882. He had been preceded, he noted, by John Ross, who had paid several visits from Newchang to Mukden and begun to create a small Christian congregation in the face of mud-slinging both metaphorical and actual. For Christie at first, the going was tough as Chinese suspicion was hard to overcome. For example, the rumour circulated that the eyes and hearts of children were cut out for use in photography as well as medicine. But by 1887 trust had increased sufficiently for a new dispensary to be opened in Mukden by a high-ranking Manchu official in the presence of the city's leading mandarins. Dr Ross was evidently paying the kind of attention to the upper ranks of Chinese society that Francis Younghusband had noted a few months previously.

In 1894, Japan won a conclusive victory over China and would have taken a great chunk of Manchuria if Russia had not persuaded other great powers to oppose this incursion. In apparent gratitude, China gave permission for Russia to run a railway across the north of Manchuria. According to Dugald Christie, 'Russian engineers surveyed and made maps and went away again, and it was reported that they were making a railway over the desert mountains in the far north.'[39]

However, when Port Arthur and Dalny (Dal'nii, Dalian) were leased to Russia for an extension of the railway, while the Germans and British infiltrated the Shantung (Shandong) peninsula to take Kiachow (Kiautschou) and Wei-hai-wei (Weihai) respectively, Chinese resentment was aroused, some more mild hoping for modernizing reform, some harbouring hatred for foreigners and all their works. To begin with, proposals among others for the construction of more railways and the establishment of a Western-style university, for new law courts and even a parliament, appeared to be winning the day until towards the end of September 1898, when the old Dowager Empress took over and the young Emperor was immured. Six young reformers were summarily executed while others fled the country. On 23 October, Chinese soldiers attacked British railway engineers on the line under construction between Peking and Tientsin. On 5 November, the day after a missionary was murdered in a south-western province, an edict stated that, 'The whole country can then be turned into a great armed camp, to fight for their homes', at which point volunteer military organizations were formed in towns and villages.[40] Early in June 1899, the railway service on the Peking to Tientsin line was discontinued and

---

[39] Dugald Christie, C. M. G., *Thirty Years in Moukden, 1883–1913*, London, 1914, p. 124.
[40] Ibid., p. 127.

missionaries sought safety in the legations in Peking after two of them were murdered.

In Manchuria, there was little anti-foreign feeling to begin with. Missionaries had been looked upon as good rather than bad, Christie observed. As for the railway:

> Superstitious prejudices had prevented its coming closer to Moukden than about ten miles, lest the Imperial Tombs be disturbed and the prosperity of the dynasty destroyed. The Russian railway and the presence of Russians were sullenly accepted as facts which could be neither denied nor altered. The only thing to be done was to make best use of them possible, and take one's journeys by train.[41]

Then, after a terrible explosion in the barracks to the west of Mukden at the end of May 1899, there was much more talk of the Boxers and on 10 June the cry went up that they had come and were looking for recruits. Peace and quiet were not immediately shattered, but Dugald Christie considered that there were two reasons why they could not be maintained: the occult nature of the Boxer movement; and the support given to it by the Dowager Empress. He detected mesmerism:

> Strange movements, passes, and contortions were practised until the devotee fell down in a fit or trance, sometimes uttering unknown words and uncouth sounds, said to be the language of the spirits which now entered into him. When he rose he was a true Boxer, and invulnerable. Superstition worked also on the susceptible nervous temperature of the Chinese, and many fell down because they believed they would, and because their neighbours did.[42]

The Boxer movement spread along with suspicion of all things foreign. For example, buttons of German manufacture were believed to be bewitched because they could burn whereas true buttons were made of metal or bone. Posters with vile charges such as the import of opium or the murder of children were put up throughout the town. As the news from Peking worsened, too, the decision was taken to evacuate, although Christie stayed on to participate in a final service where the last hymn was 'Soldiers of the Lord, arise!' adapted from 'Scots wha hae'.

What followed had to be reconstructed from the accounts of Chinese Christians who remained in the city. Scottish Protestant and French Roman Catholic missions alike were sacked. An articulated skeleton

[41] Ibid., p. 130.
[42] Ibid., pp. 134–35.

that Christie had bought in Edinburgh was paraded around the streets as if it were human remains while a button presented to him along with the Order of the Double Dragon was said to be all that remained of a murdered official. The Russian railwaymen were completely taken by surprise and many were killed, although to the north, missionaries had been helped to escape by the Russians. Throughout July and into August, hundreds, even thousands of Chinese Christians were put to death either by the Boxers or in fear of them. Then, however, the Boxers were defeated by armies both foreign and Chinese, and order was restored by the middle of August.

In the immediate aftermath, Christie observed, while allied forces were restoring order in Peking, 'it fell naturally to the Russians to re-conquer their railway area and drive back all opposing forces in Manchuria'.[43] Before this aim was accomplished, however, soldiers who had supported the Boxers and were incensed by defeat at the hands of the Russians, sacked Mukden. Then, after a band of about three hundred Cossacks had re-taken the city, on 1 October the main contingent of Russians arrived. They were accompanied by Dr A. Macdonald Westwater, a Red Cross surgeon, who knew both the people and the country well while having some acquaintance with Russians, and could therefore act as intermediary. A few days later, the Russian armies from the north met their counterparts from the south, creating a line of tsarist rule from Siberia to the Pacific Ocean. Christie returned to Mukden to find his hospital in ruins. One of his few surviving personal possessions, recovered by a Russian soldier, was *The Intellectual Life* by Philip Hamerton, published in 1873 and presented by the author himself to an aunt of Christie's in the Scottish Highlands.

In January 1901, while attempting to return to Mukden before going home on furlough, Christie found himself on the wrong train of a still to be fully-restored railway service. Ejected with his baggage into a blinding snowstorm, he knew there must be Russians around somewhere, and was greatly relieved when a man with a lantern appeared, exclaiming in an excited tone 'Newcastle! Angliské! Newcastle!'[44] — a bizarre reminder of some contact between Russia and the industrial English north-east. Later, Christie managed to make his way to Mukden, and found the city more peaceful than before, although the 'former general friendliness to Christianity had quite passed away', and Christians were obliged to do much of their own reconstruction. Throughout Manchuria, 'except along the railway line, there was still anarchy, brigands, blackmailing

[43] Ibid., p. 151.
[44] Ibid., p. 159.

and pillaging on all hands', and missionary work in the country had to be suspended 'partly because it was really unsafe, partly because the Russians considered it so, and refused to allow foreigners to travel'.[45]

*   *   *

Of the three missionaries met in 1886 by Francis Younghusband, Messrs Ross and Webster and Dr Christie, James Webster must be dealt with in the present context least, since his major publication, *Times of Blessing in Manchuria*, has virtually nothing to say about secular matters, concentrating on 'The Manchurian Revival' of 1908, which is in any case several years beyond the purview of this essay, which terminates at the end of the nineteenth century.

In 1900, a *Guide to the Great Siberian Railway* proclaimed:

> The civilizing policy of Russia in the East, which may be regarded as an exception to that of other countries, was guided by other principles and was directed to the mutual welfare of nations by the maintenance of peace throughout the immense extent of her dominions. The honour of having planted the flag of Christianity and civilization in Asia is due to Russia. The near future will show the results of the activity of our Government and our civilizing enterprises, which will add to the glory and power of Russia and her Sovereign Chief.[46]

While British missionaries, however charitable, would almost certainly have disagreed with this statement, B. L. Putnam Weale, a British traveller in Manchuria early in the twentieth century, was much more vehement than they would have been, declaring:

> Until the British Government decides that England's only policy is to insist that her interests extend right up to the actual frontier-stones of the Russian Empire, and promptly retaliates, should a Cossack be moved past these frontier-stones, we will continue to present the ridiculous and unmanly figure we do to-day in the Far East.[47]

The 'Great Game' was still alive, indeed had become more intense with the arrival of the railway.

---

[45] Ibid., pp. 159, 161.
[46] *Guide to the Great Siberian Railway* quoted by Ian Nish, *Origins of the Russo-Japanese War*, London, 1985, p. 17.
[47] B. L. Putnam Weale, *Manchu and Muscovite*, London, 1907, p. 531.

John Ross and Dugald Christie bore witness not only to their faith but also to secular developments at the end of the nineteenth century, from the war between China and Japan to the Boxer Rebellion, in a more restrained manner then Putnam Weale. In the estimate of a leading authority, while drawing an accurate picture of Manchuria and its origins, Ross saw the region 'as playing a historically pivotal role in the geopolitics of Northeast Asia'.[48] However, although he shared some of Chekhov's enthusiasm for the empire builder, he was far from an enthusiastic British flag waver and went beyond Przheval'skii's claim that the 'Chinese people are a nation long past its prime' to the assertion that the dynasty, not the people, was past its prime.

Dugald Christie may not have admired the Russians, but he certainly accepted their presence in Manchuria and benefited from their railway. Writing just before the arrival of the First World War, he observed:

> There are few parts of the world where the modern change in ease of access has been more marked than in Manchuria. One can now leave London at nine o'clock on a Monday morning, and after a comfortable sleeping-car journey drive through the Moukden streets in the afternoon of Friday, eleven days later. The contrast with thirty years ago, and indeed with thirteen years ago, is greater than the contrast between that time and the days of the sailing ships.

John Ross and Dugald Christie began their lives speaking Gaelic. We can only speculate, but this experience must have given them a perspective on languages and cultures in the Far East. Ross translated the Bible into Korean and made the close acquaintance of the Manchu dynasty in China as well as the people of Manchuria. Christie made the effort to understand Chinese medicine as well as to understand Chinese society in both its upper and lower ranks.

Both of them provide helpful evocations of Manchuria in the last years of the nineteenth century before and immediately after the arrival of the Russian railway, catching in particular Chinese reactions to the arrival of the 'iron horse' as well as to foreigners in general. But they both decided to retire not in Manchuria, where they had spent the best part of their careers, nor to Gaelic-speaking Scotland, where they had been born, but to Edinburgh where they both died, Ross in 1915, Christie in 1936.

---

[48] James H. Grayson, 'The Legacy of John Ross', *International Bulletin of Missionary Research*, 23, 1999, p. 169.

Publications of Will Ryan

Books

Penguin Russian Dictionary (with Peter Norman), London and New York, 1995 (hardback); 1996 (paperback).

Jerusalem Pilgrimage 1099–1185, ed. John Wilkinson with Joyce Hill and W. F. Ryan, Hakluyt Society, series 2, 167, London, 1988.

The Bathhouse at Midnight: An Historical Survey of Magic and Divination in Russia, Stroud and University Park, PA, 1999.

Russian Magic at the British Library: Books, Manuscripts, Scholars, Travellers (The Panizzi Lectures 2005), British Library, London, 2006.

[V. Raian] *Bania v polnoch': Istoricheskii obzor magii i gadanii v Rossii*, Moscow, 2006.

Maimonides' On Coitus, ed. Gerrit Bos, with medieval Latin texts and translations by Charles Burnett and the Slavonic text and translation by Will Ryan and Moshe Taube, Leiden, 2018.

The Secret of Secrets: The East Slavic Version, with introduction, text, annotated translation, Slavic index, ed. W. F. Ryan and Moshe Taube. Warburg Institute Studies and Texts 7, London, 2019.

Books edited or jointly edited (other than as series editor)

Oxford Russian-English Dictionary, ed. M. Wheeler, general editors B. O. Unbegaun and W. F. Ryan, Oxford, 1972.

Pseudo-Aristotle, The Secret of Secrets. Sources and Influences, ed. W. F. Ryan and Charles B. Schmitt. Warburg Institute Surveys 9, London, 1982.

Pseudo-Aristotle in the Middle Ages: The Theology and Other Texts, ed. Jill Kraye, W. F. Ryan and C. B. Schmitt, Warburg Institute Surveys and Texts 11, London, 1986.

Union Catalogue of Cyrillic Manuscripts in British and Irish Collections, compiled by R. Cleminson, general editors Veronica Du Feu and W. F. Ryan, London, 1988.

Making Instruments Count: Essays on Historical Scientific Instruments presented to Gerard L'Estrange Turner, ed. R. G. W. Anderson, J. A. Bennett, W. F. Ryan, Aldershot, 1993.

Britain and Russia in the Age of Peter the Great: Historical Documents, London, 1998 (as joint editor and translator).

Magic and the Classical Tradition, ed. Charles Burnett and W. F. Ryan, Warburg Institute Colloquia 7, London, 2005.

The Power of Words: Studies on Charms and Charming in Europe, ed. James Kapaló, Éva Pócs and William Ryan, Budapest and New York, 2013.

Articles and chapters

'Rathborne's *Surveyor* (1616/1625): the first Russian Translation from English?', *Oxford Slavonic Papers*, 11, 1964, pp. 1–7.

'A Russian Version of the *Secreta Secretorum* in the Bodleian Library', *Oxford Slavonic Papers*, 12, 1965, pp. 40–48.

'Science in Medieval Russia', *History of Science*, 5, 1966, pp. 52–61.

'John Russell RA and Early Lunar Mapping', *Smithsonian Journal of History*, 1, 1966, pp. 27–48.

'Some Russian Contributions to the History of the Microscope', *Proceedings of the Royal Microscopical Society*, 2, 1967, 3, pp. 362–65.

'Some Observations on the History of the Astrolabe and of Two Russian Words: *astrolabija* and *matka*', in *Studies in Slavic Linguistics and Poetics in Honor of Boris O. Unbegaun*, New York and London, 1968, pp. 155–64.

'Aristotle in Old Russian Literature', *Modern Language Review*, 63, 1968, 3, pp. 650–68.

[V. Raien]'Drevnerusskii perevod zhizneopisaniia Aristotelia Diogena Laertskogo', *Slavia*, 37, Prague, 1968, 2, pp. 348–55.

[U. Raian], 'Ob odnoi rukopisi Kosmografii Publichnoi biblioteki v Leningrade', *Trudy Otdela drevnerusskoi literatury*, 24, Leningrad, 1969, pp. 392–93.

'The Onomantic Table in the Old Russian *Secretum secretorum*', *Slavonic and East European Review*, 50, 1971, 17, pp. 392–93.

'The Oriental Duodenary Animal Cycle in Old Russian Manuscripts', *Oxford Slavonic Papers*, new series, 4, 1971, pp. 12–20.

'John Tradescant's Russian Abacus', *Oxford Slavonic Papers*, new series, 5, 1972, pp. 83–88.

'Curious Star Names in Slavonic Literature', *Russian Linguistics*, 1, 1974, 2, pp. 137–50.

[V. Raien], 'Russkii rukopisnyi uchebnik korablevozhdeniia 1703 goda', in *Trudy XIII Mezhdunarodnogo kongressa po istorii nauki,* sektsiia 6, Moscow, 1974, pp. 233–36 (also published in *Istoriko-astronomicheskie issledovaniia*, 12, 1975, pp. 121–26).

'The Old Russian Version of the Pseudo-Aristotelian *Secretum secretorum*', *Slavonic and East European Review*, 56, 1978, 2, pp. 242–60.

'Peter the Great's English Yacht', *Newsletter of the Study Group on Eighteenth-Century Russia*, 7, 1979.

Chairman's afterword in *Great Britain and Russia in the Eighteenth Century: Contacts and Comparisons*, ed. A. G. Cross, Newtonville, MA, 1979, pp. 225–27.

'Science in 17th-century Muscovy: Texts and Terminology', *Newsletter of the Study Group on Eighteenth-Century Russia*, 8, 1980.

'The *Secretum secretorum* and the Muscovite Autocracy', in *Pseudo-Aristotle: The* Secret of Secrets*: Sources and Influences*, ed. W. F. Ryan and Charles B. Schmitt, Warburg Institute Surveys 9, London, 1982, pp. 114–23.

'Peter the Great's English Yacht: Admiral Lord Carmarthen and the Russian Tobacco Monopoly', *The Mariner's Mirror*, 69, 1983, 1, pp. 65–87.

'Bead Calculator', in *Tradescant's Rarities*, ed. A. MacGregor, Oxford, 1983, p. 253.

'Astronomy in Church Slavonic: Linguistic Aspects of Cultural Transmission', in *The Formation of the Slavonic Literary Languages*, UCLA Slavic Studies 11, Columbus, 1985, pp. 53–60.

'The Passion of St Demetrius and the *Secret of Secrets*. An Onomantic Interpolation', *Cyrillomethodianum*, 8–9, 1984–5 (1986), pp. 59–65.

'Solomon, SATOR, Acrostics and Leo the Wise in Russia', *Oxford Slavonic Papers*, new series, 19, 1986, pp. 46–61.

'Limelight on Eastern Europe: The Great Dissolving Views at the Royal Polytechnic', *The New Magic Lantern Journal*, 4 (The Ten Year Book), London, 1986, pp. 48–55.

'Aristotle and Pseudo-Aristotle in Kievan and Muscovite Russia', in *Pseudo-Aristotle in the Middle Ages: The* Theology *and Other Texts*, ed. Jill Kraye, W. F. Ryan and C. B. Schmitt, Warburg Institute Surveys and Texts 11, London, 1986, pp. 97–109.

'Maimonides in Muscovy: Medical Texts and Terminology', *Journal of the Warburg and Courtauld Institutes*, 51, 1989, pp. 43–65.

'Problèmes de traduction scientifique en vieux-russe: le *Secretum secretorum*', in *La Traduction au moyen âge*, Paris, 1989, pp. 85–95.

'Navigation and the Modernization of Petrine Russia: Teachers, Textbooks, Terminology', in *Russia in the Age of the Enlightenment: Essays for Isabel de Madariaga*, ed. Roger Bartlett, Janet M. Hartley, London, 1991, pp. 75–105.

'Alchemy, Magic, Poisons and the Virtues of Stones in the Old Russian *Secretum Secretorum*', *Ambix*, 1991, pp. 46–54.

'Scientific Instruments in pre-Petrine and Petrine Russia', *Annals of Science*, 1991, pp. 367–84.

'What was the *Volkhovnik*? New Light on a Banned Book', *Slavonic and East European Review*, 68, 4, 1991, 4, pp. 718–23.

'The Great Beast in Russia: Aleister Crowley's Theatrical Tour in 1913 and his Beastly Writings on Russia', in *Symbolism and After. Essays on Russian Poetry in Honour of Georgette Donchin*, ed. Arnold McMillin, Bristol, 1992, pp. 137–61.

(with Faith Wigzell), 'Gullible Girls and Dreadful Dreams: Zhukovskii, Pushkin and Popular Divination', *Slavonic and East European Review*, 70, 1992, 4, pp. 647–69.

'Alchemy and the Virtues of Stones in Muscovy', in *Alchemy and Chemistry in the 16th and 17th Centuries*, ed. P. Rattansi and A. Clericuzio, Dordrecht, 1994, pp. 149–159.

'The "Hand of Glory" and "Dead Candles"', *FLS News: The Newsletter of the Folklore Society*, 21, June, 1995, p. 6.

'Magic and Divination: Old Russian Sources', in *The Occult in Russian and Soviet Culture*, Cornell NY, 1997, pp. 35–58.

'The Witchcraft Hysteria in Early Modern Europe: Was Russia an Exception?', *Slavonic and East European Review*, 76, 1998, 1, pp. 1–36.

(with Charles Burnett), 'Abacus (Western)', in *Instruments of Science: An Historical Encyclopedia*, London, 1998, pp. 5–7.

'Peter I and English Maritime Technology', in *Peter the Great and the West: New Perspectives*, ed. Lindsey Hughes, Basingstoke and New York, 2001, pp. 130–58.

'Magic and the Military in Russia', in *Reflections on Russia in the Eighteenth Century*, ed. Joachim Klein, Simon Dixon, Maarten Fraanje, Cologne, Weimar and Vienna, 2001, pp. 84–95.

'Eclecticism in the Russian Charm Tradition', in *Charms and Charming in Europe*, ed. Jonathan Roper, London, 2004, pp. 113–27.

'Ancient Demons and Russian Fevers', in *Magic and the Classical Tradition*, ed. Charles Burnett and W. F. Ryan, Warburg Institute Colloquia 7, London, 2005, pp. 37–58.

'Russia and the Magic of Cats', *Solanus*, new series, 19, 2005, pp. 7–13.

'The Magic of the Law in Russia', in *'Forging a Common Destiny', Liber Amicorum in Honour of William E. Butler*, ed. Natalia Iu. Erpylova, Maryann E. Gashi Butler, Jane E. Henderson, London, 2005, pp. 32–43.

Articles on 'The Evil Eye', 'Hand of Glory', 'Amulets', 'Witchcraft and Orthodoxy', in *Encyclopedia of Witchcraft*, ABC-CLIO, 2005.

'Peter the Great's Magician' (essay review), *Kritika*, new series, 6, 2005, 1, pp. 217–21.

'Slavonic Studies', in *A Century of British Medieval Studies*, The British Academy, Oxford, 2007, pp. 283–300.

'Games, Pastimes and Magic in Russia', *Folklore*, 119, 2008, pp. 1–13.

'Witchcraft and the Russian State', in *Hexenprozess und Staatsbildung*, Bielefeld, 2008, pp. 135–47.

'W. R. S. Ralston and the Russian Folktale', *Folklore*, 120, 2009, pp. 123–32.

'Reply to Andrei Toporkov', *Forum for Anthropology and Culture*, 5, 2009, pp. 445–47.

'Ivan the Terrible's Malady and Its Magical Cure', *Incantatio*, 2, 2012, pp. 23–32.

'The *Gates of Aristotle* — A Strange Title with a Curious History', in *Russkii srednevekovyi gorod. Arkheologiia. Kul'tura. K Iubileiu A. V. Chernetsova* (forthcoming).

(with Moshe Taube), 'Chancellor Timofej Kamenevič and the Russification of the *Тайная тайных*', forthcoming.

Translations

Translator, editor and reviser of V. L. Chenakal, *Watchmakers and Clockmakers in Russia from 1400 to 1850*, Antiquarian Horological Society Monograph 6, London, 1972.

V. L. Chenakal, 'The Astronomical Instruments of John Rowley in 18th-century Russia', *Journal for the History of Astronomy*, 3, 1972, pp. 119–35.

I. G. Spassky, 'Numismatic Research in Russia, the Ukraine, and Byelorussia in the Period 1917–1967', *Numismatic Chronicle*, 1972, pp. 247–73.

V. L. Chenakal, 'John Bradlee and his Sundials', *Journal for the History of Astronomy*, 4, 1973, pp. 159–67.

Series editorships

Former joint series editor of Warburg Colloquia, Warburg Surveys and Texts, and Warburg Studies and Texts.

Former series editor of The Hakluyt Society.

Index

Milton Keynes UK
Ingram Content Group UK Ltd.
UKHW020955090124
435730UK00007B/308

9 780950 331485